The
European Union

History, Institutions, Economics and Policies

....

The
European Union

History, Institutions, Economics and Policies

ALI M. EL-AGRAA

WITH EDITED CONTRIBUTIONS

FIFTH EDITION OF
THE ECONOMICS OF THE EUROPEAN COMMUNITY

PRENTICE HALL

LONDON ● NEW YORK ● TORONTO ● SYDNEY ● TOKYO ●

SINGAPORE ● MADRID ● MEXICO CITY ● MUNICH ● PARIS

First published 1980 by
Philip Allan
Second edition 1983
Third edition 1990
Fourth edition published 1994 by
Harvester Wheatsheaf
This fifth edition published1998 by
Prentice Hall
A Pearson Education company
Edinburgh Gate Harlow,
Essex CM20 2JE, England

Typeset in 9.25/12pt Stone Serif by Fakenham Photosetting Ltd, Fakenham, Norfolk

Printed in Great Britain by Redwood Books Ltd, Trowbridge, Wiltshire

Library of Congress Cataloging-in-Publication Data

Available from the publisher

British Library Cataloguing in Publication Data

A catalogue record for this book is available from
the British Library

ISBN 0–13–916263–1

2 3 4 5 02 01 00 99

To Diana, Mark, Frances
and German Chancellor Helmut Köhl
for never losing sight of his vision for Europe

Lest it be forgotten, the European Union stands for the harmonized integration of some of the oldest countries in the world with very diverse cultures and extremely complicated economic systems. The European Union is about unity within diversity.

Contents

part three **Major EU policies** 169

List of figures

List of tables

List of contributors

Mr Harvey W. Armstrong is Professor of Economic Geography, Department of Geography, University of Sheffield, UK.

Dr Marius Brülhart is Lecturer in Economics, Trinity College, Dublin, Ireland.

Dr C. Doreen E. Collins was Senior Lecturer in Social Policy and Administration, University of Leeds, UK, before taking early retirement in 1985.

Dr Dermot McAleese is Whately Professor of Political Economy, Trinity College, Dublin, Ireland.

Mr Francis McGowan is Lecturer in Politics, Sussex European Institute, University of Sussex, UK.

Mr Alan Marin is Lecturer in Economics, London School of Economics and Political Science, University of London, UK.

Dr David G. Mayes is Adviser to the Board of the Bank of Finland.

Preface

Since the publication of the fourth edition of *The Economics of the European Community*, the most significant developments in the European Union's integrative process have been the efforts to accommodate the central and eastern European countries (CEECs) and the signing in June 1997 of the Amsterdam Treaty. The first development led to many association treaties, extensive aid, the invitation, with Russian endorsement, of the Czech Republic, Hungary and Poland to join NATO and applications for full membership by practically all the CEECs. The Amsterdam Treaty fully endorses the Maastricht Treaty (as adjusted in the Edinburgh summit of December 1992 and later in terms of waiving the earlier date of the end of 1997 for the adoption of the single currency – the *Euro*) by adhering to the convergence criteria (on inflation, currency stability, interest rates, budgetary deficits and public borrowing) for the introduction of the Euro on 1 January 1999.

Although the Amsterdam Treaty comes as somewhat of a disappointment in that the fifteen EU member nations could not agree on institutional changes, including representation in the Commission and the number needed for qualified majority as well as its wider use, it is nonetheless a major development when seen within the context of wavering support at the time for the European venture at both the governmental and popular levels: the French voted in a new government which they believed would sacrifice the Euro for commitment to lowering unemployment; the Germans feared the Euro would be weaker and less stable than their Mark and Chancellor Köhl was being reprimanded for trying to raise the value of gold deposits with the Bundesbank to enable Germany to pass the public debt criterion; the British Conservative Party was split down the middle on Europe and although the new Labour government has decided to sign Maastricht Treaty's social chapter, it has promised to conduct referenda on all EU major issues, including most immediately the adoption of the Euro; etc.

These developments and the need to update the extensive data employed throughout the book and to incorporate new initiatives in the various EU policy areas fully justify the production of a new edition. Indeed, one could argue that the updating alone would necessitate annual new editions, but given the cost implications, the publisher has decided to offer new editions on a biannual basis. This should prove helpful for those who continue to use the book as their basic text in terms of assurance on frequency and reasonable pricing. This new edition is also uniquely justified since, as promised in the fourth edition, it is high time to give the book a title which reflects both the change from EC to EU and the content of the book: the book is not limited to just the economics of the Union. At this juncture, one should inform the reader that the acronym EU is used throughout the book unless there is a compelling reason for referring to the EC or EEC. I hope the new title is appropriate, but I should be grateful for suggestions for a more suitable title.

The approach in this book continues to be one of perceiving the EU as an evolving and dynamic institution whose integrative process will not cease until the realization of the founding fathers' dream: the establishment of a United States of Europe. This new edition continues to treat these new developments within precisely this context. Thus the Single Market, the Maastricht Treaty and the Amsterdam Treaty are regarded as no more than long strides in the process of European integration.

Contrary to previous editions, I have made no rearrangements and have kept the same contributors, except for the addition of Dr Marius Brülhart of Trinity College Dublin as co-author with Professor Dermot McAleese, since I believe changes are not warranted this time. I welcome Marius to our team and thank all my contributors for their continued collaboration and support. Here, I should draw the reader's attention to some changes concerning some of the contributors: Professor David Mayes is now Adviser to the Board of the Bank of Finland and Harvey Armstrong has assumed the Chair of Economic Geography at the University of Sheffield, UK.

Finally, as in the previous edition, I would like to express my gratitude to all the universities and institutions which continue to use this book as their main guide to the teaching of the EU. I would also like to thank all those who have written formal and informal reviews of the book, not only for their generous praise but also for their constructive suggestions, and add that I am always looking forward to receiving criticisms and suggestions for improvement from all concerned.

Ali M. El-Agraa

University of Fukuoka
Japan
August 1997

List of abbreviations

AAMS	Association of African and Malagasy States
AAU	Arab African Union
ACC	Arab Cooperation Council
ACM	Arab Common Market
ACP	African, Caribbean and Pacific countries party to the Lomé Convention
AEC	Arab Economic Council
AIM	Advanced informatics in medicine
AL	Arab League
ALADI	Association for Latin American Integration
AMU	Arab Maghreb Union
ANZCERTA	Australia and New Zealand Closer Economic Relations and Trade Agreement
ASEAN	Association of South-East Asian Nations
BAP	Biotechnology action programme
BATNEEC	Best available technology not entailing excessive cost
BC-NET	Business Cooperation Network
BCR	Community Bureau of References
BEP	Biomolecular engineering programme
BRAIN	Basic research in adaptive intelligence and neurocomputing
BRITE/EURAM	Basic research in industrial technologies for Europe/raw materials and advanced materials
BU	Benin Union
CAA	Civil Aviation Authority
CACM	Central American Common Market
CADDIA	Cooperation in automation of data and documentation for imports/exports and agriculture
CAEU	Council for Arab Economic Unity
CAP	Common Agricultural Policy
CARICOM	Caribbean Community
CARIFTA	Caribbean Free Trade Association
CCP	Common Commercial Policy

CCT	Common Customs Tariff
CEAO	Communauté Economique de l'Afrique de l'Ouest
CEC	Commission of the European Communities
CEDB	Component event data bank
CEDEFOP	European Centre for Development of Vocational Training
CEN	European Committee for Standardization
CENELEC	European Committee for Electrotechnical Standardization
CEP	Common energy policy
CEPGL	Economic Community of the Countries of the Great Lakes
CER	Closer Economic Relations
CET	Common external tariff
CFP	Common Fisheries Policy
CFSP	Common Foreign and Security Policy
CI	Community Initiative
CIS	Commonwealth of Independent States
CM	Common market
CMEA	Council for Mutual Economic Assistance
CN	Combined Nomenclature
CODEST	Committee for the European Development of Science and Technology
COMECON	see CMEA
COMETT	Community programme in education and training for technology
CORDIS	Community research and development information service
COREPER	Committee of Permanent Representatives
CORINE	Coordination of information on the environment in Europe
COSINE	Cooperation for open systems interconnection networking in Europe
COST	European cooperation on scientific and technical research
CREST	Scientific and Technical Research Committee
CRS	Computerised Reservation System
CSCE	Conference on Security and Cooperation in Europe
CSF	Community support framework
CSTID	Committee for Scientific and Technical Information and Documentation
CTP	Common Transport Policy
CTS	Conformance testing services
CU	Customs union
DAC	Development Assistance Committee (OECD)
DELTA	Development European learning through technological advance
DG4	Directorate General Four
DI	Divergence indicator
DRIVE	Dedicated road infrastructure for vehicle safety in Europe

DV	Dummy variable
EAC	East African Community
EAGGF	European Agricultural Guidance and Guarantee Fund
EC	European Community
ECB	European Central Bank
ECJ	European Court of Justice
ECLAIR	European collaborative linkage of agriculture and industry through research
ECOFIN	European Council of Ministers for Financial Affairs
ECOSOC	Economic and Social Committee
ECOWAS	Economic Community of West African States
ECSC	European Coal and Steel Community
ECU	European currency unit
EDC	European Defence Community
EDF	European Development Fund
EDIFACT	Electronic data interchange for administration, commerce and transport
EEA	European Economic Area
EFTA	European Free Trade Association
EIB	European Investment Bank
EMCF	European Monetary Cooperation Fund
EMF	European Monetary Fund
EMI	European Monetary Institute
EMS	European Monetary System
EMU	European monetary union or economic and monetary union
EP	European Parliament
EPC	European political cooperation
EPOCH	European programme on climatology and natural hazards
EQS	Environmental quality standard
Erasmus	European Community action scheme for the mobility of university students
ERDF	European Regional Development Fund
ERM	Exchange-rate mechanism
ESCB	European System of Central Banks
ESF	European Social Fund
ESI	Electricity supply industry
ESPRIT	European strategic programme for research and development in information technology
EU	Economic union
EUA	European Unit of Account
Euratom	European Atomic Energy Commission
EUREKA	European Research Cooperation Agency
EURONET-DIANE	Direct information access network for Europe
EVCA	European Venture Capital Association

FADN	EEC farm accountancy data network
FAO	Food and Agriculture Organization of the United Nations
FAST	Forecasting and assessment in the field of science and technology
FCO	Foreign and Commonwealth Office
FEER	Fundamental Equilibrium Exchange Rate
FEOGA	Fonds Européen d'Orientation et de Garantie Agricole
FIFG	Instrument for Fisheries Guidance
FLAIR	Food-linked agro-industrial research
FTA	Free trade area
GATT	General Agreement on Tariffs and Trade (UN)
GCC	Gulf Cooperation Council
GDP	Gross domestic product
GNP	Gross national product
GSP	Generalized system of preferences
HDTV	High-definition television
HELIOS	Action programme to promote social and economic integration and an independent way of life for disabled people
HS	Harmonized Commodity Description and Coding System
IAEA	International Atomic Energy Agency (UN)
IATA	International Air Transport Association
IBRD	International Bank for Reconstruction and Development (World Bank) (UN)
ICONE	Comparative index of national and European standards
IDA	International Development Association (UN)
IDB	Inter-American Development Bank
IDO	Integrated development operation
IEA	International Energy Agency (OECD)
IEM	Internal energy market
IGC	Intergovernmental conference
IMF	International Monetary Fund (UN)
IMP	Integrated Mediterranean programme
IMPACT	Information market policy actions
INSIS	Inter-institutional system of integrated services
IRCC	International Radio Consultative Committee
IRIS	Network of demonstration projects on vocational training for women
IRTE	Integrated road transport environment
ISIS	Integrated standards information system
ITER	International thermonuclear experimental reactor
JET	Joint European Torus
JHA	Judicial and home affairs
JOULE	Joint opportunities for unconventional or long-term energy supply

JRC	Joint Research Centre
LAFTA	Latin American Free Trade Area
LDC	Less-developed country
LEDA	Local employment development action programme
LLDC	Least-developed country
MAST	Marine science and technology
MB	Marginal benefit
MC	Marginal cost
MCA	Monetary compensatory amount
MEDIA	Measures to encourage the development of the audio-visual industry
MEP	Member of the European Parliament
MERM	Multilateral exchange rate model
MFA	Multifibre Arrangement (arrangement regarding international trade in textiles)
MFT	Multilateral free trade
MISEP	Mutual information system on employment policies
MONITOR	Research programme on strategic analysis, forecasting and assessment in research and technology
MP	Marginal productivity
MRU	Mano River Union
NAFTA	North Atlantic Free Trade Agreement; New Zealand Australia Free Trade Area
NATO	North Atlantic Treaty Organisation
NCI	New Community Instrument
NEAFC	North-East Atlantic Fisheries Commission
NET	Next European Torus
NETT	Network for environmental technology transfer
NGO	Non-governmental organisation
NIC	Newly industrialising country
NIE	Newly industrialising economy
NIEO	New International Economic Order
NPCI	National programme of Community interest
NTB	Non-tariff barrier
NTM	Non-tariff measure
NUTS	Nomenclature of Territorial Units for Statistics
OAPEC	Organisation of Arab Petroleum Exporting Countries
OAU	Organisation for African Unity
OCTs	Overseas countries and territories
OECD	Organisation for Economic Cooperation and Development
OEEC	Organisation for European Economic Cooperation
OPEC	Organisation of Petroleum Exporting Countries
OSI	Open systems interconnection
PAFTAD	Pacific Trade and Development Conference

PBEC	Pacific Basin Economic Council
PECC	Pacific Economic Cooperation Conference
PEDIP	Programme to modernise Portuguese industry
PETRA	Action programme for the vocational training of young people and their preparation for adult and working life
POSEIDOM	Programme of options specific to the remote and insular nature of the overseas departments
PPP	Polluter pays principle
PTA	Preferential trade area
PTC	Pacific Telecommunications Conference
PTT	Posts, Telegraphs and Telecommunications
QMV	Qualified Majority Voting
RACE	Research and development in advanced communication technologies for Europe
RARE	Réseaux associés pour la recherche européenne
R&TD	Research and technological development
RCD	Regional Cooperation for Development
REIMEP	Regular European interlaboratory measurements evaluation programme
RENAVAL	Programme to assist the conversion of shipbuilding areas
RESIDER	Programme to assist the conversion of steel areas
RIA	Regional impact assessment
SACU	Southern African Customs Union
SAP	Social action programme
SAST	Strategic analysis in the field of science and technology
SCENT	System for a customs enforcement network
SCIENCE	Plan to stimulate the international cooperation and interchange necessary for European researchers
SDR	Special drawing rights
SEA	Single European Act
SEDOC	Inter-state notification of job vacancies
SEM	Single European Market
SPD	Single Programme Documents
SPEAR	Support programme for a European assessment of research
SPES	Stimulation plan for economic science
SPRINT	Strategic programme for innovation and technology transfer
STABEX	System for the stabilization of ACP and OCT export earnings
STAR	Community programme for the development of certain less-favoured regions of the Community by improving access to advanced telecommunications services
STEP	Science and technology for environmental protection
SYSMIN	Special financing facility for ACP and OCT mining products
TAC	Total allowable catch
TARIC	Integrated Community tariff

TEDIS	Trade electronic data interchange systems
TELEMAN	Research and training programme on remote handling in nuclear hazardous and disordered environments
t/t	Terms of trade
TVA	*Tax sur la valeur ajoutée*
TUC	Trades Union Congress
UDEAC	Union Douanière et Economique de l'Afrique Centrale
UES	Uniform emission standards
UN	United Nations
UNCLOS	United Nations Conference on the Law of the Sea
UNCTAD	United Nations Conference on Trade and Development
UNECA	United Nations Economic Commission for Africa
UNEP	United Nations Environment Programme
UNESCO	United Nations Educational, Scientific and Cultural Organization
UNHCR	United Nations High Commissioner for Refugees
UNIDO	United Nations Industrial Development Organization
UNRWA	United Nations Relief and Works Agency for Palestine Refugees in the Near East
UTR	Unilateral tariff reduction
VALOREN	Community programme for the development of certain less-favoured regions of the Community by exploiting endogenous energy potential
VALUE	Programme for the dissemination and utilization of research results
VAT	Value-added tax
VER	Voluntary export restraint
VSTF	Very short-term financing facility
WEU	Western European Union
WFC	World Food Council (UN)
WFP	World Food Programme (UN)
WIPO	World Intellectual Property Organization (UN)
YES	'Youth for Europe' programme (youth exchange scheme)

chapter one

General introduction

A. M. EL-AGRAA

1.1 What is economic integration?

'International economic integration' (hereafter, simply economic integration) is one aspect of 'international economics' which has been growing in importance for well over four decades. The term itself has a rather short history; indeed, Machlup (1977a) was unable to find a single instance of its use prior to 1942. Since then the term has been used at various times to refer to practically any area of international economic relations. By 1950, however, the term had been given a specific definition by economists specializing in international trade to denote a state of affairs or a process which involves the amalgamation of separate economies into larger free trading regions. It is in this more limited sense that the term is used today. However, one should hasten to add that economists not familiar with this branch of international economics have for quite a while been using the term to mean simply increasing economic interdependence between nations.

More specifically, economic integration is concerned with the discriminatory removal of all trade impediments between at least two participating nations and with the establishment of certain elements of cooperation and coordination between them. The latter depends entirely on the actual form that integration takes. Different forms of economic integration can be envisaged and many have actually been implemented (see Table 1.1 for schematic presentation):

1. *Free trade areas*, where the member nations remove all trade impediments among themselves but retain their freedom with regard to the determination of their own policies *vis-à-vis* the outside world (the non-participant – for example, the European Free Trade Association (EFTA) and the demised Latin American Free Trade Area (LAFTA)).

2. *Customs unions*, which are very similar to free trade areas except that member nations must conduct and pursue common external commercial relations – for instance, they must adopt common external tariffs (CETs) on imports from the non-participants as is the case in, *inter alia*, the European Union (EU, which is in this particular sense a customs union, but, as we shall presently see, it is more

than that), the Central American Common Market (CACM) and the Caribbean Community and Common Market (CARICOM).

3. *Common markets*, which are custom unions that allow also for free factor mobility across national member frontiers, i.e. capital, labour, technology and enterprises should move unhindered between the participating countries – for example, the EU (but again it is more complex).

4. *Complete economic unions*, which are common markets that ask for complete unification of monetary and fiscal policies, i.e. the participants must introduce a central authority to exercise control over these matters so that member nations effectively become regions of the same nation – the EU is heading in this direction.

5. *Complete political unions*, where the participating countries become literally one nation, i.e. the central authority needed in complete economic unions should be parallelled by a common parliament and other necessary institutions needed to guarantee the sovereignty of one state – an example of this is the unification of the two Germanies in 1990.

Table 1.1 ⬭ Schematic presentation of economic integration schemes

Scheme	Free intrascheme trade	Common commercial policy	Free factor mobility	Common monetary and fiscal policy	One government
Free trade area	Yes	No	No	No	No
Customs union	Yes	Yes	No	No	No
Common market	Yes	Yes	Yes	No	No
Economic union	Yes	Yes	Yes	Yes	No
Political union	Yes	Yes	Yes	Yes	Yes

However, one should hasten to add that political integration need not be, and in the majority of cases will never be, part of this list. Nevertheless, it can of course be introduced as a form of unity and for no economic reason whatsoever, as was the case with the two Germanies and as is the case with the pursuit of the unification of the Korean Peninsula, although one should naturally be interested in its economic consequences (see below). More generally, one should indeed stress that each of these forms of economic integration can be introduced in its own right; hence they should not be confused with *stages* in a *process* which eventually leads to either complete economic or political union.

It should also be noted that there may be *sectoral* integration, as distinct from general across-the-board integration, in particular areas of the economy as was the case with the European Coal and Steel Community (ECSC), created in 1950, but sectoral integration is a form of cooperation not only because it is inconsistent with the accepted definition of economic integration but also because it may contravene the rules of the General Agreement on Tariffs and Trade (GATT), now called the World Trade Organization (WTO) – see below. Sectoral integration may also occur within any of the mentioned schemes, as is the case with the EU's Common Agricultural Policy (CAP), but then it is nothing more than a 'policy'.

One should further point out that it has been claimed that economic integration can be *negative* or *positive*. The term negative integration was coined by Tinbergen (1954) to refer to the removal of impediments on trade between the participating nations or to the elimination of any restrictions on the process of trade liberalization. The term positive integration relates to the modification of existing instruments and institutions and, more importantly, to the creation of new ones so as to enable the market of the integrated area to function properly and effectively and also to promote other broader policy aims of the scheme. Hence, at the risk of oversimplification, according to this classification, it can be stated that sectoral integration and free trade areas are forms of economic integration which require only negative integration, while the remaining types require positive integration, since, as a minimum, they need the positive act of adopting common relations. However, in reality this distinction is oversimplistic not only because practically all existing types of economic integration have found it essential to introduce some elements of positive integration, but also because theoretical considerations clearly indicate that no scheme of economic integration is viable without certain elements of positive integration, for example, even the ECSC deemed it necessary to establish new institutions to tackle its specified tasks – see below.

1.2   Economic integration and WTO rules

The rules of WTO, GATT's successor, allow the formation of economic integration schemes on the understanding that, although free trade areas, customs unions, etc. are discriminatory associations, they may not pursue policies which increase the level of their discrimination beyond that which existed prior to their formation, and that tariffs and other trade restrictions (with some exceptions) are removed on *substantially* all the trade among the participants. Hence, once allowance was made for the proviso regarding the external trade relations of the economic integration scheme (the CET level, or the common level of discrimination against extra-area trade, in a customs union, and the average tariff or trade discrimination level in a free trade area), it seemed to the drafters of Article XXIV (see Appendix to this chapter) that economic integration did not contradict the basic principles of WTO – trade *liberalization* on a most-favoured-nation (MFN) basis, *non-discrimination, transparency* of instruments used to restrict trade and the promotion of *growth and stability* of the world economy – or more generally the principles of *non-discrimination, transparency* and *reciprocity*.

There are more serious arguments suggesting that Article XXIV is in direct contradiction to the spirit of WTO – see Chapter 4 and, *inter alia*, Dam (1970). However, Wolf (1983, p. 156) argues that if nations decide to treat one another as if they are part of a single economy, nothing can be done to prevent them, and that economic integration schemes, particularly like the EU at the time of its formation in 1957, have a strong impulse towards liberalization; in the case of the EU at the mentioned time, the setting of the CETs happened to coincide with GATT's Kennedy Round of tariff reductions. However, recent experience, especially in the case of the EU, has proved otherwise since there has been a proliferation of non-tariff barriers, but the point about WTO not being able to deter countries from pursuing economic integration has general validity: WTO has no means for enforcing its rules; it has no coercion powers.

Of course, these considerations are more complicated than is suggested here, particularly since there are those who would argue that nothing could be more discriminatory than for a group of nations to remove all tariffs and trade impediments on their mutual trade while *at the same time* maintaining the initial levels against outsiders. Indeed, it would be difficult to find 'clubs' which extend equal privileges to non-subscribers. Moreover, as we shall see in Chapter 4, economic integration schemes may lead to resource reallocation effects which are economically undesirable. However, to have denied nations the right to form such associations, particularly when the main driving force may be political rather than economic, would have been a major setback for the world community. Hence, all that needs to be stated here is that as much as Article XXIV raises serious problems regarding how it fits in with the general spirit of WTO, it also reflects its drafters' deep understanding of the future development of the world economy.

1.3 The global experience

Although this book is concerned with the EU alone, it is important to view the EU within the context of the global experience of economic integration. This section provides a brief summary of this experience – see El-Agraa (1997) for a full and detailed coverage.

Since the end of the Second World War various forms of economic integration have been proposed and numerous schemes have actually been implemented. Even though some of those introduced were later discontinued or completely reformulated, the number adopted during the decade commencing in 1957 was so great as to prompt Haberler in 1964 to describe that period as the 'age of integration'. After 1964, however, there has been such a proliferation of integration schemes that Haberler's description may be more apt for the post-1964 era.

The EU is the most significant and influential of these arrangements since it comprises some of the most advanced nations of Western Europe: Austria, Belgium,

Denmark, Finland, France, Germany, Greece, Ireland, Italy, Luxemburg, the Netherlands, Portugal, Spain, Sweden and the United Kingdom (UK). The EU was founded by six (not quite since Germany was then not yet united) of these nations (Belgium, France, West Germany, Italy, Luxemburg and the Netherlands, usually referred to as the *Original Six*, simply the Six hereafter) by two treaties, signed in Rome on the same day in 1957, creating the *European Economic Community* (EEC) and the *European Atomic Energy Community* (Euratom). However, the Six had then been members of the *European Coal and Steel Community* (ECSC) which was established by the Treaty of Paris in 1951. Thus, in 1957 the Six belonged to three communities, but in 1965 it was deemed sensible to merge the three entities into one and to call it the *European Communities* (EC). Three of the remaining nine (Denmark, Ireland and the UK) joined later in 1973. Greece became a full member in January 1981, Portugal and Spain in 1986, and Austria, Finland and Sweden in 1995.

At present, the EU is in receipt of applications for membership from Cyprus, Hungary, Malta, Poland, Turkey and Switzerland. Also, most of the remaining Eastern European nations have not only signed *Agreements of Association* with the EU, but also intend to join as soon as possible, especially the Czech and Slovak Republics. Moreover, the EU, Iceland, Liechtenstein and Norway belong to the *European Economic Area* (EEA), a scheme which provides Iceland and Norway with virtual membership of the EU, but without having a say in EU decisions; indeed the EEA is seen as stepping stone in the direction of full EU membership. Thus, if all goes according to plan, the EU is set to comprise the whole of Europe.

Although the EEC Treaty relates simply to the formation of a customs union and provides the basis for a common market in terms of free factor mobility, many of the originators of the EEC saw it as a phase in a process culminating in complete economic and political union. Thus the *Treaty on European Union* (the Maastricht Treaty), which transformed the EC into the EU in 1994 and which intends, *inter alia*, to provide the EU with a single central bank, a single currency, and common foreign and defence policies by the end of this century, should be seen as positive steps towards the attainment of the founding fathers' desired goal.

EFTA is the other major scheme of international economic integration in Europe. To understand its membership one has to learn something about its history. In the mid-1950s when an EEC of the Six plus the UK was being contemplated, the UK was unprepared to commit itself to some of the economic and political aims envisaged for that community. For example, the adoption of a common agricultural policy and the eventual political unity of Western Europe were seen as aims which were in direct conflict with the UK's powerful position in the world and its interests in the Commonwealth, particularly with regard to 'Commonwealth preference' which granted special access to the markets of the Commonwealth. Hence the UK favoured the idea of a Western Europe which adopted free trade in industrial products only, thus securing for itself the advantages offered by the Commonwealth as well as opening up Western Europe as a free market for its industrial goods. In short, the UK sought to achieve the best of both worlds for itself, which is of course quite understandable. However, it is equally understandable that such an arrangement was not acceptable to those seriously contemplating the formation of the EEC, especially France which stood to lose in an arrangement excluding a common policy for agriculture. As a result the UK approached those Western European nations who had similar interests with the purpose of forming an alternative scheme of economic integration to counteract any possible damage due to the formation of the EEC. The outcome was EFTA which was established in 1960 by the Stockholm Convention with the object of creating a free market for industrial products only; there were some agreements on non-manufactures but these were relatively unimportant.

The membership of EFTA consisted of Austria, Denmark, Norway, Portugal, Sweden, Switzerland (and Liechtenstein) and the UK. Finland became an associate member in 1961, and Iceland joined in 1970 as a full member. But, as already stated, Denmark and the UK (together with Ireland) joined the EC in 1973; Portugal (together with Spain) joined in 1986; Austria, Finland and Sweden joined the EU in 1995. This left EFTA with a membership consisting mainly of a few and relatively smaller nations of Western Europe.

Until recently, economic integration schemes in Europe were not confined to the EU and EFTA. Indeed, before the dramatic events of 1989–90, the socialist planned economies of Eastern Europe had their own arrangement which operated under the CMEA, or COMECON as it was generally known in the West. The CMEA was formed in 1949 by Bulgaria, Czechoslovakia, the German Democratic Republic, Hungary, Poland, Romania and the USSR; they were later joined by three non-European countries: Mongolia (1962), Cuba (1972) and Vietnam (1978). In its earlier days, before the death of Stalin, the activities of the CMEA were confined to the collation of the plans of the member states, the development of a uniform system of reporting statistical data and the recording of foreign trade statistics. However, during the 1970s a series of measures was adopted by the CMEA to implement their 'Comprehensive Programme of Socialist Integration', hence indicating that the organization was moving towards a form of integration based principally on methods of plan coordination and joint planning activity, rather than on market levers (Smith, 1977). Finally, attention should be drawn to the fact that the CMEA comprised a group of relatively small countries and one 'super power' and that the long-term aim of the association was to achieve a highly organized and integrated bloc, without any agreement ever having been made on how or when that was to be accomplished.

The dramatic changes that have recently taken place in Eastern Europe and the former USSR have inevitably led to the demise of the CMEA. This, together with the fact that the CMEA did not really achieve much in the nature of economic integration, indeed some analysts have argued that the entire organization was simply an instrument for the USSR to dictate its wishes on the rest, are the reasons why El-Agraa's (1997) book does not contain a chapter on the CMEA; the interested reader will find a chapter in El-Agraa (1988b). However, one should hasten to add that soon after the demise of the USSR, Russia and seventeen former USSR republics formed the Commonwealth of Independent States (CIS) which makes them effectively one nation.

Before leaving Europe it should be mentioned that another scheme exists in the form of a regional bloc between the five Nordic countries (the Nordic Community): Denmark, Finland, Iceland, Norway and Sweden. However, in spite of claims to the contrary (Sundelius and Wiklund, 1979), the Nordic scheme is one of cooperation rather than economic integration since its members belong to either the EU or EFTA, and, as we have seen, the EU and EFTA are closely linked through the EEA.

In Africa, there are numerous schemes of economic integration. The *Union Douaniére et Economique de l'Afrique Centrale* (UDEAC), a free trade area, comprises the People's republic of the Congo, Gabon, Cameroon and the Central African Republic. Member nations of UDEAC plus Chad, a former member, constitute a monetary union. The *Communauté Economique de l'Afrique de l'Ouest* (CEAO), which was formed under the Treaty of Abidjan in 1973, is a free trade area consisting of the Ivory Coast (Cote d'Ivoire), Mali, Mauretania, Niger, Senegal and Upper Volta (now Burkina Faso); Benin joined in 1984. Member countries of the CEAO, except for Mauretania, plus Benin and Togo, have replaced the CEAO by an Act constituting an economic and monetary union. In 1973 the *Mano Riven Union* (MRU) was established between Liberia and Sierra Leone; they were joined by Guinea in 1980. The MRU is a customs union which involves a certain degree of cooperation particularly in the industrial sector. The *Economic Community of West African States* (ECOWAS) was formed in 1975 with fifteen signatories: its membership consists of all those countries participating in UDEAC, CEAO, MRU plus some other West African States. Despite its name, ECOWAS is a free trade area. Its total membership today is seventeen.

In 1969 the *Southern African Customs Union* (SACU) was established between Botswana, Lesotho, Swaziland and the Republic of South Africa; they were later joined by Namibia. The *Economic Community of the Countries of the Great Lakes* (CEPGL), a free trade area, was created in 1976 by Rwanda, Burundi and Zaire. Until its collapse in 1978, there was the *East African Community* (EAC) between Kenya, Tanzania and Uganda. In 1981 the *Preferential Trade Area* (PTA), a free trade area, was created by fifteen nations from Eastern and Southern Africa: Angola, Botswana, the Comoros, Djibouti, Ethiopia, Kenya, Losetho, Malawai, Mauritius, Mozambique, Swaziland, Tanzania, Uganda, Zambia and Zimbabwe; they were later joined by another five nations. The PTA has been replaced by the much more ambitious *Common Market for Eastern and Southern Africa* (COMESA). In 1983 the *Economic Community of Central African States* (EEAC, the acronym is from French) was created by eleven nations in Equatorial and Central Africa. In 1985 the *Benin Union* (BU) was formed by Benin, Ghana, Nigeria and Togo. In 1980, the *Lagos Plan of Action* was inaugurated with a membership which included practically the whole of Africa. There are also many smaller subregional groupings such as the Kagera River Basin organization (KBO), the Lake Tanganyika and Kivu Basin organization (LTKBC) and the Southern African Development Coordination Council (SADCC).

Moreover, there are schemes involving the Northern African nations. In August 1984 a Treaty was signed by Libya and Morocco to establish the *Arab-African Union*, whose main aim is to tackle their political conflicts in the Sahara Desert. In 1989 the

Arab Maghreb Union (AMU), a common market, was created by Algeria, Libya, Morocco and Tunisia. Egypt participates in the *Arab Cooperation Council* (ACC) which was formed in 1990 (see below).

Hence, a unique characteristic of economic integration in Africa is the multiplicity and overlapping of its schemes. For example, in the West alone, there was a total of thirty-three schemes and intergovernmental cooperation organizations, which is why the United Nations Economic Commission for Africa (UNECA) recommended in 1984 that there should be some rationalization in the economic cooperation attempts in West Africa. However, the diversity and overlapping are not confined to West Africa alone. Needless to add, the Lagos Plan of Action is no solution since, apart from encompassing the whole of Africa and being a weaker association, it exists on top of the other schemes. When this uniqueness is combined with proliferation in schemes, one cannot disagree with Robson (1997) when he declares that

> *Reculer pour mieux sauter* is not a dictum that seems to carry much weight among African governments involved in regional integration. On the contrary, if a certain level of integration cannot be made to work, the reaction of policy makers has typically been to embark on something more elaborate, more advanced and more demanding in terms of administrative requirements and political commitment.

Economic integration in Latin America has been too volatile to describe in simple terms since the post-1985 experience has been very different from that in the 1960s and 1970s. At the risk of misleading, one can state that there are four schemes of economic integration in this region. Under the 1960 Treaty of Montevideo, the *Latin American Free Trade Association* (LAFTA) was formed between Mexico and all the countries of South America except for Guyana and Surinam. LAFTA came to an end in the late 1970s but was promptly succeeded by the *Association for Latin American Integration* (ALADI or LAIA) in 1980. The Managua Treaty of 1960 established the *Central American Common Market* (CACM) between Costa Rica, El Salvador, Guatemala, Honduras and Nicaragua. In 1969 the *Andean Pact* (AP) was established under the Cartegena Agreement between Bolivia, Chile, Colombia, Ecuador, Peru and Venezuela; the AP forms a closer link between some of the least developed nations of LAFTA, now LAIA.

Since the debt crisis in the 1980s, economic integration in Latin America has taken a new turn with Mexico joining Canada and the US (see below) and Argentina, Brazil, Paraguay and Uruguay, the more developed nations of LAIA, creating *MERCOSUR* in 1991. MERCOSUR became a customs union by 1 January 1995 but aimed to become a common market by 1995. Bolivia and Chile became associate members in mid-1995, a move which Brazil sees as merely a first step towards the creation of a *South American Free Trade Area* (SAFTA), a counterweight to the efforts in the north (see below).

There is one scheme of economic integration in the Caribbean. In 1973 the *Caribbean Community* (CARICOM) was formed between Antigua, Barbados, Belize, Dominica, Grenada, Guyana, Jamaica, Montserrat, St Kitts–Nevis–Anguilla, St Lucia,

St Vincent, and Trinidad and Tobago. CARICOM replaced the *Caribbean Free Trade Association* (CARIFTA) which was established in 1968.

In 1988 Canada and the United States established the *Canada–US Free Trade Agreement* (CUFTA), and, together with Mexico, they formed the *North American Free Trade Agreement* (NAFTA) in 1993 which started to operate from 1 January 1994. Despite its name, NAFTA also covers investment. The enlargement of NAFTA to include the rest of the Western Hemisphere was suggested by George Bush while US President who hoped to construct what is now referred to as the *Free Trade Area of the Americas* (FTAA) which is under negotiation, aiming for a conclusion by 2005. Chile has been negotiating membership of NAFTA.

Asia does not figure prominently in the league of economic integration schemes, but this is not surprising given the existence of such large (if only in terms of population) countries as China and India. The *Regional Cooperation for Development* (RCD) was a very limited arrangement for sectoral integration between Iran, Pakistan and Turkey. The *Association for South-East Asian Nations* (ASEAN) comprises seven nations: Brunei, Indonesia, Malaysia, the Philippines, Singapore, Thailand and Vietnam. ASEAN was founded in 1967 by these countries minus Brunei and Vietnam in the shadow of the Vietnam War. Brunei joined in 1984 and Vietnam in July 1995. After almost a decade of inactivity 'it was galvanized into renewed vigour in 1976 by the security problems which the reunification of Vietnam seemed to present to its membership' (Arndt and Garnaut, 1979). The drive for the establishment of ASEAN and for its vigorous reactivation in 1976 was both political and strategic. However, right from the start, economic cooperation was one of the most important aims of ASEAN, indeed most of the vigorous activities of the group since 1976 have been predominantly in the economic field, and the admission of Vietnam in 1995 is a clear manifestation of this. Moreover, ASEAN has recently been discussing proposals to accelerate its own plan for a free trade area to the year 2000 from 2003, itself an advance on the original target of 2008.

In 1965 Australia and New Zealand entered into a free trade arrangement called the *New Zealand Australia Free Trade Area*. This was replaced in 1983 by the more important *Australia New Zealand Closer Economic Relations and Trade Agreement* (CER, for short): not only have major trade barriers been removed, but significant effects on the New Zealand economy have been experienced as a result.

A scheme for the Pacific Basin integration-cum-cooperation was being hotly discussed during the 1980s. In the late 1980s I (El-Agraa, 1988a, 1988b) argued that 'given the diversity of countries within the Pacific region, it would seem highly unlikely that a very involved scheme of integration would evolve over the next decade or so'. This was in spite of the fact that there already existed:

1. The *Pacific Economic Cooperation Conference* (PECC) which is a tripartite structured organization with representatives from governments, business and academic circles and with the secretariat work being handled between general meetings by the country next hosting a meeting;

2. The *Pacific Trade and Development Centre* (PAFTAD) which is an academically oriented organization;

3. The *Pacific Basin Economic Council* (PBEC) which is a private-sector business organization for regional cooperation; and

4. The *Pacific Telecommunications Conference* (PTC)) which is a specialized organization for regional cooperation in this particular field.

The reason for the pessimism was that the

> region under consideration covers the whole of North America and Southeast Asia, with Pacific South America, the People's Republic of China and the USSR all claiming interest since they are all on the Pacific. Even if one were to exclude this latter group, there still remains the cultural diversity of such countries as Australia, Canada, Japan, New Zealand and the USA, plus the diversity that already exists within ASEAN. It would seem that unless the group of participants is severely limited, Pacific Basin *cooperation* will be the logical outcome. (El-Agraa, 1988a, p. 8)

However, in an attempt to provide a rational basis for resolving Japan's trade frictions, I may appear to have contradicted myself:

> it may be concluded that ... Pacific Basin cooperation-cum-integration is the only genuine solution to the problems of Japan and the USA (as well as the other nations in this area). Given what is stated above about the nature of the nations of the Pacific Basin, that would be a broad generalisation: what is needed is a very strong relationship between Japan and the USA within a much looser association with the rest of SE Asia. Hence, what is being advocated is a form of involved economic integration between Japan and the USA (and Canada, if the present negotiations for a free trade area of Canada and the USA lead to that outcome), within the broad context of 'Pacific Basin Cooperation', or, more likely, within a free trade area with the most advanced nations of SE Asia: Australia, New Zealand, South Korea, the nations of ASEAN, etc. (El-Agraa, 1988b, pp. 203–4)

I added that the proposed scheme should not be a protectionist one. Members of such a scheme should promote cooperation with the rest of the world through their membership of GATT (now WTO) and should coordinate their policies with regard to overseas development assistance, both financially and in terms of the transfer of technology, for the benefit not only of the poorer nations of SE Asia, but also for the whole developing world.

Thus the *Asia Pacific Economic Cooperation* (APEC) forum can be considered as the appropriate response to my suggestion. It was established in 1989 by ASEAN plus Australia, Canada, Japan, New Zealand, South Korea, the US. These were joined by China, Hong Kong and Taiwan in 1991. In 1993 President Clinton galvanized it into its present form and size of eighteen nations. In Bogor, Indonesia, in 1994 APEC declared its intention (vision) to create a free trade and investment area by the year 2010 by its advanced members, with the rest to follow suit ten years later. APEC tried to chart the route for realizing this vision in Osaka, Japan, in November 1995, and came up with the interesting resolution that each member nation should unilaterally declare its own measures for freeing trade and investment, with agriculture completely left out of the reckoning.

There are several schemes in the Middle East, but some of them extend beyond the geographical area traditionally designated as such. This is natural since there are nations with Middle Eastern characteristics in parts of Africa. The *Arab League* (AL) clearly demonstrates this reality since it comprises 22 nations, extending from the Gulf in the East to Mauritania and Morocco in the West. Hence the geographical area covered by the scheme includes the whole of North Africa, a large part of the Middle East, plus Djibouti and Somalia. The purpose of the AL is to strengthen the close ties linking Arab states, to coordinate their policies and activities and to direct them to their common good and to mediate in disputes between them. These may seem like vague terms of reference, but the *Arab Economic Council*, whose membership consists of all Arab Ministers of Economic Affairs, was entrusted with suggesting ways for economic development, cooperation, organization and coordination. The *Council for Arab Economic Unity* (CAEU), which was formed in 1957, had the aim of establishing an integrated economy of all AL states. Moreover, in 1964 the *Arab Common Market* was formed (but practically never got off the ground) between Egypt, Iraq, Jordan and Syria, and in 1981 the *Gulf Cooperation Council* (GCC) was established between Bahrain, Kuwait, Oman, Qatar, Saudi Arabia and United Arab Emirates to bring together the Gulf states and to prepare the ground for them to join forces in the economic, political and military spheres.

The latest schemes of economic integration in the Middle East have already been mentioned, but only in passing in the context of Africa. The ACC was founded on 16 February 1989 by Egypt, Iraq, Jordan and the Arab Yemen Republic with the aim of boosting Arab solidarity and acting as 'yet another link in the chain of Arab efforts towards integration'. Moreover, on 18 February 1989 the AMU was formed by Algeria, Libya, Mauritania, Morocco and Tunisia. The AMU aims to create an organization similar to the EU.

There are two schemes of sectoral economic integration which are not based on geographical proximity. The first is the *Organization for Petroleum Exporting Countries* (OPEC), founded in 1960 with a truly international membership. Its aim was to protect the main interest of its member nations: petroleum. After verging close to liquidation, OPEC seems to have been revived, but it has lost some of its political clout. The second is the *Organization for Arab Petroleum Exporting Countries* (OAPEC), established in January 1968 by Kuwait, Libya and Saudi Arabia. These were joined in May 1970 by Algeria, and the four Arab Gulf Emirates: Abu Dhabi, Bahrain, Dubai and Qatar. In March 1972 Egypt, Iraq and Syria became members. OAPEC was temporarily liquidated in June 1971 and Dubai is no longer a member. The agreement establishing OAPEC states that the

> principal objective of the Organization is the cooperation of the members in various forms of economic activity … the realization of the closest ties among them … the determination of ways and means of safeguarding the legitimate interests of its members … the unification of efforts to ensure the flow of petroleum to its consumption markets on equitable and reasonable terms and the creation of a suitable climate for the capital and expertise invested in the petroleum industry in the member countries. (*Middle East Economic Survey*, 1968)

However, in the late 1960s OAPEC flexed its muscle within OPEC to force the latter to use petroleum as a weapon against Israeli occupation of certain Arab areas. Many analysts would argue that the tactic was to no avail; indeed many believe that it accomplished no more than to undermine OAPEC's reputation, especially since there is nothing in the aims quoted above to vindicate such action. Since then, OAPEC has undertaken a number of projects both within and outside the organization – see, for example, Mingst (1977/78).

Finally, there are also the *Organization for African Unity* (OAU), *Organization for Economic Cooperation and Development* (OECD) and the *World Trade Organization* (WTO). However, these and the above are schemes for intergovernmental cooperation rather than for economic integration. Therefore, except where appropriate, nothing more shall be said about them.

1.4 The EU

Since this book is devoted to the EU, it is important to establish the nature of the EU within the context of the different types of economic integration discussed at the beginning of the chapter – readers interested in the other schemes will find a full discussion of them in El-Agraa (1997).

Article 2 of the treaty establishing the EEC pronounces that:

> The Community shall have as its task, by setting up a common market and progressively approximating the economic policies of Member States, to promote throughout the Community an harmonious development of economic activities, a continuous and balanced expansion, an increase in stability, an accelerated raising of the standard of living and closer relations between the Member States belonging to it. (Article 2, p. 3)

Article 3 then states that for the purposes set out in Article 2:

> The activities of the Community shall include, on the conditions and in accordance with the time-table provided in this Treaty:
>
> (a) the elimination, as between Member States, of customs duties and of quantitative restrictions in regard to the import and export of goods, as well as of all other measures having equivalent effect;
> (b) the establishment of a common customs tariff and a common commercial policy towards third countries;
> (c) the abolition, as between Member States, of obstacles to the freedom of movement for persons, services and capital;
> (d) the establishment of a common policy in the sphere of agriculture;
> (e) the adoption of a common policy in the sphere of transport;
> (f) the establishment of a system ensuring that competition in the common market is not distorted;
> (g) the application of procedures by which the economic policies of Member States can be co-ordinated and disequilibria in their balances of payments can be remedied;
> (h) the approximation of the laws of Member States to the extent required for proper functioning of the common market;

(i) the creation of a European Social Fund in order to improve the possibilities of employment for workers and to contribute to the raising of their standard of living;

(j) the establishment of a European Investment Bank to facilitate the economic expansion of the Community by opening up fresh resources; and

(k) the association of overseas countries and territories with a view to increasing trade and to promoting jointly economic and social development. (*Treaty of Rome*, pp. 3–4)

These elements are stated more elaborately in later articles. For instance, Article 9(1) states:

> The Community shall be based upon a customs union which shall cover all trade in goods and which shall involve the prohibition between Member States of customs duties on imports and exports and of all charges having equivalent effect, and the adoption of a common customs tariff in their relation with third countries. (*Treaty of Rome*, p. 6)

Articles 35–7 elaborate on the common agricultural policy (CAP), Articles 48–73 on the conditions for freedom of movement of factors of production, Articles 74–84 on the common transport policy (CTP) and Articles 99 and 100 on the harmonization of certain taxes.

The Treaty of Rome provisions should, however, be considered in conjunction with later developments. These have been incorporated into the Single European Act (SEA) which includes the European Monetary System (EMS), the creation of a true single market by the end of 1992 and the Maastricht Treaty which, when fully implemented by all the member countries, will realize the 'European Union', with a single currency (the Euro), a common central bank, a common monetary policy, a common defence policy and a common foreign policy by the beginning of 1999 – these are fully discussed in Chapter 2. Here, it can be categorically stated that the *EU is at present more than a common market but falls short of being a complete economic union, but it is aspiring to achieve the latter as well as political union.*

1.5 The possible gains from economic integration

We shall see in Chapters 2 and 5 that the driving force behind the formation of the EU, the earliest and most influential of all existing integration schemes, was the political unity of Europe with the aim of realizing eternal peace in the Continent. Some analysts would also argue that the recent attempts by the EU for more intensive economic integration can be cast in the same vein, especially since they are accompanied by common foreign and defence policies. At the same time, during the late 1950s and early 1960s economic integration among developing nations was perceived as the only viable way for them to make some real economic progress; indeed that was the rationale behind the United Nation's encouragement and support of such efforts. However, no matter what the motives for economic integration may be, it is still necessary to analyse the economic implications of such geographically discriminatory associations; that is one of the reasons why I have included political unification as one of the possible schemes.

At the customs union (CU) and free trade area (FTA) levels, the possible sources of economic gain from economic integration can be attributed to:

1. enhanced efficiency in production made possible by increased specialization in accordance with the law of comparative advantage, due to the liberalized market of the participating nations;

2. increased production levels due to better exploitation of economies of scale made possible by the increased size of the market;

3. an improved international bargaining position, made possible by the larger size, leading to better terms of trade (cheaper imports from the outside world and higher prices for exports to them);

4. enforced changes in efficiency brought about by intensified competition between firms;

5. changes affecting both the amount and quality of the factors of production due to technological advances, themselves encouraged by (4).

If the level of economic integration is to go beyond the free trade area and customs union levels, then further sources of economic gain also become possible:

6. factor mobility across the borders of the member nations will materialize only if there is a net economic incentive for them, thus leading to higher national incomes;

7. the coordination of monetary and fiscal policies may result in cost reductions since the pooling of efforts may enable the achievement of economies of scale;

8. the unification of efforts to achieve better employment levels, lower inflation rates, balanced trade, higher rates of economic growth and better income distribution may make it cheaper to attain these targets.

It should be apparent that some of these possible gains relate to static resource reallocation effects while the rest relate to long-term or dynamic effects. It should also be emphasized that these are *possible* economic gains, i.e. there is no guarantee that they can ever be achieved; everything would depend on the nature of the particular scheme and the type of competitive behaviour prevailing prior to integration. Indeed, it is quite feasible that in the absence of 'appropriate' competitive behaviour, economic integration may worsen the situation. Thus the possible attainment of these benefits must be considered with great caution:

> Membership of an economic grouping cannot of itself guarantee to a member state or the group a satisfactory economic performance, or even a better performance than in the past. The static gains from integration, although significant, can be – and often are – swamped by the influence of factors of domestic or international origin that have nothing to do with integration. The more fundamental factors influencing a country's economic performance (the dynamic factors) are unlikely to be affected by integration except in the long run. It is clearly not a necessary condition for economic success that a country should be a member of an economic community as the experience of several small countries confirms, although such

countries might have done better as members of a suitable group. Equally, a large integrated market is in itself no guarantee of performance, as the experience of India suggests. However, although integration is clearly no panacea for all economic ills, nor indispensable to success, there are many convincing reasons for supposing that significant economic benefits may be derived from properly conceived arrangements for economic integration. (Robson, 1985)

However, in the case of the EU, one should always keep in mind that the 'founding fathers' had the formation of a United States of Western (hopefully all) Europe as the ultimate goal and that economic integration became the immediate objective so as to facilitate the attainment of political unity via the back door (see Chapter 2). Those who fail to appreciate this will always undermine the EU's serious attempts at the achievement of economic and monetary union via the Maastricht Treaty as the ongoing discussion clearly demonstrates – see Chapter 5.

1.6 Areas of enquiry

The necessary areas of enquiry, emphasizing the economic aspects, are quite apparent now that we have established the nature of the EU. It is necessary to analyse the effects and consequences of the removal of trade impediments between the participating nations and to make an equivalent study of the establishment of the common external relations. These aspects are tackled in Chapters 4 and 6. It is also extremely important to discuss the role of competition and industrial policies and the presence of multinational firms. These aspects are covered in Chapters 8 and 9. Moreover, it is vital to analyse the implications and consequences of a special provision for the CAP (Chapter 10), the fisheries policy (Chapter 11), transport policy (Chapter 12), EMU (Chapter 5), EMS (Chapter 16), the fiscal policy (Chapters 14 and 15), the regional policy (Chapter 17), the energy policy (Chapter 13), the social policy (Chapter 18), factor mobility (Chapter 20), environmental policy (Chapter 19) and external trade and aid policies (Chapters 21 and 22). The book also contains chapters on the development of the EU (Chapter 23) and the future of the EU (Chapter 24) as well as a chapter on the 'economics of the single market' (Chapter 7).

1.7 About this book

This book offers, more or less, a comprehensive but brief coverage of the theoretical issues: trade creation, trade diversion and the Cooper–Massell criticism; the domestic distortions argument; the terms of trade effects; the economies of scale argument. It also offers a fresh look at the different attempts at the economic justification of customs union formation. A full chapter deals with the methodology and results of the measurements of the effects of the EU formation on the member states and the outside world. These are discussed briefly since a comprehensive book on them is available – see El-Agraa (1989a). There is also a full treatment of all major policy considerations – see previous section.

Although chapters on EU political cooperation, distributional problems and political and legal considerations may seem to be absent, these aspects have not been omitted: some elements of political cooperation are discussed in Chapters 2 and 23, while some of the most significant elements of the distribution problem are tackled in the chapters on the role of the EU budget, fiscal harmonization, social policies and regional policies. This does not imply that these aspects are not worthy of separate chapters, as one could in fact argue that these are the most important issues facing the EU. The treatment given to them in this book is such that the significant aspects of these policies are tackled where they are particularly relevant. Moreover, with regard to some of these policies, the EU is not yet certain in which direction it is heading, and this in spite of the adoption and endorsement of the Maastricht Treaty, which specifies certain details. The wider political considerations lie outside our scope.

Appendix: WTO's Article XXIV

Territorial application – frontier traffic – customs unions and free trade areas

1. The provisions of this Agreement shall apply to the metropolitan customs territories of the contracting parties and to any other customs territories in respect of which this Agreement has been accepted under Article XXVI or is being applied under Article XXXIII or pursuant to the Protocol of Provisional Application. Each such customs territory shall, exclusively for the purposes of the territorial application of this Agreement, be treated as though it were a contracting party; *Provided* that the provisions of this paragraph shall not be construed to create any rights or obligations as between two or more customs territories in respect of which this Agreement has been accepted under Article XXVI or is being applied under Article XXXIII or pursuant to the Protocol of Provisional Application by a single contracting party.
2. For the purposes of this Agreement a customs territory shall be understood to mean any territory with respect to which separate tariffs or other regulations of commerce are maintained for a substantial part of the trade of such territory with other territories.
3. The provisions of this Agreement shall not be construed to prevent:
    (a) Advantages accorded by any contracting party to adjacent countries in order to facilitate frontier traffic;
    (b) Advantages accorded to the trade with the Free Territory of Trieste by countries contiguous to that territory, provided that such advantages are not in conflict with the Treaties of Peace arising out of the Second World War.
4. The contracting parties recognize the desirability of increasing freedom of trade by the development, through voluntary agreements, of closer integration between the economies of the countries parties to such agreements. They also recognize that the purpose of a customs union or of a free-trade area should be to facilitate trade between the constituent territories and not to raise barriers to the trade of other contracting parties with such territories.
5. Accordingly, the provisions of this Agreement shall not prevent, as between the territories of contracting parties, the formation of a customs union or of a free-trade area of

the adoption of an interim agreement necessary for the formation of a customs union or of a free-trade area; *Provided* that:

(a) with respect to a customs union, or an interim agreement leading to the formation of a customs union, the duties and other regulations of commerce imposed at the institution of any such union or interim agreement in respect of trade with contracting parties not parties to such union or agreement shall not on the whole be higher or more restrictive than the general incidence of the duties and regulations of commerce applicable in the constituent territories prior to the formation of such union or the adoption of such interim agreement, as the case may be;

(b) with respect to a free-trade area, or an interim agreement leading to the formation of a free-trade area, the duties and other regulations of commerce maintained in each of the constituent territories and applicable at the formation of such free-trade area or the adoption of such interim agreement to the trade of contracting parties not included in such area or not parties to such agreement shall not be higher or more restrictive than the corresponding duties and other regulations of commerce existing in the same constituent territories prior to the formation of the free-trade area, or interim agreement, as the case may be; and

(c) any interim agreement referred to in sub-paragraphs (a) and (b) shall include a plan and schedule for the formation of such a customs union or of such a free-trade area within a reasonable length of time.

6. If, in fulfilling the requirements of sub-paragraph 5(a), a contracting party proposes to increase any rate of duty inconsistently with the provisions of Article II, the procedure set forth in Article XXVIII shall apply. In providing for compensatory adjustment, due account shall be taken of the compensation already afforded by the reductions brought about in the corresponding duty of the other constituents of the union.

7. (a) Any contracting party deciding to enter into a customs union or free-trade area, or an interim agreement leading to the formation of such a union or area, shall promptly notify the CONTRACTING PARTIES and shall make available to them such information regarding the proposed union or area as will enable them to make such reports and recommendations to contracting parties as they may deem appropriate.

(b) If, after having studied the plan and schedule included in an interim agreement referred to in paragraph 5 in consultation with the parties to that agreement and taking due account of the information made available in accordance with the provisions of sub-paragraph (a), the CONTRACTING PARTIES find that such agreement is not likely to result in the formation of a customs union or of a free-trade area within the period contemplated by the parties to the agreement or that such period is not a reasonable one, the CONTRACTING PARTIES shall make recommendations to the parties to the agreement. The parties shall not maintain or put into force, as the case may be, such agreement if they are not prepared to modify it in accordance with these recommendations.

(c) Any substantial change in the plan or schedule referred to in paragraph 5(c) shall be communicated to the CONTRACTING PARITIES, which may request the contracting parties concerned to consult with them if the change seems likely to jeopardize or delay unduly the formation of the customs union or of the free-trade area.

8. For the purposes of this Agreement:

(a) A customs union shall be understood to mean the substitution of a single customs territory for two or more customs territories, so that

(i) duties and other restrictive regulations of commerce (except, where necessary, those permitted under Articles XI, XII, XIII, XIV, XV and XX) are eliminated with respect to substantially all the trade between the constituent territories of the union or at least with respect to substantially all the trade in products originating in such territories, and,

(ii) subject to the provisions of paragraph 9, substantially the same duties and other regulations of commerce are applied by each of the members of the union to the trade territories not included in the union;

(b) A free-trade area shall be understood to mean a group of two or more customs territories in which the duties and other restrictive regulations of commerce (except, where necessary, those permitted under Articles XI, XII, XIII, XIV, XV and XX) are eliminated on substantially all the trade between the constituent territories in products originating in such territories.

9. The preferences referred to in paragraph 2 of Article I shall not be affected by the formation of a customs union or of a free-trade area but may be eliminated or adjusted by means of negotiations with contracting parties affected. This procedure of negotiations with affected contracting parties shall, in particular, apply to the elimination of preferences required to conform with the provisions of paragraph 8(a)(i) and paragraph 8(b).

10. The CONTRACTING PARTIES may by a two-thirds majority approve proposals which do not fully comply with the requirements of paragraphs 5 to 9 inclusive, provided that such proposals lead to the formation of a customs union or a free-trade area in the sense of this Article.

11. Taking into account the exceptional circumstances arising out of the establishment of India and Pakistan as independent States and recognizing the fact that they have long constituted an economic unit, the contracting parties agree that the provisions of this Agreement shall not prevent the two countries from entering into special arrangements with respect to the trade between them, pending the establishment of their mutual trade relations on a definitive basis.

12. Each contracting party shall take such reasonable measures as may be available to it to ensure observance of the provisions of this Agreement by the regional and local governments and authorities within its territory.

part one

Historical, institutional and statistical background

The aim of this section is to provide the reader with a general background to the EU. Chapter 2 gives a short account of the historical development of the EU and describes its institutions and their functioning. Chapter 3 is a general statistical survey of the major economic indicators for members of the EU, but it also provides relevant information concerning the potential members of the EU and compares the state of the fifteen nations plus the potential members with that of Canada, Japan, the United States and the Russian Federation.

chapter two

History and institutions of the EU

C. D. E. COLLINS

2.1 Organizing Western Europe

The European Union (EU) is a unique political institution and this makes it difficult to analyse and understand. The usual political models relate either to nation states, whether unitary or federal, or to traditional international organizations and the Union has elements drawn from all these strands. Furthermore, it is constantly evolving, often in very controversial ways. It is helpful to bear in mind the broader political environment within which the EU operates for this helps to explain many of the disagreements about its internal structure and future development. In the last analysis, the objectives of the Union are political rather than economic and, in the words of the preamble of the Treaty of Rome, are to 'lay the foundations of an ever closer union among the peoples of Europe' and by 'pooling their resources to preserve and strengthen peace and liberty'.

Historically, the aim of political union in western Europe is an old one and although, in the past, it has failed to match the strength of nationalist feelings, beliefs in a common history, culture and destiny have helped to keep alive the view that a common political framework may one day be found. As the Second World War came to an end, the task appeared more urgent for Europe was physically devastated, was too weak to restore itself without aid from the United States of America and was shortly to be divided as the cold war began. Such circumstances made it possible to breach the psychological barriers preventing moves towards greater integration. There have remained, however, divergent views about how to proceed. A major divide soon appeared between those who wished to develop on the basis of very close interstate cooperation and those who wished to take the plunge of moving towards a political entity of a federal nature and the fierce debates of the time, and more recently over the Maastricht Treaty and beyond, reflect the fact that there is still no agreement on a suitable future political shape for western Europe.

It was in 1947 that General Marshall launched the plan of aid from the United States to revitalize the European economy, provided assistance programmes were organized on a continental and not a state basis. The following years saw the creation of the Organization for European Economic Cooperation (OEEC) to control a joint recovery programme and to work for the establishment of freer trade, although this was limited to western Europe only. Its later expansion into the Organization for Economic Cooperation and Development (OECD) brought worldwide membership and this gave expression to the world liberal trading area which forms part of the environment in which the EC (now the EU) has taken root. It continues to be an organization whose views on the activities of member states and the way they handle their economies have considerable influence.

Defence problems demanded special arrangements. The Brussels Treaty of 1948 was a pact of mutual assistance between the United Kingdom, France and the Benelux countries and was neatly balanced in aim between the perpetuation of the wartime alliance against Germany and the realization of a newer threat from the USSR. Recognition of the interdependence of the defence of western Europe and wider defence needs was marked by the signature of the North Atlantic Treaty in 1949 by the Brussels Treaty powers in association with the United States and Canada, Denmark, Iceland, Italy, Norway and Portugal. This move brought a new dimension into European integration by recognizing that western Europe was part of a larger military grouping but kept defence arrangements away from subsequent political and economic developments.

The same period saw yet another attempt to express the unity of Europe with the creation of the Council of Europe in 1949. This body has very broad political and cultural objectives, including the notable contribution of protecting the individual through the Convention for the Protection of Human Rights and Fundamental Freedoms. Its statute expresses a belief in a common political heritage based on accepted spiritual and moral values, political liberty, the rule of law and the maintenance of democratic forms of government. The Council of Europe was able to obtain wide support in western Europe but it contained no real drive towards unification. It was impatience with this omission that led activists to try a new approach which was to result in the setting up of three European Communities and it was not long before an opportunity arose.

The establishment of a working relationship between the western alliance and West Germany was becoming urgent. The old Germany was now, in practice, divided but the western half was not accepted as a fully independent state. However, West Germany's economic recovery had begun and with the onset of the cold war it was needed as a contributor to the defence and prosperity of the west. A way had therefore to be found to re-establish West Germany without arousing the fears of its recent enemies and, in particular, of France.

The beauty of the proposal for the European Coal and Steel Community (ECSC) was its ability to appeal to many interests. It seemed rational to treat the coal and steel industries of the area as a single whole; greater efficiency and control of war-making capacity would thus be gained and it would be physically impossible for France and Germany to go to war with each other again. It was to be the first stone in the sound and practical foundation of a united Europe creating a base for economic unity under the guidance of a strong executive. Integration was here founded on a sectoral approach allowing for functional integration based on the belief that common solutions could be found for common problems. This approach, so different from classical diplomacy, formed the basis of what was to become known as the Community method. The ECSC was rapidly launched and, at any rate initially, appeared to work well so it was not long before a new project was launched based upon the same approach.

The outbreak of the Korean war in 1950 resulted in American pressure on the west Europeans to do more to defend themselves against possible Soviet attack. This raised the issue of a military contribution from West Germany. Since the situation bore some resemblance to that which had made the launching of the ECSC possible, a similar attempt was made. The proposal was for a European Defence Community (EDC) and the six members of the ECSC initialled a treaty in 1952. As before, the EDC was intended to kill several birds with one stone. It would be a further move to attach West Germany and the Germans to the West, in both a political and a psychological sense; it would produce the needed military contribution and it would introduce institutional controls. The novel feature was to be a European army, in which small national units would be merged into an integrated force which, in turn, would be subordinated to the NATO command. The whole structure bore a striking similarity to the ECSC arrangements.

However, it required a further element. A unified army made no sense if member states went their own ways in foreign policy or controlled their own defence efforts and a method of democratic control over the army would need to be found. Almost inevitably, therefore, the project had to be enlarged with a proposal for a parallel European political authority whose institutions would ultimately absorb those of the ECSC and EDC and which would push forward towards more general economic integration.

The project was larger and more sensitive than the ECSC and it failed to be accepted with the result that the next move in European integration, the European Economic Community (EEC), steered very clear of foreign and defence policy and even under the Maastricht terms these remain apart from the Community structures (see section 2.5). Meanwhile alternative solutions to immediate problems had to be found. The Brussels Treaty Organization was merged into a new body, the Western European Union; West Germany and Italy became members of WEU and it was agreed that West Germany should become a member of NATO (Italy was already a member). Other measures were agreed to clear up the aftermath of the Second World War and so, although formally the cause of European unity had received a setback, a line had been drawn under the past, means found whereby West Germany could become a full member of the western community and the states of the area could concentrate upon the future.

A new attempt at integration was soon made and in June 1955 the foreign ministers of the six ECSC countries met at Messina. They discussed the possibility of pursuing general integration but also the idea of creating further functional organizations for transport and for the peaceful exploitation of atomic energy. Although general integration was seen as the way towards political unity this goal was not unduly stressed for fear of running into further antagonism so it became an aspiration, relegated to a distant future. The meeting set up an intergovernmental committee under the chairmanship of Paul-Henri Spaak, then Foreign Minister of Belgium, and this committee produced the blueprint which was to form the Treaty of Rome creating the European Economic Community. A second Treaty of Rome set up Euratom but the proposed transport community was not adopted.

Underlying the detail of the report is a vision of a revitalized western Europe, able to deal on equal terms with the superpowers and to influence world events. It looked for ways of liberating the abilities of the European people and of improving the foundations of European society. The chosen method was to be the setting up of a common market to provide the necessary productive base; this would require some collective measures, broadly common economic policy to ensure economic expansion and higher living standards and measures to utilize, and develop, European resources, including labour reserves. The resulting treaty contained the necessary detail with a heavy emphasis upon the measures immediately required to create the common market but leaving a great deal to be decided in the future as the project unfolded. It was thus necessary for the new organization to have a general capacity to act. The treaty also set up the necessary institutions but these were politically cautious in their powers and it was generally held that the new organization was less supranational than the ECSC. Partly this reflected a change of mood, partly an unwillingness to run into more political controversy and partly a realization that the task of integrating whole economies was larger, more difficult and uncertain, than handling a single sector. The price paid for the new venture was therefore caution in the political sphere and the institutions of the EEC left a great deal of power to the member states. It provided, however, a unique cooperative framework in which the clash of national interests could occur without being pushed to the point of mutual destruction. Unless they wished to break the edifice, member states were forced to find agreement.

2.2 The development of the EC

The EEC (which later adopted the title European Community to embrace the work of the three Communities) created a special set of institutions to handle its affairs. These centred on a Council of Ministers and a Commission, backed by a Parliament and a Court of Justice (see section 2.4). By the 1970s, however, it was clear that the EC needed institutional strengthening. The early tasks laid down in the Treaty of Rome had been completed, further internal objectives had to be formulated and a way found to ensure that the EC could act more effectively on the international stage. The result was to bring national political leaders more closely into EC affairs by the introduction of summit meetings. These were formalized under the name of the European Council in 1974 but the first major summit meeting was in 1969 when member states agreed that they were now so interdependent that they had no choice but to continue with the EC. This decision provided the necessary political will to reach agreement on the development of the common agricultural policy (CAP), on budgetary changes and, most importantly, on the need to work for enlargement. At the time, this meant settling the question of relations with the United Kingdom which had vexed the EC from the beginning.

Additionally, it was recognized that the EC needed institutional development to match its growing international stature. Its existing international responsibilities neither matched its economic weight nor allowed effective consideration of the political aspects of external economic relations. Individual members still conducted most of their external affairs themselves and could easily cut across EC interests and this was apart from the issue of whether the EC should begin to move into the field of wider foreign affairs. Since member states had very different interests, and often different views on relations with the United States of America, with the USSR and on defence, it was clear that the EC was not ready to take over full competences. However, the foreign ministers were asked to study the means of achieving further political integration, on the assumption of enlargement, and to present a report. As a result, the EC began, in a gingerly fashion, to move into political cooperation with an emphasis on foreign affairs. This did not lead to a common foreign policy but it did mean efforts to identify common aims and it led to further institutional innovation alongside the institutions of the EC rather than as part of them although old and new gradually came closer together.

A second landmark summit meeting was held in 1972 and attended by three new members, Denmark, Ireland and the United Kingdom. It devoted considerable attention to internal affairs and notably to the need to strengthen the social and regional aims of the EC as part of an ambitious programme designed to lead to a full European Union. It also saw a continuing need to act externally to maintain a constructive dialogue with the United States, Canada and Japan and for member states to make a concerted contribution to the Conference on Security and Cooperation in Europe. Foreign ministers were to meet more frequently to discuss this last issue. This meeting marked the realization that heads of governments would have to meet more frequently than in the past. At first sight this seemed to strengthen the intergovernmental structure of the EC at the expense of the supranational element but this was not really so. Rather it showed that the future was a joint one, that the international climate was changing and often bleak and that, if members dealt with their internal economic difficulties alone, then this could undermine the efforts of the EC to strengthen the economies. Informal discussion of general issues, whether economic or political, domestic or worldwide, was a necessary preliminary to action which often seemed stronger if it were to be EC based. Through the summit meetings and the political cooperation procedure (EPC) the subject matter coming to the EC steadily enlarged.

By the 1980s it was clear that the political and economic environment in which the EC operated was changing fast. Tumultuous events in the previous Soviet Union and the countries of the Warsaw pact threw the institutional arrangements of western Europe into disarray and brought the need to reassess defence requirements, the role of NATO and the continuance of the American defence presence. The unsolved issue of whether the EC needed a foreign and defence policy, or at least some halfway house towards one, was bound to be raised once more. Meanwhile, the economic base upon which the EC had been able to develop had become much more uncertain. Recession, slow growth, industrial change, higher unemployment and worries about European competitiveness undermined previous confidence.

The twin issues of constitutional development and institutional reform continued to exercise EC circles but little progress was possible and the EC seemed to be running out of steam. The deepening of the integrative process required action which governments found controversial and the new members, now including Greece, Spain and Portugal, inevitably made for a less cohesive group while the recession hardened national attitudes towards the necessary give and take required for cooperative solutions. EC finances were constrained with the result that new policies could not be developed and this, in turn, led to bitter arguments about the resources devoted to the CAP. Internal divisions were compounded by fears of a lack of dynamism in the EC economy threatening a relative decline in world terms. Such worries suggested that a significant leap forward was required to ensure a real common market, to encourage new growth and at the same time to modernize the institutions of the EC.

As the debate progressed, a major division emerged between those who were primarily interested in the political ideal of political union and who wished to develop the EC institutions accordingly and those, more pragmatic in approach, who stressed the need for new policies. It was not until December 1985 that the lines of agreement could be settled. These were brought together in the Single European Act (SEA) which became operative on 1 July 1987. The key policy development was to establish a true single market by the end of 1992 with free movement of capital, labour, services and goods. This was supported by other policy goals including responsibilities towards the environment, more encouragement of health and safety at work, technological research and development and cooperation in economic and monetary policy. The SEA also accepted that a policy of economic and social cohesion would be required to help the weaker states to develop so that they could participate fully in the single market. Foreign policy cooperation was brought more closely into the mainstream and given a stronger support structure. Institutionally, it was agreed that the Council of Ministers should take decisions by qualified majority vote in relation to the internal market, research, cohesion and improved working conditions and that, in such cases, Parliament should share in decision making.

The single market provided a goal for the next few years and the EC busied itself with the necessary preparation, giving evidence of its ability to work as a unit. But it brought new complications. It raised the question of how much power should be held by the EC institutions, presented member states with heavy internal programmes to complete the changes necessary for the single market and exposed the very different economic conditions in member states which were bound to affect their fortunes in the single market. Meanwhile the unification of Germany fundamentally changed its position within the EC by giving it more political and economic weight but at the same time it was required to expend considerable effort eastwards.

A further challenge of the time came from new bids for membership. (So far there has been one withdrawal. The position of Greenland was renegotiated in 1984 but it remains associated and has a special agreement to regulate mutual fishing interests.) The single market policy finally convinced the doubters in western Europe that they should try to join. This was both a triumph and an embarrassment for the EC in that it was preoccupied with its own internal changes and a belief that it had not yet fully come to terms with the southern enlargement which had brought in Greece, Spain and Portugal. An uncertain reaction was shown in that some member states wished to press on with enlargement as a priority while others wished to complete the single market and to tighten internal policies before opening the doors. A closer economic relationship was negotiated between the EC and the EFTA countries other than Switzerland (i.e. Austria, Sweden, Finland, Norway, Iceland, Lichtenstein) to form a European Economic Area and this was assumed to be a preliminary step towards membership, a step taken in 1995 by Austria, Sweden and Finland. Ten states from central and eastern Europe have now put in formal applications (Czech Republic, Hungary, Poland, Slovenia, Estonia, Lithuania, Latvia, Slovakia, Bulgaria and Romania). Of this group, the first three are likely to succeed first, probably in the early years of the next century. Cyprus and Malta applied in 1990 but the latter has since said that it prefers a form of close association while Switzerland has never formally withdrawn the application it made some years ago. Turkey has a longstanding association agreement but the EU remains reluctant to go further with it.

It is not easy to generalize about the issues involved in admitting such a variety of states to membership. The EU has a series of agreements with applicants through which it provides aid and advice on development and reform. In particular, it is looking for economic reform, the development of democratic political institutions and the protection of minority and human rights as necessary preconditions for closer relationships with the EU and, finally, full membership. Partnership and co-operation agreements with Russia and the newly independent states exist also but have no membership goal.

Clearly, an organization with such a large and varied membership would be very different from the original EEC of six and the applications challenge received wisdom as to its nature. They necessarily demand institutional change as it is accepted that the major institutions will become unworkable with such large numbers and this is one reason why pursuing the question of enlargement was made consequent upon the finalizing of the Maastricht Treaty and agreement upon new financial and budgetary arrangements for the existing members. Continuing issues about defence and the appropriate reaction to conditions in central and eastern Europe, the war with Iraq and the collapse of Yugoslavia all suggested that further consideration of foreign and defence capabilities was important.

It was, therefore, against a troubled background that the EC set up two intergovernmental conferences to prepare the way for a meeting of the European Council at Maastricht in December 1991 which produced a new blueprint for the future. It aimed to integrate the EC further through setting out a timetable for full economic and monetary union, introduced institutional changes and developed political competences, the whole being brought together in a Treaty on European Union of which the Economic Community should form a part. It is not surprising that the ratification process, for which not a great deal of time was allowed, produced furious argument across western Europe. Although each nation had its own particular worries, a general characteristic which the treaty made obvious was the width of the gap between political elites and the voters in modern society. Although political leaders rapidly expressed contrition that they had failed to provide adequate explanation for their moves they seemed less able to accept that there were strong doubts about many of the proposed new arrangements as being the best way forward and that a period of calm thinking, with less frenetic development, might in the end serve the EC and its people better.

2.3 The European Union

The EC was originally set up as three separate entities but with some sharing of institutions. Although there are some differences of legal competences, it became convenient to consider the ECSC, Euratom and EEC as branches of the same whole and, in this, the EEC became the dominant partner. Since 1965, when a merger treaty was passed, it has seemed more logical to refer to the whole structure as the European Community (EC) whose main constitutional base was the Treaty of Rome creating the EEC. The basic treaties have steadily become overlain with later texts, the most important of which are incorporated in treaties which must be ratified by each member state in accordance with its own legal processes. Thus changes in budget procedures, agreements to admit new members and the single market policy have all formed the subject of special treaty instruments. Overlying these is the Treaty on European Union agreed at Maastricht in December 1991, the final version being signed by the foreign ministers in February 1992. Fourteen signatories were bound by an attached agreement and protocol on social policy (Chapter 18). In addition to the treaties, there is a host of secondary legislation resulting from the decisions taken under the treaties and the rulings of the Court of Justice and all together they form the constitution of the EU. The EC forms the most developed section of the Union and its legislation takes precedence over national decisions in the appropriate field. A moment's reflection will show that this is a necessary precondition for the EC to work at all; it would otherwise be impossible to create a single economic unit, to establish the confidence necessary between the members or to handle external economic relations.

The Treaty on European Union, which is a complicated document, can perhaps be best understood as a treaty with five sections. The first sets out the principles of the European Union (EU) and the second is concerned with amendments to the EEC, ECSC and Euratom treaties. In the course of amendment, the treaty formally accepts the name of the European Community, thus signalling an increased importance for non-economic functions. Thirdly, it develops EPC by introducing provisions for a common foreign and security policy and, fourthly, lays down the aims and procedures for cooperation in the fields of justice and home affairs. It is very important to note that both these sections are based on the principle of inter-state cooperation and are not brought directly under the same procedures as those for the EC itself. This explains why the treaty is often referred to as being built on three pillars, the EC proper and cooperation in foreign and judicial affairs. However, the last two form an integral part of the treaty, their work is coordinated by the main EC institutions, notably the Council of Ministers and the Commission, and the possibility of drawing some judicial and home affairs functions into the main working of the EC remains open. Fifthly, there are a number of provisions dealing with miscellaneous matters. Finally, there are 17 protocols and 33 declarations attached to the treaty. Although it is not possible to classify the questions covered in the last two groups, some of them contain important principles on running the Union.

The complexity of the structure itself suggests that the treaty represents a fundamental step, taking the EU significantly down the road to statehood although it has not yet arrived. It represents an uneasy balance between the two opposing views on how to organize western Europe which have been so eloquently expressed since the end of the Second World War. It can be thought of as the penultimate step towards a federal Europe but also as a means of checking this drive by keeping certain essential functions outside the competence of the Community institutions and under the control of national governments. Only the future can say whether one of these drives will eventually prevail or whether a stable balance between them can be found. A further intergovernmental conference held in June 1997 brought minor integrative and institutional changes embodied in the Treaty of Amsterdam which was signed in June 1997 and published in October 1997.

The European Union (EU) has broad objectives. It promotes economic and social progress, an aim which includes the abolition of internal frontiers, better economic and social cohesion, an economic and monetary union and a single currency. It wishes to assert an international identity through a common foreign and defence policy, it introduces a formal union citizenship and close cooperation in justice and home affairs and it maintains, and builds upon, the *acquis communautaire* (i.e. the achievements to date). An overarching institutional framework is intended to ensure some consistency between the many different branches; the treaty modifies the balance of power between the Council of Ministers, European Commission and European Parliament as well as that between the Community and the member states in favour of the former. The European Council, which brings together the heads of state or government, is recognized as a source of impetus and of policy guidelines but it has to report to Parliament thus providing some check on a possible tendency to represent national, rather than Community, views (EU Treaty Article D).

The objectives of the Community are now more broadly defined than before, some are firmed up and some appear for the first time although not necessarily as matters for an exclusive competence. In addition to the economic objectives relating to the internal market and agricultural and transport objectives, the aims of economic and social cohesion, of an environmental policy and of greater scope for the European Social Fund were added while in 1997 the Amsterdam conference agreed that a new emphasis should be given to employment as a treaty goal and that the essential commitment to the basic principles of liberty, human rights and the rule of law should be given new stress. The need for greater competitiveness for Community industry, the promotion of R&D, the construction of trans-European infrastructure, the attainment of a high level of health protection, better education, training and cultural development all find their place. Recognition is given to development policies, consumer protection and measures in energy policy, consumer protection and tourism.

A new arrangement was set up in 1997 to allow for the further development of policies. A group of states will be able to join together for a special goal, provided that it does not adversely affect the operation of the single market or other existing policies and which can be agreed by a qualified majority vote in the Council among participating states. This can later be vetoed by a dissenting state whose national interests would be badly damaged so that the European Council may look at the matter afresh. This is an attempt to meet ideas of 'flexible integration' whereby states keenest on greater unity are not constantly thwarted but there is much room for dissent inherent in this arrangement.

The Maastricht enlargement of powers touched fears of the creation of a super-state and there is a general stress in the treaty on the importance of respecting national identities and the fundamental rights of persons as well as on the principle of subsidiarity. It is obvious that, as the Community increases its power, some clarification of function between it and the member states is essential but a good deal more work will be needed before the principle of subsidiarity can be said to have clarified the position. Article 3b asserts that, in areas which do not fall within its exclusive competence, the EC shall act only as far as it is necessary to achieve the objective, either because member states cannot do so adequately or because the scale and effects would be such that the EC can achieve the objects more effectively. Unfortunately, this leaves wide open for continuing argument whether the EC would indeed do the job better, provides no protection against a move to give the EC more powers and gives no guidance on how the EC should proceed in matters where it already possesses exclusive competence. It is not so much a legal check upon centralizing tendencies as a well-intentioned effort to provide reassurance that the EC will 'play fair'. At Edinburgh, in December 1992, the heads of state or government adopted further guidelines on the working of the principle while further clarification was sought in 1997 in the form of a new protocol for the Amsterdam Treaty. This spells out in considerable detail how the principle should be applied by the Community institutions. The difficulty is always to provide rules governing the use of EC powers and thus to prevent an insidious slippage of power in a direction which has never been consciously agreed. Another check is that member states should be able to bring a case in the European Court of Justice (ECJ) arguing that the EC is extending its powers unjustifiably but it is clear that the last word has not been said on the vexed questions of the relationship between member states and the central institutions and of their respective competences.

An element in the debate about subsidiarity is doubt concerning the remoteness of decision taking in Brussels, the need to make the Community more responsive to the needs of the general public and more sensitive to the effects of the intrusiveness that EC legislation appears to bring. A particular issue is the undermining of national parliaments, especially those which have an important legislative function and which have found it hard to find ways of exercising control over the EC. In practice, they have been limited to scrutiny of proposals which, once they are in an advanced stage, are very difficult to change. Some efforts have also been made, through scrutiny committees, to discuss general issues, thus helping to suggest policy positions for the future, while Denmark, in particular, has tried to define the parameters within which ministers may negotiate. The 'democratic deficit' has been discussed for many years and steps were taken at Maastricht to diminish it. The European Parliament (EP) was given more power, a Declaration was attached calling for a greater involvement of national parliaments through better contacts with the EP and a conference of parliaments was held to discuss the main features of the EU while the general decision-making function was to become more open by providing the public with more information. The right of individuals to petition the EP was buttressed by the establishment of an Ombudsman, appointed by the EP but independent in investigations. A further change, directly affecting individuals, was to confer the citizenship of the Union on the nationals of member states (see Chapter 18). The Amsterdam conference recognized that individuals need a right of access to documents and brought some timetable changes for the taking of decisions which are intended to give better opportunities for national parliaments to consider Union issues. It accepted, too, that the quality of drafting of legislation must be improved. Such changes are intended to encourage a greater openness in decision making but it will take time for them to be implemented. Actual decision taking in the Council of Ministers will, however, remain private.

2.4 The European institutions

The institutions of the Union have their functions under the respective sections of the treaties but their most comprehensive use is under the first pillar which deals with the work of the European Community and the institutions are therefore explained within this context. However, in the Maastricht Treaty, the *European Council* was given a formal status and directed to provide the impetus for development and political guidance for the Union as a whole. The working institutions operate on a *modus vivendi* which has developed over the years which enables business to be carried on. In practice, tensions exist which can develop into a power struggle between them as happens between national governments and the Union itself. A critical example was the conflict between the Council and the Commission in 1965–6 which curbed the development of the Commission's powers and another period of difficulty appeared in the late 1970s when the Parliament tried to obtain greater power, especially over the budget. Both episodes contributed to periods of political stagnation and led to uneasy compromises.

Formally, a Community decision results in a regulation, directive, a decision, a recommendation or an opinion. A *regulation* is generally and directly applicable as it stands, a *directive* is binding in objective on the member states but not in method of achievement and a *decision* is binding on those to whom it is addressed while *recommendations* and *opinions* have no binding force (Article 189). These formal acts, notably the regulations and directives, are constantly adding to EC law. Decisions normally emanate from the Council of Ministers which decides the issue on procedures as laid down for the particular subject matter. Before reaching this stage, however, a complex process has been undertaken.

The Council of Ministers consists of representatives of member governments. Its decisions are taken by unanimous, simple or qualified majority voting and, when the last method is used, the votes are weighted so that at least some of the smaller members must assent. It is thereby hoped to arrive at a decision supported by a wide spectrum of opinion. The original intention was for the Council to move towards the use of majority voting and, although this has happened, it has been a slow and bumpy ride. The SEA extended the use of qualified majority voting (QMV) to a wide range of decisions relating to the completion of the single market, research and development and the improvement of working conditions and the EU and Amsterdam treaties go even further along this road. Nevertheless, some matters remain subject to the unanimity rule. These include treaty amendments, the accession of new members, the future extension of citizen's rights, the principles of foreign policy and the possibility of permitting derogations. Unanimity also comes into play, along with absolute majority, in some procedural mechanisms for reaching final conclusions on proposals as they pass between Council, Parliament and Commission. However, the broad flow of policy now comes under QMV.

The Commission also attends Council meetings and plays an active part in helping to reach a decision, although it has no voting rights. It is here, however, that it can perform an important mediatory function between national viewpoints and its own, which is intended to represent the general community interest.

The presidency of the Council is held by each member state in turn for a six month period and the chairmanship of the many committees alters correspondingly. To achieve continuity, a troika of the immediate past, present and immediate future presidents also meets. It has become the practice for each member state to try to establish a particular style of working and to single out certain matters to which it wishes to give priority. Since any chairman can influence business significantly, the president may occupy an important, albeit temporary, role. The president also fulfils some representational functions both towards other EC institutions, notably the European Parliament, and in external negotiations where the presidents of the Council and Commission may act in association.

Membership of the Council varies according to the subject matter under review and this growth has brought its own problems at home. As Community issues are handled by various ministers, briefed by their own civil servants, so it becomes harder for any government to see its European policy as a coherent whole. In turn, coordination within the government machine becomes important. For the Community, too, the greater specialization of business creates difficulties for it has become far harder to negotiate a package deal whereby a set of decisions can be agreed and each member has gains to set off against its losses although the European Council may act in this way.

The Council has its own secretariat and is also supported by a most important body, the *Committee of Permanent Representatives* (COREPER). Members of this committee, drawn from national administrations, are of ambassadorial rank and are the pinnacle of a structure of specialist and subordinate committees, often including members of home departments who travel to Brussels as required. COREPER prepares Council meetings and handles a great deal of work on behalf of the Council. It serves as an essential link between national bureaucracies, is in touch with the Commission during the process of formulating an intended proposal and is, in practice, involved in all major stages of policy making, ranging from early discussion to final Council decision taking. Many policy matters are, in reality, agreed by COREPER and reach the Council of Ministers only in a formal sense.

While this is one way of keeping business down to manageable proportions, it has meant that the Council itself has become concerned only with the most important matters or those which may not be of great substance but are nevertheless politically sensitive. This has encouraged domestic media to present Council meetings as national battles in which there has to be victory or defeat and politicians, too, have become extremely adept at using publicity to rally support to their point of view. As a result, the effect has become the opposite of that originally intended when it was thought that the experience of working together would make it progressively easier to find an answer expressive of the general good and for which majority voting would be a suitable tool. Instead, conflict of national interests is often a better description. Practical problems, too, are encountered by the Council. The great press of business, the fact that ministers can only attend to Council business part time, the highly sensitive nature of their activities and the larger number of members all contribute to a grave time lag in reaching policy decisions and the move towards QMV to settle matters relating to the single market was one measure designed to overcome this difficulty.

The Council is charged with the coordination of general economic policies of the members and as power is transferred to the Community from the states, as in the establishment of economic and monetary union, so its powers must grow. The EU treaty has also given it power to fine member states or to impose other sanctions with regard to government deficits (Article 104(c)11). These measures suggest it is gaining in power *vis-à-vis* member states but, on the other hand, it is more circumscribed in other directions by the growing powers of the European Parliament.

The second essential element in the making of EC policy is the *Commission*. This consists of twenty members, all nationals of the fifteen member states and chosen on the grounds of competence and capacity to act independently in the interest of the EC itself. They are thus charged not to take instructions from governments. They do, however, need to be people familiar with the political scene, able to meet senior politicians on equal terms, for without this stature and ability to understand political pressures they would lose the senses of touch and timing which are essential for effective functioning. A few women have achieved Commissioner rank but it remains largely a male preserve as do the top levels of the Commission's staff although efforts are being made to change this imbalance.

France, Germany, Italy, Spain and the United Kingdom have two members each; the remaining states have one each. It has been known for some time that the Commission is too large a body for its tasks, a problem which enlargement will exacerbate, and a number of ideas exist for getting round this difficulty such as senior and junior commissioners or shared portfolios. National pride stands in the way of reform. The latest agreement is that, at the time of the first enlargement after 1997, the major powers should lose their second Commissioner in exchange for a changed weighting of votes in the Council of Ministers in order to represent better their population strengths. Should the next enlargement cover more than five states, or at the time of the second post-1997 enlargement, then a wholesale reorganization is intended.

A new-style Commission took office in January 1995. Tenure now extends to five years and the period coincides with the life of the European Parliament; governments continue to appoint the president of the Commission by common accord but consult the Parliament about the decision. After 1997, Parliament will have to approve the nomination. Governments then, in consultation with the presidential nominee, nominate the other members of the Commission. The whole team must be approved by the European Parliament before being formally confirmed in office. The procedures have enhanced Parliament's powers considerably since it can satisfy itself about the Commission's programme and intended initiatives before giving its approval.

Each Commissioner has responsibility for one, or more, major areas of EC policy and, although in form the Commission is a collegiate body accepting responsibility as a group, in practice policy rests mainly with the responsible Commissioner, perhaps in association with two or more colleagues. Adoption by the full Commission is often a formality but, unlike the Council, it has always used majority voting and no other method would enable it to get through the volume of work. At all stages of its work, it consults closely with the Council and is further developing its working relationships with the Parliament.

The Commissioners are supported in two ways. Each Commissioner has a private office, under a *chef de cabinet*, and these officers take many decisions on behalf of their chiefs. Secondly, there is the Commission staff itself. This is organized into *general directorates* corresponding to the main areas of EC policy. In total there are about fifteen thousand civil servants of whom about 15% are necessary because of the heavy linguistic burden resulting from the use of eleven official EC languages. Often the work of the Commission seems rather slow but integrating the detail of national economies and undertaking the necessary consultations and translations are time consuming. Although the directorates are staffed by various nationalities, it is important to try to ensure that no one national viewpoint predominates, especially amongst the more senior staff. Over time, some directorates have acquired greater prestige than others; not surprisingly, those that deal with core Community policies count for most and, as the EC has developed, so the possibility of conflict between directorates over policy matters can arise. Competition and regional policy, Third World imports and agricultural policy are obvious examples. A fundamental internal reorganization of the Commission is intended for the future.

The directorates are responsible for the initiation of proposals leading to a formal Commission proposal and they also administer agreed policy. The significance of this varies since a great deal of EC policy is administered nationally with the Commission employed more in monitoring and evaluation. Competition policy, however, requires direct contact with individual firms as do some functions relating to the coal and steel industries.

In recent years, the Commission has become more involved with the operation of the structural funds. It has considerable discretion in the allocation of monies, within broad guidelines, and has a series of advisory committees to assist it. Grants go through national administrations and there is close contact with them and with lesser authorities over planning programmes and deciding which schemes will fit in best with the overall framework.

The implementation of the single market inevitably meant an active role for the Commission which began a heavy programme of harmonizing directives and other legislation. This has led to considerable unease, not just on the part of national governments who are constantly being asked to change established rules and see power slipping away. The European Parliament and politically concerned groups also worry about the Commission's lack of accountability and the difficulty of keeping abreast of its activities. The new arrangements brought by the EU treaty for the EC to work on the principle of subsidiarity and for the EP to share in the appointment of Commissioners were one response to these fears.

An important function of the Commission is to ensure that the members abide by their obligations or, as it is normally described, to act as the guardian of the treaties. It is essential that the rules are actively, and correctly, applied in member states or mutual confidence in the edifice will begin to slip. In many cases, keeping states and firms up to the mark results simply from day to day business and normal liaison but there are occasions when more formal steps are necessary. The Commission can investigate a suspected breach of obligation and issue a *reasoned opinion*. If matters are not set right, the Commission may refer the matter to the Court of Justice and this may, ultimately, lead to a fine (Article 171(2)). Although the Commission has few direct sanctions, it has the power to fine firms which breach certain operational rules while member states have, so far, generally accepted their obligation to abide by EC rules. Recent evidence has suggested that states are beginning to resist implementation, and there has been considerable slippage on matters relating to the single market which has increased the argument that it would be better if the EC did less.

Considerable interest attaches to the functions of the Commission as initiator of policy and exponent of the EC interest. These responsibilities explain why it is the Commission which must initiate the policy proposals which go to the Council for decision (but see below for Parliament's role). Thus the working of the EU largely depends on the activity of the Commission and the quality of its work. With the need to develop a range of policies the Commission's role is crucial. However, in working out its proposals, the Commission is subject to a number of influences. It has to take Parliament's view into account while the regular meetings of the European Council provide broad guidelines for policy. In preparing a proposal, the appropriate directorate undertakes extensive discussions with COREPER, government departments and representatives of interested firms and other groups. It carries out, or more frequently commissions, initial studies and all this knowledge will contribute to a Commission proposal which will be further discussed by the European Parliament, the Economic and Social Committee and the Committee on the Regions after which it will probably be amended. These extensive and lengthy discussions, taken both before and after a proposal is formalized, are part of a process designed to obtain the highest level of agreement and acceptability to member states and, at the same time, to enhance the process of European integration.

To sum up, the Commission has a number of responsibilities. Some are executive in nature but its functions extend to the initiation of policy, the protection of EU interests, the mediation between national interests and the protection of the treaty structure. It also has the power to raise loans for agreed purposes. Thus the Commission cannot be equated with any equivalent national body. At one time it was thought that the Commission might simply become an organization for implementing decisions of the Council but its powers and its links with Parliament prevent this happening. While the EU Treaty, by increasing the powers of Parliament, seems to curtail those of the Commission, it has a new position in the pillars for a common foreign and security policy (CFSP) and judicial and home affairs (JHA) and thus it seems bound to remain as the driving force for change and development.

The *Court of Justice* is an integral part of the institutional structure. The Community is a highly complex body, created by treaties which lay down the operating rules for the various institutions and the basic rules for economic integration but which can also introduce general ideas for later clarification by the Court. Thus it is necessary for several reasons. It must ensure that the institutions act constitutionally, fulfilling their treaty obligations, but it must also help to ensure the observance of an ever-growing volume of EU rules by member states, firms and individuals. This is not just a matter of pronouncing upon any possible infringements of the EU legal system, although these may range from neglecting to implement a rule to slow and lax administration. It includes the need to guide national courts in their interpretation of EU law. A uniform application of the law is a slow business and difficult to achieve since it has to be incorporated into fifteen legal systems, each with its own norms and methods of work. The difficulty is compounded since EU rules often operate alongside national ones where responsibilities are shared. It is not surprising that a great many Court cases arise from policies for agriculture, competition and social security for migrants where states have their own pre-existing policies and national and EU interests overlap.

The Court consists of fifteen judges and nine advocates-general, the latter being responsible for preliminary investigation and for submitting a reasoned opinion to the Court to help it to come to a decision. In its method of working, the Court is heavily influenced by the legal systems of the members and particularly of the original six. It will hear cases brought by a Community institution, member state or directly concerned individual against the decisions of a Community institution or a national government which are thought incompatible with Community law, including a failure to act. It may impose penalties for infringements. States agreed they would abide by the decisions and the fact that, in practice, they mainly do so is an important factor in maintaining the validity of the system.

As the EC developed, the Court became worried about its ability to keep up and a backlog of cases developed. It is important that there should be no serious delay in making judgements since large business and commercial decisions may be at stake and the single market could be prejudiced if firms do not know where they stand. Similarly, if the Court delays, national courts will become chary of seeking rulings and will go their own way in interpreting the rules. The SEA, therefore, allowed for the setting up of a *Court of First Instance* to handle cases on the business side, including competition policy, together with staff cases and subject to a right of appeal. The EU treaty also introduced the notion of a chamber of judges to deal with particular categories of cases and allows the Council to increase the number of judges if the Court so wishes (Article 165).

The EU Treaty did not greatly change the powers of the ECJ and it was excluded from the EU common provisions, CFSP and JHA (apart from one special case). However, its remit will enlarge in the future as more JHA matters pass to the control of the Community institutions as was agreed in 1997. It does now have power to fine a member state in some circumstances and Parliament's right to bring actions against the Council and Commission has been extended.

A relatively young institution is the *Court of Auditors* which the EU Treaty established as a major Community institution. It resulted from growing demands, notably from Parliament, for better external auditing of the budget and its clarification. Its work includes investigating the operations carried out in member states, pronouncing upon their effectiveness and publishing a report on its work in the Official Journal. Its influence grows along with EC business. Some concern exists about the fraudulent use of Community funds and member states are expected to tighten up their control measures.

It is now time to turn to the place of the *European Parliament* (EP) whose powers have steadily, but slowly, grown over the years. It has also become more adroit at exploiting its powers to gain a stronger position. A prime function is, of course, as a debating chamber and annual reports are submitted to it by the other major institutions for this purpose. Much detailed work on matters of interest, and on legislative proposals, is carried out through a committee system and the EP formulates its views through debates on the Committee reports. An important function is exercised in relation to the Commission especially since the EU Treaty made the appointments of President and Commission subject to Parliamentary approval. It has always had a formal control mechanism in the right to dismiss the whole Commission; this has been considered as rather impractical as it would bring the Community process to a halt but votes of censure have been used occasionally to express strong disapproval of a policy line. It is possible to imagine that this may be used more readily now that the EP can influence the composition of any re-appointed Commission. Parliament has also become better in the use of its power to ask questions, both verbally and in writing, as a means of keeping the Council and Commission up to the mark. Foreign policy discussions are held with the foreign ministers by the Political Committee and this work is also subject to question time.

It has the right to set up committees of inquiry and to appoint an Ombudsman and may be petitioned by any EU citizen or other resident. It must also draw up proposals for a uniform procedure for the electoral process which the Council is to recommend to members for adoption. Finding a solution to this problem has exercised the EC for many years and the anomalies extend to include severe imbalances of size and population between constituencies. A Declaration attached to the EU Treaty asked for changes in seat allocations to member states, primarily to allow for an increase in German representation following her unification, but any further enlargement will require more members so there is a case for fundamental re-examination. In 1997, the maximum membership was set at 700 members.

A vexed question has been that of the site of Parliament. Plenaries are divided between Brussels and Strasbourg, most committee work is carried out in Brussels and a large part of the secretariat is based in Luxemburg. This arrangement has been confirmed although a more rational arrangement would ease many practical difficulties and help Parliament to become a more coherent and effective organization.

The European Parliament is remarkable for having achieved the first international election in June 1979 and members (MEPs) are elected every five years. Once elected, MEPs are organized in political, rather than national, groups and the EU Treaty gave formal recognition to parties and their importance to the integrative process (Article 138(a)). However, the groups still often consist of a collection of loosely cooperating national parties rather than forming a single coherent unit. It is important, however, for Parliamentarians to be members of a group since the business of Parliament is conducted through them. There are 626 members in all; 99 for Germany, 87 for France, Italy and the United Kingdom, 64 for Spain, 31 for the Netherlands, 25 for Belgium, Greece and Portugal, 22 for Sweden, 21 for Austria, 16 for Denmark and Finland, 15 for Ireland and 6 for Luxemburg.

Following the 1994 election, the Socialists were returned with the largest number of seats (214) and the European Peoples Party (mainly Christian Democrat) were second with 181. The other groupings are considerably smaller. The Group for Europe has 56 members, the Group of European Liberal, Democrat and Reform Party 43, the Confederal Group of the European United Left has 33, the Green

Group 28, the Group of the European Radical Alliance 20, the Group of Independents for a Europe of Nations 18 and the Non-attached 33.

The key question for the EP has always been its role in the legislative process. The original treaties laid down occasions upon which the EP must be consulted and, in practice, its opinion has been sought on all important issues. It could, nevertheless, be legally disregarded. However, consultation meant that the committees were able to build up close relations with the Commission while working on their reports. An important change came with the SEA which gave the EP a limited, but real, place in the legislative process under the 'cooperation procedure' (Article 189(c)). Decisions eligible for this procedure are taken by the Council on QMV and Parliament may accept, reject or amend this common position. Although there are procedures for reconsideration, ultimately the Council may, by unanimity, override the EP's wishes if they differ from its own. More significantly, the EU Treaty introduced a new procedure of 'co-decision' (Article 189(b)) which covers some very important issues, including the internal market, free movement and establishment, education, culture and public health. The Treaty of Amsterdam intends to add to the list to include elements of social policy, transport, the combating of fraud, statistical matters, public health and the openness of the institutions and also passes a number of existing responsibilities into the co-decision category. The cooperation procedure will rarely be necessary.

Co-decision requires the Council of Ministers to adopt a common position by QMV (or unanimity if appropriate) which the EP can again approve, express no opinion on, reject or amend. The Council may, of course, accept the amendments but, if it rejects the EP's position, a joint conciliation committee comes into play to try to get a text agreeable to both sides. Should it fail then the proposal is lost unless the Council returns to its original position and Parliament fails to veto this latest move. Here, then, Parliament has the last word through a blocking mechanism. It should be noted that, in these complex passages between institutions, timetables for action apply. When the Treaty of Amsterdam is operating, these procedures will be simplified. The Council will always act on QMV under co-decision and the Parliament will accept or reject the common position of the Council in order to transact the increased volume of business more efficiently. Conciliation procedures will still be used.

Two other ways in which the EP has a part to play in the decision-making process are assent and information. The Council may only go forward with assent on the free movement of citizens (Article 8a), on the tasks of the structural funds (Article 130d), on recommending to states a uniform electoral procedure (Article 138(3)) and on some international agreements (Article 228(3)). There are some measures for which the Council must inform Parliament of action taken.

Finally, passing the budget has its own special procedures. Once it had been agreed that the EC should be responsible for its own monies, some degree of parliamentary control was required. A treaty to start the process was signed in 1970, and amended subsequently.

A draft budget is made up by the Commission by September for expenditure the following year. This is then adopted by the Council on QMV and sent to Parliament for discussion. The key to understanding Parliament's budgetary control lies in the distinction between 'compulsory' and 'non-compulsory' expenditure. The former derives from treaty obligations and the bulk has always consisted of CAP expenditure. Compulsory expenditure may be modified in the first instance by a majority of votes cast, but these changes must subsequently be agreed, or rejected, by the Council. Non-compulsory expenditure may be modified by a majority of all members of Parliament but there is a given limit beyond which Parliament may not go. Although the Council may subsequently amend Parliament's decision, the total draft budget must return for a second parliamentary reading and, at this point, Parliament may reject the Council's changes in non-compulsory expenditure. Finally, Parliament is entitled to reject the draft budget entirely and to demand a new one or, alternatively, it must formally approve the final form. Parliament has made full use of the procedural powers thus given to it to try to force changes in budget expenditure.

Once both Council and Parliament had been given budgetary powers, it was necessary to strengthen procedures for consultation between them. Procedural matters are dealt with through the concertation procedure and policy issues through the conciliation procedure, both designed to resolve disagreements through mutual discussion and compromise and to allow for early discussion of proposals likely to give rise to future expenditure.

An innovation in the EU Treaty was to give Parliament the right to ask the Commission to submit a proposal leading to a Community act. This was the first amendment made to the Commission's sole right of initiative and may well produce significant changes in the subject matter of decisions.

Parliament is still in an evolutionary stage and cannot be expected to follow the path of national parliaments which, in any case, differ between themselves. It operates in a different environment and its power struggles, so far, have been with the Council and Commission rather than national parliaments.

A considerable problem for the EC has always been that of keeping in touch with citizens and ensuring they are adequately consulted and informed. Parliament, of course, is one way of making public opinion more aware of EC activity and it is an important channel through which information and knowledge are fed back to member states. Additionally, there is a vast battery of machinery which acts as another link in the communications chain and which plays its part in shaping EC decisions. One of the formal mechanisms is the *Economic and Social Committee*, which has advisory status, and is designed to represent the various categories of economic and social activity such as employers, unions, farmers and the self-employed together with representatives from community and social organizations. It has 222 members, appointed by the Council on the basis of national lists, each member appointed for four years and acting in a personal capacity. In practice, members are considered as coming from three main groups, namely employers, unions and representatives of the general interest and national delegations reflect this tripartite composition. It is usual to seek the opinion of the committee on all major policy proposals and the committee will also formulate its own opinion on subjects it considers important. Like many advisory bodies, the committee has found it hard to establish an effective voice but it is, nevertheless, helpful to the Council and Commission to have group views available before policy has hardened and discussions in the committee provide this information. Meetings also enable like-minded people throughout the EC to meet and discuss so that it helps to build up a core of people in the EC who are knowledgeable about EC affairs.

In addition, the Commission is supported by a set of advisory committees for its funding operations and by a range of working parties and committees for particular industries and problems. It freely uses outside experts and organizations to provide services while Brussels is famous for the amount of pressure group lobbying that occurs. A *Standing Committee of Employment*, representing national employment ministers, employers and unions as well as the Commission, is a reflection of concern with the economy, the effect of inflation and structural change on employment levels and the difficulties experienced by workers in declining industries. The meetings of employers and unions in the *social dialogue* are another way in which the Commission pursues consultation.

In some ways, both for interest groups and for the man or woman in the street who wishes to make the effort, the Commission is more accessible than national administrations. This is in part because the consultation processes, although clumsy, do bring a wide range of people into touch with EC affairs. It is also the result of a well-established Commission policy of informing and educating the public in order to mobilize public opinion behind the integration process. Nevertheless, considerable unease remains and its relative success in establishing relations with bankers, organizational representatives, industrialists and other power groups has contributed to a widespread belief that the EC is an elitist institution far away from the ordinary citizen. Hence a new drive towards better information, and public access to it, was promised in the Maastricht Treaty and is continuing.

The EU Treaty also created a further advisory committee, the *Committee of the Regions* representing regional and local bodies and also with 222 members. It has to be consulted by both Council and Commission on some matters and can submit its own opinions. Its creation reflects the growing interest of authorities, such as the German Lander, and of national groups, including the Scots, Flemings and Catalans, in the work of the EC and their wish to influence its decisions directly but whether the committee will be able to develop a significant role, as many hope, remains a matter for the future. The danger in this web of machinery and consultation is indecision and slowness of action while it puts a premium on the views of those who are effectively organized. Some members have a powerful regional structure and others none at all and the Committee has not yet become an effective political player on the European stage.

Standing apart from these institutions is the *European Investment Bank* (EIB) which was given the task of contributing to the balanced and steady development of the common market in the interests of the EC. It has three main fields of operation: to aid regional development, to help with projects made necessary by the establishment of the common market for which normal financial means are lacking and to assist projects of common interest. It is not a grant-aiding fund but a bank operating normal banking criteria whose capital is contributed by member states and by the money it can raise on normal markets. In addition to its lending operations, it is used as a channel for loans guaranteed by the EC budget and this is especially important for loans to the Third World and Mediterranean countries. Finally, the EU Treaty set out the arrangements of the institutions necessary for economic and monetary union. These are the European System of Central Banks and the European Central Bank. The European Monetary Institute operates only in the second stage towards economic and monetary union with the task of preparing the entry of the third, and final, stage.

2.5 Foreign and security policies

The EU Treaty brought the EPC procedure firmly within its orbit as the means through which the Union is to 'assert its identity on the international scene'. Although CFSP is intergovernmental in character, it nevertheless uses the Community institutions other than the Court of Justice. Broad objectives are laid down in the treaty and further guidelines are laid down by the European Council. It will be possible, in the future, for the Council to go further in developing common strategies where member states have important shared interests, e.g. the Middle East, while the Council of Ministers takes more specific implementing decisions on a majority vote subject to a veto by a member who has special interests at stake. The Council is helped by a political committee, drawn from member states, which monitors the international scene and helps to define policy while the creation of a permanent planning unit to strengthen the analysis and definition of the Union's foreign policy has been agreed. It will also act as an early warning unit. Although the EP has no formal power, it must be consulted and its views, which are actively expressed, taken into account. The Commission is brought fully into the structure and is involved at all stages. It has a right of initiative but shares this with member states who may also bring matters to Council attention. The lack of a central focal point for foreign policy led some states to advocate the creation of a new appointment whose holder would act as the 'foreign minister' for Europe and a first step was taken at Amsterdam by making the Secretary-General of the Council of Ministers into a 'high representative'. The challenges faced by the EU in formulating foreign policy were amply demonstrated by events in Yugoslavia and Albania and it is to be hoped that the steps taken in 1997 to strengthen the arrangements prove more adequate. In particular, it is hoped that the EU will be able to react to sudden crises more effectively and to appoint a special representative when occasion demands while it has been agreed that operational costs will be carried on the Community budget. By this decision, the EP will acquire a greater voice in foreign affairs.

At present, security policy simply envisages the possibility of an eventual framing of a common defence policy and that, in time, a common defence may emerge, a form of words which glosses over differences of view and the neutral status held by some members. However, the Western European Union (WEU) has become an integral part of the Union in order to handle defence matters and a special Declaration of the TEU is concerned with its position. In order to become the defence arm of the Union, with responsibility to elaborate and execute defence policies, it has to develop close relationships with Community institutions and to strengthen its operational role. It has a planning cell and military units answerable to WEU. At the same time, it is seen as the European pillar of the Atlantic alliance and it will not cut across NATO obligations. Although all members of WEU belong to the EU the converse is not true, although the non-members may, of course, change their minds in the future and there are many awkwardnesses to be worked out consequent upon the dual position held by WEU in NATO and the EU and the reluctance of neutral members of the EU to find themselves committed to future action. However, serious defence decisions were postponed by the Maastricht Treaty which gave only an outline of a new position. The situation is complicated by the concurrent discussions of the future role and membership of NATO since the functions of WEU are inevitably affected by these. It may, however, be possible to agree on WEU's responsibilities in peace keeping, crisis management and the protection of humanitarian operations but the relationship to the EU is very controversial. The WEU treaty is due for revision in 1998 and the Amsterdam discussions postponed any major decision on further integration with the EU although approving closer cooperation between the two organizations.

Other difficulties stem from the problem of separating external economic relations, which are covered by the Treaty of Rome and the EC procedures, from other elements of foreign policy.

2.6 Judicial and Home Affairs

The Maastricht arrangements did not appear out of the blue. Collaboration had been developing steadily over matters such as the apprehension of terrorists and drug pedlars, judicial cooperation in matters of mutual interest and the implications of the abolition of internal frontiers for the free movement of goods and people. Under the EU Treaty such collaboration is brought within the Community umbrella but, like foreign and security policy, remains for intergovernmental cooperation. It is possible, however, for the Council to pass many matters over to the EU institutions in the future (Article K.9).

One question, visa policy, was put into the EC structure straightaway (Article 100(c)). The Council determines which state's nationals require visas to pass the external border and now acts upon QMV. Temporary arrangements may be made in emergencies. Other objectives of JHA cooperation concerned free movement issues such as asylum policy, controls at external borders, immigration policy, the entry and residence of third-country nationals, illegal immigration, control of drugs and international fraud. Judicial and customs cooperation is specifically covered as is police cooperation to combat terrorism, drug trafficking and other international crimes. In 1997, states agreed to create an area of freedom, security and justice but over a period of years. This will start the process of passing some JHA matters such as external border controls, asylum and immigration policies, judicial and police co-operation to combat crime to the EC institutions although unanimous voting will normally prevail. The Schengen agreement will be incorporated into the treaty and special arrangements made for the Nordic Passport Union. A formal agreement will allow the UK and Ireland to retain their own rights to border control and Denmark also has a partially independent position. A European Police Office (Europol) was set up some years ago. In this work, states commit themselves to respect the European Convention for the Protection of Human Rights and Fundamental Freedoms and the Convention on the Status of Refugees.

In practical terms, these objectives lead to administrative collaboration and a general agreement by governments to inform and consult each other. A coordinating committee of senior officials supervises the daily work and prepares the ground for the Council meetings. The Council, in turn, may adopt a joint position on a subject and decide joint action. Member states may bring matters to the Council and the Commission may do likewise but not on the full range of subjects. The EP must be kept informed and may ask questions of the Council and make recommendations to it.

2.7 Conclusion

It is still early to provide a full assessment of the EU Treaty for the changes brought in by the Maastricht Treaty need time to take effect and Amsterdam is bringing further amendments. Overall, however, it was an important stage in EU integration and was meant as such. Much has been made in countries, such as the United Kingdom, which are suspicious of its terms, of the pillar structure and the principle of subsidiarity as bulwarks against integration but the discussion above suggests that the balance has been shifted away from member states and towards the Community institutions. The competence of the EU and the use of QMV in the Council are both extended, the EP has greater powers and the Commission is drawn closer to the EP and thus away from governments while the concept of a Union was introduced. Foreign and security policy, judicial and home affairs cooperation have been brought more closely into the structure than before. The Amsterdam decisions accentuate these trends. However, the Community has always known that it needs to work on consensus, sometimes difficult to achieve but in the end acceptable to all on the grounds of the overall benefits of membership. It is too simple, therefore, to suggest that reluctant states will, in future, simply be forced into line, hence the current discussions about flexibility or inner and outer circles as possible ways of deepening the integrative process. They present a challenge to statesmanship to find a way through the difficulties so that the EU can continue to express the belief in common interests and likemindedness on which it was founded and which persists.

It was, indeed, not long before a re-evaluation began. The need to ratify the

Maastricht agreement unleashed a storm of argument across Europe about the future. Denmark, France and Ireland held referendums. In the first, the treaty terms were narrowly rejected and in the second accepted by a slim margin. Only in Ireland did they appear generally acceptable. As doubts grew about the objective of economic and monetary union, financial turmoil shook the European exchange rate mechanism, the United Kingdom delayed ratification and Germany qualified its acceptance of the treaty. Agreement was here made conditional on an addition to the constitution that any transfer of German sovereignty must be agreed by a two-thirds majority of both houses of parliament. In future, the government is bound to consult the Bundestag before accepting any new European legislation and to respect its views during any negotiations while the German parliament now holds a veto over entry into a single European currency.

A summit meeting at Edinburgh in December 1992 reached a set of agreements adequate for the organization to claim that it was back on track but not enough for the Maastricht goals to emerge unscathed. In order to allow Denmark to hold a second referendum with a reasonable chance of obtaining a favourable result, a series of legally binding opt-outs for Denmark were agreed. These cover exemptions from the third phase of monetary union, the common defence policy and European citizenship, and the right to continue to cooperate on justice and immigration policy on an interstate rather than a Community basis. For these reasons alone, the EU cannot advance to a single currency for all by the year 2000 or a single defence policy without further agreement. The opt-outs appear to have taken a step towards a more differentiated Community than before.

Other matters were also agreed. Extra parliamentary seats were allocated as mentioned earlier and it was decided to open enlargement talks with Austria, Finland and Sweden. All three are net contributors to the budget so the existing paymasters felt able to accept a phased increase in the size of the structural and cohesion funds necessary to obtain the agreement of the southern members to the enlargement negotiations. A budget compromise covered a seven year period. The budget is kept at a ceiling of 1.2% GNP for two years with phased increases to reach 1.277% GNP by 1999. Guidelines to implement the principle of subsidiarity and to improve the openness of decision making were accepted. Stimulation for the economy was announced. The EIB was given a temporary lending facility to help with roads and telecommunications while a new European Investment Fund provides guarantees for small and medium-sized businesses. Finally, a set of declarations covered major external issues.

There was little time to consolidate these changes for an intergovernmental conference was arranged for 1996 to consider what further alterations were necessary after which a new round of enlargement negotiations could begin. The IGC ended in 1997 but it will take some time for the resulting treaty to be ratified and put in place while some unsolved problems still remain, notably concerning institutional changes.

There are serious problems in running such an unwieldy organization without more effective institutional arrangements; the lack of definition of the foreign policy role of the EU and of its corresponding security and defence function are complicating relations with NATO and inhibiting its responsibilities for peace and security in Europe, although the modest changes agreed at Amsterdam will help. Many practical difficulties arise consequent upon the greater mobility of people within the EU. Underlying these issues are different ideas about the nature of the EU enterprise, how best to proceed for the future and how to handle the relationships between the EU and its constituent member states.

Suggestions for institutional change which, in themselves, seem no more than what is necessary for efficiency normally raise basic questions about the future of the EU. For example, the Council of Ministers will not be able to function in its old way with twenty or more members, and thus there is an argument for extending the use of QMV, perhaps balanced by the need to achieve supermajorities in important issues. Another suggestion is to change the weights given to the votes held by states in order to protect the position of the larger states as an increase in membership will bring in several smaller ones. A major criticism of the Council remains its lack of openness and the failure of existing democratic institutions to control the decisions taken but no clear view has emerged as to the remedy. A second issue is the number of Commissioners which is thought to be too large and cannot be allowed to grow indefinitely. The same criticism is made of the European Parliament for which a maximum of 700 members is now agreed. There is still a reluctance to see the EP's powers increased but the variety of procedures used by the EP was reduced at Amsterdam and this should help public understanding of its work. Similarly, reform of the foreign policy arm and the clarification of the security and defence function, the relationship with NATO and the position of the neutrals are all matters which require resolution but raise the most fundamental questions about the future of the EU. The prevailing orientation may still be economic but the momentum for change has spilled over into other areas so that, albeit gradually and untidily, the EU is obtaining functions which traditionally were essential attributes of statehood. If this remains unwelcome to large bodies of opinion then the EU may continue in a form which allows for much ambiguity to persist but which keeps the door open for future action should a new favourable moment occur.

Guide to references

Sweet and Maxwell, *European Community Treaties*, is regularly updated but the EU badly needs a consolidated text to serve as a constitution.

Many authors have dealt with the post-war organization of western Europe. These include Haas (1958) and Palmer and Lambert (1968). Wallace (1990) discusses more modern issues.

EC developments may be traced through EC *Bulletin* and its supplements.

chapter three

The basic statistics of the EU

A. M. EL-AGRAA

The purpose of this chapter is to provide the reader with a brief summary of the basic economic statistics of the EU which are used in the analytical chapters. For comparative purposes and in order to preserve a general sense of perspective, similar information is given for Canada, Japan, the United States, the Russian Federation and for the immediate potential EU member countries: the member nations of EFTA, not only because they, except Switzerland, have signed to join the European Economic Area (EEA), but also because some of them are in the process of negotiating EU membership; Bulgaria, Cyprus, the Czech Republic, Estonia, Hungary, Latvia, Lithuania, Malta, Poland, Romania, the Slovak Republic and Slovenia because they have applied for EU membership (but for some of which most data is not available); Turkey because its application for joining the EU has been on the table for a very long time.

The main purpose of this chapter is to provide information; the analysis of most of these statistics and the economic forces that determine them is one of the main tasks of the rest of this book. For example, the analysis of the composition and pattern of trade prior to the inception of the EU and subsequent to its formation is the basic aim of the theoretical and measurement section of the book. Moreover, the policy chapters are concerned with the analysis of particular areas of interest: the Common Agricultural Policy (CAP), the role of the EU general budget, competition and industrial policies, the EU regional policy, etc., and these specialist chapters contain further relevant information.

3.1 The basic statistics

3.1.1 Area, population and life expectancy

Table 3.1 (the tables may be found in the appendix at the end of the chapter) gives information about area, population and life expectancy at birth. The data are more or less self-explanatory but a few points warrant particular attention.

The EU of fifteen has a larger population (about 372 million) than any country in the advanced Western world. This population exceeds that of the Russian Federation (about 148 million) and of the United States (about 263 million) and is only just short of being three times that of Japan. It exceeds the combined population of the United States and Canada (member nations of the North American Free Trade Agreement, NAFTA) by about 80 million, is about 4 million short of the combined population of all three NAFTA nations (Mexico has a population of 91.8 million), and is only about 12 million less than the combined population of the United States and Japan, the world's two largest economies.

A quick comparison of the first two columns of Table 3.1 reveals that the EU member nations have higher population densities than Canada and the United States. However, the population densities within the EU exhibit great diversity with the Netherlands and Belgium at the top of the league and Spain, Greece and Ireland at the bottom. It should be stressed that population density has important implications for the potential economic growth and the future of the social policies of the EU.

The average rate of increase of population between 1965 and 1980 was quite variable for the member nations of the EU. It was low in West Germany (0.2%), the United Kingdom (0.2%), Austria (0.3%), Belgium (0.3%), Finland (0.3%) and Portugal (0.4%), but high in the Netherlands (0.9%), Spain (1.0%) and Ireland (1.2%). The remaining EU nations occupied the middle ground. For the same period, among the three EFTA countries, Norway and Switzerland had roughly the same rates as Denmark, Italy and Sweden, which are near the average for the EU as a whole. All the other countries shown in the table had high rates, with Turkey being completely out of line with a rate of 2.4%. For the period 1980–90, the rates declined for virtually all the countries except for Finland, Switzerland and Latvia, where it increased by about one tenth of a percentage point, and the United Kingdom where it remained at the previous rate. For the 1990–95 period, the change is dramatic in both directions, but, since this is a shorter period, no serious comparison can be made. However, Turkey continued to be the only country out of line within this group of nations.

Note that for the majority of the countries listed in the table, life expectancy at birth is 70 years or over, except for Latvia (69), Lithuania (69) and Turkey (67); thus health provision (Table 3.22) may be irrelevant. For the EU nations, the range is between 75 (Denmark and Portugal) and 79 (Sweden) years, and the EFTA nations are at the top of this range, with Iceland on 79. For the Central and Eastern European potential EU members, the range is 69–74. Although these figures do not seem far apart, a difference in life expectancy of about five years is in reality quite substantial in terms of the required provision for old age, a question that is becoming a real headache for countries such as Japan, but many EU nations are only one year behind Japan.

However, one should be careful not to read too much into such comparisons – there is always the danger that they may distract the reader from some obvious and basic realities of life: the cultural diversity of the member nations of the EU relative to the almost common historical evolution and economic development of the United States, the contrasting political systems of the countries compared, the frequency of natural disasters, etc.

3.1.2 GNP and inflation

Table 3.2 gives per capita GNP (total GDP is provided in Table 3.5) and its average annual rate of growth between 1985 and 1995. The table also provides the annual inflation rates for the period 1985–95. One of the salient features of this table is the disparity between the member nations of the EU in terms of per capita GNP: Greece ($8,210), Portugal ($9,740), Spain ($13,580), and Ireland ($14,710) lag far behind the rest, with Germany on $27,510, Denmark on $29,890 and Luxemburg on $41,210. All three member countries of EFTA have per capita incomes exceeding the average for the EU, while all the EU potential partners, with the exception of Cyprus and Slovenia, have per capita GNPs in the range of 16–50% that of Greece. Note that in this respect Luxemburg, Denmark and Germany are ahead of the United States.

For the period 1958–64, the United Kingdom showed the slowest rate of growth of GDP in comparison with the original six member nations of the EC (this information is not provided in the table). Indeed, if a longer period is considered (1953–64), the average exponential growth rate of the United Kingdom was only 2.7%, with the United States next with 3.1% (Kaldor, 1966, p. 5). On the other hand, Japan had exceptionally high growth rates – for the period 1953–64 the average exponential growth rate was 9.6%. Although during 1965–80 (Table 3.6) these rates declined for all the countries concerned, relative performance did not change much, but during 1990–95 dramatic changes were beginning to happen, with the United States and Ireland being the stars and the United Kingdom not so far behind its EU partners and exceeding the performance of some of them.

With regard to the rate of growth of GNP per capita for the period 1965–90 (not given in the table), except for the fact that the rates declined overall and that the United Kingdom's position was taken over by Switzerland, the Netherlands, the United States and Sweden (in that order), the United Kingdom occupied the fourth lowest position. However, during 1985–95, although the United Kingdom did a little better than the United States and was on par with Italy, its overall performance within the EU ranked tenth (equal).

Table 3.2 also provides information on the annual inflation rates for 1984–95. During this period Greece and Portugal had exceptionally high rates; they are the only two EU member nations with double-digit rates (15.4% and 11.1% respectively). Although the Netherlands and Ireland had impressive low rates (1.7% and 2.5% respectively), taking the rate for the United States as the standard, five EU nations did better and two equalled it. Note that Japan continues to occupy the bottom of this league with a low rate of 1.4%. Thus the data clearly demonstrate the disparity of performance by the member nations of the EU in this respect.

3.1.3 Work

Table 3.3 provides data on the percentage of civilian working population, the unemployment rates and the sectoral distribution of the labour force in terms of the broad categories of agriculture, industry and services. Of course, from this information and the total population figures given in Table 3.1, one can easily arrive at the absolute total for the labour force.

With regard to the percentage of civilian working population, there was no striking difference between the member nations of the EU in 1965 except for the fact that Ireland (with 57%) stood below the 62–66% range that covered the rest. For the same year, of all the relevant nations in the table, Turkey stood out with a figure of 53–55%. In 1993, this rate declined for all the countries in the table, and, except for Denmark, the rate was below 50% for the EU nations. Note that Ireland still occupied the bottom position within the EU with about 39%, but this time it was joined by Spain, and Turkey was still far below the rest, being the only country with less than 35%. However, one should again be careful with regard to this information since it does not include those employed in the military field, and the decline in rates may reflect an increase in the number of those going for higher education as well as lengthening of the duration of such education; the reader is advised to glance at Table 3.20 on education which may prove helpful in this respect.

The unemployment rates were high for all the member countries of the EU except for Luxemburg, Austria and Portugal (in that order), if one were again to adopt the rate for the United States as the norm. Since by present standards any rate below 3% can be regarded as exceptionally good, Luxemburg would stand out. However, Luxemburg is so small and so dominated by EU bureaucrats and parliamentarians that it should be discounted in any serious comparison. Belgium, Denmark, Finland, France, Ireland, Italy and Spain had double-digit rates and hence can be classified as EU countries with extremely worrying unemployment rates. Given this arbitrary classification, Austria can claim to have performed extremely well while Portugal, Germany and Greece (in that order) can be regarded as nations with unsatisfactory yet not worrying rates. All three member nations of EFTA registered good rates, especially Iceland with 3%. Of the 'other countries', Japan passes as exceptionally good.

Of particular interest is the relative size of the services sector. This is mainly the tertiary sector (it comprises such divergent items as banking, distribution, insurance, transport, catering and hotels, laundries and hairdressers, professional services of a more varied kind, publicly and privately provided, etc.) and was, for all the EU, EFTA and Other Countries, the largest in 1994, exceeding 60% in the majority of them. This is a significant point, particularly since it has frequently been alleged in the past that the size of this sector was the cause of the slow rate of growth of the UK economy; there is nothing in the data to suggest that the UK is unique in this respect. Moreover, the increasing size of this sector over time has led to the doctrine of 'deindustrialization': as this sector grows in percentage terms, it automatically follows that the other sectors, especially industry, must decline in relative terms.

As one would expect (since it is a natural characteristic of development), all the countries considered show a decline in the percentage of the labour force engaged in agriculture, even for the United Kingdom whose percentage has remained consistently near the 2–3% level: when the percentage is so low it is difficult for it to fall further especially when most countries deem some agriculture to be necessary for food security. However, Greece, Ireland, Portugal and Spain were the only EU countries with double-digit percentages. Again, note that Turkey, with 53%, is in a league of its own.

3.1.4 Employment and unemployment

Although some aspects of EU employment and unemployment are tackled in various chapters of the book, especially those on the social and competition and industrial policies, this may be the appropriate point to consider briefly certain aspects of this topic which are not tackled in those chapters. Employment is a political and socioeconomic issue which needs to be tackled in all its manifestations, and that is why, at the particular insistence of France, the Amsterdam Treaty incorporates it as a new policy area. It is quite obvious that the solution to the unemployment problem necessitates a close integration of economic policies as well as social and manpower policies. The unemployment problem has two basic features. First, there is the transitional problem: given existing levels of unemployment and possible rates of growth of population, the achievement of acceptable levels of manpower utilization will inevitably be slow and in some countries may take many years. In addition, there is the longer-term problem: the effect of evolving structures of the labour force, attitudes to work and changing social objectives which may affect employment in a fundamental sense.

Table 3.4 gives a longer-term perspective for manpower utilization and unemployment rates. It should be noted that between 1973 and 1975 unemployment grew steadily in all the countries included in the table and that the rates of growth were much higher than during the boom years of the 1960s. In terms of employment, the maximum declines in the 1973–5 recession were much greater than any that had occurred in the 1960s. However, the reader should note that the absolute levels of unemployment for these countries are not strictly comparable owing to differences in measurement techniques. For example, some of those considered as fully employed in Japan will not pass as such elsewhere.

In spite of the above observation, a great deal of the slack in manpower utilization which developed during the period 1973–5 was absorbed by various measures which diverted the growth of overt unemployment. Working hours fell in a number of countries and jobs were preserved by subsidies to employers, by restrictions on dismissals or by deterrents such as redundancy payments which made employers reluctant to dismiss labour. As a result, output per employee fell in many cases.

The table also gives some indication of the change in working hours in the major countries. Many of the figures refer only to manufacturing and may therefore be more sensitive to a recession than those for the economy as a whole, but they do indicate that working hours dropped more than the 1960–70 trend would have suggested. The biggest fall was in Japan. This explains some of the fall in output per employee, but the reduction in working hours does not by any means explain the whole of this decline.

The bottom half of the table gives recorded unemployment for the EU countries for various years. It should be apparent that, on the whole and with the exception of 1994, Germany remained the country with the lowest unemployment rate, albeit the rate had been increasing even before unification.

3.1.5 Demand

Tables 3.7–3.9 give information on the structure of demand in 1995, i.e. on the distribution of GDP between private consumption, collective consumption of the general government, investment expenditure, savings, the export of goods and non-factor services and resource balance. With regard to private consumption, the lowest percentage within the EU belonged to Denmark and Finland (54%) and the highest was that of Greece (73%). As to gross domestic investment, the lowest percentage belonged to Ireland (13%) and the highest was that of Portugal (28%). The percentages for savings showed a larger divergence between the lowest (7% for Greece) and the highest (29% for the Netherlands). Note that no single EU nation had an equality between the percentages devoted to savings and domestic investment, and four EU countries (Austria, Greece, Portugal and the United Kingdom) spent a higher percentage on domestic investment than on savings; thus, eleven EU nations did the opposite. Exports of goods and non-factor services loomed large in the case of Ireland (75%), Belgium (74%) and the Netherlands (53%) but varied between 19% and 38% for the rest. Norway and Switzerland fitted into the general picture for the EU, but the divergence was somewhat wider for the remaining nations, with the United States being in a league of its own in terms of savings and exports as well as Japan with its very high savings and domestic investment rates and low exports rate. Note that all these comparisons relate to 1995 data; longer-term data can be guessed from the growth rates for 1965–80 and 1990–95 given in Table 3.6. Here, it suffices to state that the excess of domestic savings over investment in Japan is far in excess of the 2% given in 1990, and the same qualification applies to the opposite relationship between investment and savings in the United States.

3.1.6 Government sector

Tables 3.10–3.13 provide data on what can loosely be referred to as the 'government sector'. They give information about current government revenue and expenditure as a percentage of GDP, net official development assistance to developing countries and multilateral agents, total official reserves, money and interest rates, etc.

There was a dissimilarity between the member nations of the EU with respect to both their current government expenditure and revenue as percentages of their GDPs. In terms of total current expenditure, the range was between 32.2% for Germany and 48.3% for the Netherlands. This was in stark contrast to those for Japan (14.8%), Canada (21.6%), the United States (22.2%) and Switzerland (25.8%). A wider range (20.9–50.6%) existed between the potential EU nations. With regard to total capital expenditure, the ranges are also wide, but the percentages are smaller. There were also wide ranges in terms of total expenditure on defence and social services. Of particular interest in the case of the EU is the variation in the size of the overall budget deficit since it is one of the criteria set for the introduction of the single currency (see Chapter 5); only three countries would have passed this criterion were the test set for 1994.

A particularly interesting feature is the percentage of GDP spent on net official assistance extended to developing countries and multilateral agents. Denmark (1.03%), Norway (1.01%) and Sweden (0.98%) came at the top of the league while the United States (0.15%) and Japan (0.26%) came at the bottom if one rightly excluded Greece (0.10%) and Ireland (0.20%) from this comparison since their level of development does not match that of this group of countries. One does not want to dwell too much on this matter, but the information suggests that the advanced world, in resisting the demands made by the developing world, is more concerned about absolute figures than about percentages. The latter clearly indicate the significant implications for official development assistance of the developing countries' plea (through UNCTAD) that this figure should be raised to 0.5% (originally 1.0%) of the major donor countries' GDP: Germany, Japan, the United Kingdom and the United States. Therefore, as far as developing countries are concerned, only Denmark, Norway, Sweden, the Netherlands and France will be applauded.

For a proper and detailed discussion of the role played by the governments' budgets, the reader is advised to turn to the chapters on the role of the EU general budget and on fiscal harmonization.

3.1.7 Exports, imports and balance of payments

Tables 3.14–3.19 give information on merchandise exports and imports, the terms of trade and export concentration ratios, imports from and exports to the EU nations and the balance of payments and reserves.

All these tables are more or less self-explanatory, but Tables 3.17 and 3.18 warrant particular attention. They should be considered together since they give the percentages for the share of imports of the importing country coming from the EU and the share of exports of the exporting country going to the EU. The reader should be warned that these percentages are not strictly comparable, because for the year 1957 the EU refers to the original six, while for 1974 it refers to the nine, for 1981 to the ten, and for 1986, 1990 and 1993 to the twelve. For an analysis of the proper trends, the reader should consult Chapter 6, and for a full analysis consult El-Agraa (1989b).

The tables show that, in 1993, EU member nations' imports from each other varied from almost 49% for the United Kingdom to about 95% for Ireland. The percentages for exports varied less, with the lowest being over 45% for Finland and the highest over 75% for Portugal. Thus, on average, Ireland comes at the top. This should not come as a surprise, given the close ties between it and the United Kingdom. Of the potential EU partners, all three member nations of EFTA conducted more than half of their total trade (both exports and imports) with the EU, and Turkey comes close to Finland (with the lowest percentages in the EU) in this respect.

3.1.8 Education

Table 3.20 gives the enrolment rates at the primary, secondary and tertiary levels of education, the percentage of cohort reaching grade 4 and the adult illiteracy rate. The table shows that for 1993 there were on the whole no drastic differences between the countries compared with regard to the primary levels, but that major deviations are noticeable at the secondary and tertiary levels. However, the table also reveals that five EU nations did not provide primary education to every child, and that Italy failed likewise with regard to secondary education.

At the tertiary level, Canada (103%), the United States (81%) and Finland (63%) stand out while Portugal (23%) recorded the lowest percentage within the EU, but much lower rates can be seen in many of the countries within the EU potential members. These rates may suggest that a general positive relationship exists between economic development and high rates of enrolment at the tertiary level, but there is no such relationship if one concentrates on the most advanced of the nations in the table; for example, Japan and Switzerland are the two countries with the highest per capita GNP in the world yet their enrolment rate at the tertiary level is only higher than that of Portugal. Moreover, the data are not strictly comparable since what is deemed to be university education in one country may not pass as such in others.

3.1.9 Income–consumption distribution

Table 3.21 gives some information on the distribution of income and consumption. The table shows that, within the EU and EFTA nations, Canada, Japan and the United States, the highest 20% received a share of between 36.0% and 41.6% of income while the lowest 20% received only between 4.6% and 8.7%, i.e. the shares were, respectively, about double and less than a half. It is interesting to note that the gap is widest for Russia (but in terms of expenditure) and narrowest for Sweden, followed by Spain and Japan.

3.1.10 Tariffs

Table 3.23 provides information on the average tariff levels in the original six as well as in Denmark, the United Kingdom, Canada and the United States. To see how these compare with the tariff levels that are at present in existence, one should turn to Chapter 21 on EU external trade policy.

3.2 Conclusion

As stated at the beginning of this chapter, there are no conclusions to be drawn from this general statistical survey; the information is provided only for the purpose of giving a general sense of perspective. The reader who is seeking conclusions should turn to the relevant specialist chapter or chapters.

Appendix: The statistical tables

In all tables, na means not available. Unless otherwise stated, the sources for all the tables are the World Bank's *World Development Report*, Eurostat's *Basic Statistics of the EU* and *Statistical Review*, and OECD publications for various years. The data are subject to technical explanations as well as to some critical qualifications; hence the reader is strongly advised to turn to the original sources for these.

Table 3.1 ⬤ Area and population.

	Area (000 km^2)	Population (millions) mid-1995	Average annual growth of population (%)			Life expectancy at birth (years) 1995
			1965–80	1980–90	1990–95	
EU countries						
Austria	84	8.1	0.3	0.2	0.5	77
Belgium	31	10.1	0.3	0.1	0.4	77
Denmark	43	5.2	0.5	0.0	0.3	75
Finland	338	5.1	0.3	0.4	0.5	76
France	552	58.1	0.7	0.5	0.5	78
Germany	357	81.9	0.2	0.1	0.6	76
Greece	132	10.5	0.7	0.5	0.6	78
Ireland	70	3.6	1.2	0.3	0.5	77
Italy	301	57.2	0.5	0.1	0.2	78
Luxemburg	3	0.4	na	na	na	76
Netherlands	37	15.5	0.9	0.6	0.7	78
Portugal	92	9.9	0.4	0.1	0.1	75
Spain	505	39.2	1.0	0.4	0.2	77
Sweden	450	8.8	0.5	0.3	0.6	79
United Kingdom	245	58.5	0.2	0.2	0.3	77
EU (15)	3,240	372.1				
EFTA countries						
Iceland	103	0.27	na	na	na	79
Norway	324	4.4	0.6	0.4	0.5	78
Switzerland	41	7.0	0.5	0.6	1.0	78
EU potential members						
Bulgaria	111	8.4	0.4[a]	−0.2	−0.7	71
Cyprus	9	0.73	na	na	na	78
Czech Republic	79	10.3	0.5[a]	0.1	−0.1	73
Estonia	45	1.5	0.8[a]	0.6	−1.1	70
Hungary	93	10.2	0.4[a]	−0.3	−0.3	70
Latvia	64	2.5	0.4	0.5	−1.2	69
Lithuania	65	3.7	na	0.9	0.0	69
Malta	0.3	0.37	na	na	na	77
Poland	313	38.6	0.8	0.7	0.3	70
Romania	238	22.7	na	0.4	−0.4	70
Slovak Republic	49	5.4	0.9[a]	0.6	0.3	72
Slovenia	20	2.0	0.9[a]	0.5	−0.1	74
Turkey	779	61.1	2.4	2.3	1.7	67
Other countries						
Canada	9,976	29.6	1.3	1.2	1.3	78
Japan	378	125.2	1.2	0.6	0.3	80
Russian Federation	17,075	148.2	0.6[a]	0.6	0.0	65
United States	9,364	263.1	1.0	0.9	1.0	77

[a]The rate is for 1970–80.

Table 3.2 ⬭ GNP per capita and inflation rates.

	US$ 1995	GNP per capita Average annual growth rate (%) 1985–95	Average annual inflation (%) 1985–95
EU countries			
Austria	26,890	1.9	3.2
Belgium	24,710	2.2	3.2
Denmark	29,890	1.5	2.8
Finland	20,580	−0.2	3.8
France	24,990	1.5	2.8
Germany	27,510	na	na
Greece	8,210	1.3	15.4
Ireland	14,710	5.2	2.5
Italy	19,020	1.4	6.0
Luxemburg	41,210	0.9	na
Netherlands	24,000	1.9	1.7
Portugal	9,740	3.6	11.1
Spain	13,580	2.6	6.3
Sweden	23,750	−0.1	5.5
United Kingdom	18,700	1.4	5.1
EFTA countries			
Iceland	24,950	1.0	na
Norway	31,250	1.7	3.0
Switzerland	40,630	0.2	3.4
EU potential members			
Bulgaria	1,330	−2.6	45.9
Cyprus[a]	10,260	na	na
Czech Republic	3,870	−1.8	12.2
Estonia	2,860	−4.3	77.2
Hungary	4,120	−1.0	19.9
Latvia	2,270	−6.6	72.5
Lithuania	1,900	−11.7	102.3[c]
Malta	[b]	na	na
Poland	2,790	1.2	91.8
Romania	1,480	−3.8	68.7
Slovak Republic	2,950	−2.8	10.6
Slovenia	8,200	na	na
Turkey	2,790	1.2	64.6
Other countries			
Canada	19,380	0.4	2.9
Japan	39,640	2.9	1.4
Russian Federation	2,240	−5.1	148.9
United States	26,980	1.3	3.2

[a]Estimated to be high income ($9,386 or more).
[b]Upper middle income ($3,036 to $9,385).
[c]The rate is for 1984–94.

Table 3.3 ⬤ Labour force and unemployment rates.

	Civilian working population (% of total population)		Agriculture		Industry		Services		Unemployment rates (annual averages in %)
	1965	1993	1965	1993	1965	1995	1965	1995	1994
EU countries									
Austria	63	47	19	8	45	37	36	55	4.4[a]
Belgium	63	41	6	3	46	28	48	69	10.0
Denmark	64	56	14	6	37	28	49	66	10.3[a]
Finland	65	49	24	8	35	31	41	61	17.3[a]
France	62	44	18	5	39	29	43	66	10.8[a]
Germany	65	49	11	4	48	38	41	59	7.2[a]
Greece	65	41	47	23	24	28	41	58	7.7[b]
Ireland	57	39	31	14	28	29	41	58	17.7
Italy	66	40	25	9	42	32	34	59	11.8
Luxemburg	na	43	na	3	na	26	na	70	2.6[a]
Netherlands	62	47	9	5	41	26	51	69	8.8[a]
Portugal	62	48	38	18	30	34	32	48	6.1
Spain	64	39	34	12	35	33	32	55	23.0
Sweden	66	49	11	4	43	25	46	71	7.7[a]
United Kingdom	65	49	3	2	47	29	50	69	9.6
EU (15)									
EFTA countries									
Iceland	na	55	na	11	na	26	na	63	3.0[c]
Norway	63	49	16	6	37	25	48	69	6.2[a]
Switzerland	65	52	9	6	49	35	41	59	4.4[a]

EU potential members

Bulgaria	na	na	na	14	na	50	na	36	na
Cyprus	na	na	na	na	na	na	na	na	na
Czech Republic	na	na	na	11	na	45	na	44	na
Estonia	na	na	na	14	na	41	na	45	na
Hungary	na	na	na	15	na	38	na	47	na
Latvia	na	na	na	16	na	42	na	42	na
Lithuania	na	na	na	18	na	41	na	41	na
Malta	na	na	na	na	na	na	na	na	na
Poland	na	na	na	27	na	36	na	37	na
Romania	na	na	na	24	na	47	na	29	na
Slovak Republic	na	na	na	12	na	32	na	56	na
Slovenia	na	na	na	5	na	44	na	51	na
Turkey	53	34	75	53	35	18	14	29	6.8[a]
Other countries									
Canada	59	49	10	3	33	25	57	72	11.6[a]
Japan	67	53	26	7	32	34	42	59	2.5[a]
Russian Federation	62	57	34	14	33	42	33	44	1.0[a]
United States	60	50	5	3	35	28	60	69	6.8[a]

[a]The rate is for 1993.
[b]The rate is for 1991.
[c]The rate is for 1992.

Table 3.4 💬 Manpower utilization, unemployment rates and recorded unemployment

	Employment		Hours worked per person		Output per man-hour		Unemployment % of labour	
	1960–73	1973–75	1960–73	1973–75	1960–73	1973–75	1960–73	1974
EC countries								
Belgium[a]	0.7	na	−1.2	na	5.4	na	2.2	2.6
Denmark	1.3	na	−1.5	na	5.0	na	1.1	2.1
France	0.7	−0.5	−0.5	−2.1	5.5	3.6	1.6	2.3
Germany	0.1	−2.8	−0.9	−2.7	5.5	4.0	0.8	2.2
Ireland	na	na	na	na	na	na	na	na
Italy	−0.7	1.2	1.9	na	7.8	na	3.3	2.9
Netherlands	0.9	na	na	na	na	na	1.3	3.0
United Kingdom	0.1	0.0	−0.5	−0.8	3.4	0.1	1.9	2.1
Other countries								
Canada	2.9	3.1	−0.3	−1.4	−2.8	−0.8	5.3	5.4
Japan	1.2	−0.8	−1.0	−5.3	10.1	6.2	1.3	1.4
United States	1.9	0.1	0.1	−0.2	2.3	−2.4	4.8	5.4

	Unemployment (annual average % of labour force)					Estimated number (annual averages in 1,000)
	1973	1979	1985	1991	1994	1994
Austria	na	na	na	3.5	4.4[b]	na
Belgium[a]	3	8	14	8.3	10.0	413
Denmark	1	5	12	8.6	10.3[b]	304[b]
Finland	na	na	na	7.6	17.3[b]	na
France	2	6	12	9.7	10.8[b]	2,679[b]
Germany	1	3	7	4.3	7.2[b]	2,870[b]
Greece	na	na	8	7.0	7.7[b]	303[b]
Ireland	6	8	15	16.1	17.7	244
Italy	5	7	12	10.3	11.8	2,883
Netherlands	2	4	12	7.0	8.8[b]	622[b]
Portugal	na	na	na	4.0	6.1	317
Spain	na	na	na	16.4	23.0	3,760
Sweden	na	na	na	2.7	7.7[b]	na
United Kingdom	2	5	16	9.4	9.6	2,778
EU12	na	na	na	na	na	16,932[b]

[a] Includes Luxemburg.
[b] The rate is for 1993.

Table 3.5 ⬤ Structure of production, 1995.

	GDP (million US$)	Distribution of gross domestic product (%)			
		Agriculture	Industry	(of which manufacturing)	Services etc.
EU countries					
Austria	233,427	2	34	24	63
Belgium	269,081	2[a]	30[a]	20[a]	68[a]
Denmark	172,220	4	29	21	67
Finland	125,432	6	37	28	57
France	1,536,089	2	27	19	71
Germany	2,415,764	1[a]	38[b]	27[b]	61[b]
Greece	90,550	21	36	218	43
Ireland	60,780	8[c]	9[c]	3[c]	83[c]
Italy	1,086,932	3	31	21	66
Luxemburg	na	2[a]	36[a]	na	62[a]
Netherlands	395,900	3	2	18	70
Portugal	102,337	6[a]	39[a]	na	55[a]
Spain	558,617	4[a]	34[a]	na	62[a]
Sweden	228,679	2	32	23	66
United Kingdom	1,105,822	2	32	21	66
EU (15)	7,312,533				
EFTA countries					
Iceland	na	na	na	na	na
Norway	109,568	3[c]	35[c]	14[c]	62[c]
Switzerland	260,352	4[a]	40[a]	na	56[a]
EU potential members					
Bulgaria	12,366	13	34	na	53
Cyprus	na	na	na	na	na
Czech Republic	44,772	6	39	na	55
Estonia	4,007	8	28	17	64
Hungary	43,712	8	33	24	59
Latvia	6,034	9	31	18	60
Lithuania	7,089	11	36	30	53
Malta	na	na	na	na	na
Poland	117,663	6	39	26	54
Romania	35,533	21	40	na	39
Slovak Republic	17,414	6	33	na	61
Slovenia	18,550	5	39	1	57
Turkey	164,789	16	31	21	53
Other countries					
Canada	568,928	3[a]	40[a]	na	57[a]
Japan	5,108,540	2	38	24	60
Russian Federation	344,711	7	38	31	55
United States	6,952,020	2	26	18	72

[a] The rate is for 1992.
[b] The rate is for 1993.
[c] The rate is for 1994.

Table 3.6 Growth of production.

	GDP 1965–1980	GDP 1990–1995	Agriculture 1980–1990	Agriculture 1990–1995	Industry 1980–1990	Industry 1990–1995	Services 1980–1990	Services 1990–1995
				Average annual growth rate (%)				
EU countries								
Austria	4.1	1.9	1.1	−1.8	1.9	1.7	2.3	2.2
Belgium	3.8	1.1	1.8	4.0	2.2	na	1.8	na
Denmark	2.7	2.0	3.1	0.3	2.9	1.6	2.1	1.3
Finland	4.0	−0.5	−0.2	0.0	3.3	−1.2	3.7	−2.7
France	4.0	1.0	2.0	1.1	1.1	−1.0	3.0	1.5
Germany	3.3[a]	1.1	1.7	1.6[b]	1.2	1.1[b]	2.9	3.0[b]
Greece	5.6	1.1	−0.1	3.1	1.3	−0.8	2.3	0.6
Ireland	5.0	4.7	na	−6.2[c]	na	na	na	3.8[c]
Italy	4.3	1.0	0.6	2.1	2.2	−0.5	2.7	0.9
Luxemburg	na	na	na	na	na	na	na	na
Netherlands	3.8	1.8	4.1[d]	2.6	0.8[d]	−0.4	1.6[d]	1.9
Portugal	5.3	0.8	−0.9[d]	na	1.0[d]	na	1.3[d]	na
Spain	4.6	1.1	0.9[d]	−1.0	0.4[d]	na	2.1[d]	na
Sweden	2.9	−0.1	1.5	−1.9	2.8	−0.7	2.1	−0.1
United Kingdom	2.4	1.4	3.1[d]	na	1.3[d]	na	3.0[d]	na
EFTA countries								
Iceland	na	na	na	na	na	na	na	na
Norway	4.4	3.5	0.9	1.2[e]	3.5	5.3[e]	2.6	1.5[e]
Switzerland	2.0	0.1	na	na	na	na	na	na
EU potential members								
Bulgaria	na	−4.3	−2.1	−1.9	5.2	−7.5	4.8	−20.7
Cyprus	na	na	na	na	na	na	na	na
Czech Republic	na	−2.6	−0.4[f]	na	0.3[f]	na	1.2[f]	na
Estonia	na	−9.2	−1.9	−8.9	1.6	−14.9	−0.5	−3.8
Hungary	5.6	−1.0	0.6	−7.0	−2.6	−0.5	4.8	−4.6
Latvia	na	−13.7	2.3	−16.4	4.3	−25.1	3.1	−2.1
Lithuania	na	−9.7	na	0.3[b]	na	4.4[b]	na	−0.1[b]
Malta	na	na	na	na	na	na	na	na
Poland	na	2.4	0.7	−2.0	0.1	3.7	2.2	2.4
Romania	na	−1.4	na	−0.4	na	−2.1	na	−2.8
Slovak Republic	na	−2.8	0.6	1.0	2.2	−10.4	1.7	6.2
Slovenia	na	na	na	na	na	na	na	na
Turkey	6.2	3.2	4.4	0.9	6.4	4.2	5.5	3.3
Other countries								
Canada	4.8	1.8	1.5	0.3	2.9	1.2	3.6	1.8
Japan	6.4	1.0	1.1	−2.2	4.9	0.0	3.7	2.3
Russian Federation	na	−1.6	na	0.9[e]	na	0.2	na	2.0[e]
United States	2.6	2.5	4.0	3.6	2.8	1.2	3.1	2.1

[a] The figure is for West Germany. [b] The percentage is for 1980–92.
[c] The percentage is for 1980–90. [d] The percentage is for 1980–88.
[e] The percentage is for 1980–93. [f] The percentage is for Czechoslovakia for 1980–91.
[g] The percentage is for 1970–80.

Table 3.7 ◯ Structure of demand, 1995.

	Distribution of gross domestic product (%)					
	General government consumption	Private consumption etc.	Growth domestic investment	Growth domestic savings	Exports of goods and non-factor services	Resource balance
EU countries						
Austria	19	55	27	26	38	−1
Belgium	15	62	18	24	74	6
Denmark	25	54	16	21	35	6
Finland	21	54	16	24	38	8
France	20	60	18	20	23	2
Germany	20	58	21	23	23	1
Greece	19	73	19	7	22	−12
Ireland	15	57	13	27	75	15
Italy	16	60	18	22	26	3
Luxemburg	na	na	na	na	na	na
Netherlands	14	57	22	29	53	7
Portugal	17	65	28	18	28	−9
Spain	16	62	21	22	24	0
Sweden	26	55	14	19	41	4
United Kingdom	21	64	16	15	28	−1
EFTA countries						
Iceland	na	na	na	na	na	na
Norway	21	50	23	29	38	6
Switzerland	14	59	23	27	36	4
EU potential members						
Bulgaria	15	61	21	25	49	2
Cyprus	na	na	na	na	na	na
Czech Republic	20	60	25	20	52	−5
Estonia	23	58	27	18	75	−9
Hungary	11	68	23	21	35	−2
Latvia	20	65	21	16	43	−5
Lithuania	20	73	19	16	58	−3
Malta	na	na	na	na	na	na
Poland	18	63	17	19	28	2
Romania	12	66	26	21	28	−5
Slovak Republic	20	50	28	30	63	2
Slovenia	21	58	22	21	56	−1
Turkey	10	70	25	20	20	−5
Other countries						
Canada	19	60	19	21	37	2
Japan	10	60	29	31	9	2
Russian Federation	16	58	25	26	22	3
United States	16	68	16	15	11	−2

Table 3.8 ⬤ Structure of manufacturing, 1992.

	Value added in manufacturing (US$m)	Distribution of manufacturing value added (%)				
		Food, beverages and tobacco	Textiles and clothing	Machinery and transport equipment	Chemicals	Other
EU countries						
Austria[a]	46,739	15	6	28	8	43
Belgium[a]	43,280[b]	17	8	22	14	39
Denmark	23,478	23	4	23	12	38
Finland	20,785	14	3	23	8	51
France[a]	271,133	14	6	30	9	42
Germany[a,c]	565,603	10	4	41	12	33
Greece	12,389	26	17	12	9	35
Ireland	1,511	27	3	27	21	22
Italy[a]	250,345	10	14	33	6	38
Luxemburg	na	na	na	na	na	na
Netherlands[a]	58,476	21	3	24	16	36
Portugal	na	20	23	12	10	35
Spain[a]	100,672	18	8	26	10	38
Sweden	43,605	11	2	33	10	44
United Kingdom	201,859	15	5	30	13	37
EFTA countries						
Iceland	na	na	na	na	na	na
Norway	14,282	23	2	27	8	40
Switzerland[a]	na	10	4	14	na	72
EU potential members						
Bulgaria	na	na	na	na	na	na
Cyprus	na	na	na	na	na	na
Czech Republic	na	na	na	na	na	na
Estonia[a]	1,265	na	na	na	na	na
Hungary[a]	7,381	11	9	27	14	40
Latvia	1,738	na	na	na	na	na
Lithuania	na	na	na	na	na	na
Malta	na	na	na	na	na	na
Poland	na	21	9	26	7	37
Romania	10,623	19	15	12	6	47
Slovak Republic[a]	na	na	na	na	na	na
Slovenia	3,670	16	16	23	10	35
Turkey	27,465	18	14	19	9	40
Other countries						
Canada	na	17	5	26	10	41
Japan[a]	1,023,048	10	5	38	10	38
Russian Federation[a]	200,237	na	na	na	na	na
United States[a]	na	13	5	31	12	38

[a] Data are at purchaser values.   [b] Data are for 1991.
[c] Data are for West Germany before unification, and all the percentages are for 1991.

Table 3.9 ⬭ Growth of consumption and investment.

	General government consumption			Private consumption, etc.			Gross domestic investment		
	1965–80	1980–90	1990–93	1965–80	1980–90	1990–93	1965–80	1980–90	1990–95
EU countries									
Austria	3.7	1.3	1.4	4.4	2.4	2.5	4.5	2.5	3.6
Belgium	4.6	0.4	0.7	4.3	1.7	1.9	2.9	3.2	−0.9
Denmark	4.8	0.9	0.9	2.3	1.9	1.7	1.2	4.0	−1.1
Finland	5.3	3.6	2.7	3.8	4.6	3.3	2.9	3.0	−8.3
France	3.6	2.2	2.2	4.7	4.1	2.2	3.9	2.8	−2.8
Germany[a]	3.5	1.4	1.3	4.0	1.9	2.6	1.7	2.0	2.4[b]
Greece	6.6	2.8	2.4	4.9	3.4	3.3	5.3	−0.9	1.9
Ireland	6.1	−0.4	0.2	4.3	1.8	3.3	6.3	na	−3.8
Italy	3.4	2.7	2.3	4.1	3.0	2.7	3.4	2.1	−3.2
Luxemburg	na	na	na	na	na	na	na	na	na
Netherlands	2.9	1.0	1.5	4.8	1.6	2.0	1.8	3.1	−0.3
Portugal	8.1	2.5	4.5	6.7	5.0	2.9	4.6	na	4.1[b]
Spain	5.1	5.1	5.4	4.8	3.0	2.7	3.7	5.7	−2.6
Sweden	4.0	1.5	1.6	2.5	2.1	1.5	0.9	4.3	−7.2
United Kingdom	2.3	1.1	1.2	2.2	4.0	3.3	0.6	6.4	4.0[b]
EFTA countries									
Iceland	na	na	na	na	na	na	na	na	na
Norway	5.5	3.0	2.8	3.9	1.6	1.6	4.2	0.6	−1.0[b]
Switzerland	2.7	2.9	2.7	2.5	1.7	1.4	0.8	4.9	0.0
EU potential members									
Bulgaria	na	na	9.9	na	na	0.3	na	2.4	−7.1
Cyprus	na	na	na	na	na	na	na	na	na
Czech Republic	na	na	na	na	na	na	na	2.3	0.9
Estonia	na	na	na	na	na	na	na	0.5	−13.4
Hungary	na	na	na	na	na	na	na	−0.4	6.6
Latvia	na	na	na	na	na	na	na	3.4	−37.1
Lithuania	na	na	na	na	na	na	na	na	na
Malta	na	na	na	na	na	na	na	na	na
Poland	na	na	na	na	na	na	na	0.9	1.1
Romania	na	na	na	na	na	na	na	na	−10.0
Slovak Republic	na	na	na	na	na	na	na	1.1	7.7
Slovenia	na	na	na	na	na	na	na	na	na
Turkey	6.1	3.1	3.3	5.7	5.9	5.1	8.8	5.3	2.0
Other countries									
Canada	4.8	2.3	2.5	4.9	3.6	2.8	5.1	5.2	2.3
Japan	5.1	2.4	2.3	6.0	3.7	3.5	6.7	5.3	0.8
Russian Federation	na	na	−2.0	na	na	−3.5	na	na	−0.1[b]
United States	1.2	3.3	2.4	3.1	3.4	2.9	2.6	3.4	4.1

[a] Data are for West Germany before unification.
[b] Data are for 1980–93.

Table 3.10 ⬤ Central government expenditure, 1995.

	Total expenditure (% of GDP)		Percentage of total expenditure on		Overall deficit/surplus[b] (% of GNP)
	Current	Capital	Defence	Social services[c]	
EU countries					
Austria	37.5	2.9	3.7	77.8	−0.1
Belgium	47.9	5.5	7.0	7.2	−0.5
Denmark	42.0	1.5	4.0	56.9	−2.0
Finland	42.0	1.7	3.9	63.5	−13.4
France	44.4	2.4	5.6[e]	72.5	−5.5
Germany	32.2	1.7	na	na	−2.5
Greece	38.8	4.4	8.9	34.1	−15.7
Ireland	39.3	3.2	3.0	57.5	−0.2
Italy	48.0	1.9	na	na	−10.5
Luxemburg	na	na	na	na	na
Netherlands	48.3	2.5	3.9	68.7	−4.9
Portugal	37.7	5.4[e]	na	na	−2.2[e]
Spain	36.8	2.6	6.8	54.0	0.0
Sweden	43.6	1.4	5.6	64.6	−6.9
United Kingdom	39.6	4.4	10.4[e]	54.5	0.1
EFTA countries					
Iceland	na	na	na	na	na
Norway	39.1	1.9[e]	6.5[e]	51.1	−7.5[e]
Switzerland[d]	25.9	1.2	15.2	75.2	−0.1
EU potential members					
Bulgaria	41.4	1.6	6.3	35.0	−5.5
Cyprus	na	na	na	na	na
Czech Republic	36.9	5.1	5.7	65.7	0.5
Estonia	na	na	3.1	56.4[e]	1.4
Hungary[d]	50.6[e]	7.7[e]	4.3	26.7	−2.9[e]
Latvia	29.2	1.2	2.6	63.7	−4.2
Lithuania	24.7	2.7	1.9	53.2	na
Malta	na	na	na	na	na
Poland	41.9	1.5	na	na	−2.3
Romania	27.7	4.3	6.2	54.8	0.0
Slovak Republic	na	na	na	na	na
Slovenia	na	na	na	na	na
Turkey	20.9	6.1	15.8	21.6	0.0
Other countries					
Canada	21.6[d]	0.3[d]	10.8	51.4[e]	−4.5[e]
Japan	14.8[d]	3.6[d]	4.1	59.2[e]	0.0
Russian Federation	25.8	1.3	16.4	34.6	−10.5
United States	22.1	0.8	18.1	55.0	−2.3

[a] Includes lending minus repayments.   [b] Includes grants.
[c] Refers to education, health, social security, welfare, housing and community amenities.
[d] The figure(s) is (are) for 1980.   [e] The figure is for 1994.

Table 3.11 ⬤ Central government revenue, 1980 and 1995.

	Total revenue[a] Tax		(% of GDP) Non-tax	
	1980	1994	1980	1994
EU countries				
Austria	32.0	32.9	8.8	9.1
Belgium	41.7	43.7	10.5	11.4
Denmark	31.3	35.4	16.7	16.5
Finland	25.1	29.3	13.3	14.2
France	36.7	38.1	12.2	11.5
Germany	na	30.0	na	7.3
Greece	27.4	26.0	9.7	17.8
Ireland	30.9	35.1	10.4	11.4
Italy	29.1	38.4	7.7	11.2
Luxemburg	na	na	na	na
Netherlands	44.2	42.9[b]	10.3	10.5
Portugal	24.3	30.9	8.8	12.8
Spain	22.2	28.7	3.1	6.5
Sweden	30.1	32.8	10.2	11.2
United Kingdom	30.6	33.5	9.8	11.8
EFTA countries				
Iceland	na	na	na	na
Norway	33.9	31.6	14.8	15.4
Switzerland	18.3	21.5	3.8	3.4
EU potential members				
Bulgaria	na	29.0	na	10.4
Cyprus	na	na	na	na
Czech Republic	na	37.5	na	13.0
Estonia	na	33.2	na	13.6
Hungary	44.9	na	20.5	na
Latvia	na	23.1	na	10.9
Lithuania	na	24.4	na	12.6
Malta	na	na	na	na
Poland	na	36.7	na	11.6
Romania	10.1	26.3	0.0	6.9
Slovak Republic	na	na	na	na
Slovenia	na	na	na	na
Turkey	14.3	14.3	3.6	7.3
Other countries				
Canada	16.2	19.5[b]	3.1	2.5[b]
Japan	11.0	17.6	14.8	15.4
Russian Federation	na	16.1	na	6.3
United States	18.4	19.0	0.9	0.8

[a] Refers to current revenue.
[b] The figure is for 1994.

Table 3.12 ● Official development assistance.

	Amount in US$m[a]				% of donor country GNP			
	1965	1975	1985	1993	1965	1975	1985	1993
EU countries								
Austria	10	79	248	544	0.11	0.21	0.38	0.33
Belgium	102	378	440	808	0.60	0.59	0.55	0.39
Denmark	13	205	440	1,340	0.13	0.58	0.80	1.03
Finland	2	48	211	355	0.02	0.18	0.40	0.46
France	752	2,093	3,995	7,915	0.76	0.62	0.78	0.63
Germany[a]	456	1,689	2,942	6,954	0.40	0.40	0.47	0.37
Greece	na	na	−11	na	na	na	0.10	0.10
Ireland	0	8	39	81	0.00	0.09	0.24	0.20
Italy	60	182	1,098	3,043	0.10	0.11	0.26	0.31
Netherlands	70	608	1,136	2,525	0.36	0.75	0.91	0.82
Portugal	na	na	−101	na	na	na	0.50	na
Spain	na	na	0	na	na	na	0.00	na
Sweden	38	566	840	1,769	0.19	0.82	0.86	0.98
United Kingdom	472	904	1,530	2,908	0.47	0.39	0.33	0.31
EFTA countries								
Iceland	na	na	na	na	na	na	na	na
Norway	11	184	574	1,014	0.16	0.66	1.01	1.01
Switzerland	12	104	302	793	0.09	0.19	0.31	0.33
EU potential members								
Bulgaria	na	na	na	na	na	na	na	na
Cyprus	na	na	na	na	na	na	na	na
Czech Republic	na	na	na	na	na	na	na	na
Estonia	na	na	na	na	na	na	na	na
Hungary	na	na	na	na	na	na	na	na
Latvia	na	na	na	na	na	na	na	na
Lithuania	na	na	na	na	na	na	na	na
Malta	na	na	na	na	na	na	na	na
Poland	na	na	na	na	na	na	na	na
Romania	na	na	na	na	na	na	na	na
Slovak Republic	na	na	na	na	na	na	na	na
Slovenia	na	na	na	na	na	na	na	na
Turkey	na	na	−175	na	na	na	0.60	0.10
Other countries								
Canada	96	880	1,631	2,373	0.19	0.54	0.49	0.45
Japan	244	1,148	3,797	11,259	0.27	0.23	0.49	0.26
Russian Federation	na	na	na	na	na	na	na	na
United States	4,023	4,161	9,403	9,721	0.58	0.27	0.24	0.15

[a] Data refer to West Germany before unification.

Table 3.13 ⬤ Money and interest rates.

| | Money and quasi money | | | | Nominal bank interest rates (average annual %) | |
| | Average annual nominal growth (%) | | Average outstanding (% of GDP) | | Deposit rate | Lending rate |
	1985–95	1965	1980	1995	1995	1995
EU countries						
Austria	7.0	49.0	72.6	89.5	2.2	na
Belgium	13.0	59.2	45.0	80.2	4.0	8.4
Denmark	4.4	45.9	42.6	57.8	3.9	10.3
Finland	6.6	39.1	39.8	56.7	3.2	7.7
France	3.7	53.7	71.6	64.4	4.5	8.1
Germany	8.1	46.1	na	62.0	3.9	10.9
Greece	15.1[a]	35.0	50.5	53.0	15.8	23.1
Ireland	11.4	na	43.8	50.1	0.4	6.6
Italy	7.9[a]	68.8	70.9	62.5	6.4	12.5
Luxemburg	na	na	na	na	na	na
Netherlands	5.6	54.5	67.3	82.0	4.4	7.2
Portugal	15.5	77.7	70.1	78.1	8.4	13.8
Spain	11.2	58.5	75.4	78.6	7.7	10.0
Sweden	na	46.5	54.0	47.5[b]	6.2	11.1
United Kingdom	16.3[a]	48.4	29.8	na	4.1	6.7
EFTA countries						
Iceland	na	na	na	na	na	na
Norway	5.9	51.9	47.1	55.6	5.0	7.8
Switzerland	4.6	101.1	107.4	126.3	1.3	5.5
EU potential members						
Bulgaria	44.7[a]	na	33.4[b]	15.2[b]	na	na
Cyprus	na	na	na	na	na	na
Czech Republic	na	na	na	81.0	7.0	12.8
Estonia	na	na	na	22.5	8.7	16.0
Hungary	18.2[a]	na	na	43.0	26.1	32.6
Latvia	na	na	na	11.6	102.0	319.5
Lithuania	na	na	na	22.6	8.4	27.1
Malta	na	na	na	na	na	na
Poland	87.2	na	57.0	31.8	26.8	33.5
Romania	51.3	na	33.4	19.9	na	na
Slovak Republic	na	na	na	62.9	9.0	15.6
Slovenia	na	na	na	32.5	15.3	24.8
Turkey	73.9	23.0	14.2	24.8	76.1	na
Other countries						
Canada	8.9	40.5	45.1	59.3	7.1	8.6
Japan	5.9	106.9	83.4	112.7	0.7	3.4
Russian Federation	na	na	na	13.7	na	na
United States	3.9	63.8	60.4	59.4	5.9[d]	8.8

[a] The figure is for 1985–94.   [b] The figure is for 1994.
[c] The figure is for 1980.   [d] Certificate of deposit rate.

Table 3.14 ⬭ Merchandise exports.

	Total (US$m)		Manufactures (% of total)		Average annual volume growth (%)	
	1980	1995	1980	1995	1980–90	1990–95
EU countries						
Austria	17,500	45,200	83	89	6.4	3.9
Belgium[a]	64,500	136,864	74[b]	81	4.4	4.2
Denmark	16,700	49,036	56	66	4.4	5.4
Finland	14,200	39,573	70	83	2.3	8.7
France	116,000	286,738	74	78	4.1	2.3
Germany[c]	193,000	523,743	86	90	4.6	2.2
Greece	5,150	9,384	47	53	5.1	11.9
Ireland	8,400	44,191	58	75	9.3	11.4
Italy	78,100	231,336	85	89	4.3	6.0
Netherlands	74,000	195,912	51	63	4.5	5.8
Portugal	4,640	22,621	72	84	12.2	0.5
Spain	20,700	91,716	72	78	6.9	11.2
Sweden	30,900	97,908	79	85	4.6	7.4
United Kingdom	110,000	242,042	74	82	4.4	1.8
EFTA countries						
Iceland	na	na	na	na	na	na
Norway	18,600	41,764	32	31	6.8	6.5
Switzerland	29,600	77,649	91	94	6.0	3.3
EU potential members						
Bulgaria	10,400	5,100	na	na	na	na
Cyprus	na	na	na	na	na	na
Czech Republic	na	21,654	na	na	na	na
Estonia	na	1,847	na	na	na	na
Hungary	8,670	12,540	66	68	3.0	−1.8
Latvia	na	967	na	na	na	na
Lithuania	na	1,305	na	64	na	na
Malta	na	na	na	na	na	na
Poland	14,200	22,892	71	68	4.8	3.9
Romania	11,200	7,548	na	76	−6.8	−4.7
Slovak Republic	na	8,585	na	na	na	na
Slovenia	na	8,286	na	86	na	na
Turkey	2,910	21,600	27	72	12.0	8.8
Other countries						
Canada	67,700	192,198	49	66	5.7	8.4
Japan	130,000	443,116	96	97	5.0	0.4
Russian Federation[d]	na	81,500	na	na	na	na
United States	226,000	584,473	68	82	3.6	5.6

[a] Includes Luxemburg.   [b] The figure is for 1994.
[c] Data prior to 1990 refer to West Germany before unification.
[d] Excludes trade with other members of the Commonwealth of Independent States.

Table 3.15 ⬤ Merchandise imports.

	Total (US$m)		Food (% of total)		Fuel (% of total)		Average annual volume growth (%)	
	1980	1995	1980	1993	1980	1993	1980–90	1990–95
EU countries								
Austria	24,400	55,300	6	5	16	5	5.8	1.9
Belgium[a]	71,900	125,297	11	11	17	8	4.0	0.3
Denmark	19,300	43,223	12	13	22	6	3.6	3.4
Finland	15,600	28,114	7	7	29	13	4.4	−1.9
France	135,000	275,275	10	11	27	9	5.0	0.8
Germany[b]	188,000	464,220	12	10	23	8	4.9	2.9
Greece	10,500	21,466	9	14	23	25	5.8	12.8
Ireland	11,200	32,568	12	10	15	5	4.7	5.6
Italy	101,000	204,062	13	13	28	10	5.3	−1.7
Netherlands	76,600	176,420	15	15	24	9	4.6	4.3
Portugal	9,310	32,339	14	19	24	24	9.8	2.4
Spain	34,100	115,019	13	14	39	11	10.1	5.3
Sweden	33,400	64,438	7	8	24	9	4.9	5.0
United Kingdom	116,000	263,719	13	11	14	5	6.3	0.9
EFTA countries								
Iceland	na	na	na	na	na	na	na	na
Norway	16,900	32,702	8	7	17	3	4.2	0.7
Switzerland	36,300	76,985	8	7	11	4	4.9	−6.7
EU potential members								
Bulgaria	9,650	5,015	na	8	na	36	na	na
Cyprus	na	na	na	na	na	na	na	na
Czech Republic	na	26,523	na	na	na	na	na	na
Estonia	na	2,539	na	na	na	na	na	na
Hungary	9,220	15,073	8	na	na	na	na	7.9
Latvia	na	1,818	na	6	16	13	0.7	na
Lithuania	na	3,083	na	11	na	45	na	na
Malta	na	na	na	na	na	na	na	na
Poland	16,700	29,050	14	12	18	17	1.5	26.4
Romania	12,800	9,424	na	14	na	26	−0.9	−5.3
Slovak Republic	na	9,070	na	na	na	na	na	na
Slovenia	na	9,452	na	8	na	11	na	na
Turkey	7,910	35,710	4	6	48	14	11.3	11.2
Other countries								
Canada	62,500	168,426	8	6	12	4	6.2	6.3
Japan	141,000	335,882	12	18	50	21	6.5	4.0
Russian Federation[c]	na	58,900	na	na	na	na	na	na
United States	257,000	770,852	8	5	33	10	7.2	7.4

[a] Includes Luxemburg.
[b] Data prior to 1990 refer to West Germany before unification.
[c] Excludes trade with other members of the Commonwealth of Independent States.

Table 3.16 ⬤ Terms of trade and export concentration index.

	Trade % of GDP		Net barter terms of trade (1987 = 100)		Export concentration index	
	1985	1995	1985	1995	1984	1992
EU countries						
Austria	76	77	92	87	0.078	0.061
Belgium[a]	128	143	96	101	0.115	0.106
Denmark	66	64	91	100	0.087	0.077
Finland	67	68	88	95	0.210	0.230
France	44	43	89	106	0.085	0.064
Germany	na	46	84[b]	96	0.136	0.084
Greece	47	57	96	111	0.127	0.118
Ireland	108	136	96	90	0.161	0.125
Italy	47	49	84	100	0.100	0.056
Netherlands	103	99	101	103	0.137	0.061
Portugal	61	66	117	92	0.144	0.106
Spain	34	47	82	114	0.120	0.142
Sweden	61	77	92	102	0.151	0.110
United Kingdom	52	57	104	102	0.152	0.063
EFTA countries						
Iceland	na	na	na	na		
Norway	81	71	142	95	0.345	0.366
Switzerland	77	68	85	60	0.119	0.102
EU potential members						
Bulgaria	66	94	95	106	na	na
Cyprus	na	na	na	na	na	na
Czech Republic	na	108	98	86	na	na
Estonia	na	160	na	na	na	na
Hungary	80	67	103	97	na	na
Latvia	na	91	na	na	na	na
Lithuania	na	108	na	na	na	na
Malta	na	na	na	na	na	na
Poland	59	53	95	109	na	na
Romania	75	60	66	111	na	na
Slovak Republic	na	124	98	86	na	na
Slovenia	na	113	na	na	na	0.083
Turkey	17	45	82	109	0.159	0.119
Other countries						
Canada	55	71	99	107	0.225	0.125
Japan	28	17	73	127	0.209	0.140
Russian Federation	na	44	na	na	na	na
United States	21	24	101	102	0.110	0.080

[a] Includes Luxemburg.
[b] Data prior to 1990 refer to West Germany before unification.

Table 3.17 ● Imports from EU(12) countries.

Importing country	% share of total imports of importing country					
	1957	1974	1981	1986	1990	1993
EU countries						
Austria	na	na	na	66.9	68.6	66.6
Belgium*a*	43.5	66.1	59.3	69.9	70.7	71.4
Denmark	31.2	45.5	47.9	53.2	53.7	54.3
Finland	na	na	na	43.1	46.3	45.6
France	21.4	47.6	48.2	64.4	64.8	64.0
Germany	23.5	48.1	48.2	54.2	54.1	51.2
Greece	40.8	43.3	50.0	58.3	64.1	60.3
Ireland	na	68.3	74.7	73.0	70.8	94.5
Italy	21.4	42.4	40.7	55.4	57.4	55.4
Netherlands	41.1	57.4	52.4	61.0	59.9	66.1
Portugal	37.1	43.5	38.0	58.8	69.1	71.9
Spain	21.3	35.8	29.0	51.3	59.1	61.3
Sweden	na	na	na	57.2	55.3	55.0
United Kingdom	12.1	30.0	39.4	50.4	51.0	48.9
EFTA countries						
Iceland	na	na	na	na	na	na
Norway	na	na	na	50.1	45.8	48.7
Switzerland	na	na	na	73.0	71.7	72.6
EU potential members						
Bulgaria	na	na	na	na	na	na
Cyprus	na	na	na	na	na	na
Czech Republic	na	na	na	na	na	na
Estonia	na	na	na	na	na	na
Hungary	na	na	na	na	na	na
Latvia	na	na	na	na	na	na
Lithuania	na	na	na	na	na	na
Malta	na	na	na	na	na	na
Poland	na	na	na	na	na	na
Romania	na	na	na	na	na	na
Slovak Republic	na	na	na	na	na	na
Slovenia	na	na	na	na	na	na
Turkey	na	na	na	41.0	41.9	45.5
Other countries						
Canada	4.2	6.9	8.0	11.3	11.5	8.4
Japan	na	6.4	6.0	11.1	15.0	12.6
Russian Federation	na	na	na	na	na	34.7
United States	11.7	9.0	16.0	20.5	18.6	16.8

*a*Includes Luxemburg.

Table 3.18 ⬭ Exports to EU(12) countries.

Exporting country	% share of total exports of exporting country					
	1957	1974	1981	1986	1990	1993
EU countries						
Austria	na	na	na	60.1	65.2	60.3
Belgium[a]	46.1	69.9	70.0	72.9	75.1	73.6
Denmark	31.2	43.1	46.7	46.8	52.1	54.2
Finland	na	na	na	38.3	46.9	45.4
France	25.1	53.2	48.2	57.8	62.7	61.2
Germany	29.2	53.2	46.9	50.8	53.6	49.8
Greece	52.5	50.1	43.3	63.5	64.0	55.9
Ireland	na	74.1	69.9	71.9	74.8	69.1
Italy	24.9	45.4	43.2	53.5	58.2	53.3
Netherlands	41.6	70.8	71.2	75.7	76.5	73.9
Portugal	22.2	48.2	53.7	68.0	73.5	75.3
Spain	29.8	47.4	43.0	60.9	64.9	62.3
Sweden	na	na	na	50.0	54.3	53.0
United Kingdom	14.6	33.4	41.3	47.9	52.6	52.5
EFTA countries						
Iceland	na	na	na	na	na	59.8
Norway	na	na	na	65.1	64.9	66.6
Switzerland	na	na	na	54.9	58.1	56.7
EU potential members						
Bulgaria	na	na	na	na	na	na
Cyprus	na	na	na	na	na	na
Czech Republic	na	na	na	na	na	na
Estonia	na	na	na	na	na	na
Hungary	na	na	na	na	na	na
Latvia	na	na	na	na	na	na
Lithuania	na	na	na	na	na	na
Malta	na	na	na	na	na	na
Poland	na	na	na	na	na	na
Romania	na	na	na	na	na	na
Slovak Republic	na	na	na	na	na	na
Slovenia	na	na	na	na	na	na
Turkey	na	na	na	44.0	53.3	45.9
Other countries						
Canada	9.3	12.6	10.7	6.8	8.1	5.5
Japan	na	10.7	12.4	14.8	18.8	15.6
Russian Federation	na	na	na	na	na	36.3
United States	15.3	21.9	22.4	24.5	25.0	13.3

[a] Includes Luxemburg.

Table 3.19 ● Balance of payments and reserves, 1995 (US$million).

	Exports of goods, services and income	Imports of goods, services and income	Current transfers Net workers' remit- tances	Other net transfers	Current account balance	Gross inter- national reserves
EU countries						
Austria	106,474	110,085	28	−1,531	−5,113	23,396
Belgium*a*	305,010	286,809	−393	−2,848	14,960	24,120
Denmark	92,772	90,398	0	−961	1,413	11,652
Finland	50,798	44,813	na	−343	5,642	10,657
France	498,203	475,234	−1,364	−5,162	16,443	58,510
Germany*b*	706,502	686,512	−5,305	−35,661	−20,976	121,816
Greece	16,835	27,707	2,982	5,026	−2,864	16,119
Ireland	53,126	53,530	na	1,782	1,379	8,770
Italy	330,286	299,954	98	−4,724	25,706	60,690
Netherlands	250,990	228,460	−423	−5,916	16,191	47,162
Portugal	35,666	43,026	3,348	3,783	−229	22,063
Spain	146,042	149,863	2,119	2,983	1,280	40,531
Sweden	109,063	101,439	106	−3,098	4,633	25,909
United Kingdom	458,728	452,359	na	−11,001	−4,632	49,114
EFTA countries						
Iceland	na	na	na	na	na	na
Norway	50,837	45,573	−236	−1,384	3,645	22,976
Switzerland	154,840	129,113	−2,519	−1,586	21,622	68,620
EU potential members						
Bulgaria	6,680	6,478	0	132	334	na
Cyprus	na	na	na	na	na	na
Czech Republic	29,399	31,345	0	572	−1,374	14,613
Estonia	2,801	3,112	−1	127	−184	583
Hungary	17,933	21,528	−14	1,073	−2,535	12,095
Latvia	2,151	2,246	na	68	−27	602
Lithuania	3,242	3,966	1	109	−614	829
Malta	na	na	na	na	na	na
Poland	33,169	36,929	35	−520	−4,245	14,597
Romania	9,094	10,799	3	360	−1,342	2,624
Slovak Republic	11,185	10,629	0	93	648	3,863
Slovenia	10,731	10,812	53	−8	−37	1,821
Turkey	38,069	44,904	3,327	1,169	−2,339	13,891
Other countries						
Canada	224,135	232,458	na	−370	−8,693	13,369
Japan	687,136	568,143	0	−7,747	111,246	192,620
Russian Fed.	95,100	85,800	na	304	9,604	18,024
United States	969,220	1,082,260	−12,230	−22,960	−148,230	175,996

a Includes Luxemburg.
b Data prior to 1990 refer to West Germany before unification.

Table 3.20 ⬭ Education.

	School enrolment as a % of age group					Percentage of cohort reaching grade 4		Adult illiteracy (%)	
	Primary		Secondary						
	Female 1993	Male 1993	Female 1993	Male 1993	Tertiary 1993	Female 1990	Male 1990	Female 1995	Male 1995
EU countries									
Austria	103	103	104	109	43	99	97	a	a
Belgium	100	99	104	103	na	na	na	a	a
Denmark	98	97	115	112	41	98	98	a	a
Finland	100	100	130	110	63	98	98	a	a
France	105	107	107	104	50	95	100	a	a
Germany	98	97	100	101	36	99	97	a	a
Greece	na	na	na	na	na	99	98	na	na
Ireland	103	103	110	101	34	99	98	a	a
Italy	99	98	82	81	37	na	na	a	a
Luxemburg	na	na	na	na	na	na	na	na	na
Netherlands	99	96	120	126	45	na	na	a	a
Portugal	118	122	na	na	23	na	na	na	na
Spain	105	104	120	107	41	95	94	na	na
Sweden	100	100	100	99	38	na	na	a	a
United Kingdom	113	112	94	91	37	na	na	a	a
EFTA countries									
Iceland	na	na	na	na	na	na	na	na	na
Norway	99	99	114	118	54	na	na	a	a
Switzerland	102	100	89	93	31	na	na	a	a
EU potential members									
Bulgaria	84	87	70	66	23	91	93	na	na
Cyprus	na	na	na	na	na	na	na	na	na
Czech Republic	100	99	88	85	16	na	na	na	na
Estonia	83	84	96	87	38	na	na	na	na
Hungary	95	95	82	79	17	97	97	na	na
Latvia	82	83	90	84	39	na	na	na	na
Lithuania	90	95	79	76	39	na	na	na	na
Malta	na	na	na	na	na	na	na	na	na
Poland	97	98	87	82	26	97	98	na	na
Romania	86	87	82	83	12	94	93	na	na
Slovak Republic	101	101	90	87	17	na	na	na	na
Slovenia	97	97	90	88	28	na	na	na	na
Turkey	98	107	48	74	16	98	98	28	8
Other countries									
Canada	104	106	103	104	103	98	95	a	a
Japan	102	102	97	95	30	100	100	a	a
Russian Federation	107	107	91	84	45	na	na	na	na
United States	106	107	97	98	81	na	na	a	a

aAccording to UNESCO, illiteracy is less than 5%.

Table 3.21 ⬤ Distribution of income or consumption.

| | Survey year | Gini index | \| % share of income or consumption | | | | | |
			Lowest 20%	Second quantile	Third quantile	Fourth quantile	Highest 20%	Highest 10%
EU countries								
Austria	na	na	na	na	na	na	na	na
Belgium	1978–79[a]	na	7.9	13.7	18.6	23.8	36.0	21.5
Denmark	1981[a]	na	5.4	12.0	18.4	25.6	38.6	22.3
Finland	1981[a]	na	6.3	12.1	18.4	25.5	37.6	21.7
France	1989[a]	na	5.6	11.8	17.2	23.5	41.9	26.1
Germany	1988[a]	na	7.0	11.8	17.1	23.9	40.3	24.4
Greece	na	na	na	na	na	na	na	na
Ireland	na	na	na	na	na	na	na	na
Italy	1986[a]	na	6.8	12.0	16.7	23.5	41.0	25.3
Luxemburg	na	na	na	na	na	na	na	na
Netherlands	1988[a]	na	8.2	13.1	18.1	23.7	36.9	21.9
Portugal	na	na	na	na	na	na	na	na
Spain	1988[a]	na	8.3	13.7	18.1	23.4	36.6	21.8
Sweden	1981[a]	na	8.0	13.2	17.4	24.5	36.9	20.8
United Kingdom	1988[a]	na	4.6	10.0	16.8	24.3	44.3	27.8
EFTA countries								
Iceland	na	na	na	na	na	na	na	na
Norway	1979[a]	na	6.2	12.8	18.9	25.3	36.7	21.2
Switzerland	1982[a]	na	5.2	11.7	16.4	22.1	44.6	29.8
EU potential members								
Bulgaria	1992[b]	30.8	8.3	13.0	17.0	22.3	39.3	24.7
Cyprus	na	na	na	na	na	na	na	na
Czech Republic	1993[b]	26.6	10.5	13.9	16.9	21.3	37.4	23.5
Estonia	1993[b]	39.5	6.6	10.7	15.1	21.4	46.3	31.3
Hungary	1993[c]	27.0	9.5	14.0	17.6	22.3	36.6	22.6
Latvia	1993[b]	27.0	9.6	13.6	17.5	22.6	36.7	22.1
Lithuania	1993[b]	33.6	8.1	12.3	16.2	21.3	42.1	28.0
Malta	na	na	na	na	na	na	na	na
Poland	1992[c]	27.2	9.3	13.8	17.7	22.6	36.6	21.1
Romania	1992[b]	25.5	9.2	14.4	18.4	23.2	34.8	20.2
Slovak Republic	1992[b]	19.5	11.9	15.8	18.8	22.2	31.4	18.2
Slovenia	1993[b]	28.2	9.5	13.5	17.1	21.9	37.9	23.8
Turkey	na	na	na	na	na	na	na	na
Other countries								
Canada	1987[a]	na	5.7	11.8	17.7	24.6	40.2	24.1
Japan	1979[a]	na	8.7	13.2	17.5	23.1	37.5	22.4
Russian Federation	1993[c]	49.6	3.7	8.5	13.5	20.4	53.8	38.7
United States	1985[a]	na	4.7	11.0	17.4	25.0	41.9	25.0

[a] Refers to income shares by percentiles of households, and ranked by household income.
[b] Refers to income shares by percentiles of persons, and ranked by per capita income.
[c] Refers to expenditure shares by percentiles of persons, and ranked by per capita expenditure.

Table 3.22 ⬭ Health.

		Percentage of total population with access to		Infant mortality rate (per 1,000 live births)		Total fertility rate		Maternal mortality rate (per 100,000 live births)
		Health care 1993	Safe water 1994–5	Sanitation 1994–5	1980	1995	1980	1995	1989–95
EU countries									
Austria	na	100[a]	100	14	6	1.5	na	
Belgium	na	100[a]	100	12	8	1.7	1.6	na
Denmark	na	100	100	8	6	1.5	1.8	na
Finland	na	100	100	8	5	1.6	1.8	na
France	na	100	96	10	6	1.9	1.7	na
Germany	na	na	100	12	6	1.6	1.2	na
Greece	na	100[a]	96	18	8	2.2	1.4	na
Ireland	na	100[a]	100	11	6	3.2	1.9	na
Italy	na	100[a]	100	15	7	1.6	1.2	na
Luxemburg	na	na	na	na	85	na	na	na
Netherlands	na	100	100	9	6	1.6	1.6	na
Portugal	na	100[a]	100	24	7	2.2	1.4	na
Spain	na	99	97	12	7	2.2	1.2	na
Sweden	na	100[a]	100	7	4	1.7	1.7	na
United Kingdom	na	100	96	12	6	1.9	1.7	na
EFTA countries									
Iceland	na	na	na	na	na	na	na	na
Norway	na	100	100	8	6	1.7	1.9	na
Switzerland	na	100	100	9	6	1.6	1.5	na
EU potential members									
Bulgaria	na	100[a]	99	20	15	2.1	1.2	na
Cyprus	na	na	na	na	na	na	na	na
Czech Republic	na	na	na	16	8	2.1	1.3	na
Estonia	na	na	na	17	14	2.0	1.3	41
Hungary	na	100[a]	94	23	11	1.9	1.6	na
Latvia	na	na	na	20	16	2.0	1.3	na
Lithuania	na	na	na	20	14	2.0	1.5	29
Malta	na	na	na	na	na	na	na	na
Poland	na	100[a]	100	21	14	2.3	1.6	na
Romania	na	100[a]	49	29	23	2.4	1.4	na
Slovak Republic	na	77[a]	51	21	11	2.3	1.5	na
Slovenia	na	na	90	15	7	2.1	1.3	na
Turkey	na	92	94	109	48	4.3	2.7	183[b]
Other countries									
Canada	na	100	85	10	6	1.7	1.7	na
Japan	100	95	85	8	4	1.8	1.5	64[c]
Russian Federation	na	na	na	22	18	1.9	1.4	52
United States	na	90	85	13	8	1.8	2.1	na

[a] The figure is for 1993.
[b] UNICEF–WHO estimate.
[c] Official estimation.

Table 3.23 ● Average tariffs (%), 1958[a].

	Benelux	France	West Germany	Italy	EC(6)	Denmark	United Kingdom	Canada	United States
Instruments (86)	13	22	8	17	16	3	27	19	29
Footwear (851)	20	21	10	21	19	19	25	24	19
Clothing (84)	20	26	13	25	21	19	26	25	32½
Furniture (821)	13	23	8	21	17	11	20	25	24
Building parts and fittings (81)	15	19	8	25	17	8	15	16	20
Transport equipment (73)	17	29	12	34	22	8	25	17	13
Electric machinery, etc. (72)	11	19	6	21	15	8	23	18	20
Machinery other than electric (71)	8	18	5	20	13	6	17	9	12
Manufactures of metals (699)	11	20	10	23	16	6	21	18	23
Ordnance (691)	9	14	7	17	11	1	22	13	26
Iron and steel (681)	5	13	7	17	10	1	14	12	13
Silver, platinum, gems, jewellery (67)	5	13	3	7	6	5	11	13	29
Non-metallic mineral manufactures (66)	12	16	6	21	13	5	17	21	13
Textiles, etc. except clothing (65)	14	19	11	20	16	9	23	21	26
Paper, paperboard, etc. (54)	14	16	8	18	15	6	13	17	10½
Wood manufactures, etc. except furniture (63)	11	19	7	22	16	4	15	12	18
Rubber manufactures (62)	17	17	10	19	18	8	21	18	18
Leather, etc. (61)	11	11	12	18	12	11	16	17	17
Chemicals (59)	7	16	8	17	12	4	15	11	24

[a] The figures are subject to the reservations stated in the source. The figures in parentheses refer to SITC classification.
Source PEP (1962).

Theory and measurement

This section of the book is devoted to the discussion of the theoretical aspects of the EU and to the measurement of the impact of the formation of the EU on trade, production and factor mobility (the policy aspects of this are discussed in Chapter 20).

The whole section is basically concerned with two concepts: 'trade creation' and 'trade diversion'. These can be illustrated rather simplistically as follows. In Table II.1 the cost of beef per kg is given in pence for the United Kingdom, France and New Zealand. With a 50% non-discriminatory tariff rate the cheapest source of supply of beef for the United Kingdom is the home producer. When the United Kingdom and France form a customs union, the cheapest source of supply becomes France. Hence the United Kingdom saves 10p per kg of beef making a total saving of £1 million for ten million kg (an arbitrarily chosen quantity). This is 'trade creation': *the replacement of expensive domestic production by cheaper imports from the partner.*

In Table II.2 the situation is different as a result of a lower initial non-discriminatory tariff rate (25%) by the United Kingdom. Before the customs union, New Zealand is the cheapest source of supply. After the customs union, France becomes the cheapest source. There is a total loss to the United Kingdom of £1 million, since the tariff revenue is claimed by the government. This is 'trade diversion': *the replacement of cheaper initial imports from the outside world by expensive imports from the partner.*

In Tables II.3 and II.4 there are two commodities: beef and butter. The cost of beef per kg is the same as in the previous examples and so is the cost of butter per kg. Note that

Table II.1 ⬤ Beef.

	United Kingdom	France	New Zealand
The cost per unit (p)	90	80	70
UK domestic price with a 50% tariff rate (p)	90	120	105
UK domestic price when the UK and France form a customs union (p)	90	80	105

Total cost before the customs union = 90p × 10 million kg = £9 million
Total cost after the customs union = 80p × 10 million kg = £8 million
Total savings for the UK consumer = £1 million

Table II.2 ⬤ Beef.

	United Kingdom	France	New Zealand
The cost per unit (p)	90	80	70
UK domestic price with a 25% tariff rate (p)	90	100	87½
UK domestic price when the UK and France form a customs union (p)	90	80	87½

Total cost to the UK government before the customs union = 70p × 10 million kg = £7 million
Total cost to the UK after the customs union = 80p × 10 million kg = £8 million
Total loss to the UK government = £1 million

Table II.3 starts from the same position as Table II.1 and Table II.4 from the same position as Table II.2. Here the United Kingdom does not form a customs union with France; rather, it reduces its tariff rate by 80% on a non-discriminatory basis.

Now consider Tables II.3 and II.4 in comparison with Tables II.1 and II.2. The total cost for Tables II.1 and II.2 before the customs union is £9 million + £7 million = £16 million.

Table II.3 Beef.

	United Kingdom	France	New Zealand
The cost per unit (p)	90	80	70
UK domestic price with a 50% tariff rate (p)	90	120	105
UK domestic price with a non-discriminatory tariff reduction of 80% (i.e. tariff rate becomes 10%) (p)	90	88	77

Total cost to the UK before the tariff reduction = 90p × 10 million kg = £9 million
Total cost to the UK after tariff reduction = 70p × 10 million kg = £7 million
Total savings for the UK = £2 million

Table II.4 Butter.

	United Kingdom	France	New Zealand
The cost per unit (p)	90	80	70
UK domestic price with a 25% tariff rate (p)	90	100	87½
UK domestic price with a non-discriminatory tariff reduction of 80% (i.e. tariff rate becomes 5%) (p)	90	84	73½

Total cost to the UK before the tariff reduction = 70p × 10 million kg = £7 million
Total cost to the UK after the tariff reduction = 70p × 10 million kg = £7 million
Total savings for the UK = nil

The total cost for Tables II.1 and II.2 after the customs union = £8 million + £8 million = £16 million.

The total cost for Tables II.3 and II.4 after the customs Union = £7 million + £7 million = £14 million.

This gives a saving of £2 million in comparison with the customs union situation. Hence, a non-discriminatory tariff reduction is more economical for the United Kingdom than the formation of a customs union with France. Therefore, a *non-discriminatory tariff reduction is superior to customs union formation.*

This dangerously simple analysis (since a number of simplistic assumptions are implicit in the analysis and all the data are chosen to prove the point) has been the inspiration of a massive literature on customs union theory. Admittedly, some of the contributions are misguided in that they concentrate on a non-problem.

Chapter 4 tackles the basic concepts of trade creation and trade diversion, considers the implications of domestic distortions and scale economies for the basic analysis and discusses the terms of trade effects. Chapter 5 contains an analysis of the vital issue of monetary integration. Chapter 6 discusses the measurement of the theoretical concepts discussed in Chapter 4. Finally, Chapter 7 concentrates on the specific issues of the 'internal market'.

chapter four

The theory of economic integration

A. M. EL-AGRAA

In reality, almost all existing cases of economic integration were either proposed or formed for political reasons even though the arguments popularly put forward in their favour were expressed in terms of possible economic gains. However, no matter what the motives for economic integration are, it is still necessary to analyse the economic implications of such geographically discriminatory groupings.

As mentioned in the introduction, at the customs union (and free trade area) level, the *possible* sources of economic gain can be attributed to the following:

1. Enhanced efficiency in production made possible by increased specialization in accordance with the law of comparative advantage.

2. Increased production level due to better exploitation of economies of scale made possible by the increased size of the market.

3. An improved international bargaining position, made possible by the larger size, leading to better terms of trade.

4. Enforced changes in economic efficiency brought about by enhanced competition.

5. Changes affecting both the amount and quality of the factors of production arising from technological advances.

If the level of economic integration is to proceed beyond the customs union (CU) level, to the economic union level, then further sources of gain become *possible* as a result of:

6. Factor mobility across the borders of member nations.

7. The coordination of monetary and fiscal policies.

8. The goals of near full employment, higher rates of economic growth and better income distribution becoming unified targets.

I shall now discuss these considerations in some detail.

4.1 The customs union aspects

4.1.1 The basic concepts

Before the theory of second best was introduced, it used to be the accepted tradition that CU formation should be encouraged. The rationale for this was that since free trade maximized world welfare and since CU formation was a move towards free trade, CUs increased welfare even though they did not maximize it. This rationale certainly lies behind the guidelines of the GATT–WTO Article XXIV (see appendix to Chapter 1) which permits the formation of CUs and free trade areas as the special exceptions to the rules against international discrimination.

Viner (1950) and Byé (1950) challenged this proposition by stressing the point that CU formation is by no means equivalent to a move to free trade since it amounts to free trade *between* the members and *protection vis-à-vis* the outside world. This combination of free trade and protectionism could result in trade creation and/or trade diversion. Trade creation (TC) is the replacement of expensive domestic production by cheaper imports from a partner and trade diversion (TD) is the replacement of cheaper initial imports from the outside world by more expensive imports from a partner. Viner and Byé stressed the point that trade creation is beneficial since it does not affect the rest of the world, while trade diversion is harmful; it is the relative strength of these two effects that determines whether or not CU formation should be advocated. It is therefore important to understand the implications of these concepts.

Assuming perfect competition in both the commodity and factor markets, automatic full employment of all resources, costless adjustment procedures, perfect factor mobility nationally but perfect immobility across national boundaries, prices determined by cost, three countries H (the home country), P (the potential customs union partner) and W (the outside world), plus all the traditional assumptions employed in tariff theory, we can use a simple diagram to illustrate these two concepts.

In Figure 4.1 I use partial-equilibrium diagrams because it has been demonstrated that partial- and general-equilibrium analyses are, under certain circumstances, equivalent – see El-Agraa and Jones (1981). S_W is W's perfectly elastic tariff-free supply curve for this commodity; S_H is H's supply curve while S_{H+P} is the joint H and P tariff-free supply curve. With a non-discriminatory tariff (t) imposition by H of AD ($=t_H$), the effective supply curve facing H is $BREFQT$, i.e. its own supply curve up to E and W's, subject to the tariff $[S_W(1 + t_H)]$ after that. The domestic price is therefore OD, which gives domestic production of Oq_2, domestic consumption of Oq_3 and imports of $q_2 q_3$. H pays $q_2 LMq_3$ ($=a$) for the imports while the domestic consumer pays $q_2 EFq_3$ ($a + b + c$) with the difference ($LEFM = b + c$) being the tariff revenue which accrues to the H government. This government revenue can be viewed as a transfer from the consumers to the government with the implication that, when the government spends it, the marginal valuation of that expenditure should be exactly equal to its valuation by the private consumers so that no distortions should occur.

If H and W form a CU, the free trade position will be restored so that Oq_5 will be

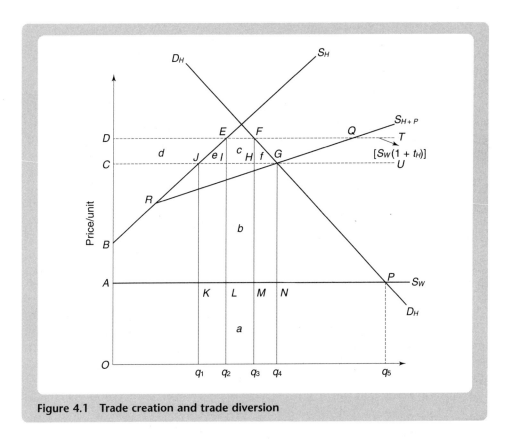

Figure 4.1 Trade creation and trade diversion

consumed in H and this amount will be imported from W. Hence free trade is obviously the ideal situation. But if H and P form a CU, the tariff imposition will still apply to W while it is removed from P. The effective supply curve in this case is $BRGQT$. The union price falls to OC resulting in a fall in domestic production to Oq_1, an increase in consumption to Oq_4 and an increase in imports to q_1q_4. These imports now come from P.

The welfare implications of these changes can be examined by employing the concepts of consumers' and producers' surpluses. As a result of increased consumption, consumers' surplus rises by $CDFG$ ($= d + e + c + f$). Part of this (d) is a fall in producers' surplus due to the decline in domestic production and another part (c) is a portion of the tariff revenue now transferred back to the consumer subject to the same condition of equal marginal valuation. This leaves e and f as gains from CU formation. However, before we conclude whether or not these triangles represent *net* gains we need to consider the overall effects more carefully.

The fall in domestic production from Oq_2 to Oq_1 leads to increased imports of q_1q_2. These cost q_1JIq_2 to import from P while they originally cost q_1JEq_2 to produce domestically. (Note that these resources are assumed to be employed elsewhere in the economy without any adjustment costs or redundancies.) There is therefore a saving of e. The increase in consumption from Oq_3 to Oq_4 leads to new imports of q_3q_4 which cost q_3HGq_4 to import from P. These give a welfare satisfaction to the consumer equal to q_3FGq_4. There is therefore an increase in satisfaction of f. However, the *initial* imports of q_2q_3 cost the country a, but these imports now come from P costing $a + b$. Therefore these imports lead to a loss in government revenue of b (c being a retransfer). It follows that the triangle gains ($e + f$) have to be compared with the loss of tariff revenue (b) before a definite conclusion can be made regarding whether or not the net effect of CU formation has been one of gain or loss.

It should be apparent that q_2q_3 represents, in terms of our definition, trade diversion, and $q_1q_2 + q_3q_4$ represents trade creation, or alternatively that areas $e + f$ are trade creation (benefits) while area b is trade diversion (loss). (The reader should note that I am using Johnson's 1974 definition so as to avoid the unnecessary literature relating to a trade-diverting welfare-improving CU promoted by Gehrels (1956–7), Lipsey (1960) and Bhagwati (1971)). It is, then, obvious that trade creation is economically desirable while trade diversion is undesirable: hence Viner and Byé's conclusion that it is the relative strength of these two effects which should determine whether or not CU formation is beneficial or harmful.

The reader should note that if the initial price is that given by the intersection of D_H and S_H (due to a higher tariff rate), the CU would result in pure trade creation since the tariff rate is prohibitive. If the price is initially OC (due to a lower tariff rate), then CU formation would result in pure trade diversion. It should also be apparent that the size of the gains and losses depends on the price elasticities of $S_{H'}$ and S_{H+P} and D_H and on the divergence between S_W and S_{H+P}, i.e. cost differences.

4.1.2 The Cooper–Massell criticism

Viner and Byé's conclusion was challenged by Cooper and Massell (1965a). They suggested that the reduction in price from OD to OC should be considered in two stages: firstly, reduce the tariff level indiscriminately (i.e. for both W and P) to AC which gives the same union price and production, consumption and import changes; secondly, introduce the CU starting from the new price OC. The effect of these two steps is that the gains from the trade creation ($e + f$) still accrue while the losses from trade diversion (b) no longer apply since the new effective supply curve facing H is $BJGU$ which ensures that imports continue to come from W at the cost of a. In addition, the new imports due to trade creation ($q_1q_2 + q_3q_4$) now cost less, leading to a further gain of $KJIL$ plus $MHGN$. Cooper and Massell then conclude that *a policy of unilateral tariff reduction (UTR) is superior to customs union formation.*

4.1.3 Further contributions

Following the Cooper–Massell criticism have come two independent but somewhat similar contributions to the theory of CUs. The first development is by Cooper and Massell (1965b) themselves, the essence of which is that two countries acting together can do better than each acting in isolation. The second is by Johnson (1965b) which is a private plus social costs and benefits analysis expressed in political economy terms. Both contributions utilize a 'public good' argument, with Cooper and Massell's expressed in practical terms and Johnson's in theoretical terms. However, since the Johnson approach is expressed in familiar terms this section is devoted to it – space limitations do not permit a consideration of both.

Johnson's method is based on four major assumptions:

1. Governments use tariffs to achieve certain non-economic (political, etc.) objectives.

2. Actions taken by governments are aimed at offsetting differences between private and social costs. They are, therefore, rational efforts.

3. Government policy is a rational response to the demands of the electorate.

4. Countries have a preference for industrial production.

In addition to these assumptions, Johnson makes a distinction between private and public consumption goods, real income (utility enjoyed from both private and public consumption, where consumption is the sum of planned consumption expenditure and planned investment expenditure) and real product (defined as total production of privately appropriable goods and services).

These assumptions have important implications. Firstly, competition among political parties will make the government adopt policies that will tend to maximize consumer satisfaction from both 'private' and 'collective' consumption goods. Satisfaction is obviously maximized when the *rate of satisfaction per unit of resources is the same in both types of consumption goods*. Secondly, 'collective preference' for industrial production implies that consumers are willing to expand industrial production (and industrial employment) beyond what it would be under free international trade.

Tariffs are the main source of financing this policy simply because GATT–WTO regulations rule out the use of export subsidies, and domestic political considerations make tariffs, rather than the more efficient production subsidies, the usual instruments of protection.

Protection will be carried to the point where *the value of the marginal utility derived from collective consumption of domestic and industrial activity is just equal to the marginal excess private cost of protected industrial production.*

The marginal excess cost of protected industrial production consists of two parts: the marginal production cost and the marginal private consumption cost. The marginal production cost is equal to the proportion by which domestic cost exceeds world market costs. In a very simple model this is equal to the tariff rate. The marginal private consumption cost is equal to the loss of consumer surplus due to the fall in consumption brought about by the tariff rate which is necessary to induce the marginal unit of domestic production. This depends on the tariff rate and the price elasticities of supply and demand.

In equilibrium, the proportional marginal excess private cost of protected production measures the marginal 'degree of preference' for industrial production. This is illustrated in Figure 4.2 where S_W is the world supply curve at world market prices; D_H is the constant-utility demand curve (at free trade private utility level); S_H is the domestic supply curve; S_{H+u} is the marginal private cost curve of protected industrial production, including the excess private consumption cost (FE is the first component of marginal excess cost – determined by the excess marginal cost of domestic production in relation to the free trade situation due to the tariff imposition (AB) – and the area GED (= IHJ) is the second component which is the dead loss in consumer surplus due to the tariff imposition); the height of vv above S_W represents the marginal value of industrial production in collective consumption and vv represents the preference for industrial production which is assumed to yield a diminishing marginal rate of satisfaction.

The maximization of *real* income is achieved at the intersection of vv with S_{H+u} requiring the use of tariff rate AB/OA to increase industrial production from Oq_1 to Oq_2 and involving the marginal degree of preference for industrial production v.

Note that the higher the value of v, the higher the tariff rate, and that the degree

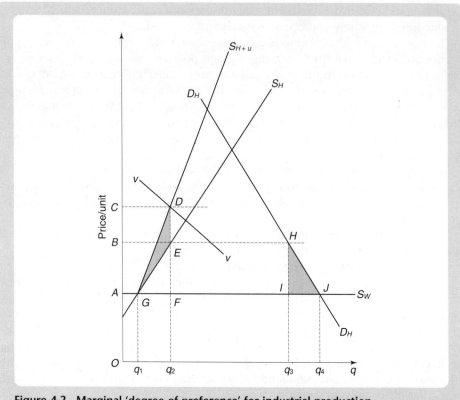

Figure 4.2   Marginal 'degree of preference' for industrial production

of protection will tend to vary inversely with the ability to compete with foreign industrial producers.

It is also important to note that, in equilibrium, the government is maximizing real income, not real product: maximization of real income makes it necessary to sacrifice real product in order to gratify the preference for collective consumption of industrial production.

It is also important to note that this analysis is not confined to net importing countries. It is equally applicable to net exporters, but lack of space prevents such elaboration – see El-Agraa (1984a) for a detailed explanation.

The above model helps to explain the significance of Johnson's assumptions. It does not, however, throw any light on the CU issue. To make the model useful for this purpose it is necessary to alter some of the assumptions. Let us assume that industrial production is not one aggregate but a variety of products in which countries have varying degrees of comparative advantage, that countries differ in their overall comparative advantage in industry as compared with non-industrial production, that no country has monopoly–monopsony power (conditions for optimum tariffs do not exist) and that no export subsidies are allowed (GATT–WTO).

The variety of industrial production allows countries to be both importers and exporters of industrial products. This, in combination with the 'preference for industrial production', will motivate each country to practise some degree of protection.

Given the third assumption; a country can gratify its preference for industrial production only by protecting the domestic producers of the commodities it imports (import-competing industries). Hence the condition for equilibrium remains the same: $vv = S_{H+u}$. The condition must now be reckoned differently, however: S_{H+u} is slightly different because, firstly, the protection of import-competing industries will reduce exports of both industrial and non-industrial products (for balance of payments purposes). Hence, in order to increase total industrial production by one unit it will be necessary to increase protected industrial production by more than one unit so as to compensate for the induced loss of industrial exports. Secondly, the protection of import-competing industries reduces industrial exports by raising their production costs (because of perfect factor mobility). The stronger this effect, *ceteris paribus*, the higher the marginal excess cost of industrial production. This will be greater the larger the industrial sector compared with the non-industrial sector and the larger the protected industrial sector relative to the exporting industrial sector.

If the world consists of two countries, one must be a net exporter and the other necessarily a net importer of industrial products and the balance of payments is settled in terms of the non-industrial sector. Therefore for each country the prospective gain from reciprocal tariff reduction must lie in the expansion of exports of industrial products. The reduction of a country's own tariff rate is therefore a source of loss which can be compensated for only by a reduction of the other country's tariff rate (for an alternative, orthodox, explanation see El-Agraa, 1979b).

What if there are more than two countries? If reciprocal tariff reductions are arrived at on a 'most-favoured nation' basis, then the reduction of a country's tariff

rate will increase imports from *all* the other countries. If the tariff rate reduction is, however, discriminatory (starting from a position of non-discrimination), then there are two advantages: firstly, a country can offer its partner an increase in exports of industrial products without any loss of its own industrial production by diverting imports from third countries (trade diversion); secondly, when trade diversion is exhausted, any increase in partner industrial exports to this country is exactly equal to the reduction in industrial production in the same country (trade creation), hence eliminating the gain to third countries.

Therefore, discriminatory reciprocal tariff reduction costs each partner country less, in terms of the reduction in domestic industrial production (if any) incurred per unit increase in partner industrial production, than does non-discriminatory reciprocal tariff reduction. On the other hand, preferential tariff reduction imposes an additional cost on the tariff-reducing country: the excess of the costs of imports from the partner country over their cost in the world market.

The implications of this analysis are as follows:

1. Both trade creation and trade diversion yield a gain to the CU partners.
2. Trade diversion is preferable to trade creation for the preference-granting country since a sacrifice of domestic industrial production is not required.
3. Both trade creation and trade diversion may lead to increased efficiency due to economies of scale.

Johnson's contribution has not achieved the popularity it deserves because of the alleged nature of his assumptions. However, a careful consideration of these assumptions indicates that they are neither extreme nor unique: they are the kind of assumptions that are adopted in any analysis dealing with differences between social and private costs and benefits. It can, of course, be claimed that an

> economic rationale for customs unions on public goods grounds can only be established if for political or some such reasons governments are denied the use of direct production subsidies – and while this may be the case in certain countries at certain periods in their economic evolution, there would appear to be no acceptable reason why this should generally be true. Johnson's analysis demonstrates that customs union and other acts of commercial policy may make economic sense under certain restricted conditions, but in no way does it establish or seek to establish a general argument for these acts. (Krauss, 1972)

While this is a legitimate criticism it is of no relevance to the world we live in: subsidies are superior to tariffs, yet all countries prefer the use of tariffs to subsidies! It is a criticism related to a first best view of the world. It therefore seems unfair to criticize an analysis on grounds which do not portray what actually exists; it is what prevails in practice that matters. That is what Johnson's approach is all about and that is what the theory of second best tries to tackle. In short, the lack of belief in this approach is tantamount to a lack of belief in the validity of the distinction between social and private costs and benefits.

4.1.4 Dynamic effects

The so-called dynamic effects (Balassa, 1961) relate to the numerous means by which economic integration may influence the rate of growth of GNP of the participating nations. These ways include the following:

1. Scale economies made possible by the increased size of the market for both firms and industries operating below optimum capacity before integration occurs.
2. Economies external to the firm and industry which may have a downward influence on both specific and general cost structures.
3. The polarization effect, by which is meant the cumulative decline either in relative or absolute terms of the economic situation of a particular participating nation or of a specific region within it due either to the benefits of trade creation becoming concentrated in one region or to the fact that an area may develop a tendency to attract factors of production.
4. The influence on the location and volume of real investment.
5. The effect on economic efficiency and the smoothness with which trade transactions are carried out due to enhanced competition and changes in uncertainty.

Hence these dynamic effects include various and completely different phenomena. Apart from economies of scale, the possible gains are extremely long term and cannot be tackled in orthodox economic terms: for example, intensified competition leading to the adoption of best business practices and to an American type of attitude, etc. (Scitovsky, 1958), seems like a naïve sociopsychological abstraction that has no solid foundation with regard to either the aspirations of those countries contemplating economic integration or to its actually materializing.

Economies of scale can, however, be analysed in orthodox economic terms. In a highly simplistic model, like that depicted in Figure 4.3 where scale economies are internal to the industry, their effects can easily be demonstrated – a mathematical discussion can be found in, *inter alia*, Choi and Yu (1984), but the reader must be warned that the assumptions made about the nature of the economies concerned are extremely limited, e.g. H and P are 'similar'. $D_{H,P}$ is the identical demand curve for this commodity in both H and P and D_{H+P} is their joint demand curve; S_W is the world supply curve; AC_P and AC_H are the average cost curves for this commodity in P and H respectively. Note that the diagram is drawn in such a manner that W has constant average costs and is the most efficient supplier of this commodity. Hence free trade is the best policy resulting in price OA with consumption that is satisfied entirely by imports of Oq_4 in each of H and P giving a total of Oq_6.

If H and P impose tariffs, the only justification for this is that uncorrected distortions exist between the privately and socially valued costs in these countries – see Jones (1979) and El-Agraa and Jones (1981). The best tariff rates to impose are Corden's (1972a) made-to-measure tariffs which can be defined as those that encourage domestic production to a level that just satisfies domestic consumption

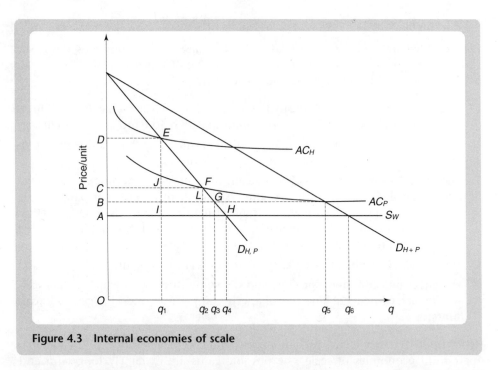

Figure 4.3   Internal economies of scale

without giving rise to monopoly profits. These tariffs are equal to AD and AC for H and P respectively, resulting in Oq_1 and Oq_2 production in H and P respectively.

When H and P enter into a CU, P, being the cheaper producer, will produce the entire union output – Oq_5 – at a price OB. This gives rise to consumption in each of H and P of Oq_3 with gains of $BDEG$ and $BCFG$ for H and P respectively. Parts of these gains, $BDEI$ for H and $BCFL$ for P, are 'cost-reduction' effects. There also results a production gain for P and a production loss in H due to abandoning production altogether.

Whether or not CU formation can be justified in terms of the existence of economies of scale will depend on whether or not the net effect is a gain or a loss, since in this example P gains and H loses, as the loss from abandoning production in H must outweigh the consumption gain in order for the tariff to have been imposed in the first place. If the overall result is net gain, then the distribution of these gains becomes an important consideration. Alternatively, if economies of scale accrue to an integrated industry, then the locational distribution of the production units becomes an essential issue.

4.1.5 Domestic distortions

A substantial literature has tried to tackle the important question of whether or not the formation of a CU may be economically desirable when there are domestic distortions. Such distortions could be attributed to the presence of trade unions which negotiate wage rates in excess of the equilibrium rates or to governments introduc-

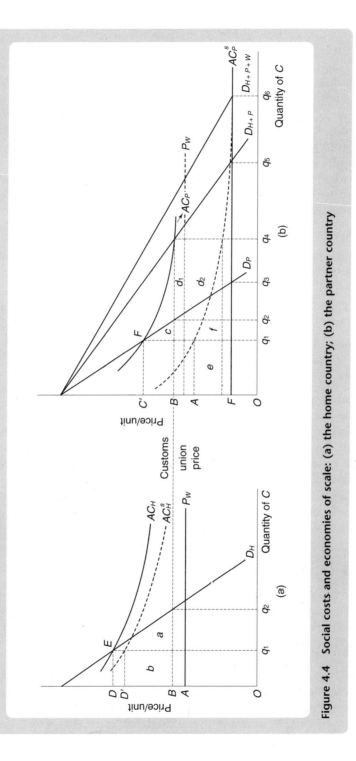

Figure 4.4   Social costs and economies of scale: (a) the home country; (b) the partner country

ing minimum wage legislation – both of which are widespread activities in most countries. It is usually assumed that the domestic distortion results in a *social* average cost curve which lies below the private one. Hence, in Figure 4.4, which is adapted from Figure 4.3, I have incorporated AC^s_H and AC^s_P as the *social* curves in the context of economies of scale and a separate representation of countries H and P.

Note that AC^s_H is drawn to be consistently above AP_W, while AC^s_P is below it for higher levels of output. Before the formation of a CU, H may have been adopting a made-to-measure tariff to protect its industry, but the first best policy would have been one of free trade, as argued in the previous section. The formation of the CU will therefore lead to the same effects as in the previous section, with the exception that the cost-reduction effect (Figure 4.4(a)) will be less by DD' times Oq_1. For P, the effects will be as follows:

1. As before, a consumption gain of area c.
2. A cost-reduction effect of area e due to calculations relating to social rather than private costs.
3. Gains from sales to H of areas d_1 and d_2, with d_1 being an income transfer from H to P, and d_2 the difference between domestic social costs in P and P_W – the world price.
4. The social benefits accruing from extra production made possible by the CU – area f – which is measured by the extra consumption multiplied by the difference between P_W and the domestic social costs.

However, this analysis does not lead to an economic rationale for the formation of CUs, since P could have used first best policy instruments to eliminate the divergence between private and social cost. This would have made AC^s_P the operative cost curve, and, assuming that D_{H+P+W} is the world demand curve, this would have led to a world price of OF and exports of q_3q_5 and q_5q_6 to H and W respectively, with obviously greater benefits than those offered by the CU. Hence the economic rationale for the CU will have to depend on factors that can explain why first best instruments could not have been employed in the first instance (Jones, 1980). In short, this is not an absolute argument for CU formation.

4.1.6 Terms of trade effects

So far the analysis has been conducted on the assumption that CU formation has no effect on the terms of trade (t/t). This implies that the countries concerned are too insignificant to have any appreciable influence on the international economy. Particularly in the context of the EU and groupings of a similar size, this is a very unrealistic assumption.

The analysis of the effects of CU formation on the t/t is not only extremely complicated but is also unsatisfactory since a convincing model incorporating tariffs by all three areas of the world is still awaited – see Mundell (1964), Arndt (1968, 1969) and Wonnacott and Wonnacott (1981). To demonstrate this, let us consider Arndt's analysis, which is directly concerned with this issue, and the Wonnacotts' analysis, whose main concern is the Cooper–Massell criticism but which has some bearing on this matter.

In Figure 4.5, O_H, O_P and O_W are the respective offer curves of H, P and W. In sec-

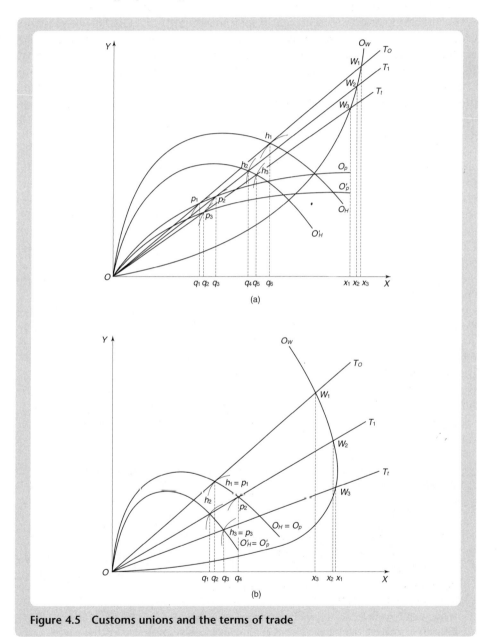

Figure 4.5   Customs unions and the terms of trade

tion (a) of the figure, H is assumed to be the most efficient producer of commodity Y, while in section (b), H and P are assumed to be equally efficient. Assuming that the free trade t/t are given by OT_0, H will export q_6h_1 of Y to W in exchange for Oq_6 imports of commodity X, while P will export q_1p_1 of Y in exchange for Oq_1 of commodity X, with the sum of H and P's exports being exactly equal to OX_3.

When H imposes an *ad valorem* tariff (percentage tariff), its tariff revenue-distributed curve is assumed to be displaced to $O'H$ altering the t/t to OT_1. This leads to a contraction of H's trade with W and, at the same time, increases P's trade with W. In section (a) of the figure, it is assumed that the net effect of H and P's trade changes (contraction in H's exports and expansion in P's) will result in a contraction in world trade. It should be apparent that, from H's point of view, the competition of P in its exports market has reduced the appropriateness of the Cooper–Massell alternative of a (non-discriminatory) UTR.

Note, however, that H's welfare may still be increased in these unfavourable circumstances, provided that the move from h_1 to h_2 is accompanied by two conditions. It should be apparent that the larger the size of P relative to H and the more elastic the two countries' offer curves over the relevant ranges, the more likely it is that H will lose as a result of the tariff imposition. Moreover, given the various offer curves and H's tariff, H is more likely to sustain a loss in welfare, the lower her own marginal propensity to spend on her export commodity, X. If, in terms of consumption, commodity Y is a 'Giffen' good in country H, h_2 will be inferior to h_1.

In this illustration, country H experiences a loss of welfare in case (a) but an increase in case (b), while country P experiences a welfare improvement in both cases. Hence, it is to H's advantage to persuade P to adopt restrictive trade practices. For example, let P impose an *ad valorem* tariff and, in order to simplify the analysis, assume that in section (b) H and P are identical in all respects such that their revenue-redistributed offer curves completely coincide. In both sections of the figure, the t/t will shift to $OT_{t'}$ with h_3, P_3 and w_2 being the equilibrium trading points. In both cases, P's tariff improves H's welfare but P gains only in case (b), and is better off with unrestricted trade in case (a) in the presence of tariff imposition by H.

The situation depicted in Figure 4.5 illustrates the fundamental problem that the interests, and hence the policies, of H and P may be incompatible:

> Country [H] stands to gain from restrictive trade practices in [P], but the latter is better off without restrictions – provided that [H] maintains its tariff. The dilemma in which [H] finds itself in trying to improve its terms of trade is brought about by its inadequate control of the market for its export commodity. Its optimum trade policies and their effects are functions not only of the demand elasticity in [W] but also of supply conditions in [P] and of the latter's reaction to a given policy in [H].
>
> Country [H] will attempt to influence policy making in [P]. In view of the fact that the latter may have considerable inducement to pursue independent policies, country [H] may encounter formidable difficulties in this respect. It could attempt to handle this problem in a relatively loose arrangement along the lines of international commodity agreements, or in a tightly controlled and more restrictive set-up involving an international cartel. The difficulty is that neither alternative may provide effective control over the maverick who

stands to gain from independent policies. In that case a [CU] with common tariff and sufficient incentives may work where other arrangements do not. (Arndt, 1968, p. 978)

Of course, the above analysis relates to potential partners who have similar economies and who trade with W, with no trading relationships between them. Hence, it could be argued that such countries are ruled out, by definition, from forming a CU. Such an argument would be misleading since this analysis is not concerned with the static concepts of TC and TD; the concern is entirely with t/t effects, and a joint trade policy aimed at achieving an advantage in this regard is perfectly within the realm of international economic integration.

One could ask about the nature of this conclusion in a model which depicts the potential CU partners in a different light. Here, Wonnacott and Wonnacott's (1981) analysis may be useful, even though the aim of their paper was to question the general validity of the Cooper–Massell criticism, when the t/t remain unaltered as a result of CU formation. However, this is precisely why it is useful to explain the Wonnacotts' analysis at this junction: it has some bearing on the t/t effects and it questions the Cooper–Massell criticism.

The main point of the Wonnacotts' paper was to contest the proposition that UTR is superior to the formation of a CU; hence the t/t argument was a side issue. They argued that this proposition does not hold generally if the following assumptions are rejected:

1. That the tariff imposed by a partner (P) can be ignored.
2. That W has no tariffs.
3. That there are no transport costs between members of the CU (P and H) and W.

Their approach was not based on t/t effects of economies of scale and, except for their rejection of these three assumptions, their argument is also set entirely in the context of the standard two-commodity, three-country framework of CU theory.

The basic framework of their analysis is set out in Figure 4.6. O_H and O_p are the free trade offer curves of the potential partners while O_H^t and O_p^t are their initial tariff-inclusive offer curves. O_W^1 and O_W^2 are W's offer curves depending on whether the prospective partners wish to import commodity X (O_W^1) or to export it (O_W^2). The inclusion of both O_H^t and O_p^t meets the Wonnacott's desire to reject assumption (1) while the gap between O_W^1 and O_W^2 may be interpreted as the rejection of (2) and/or (3) – see Wonnacott and Wonnacott (1981, pp. 708–9).

In addition to these offer curves, I have inserted in Figure 4.6 various trade indifference curves for countries H and P ($T_{H...}$ and $T_{P...}$ respectively) and the pre-CU domestic t/t in H (O_t). $O_W^{2'}$ is drawn parallel to O_W^2 from the point c where O_p intersects O_t.

The diagram is drawn to illustrate the case where a CU is formed between H and P with the CET set at the same rate as H's initial tariff on imports of X and where the domestic t/t in H remain unaltered so that trade with W continues after the formation of the CU. With its initial non-discriminatory tariff, H will trade along O_W^2 with both P (Oa) and with W (ab). The formation of the CU means that H and P's

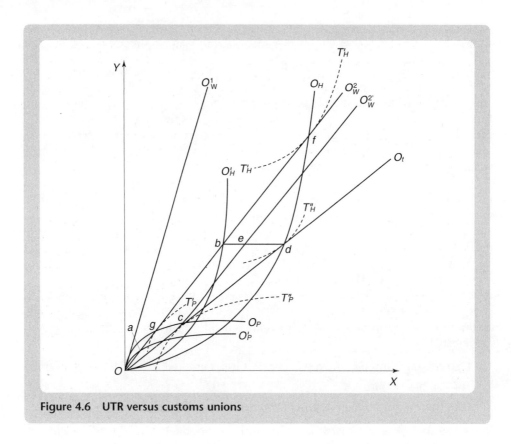

Figure 4.6   UTR versus customs unions

trade is determined by where O_p intersects O_t (i.e. at c) and that H will trade with W along $cO_W^{2'}$ (drawn parallel to OO_W^2). The final outcome for H will depend on the choice of assumptions about what happens to the tariff revenue generated by the remaining external trade. If there is no redistribution of tariff revenue in H, then traders in that country will remain at point d. The tariff revenue generated by the external trade of the CU with W is then shown to be equal to ed (measured in units of commodity X) which represents a reduction of be compared with the pre-CU tariff revenue in H. Further, if procedures similar to those of the European Union were adopted, the revenue ed would be used as an 'own resource' (see Chapter 15) to be spent–distributed for the benefit of both members of the CU whereas the pre-union tariff (bd) would be kept by country H.

It can be seen that country P will benefit from the formation of the CU even if it receives none of this revenue, but that H will undoubtedly lose even if it keeps all the post-union tariff revenue. This is the case of pure TD (trade diversion) and, in the absence of additional income transfers from P, H clearly cannot be expected to join the CU even if it considers that this is the only alternative to its initial tariff policy. There is no rationale, however, for so restricting the choice of policy alternatives. UTR is unambiguously superior to the initial tariff policy for both H and P and, compared with the non-discriminatory free trade policies available to both countries (which take country H to T'_H at f and country P to T'_P at g), there is no possible system of income transfers from P to H which can make the formation of a CU Pareto-superior to free trade for both countries. It remains true, of course, that country P would gain more from membership of a CU with H than it could achieve by UTR but, provided that H pursues its optimal strategy, which is UTR, country P itself can do no better than follow suit so that the optimal outcome for both countries is multilateral free trade (MFT).

Of course, there is no *a priori* reason why the CU, if created, should set its CET at the level of country H's initial tariff. Indeed, it is instructive to consider the consequences of forming a CU with a lower CET. The implications of this can be seen by considering the effect of rotating O_t anticlockwise towards O^t_W. In this context, the moving O_t line will show the post-union t/t in countries H and P. Clearly, the lowering of the CET will improve the domestic t/t for H compared with the original form of the CU and it will have a trade-creating effect as the external trade of the CU will increase more rapidly than the decline in intraunion trade. Compared with the original CU, H would gain and P would lose. Indeed, the lower the level of the CET, the more likely is H to gain from the formation of the CU *compared with the initial non-discriminatory tariff*. As long as the CET remains positive, however, H would be unambiguously worse off from membership of the CU than from UTR and, although P would gain from such a CU compared with any initial tariff policy it may adopt, it remains true that there is no conceivable set of income transfers associated with the formation of the CU which would make both H and P simultaneously better off than they would be if, after H's UTR, P also pursued the optimal unilateral action available – the move to free trade.

It is of course true that, if the CET is set to zero, so that the rotated O_t coincides with $O^{2'}_W$ then the outcome is identical with that for the unilateral adoption of free trade for both countries. This, however, merely illustrates how misleading it would be to describe such a policy as 'the formation of a CU'; a CU with a zero CET is indistinguishable from a free-trade policy by both countries and should surely be described solely in the latter terms.

One can extend and generalize this approach beyond what has been done here – see El-Agraa (1989) and Berglas (1983). The important point, however, is what the analysis clearly demonstrates: the assumption that the t/t should remain constant for members of a CU, even if both countries are 'small', leaves a lot to be desired. But it should also be stressed that the Wonnacotts' analysis does not take into consideration the tariffs of H and P on trade with W nor does it deal with a genuine three-country model since W is assumed to be very large: W has constant t/t.

4.2 Customs unions versus free trade areas

The analysis so far has been conducted on the premise that differences between CUs and free trade areas can be ignored. However, the ability of the member nations of free trade areas to decide their own commercial policies *vis-à-vis* the outside world raises certain issues. Balassa (1961) pointed out that free trade areas may result in deflection of trade, production and investment. Deflection of trade occurs when imports from W (the cheapest source of supply) come via the member country with the lower tariff rate, assuming that transport and administrative costs do not outweigh the tariff differential. Deflection of production and investment occur in commodities whose production requires a substantial quantity of raw materials imported from W – the tariff differential regarding these materials might distort the true comparative advantage in domestic materials, therefore resulting in resource allocations according to overall comparative disadvantage.

If deflection of trade does occur, then the free trade area effectively becomes a CU with a CET equal to the lowest tariff rate which is obviously beneficial for the world – see Curzon Price (1974). However, most free trade areas seem to adopt 'rules of origin' so that only those commodities which originate in a member state are exempt from tariff imposition. If deflection of production and investment does take place, we have the case of the so-called 'tariff factories'; but the necessary conditions for this to occur are extremely limited – see El-Agraa in El-Agraa and Jones (1981, Chapter 3) and El-Agraa (1984b, 1989a).

4.3 Economic unions

The analysis of CUs needs drastic extension when applied to economic unions. Firstly, the introduction of free factor mobility may enhance efficiency through a more rational reallocation of resources but it may also result in depressed areas, therefore creating or aggravating regional problems and imbalances – see Mayes (1983a) and Robson (1985). Secondly, fiscal harmonization may also improve efficiency by eliminating non-tariff barriers (NTBs) and distortions and by equalizing their effective protective rates – see Chapter 14. Thirdly, the coordination of monetary and fiscal policies which is implied by monetary integration may ease unnecessarily severe imbalances, hence resulting in the promotion of the right atmosphere for stability in the economies of the member nations.

These economic union elements must be tackled *simultaneously* with trade creation and diversion as well as economies of scale and market distortions. However, such interactions are too complicated to consider here: the interested reader should consult El-Agraa (1983a, 1983b, 1984a, 1989a). This section will be devoted to a brief discussion of factor mobility. Since monetary integration is probably the most crucial of commitments for a regional grouping and because it is one of the immediate aspirations of the EU, the following chapter is devoted to it.

With regard to *factor mobility*, it should be apparent that the removal (or harmonization) of all barriers to labour (L) and capital (K) will encourage both L and K to move. L will move to those areas where it can fetch the highest possible reward, i.e. 'net advantage'. This encouragement need not necessarily lead to an increase in actual mobility since there are sociopolitical factors which normally result in people remaining near their birthplace – social proximity is a dominant consideration, which is why the average person does not move. If the reward to K is not equalized, i.e. differences in marginal productivities (MPs) exist before the formation of an EU, K will move until the MPs are equalized. This will result in benefits which can be clearly described in terms of Figure 4.7, which depicts the production characteristics in H and P. M_H and M_P are the schedules which relate the K stocks to their MPs in H and P respectively, given the quantity of L in each country (assuming two factors of production only).

Prior to formation of an economic union, the K stock (which is assumed to remain constant throughout the analysis) is Oq_2 in H and Oq_1^* in P. Assuming that K is immobile internationally, all K stocks must be nationally owned and, ignoring taxation, profit per unit of K will be equal to its MP, given conditions of perfect competition. Hence the total profit in H is equal to $b + e$ and $i + k$ in P. Total output is, of course, the whole area below the M_p curve but within Oq_2 in H and Oq_1^* in P, i.e. areas $a + b + c + d + e$ in H and $j + i + k$ in P. Therefore, L's share is $a + c + d$ in H and j in P.

Since the MP in P exceeds that in H, the removal of barriers to K mobility or the harmonization of such barriers will induce K to move away from H and into P. This is because nothing has happened to affect K in W. Such movement will continue until the MP of K is the same in both H and P. This results in q_1q_2 ($= q_1^*q_2^*$) of K moving from H to P. Hence the output of H falls to $a + b + d$ while its *national* prod-

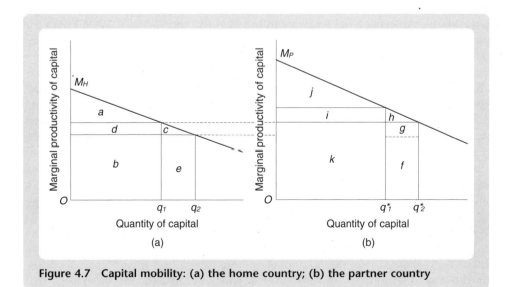

Figure 4.7 Capital mobility: (a) the home country; (b) the partner country

uct including the return of the profit earned on K in $P (= g + f)$ increases by $(g - c)$. In P, *domestic* product rises by $(f + g + h)$ while *national* product (excluding the remittance of profits to H) increases by area h only. Both H and P experience a change in the relative share of L and K in national product, with K owners being favourably disposed in H and unfavourably disposed in P.

Of course, the analysis is too simplistic since, apart from the fact that K and L are never perfectly immobile at the international level and multinational corporations have their own ways of transferring K (see McManus, 1972; Buckley and Casson, 1976; Dunning, 1977), the analysis does not take into account the fact that K may actually move to areas with low wages after the formation of an economic union. Moreover, if K moves predominantly in only one direction, one country may become a depressed area; hence the 'social' costs and benefits of such an occurrence need to be taken into consideration, particularly if the economic union deems it important that the economies of both H and P should be balanced. Therefore, the above gains have to be discounted or supplemented by such costs and benefits.

4.4   Macroeconomics of integration

We have seen that trade creation and trade diversion are the two concepts most widely used in international economic integration. We have also seen that their economic implications for resource reallocation are usually tackled in terms of particular commodities under conditions of global full employment. However, the economic consequences for the outside world and their repercussions on the integrated area are usually left to intuition. Moreover, their implications for employment are usually ruled out by assumption.

In an effort to rectify these serious shortcomings, I have used a macroeconomic model (see chapters 6–8 of El-Agraa and Jones, 1981, and El-Agraa, 1989a) with the purpose of investigating these aspects; the model has been refined (see A. J. Jones, 1983). However, even the crude model indicates that the advantages of using a macro model are that it clearly demonstrates the once and for all nature of trade creation and trade diversion. It also shows the insignificance of their overall impact given realistic values of the relevant coefficients: marginal propensities to import, marginal propensities to consume, tariff rates, etc. The model also demonstrates that trade creation is beneficial for the partner gaining the new output and exports but is detrimental to the other partner and the outside world and that trade diversion is beneficial for the partner now exporting the commodity but is detrimental for the other partner and the outside world.

4.5   Economic integration in developing countries

It has been claimed that the body of economic integration theory as so far developed has no relevance for the Third World. This is because the theory suggests that there would be more scope for trade creation if the countries concerned were initially very competitive in production but potentially very complementary and that a CU would be more likely to be trade creating if the partners conducted most of their foreign trade among themselves – see Lipsey (1960) and Meade (1980). These conditions are unlikely to be satisfied in the majority of the developing nations. Moreover, most of the effects of integration are initially bound to be trade diverting, particularly since most of the Third World seeks to industrialize.

On the other hand, it was also realized that an important obstacle to the development of industry in these countries is the inadequate size of their individual markets – see Brown (1961), Hazlewood (1967, 1975) and Robson (1980, 1983, 1985). It is therefore necessary to increase the market size so as to encourage optimum plant installations: hence the need for economic integration. This would, however, result in industries clustering together in the relatively more advanced of these nations – those that have already commenced the process of industrialization.

I have demonstrated elsewhere (El-Agraa, 1979a) that there is essentially *no theoretical difference* between economic integration in the advanced world and the Third World but that there is a major difference in terms of the *type* of economic integration that suits the particular *circumstances* of developing countries and that is politically feasible: the need for an equitable distribution of the gains from industrialization and the location of industries is an important issue (see above). This suggests that any type of economic integration that is being contemplated must incorporate as an essential element a common fiscal authority and some coordination of economic policies. But then one could equally well argue that *some degree* of these elements is necessary in *any* type of integration – see the Raisman Committee recommendations for the EAC (1961).

4.6 Economic integration among communist countries

The only example of economic integration among communist countries was the CMEA. However, there the economic system perpetuated a fundamental lack of interest of domestic producers in becoming integrated with both consumers and producers in other member countries. As Marer and Montias (1988) emphasize, the integration policies of member nations must focus on the mechanism of state to state relations rather than on domestic economic policies which would make CMEA integration more attractive to producers and consumers alike. That is, integration must be planned by the state at the highest possible level and imposed on ministries, trusts and enterprises. It should also be stated that the CMEA operated different pricing mechanisms for intra- and extra-area trade. Moreover, the attitude of the former USSR was extremely important since the policies of the East European members of the CMEA were somewhat constrained by the policies adopted by the organization's most powerful member, for economic as well as political reasons. CMEA integration, therefore, had to be approached within an entirely different framework but this is not the appropriate place for discussing it, especially since the

CMEA met its demise soon after the collapse of socialism in the former USSR and Eastern Europe.

4.7 Conclusions

The conclusions reached here are consistent with my 1979 and 1989a conclusions and with those of Jones in El-Agraa and Jones (1981). They are as follows.

First, the rationale for regional economic integration rests upon the existence of constraints on the use of first best policy instruments. Economic analysis has had little to say about the nature of these constraints, and presumably the evaluation of any regional scheme of economic integration should incorporate a consideration of the validity of the view that such constraints do exist to justify the pursuit of second rather than first best solutions.

Second, even when the existence of constraints on superior policy instruments is acknowledged, it is misleading to identify the results of regional economic integration by comparing an arbitrarily chosen common policy with an arbitrarily chosen national policy. Of course, ignorance and inertia provide sufficient reasons why existing policies may be non-optimal; but it is clearly wrong to attribute gains which would have been achieved by appropriate unilateral action to a policy of regional integration. Equally, although it is appropriate to use the optimal common policy as a point of reference, it must be recognized that this may overstate the gains to be achieved if, as seems highly likely, constraints and inefficiencies in the political processes by which policies are agreed prove to be greater among a group of countries than within any individual country.

Although the first two conclusions raise doubts about the case for regional economic integration, in principle at least, a strong general case for economic integration does exist. In unions where economies of scale may be in part external to national industries, the rationale for unions rests essentially upon the recognition of the externalities and market imperfections which extend beyond the boundaries of national states. In such circumstances, unilateral national action will not be optimal while integrated action offers the scope for potential gain.

As with the solution to most problems of externalities and market imperfections, however, customs union theory frequently illustrates the proposition that a major stumbling block to obtaining the gains from joint optimal action lies in agreeing an acceptable distribution of such gains. Thus the fourth conclusion is that the achievement of the potential gains from economic integration will be limited to countries able and willing to cooperate to distribute the gains from integration so that all partners may benefit compared with the results achieved by independent action. It is easy to argue from this that regional economic integration may be more readily achieved than global solutions but, as the debate about monetary integration in the EU illustrates (see Chapter 5), the chances of obtaining potential mutual gain may well founder in the presence of disparate views about the distribution of such gains and weak arrangements for redistribution.

chapter five

European monetary integration

A. M. EL-AGRAA

The previous chapter was devoted to a discussion of the economic consequences of tariff removal and the establishment of the common external tariff (CET), i.e. the chapter was concerned mainly with the customs union (CU) and some of the economic union aspects of the EU. However, it is now well recognized that monetary integration, more precisely economic and monetary union (EMU), is by far the most challenging feature of the EU, or any scheme of economic integration that may decide to embrace it. The aim of this chapter is to explain the reasons for the challenge as well as to trace the EU endeavours in this respect. Before doing so, however, one needs to explain what monetary integration means.

5.1 What is monetary integration?

Monetary integration has two essential components: an exchange-rate union and capital (K) market integration. An exchange-rate union is established when member countries have what is in effect one currency. The actual existence of one currency is not necessary, however, because, if member countries have *permanently* and *irrevocably* fixed exchange rates among themselves, the result is effectively the same. Of course, one could argue that the adoption of a single currency would guarantee the irreversibility of undertaking membership of a monetary union, which would have vast repercussions for the discussion in terms of actual unions; but one could equally well argue that if a member nation decided to opt out of a monetary union, it would do so irrespective of whether or not the union entailed the use of a single currency.

Convertibility refers to the *permanent* absence of all exchange controls for both current and K transactions, including interest and dividend payments (and the harmonization of relevant taxes and measures affecting the K market) within the union. It is, of course, absolutely necessary to have complete convertibility for trade transactions, otherwise an important requirement of CU formation is threatened, namely the promotion of free trade among members of the CU, which is an integral part of an economic union – see Chapter 1. That is why this aspect of monetary integration does not need any discussion; it applies even in the case of a free trade area

(FTA). Convertibility for K transactions is related to free factor mobility and is therefore an important aspect of K market integration which is necessary in common markets (CMs), not in CUs or FTAs.

In practice, this definition of monetary integration should specifically include the following:

1. An explicit harmonization of monetary policies.
2. A common pool of foreign exchange reserves.
3. A single central bank.

There are important reasons for including these elements. Suppose union members decide either that one of their currencies will be a reference currency or that a new unit of account will be established. Also assume that each member country has its own foreign exchange reserves and conducts its own monetary and fiscal policies. If a member finds itself running out of reserves, it will have to engage in a monetary and fiscal contraction sufficient to restore the reserve position. This will necessitate the fairly frequent meeting of the finance ministers or central bank governors, to consider whether or not to change the parity of the reference currency. If they do decide to change it, then all the member currencies will have to move with it. Such a situation could create the sorts of difficulty which plagued the Bretton Woods System:

1. Each finance minister might fight for the rate of exchange that was most suitable for his/her country. This might make bargaining hard; agreement might become difficult to reach and the whole system might be subject to continuous strain.
2. Each meeting might be accompanied by speculation about its outcome. This might result in undesirable speculative private K movements into or out of the union.
3. The difficulties that might be created by (1) and (2) might result in the reference currency being permanently fixed relative to outside currencies, e.g. the US dollar.
4. However, the system does allow for the possibility of the reference currency floating relative to non-member currencies or floating within a band. If the reference currency does float, it might do so in response to conditions in its own market. This would be the case, however, only if the union required the monetary authorities in the partner countries to vary their exchange rates so as to maintain constant parities relative to the reference currency. They would then have to buy and sell the reserve currency so as to maintain or bring about the necessary exchange-rate alteration. Therefore, the monetary authorities of the reference currency would, in fact, be able to determine the exchange rate for the whole union.
5. Such a system does not guarantee the permanence of the parities between the union currencies that is required by the appropriate specification of monetary

integration. There is the possibility that the delegates will not reach agreement, or that one of the partners might finally choose not to deflate to the extent necessary to maintain its rate at the required parity or that a partner in surplus might choose neither to build up its reserves nor to inflate as required and so might allow its rate to rise above the agreed level.

In order to avoid such difficulties, it is necessary to include in monetary integration the three elements specified. The central bank would operate in the market so that the exchange parties were permanently maintained among the union currencies and, at the same time, it would allow the rate of the reference currency to fluctuate, or to alter intermittently, relative to the outside reserve currency. For instance, if the foreign exchange reserves in the common pool were running down, the common central bank would allow the reference currency, and with it all the partner currencies, to depreciate. This would have the advantage of economizing in the use of foreign exchange reserves, since all partners would not tend to be in deficit or surplus at the same time. Also surplus countries would automatically be helping deficit countries.

However, without explicit policy coordination, a monetary union would not be effective. If each country conducted its own monetary policy, and hence could engage in as much domestic credit as it wished, surplus countries would be financing deficit nations without any incentives for the deficit countries to restore equilibrium. If one country ran a large deficit, the union exchange rate would depreciate, but this might put some partner countries into surplus. If wage rates were rising in the member countries at different rates, while productivity growth did not differ in such a way as to offset the effects on relative prices, those partners with the lower inflation rates would be permanently financing the other partners.

In short,

> Monetary integration, in the sense defined, requires the unification and joint management both of monetary policy and of the external exchange-rate policy of the union. This in turn entails further consequences. First, in the monetary field the rate of increase of the money supply must be decided jointly. Beyond an agreed amount of credit expansion, which is allocated to each member state's central bank, a member state would have to finance any budget deficit in the union's capital market at the ruling rate of interest. A unified monetary policy would remove one of the main reasons for disparate movements in members' price levels, and thus one of the main reasons for the existence of intra-union payment imbalances prior to monetary union. Second, the balance of payments of the entire union with the rest of the world must be regulated at union level. For this purpose the monetary authority must dispose of a common pool of exchange reserves, and the union exchange rates with other currencies must be regulated at the union level. (Robson, 1980)

Monetary integration which explicitly includes the three requirements specified will therefore enable the partners to do away with all these problems right from the start. Incidentally, this also suggests the advantages of having a single currency.

5.2 The gains and losses

The gains due to membership of a monetary union could be both economic and non-economic, e.g. political. The non-economic benefits are too obvious to warrant space; for example, it is difficult to imagine that a complete political union could become a reality without the establishment of a monetary union. The discussion will therefore be confined to the economic benefits, which can be briefly summarized as follows:

1. The common pool of foreign exchange reserves already discussed has the incidental advantage of economizing in the use of foreign exchange reserves in terms of the facts both that member nations will not likely go into deficit *simultaneously* and that intraunion trade transactions will no longer be financed by foreign exchange. In the context of the EU this will reduce the role of the US dollar or reduce the EU's dependence on the dollar.

2. In the case of forms of economic integration like the EU, the adoption of a common currency would transform that currency into a major world medium able to compete with the US dollar or Japanese yen on equal terms. The advantages of such a currency are too well established to discuss here. However, the use of an integrated area's currency as a major reserve currency doubtless imposes certain burdens on the area; but, in the particular case of the EU, it would create an oligopolistic market situation which could either lead to collusion, resulting in a stable international monetary system, or intensify the reserve currency crisis and lead to a complete collapse of the international monetary order. The latter possibility is, of course, extremely likely to result in the former outcome; it is difficult to imagine that the leading nations in the world economy would allow monetary chaos to be the order of the day; indeed, the group of seven (G7) was created in 1986 to establish a system of international coordination between the most advanced nations in the world for precisely such a reason.

3. Another source of gain could be a reduction in the cost of financial management. Monetary integration should enable the spreading of overhead costs of financial transactions more widely. Also, some of the activities of the institutions dealing in foreign exchanges might be discontinued, leading to a saving in the use of resources.

4. There also exist the classical advantages of having permanently fixed exchange rates (or one currency) among members of a monetary union for free trade and factor movements. Stability of exchange rates enhances trade, encourages K to move to where it is most productively rewarded and ensures that labour (L) will move to where the highest rewards prevail. It seems unnecessary to emphasize that this does not mean that *all L* and *all K* should be mobile, but simply enough of each to generate the necessary adjustment to any situation. Nor is it necessary to stress that hedging can tackle the problem of exchange-rate fluctuations only at a cost, no matter how low that cost may be.

5. The integration of the K market has a further advantage. If a member country of a monetary union is in deficit (assuming that countries can be recognized within such a union), it can borrow directly on the union market or raise its rate of interest to attract K inflow and therefore ease the situation. However, the integration of economic policies within the union ensures that this help will occur automatically under the auspices of the common central bank. Since no single area is likely to be in deficit permanently, such help can be envisaged for all the members. Hence, there is no basis for the assertion that one country can borrow indefinitely to sustain real wages and consumption levels that are out of line with that nation's productivity and the demand for its products.

6. When a monetary union establishes a central fiscal authority with its own budget, then the larger the size of this budget, the higher the degree of fiscal harmonization (the *McDougall Report*, CEC, 1977). This has some advantages: regional deviations from internal balance can be financed from the centre and the centralization of social security payments financed by contributions or taxes on a progressive basis would have some stabilizing and compensating effects, modifying the harmful effects of monetary integration.

7. There are negative advantages in the case of the EU in the sense that monetary integration is necessary for maintaining the EU as it exists; for example, realizing the 'single market' would become more difficult to achieve and the common agricultural prices enshrined in the *Common Agricultural Policy* (CAP – see Chapter 10) would be undermined if exchange rates were to be flexible.

These benefits of monetary integration are clear and there are few economists who would question them. However, there is no consensus of opinion with regard to its costs.

The losses from membership of a monetary union are emphasized by Fleming (1971) and Corden (1972a). Assume that the world consists of three countries: the home country (H), the potential partner country (P) and the rest of the world (W). Also assume that, in order to maintain both internal and external equilibrium, one country (H) needs to devalue its currency relative to W, while P needs to revalue vis-à-vis W. Moreover, assume that H and P use fiscal and monetary policies for achieving internal equilibrium. If H and P were partners in an exchange-rate union, they would devalue together – which is consistent with H's policy requirements in isolation – or revalue together – which is consistent with P's requirements in isolation – but they would not be able to alter the rate of exchange in a way that was consistent with both. Under such circumstances, the alteration in the exchange rate could leave H with an external deficit, forcing it to deflate its economy and to increase–create unemployment, or it could leave it with a surplus, forcing it into accumulating foreign reserves or allowing its prices and wages to rise. If countries deprive themselves of rates of exchange (or trade impediments) as policy instruments, they impose on themselves losses that are essentially the losses emanating from *enforced departure from internal balance* (Cordon, 1972a).

In short, the rationale for retaining flexibility in the rates of exchange rests on the assumption that governments aim to achieve both internal and external balance, and, as Tinbergen (1952) has shown, to achieve these *simultaneously* at least an equal number of instruments is needed. This can be explained in the following manner. Orthodoxy has it that there are two macroeconomic policy targets and two policy instruments. Internal equilibrium is tackled via financial instruments, which have their greatest impact on the level of aggregate demand, and the exchange rate is used to achieve equilibrium. Of course, financial instruments can be activated via both monetary and fiscal policies and may have a varied impact on both internal and external equilibria. Given this understanding, the case for maintaining flexibility in exchange rates depends entirely on the presumption that the loss of one of the two policy instruments will conflict with the achievement of both internal and external equilibria.

With this background in mind, it is vital to follow the Corden–Fleming explanation of the enforced departure from internal equilibrium. Suppose a country is initially in internal equilibrium but has a deficit in its external account. If the country were free to vary its rate of exchange, the appropriate policy for it to adopt to achieve overall balance would be a combination of devaluation and expenditure reduction. When the rate of exchange is not available as a policy instrument, it is necessary to reduce expenditure by more than is required in the optimal situation, with the result of extra unemployment. The *excess* unemployment, which can be valued in terms of output or whatever, is the cost to that country of depriving itself of the exchange rate as a policy instrument. The extent of this loss is determined, *ceteris paribus*, by the marginal propensity to import and to consume exportables, or, more generally, by the marginal propensity to consume tradables relative to non-tradables.

The expenditure reduction which is required for eliminating the initial external account deficit will be smaller the higher the marginal propensity to import. Moreover, the higher the marginal propensity to import, the less the effect of that reduction in expenditure on demand for domestically produced commodities. For both reasons, therefore, the higher the marginal propensity to import, the less domestic unemployment will result from abandoning the devaluation of the rate of exchange as a policy instrument. If the logic of this explanation is correct, it follows that as long as the marginal propensity to consume domestic goods is greater than zero, there will be some cost due to fixing the rate of exchange. A similar argument applies to a country which cannot use the exchange-rate instrument when it has a surplus in its external account and internal equilibrium: the required excess expenditure will have little effect on demand for domestically produced goods and will therefore exert little inflationary pressure if the country's marginal propensity to import is high.

This analysis is based on the assumption that there exists a trade-off between rates of change in costs and levels of unemployment – the Phillips curve. Assuming that there is a Phillips (1958) curve relationship (a negative response of rates of change in money wages – $\dot{W}$ – and the level of unemployment – U), Fleming's (1971) and Corden's (1972a) analysis can be explained by using a simple diagram devised by de

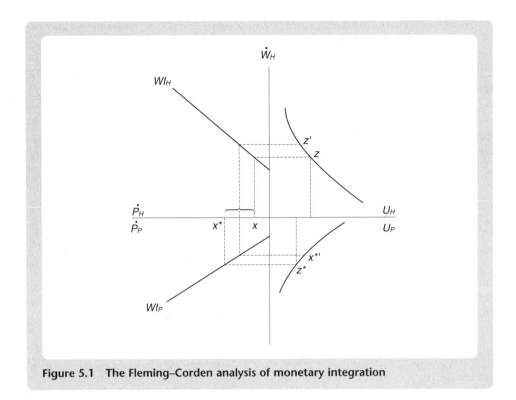

Figure 5.1   The Fleming–Corden analysis of monetary integration

Grauwe (1978). Hence, in Figure 5.1, the top half depicts the position of H while the lower half depicts that of P. The top right and the lower right corners represent the two countries' Phillips curves, while the remaining quadrants show their inflation rates corresponding to the rates of change in wages – $\dot{P}$. WI_H (which stands for *wage-rate change* and corresponding *inflation*) and WI_P, are, of course, determined by the share of L in total GNP, the rate of change in the productivity of L and the degree of competition in both the factor and the commodity markets, with perfect competition resulting in the WIs being straight lines. Note that the intersection of the WIs with the vertical axes will be determined by rates of change of L's share in GNP and its rate of productivity change. The diagram has been drawn on the presumption that the L productivity changes are positive.

The diagram is drawn in such a way that countries H and P differ in all respects: the positions of their Phillips curves, their preferred trade-offs between $\dot{W}$ and $\dot{P}$, and their rates of productivity growth. H has a lower rate of inflation, x, than P, x^* (equilibria being at z and z^*); hence, without monetary integration, P's currency should depreciate relative to H's; note that it is only a chance in a million that the two countries' inflation rates would coincide. Altering the exchange rates would then enable each country to maintain its preferred internal equilibrium: z and z^* for countries H and P, respectively.

When H and P enter into an exchange-rate union, i.e. have irrevocably fixed exchange rates *vis-à-vis* each other, their inflation rates cannot differ from each other, given a model without traded goods. Each country will therefore have to settle for a combination of U and $\dot{P}$ which is different from what it would have liked. The Fleming–Corden conclusion is thus vindicated.

However, this analysis rests entirely on the acceptance of the Phillips curve. The controversy between Keynesians and monetarists, although still far from being resolved, has at least led to the consensus that the form of the Phillips curve just presented is too crude. This is because many economists no longer believe that there is a trade-off between unemployment and inflation; if there is any relationship at all, it must be a short-term one such that the rate of unemployment is in the long term independent of the rate of inflation: there is a 'natural rate' (now referred to as NAIRU, which stands for non-accelerating inflation rate of unemployment) of unemployment which is determined by rigidities in the market for L. The crude version of the Phillips curve has been replaced by an expectations-adjusted one along the lines suggested by Phelps (1968) and Freidman (1975), i.e. the Phillips curves become vertical in the long run. This position can be explained with reference to Figure 5.2 which depicts three Phillips curves for one of the two countries. Assume that unemployment is initially at point U_2, i.e. the rate of inflation is equal to zero,

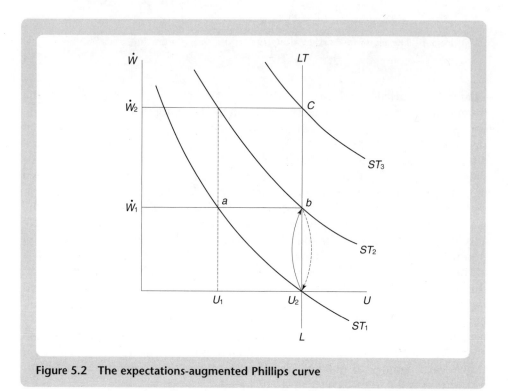

Figure 5.2   The expectations-augmented Phillips curve

given the short-term Phillips curve indicated by ST_1. The expectations-augmented Phillips curve suggests that, if the government tries to lower unemployment by the use of monetary policy, the short-term effect would be to move to point a, with positive inflation and lower unemployment. However, in the long term, people would adjust their expectations, causing an upward shift of the Phillips curve to ST_2 which leads to equilibrium at point b. The initial level of unemployment is thus restored but with a positive rate of inflation. A repetition of this process gives the vertical long-term curve labelled LT.

If both partners H and P have vertical LT curves, Figure 5.1 will have to be adjusted to give Figure 5.3. The implications of this are that:

1. Monetary integration will have no long-term effect on either partner's rate of unemployment since this will be fixed at the appropriate NAIRU for each country – U_H, U_P.

2. If monetary integration is adopted to bring about balanced growth as well as equal NAIRU, this can be achieved only if other policy instruments are introduced to bring about uniformity in the two L markets.

Therefore, this alternative interpretation of the Phillips curve renders the Fleming–Corden conclusion invalid.

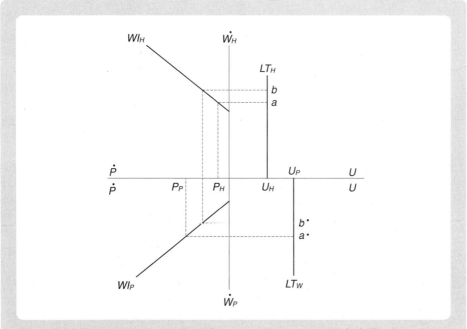

Figure 5.3   Monetary integration with expectations augmented Phillips curves

Be that as it may, it should be noted that Allen and Kenen (1980) and P. R. Allen (1983) have demonstrated, using a sophisticated and elaborate model with financial assets, that, although monetary policy has severe drawbacks as an instrument for adjusting cyclical imbalances within a monetary union, it may be able to influence the demand for the goods produced by member countries in a differential manner within the short term, provided that the markets of the member nations are not too closely integrated. Their model indicates that economic integration, in this sense, can come about as a consequence of the substitutability between nations' commodities, especially their financial assets, and of country biases in the purchase of commodities and financial assets. The moral of this is that the central bank of a monetary union can operate disparate monetary policies in the different partner countries without compromising their internal and external equilibria – a severe blow to those who stress the costs from monetary integration.

Moreover, once non-traded goods are incorporated into the model and/or K and L mobility is allowed for, it follows that the losses due to deviating from internal equilibrium vanish into oblivion, a point which Corden (1972a, 1977) readily accedes to. Finally, this model does not allow for the fact that monetary integration involves at least three countries; hence W has to be explicitly included in the model. Allen and Kenen (1980) tried to develop a model along these lines, but their model is not a straightforward extension of that depicted in Figure 5.1.

In concluding this section, it may be appropriate to highlight the limitations in the argument put forward by Fleming and Corden:

1. It is clearly stated in the definition of monetary integration that the fixity of exchange-rate parities within a monetary union (or the adoption of one currency) does not mean that the different member currencies cannot vary in unison relative to extraunion currencies. Hence the monetary union is not forgoing the availability of exchange rate variations relative to the outside world.

2. In a proper monetary union, an extra deficit for one region can come about only as a result of a revaluation of the union currency – the union as a whole has an external surplus *vis-à-vis* the outside world. Such an act would increase the foreign exchange earnings of the surplus region, and therefore of the union as a whole, provided that the conditions for a successful revaluation exist. The common central bank and the integration of monetary policies will ensure that the extra burden on the first region is alleviated: the overall extra earnings will be used to help the region with the extra deficit. Needless to say, such a situation does not lead to surplus regions financing deficit regions indefinitely because no single region is likely to be in deficit or surplus permanently and because the policy coordination will not allow one region to behave in such a manner unless there are reasons of a different nature which permit a situation to be sustained.

3. Even if one accepts the Fleming–Corden argument at its face value, the assumptions are extremely controversial. For instance, devaluation can work effectively only when there is 'monetary illusion'; otherwise it would be pointless since it would not work. Is it really permissible to assume that trade unionists,

wherever they may be, suffer from money illusion? Many authors have disputed this assumption, but Corden's response has been to suggest that exchange-rate alterations may work if money wages are forced up because the catching-up process is never complete. Such an argument is far from convincing simply because the catching-up process has no validity as a true adjustment; it cannot be maintained indefinitely because, sooner or later, trade unionists will allow for it when negotiating money wage increases.

4. One must remember that in practice there would never be a separation between the exchange-rate union and K market integration. Once one allows for the role of convertibility for K transactions, K will always come to the rescue. Corden has reservations about this too since he argues that K integration can help in the short run, but, in the long term, while it has its own advantages, it cannot solve the problem. The rationale for this is that no region can borrow indefinitely on a private market, no matter how efficient and open the market is, to sustain levels of real wages, and hence real consumption levels, which are too high, given the productivity level in the region. Clearly, this is a switching of grounds: devaluation is nothing but a temporary adjustment device as the discussion of the monetary approach to the balance of payments has shown. Why then should devaluation be more desirable than short-term K adjustment? Moreover, for a region that is permanently in deficit, all economists would agree that devaluation is no panacea.

5. We have seen that monetary integration can be contemplated only when the countries concerned have an economic union in mind. In such conditions, the mobility of L will also help in the adjustment process. This point is conceded by Corden, but he believes that L mobility may help only marginally since it would take prolonged unemployment to induce people to emigrate, and, if monetary integration proceeded far in advance of 'psychological integration' (defined as the suppression of existing nationalisms and a sense of attachment to place in favour of an integrated community nationalism and an American-style geographic rootedness), nationalistic reactions to any nation's depopulation may become very intense. This reasoning is similar to that in the previous case since it presupposes that the problem region is a *permanently* depressed area. Since no region in the union is ever likely to experience chronic maladjustments, L mobility needs only to be marginal and national depopulation is far from the truth.

6. Finally, and more fundamentally, a very crucial element is missing from the Fleming–Corden argument. Their analysis relates to a country in internal equilibrium and external deficit. If such a country were outside a monetary union, it could devalue its currency. Assuming that the necessary conditions for effective devaluation prevailed, then devaluation would increase the national income of the country, increase its price level, or result in some combination of the two. Hence a deflationary policy would be required to restore the internal balance. However, if the country were to lose its freedom to alter its exchange rate, it would have to deflate in order to depress its imports and restore external

balance. According to the Fleming–Corden analysis, this alternative would entail unemployment in excess of that prevailing in the initial situation. The missing element in this argument can be found by specifying how devaluation actually works. Devaluation of a country's currency results in changes in relative price levels and is price inflationary for, at least, both exportables and importables. These relative price changes, given the necessary stability conditions, will depress imports and (perhaps) increase exports. The deflationary policy which is required (to accompany devaluation) in order to restore internal balance should therefore eliminate the *newly injected* inflation as well as the *extra* national income. By disregarding the 'inflationary' implications of devaluation, Fleming and Corden reach the unjustifiable *a priori* conclusion that membership of a monetary union would necessitate extra sacrifice of employment in order to achieve the same target. Any serious comparison of the two situations would indicate that no such *a priori* conclusion can be reached – one must compare like with like.

In addition to the above limitations, one should point out a fundamental contradiction in the analysis of those who exaggerate the costs. If a nation decides to become a member of a monetary union, this implies that it accedes to the notion that the benefits of such a union must outweigh any possible losses and/or that it feels that a monetary union is essential for maintaining a rational economic union. It will want to do so because its economy is more interdependent with its partners than with *W*. Why then would such a country prize the availability of the exchange rate as a policy instrument for its own domestic purposes? The answer is that there is no conceivable rational reason for its doing so: it will want to have an inflation rate, monetary growth target and unemployment rate which are consistent with those of its partners. Also, the use of an economic union's rate of exchange *vis-à-vis* *W*, plus the rational operations of the common central bank and its general activities, should ensure that any worries on the part of the home country are alleviated. For such a country to feel that there is something intrinsically good about having such a policy instrument at its own disposal is tantamount to its not having any faith in or a true commitment to the economic union to which it has voluntarily decided to belong.

Expressed in terms of Tinbergen's criterion of an equal number of policy instruments and objectives, it should be remembered that the formation of a *complete* economic union is effectively just a step short of complete political union. However, given that the necessary conditions for an effective economic union require a great deal of political unification, economic union and complete political integration are hardly distinguishable in a realistic situation. In forming an economic union, the countries concerned will actually be acquiring a free policy instrument: they will have two instruments for internal policy adjustments and one for external (joint) adjustment when all they effectively need is only one of the former instruments. Therefore, an analysis which does not explicitly incorporate this dimension can hardly claim to have any relevance to the situation under consideration.

Lest one is misunderstood, one should stress that the argument is not that there are *no costs* to EMU, only that the benefits seem to be far in excess of the costs, but that there are influential economists who hold the opposite view. However, a somewhat supportive explanation for the position taken in this chapter is provided by Krugman (1990), who adopts a longer time perspective. Krugman examines EMU in cost–benefit terms, where the costs are represented by *CC* and the benefits by *BB* in Figure 5.4; both costs and benefits are expressed in relation to GDP. The benefits from the single currency (given above) are shown to rise with integration, since, for example, intra-EU trade, which is expected to increase, and has been doing so (see Chapter 3), with integration over time, will be conducted at lesser costs, while the losses from giving up the exchange rate variable (explained above) decline with time. To put it in modern jargon, changes in the exchange rate are needed to absorb *asymmetric* shocks (those that affect the member economies differently), but these will decline with time, owing to the shocks becoming less asymmetric as integration proceeds and becomes more intensive. These modern macroeconomic concepts are explained in standard texts, and hence all that one needs to emphasize here is that the essence of the Krugman analysis is that, as the member economies become more integrated, the use of the exchange rate instrument for variations against member nations' currencies would become less and less desirable. Thus, for countries seriously and permanently involved in an EMU, sooner or later, a time will come when the benefits will exceed the costs: the two lines are bound to intersect at some future point in time, indicating 'bliss' thereafter. Nevertheless, one should stress that, although this analysis is reassuring for countries committed to EMU, it is not

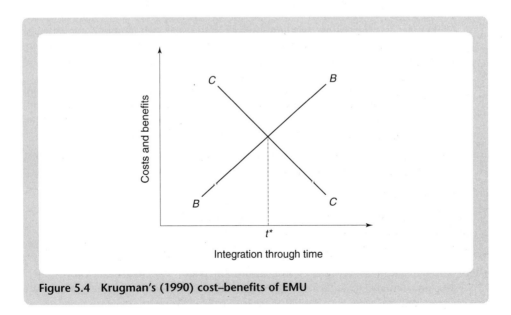

Figure 5.4 Krugman's (1990) cost–benefits of EMU

helpful for those wishing to use it to guide them in reaching a decision regarding whether or not to join or form EMUs since the empirical estimation of the two lines is practically impossible (see Chapter 6), making it difficult to determine the position of the point of bliss.

5.3 The road to EMU

The aim of achieving EMU, although enshrined in the Maastricht Treaty, is not a new phenomena for the EU – see Chapters 2 and 23. This section provides a historical perspective by travelling, albeit along the fast lanes, on the route taken by the EU in this direction.

5.3.1 The Werner Report

In 1969, during The Hague summit (see Chapters 2 and 24), the Six decided that the EC should progressively transform itself into an EMU, and set up a committee, led by Pierre Werner, then Prime Minister of Luxemburg, to consider the issues involved. The Werner Committee presented an interim report in June 1970 and a final report in October of the same year. The latter became generally known as the 'Werner Report', and was endorsed by the Council in February 1971.

According to the Council resolution, the EC would:

1. Constitute a zone where persons, goods, services and capital would move freely – but without distorting competition, or creating structural and regional imbalances – and where economic undertakings could develop their activities on a Community scale;
2. Form a single monetary entity within the international monetary system, characterised by the total and irreversible convertibility of currencies; the elimination of fluctuation margins of exchange rates between the [members]; the irrevocable fixing of their parity relationships. These steps would be essential for the creation of a single currency, and they would involve a Community-level organisation of central banks;
3. Hold the powers and responsibilities in the economic and monetary field that would enable its institutions to ensure the administration of the economic union. To this end, the necessary economic policy decisions would be taken at Community level and the necessary powers would be attributed to community institutions.

The Community organisation of central banks would assist, in the framework of its own responsibilities, in achieving the objectives of stability and growth in the Community.

These three principles would apply to:

(a) The internal monetary and credit policies of the union;
(b) Monetary policy *vis-à-vis* the rest of the world;
(c) Policy on a unified capital market and capital movements to and from non-member countries;
(d) Budgetary and taxation policies, as related to the policy for stability and growth ...;
(e) Structural and regional action needed to contribute to the balanced development of the Community.

As progress was made in moving closer to the final objectives, Community instruments would be created whenever they seemed necessary to replace or complement the action of national instruments. All actions would be interdependent; in particular, the development of monetary unification would be backed by parallel progress in the convergence, and then the unification of economic policies.

The Council decided that EMU could be attained during that decade, if the plan had the permanent political support of the member governments. Implementation was envisaged to be in three stages, with the first beginning in 1971 and the final completed by 1980. The Council made quite clear how it envisaged the process leading to full EMU (emphasis added):

(a) The first phase should begin on January 1, 1971, and could technically be completed within three years. This phase would be used to make the Community instruments more operational and to mark the beginnings of the Community's individuality within the international monetary system;

(b) The first phase should not be considered as an objective in itself; it should be associated with the complete process of economic and monetary integration. *It should therefore be launched with the determination to arrive at the final goal*;

(c) In the first phase consultation procedures should be strengthened; the budgetary policies of the member states should accord with Community objectives; some taxes should be harmonised; monetary and credit policies should be coordinated; and integration of financial markets should be intensified.

Thus, it should be clear that the EMU launched by the EC in 1971 was consistent with and satisfied all the above requirements for a proper EMU. What is of significance for our purposes, however, is that EMU is not a new venture for the EC since it goes back to more than two decades. Yet, the 1971 venture did fail after an earlier than expected successful negotiation of the first phase and some progress during the second, but the failure was not due to lack of commitment, determination or both: the Nixon shock, the first oil shock and the enlargement shock (the admission of three new members, each bringing with it its own unique problems) were the real culprits.

5.3.2 The EMS

In some quarters, the European Monetary System (EMS) has been considered as the next EC attempt at EMU, but in reality the EMS was no more than a mechanism devised to check the monetary upheavals of the 1970 by creating a 'zone of monetary stability'. Although Chapter 16 is devoted to a full coverage of the EMS, here a few words on the EMS are in order.

The route to EMS was a fairly short one: the Bremen Declaration on 6 and 7 July 1978 was followed by its affirmation in Bonn on 16 and 17 July and then by its adoption by the Council, in the form of a resolution 'on the establishment of the European Monetary System (EMS) and related matters', on 5 December of the same year.

The EMS was introduced with the immediate support of six of the EC nations at the time. Ireland, Italy and United Kingdom adopted a wait-and-see attitude; 'time for reflection' was needed by Ireland and Italy and a definite reservation was expressed by the United Kingdom. Later, Ireland and Italy joined the system, while the United Kingdom expressed a 'spirit of sympathetic cooperation'. The EMS was to start operating on 1 January 1979, but France, who wanted assurances regarding the MCA system (see Chapter 10), delayed that start to 13 March 1979.

The main features of the EMS are given in the annex to the conclusions of the EC presidency (*Bulletin of the European Communities*, no. 6, 1978, pp. 20–1):

1. In terms of exchange rate management, the ... (EMS) will be at least as strict as the 'snake'. In the initial stages of its operation and for a limited period of time, member countries currently not participating in the 'snake' may opt for somewhat wider margins around central rates. In principle, intervention will be in the currencies of participating countries. Changes in central rates will be subject to mutual consent. Non-member countries with particularly strong economic and financial ties with the Community may become associate members of the system. The European Currency Unit (ECU) will be at the centre of the system; in particular, it will be used as a means of settlement between EEC monetary authorities.

2. An initial supply of ECUs (for use among Community central banks) will be created against deposit of US dollars and gold on the one hand (e.g. 20% of the stock currently held by member central banks) and member currencies on the other hand in an amount of a comparable order of magnitude.

   The use of ECUs created against member currencies will be subject to conditions varying with the amount and the maturity; due account will be given to the need for substantial short-term facilities (up to 1 year).

3. Participating countries will coordinate their exchange rates policies *vis-à-vis* third countries. To this end, they will intensify the consultations in the appropriate bodies and between central banks participating in the scheme. Ways to coordinate dollar interventions should be sought which avoid simultaneous reserve interventions. Central banks buying dollars will deposit a fraction (say 20%) and receive ECUs in return; likewise, central banks selling dollars will receive a fraction (say 20%) against ECUs.

4. Not later than two years after the start of the scheme, the existing arrangements and institutions will be consolidated in a European Monetary Fund.

5. A system of closer monetary cooperation will only be successful if participating countries pursue policies conducive to greater stability at home and abroad; this applies to deficit and surplus countries alike.

Thus, in essence, the EMS is concerned with the creation of an EC currency zone within which there is discipline for managing exchange rates. This discipline is known as the 'exchange rate mechanism' (ERM), which asks a member nation to intervene to reverse a trend when 75% of the allowed exchange rate variation of $\pm 2.25\%$ is reached; this is similar to that which was practised within the 'snake' arrangements that preceded the EMS. The ERM, however, did not apply to all the member nations of the EMS, since wider margins of fluctuation for those not participating in the snake were allowed for ($\pm 6\%$). The ECU, which is similar to the European Unit of Account in that it is a basket of *all* EC currencies, lies at the heart of the system; it is the means of settlement between the EC central banks. The EMS is supported by a European Monetary Fund (EMF) which (supposedly within two years) was to absorb the short-term financing arrangement operating within the snake, the short-term monetary support agreement which was managed by the European Monetary Cooperation Fund (EMCF) and the medium-term loan facilities for balance of payments assistance (*Bulletin of the European Communities*, no. 12, 1978). The EMF is backed by approximately 20% of national gold and US dollar reserves and by a similar percentage in national currencies. The EMF issues ECUs which are used as new reserve assets. An exchange-stabilization fund able to issue about 50 billion US dollars was to be created (*Bulletin of the European Communities*, no. 12, 1978).

It is clear from the above that the EMS asks neither for permanently and irrevocably fixed exchange rates between the member nations nor for complete capital convertibility. Moreover, it does not mention the creation of a common central bank to be put in charge of the member nations' foreign exchange reserves and to be vested with the appropriate powers. Hence, the EMS is not EMU, and although it could be seen as paving the way for one, the 1992 crisis, which resulted in the complete withdrawal of the United Kingdom from the ERM and the widening of the margin of exchange rate fluctuations to ±15%, completely erases such a vision.

5.3.3 The Delors Report and the Maastricht Treaty

The EC summit which was held in Hanover on 27 and 28 June 1988 decided that, in adopting the Single Act, the EC member states had confirmed the objective of 'progressive realisation of economic and monetary union'. The heads of state agreed to discuss the means of achieving this in their meeting in Madrid in June of the following year, and to help them in their deliberations then they entrusted to a committee of central bankers and others, chaired by Mr Jacques Delors, then President of the EC Commission, the 'task of studying and proposing concrete stages leading towards this union'. The committee reported just before the Madrid summit and its report is referred to as the Delors Report on EMU.

The committee was of the opinion that the creation of the EMU must be seen as a single process, but that this process should be in stages which progressively led to the ultimate goal; thus the decision to enter upon the first stage should commit a member state to the entire process. Emphasizing that the creation of the EMU would necessitate a common monetary policy and require a high degree of compatibility of economic policies and consistency in a number of other policy areas, particularly in the fiscal field, the Report pointed out that the realization of the EMU would require new arrangements which could be established only on the basis of a change in the relevant Treaty of Rome and consequent changes in national legislation.

The first stage should be concerned with the initiation of the process of creating the EMU. During this stage there would be a greater convergence of economic performance through the strengthening of economic and monetary policy coordination within the existing institutional framework. The economic measures would be concerned with the completion of the internal market and the reduction of existing disparities through programmes of budgetary consolidation in the member states involved and more effective structural and regional policies. In the monetary field the emphasis would be on the removal of all obstacles to financial integration and on the intensification of cooperation and coordination of monetary policies. Realignment of exchange rates was seen to be possible, but efforts would be made by every member state to make the functioning of other adjustment mechanisms more effective. The committee was of the opinion that it would be important to include all EC currencies in the exchange-rate mechanism of the EMS during this stage. The 1974 Council decision defining the mandate of central bank governors would be replaced by a new decision indicating that the committee itself should formulate opinions on the overall orientation of monetary and exchange-rate policy.

In the second stage, which would commence only when the Treaty had been amended, the basic organs and structure of the EMU would be set up. The committee stressed that this stage should be seen as a transition period leading to the final stage; thus it should constitute a 'training process leading to collective decision-making', but the ultimate responsibility for policy decisions would remain with national authorities during this stage. The procedure established during the first stage would be further strengthened and extended on the basis of the amended Treaty, and policy guidelines would be adopted on a majority basis. Given this understanding, the EC would achieve the following:

1. Establish 'a medium-term framework for key economic objectives aimed at achieving stable growth, with a follow-up procedure for monitoring performances and intervening when significant deviations occurred'.

2. 'Set precise, although not yet binding, rules relating to the size of annual budget deficits and their financing'.

3. 'Assume a more active role as a single entity in the discussions of questions arising in the economic and exchange rate field'.

In the monetary field, the most significant feature of this stage would be the establishment of the European System of Central Banks (ESCB) to absorb the previous institutional monetary arrangements. The ESCB would start the transition with a first stage in which the coordination of independent monetary policies would be carried out by the Committee of Central Bank Governors. It was envisaged that the formulation and implementation of a common monetary policy would take place in the final stage; during this stage exchange-rate realignments would not be allowed except in exceptional circumstances.

The Report stresses that the nature of the second stage would require a number of actions, e.g.:

1. National monetary policy would be executed in accordance with the general monetary orientations set up for the EC as a whole.

2. A certain amount of foreign exchange reserves would be pooled and used to conduct interventions in accordance with the guidelines established by the ESCB.

3. The ESCB would have to regulate the monetary and banking system to achieve a minimum harmonization of provisions (such as reserve requirements or payment arrangements) necessary for the future conduct of a common monetary policy.

The final stage would begin with the irrevocable fixing of member states' exchange rates and the attribution to the EC institutions of the full monetary and economic consequences. It is envisaged that during this stage the national currencies would eventually be replaced by a single EC currency. In the economic field, the transition to this stage is seen to be marked by three developments:

1. EC structural and regional policies may have to be further strengthened.

2. EC macroeconomic and budgetary rules and procedures would have to become binding.

3. The EC role in the process of international policy cooperation would have to become fuller and more positive.

In the monetary field, the irrevocable fixing of exchange rates would come into effect and the transition to a single monetary policy and a single currency would be made. The ESCB would assume full responsibilities, especially in four specific areas:

1. The formulation and implementation of monetary policy.

2. Exchange-market intervention in third currencies.

3. The pooling and management of all foreign exchange reserves.

4. Technical and regulatory preparations necessary for the transition to a single EC currency.

As agreed, the Report was the main item for discussion in the EC summit which opened in Madrid on 24 June 1989. In that meeting member nations agreed to call a conference which would decide the route to be taken to EMU. This agreement was facilitated by a surprisingly conciliatory Mrs Thatcher, the British Prime Minister then, on the opening day of the summit. Instead of insisting (as was expected) that the United Kingdom would join the exchange-rate mechanism of the EC 'when the time is ripe', she set out five conditions for joining:

1. A lower inflation rate in the United Kingdom, and in the EC as a whole.

2. Abolition of all exchange controls (at the time of writing, Italy, France and Spain have them).

3. Progress towards the single EC market.

4. Liberalisation of financial services.

5. Agreement on competition policy.

Since these were minor conditions relative to the demands for creating the EMU, all member nations endorsed the Report and agreed on 1 July 1990 as the deadline for the commencement of the first stage. Indeed, the economic and finance ministers of the EC at a meeting on 10 July 1989 agreed to complete the preparatory work for the first stage by December, thus giving themselves six months to accommodate the adjustments that would be needed before the beginning of the first stage.

The three-stage timetable for EMU did start on 1 July 1990 with the launching of the first phase of intensified economic cooperation during which all the member states were to submit their currencies to the EMS's *exchange-rate mechanism* (ERM) (see above and below). The main target of this activity was the United Kingdom whose currency was not subject to the ERM discipline; the United Kingdom joined in 1991 while Mrs Thatcher was still in office, but withdrew from it in 1992, and so did Italy – see Chapter 16.

The second stage is clarified in the Maastricht Treaty. It was to start in 1994. During this stage the EU was to create the *European Monetary Institute* (EMI) to prepare the way for a European Central Bank which would start operating on 1 January 1997. Although this was upset by the 1992 turmoil in the EMS, the compromises reached in the Edinburgh summit of December 1992 (deemed necessary for creating the conditions which resulted in a successful second referendum on the Treaty in Denmark and hence in ratification by the United Kingdom – see Chapter 2) did not water down the Treaty too much. Be that as it may, the Treaty already allows Denmark and the United Kingdom to opt out of the final stage when the EU currency rates will be permanently and irrevocably fixed and a single currency floated. However, in a separate protocol, all then twelve EC nations declared that the drive to a single currency this century is 'irreversible'. Denmark, which supports the decision, is an exception because its constitution demands the holding of a referendum on this issue; the United Kingdom, because, apart from its cultural and institutional differences from the rest of the EC, it has always been the black sheep of Europe – see Chapters 1, 2, 24 and 25.

A single currency (the *Euro*), to be managed by an independent European Central Bank, will be introduced as early as 1997 if seven of the then twelve EC nations pass the strict economic criteria required for its successful operation, and in 1999 at the very latest. These conditions are as follows:

1. *Price stability.* Membership requires 'a price performance that is sustainable and an average rate of inflation, observed over a period of one year before the examination, that does not exceed by more than [1.5] percentage points that of, at most, the three best performing' EC member countries. Inflation 'shall be measured by means of the consumer price index on a comparable basis, taking into account differences in national definitions'.

2. *Interest rates.* Membership requires that,

   observed over a period of one year before the examination, a Member State has had an average nominal long-term interest rate that does not exceed by more than two percentage points that of, at most, the three best performing Member States in terms of price stability. Interest rates shall be measured on the basis of long-term government bonds or comparable securities, taking into account differences in national definitions.

3. *Budget deficits.* Membership requires that a member country 'has achieved a gov-

ernment budgetary position without a deficit that is excessive' (Article 109j). However, what is to be considered excessive is determined in Article 104c(6) which simply states the Council shall decide after an overall assessment 'whether an excessive deficit exists'. Given the general trend at present, one could argue that the deficit should be less than 3% of GDP.

4. *Public debt.* The Protocol does not state anything on this, but by present standards this is interpreted to mean that membership requires a ratio not exceeding 60% of GDP.

5. *Currency stability.* Membership requires that a member country

> has respected the normal fluctuation margin provided for by the exchange-rate mechanism of the [EMS] without severe tensions for at least two years before the examination. In particular, [it] shall not have devalued its currency's bilateral central rate against any other Member State's currency on its own initiative for the same period.

One is of course perfectly justified in asking about the theoretical rationale for these convergence criteria. The answer is simply that there is not one; for example, the inflation criterion is not even based on NAIRUs (i.e. inflation bears no relationship to that consistent with a natural rate of unemployment) and there is no way to evaluate whether or not a 60% of GDP public debt is better or worse than, say, a 65% of GDP rate. The important point is that the performance of the member countries must not diverge so much as to make it difficult for the EMU to operate, and the members, in their wisdom, decided that the convergence criteria agreed upon are the ones that will insure against such an outcome.

It is interesting to note that if one conducted this test then, only France and Luxemburg would have scored full marks. The others would have scored as follows: Denmark and the United Kingdom four points each; Belgium, Germany and Ireland three points each; the Netherlands two points; Italy and Spain one point each; Greece and Portugal zero points each. Hence, the EMU cannot be introduced since seven countries need to score full marks for this purpose. The position at the end of 1996 was even worse since only Luxemburg qualified – see Figure 5.5. However, one should hasten to add three provisos regarding this test. The first is that it is an extremely severe one since it is based on the most demanding scenario stated in the protocol. The second is that not only has the text been written in a vague manner, but the vagueness has been enforced by Article 6 of the Protocol which states that the

> Council shall, acting unanimously on a proposal from the Commission and after consulting the European Parliament, the EMI or the ECB as the case may be, and the Committee referred to in Article 109c, adopt appropriate provisions to lay down the details of the convergence criteria referred to in Article 109j of the Treaty, which shall then replace this Protocol.

The third is that the day of reckoning is yet to arrive.

In the previous edition, I added that these criteria are no more than general guidelines; hence they can be eased or made more difficult, depending on the order of the

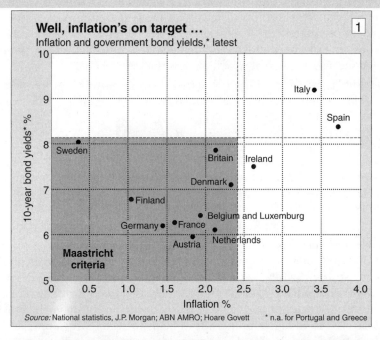

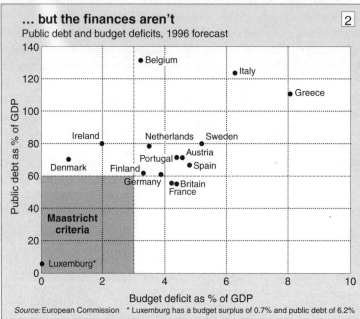

Figure 5.5 Performing to the convergence criteria, 1996

day in 1997. Indeed, it was later decided that 1 January 1999 should be the earliest day for introducing the Euro.

Thus, it should be clear that the EMU envisaged in the Delors Report and detailed and endorsed in the Maastricht Treaty is consistent with and satisfies all the requirements of a full economic and monetary union. However, I did caution in the previous edition (p. 124) that it was needless to add, 'sceptics will insist that this does not mean that the EMU will actually materialize since there is always the possibility of a loss of momentum (Delors has been both vigorous and successful), more British stalling and German vacillation, and that the process itself may take more than two decades to complete'; the continuing debate vindicates this.

5.4 The transition to EMU

It was pointed out earlier that the most pessimistic conclusion an economist can reach is that the gains from EMU must exceed any possible losses from its adoption. That being the case, why is it that the Corden–Fleming argument is still so dominant in this field, as clearly reflected by the position taken especially by the United Kingdom and Denmark?

The answer is twofold. Firstly, it is because economists had failed to point out the fallacy in their argument. Secondly, it is due to Corden's distinction between a *complete* and a *pseudo* exchange rate union and to his equating the latter with the EMU envisaged in the Werner Report, and, by extension, with the EMU enshrined in the Maastricht Treaty, since the two are more or less equivalent (see above).

The *pseudo* EMU, unlike the *complete* EMU, does not allow for economic policy coordination, a pool of foreign exchange reserves and a common central bank. It is therefore subject to the problems discussed in the definitional section. However, as we have seen, both the EMU of the Werner Report and that of the Maastricht Treaty are *complete* EMUs.

5.5 Conclusions

One need stress only two conclusions. The first is that the alleged net disadvantages of EMU apply mainly to the so-called pseudo exchange rate unions. Such unions are consistent neither with the first stage of the EMU envisaged in both the Werner Report and the Maastricht Treaty nor with their nature as processes leading to complete EMUs. All economists would concede the difficulties associated with the transitional phase, but none of them, in their strict area of competence, should interpret this to mean that the losses exceed the benefits of the Community's EMUs.

The second is that the EU, but not the entirety of its present membership, is set to achieve EMU more or less on target. The reason for the optimism is that the convergence criteria have been specified in such a way that they can always be modified to ensure that all those EU member countries who wish to join can do so on the specified day. Moreover, although the recent trend has been to emphasize the economic dimension, in reality, the driving force behind EMU has always been political (see Chapter 24), and as long as Germany and France are committed and Italy and Spain think of EMU as panacea to their ills, nothing can happen to deter the present momentum; the decision by the EU Finance Ministers on 6 April 1997 to impose fines of up to 0.5% of GDP on any member nation that undermines the Euro with slack finance and to use the proceeds to reward 'virtuous members' signifies the members' determination.

chapter six

Measuring the impact of economic integration

A. M. EL-AGRAA

A growing area of research in the field of international economic integration is concerned with the measurement of the impact of the formation of the EU, EFTA and similar associations on the economies of member states and on the outside world. The purpose of this chapter is to explain the nature of the problem and to evaluate the attempts at measurement that have so far been made. The reader who is interested in a comprehensive survey and assessment of the actual estimates that have been carried out is advised to read El-Agraa (1989a).

6.1 Nature of the problem

It is extremely important to comprehend the nature of the methodology of measuring the impact of international economic integration in order to appreciate the difficulties associated with such measurements.

Assume that the world is constituted of three mutually exclusive and collectively exhaustive areas: the EU, EFTA and the rest of the world (W). The object of the exercise is to contrast the world trade matrix[1] Y as it appears in year t (indicated by a subscript), with the situation that would have materialized in year t if the EU and EFTA had not been formed. The latter is referred to as the 'anti-monde' – alternative world in which all events except one are identical – or non-integration position. The differences between this hypothetical position and the actual position can then be attributed to the following:

1. Trade creation: the substitution of cheaper imports from the partner country for expensive domestic production.

2. Trade diversion: the replacement of cheap *initial* imports from non-partners by expensive imports from a partner country.

3. External trade creation: the replacement of expensive domestic production by cheaper imports from a non-partner country due to a reduction in the common external tariff rate which is necessary in a customs union but not in a free trade area.

4. 'Supply-side diversion'; i.e. the replacement of exports to non-partners by exports to partners.[2]

5. Balance of payments induced adjustments due to (1)–(4) which are made necessary for equilibrating purposes.

Let us adopt the notation used by Williamson and Bottrill (1971) where:

c_{ii} = intra-ith area trade creation

d_{ij} = diversion of the ith area's imports from area j

d_{ii} = $\sum_{j \neq 1} d_{ij}$ = diversion of ith's imports (to area i)

e_{ij} = increase in i's imports from j caused by external trade creation

e_i = $\sum_j e_{ij}$ = total external trade creation of area i

r_{ij} = increase in i's imports from j caused by balance of payments reactions

s_{ij} = reduction in j's exports to i caused by supply-side constraints

x_{ij} = (hypothetical) imports of area i from area j in the non-integration position

x_i = $\sum_j x_{ij}$ = (hypothetical) imports of area i in the non-integration position

y_i = $\sum_j y_{ij}$ = actual imports of area i

The world trade matrix Y is:

		Exports by			
		EU	EFTA	W	Total
	EU	y_{11}	y_{12}	y_{13}	y_1
Imports of	EFTA	y_{21}	y_{22}	y_{23}	y_2
	W	y_{31}	y_{32}	y_{33}	y_3

The world trade matrix can be disaggregated to show the various effects that followed the formation of the EU and EFTA. Both these areas could have led to internal trade creation and/or could have diverted imports from W. The EU may have been responsible for external trade creation (in the low tariff partner countries which raised their external tariff rates to the level of the common external tariff rates):

> The attractions of partners' markets may have directed some EU and EFTA exports away from non-partners' markets, but this effect may have been partially, wholly, or more than fully offset by the greater competitiveness of exports from those blocs resulting from the advantages of a larger 'home' market. (Williamson and Bottrill, 1971, pp. 324–5).

Also, every trade flow in the matrix may have been affected by reactions made necessary in order to re-equilibrate payments positions.

The Y matrix can be disaggregated to show all these changes:

$$\begin{bmatrix} y_{11} \; y_{12} \; y_{13} \\ y_{21} \; y_{22} \; y_{23} \\ y_{31} \; y_{32} \; y_{33} \end{bmatrix} =$$

$$\begin{bmatrix} x_{11} + c_{11} + d_{11} + r_{11} & x_{12} - d_{12} + e_{12} - s_{12} + r_{12} & x_{13} - d_{13} + e_{13} + r_{13} \\ x_{21} - d_{21} - s_{21} + r_{21} & x_{22} + c_{22} + d_{22} + r_{22} & x_{23} - d_{23} + r_{23} \\ x_{31} - s_{31} + r_{31} & x_{32} - s_{32} + r_{32} & x_{33} + r_{33} \end{bmatrix} \tag{6.1}$$

Most of the studies in this field have disregarded some of these effects, particularly the supply-side constraints and the balance of payments re-equilibrating reactions. This amounts to assuming that s_{ij} and v_{ij} are equal to zero. This leads to the much simpler framework:

$$\begin{bmatrix} y_{11} \; y_{12} \; y_{13} \\ y_{21} \; y_{22} \; y_{23} \\ y_{31} \; y_{32} \; y_{33} \end{bmatrix} = \begin{bmatrix} x_{11} + c_{11} + d_{11} & x_{12} - d_{12} + e_{12} & x_{13} - d_{13} + e_{13} \\ x_{21} - d_{21} & x_{22} + c_{22} + d_{22} & x_{23} - d_{23} \\ x_{31} & x_{32} & x_{33} \end{bmatrix} \tag{6.2}$$

This implies that:

$$y_i = x_i + c_{ii} + e_i \tag{6.3}$$

Even though this methodology is very useful for analyzing the *overall* effects of the formation of the EU and EFTA, it is inadequate for analyzing the effects on particular countries. For example, the method cannot provide information about the consequences for the United Kingdom of membership of the EU. In order to deal with this problem, it is necessary to alter the matrix so as to allow for at least two areas for each of the EU and EFTA. This would provide the freedom to investigate the impact of the formation of EFTA and the EU on one member of the EU (United Kingdom), on that country's relationship with EFTA, with a particular member of EFTA (Norway) and with the rest of the world. Hence, the matrix should look like this:

			Exports by					
			EU		EFTA		W	Total
			(1)	(2)	(3)	(4)		
				Rest of		Rest of		
			UK	EU	Norway	EFTA		
Imports of	EU	(1)	y_{11}	y_{12}	y_{13}	y_{14}	y_{15}	y_1
		(2)	y_{21}	y_{22}	y_{23}	y_{24}	y_{25}	y_2
	EFTA	(3)	y_{31}	y_{32}	y_{33}	y_{34}	y_{35}	y_3
		(4)	y_{41}	y_{42}	y_{43}	y_{44}	y_{45}	y_4
	W	(5)	y_{51}	y_{52}	y_{53}	y_{54}	y_{55}	y_5

Disaggregating in terms of trade creation, trade diversion and external trade creation (assuming $s_{ij} = 0$ and $r_{ij} = 0$) gives:

$$
\begin{bmatrix}
y_{11} \ y_{12} \ y_{13} \ y_{14} \ y_{15} \\
y_{21} \ y_{22} \ y_{23} \ y_{24} \ y_{25} \\
y_{31} \ y_{32} \ y_{33} \ y_{34} \ y_{35} \\
y_{41} \ y_{42} \ y_{43} \ y_{44} \ y_{45} \\
y_{51} \ y_{52} \ y_{53} \ y_{54} \ y_{55}
\end{bmatrix} =
$$

$$
\begin{bmatrix}
\underline{} & x_{12}+c_{12}+d_{12} & x_{13}-d_{13}+e_{13} & x_{14}-d_{14}+e_{14} & x_{15}-d_{15}+e_{15} \\
x_{21}+c_{21}+d_{21} & \underline{} & x_{23}-d_{23}+e_{23} & x_{24}-d_{24}+e_{24} & x_{25}-d_{25}+e_{25} \\
x_{31}-d_{31} & x_{32}-d_{22} & \underline{} & x_{34}+c_{34}+d_{34} & x_{35}-d_{35} \\
x_{41}-d_{41} & x_{42}-d_{42} & x_{43}+c_{43}+d_{43} & \underline{} & x_{45}-d_{45} \\
x_{51} & x_{52} & x_{53} & x_{54} & x_{55}
\end{bmatrix} \quad (6.4)
$$

The matrix could, of course, be made more suitable for studying the impact of the formation of the EU and EFTA on particular areas of the rest of the world, e.g. the impact of UK membership of the EU on imports from New Zealand. This can easily be done by an appropriate breakdown of W. The most significant consideration that remains is the effect of the formation of the EU and EFTA on their economies and on the outside world.

Thus the problem of measuring the impact of economic integration relates to the empirical calculation of the indicated changes in the world trade matrix. However, it seems evident that any sensible approach to the analysis of these changes should have the following characteristics:

1. It should be capable of being carried out at the appropriate level of disaggregation.

2. It should be able to distinguish between trade creation, trade diversion and external trade creation.

3. It should be capable of discerning the effects of economic growth on trade that would have taken place in the absence of economic integration.

4. It should be 'analytic': it should be capable of providing an economic explanation of the actual post-integration situation.

5. It should be a general-equilibrium approach capable of allowing for the effects of economic integration on an interdependent world.

The above approach relates to the measurement of changes in only the trade flows, but economic integration is not confined to customs unions and free trade areas. In the case of common markets, the impact of factor mobility needs to be taken into account and in economic unions so too must the effects of common policies, considerations which are especially pertinent in the case the EU (see Chapters 1 and 20). Since most of these issues are considered in, respectively, Chapter 20 and the following chapter, a brief statement on only factor mobility may be in order.

Factor mobility complicates the estimation of the impact of economic integration on goods and services since they can be both complements to and substitutes for them. A new foreign investment may require an inflow of skilled labour, imports for some of its inputs and may export part of its output. Alternatively, a firm may decide to invest in a new plant using local labour to supply the local market, both substituting for goods and services it previously supplied from its home market. These interactions are very difficult to separate, especially since the theoretical literature on factor movements is relatively undeveloped and factors may not respond to any changes that are meant to enhance their movement.

6.2 The effects on trade

The general trend of the empirical work on economic integration has been to examine various specific aspects of integration (mainly the effects on trading patterns) and to analyze them separately. The most important practical distinction made is between 'price' and 'income' effects. This is largely because the main initial instruments in economic integration are tariffs and quotas and other trade impediments which act mainly on relative prices in the first instance. However, all sources of possible economic gain (see Chapter 4) incorporate income as well as price effects.

The removal of quotas and other trade impediments is usually subsumed within the tariff changes for estimation purposes. These tariff changes are thought to result in a series of relative price changes: the price of imports from the partner countries falls, for commodities where the tariff is removed, relative to the price of the same commodity produced in the domestic country. In third countries which are excluded from the union, relative prices may change for more than one reason. They will change differently if the tariff with respect to third countries is shifted from its pre-integration level or they may change if producers in third countries have different pricing reactions to the change in price competition. Some third country producers may decide to absorb rather more of the potential change by reducing profits rather than by increasing prices relative to domestic producers. Relative prices are also likely to change with respect to different commodities and hence there is a complex set of interrelated income and substitution effects to be explained.

The immediate difficulty is thus the translation of tariff changes and other agreed measures in the customs union treaty into changes in prices and other variables which are known to have an impact on economic behaviour. Such evidence as there is suggests that there are wide discrepancies among the reactions of importers benefiting from tariff cuts and also among competitors adversely affected by them (EFTA Secretariat, 1968) and that reactions of trade to tariff changes are different from those to price changes (Kreinin, 1961). Two routes would appear to be open: one is to estimate the effect of tariff changes on prices and then to estimate the effects of these derived price changes on trade patterns; the other is to operate directly with observed relative price movements. This latter course exemplifies a problem which runs right through the estimation of the effects of economic integration and makes the obtaining of generally satisfactory results almost impossible. It is that to measure the effect of integration one must decide what would have happened if integration had not occurred (see previous section). Thus, if in the present instance any observed change in relative prices was assumed to be the result of the adjustment to tariff changes, all other sources of variation in prices would be ignored, which is clearly an exaggeration and could be subject to important biases if other factors were affecting trade at the same time.

6.3 The dynamic effects

While in the discussion of the exploitation of comparative advantage, the gains from a favourable movement in the terms of trade and often those from economies of scale are expressed in terms of comparative statics, it is difficult to disentangle them from feedback on to incomes and activity. The essence of the gains from increased efficiency and technological change is that the economy should reap dynamic gains. In other words, integration should enhance the rate of growth of GDP rather than just giving a step-up in welfare. Again it is necessary to explain how this might come about explicitly.

There are two generalized ways in which this can take place, first through increased productivity growth at a given investment ratio or secondly through increased investment itself. This is true whether the increased sales are generated internally or through the pressures of demand for exports from abroad through integration. Growth gains can, or course, occur temporarily in so far as there are slack resources in the economy. Again it is possible to observe whether the rate of growth has changed; but it is much more difficult to decide whether that is attributable to integration.

Krause (1968) attempted to apply a version of Denison's (1967) method of identifying the causes of economic growth but suggested that *all* changes in the rate of business investment were due to the formation of the EC (or EFTA in the case of those countries). Mayes (1978) showed that if the same contrast between business investment before and after the formation of the EC (EFTA) were applied to Japan a bigger effect would be observed than in any of the integrating countries. Clearly changes in the rate of business investment can occur for reasons other than integration.

6.4 Previous studies

As stated in the introduction to this chapter, a comprehensive survey of the studies covering up to the late 1980s is available in El-Agraa (1989a). There is therefore no need to go through these studies here. However, a few general comments and a short summary may be in order.

Most of the measurements can be broadly classified as *ex ante* or *ex post*. The *ex ante* estimates are based on *a priori* knowledge of the pre-integration period (i.e.

structural models), while the *ex post* studies are based on assumptions about the actual experience of economic integration (i.e. residual-imputation models). However, recall that either type can be analytic or otherwise.

There are two types of *ex ante* studies: those undertaken before the EC and EFTA were actually operative and those undertaken after they became operative.[3] The most influential studies to use this approach are those of Krause (1968), who predicted the trade diversion that would be brought about by the EC and EFTA on the basis of assumptions about demand elasticities, and Han and Leisner (1970), who predicted the effect on the United Kingdom by identifying those industries that had a comparative cost advantage/disadvantage *vis-à-vis* the EC and finding out how they were likely to be affected by membership, on the assumption that the pattern of trade prior to UK membership provided an indication of the underlying cost conditions and that this would be one of the determinants of the pattern of trade and domestic production after membership. This approach is of very limited value, however, for the simple reason that 'it does not provide a method of enabling one to improve previous estimates on the basis of new historical experience' (Williamson and Bottrill, 1971, p. 326).

The most significant studies to use the *ex post* approach are those of Lamfalussy (1963) and Verdoorn and Meyer zu Schlochtern (1964), who all use a relative shares method, Balassa (1967 and 1975), who uses an income elasticity of import demand method,[4] the EFTA Secretariat, which uses a share of imports in apparent consumption method,[5] Williamson and Bottrill, who use a more sophisticated share analysis,[6] Prewo, who uses an input–output method,[7] and Barten *et al.*, who use a medium-term macroeconomic method.[8] The advantage of the *ex post* method is that it can be constructed in such a way as to benefit from historical experience and hence to provide a basis for continuous research. However, the major obstacle in this approach concerns the difficulty regarding the construction of an adequate hypothetical post-integration picture of the economies concerned.

This section now provides an integrated summary of the studies of the impact of economic integration up to the early 1970s; later contributions are either refinements on these or too complex to go through here – the interested reader is advised to consult El-Agraa (1989b) – or relate to the internal market, in which case they are considered in the following chapter. In doing so, it is vital to bear in mind the distinction between short-term static effects, whereby changes in the impediments to trade lead to once and for all changes in the composition and pattern of trade, and longer-run dynamic effects, whereby economic integration over time leads to permanent changes in the rate of change of economic parameters. With this distinction in mind, one can classify the studies into *static* and *dynamic* along the lines suggested above.

The static studies can be put together into two major groups under the headings of *residual* and *analytic* models.

6.4.1 Residual models

These depend largely on their ability to quantify the situation in the absence of economic integration, i.e. on the construction of the *anti-monde*. It should be clear from the contributions discussed that the construction of a satisfactory *anti-monde* will depend on a thorough accounting for the omissions mentioned above. These models are set out here in order of increasing complexity.

(a) Import models

The general tendency here is to emphasize variables drawn from only the importing country. This has the advantage of easy data collection, but one must ask the question of whether or not this adequately compensates for the inaccuracy of the estimates? To answer this question meaningfully, we need to follow Mayes' (1978) classification of this category of studies.

(i) The demand for imports

These studies are based on the assumption that in the absence of economic integration imports would have grown over time as they did in the past. They have the obvious limitation that the extrapolation of trends has cryptic drawbacks for a cyclical activity such as international trade. Hence, many of the contributors assumed that imports would continue to be subject to the same linear relation to total expenditure, GDP and GNP respectively, in the *anti-monde* as they had been prior to the integration era – see, for example, Wemelsfelder (1960), Walter (1967) and Clavaux (1969). These contributions were built on the untenable premise that the marginal propensity to import remained constant throughout; evidence suggests that this parameter rises as income grows. Moreover, the estimation of the actual marginal propensity to import over the pre-integration periods would always be obscured by other changes in the international trading arrangements which had occurred then, and would not represent an *anti-monde* where no change had taken place.

The relative significance of changes in assumptions in terms of their quantitative impact is depicted in Figure 6.1 where the results of various estimates for the economic impact of the formation of the EC on trade are portrayed. Clearly, ideal comparison would require one to use each of the models with the *same* set of data, and where the quantity of recomputation was minimal, Mayes (1978) carried it out and included it in the figure. However, the data used in the various models were very different, so Mayes opted for the original results; these are also included in the figure with a time axis denoting the year for which they are estimates. The conclusion one reaches from a portrayal of the estimates is that the use of more observations tends to improve the results.

(ii) Shares in apparent consumption

Estimation can also be carried out by examining the relative share performance in total consumption, as against the absolute value of imports, of different suppliers.

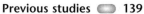

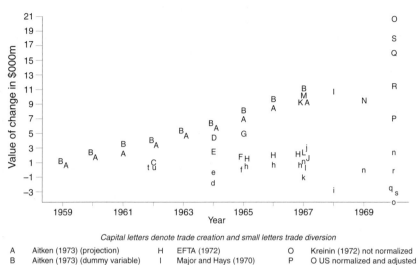

Capital letters denote trade creation and small letters trade diversion

A	Aitken (1973) (projection)	H	EFTA (1972)	O	Kreinin (1972) not normalized
B	Aitken (1973) (dummy variable)	I	Major and Hays (1970)	P	O US normalized and adjusted
C	Waelbroeck (1964) (method 1)		1958 base	Q	O UK normalized
D	Truman (1969) disaggregated	J	Resnick and Truman (1973)	R	Balassa (1964)
	1958 base	K	Truman (1972)	S	Prewo (1974)
E	as D 1960 base	L	K (adjusted)	t	Lamfalussy (1963)
F	Balassa (1967)	M	Verdoorn–Schwartz (1972)	u	C method 2
G	Clavaux (1969)	N	Williamson–Bottrill (1971)		

Values denoted   (i) Trade creation   (ii) Trade diversion

Year	Estimate	Value in $000 million	Year	Estimate	Value in $000 million	Year	Estimate	Value in $000 million
1959	A	0.9	1965	H	1.7	1962	t	0.5
	B	1.1	1966	A	8.6		u	0.5
1960	A	1.6		B	9.8	1964	d	−1.6
	B	2.5		H	2.2		e	−0.3
1961	A	2.3	1967	A	9.2	1965	f	0.1
	B	3.3		B	11.1		h	0.6
1962	A	3.2		H	2.3	1966	h	0.7
	B	4.1		J	1.8	1967	h	0.9
	C	1.0		K	9.2		j	3.0
1963	A	4.7		L	2.5		k	−1.0
	B	5.2		M	10.1		l	0.5
1964	A	5.7	1968	I	10.8		n	1.1
	B	6.4	1969	N	9.6	1968	i	−2.9
	D	4.5	1969/70	O	20.8	1969	n	0.0
	E	2.6		P	7.2	1969/70	o	−4.0
1965	A	6.9		Q	16.0		n	2.4
	B	8.2	1970	R	11.4		q	−2.8
	F	1.9		S	18.0	1970	r	0.1
	G	5.0					s	−3.1

Figure 6.1 Predictions of trade creation and diversion in the EC
Source Mayes (1978), p. 6.

Table 6.1 ⬭ Alternative estimates of aggregate effects of EFTA, 1965 ($ million).

Country	Trade creation Hypothesis		Trade diversion Hypothesis	
	(1)	(2)	(1)	(2)
Austria	−121.5	163	178.3	79
Denmark	−180.6	−122	322.1	−166
Finland	−204.9	−59	149.0	−136
Norway	−32.7	63	261.6	−73
Portugal	63.8	62	−15.1	43
Sweden	364.4	276	96.5	−110
Switzerland	−357.8	218	288.3	117
United Kingdom	831	−343	−619.1	−594
Total	361.7	258	661.6	−840

Source Mayes (1978), p. 8.

Truman (1969) adopted the simplest solution by assuming that the relative share of each supplier would remain constant over time, but, as already indicated, it would be desirable to allow changes in these ratios over time on the basis of historical experience. The studies by the EFTA Secretariat (1969, 1972) tackle this by assuming that the linear trend in relative shares during 1954–59 would have been maintained by the participating nations in the absence of economic integration. There are two objections to this premise: firstly, 1954 and 1959 may not lie on the actual trend and, secondly, the form of the trend itself is too simple. Estimation by, for example, regression analysis to improve on the results is not really worth while, given the naïvety of the original assumption.

Table 6.1 gives two alternative estimates of the impact on the aggregate trade flows for EFTA depending on whether or not one assumed a linear trend or no change in the *anti-monde*. Not only the differing results but also the almost random distribution of the negative and positive signs should be noted.

(iii) Changes in the income elasticity of demand for imports
This method tries to tackle the problem of changes in the relative shares from the opposite direction by discerning what the actual changes imply for the elasticity of demand for different types of imports with respect to income. Balassa (1967) estimates the income elasticities of demand for imports from member countries separately from those from non-participating nations. He advanced the proposition that an increase in the elasticity of demand for imports from all sources indicated 'trade creation' and that a decline in the elasticity of demand for imports from non-participants, given an increase in the elasticity for imports from the partners, indicated 'trade diversion'. The results are given in Figure 6.1. Note that the *anti-monde* here

was that these elasticities would not have changed in the absence of economic integration. To reiterate the criticism advanced in El-Agraa (1989a), Mayes (1978, pp. 8–9) argues that since the estimated elasticities 'are not unitary and not equal for imports from member and non-member countries, this means that changes in the shares of total imports in apparent consumption and imports from non-member countries (and hence member countries) in total imports can and do take place' in the *anti-monde*. Although Balassa made allowances for changes in prices, his estimates were similar to those of the general trend in Figure 6.1, but both positive and negative results were observed.

Both the Balassa (1967) and the EFTA Secretariat (1969) methods leave unanswered the question as to why the substantial liberalization in world trade prior to economic integration left unaffected the estimation of trade relationships during that period. Indeed, Clavaux (1969) showed that if this factor were taken into consideration, i.e. trade liberalization were excluded from the *anti-monde*, Balassa's calculations for trade creation by 1966 would have more than doubled. However, as Mayes (1978, p. 9) clearly argues, the most important aspect of this criticism is that price elasticities imply a level of sophistication not reflected in the methods employed: without equations depicting supply conditions, there would arise identification problems which would bias estimates of price elasticities towards zero; the neglect of supply conditions implied that the price elasticities of supply would be infinite. Note that Balassa's (1974) calculation of *ex post* income elasticities incorporated supply constraints, but for the pre-integration situation as well. Moreover, Sellekaerts (1973) demonstrated that income elasticities varied widely over both the pre- and post-integration eras. Hence, the selection of appropriate periods for comparison purposes is of the utmost importance.

(b) Inclusion of supply parameters

The explicit incorporation of supply conditions would improve the specification of models since trade between any two countries is determined by parameters within *both* of them. The simplest method dealing with this was built on the premise that, under 'normal' circumstances, trade between any two countries would be purely a function of the total trade of each of the two countries. Most particularly, the trade between any two countries would vary proportionately with the total exports of the exporting country and the total imports of the importing country in the *anti-monde*. The *RAS* advanced by Stone and Brown (1963) was the earliest input–output model to be adapted by Kouevi (1965) and Waelbroeck (1964) for this purpose. The major deficiency of this model is that total imports and exports were constrained to their actual values; hence, it was not possible to estimate trade creation.

An advance on this simple approach was the 'gravitational' method pioneered by Tinbergen and developed by Pulliainen (1963), Polyhonen (1963a, 1963b) and Linnemann (1966). The model presumed that the trade flow between any two countries would be a function of their respective national incomes, populations and the distance between them. The model was estimated by cross-section data and the economic impact of any integration scheme was calculated by the unexplained residual in the regression, or by the inclusion of dummy variables (*DVs*) for trade between participating nations as was the case in the estimates by Aitken (1973). These two methods gave very different results because of the substantial variability over time in the parameters. The estimates by Aitken (1973) gave a figure of $1264 million for trade creation by EFTA in 1967, employing the 1958 variables (this is labelled 'projection' in Figure 6.1), while the use of the 1967 values themselves together with the *DVs* made the results increase by 92%. Note that Aitken's results were the only ones to be estimated over a sequence of years; hence their great influence on the overall pattern of Figure 6.1. Even though these estimates are fairly consistent with the others, they tend to form an upper bound in some instances: for example, in 1965 they were three to four times as large as the lower bound. But one should hasten to add that the absolute magnitude of all the estimates was small. The main reason for these differences was the variability in the estimated parameters from year to year indicating that, to project with fixed parameters, one needed to take great care; this was confirmed in a disaggregated study by Bluet and Systermanns (1968). Mayes (1978, pp. 11–12) argued that much of the

> variability in the estimators occurs because a cross-section cannot represent a relationship which responds to cycles in economic activity and the very process of trade liberalisation in general. Pooling data helps to some extent but the model's main disadvantage is the omission of relative prices.

Verdoorn and Schwartz (1972) tried to tackle this drawback in their second model where they combined the advantages of the gravitational method with the effects of prices both on the overall demand for imports and the substitution between imports from different sources. While the results were mainly calculated on a residual basis, two *DVs* were used to explain some of the residual, but the explanation was statistical, not economic. The results are given in Table 6.2, and, as can be observed from Figure 6.1, they generally conform with the broad results, thus indicating that more sophisticated models do not leave us much the wiser.

(c) Incorporating information from third countries

Estimation using the share approach, without incorporating supply factors, could include third country behaviour. Lamfalussy (1963) showed that if one took into consideration the change in the shares of trade of non-participating countries and member nations of the EC in other markets, where neither was affected by economic integration, as the basis of one's expectations of how shares in the participating nations' markets would have changed in the absence of integration, one would get a different set of answers relative to those from trend extrapolation in the markets of the member countries alone. This is shown in Table 6.3, where the differences depict a fairly clear pattern: the share of EC exports in both EC and EFTA imports is much greater under the first hypothesis and the share of *W* in both markets falls under the first hypothesis but rises under the second. EFTA shares in both

Table 6.2 ⬤ Resnick and Truman's (1974) estimates (R&T) of trade creation and trade diversion in the EC and EFTA compared with those of Verdoorn and Schwartz (1972) (V&S) ($ million).

Country	Trade creation		Trade diversion	
	R&T 1968	V&S 1969	R&T 1968	V&S 1969
EC				
Belgium and Luxemburg	152	913	281	183
Netherlands	93	868	190	216
West Germany	−659	3,874	1,732	267
Italy	1,022	1,336	62	154
France	582	3,073	737	248
Total	1,190	10,064	3,002	1,068
EFTA				
UK	81	204	394	249
Other EFTA	131	161	231	547
Total	212	365	625	796
EC + EFTA	1,402	10,429	3,627	1,864

Source Mayes (1978), p. 12.

markets are greater under the second hypothesis but only very marginally so for intra-EFTA trade. As we observed earlier, it is also apparent that Lamfalussy's pessimistic conclusions were largely due to a limited period of observation; the first three years in the life of the EC. This was demonstrated by Williamson and Bottrill (1971) by using more observations and sophisticated extrapolation methods of the *anti-monde* shares. Recall, however, that their approach does not allow one to estimate trade creation and trade diversion without introducing further assumptions concerning their relative sizes.

Third countries can be used as a 'control' group or a 'normalizer' for estimating what the *anti-monde* would have been by incorporating them explicitly in the model. Kreinin (1972) does so by adapting the technique of projecting the *anti-monde* on the basis of predicted import/consumption ratios. The advantage of this method is that it allows one to observe more clearly how the normalization procedure works, and, therefore, should enable one to evaluate the tenability or otherwise of the assumptions on which it is built. However, it is an illusion to believe that a control group can be found, particularly for such schemes of integration as the EC and EFTA, since the control variables themselves are affected by the very experiment one is seeking to isolate.

Table 6.3 ⬤ A comparison of the effects of different *anti-mondes* on the imports of the EC and EFTA in 1969 ($ million).

Anti-monde	Exporter	Importer	
		EC	EFTA
(1)		5,091	−1,042
(2)	EC	1,018	−3,610
(1)/(2)		5.00	0.29
(1)		−2,258	2,542
(2)	EFTA	−1,594	2,644
(1)/(2)		1.42	0.96
(1)	W	−2,833	−1,500
(2)		576	966

(1) Share of exporter *i* in the market of importer *j* would change between 1959 and 1969 at the same linear rate as the share of *i*'s exports in the imports of rest of world (W) changed during the same period (shares constrained to sum to unity).
(2) Share of exporter *i* in the market of importer *j* would change between 1959 and 1969 at the same linear rate that it did between 1954 and 1959.
Source Mayes (1978), p. 13.

(d) Estimation of the anti-monde

We have observed that the number and range of estimates of the impact of economic integration by imputation of the unaccounted for residual are large, and it should be apparent that, the more relevant parameters are incorporated into the estimation of the *anti-monde*, the more acceptable are the results. Also, the incorporation of such refinements as disaggregation and intermediate products should lead to even more satisfactory results. However, the results of the study by Prewo (1974) depicted in Figure 6.1 give a very different pattern of estimates relative to other models, but this may be attributable to the simplicity of some of his other assumptions. Yet, as Mayes has argued, the problem of establishing a hypothetical *anti-monde* is in itself not an attractive proposition: 'While it is possible to point out the existence of biases it is not possible to know whether an unbiased estimate has been achieved, one can merely judge on the grounds of plausibility' (Mayes, 1978, p. 15). Plausibility is determined by the incorporated parameters not just in the importing and exporting countries, but also in the way they influence the trade cycle and changes in world prices. Hence, it is necessary to develop *analytic* models which are capable of explaining actual trade flows and their changes, as opposed to the estimation of *anti-mondes* and the imputation of residual differences to determine the impact of economic integration.

6.4.2 Analytic models

By *analytic* models one means methods which provide an economic rationale for the actual situation after economic integration has taken place. Such approaches are vital for all *ex ante* methods since the future values of trade flows are not known. Owing to the inherent complexity of prediction, such models are usually very simple and rely mainly on economic behaviour in the importing country. As we have seen, they assume that imports are determined by a measure of income or economic activity and the level of prices of imported and domestic products. Therefore, on the premise of a relationship between tariffs and prices, trade creation can be predicted from the change in the level of tariffs. Also, if one has knowledge about the elasticity of substitution with regard to changes in prices between member countries and the non-participants, one can estimate trade diversion.

This simple method will not provide acceptable estimates even if more sophisticated import demand functions are incorporated unless the effect of price changes on the level of prices can be explained. The EFTA Secretariat (1968) expected prices to fall by the amount of tariff changes, but it turned out that only part of the tariff changes seemed to be passed on. There is also a fair amount of evidence, at the microeconomic level, to suggest that the pricing of imports of many commodities depends mainly on the prices of existing competing domestic products. It is even suggested that the situation is far worse since importers tend to anticipate tariff changes, indicating that the growth of trade will anticipate the 'determining' tariff changes – see Walter (1967). Moreover, the attempts by Krause (1962) and Kreinin (1961) to calculate the tariff elasticities directly have not been successful; Mayes (1974) demonstrates that the estimates from this method do not correspond closely to those from the residual models.

Since different goods–nations are unlikely to behave in an identical fashion, one should expect that the greater the extent of disaggregation the more reasonable the estimates will be. Mayes (1971) uses a ninety-seven commodity breakdown of manufactures and allows for a complete system of demand equations with the volume and price of imports from each country being distinguished to give a whole matrix of direct substitution elasticities (with those of Barten, 1970) to reach estimates for a projected *Atlantic Free Trade Area* comprising Canada, EFTA, Japan and the United States. These results are given in Table 6.4. They display an expected pattern of signs for overall trade creation and trade diversion, and are also robust to quite significant changes in the variables. Other estimates utilize more global values based on either simple assumptions or crude extrapolation from calculations for the United States; the different sets of assumptions employed by Balassa (1967), Kreinin (1967) and Krause (1968) lead to estimates given respectively in columns (2), (3) and (4) of the table, as recalculated by Mayes (1978). The results are somewhat similar, but this is attributable to offsetting changes: greater trade creation being matched by greater trade diversion. However, the striking feature of these results is that they are small relative to those given by residual models; for example, Kreinin (1969) found the effect of the formation of the EC for the period 1962–65 to be less than $100 million.

Table 6.4 A comparison of *ex ante* predictions of the effects of economic integration on trade for an Atlantic free trade area[a] (effects on total exports) ($ million), 1972 (estimated).

Country	(1)[b]	(2)[c]	(3)[d]	(4)[e]
United States	2,454	2,318	2,509	2,645
Canada	2,141	2,610	2,547	2,650
Belgium–Luxemburg	−88	−124	−93	−117
France	−127	−146	−159	−199
Germany	−444	−538	−538	−673
Italy	−131	−144	−163	−204
Netherlands	−48	−56	−64	−80
Total EC	−838	−1,008	−1,017	−1,273
Denmark	22	30	24	24
Norway	15	23	18	18
Sweden	128	156	144	148
United Kingdom	607	821	726	756
Rest of EFTA	241	263	225	265
Total EFTA	1,013	1,293	1,167	1,215
Japan	1,879	2,380	2,301	2,448
Rest of the world	−646	−806	−719	−898
Total	6,002	6,786	6,786	6,786

[a] Defined here as an area comprising US, Canada, EFTA and Japan – this corresponds closely to the definitions used by Balassa (1967).
[b] Mayes (1971).
[c] Using elasticities used by Balassa (1967).[f]
[d] Using same import elasticity as Balassa but assuming elasticity of substitution is −2.5 as does Kreinin (1967).
[e] As d but assuming elasticity of substitution is −2 as does Krause (1968).
[f] Commodity categories are different so these results do not represent an exact updating of the original results.
Source Mayes (1978), p. 18.

More elaborate models (Armington, 1970; Resnick and Truman, 1975) allow for the determination of imports by a series of allocative decisions while the studies by Balassa (1967) and Kreinin (1967) use simple assumptions for supply constraints, but, as can be seen from Figure 6.1 and Table 6.2, the estimates of these models do not fit happily with those from the residual models. For example, the estimates of trade diversion from the Resnick and Truman model are only one-eighth of those from the Verdoorn and Schwartz (1972) model. Also, because the establishment of the CETs meant that West Germany had to raise its tariff levels, trade creation is negative in the analytic case but is the largest positive estimate in the residual model. This indicates that factors other than tariff changes had a very substantial and positive effect on West Germany's post-EC trade. There is, therefore, 'much more to be explained which *is not* covered by the analytic models and *cannot* be covered by the residual ones' (Mayes, 1978, p. 18).

However, the main attraction of the analytic models is that they can be tested after the event and can be used for forecasting as well as for *ex post* estimation. In this respect, the models used by Grinols (1984) and Winters (1984a), which cannot be discussed here owing to space limitations, represent a way forward.

6.4.3 Dynamic studies

The static models are predominantly concerned with the impact of price changes alone on the level, composition and pattern of trade. However, it could be argued that the static models leave out the most dominant effects of economic integration. This is due to the fact that the feedback on to incomes and the rate of economic growth or the necessity for the use of expenditure switching policies for balance of payments equilibrating purposes may be considerable and either positive or negative. For example, Kaldor (1971) not only argues that membership of the EC will inflict costs on the United Kingdom, but that the costs will be reinforced by adverse dynamic effects. However, there are very few estimates of the dynamic effects, with Krause (1968) being the exception. Krause tries to explain changes in the rate of real economic growth in the EC and EFTA by increasing business investment and efficiency. The expectation is that an increase in the ratio of investment to GDP will increase capital accumulation, and if the marginal capital/output ratios are constant, both output and the rate of growth must increase. But the fixity of the capital/output ratios automatically excludes economies of scale which lie at the very heart of the dynamic effects. The increase in efficiency is due to a decrease in input costs from imports: hence the increase in the ratio of imports to output is estimated and multiplied by the average tariff rate to calculate the income effect of the cost reduction, and this can be expressed as an annual rate.

Clearly, this method suffers from the same limitations as the static models: equating tariff changes and consequent price changes, and attributing all changes to economic integration.

6.5 A critique of previous studies

There are some general and some specific points of criticism to be made against these studies:

1. All the studies, excepting the Brada and Méndez (1985), Truman (1975) and Williamson and Bottrill (1971) studies, and to a certain extent the Aitken (1973) and Mayes (1978) estimates, assume that the formation of the EC (or EFTA) has been the sole factor to influence the pattern of trade. Since the EC and EFTA

were established more or less simultaneously (there is a year's difference between them), it is not justifiable to attribute changes in the pattern of trade to either alone. After all, the EFTA was established in order to counteract the possible damaging effects of the EC. Moreover, a few years after the establishment of these two blocs, a number of schemes were formed all over the world – see El-Agraa (1982c, 1988b, 1997) and Chapter 1 of this book for a detailed specification and discussion of these. The impact of these latter groupings should not have been ignored by studies conducted in the late 1960s and thereafter.

2. Most of the recent studies ignore the fact that Britain used to be a member of the EFTA before joining the EC. Since the United Kingdom is a substantial force as a member of either scheme, it seems misleading to attempt estimates which do not take into consideration this switch by the United Kingdom. A similar argument applies to Denmark. This point of course lends force to the previous one.

3. In the period prior to the formation of the EC and EFTA, certain significant changes were happening on the international scene. The most important of these was that the discrimination against the United States was greatly reduced. Is it at all possible that such developments had no effect whatsoever on the trade pattern of the EC and EFTA? It seems unrealistic to assume that this should have been the case.

4. All the studies, except for Truman's (1975) and to some extent Winters' (1984a), dealt with trade data in spite of the fact that a proper evaluation of the effects of economic integration requires analysis of *both* trade *and* production data. Trade creation indicates a reduction in domestic production combined with new imports of the same quantity from the partner, while trade diversion indicates new imports from the partner combined with less imports from the rest of the world (W) and a reduction in production in the W.

5. Tariffs are universally recognized as only one of the many trade impediments, yet all the studies, except Krause's (1968) and Prewo's (1974), were based on the assumption that the only effect of integration in Western Europe was on discriminatory tariff removal. This is a very unsatisfactory premise, particularly if one recalls that the EC had to resort to explicit legislation against cheaper imports of textiles from India, Japan and Pakistan in the 1960s and early 1970s. The EC later forced Japan to adopt voluntary export restraints (VERs) with regard to cars, and some unusual practices were adopted, such as France's diverting of Japanese video recorders to Poiters (poorly manned for customs inspection) to slow down their penetration of the French market – see El-Agraa (1988a) for a detailed specification of these issues. Moreover, the level of tariffs and their effective protection is very difficult to measure:

Tariff schedules are public, but their interpretation is often made difficult by peculiar institutional clauses. Furthermore, it is difficult to obtain a good measure of the restrictive impact of tariffs. Average tariff rates will not do, for, if the rate is zero on one good and prohibitive on another, the average tariff is zero. It is necessary to use *a priori* weights, which inevitably is arbitrary . . . [Others] raised a more subtle issue by proposing to use input–output analysis to measure the effective *rates of protection* achieved by tariffs on value added. This approach raises a host of problems. The assumptions of fixed technical coefficients and of perfectly competitive price adjustments are both debatable. It is clear that the concept of effective protection . . . relies on oversimplified assumptions. (Waelbroeck, 1977, p. 89)

6. The Dillon and Kennedy Rounds of tariff negotiations resulted in global tariff reductions which coincided with the first stage of the removal of tariffs by the EC. Does this not mean that any evidence of external trade creation should be devalued, and any evidence of trade diversion is an underestimate?

More specifically, however:

In all these studies, the integration effect, whether trade creation or trade diversion, is estimated by the difference between actual and extrapolated imports for a post-integration year. The extrapolation of imports is done by a time trend of imports or by relating imports with income or consumption in the importing country. The difference between the actual and estimated imports would be due to (i) autonomous changes in prices in the supplying and importing countries, (ii) changes in income, consumption or some other variable representing macroeconomic activity, (iii) changes in variables other than income/consumption and autonomous price movements, (iv) revisions of tariffs and/or other barriers as a result of integration, (v) residual errors due to the random error term in the estimating equation, misspecification of the form of the equation, errors in the data, omission or misrepresentation of certain variables, etc. The studies . . . try to segregate the effect of (ii) only. The remaining difference between the actual and estimated imports would be due to (i), (iii), (iv) and (v), but it is ascribed only to (iv), i.e. the effect of revision of tariff and/or other barriers to trade as a result of integration. Clearly, it is a totally unreliable way of estimating the integration effect on trade creation or trade diversion. Even if prices are included as an additional variable in the estimating equation, it would amount to segregating the effect of (i) and (ii), so that the difference between the actual and estimated imports would be due to (iii), (iv) and (v). It would still be wrong to ascribe it to (iv) only. The error term at (v) is often responsible for a divergence of ±10% between the actual and estimated imports, which might often overshadow the effect of integration. For this reason, the 'residual method' used by Balassa, the EFTA Secretariat and many others, is highly unreliable for estimating the trade creation and trade diversion effects of integration. (Dayal and Dayal, 1977, pp. 136–7)

Moreover, the effects of economic integration, be they trade creation or trade diversion, occur in two stages: the effects of changes in tariffs on prices and the effect of price changes on trade. These two effects have to be separately calculated before the trade creation and trade diversion effects of economic integration can be estimated. This procedure is not followed.

In addition, the accuracy of the *ex ante* forecasts of the impact of economic integration on the level and direction of trade rests on the reliability of the price elasticities utilized. Furthermore, apart from this general problem, a critical issue is whether the effect of a tariff is the same as that of an equivalent price change; tariff elasticities substantially exceed the usual import demand elasticities, and the elimination of a tariff is perceived by the business world as irreversible.

It therefore seems inevitable to conclude that:

> All estimates of trade creation and diversion by the [EC] which have been presented in the empirical literature are so much affected by *ceteris paribus* assumptions, by the choice of the length of the pre- and post-integration periods, by the choice of benchmark year (or years), by the methods to compute income elasticities, changes in trade matrices and in relative shares and by structural changes not attributable to the [EC] but which occurred during the pre- and post-integration periods (such as the trade liberalisation amongst industrial countries and autonomous changes in relative prices) that the magnitude of no ... estimate should be taken too seriously. (Sellekaerts, 1973, p. 548)

Moreover, given the validity of those criticisms, one should not take seriously such statements as:

> There are a number of studies that have reported attempts to construct ... estimates. Individually the various methods must be judged unreliable. ... But collectively the available evidence is capable of indicating conclusions of about the same degree of reliability as is customary in applied economics. That is to say, there is a wide margin of uncertainty about the correct figure, but the order of magnitude can be established with reasonable confidence. (Williamson and Bottrill, 1971, p. 323)

Since no single study can be justified in its own right and the fact that the degree of reliability in applied economics leaves a lot to be desired, it is difficult to see the collective virtue in individual misgivings.

6.6 The alternative

It seems evident that there is nothing wrong with the methodology for the empirical testing of integration effects, but that the problems of actual measurement are insurmountable. However, these difficulties are due to some basic misconceptions regarding the welfare implications of trade creation and trade diversion: trade creation is good while trade diversion is bad – using the Johnson (1974) definition.

In an interdependent macroeconomic world, trade creation is inferior to trade diversion for the country concerned – see Chapter 6 of El-Agraa (1989a) – and both are certainly detrimental to the outside world. This conclusion is also substantiated by Johnson's work which incorporates the collective consumption of a public good – see Chapter 4 of this book and Johnson (1965a). It therefore seems rather futile, for estimation purposes, to attach too much significance to the welfare implications of trade creation versus trade diversion in this respect. Lest it be misunderstood, I should hasten to add that this is not a criticism of the trade creation–trade diversion theoretical dichotomy, rather the futility–impossibility of its empirical estimation. Moreover:

> trade creation and trade diversion ... are static concepts. Their effects are once-for-all changes in the allocation of resources. At any date in the future their effects must be measured against what *would otherwise have been*, not by what is happening to trade at that time. In the economic theorist's model without adjustment lags, the introduction of a

scheme for regional integration causes a once-for-all shift to more intra-integrated area trade and less trade with the outside world, and the forces that *subsequently* influence the allocation of resources become once again cost changes due to technological advance, and demand changes due to differing income elasticities of demand as real income rises as a result of growth [,] ... call the first set of forces affecting the allocation of resources *integration induced* and the second set *growth induced* ... The two sets of forces ... are intermixed (the problem becomes even more complex conceptually if integration itself affects the growth rate). The more sudden the integration, the more likely it is that integration induced effects will dominate, at least for the first few years; but the longer the time lapse the more would normal growth-induced effects dominate. The morals are: (1) the longer the time since a relatively sudden move towards integration, the harder it is to discern the effects by studying changes in the pattern of trade; and (2) the more gradually the integration measures are introduced, the more will the effects be mixed up, even in the short term, with growth-induced effects. (Lipsey, 1977, pp. 37–8)

For all these reasons I have suggested (see the first edition of this book) that the measurement of the impact of economic integration should be confined to estimating its effect on intraunion trade and, if at all possible, to finding out whether or not any changes have been at the expense of the outside world. Although the macroeconomic framework is subject to some serious limitations, it provides, at the very least, a genuine alternative against which one can judge the quality of the estimates obtained from the previous models.

This suggestion has now been taken up by a number of leading international organizations, but has been narrowed down to a single calculation of the changes in the volume of trade between the member countries. I would go along with this for advanced nations since increased trade *may* reflect enhanced integration, but I very much doubt the usefulness of this for very poor nations where investments generated by the scheme of integration would be more important.

Notes

1. An equivalent world production matrix is also necessary, see (1)–(3).

2. It is possible that the fast growth of EEC and EFTA intra-trade in the years immediately following their formulation (and also of EC intra-trade in 1969) was particularly at the expense of slower growth in exports to [W]. There is no conclusive evidence as to whether this was an important factor. In the long run, however, one would expect supply bottlenecks to be overcome, and one might also expect their effect to be counteracted by the greater competitive strength resulting from a larger 'home market'. We therefore follow a well-established precedent in assuming $s_{ij} = 0$ (no supply-side diversion exists). (Williamson and Bottrill, 1971, p. 325)

3. See, for instance, Verdoorn (1954), Janssen (1961) and Krause and Salant (1973a).

4. Ex-post income elasticities of import demand were defined as the ratio of the average annual rate of change of imports to that of GNP, both expressed in constant prices. Under the assumption that income elasticities of import demand would have remained unchanged in the absence of integration, a rise in the income elasticity of demand for

intra-area imports would indicate gross trade creation – increases in intra-area trade – irrespective of whether this resulted from substitution for domestic or for foreign sources of supply. In turn, a rise in the income elasticity of demand for imports from all sources taken together would give expression of trade creation proper, i.e. a shift from domestic to partner-country sources, Finally, trade diversion, a shift from foreign to partner country producers, would be indicated by a decline in the income elasticity of demand for extra-area imports. (Balassa, 1975, p. 80)

5. The EFTA Secretariat's study is based on the assumption that had the EFTA not been established, the import shares in the apparent consumption of a particular commodity in any of the EFTA countries would have developed in the post-integration period in precisely the same fashion as they had during the pre-integration period 1954–59. (See EFTA Secretariat 1969 and 1972.)

6. We believe that the most promising hypothesis is that originally introduced by Lamfalussy. According to this, the share performance of the jth supplier in markets where he neither gains nor loses preferential advantages gives a good indication of his hypothetical performance in markets which were in fact being affected by integration. In terms of the present analysis, the rest of the world provides a control which indicates what share performance would have been in EEC and EFTA markets if these two organizations had not been formed. (Williamson and Bottrill, 1971, p. 333)

The methods selected are:

1. Using an *a priori* formula which ensures that the predicted gain in market shares will be small if the previous market share was either very small or very large.

2. Extrapolating from a regression of data on relative export shares.

3. Assuming that market shares would have remained constant in the absence of economic integration.

7. Prewo (1974) uses a gravitational model which links the national input–output tables of the EC countries by a system of trade equations. In this model, trade between members of the EC is assumed to be proportional to demand in the importing, and supply in the exporting, country and inversely proportional to trade impediments, whereas extra-area imports are assumed to be related to demand in the EC countries. In this model, changes in final demand have a direct effect on imports of final goods, as well as an indirect effect through their impact on the imports of inputs for domestic production.

The basis of the analysis is that the 'difference between the actual trade flows of the customs union and the hypothetical trade flows of the customs union's antimonde is taken to be indicative of the integration effects.' (Prewo, 1974, p. 380)

8. 'It basically consists of eight similarly specified country models which are linked by *bilateral trade equations* and equations specifying the formation on import and export prices.' (Barten *et al.*, 1976, p. 63)

chapter seven

The economics of the Single Market

A. M. EL-AGRAA

In this book, the Single European Act (SEA), incorporating the package proposed by the Commission in its White Paper (CEC, 1985a) for the creation of an internal market by 31 December 1992, is tackled as a natural but significant extension and development of the EU. Therefore, the reader who is interested in the details of the SEA and the internal market, and their implications for both the EU and the rest of the world, will have to go through virtually every chapter of the book for information; the implications of the Single Market are too wide and far reaching to be tackled in a vacuum. This approach may offend those who believe that the future should be highlighted and the past forgotten; but the emphasis in this book is on the evolution and dynamism of the EU. To follow the bandwagon by concentrating entirely on the economics of the Single Market or economic and monetary union (EMU) would be to negate the very foundations of our approach. However, it is appropriate to devote a chapter to the internal market and to the benefits to be expected from its creation, emphasizing its theoretical and measurement aspects: the general heading of this section of the book.

7.1 The aspirations of the White Paper

According to Lord Cockfield, then Commission Vice-President with a portfolio including the internal market, the completion of the Single Market was the first priority of the Commission to which he belonged. He went so far as to state that its accomplishment would be the greatest achievement of the Commission during its term of office. This was put more succinctly in the *Bulletin of the European Communities* (no. 6, 1985, p. 18):

> From the words of the Treaties themselves through successive declarations by the European Council since 1982, the need to complete the internal market has been confirmed at the highest level. What has been missing has been an agreed target date and a detailed programme for meeting it. The Commission has welcomed the challenge of providing the missing piece. It has interpreted the challenge in the most comprehensive way possible: the creation by 1992 of a genuine common market without internal frontiers.

According to the White Paper the completion of the internal market will become a reality when the EU has eliminated any physical, technical and fiscal barriers among its member nations. Before elaborating on these, it should be stressed that the Commission felt that the single market programme contained three main features:

> (i) there are to be no more attempts to harmonize or standardize at any price – a method originating in too rigid an interpretation of the Treaty; in most cases, an 'approximation' of the parameters is sufficient to reduce differences in rates or technical specifications to an acceptable level [see Chapter 14];
>
> (ii) the programme will propose no measures which, while supposedly facilitating trade or travel, in fact maintain checks at internal frontiers and therefore the frontiers themselves, the symbol of the Community's fragmentation; their disappearance will have immense psychological and practical importance; [and]
>
> (iii) a major factor for the success of the programme is its two-stage, binding timetable, with relatively short deadlines, relying as far as possible on built-on mechanisms; the programme is a comprehensive one, which means that it has the balance needed if general agreement is to be forthcoming. (*Bulletin of the European Communities*, no. 6, 1985, p. 18)

With regard to physical frontiers, the aim is to eliminate them altogether, not just to reduce them. The Commission argued that it is not sufficient simply to reduce the number of controls carried out at the borders because, as long as persons and goods have to stop to be checked, the main aim will not be achieved: 'goods and citizens will not have been relieved of the costly delays and irritations of being held up at frontiers, and there will still be no real Community'.

In the White Paper the Commission provided a specification of all the functions carried out at border-crossing points. It drew attention to those functions that could or should be unnecessary in a true common market. Moreover, where the function carried out at the frontier checkpoint was still deemed to be necessary, the Commission recommended alternative ways of achieving it without border-crossing points. For example, with regard to health protection, the Commission suggested that checks on veterinary and plant health should be limited to destination points, the implication being that 'national standards be as far as possible aligned on common standards'. With regard to transport, quotas had to be progressively relaxed and eliminated, and common safety standards introduced for vehicles so that systematic controls could be dispensed with.

The Commission was quick to stress that it was quite aware of the implications of the elimination of border-crossing points for such sensitive issues as tax policy and the fight against drugs and terrorism. It admitted that it 'recognises frankly that these are difficult areas, which pose real problems', but maintained its belief that the objectives justify the effort that would be needed to solve them. Thus, it promised to put forward directives regarding the harmonization of laws concerning arms and drugs.

As to the question of technical barriers, the Commission argued that the elimination of border-crossing points would be to no avail if both firms and persons inside the EC continued to be subjected to such hidden barriers. Therefore, the Commission carefully considered these technical barriers and suggested ways of eliminating them to a detailed timetable. The Commission proposals covered goods and services, freedom of movement for workers and professional persons, public procurement, capital movements and the creation of conditions for industrial co-operation.

In the case of goods, the Commission emphasized that, provided that certain health and safety-related constraints and safeguards are met, goods which are 'lawfully' made and sold in one EC member nation should be able to move freely and go on sale *anywhere* within the EC. For this purpose, the EC's new approach to technical harmonization and standards (see *Official Journal of the European Committees*, no. 136, 4 April 1985) was applied and extended.

With regard to the freedom to provide services, the Commission recognized that there had been much slower progress here than with the situation regarding goods. It claimed that the distinction between goods and services had never been a valid one and that the EC had undermined its own economic potential by retaining it. This was because the service sector was not only growing fast as a 'value-adding provider of employment in its own right', but it also gave vital support and back-up for the manufacturing sector. It stressed that this was already the case not just in such traditional services as banking, insurance and transport, but also in the new areas of information, marketing and audiovisual services. Thus the White Paper put forward proposals and a timetable for action covering all these services until 1992. The Commission concluded that, with the creation of a true common market for the services sector in mind, it should be possible to enable the exchange of 'financial products' such as 'insurance policies, home-ownership savings contracts and consumer credit, using a minimum coordination of rules as the basis of mutual recognition'. With regard to transport, proposals were to be sent to the Council for the 'phasing out of all quantitative restrictions (quotas) on road haulage and for the further liberalisation of road passenger services by 1989, of sea transport services by the end of 1986 and of competition in air transport services by 1987' (see Chapter 12).

In the case of audiovisual services, the aim should be to endeavour to create a single EC-wide broadcasting area. For this purpose, the Commission was to make specific proposals in 1985 based on its Green Paper of May 1984 on the establishment of a common market for broadcasting.

As to capital movements, the Commission stated that from 1992 onwards any residual currency control measures should be applied by means other than border controls (see Chapter 16).

The Commission stated that, in the case of employees, freedom of movement was already almost entirely complete. Moreover, the rulings of the Court of Justice restricted the right of public authorities in the EC member nations to reserve jobs for their own nationals. However, the Commission was to bring forward the necessary proposals to dismantle any obstacles that still prevailed. It was also to take measures to eliminate the cumbersome administrative procedures relating to residence permits (see Chapter 18).

With regard to the right of establishment for the self-employed, the Commission conceded that little progress has been made. This was because of the complexities involved in trying to harmonize professional qualifications: in professions such as accounting and auditing practitioners perform completely different jobs and receive completely different training in the EC member nations and hence harmonization implies a drastic change in both education and training before the profession can hope to be seen as performing the same task (see Chapter 16 of the first edition on the accounting profession). However, such efforts had led to a substantial degree of freedom of movement for those in the health sector and in 1985 the Council adopted measures which extended such freedom to architects after '18 years of protectionist pressure and exaggerated defensive arguments' (*Bulletin of the European Communities*, no. 6, 1985, p. 20). The Commission concluded by stating that, in an effort to remove obstacles to the right of establishment, it would lay before the Council (in 1985) a framework directive on a general system of recognition of degrees and diplomas (see Chapter 18), the main features of which would be:

> the principle of mutual trust between the [member nations]; the principle of comparability of university studies between the [member nations]; the mutual recognition of degrees and diplomas without prior harmonization of the conditions for access to and the exercise of professions.

Any difference between the member nations, especially with regard to training, would be compensated by professional experience.

In the field of fiscal frontiers, the Commission was of the opinion that taxation would be one of the principal areas in which the challenge of the Single Market had to be faced. It argued that the rates of indirect taxation in the EC member nations were in some cases so divergent (see Chapter 14) that they would no doubt create trade distortions, leading to loss of revenue to the exchequers of the member states. It was convinced that frontier controls could not be eliminated if substantial differences in VAT and excise duties prevailed between the member nations. Its conclusion was that, if frontiers and associated controls were to be eliminated, 'it will be necessary not only to set up a Community clearing system for VAT and a linkage system of bonded warehouses for excised products, but also to introduce a considerable measure of approximation of indirect taxes'. The first question that this raised was how close should the approximation be. As stated in Chapter 14, the 'Commission argued that the experience of countries like the United States indicated that controls could be eliminated without a complete equalisation of rates'. Variations would have to be narrowed, but 'differences of up to 5% may coexist without undue adverse effects. This would suggest a margin of 2.5% either side of whatever target rate or norm is chosen' (*Bulletin of the European Communities*, no. 6, p. 20). The Commission stated that a great deal of statistical and econometric work would have to be carried out before it could make specific proposals. However, it felt that it would be of great assistance if the Council agreed to exert extra effort to finalize work on the proposals it had already presented to it. At the same time, the Commission would propose a 'standstill clause' to guarantee that prevailing variations in the number and levels of VAT rates would not be widened, hoping that in 1986 it would propose target rates or norms and allowed ranges of variation.

However, it stressed that the approximation of indirect taxation would result in a number of problems for some of the EC member nations, and hence it might be necessary to provide for derogations. Needless to add, the discussion in Chapter 14 clearly shows that the Commission has delivered these proposals as promised.

Finally, the Commission concluded by making it clear that the proposed measures to accomplish a single EC domestic market would not become a reality without some institutional changes. It argued that in many areas the possibility of reaching decisions by majority voting must be entertained and left this issue for a separate document.

7.2 Actions promised by the Commission

The details of the actual proposals put forward by the Commission to enable the creation of the Single Market are by now not only common knowledge (see *The Economist* of 9 July 1988 and 8 July 1989), but can be found in a number of academic books (see, *inter alia*, Emerson *et al.*, 1988; Pelkmans and Winters, 1988) as well as in the majority of the chapters in this book. They therefore need not detain us here. However, in the Commission's view, the achievement of the internal market meant the enactment of 300 directives, 21 of which were quietly dropped by 1988 but a similar number of which proved necessary, thus restoring the 300 figure. By the end of December 1992, the EC was forced to concede that only 95% of the 300 directives had been launched, but all internal EC border checks were abolished by then. Indeed, Mr Jaques Delors, then President of the EC Commission, stated that as a gradual process the Single Market project was never supposed to end with a 'big bang' on 1 January 1993. However, if the discussion in Chapter 2 is recalled, it will be remembered that directives have to be incorporated into national law before they are put into practice, and some of the early directives had been in the pipeline long before the White Paper was published in 1985. Moreover, Butt Philip (1988) argues that although the *average* time taken for legislative proposals to pass through the Council is three years, many proposals have been in gestation in the Council for longer than this. He shows that, in February 1987, 126 proposals from the Commission had been part of this 'logjam for over five years. Some thirty-eight proposals had been "under consideration" for over a decade'. His main explanation (p. 2) for such legislative delays at the EC level is that the negotiators for some of the member nations, 'in anticipation of implementation problems ahead, adopt a tough stance in order to ensure that the resulting decisions can be implemented by their own national administrations', and adds that other member nations such as Italy are 'less diligent in briefing their negotiators, and more frequently encounter administrative and other difficulties' when they come to apply the rules they have already endorsed. Furthermore, many of the directives have a contingent or voluntary outcome, especially those pertaining to the harmonization of technical standards and the mutual recognition of rules. Although I added in the previous edition that be that as it may, one can still confidently assert that the internal market will be fully realized after a few months' delay, in its 1995 *General Report* the Commission stated that the 'overall rate of transposal for the 15 [members] was 93.2% at the end of the year. However, the level remained below that figure in a number of areas, such as public procurement, intellectual property rights and insurance' (p. 51).

7.3 The expected benefits

7.3.1 The Cecchini estimates

According to the Cecchini Report, which summarizes in sixteen volumes the findings of a study carried out on behalf of the EC Commission (see CEC 1988i; a popular version is to be found in Cecchini, 1988), the completion of the internal market will regenerate both the goods and services sectors of the EC. The study estimates (see below for the methodology employed and section 7.4 for theoretical analysis) the total potential gain for the EC as a whole to be in the region of 200 billion ECU, at constant 1988 prices. This would increase EC gross domestic product (GDP) by 5% or more. The gains will come not only from the elimination of the costs of barriers to intra-EC trade, but also from the exploitation of economies of scale which are expected to lower costs by about 2% of EC GDP. The medium-term impact of this on employment will be to increase it by about 2 million jobs. These estimates are considered to be minimal since the study points out that, if the governments of the member nations of the EC pursue macroeconomic policies that recognize this potential for faster economic growth, the total gains could reach 7% of EC GDP and increase employment by about 5 million jobs. If these predictions become a reality, the EC will gain a very substantial competitive edge over non-participating nations.

The summary of the Cecchini Report given in Cecchini (1988) is written for the general public. The definitive technical work is that by Emerson *et al.* (1988); Emerson is a leading economist who then worked for the Directorate-General for Economic and Financial Affairs, and in this capacity his (and his collaborators') work presents the official Commission analysis; hence the interested reader is advised to consult this work. Here it should be asked why the elimination of the various barriers mentioned above should lead to economic benefits for the EC. To answer this question meaningfully, one needs to specify the barriers, which are all of the non-tariff type, slightly differently, and in a more general context.

1. Differences in the technical regulations adopted in the various member nations which tend to increase the cost of intra-EC trade transactions.

2. Delays in the customs procedures at border-crossing points and related extra administrative tasks on both private firms and public organizations which further increase the costs of intra-EC trade transactions.

3. Public procurement procedures which effectively limit if not completely eliminate competition for public purchases to own member nation suppliers, a procedure often claimed to raise the price of such purchases.

4. Curtailment of one's ability either to transact freely in certain services, especially finance and transport, where barriers to entry are supposedly great, or to get established in them in another EC member nation.

No claim has been made to suggest that the cost of eliminating each of these barrier categories is substantial, but Emerson *et al.* (1988) have argued that the combination of these barriers, in an EC dominated by oligopolistic market structures, amounts to 'a considerable degree of non-competitive segmentation of the market', with the implication that the cost of eliminating all the barrier categories then becomes considerable. Since the emphasis is on costs (the Cecchini Report stresses them as the 'cost of non-Europe' – see Chapter 6), it follows that the elimination of these barriers will reduce the costs, i.e. increase the benefits; these are two sides of the same coin.

Here, it may be appropriate to provide a brief explanation of this methodology. Recall that the majority of the 300 or so areas of barrier identified with the cost of Europe related to differences in technical requirements, whether product standards, required qualifications for workers, location for financial services or domestic ownership for public procurement. The remainder were labelled as fiscal barriers, through the differential operation of tax systems (see Chapter 14), or physical, such as border controls. Identifying these areas was a major challenge, and trying to quantify their importance was even more so. Instead of carrying out a microeconomic exercise assessing the degree to which each measure could be translated into a value equivalent (see Chapter 5), an almost impossible task, Cecchini (or EU Commission in disguise) opted for this novel approach to examining the impact of economic integration by measuring departures from it. This inverted the procedure of trying to explain what the counterfactual might have been had economic integration not taken place. Instead the comparison became one with a specified view of what the integrated economy might have looked like. In such an economy there would be little price dispersion (see section 7.4) and firms would have operated on an EC-wide level. Thus, in setting out the potential impact, the Cecchini study looked at the extent of departures from the lowest prices and the extent to which economies of scale had not been exploited. Thus, this approach did not estimate the likely impact of economic integration; rather, it provided an estimate of the scope for gains (Mayes, 1997d).

These benefits can also be expressed forthrightly. The elimination of the costs of non-Europe is tantamount to the removal of constraints which 'today prevent enterprises from being as efficient as they could be and from employing their resources to the full' (Emerson *et al.*, 1988, p. 2). They go on to argue that since these are constraints, their removal will 'establish a more competitive environment which will incite [the enterprises] to exploit new opportunities' (p. 2). They then claim that the combination of the elimination of the constraints and the creation of a more competitive situation will have four major types of effect;

1. A significant reduction in costs due to a better exploitation of several kinds of economies of scale associated with the size of production units and enterprises.

2. An improved efficiency in enterprises, a rationalization of industrial structures and a setting of prices closer to costs of production, all resulting from more competitive markets.
3. Adjustments between industries on the basis of a fuller play of comparative advantages in an integrated market.
4. A flow of innovations, new processes and new products, stimulated by the dynamics of the internal market.

They were quick to add that these processes free resources for alternative productive uses, and, when they are so utilized, the total sustainable level of consumption and investment in the EC economy will be increased. They stressed that this was their fundamental criterion of economic gain.

Given the definitive nature of the Emerson *et al.* (1988) book, it may be useful, at the risk of duplication, to quote the estimates of the gains as presented by them. To make sense of their calculations and, of course, of the overall results given above, it has to be recalled that all the calculations relate to 1985 when the total EC GDP was 3,300 billion ECU for the twelve member nations. However, the actual calculations were made for the seven largest EC member countries (accounting for 88% of EC GDP for the twelve) with a total GDP of 2,900 billion ECU.

They claim that the overall estimates range from 70 billion ECU (2.5% of EC GDP) for 'a rather narrow conception of the benefits' of eliminating the remaining barriers to the single market, to about 125–190 billion ECUs (4.5–6.5% of EC GDP) in the case of a more competitive and integrated market. Applying the same percentages to the 1988 GDP data, the gains were estimated to be between 175 and 255 billion ECUs. These gains are expected to increase the EC's annual growth rate by about 1 percentage point for the years until 1992. Also, 'there would be good prospects that longer-run dynamic effects could sustain a buoyant growth rate further into the 1990s' (p. 5).

These gains were obtained on the understanding that it might take five or more years for the upper limits to be achieved and that policies at both the microeconomic and the macroeconomic level would ensure that the resources (basically labour) released by the savings in costs would be fully and effectively utilized elsewhere in the EC. These assumptions were made to simplify the analysis. However, in order to make the calculations look more professional, they used the estimates to generate macroeconomic simulations from macrodynamic models (see Chapter 6). For this purpose, the effects of the single market were classified into four groups according to their type of macroeconomic impact:

1. The elimination of customs delays and costs.
2. The exposing of public markets to competition.
3. The liberalization and integration of financial markets.
4. Broader supply-side effects, 'reflecting changes in the strategic behaviour of enterprises in a new competitive environment' (p. 5).

The results of the simulations are then presented according to whether or not passive macroeconomic policies are pursued.

In the case of passive macroeconomic policies, the overall impact of the measures is felt most sharply in the earlier years in reduced prices and costs; but after a modest time lag output begins to increase. It is reported that the major impact if felt in the medium term (five to six years) when a cumulative impact of 4.5% increase in GDP and a 6% reduction in the price level may be expected. The effect on employment is slightly negative at the beginning, but increases by 2 million jobs (almost 2% of the initial level of employment) by the medium term. Moreover, there is a marked improvement in the budget balance and a significant improvement in the current account.

In the case of more active macroeconomic policies, it is argued that since the main indicators of monetary and financial equilibrium would then be improved, it would be perfectly in order to 'consider adjusting medium-term macroeconomic strategy onto a somewhat more expansionary trajectory' (p. 6). Obviously, the extent of adjustment rests upon which constraint (inflation, budget or balance of payments deficit) is considered crucial. In the text, a number of variants is illustrated. For example, in the middle of the range there is a case in which the level of GDP is 2.5% higher after the medium term. Since this is additional to the 4.5% boost obtained with passive macroeconomic policies, the total effect is therefore 7%. It is pointed out that, in this instance, inflation would still be below its projected value in the absence of the Single Market, the budget balance would also be improved and the balance of payments might be worsened by a 'moderate but sustainable amount'.

Before going further, it is important to be explicit about certain assumptions behind these estimates:

> It is implicit, in order to attain the highest sustainable level of consumption and investment, that productivity and employment be also of a high order. In particular, where rationalisation efforts cause labour to be made redundant, this resource has to be successfully re-employed. Also implicit is a high rate of growth in the economy. The sustainability condition, moreover, requires that the major macroeconomic equilibrium constraints are respected, notably as regards price stability, balance of payments and budget balances. It further implies a positive performance in terms of world-wide competitivity. (Emerson *et al.*, 1988, p. 2)

Although these estimates depend largely on a number of crucial qualifications, Emerson *et al.* state that, irrespective of these qualifications, the upper limits to the gains are unlikely to be overestimates of the potential benefits of a fully integrated EC market. This is because:

> the figures exclude some important categories of dynamic impact on economic performance. Three examples may be mentioned. Firstly, there is increasing evidence that the trend rate of technological innovation in the economy depends upon the presence of competition; only an integrated market can offer the benefits both of scale of operation and competition. Secondly, there is evidence in fast-growing high technology industries of dynamic

or learning economies of scale, whereby costs decline as the total accumulated production of certain goods and services increase[s]; market segmentation greatly limits the scope of these benefits and damages performance in key high-growth industries of the future. Thirdly, the business strategies of European enterprises are likely to be greatly affected in the event of a rapid and extensive implementation of the internal market programme; a full integration of the internal market will foster the emergence of truly European companies, with structures and strategies that are better suited to securing a strong place in world market competition. (Emerson *et al.*, 1988, pp. 6–7)

7.3.2 The Baldwin estimates

Although these expected gains have generated tremendous enthusiasm for the internal market, they are not really substantial enough to cause countries such as Japan and the United States to react in a panic so as to avoid missed opportunities. However, later estimates by Baldwin (1989) may have sown the seeds for such a response. Baldwin argues that the gains may be about five times those given in Cecchini.

Baldwin's approach differs from that of Cecchini in one significant respect. He questions Cecchini for not making an allowance for an increase in the long-term rate of growth. He contends that the methodological background to the estimates in Cecchini is based on traditional growth theory which assumes that countries become wealthier because of technological change, and that the dismantling of barriers to trade and increasing the size of markets will not permanently raise the rate of technological progress. Thus, both Cecchini and the traditional methodology are built on the premise that the liberalization of markets cannot permanently raise the rates of growth of the participating countries.

Cecchini addressed the question of how the internal market will alter the *level*, not the *rate of growth*, of output. Thus, he reached the conclusion that the creation of the internal market will squeeze more output from the same resources, for reasons such as the lower costs due to economies of scale and enhanced competition, giving the predicted benefits reported by Cecchini. Note, however, that, although these expected gains will take some time to realize, the underlying methodology envisages them as a step increase; this is depicted as line 1 in Figure 7.1.

Baldwin's claim that this approach underestimates the gains rests on two distinct arguments. The first endorses the traditional approach, but asks about what the expected rise in output will do to savings and investment. He argues that, if savings and investments stay as constant percentages of national income, they will both rise in absolute terms. Consequently, the stock of physical capital will also increase, leading to a further rise in output which will raise savings and investment again; thus a virtuous cycle will set in.

The traditionalists will challenge the assertion that this burst of faster growth will continue indefinitely. They will argue that, as the capital stock rises, a larger percentage of each year's investment will simply replace existing capital owing to depreciation. Thus the capital stock will grow at a diminishing rate and, sooner or

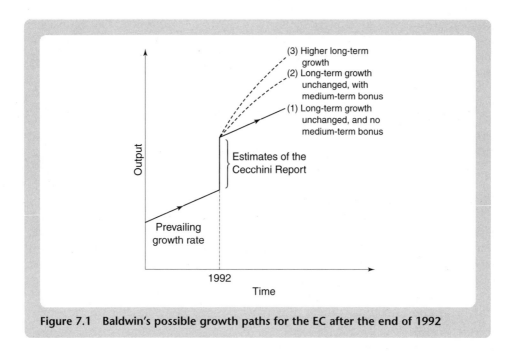

Figure 7.1   Baldwin's possible growth paths for the EC after the end of 1992

later, investment will match depreciation, bringing to a halt any further increase in the capital stock. The economy then reaches a new equilibrium with a larger capital stock and a higher level of output than initially, but with the economy once more growing at the earlier long-term rate. Therefore, it follows that, even if there is no permanent rise in the growth rate, Cecchini must have missed this vital element: the expected rise in GDP of about 6.5–7% will raise the levels of savings and investment and increase the capital stock, making the EC grow faster while this process continues. Baldwin thinks that half of this adjustment might take about ten years. He labels this a 'medium-term growth bonus'; this is depicted by line 2 in Figure 7.1. Converting this into an equivalent change in the level of output, and relying on conservative assumptions, Baldwin concludes that the gains from the internal market will be in the region of 3.5–9%, as against the 2.5–7% predicted by Cecchini.

However, Baldwin is not content with this. He declares that the medium-term bonus may be augmented by a permanent rise in growth, giving a 'long-term growth bonus'. This is because, unlike orthodox theory (which argues that there is a 'steady state' in which the capital stock grows at the same rate as the labour force, thus with the constant labour force assumed by Cecchini there will be a constant capital stock), he follows the model proposed by Romer (Chicago University) which is built on the premise that the capital stock can rise indefinitely. This leads him to believe that the increase in EC investment after 1992 will raise the growth rate for the EC permanently by something in the range of a quarter to three-quarters of a percentage point; this is depicted by line 3 in Figure 7.1. Expressed as an equivalent increase in the level of output, the total bonus (the combined bonuses from the medium and long terms) would be about 9–29% of GDP. Adding this estimate to that by Cecchini, one gets an overall figure of 11–35% increase in GDP.

The Baldwin estimates, taken at face value, should have made any non-EC country think hard about its strategy for such an expanded and more competitive EC market. Japan, which was being, and continues to be, increasingly asked by the United States to open its markets more, was even more concerned; hence it decided to enhance its investments there and in Eastern Europe (see Chapter 20).

7.4 Theoretical illustration

Before stating explicit reservations, it may be useful to provide some theoretical framework for some of the stated gains. Let us consider two cases. The first is one in which comparative advantage can be exploited by trade. The second concerns the case of enhanced competition where there is no comparative advantage between countries. The basic model behind the diagrams used below is fully set out in Chapter 4 and in standard trade theory books – see El-Agraa (1989b). No explanation will therefore be provided here.

The first case is illustrated by Figure 7.2. Because of the removal of certain market barriers and distortions, the relative price of a particular commodity is equalized throughout the entire EU market at the lower P_2 in the EU member country under consideration. As we have seen, this is because it is assumed that the presence of these barriers is costly, leading to the higher price level P_3 in that country. Since this country is a net importer from the rest of the EU, comparative advantage lies with the EU or, alternatively, this country has a comparative disadvantage.

In this member country, the removal of the barrier increases consumer surplus by areas A and B and reduces producer surplus by area A, giving a net benefit of area B. In the rest of the EU, there is an increase in producer surplus of areas C and D and a reduction in consumer surplus of area C, resulting in a net benefit of area D. Therefore, the total benefit to the EU as a whole is the sum of the two net benefits, i.e. areas B plus D. In short, the analysis in the case of the member country is the reverse of the one for tariffs considered in Chapter 10, while the analysis for the rest of the EU is exactly the same as that in the same chapter applied to agricultural surpluses.

The second case is illustrated by Figure 7.3. As barriers are removed, importers are able to reduce their prices from P_2 by the amount of direct costs saved. Domestic producers respond by reducing their own prices through reductions in their excess profits and wages or by eliminating inefficiencies of various types (overhead costs, excess manning and inventories, etc.). As prices fall, demand increases beyond Q_1 and this induces investment in productive capacity in this industry which results in economies of scale and further price reductions. However, this is not the end of the story since this more competitive market environment is supposed to make indus-

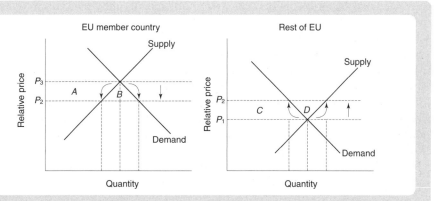

Figure 7.2   Effects of eliminating market barriers and distortions for a given commodity (the case in which comparative advantage can be exploited by trade). *Source* Emerson *et al.*, 1988, adapted.

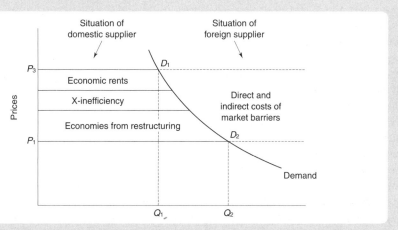

Figure 7.3   Effects of eliminating cost-increasing trade barriers (the case of enhanced competition where there are no comparative advantages between countries). Economic rents consist of the margins of excess profits or wage rates that result from market protection. X-inefficiency consists of, for example, the costs of overmanning, excess overhead costs and excess inventories (i.e. inefficiencies not related to the production technology of the firm's investments). Economies of restructuring include, for example, the greater economies of scale or scope obtained when inefficient production capacity is eliminated and new investments are made. Direct costs are those, such as delays at frontiers and the cost of differing technical regulations, that would immediately fall if the market barriers were eliminated. Indirect costs are those that would fall as foreign suppliers adjust to the more competitive situation with more efficient production and marketing. *Source* Emerson *et al..*, 1988, adapted.

tries reconsider their business strategies in a fundamental way, leading to restructuring (mergers and acquisitions, liquidations and investment) over a number of years until output increases to Q_2.

As can be seen from the diagram, there is an increase in consumer surplus equal to area $P_2D_1D_2P_1$, but what happens to producer surplus is not so clear. On the one hand, producers may be able to compensate for price cuts in terms of cost reductions; but they will lose some economic rent. On the other hand, since they have become more competitive, they may be able to sell outside the EU and so increase their output and profits. For the EU economy as a whole, it can be said that there is a net benefit since the gains to the EU consumer are in excess of the losses incurred by the EU producers. However, in the light of the discussion in Chapter 4, it must be emphasized that this analysis is extremely simple.

7.5　Reservations

There are two reservations to consider. The first is advanced by Pelkmans and Robson (1987). It is that the categorization by the EU of these three types of barriers is somewhat arbitrary. Physical barriers are concerned with frontier controls on the movement of goods and persons. Fiscal barriers consist of all impediments and substantial distortions among member states that emanate from differences in the commodity base as well as in the rates of VAT and the duties on excises (see Chapter 14). All remaining impediments fall into the category of technical barriers. Therefore, this category includes not only barriers arising from absence of technical harmonization and public procurement procedures, but also institutional impediments on the free movement of people, capital and financial services, including transport and data transmission. It also includes a miscellaneous collection of obstacles to the business environment which take the form of an inadequately harmonized company law, the lack of an EU patent and of an EU trademark, together with issues of corporate taxation and several diverse problems concerned with the national application of EU law. However, even though this categorization may make analysis more cumbersome, the approach adopted in this book shows that this is not a serious reservation.

The second reservation is more serious. It is that the estimates given in the Cecchini Report should not be taken at face value. First, in spite of the endorsement of the SEA by all the member nations, there does not seem to be a philosophy common to all of them to underpin the internal market. Second, these estimates do not take into consideration the costs to be incurred by firms, regions and governments in achieving them. Third, the internal market aims at the elimination of internal barriers to promote the efficient restructuring of supply, but it remains silent on the question of demand; thus the internal market seems to be directed mainly at the production side. Fourth, putting too much emphasis on economies of scale, when their very existence has to be proved, will encourage concentration rather than competition, and there is no evidence to support the proposition that there is a positive correlation between increased firm size and competitive success. Finally, the estimates are for the EU as a whole; thus it is likely that each member nation will strive to get the maximum gain for itself with detrimental consequences for all, i.e. this is like the classical oligopoly problem where the best solution for profit-maximization purposes is for oligopolists to behave as joint monopolists, but if each oligopolist firm tries to maximize its own share of the joint profit, the outcome may be losses all round.

Since Baldwin's estimates start from Cecchini's, these reservations apply equally to them. Moreover, not many development economists, or, for that matter, any economist, will endorse the concept of an indefinitely rising capital stock, especially when the doctrine of steady growth is built on an elegant mathematical structure, but the new theory leaves a lot to be desired in this respect. Of course, this is not meant to suggest that mathematical elegance is all that is needed in economics, rather either that some theoretical justification should be provided or that a solid and indisputable empirical foundation should be advanced.

A rigorous specification of these reservations is fully set out in Chapters 4 and 5 of this book and in El-Agraa (1989a). In the previous edition of this book, I added that here 'it is sufficient to state that such potential benefits may prove rather elusive since the creation of the appropriate environment does not guarantee the expected outcomes. However, this does not mean that the EC should not be congratulated for its genuine attempts to create the necessary competitive atmosphere, only that one should not put too much emphasis on estimates which can easily be frustrated by the realities of everyday EC economic life. However, some of the quotations given above clearly show that the experts are aware of these problems'. The part of that statement relating to the benefits expected from the internal market remains true at the time of writing.

7.6 Conclusion

The conclusion is evident: the EU has been successful not only in achieving *negative integration* (see Chapter 1), but also in adopting elements of *positive integration*. Because in the latter progress has been slow, the EU has set itself an extensive programme, with deadlines, for accomplishing a true internal market and an EMU. Only history can tell whether or not the EU has been unduly optimistic, but in terms of the philosophy of the founding fathers it could be argued that the EU is at last on target. As to the future, only politics can help, which is why it is left to the final chapter.

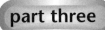

Major EU policies

The previous section of this book was devoted to the theoretical and empirical aspects of the common market elements of the EU and to an analysis of European monetary integration. This section provides an extensive discussion of virtually all the major policies of the EU.

chapter eight

EU competition policy

F. McGOWAN

If it were necessary to identify the 'rules of the game' for the EU and particularly for the Single Market, most commentators would point to the provisions of the Treaties dealing with competition policy. These establish the Community as a market within which attempts by firms to collude or abuse their power and by governments to protect or subsidize national industries are generally prohibited or closely monitored. The Community's competition policy, based on these rules, acts as a constraint on the behaviour of economic actors, albeit with certain exceptions, in defence of an integrated and liberalized European economy.

This chapter examines the development of this policy and assesses its success in 'keeping the playing field level' (Brittan, 1992). After reviewing the reasons for such a policy and some of the associated problems with it, the chapter examines national policies and the origins of EU policy, outlining the main characteristics of the competition regime. The chapter then examines a number of key issues which illustrate how the Commission has implemented competition policy, focusing on recent developments in such areas as cooperative agreements, state aids, monopoly regulation and mergers. It concludes by appraising how far the EU now has an effective competition policy.

8.1 The rationale for competition policy

Economists generally identify the market as the best mechanism for ensuring the efficient allocation of resources. In a perfect market, firms will compete with each other for the custom of buyers. Such a competitive market will be characterized by pressures towards low prices, close to a level consistent with the costs of, and profits for, manufacture and supply. Firms may go bankrupt and drop out of the market but others will enter: equally, if a firm should try to price a product too high, it is likely that it will be undercut by competitors. The market according to this view is a self-equilibrating system, good for buyers and sellers alike fostering innovation and choice, and keeping the economy as a whole efficient (Ordover, 1990).

Such a view, however, is an idealized one, as most economists admit, and the divergence of the reality from this ideal has usually been marked. Quite aside from the imperfectness of markets and market signals, however, there is also scope for firms in a particular sector to cooperate or collude or for one firm to dominate the market. Price fixing, market sharing and other forms of anti-competitive behaviour may result with the aim of securing high profits or a quiet life. For most economists, the method for countering this danger, in terms of both preventing and punishing such behaviour, has been to apply legal controls to contain anti-competitive conduct: it should be possible to correct the market's imperfections by the rule of law. Some economists have preferred an alternative means of control, through direct public ownership (Lange, 1938), but this has only been widely accepted for industries where technical factors have appeared to necessitate monopolistic structures and state control has been regarded as the lesser evil.

Competition policy, therefore, is important as a mechanism for correcting market distortions. By doing so, moreover, it also helps to maintain the overall efficiency of the economy. To the extent that an absence of such a policy or an ineffective policy would permit firms to operate anti-competitively, there may be serious productive and allocative inefficiencies (Kuhn et al., 1992).

The question of what constitutes anti-competitive conduct and what therefore requires control by competition policy is complicated in international settings. It is possible that the various phenomena identified may also operate across borders (indeed, there is a long and ignoble tradition of international cartels in many in-dustries (Mason, 1946)). However, an additional source of anti-competitive conduct rests with governments themselves: they may, through direct financial aid, favour other forms of support or restrictive rules and procedures, privilege firms from their country or exclude firms from others. Such conduct would normally be seen as a form of non-tariff barrier, to be analysed by trade economists and dealt with in a trade policy context (though the line between competition and trade policy then becomes extremely blurred (Krugman, 1986)). In a context of regional integration such as the EU, however, these issues become competition problems. Where a gov-ernment seeks to support firms in a customs union its conduct may be as anti-com-petitive as a cartel fixing prices. Thus a competition policy straddling more than one country must deal with the behaviour of governments as well as firms (Swann, 1983).

As well as being a possible agent of unfair competition, of course, the state is usually the focus for the development, implementation and enforcement of com-petition rules. In competition policy literature, an explicit role for the public auth-ority is envisaged and any sophisticated analysis must take account of its capabilities and the signals it sends to the firms it is scrutinizing. The effectiveness of control is an important dimension of any assessment of competition policy, national or EU. Enforcing competition policy is essentially a regulatory task, and in appraising it we need to take account of such factors as the resources, responsibilities and powers of the regulator as well as the problems of credibility and information which are raised in such a task (Gatsios and Seabright, 1989). Again, however, we should note that while such factors are hard to perfect in a national context, they become even more complex in a context such as the EU.

There are some persisting problems in relating the reality of competition policy to the traditional view proffered by economists. In particular there is a need to distinguish what might be plausible or preferable in an ideal setting and what is possible in real life. Indeed, the textbook case for competition policy may not take full account of the complexity of markets, firms or governments, rooted as it still is in an ideal view of how markets should be organized and how governments or authorities should regulate them. There may be trade-offs between the efficiencies wrought by competition among many firms and those achieved by large-scale and therefore concentrated operations (Asch, 1970; Williamson, 1987). Policy is often motivated by wider political and economic objectives which could affect both the tone of overall competition regulation and the exceptions which may be made.

8.2 The development of EU competition policy

Although the pitfalls of monopoly and anti-competitive conduct have long been recognized by economists, the application of policies to curb such behaviour is relatively recent – if we disregard the claims of Magna Carta (Frazer, 1992) and various principles of English common law (Whitney, 1958; George, 1990) to promote competition. The oldest tradition of anti-trust is in the US where the first explicit legislation, the Sherman Act, was passed in 1890, reinforced by subsequent laws such as the Clayton Act of 1914 and the Federal Trade Commission Act of 1917. These laws, which collectively address most aspects of what we would understand as competition policy, were initiated at a time of considerable concern over the concentration of economic power and the growth of a political movement to combat that trend (Hofstadter, 1965; Shonfield, 1965). The original concerns of the American approach and its highly legalistic system (the focus for policy is the Department of Justice) have persisted over the subsequent hundred years, although the strength of sentiment and action has ebbed and flowed over time. In recent years, a weaker anti-trust approach has been applied as 'efficiency' became the prevailing determinant of policy (Bork, 1978). Arguments over competitiveness and the perceived need for US firms to collaborate more closely may lead to a continuation of a hands-off anti-trust policy, although for rather different reasons from those prevailing in the 1980s (Comanor, 1990; Jacquemin, 1986; Audretsch, 1988). However, the United States system of anti-trust remains much more rigorous and restrictive of firms' behaviour than that applied in other countries.

In Europe, the enthusiasm of policy makers to tackle issues of competition has been rather less vigorous. In many respects, policy, where it existed, was characterized by very different approaches, and concerns to those prevailing in the United States, often ignoring or condoning collusive behaviour on the grounds of national economic development: in the interwar period many countries instituted legislation encouraging cartels (Lister, 1960). However, while this has been a common element in national policies, there have been some important differences between states, some of which are important for understanding how EU policies have developed and operated in the last forty years. Of these, the most important has been a certain equivocation over the benefits of 'competitive' versus 'managed' markets. Such views not only matter *vis-à-vis* the development of EU policy, but also affect the on-going relationship between national and EU policies.

Historically, member states have been varied in their responses towards competition policy (in most cases, explicit policies were only agreed in the post-war period and were fiercely debated in most countries). Indeed, given the prevailing national approaches and economic conditions in post-war Europe, it is remarkable that the members of the European Coal and Steel Community (ECSC) were prepared to agree on such a policy. How was it that the first Community Treaty embodied such a tough anti-trust approach? Undoubtedly, the influence of the United States was very significant at this time. In Germany, American administrators were pushing very strongly to control the re-emergence of interwar cartels, particularly in the coal and steel industries (Gillingham, 1991). As the idea of a European Coal and Steel Community took shape, the Americans actively supported the inclusion of a set of controls on restrictive practices, mergers and government aid (Diebold, 1959), although the initiative was led by Jean Monnet and supported by the French on the grounds that it would contain the concentration and revival of German economic power (Allen, 1983).

To some extent an aspect of the motivation for the anti-trust provisions of the Paris Treaty – fear of German expansionism – had dissipated by the mid-1950s when the negotiations for an Economic Community took place. Nor had the traditional attitudes on the merits of cooperation over competition been expunged from most European states. Nonetheless, the preparations for the new Treaty reiterated the commitment to competition. The Spaak Report which acted as a blueprint for the Rome Treaty (EEC) stressed the importance of competition while the subsequent negotiations for the EEC were aided by the liberal bias in German policy at the time: 'the view of competition which is generally accepted as the Community view is in practice largely a German one and is particularly strongly held by German members of the EC Commission' (MacLachan and Swann, 1967; Majone, 1991). The provisions which were finally agreed in the Treaty of Rome did not, however, set as rigid a structure as in the Paris Treaty, nor did they provide so much scope for Community authorities to intervene as was the case in the ECSC (hardly surprising given the special characteristics of the industries covered by that Treaty).

The authors of the Treaty did, however, establish a framework within which controls over cartels, the abuse of market power, government aids and public services could be regulated. The policy that was agreed was, moreover, one which focused on promoting competition and took a largely economic view of that task. However, in important respects, the Community's competition policy also took account of wider concerns, most notably that of fostering European integration. These other objectives on occasion shift the terms of specific Commission and Court decisions quite markedly.

8.3 EU competition rules and procedures

EU competition policy is driven by the EEC Treaty Provisions. Article 3(f) of the Treaty sets the objective of ensuring that competition in a common market is not distorted. This objective is implemented through the rules on competition contained in Articles 85–94. It is a measure of the role of competition policy in making the EU work and of the importance which the architects of the EEC Treaty attached to it, that it should be so rooted in the Treaty and that those provisions should have driven policy ever since. Indeed, a distinguishing characteristic of the EU system is its strong reliance on legal process: competition law and competition policy are intertwined.

The competition rules apply to firms and governments, with Articles 85–90 mainly addressed to the former and Articles 92–94 to the latter. The core of policy is to be found in Article 85 (covering agreements between firms and other concerted practices which might affect trade or by aim or effect distort competition), Article 86 (covering abuses of dominant positions within markets) and Article 92 (covering government aids to firms). The other provisions largely cover implementation and transitional measures.

Article 85's coverage extends across a wide range of economic activities and forms of conduct, information sharing, restricting markets and production, technical standards, joint purchasing and selling, promotion and advertising. If the economic effect or objective of these is to restrict trade, then it is illegal and void under conditions of Article 85(2). It is, however, possible that some forms of agreement may be exempted under Article 85(3) from this provision if they are seen as contributing to the production or distribution of product or to technical or economic progress. This can be done either through a block exemption, which excludes a defined type of agreements, or by individual Commission decision.

Article 86 tackles instances where a firm or firms with a dominant position in a market uses that market power to distort competition and affect trade. This can be done through such means as imposing unfair prices, limiting production, discriminating between customers and applying specific conditions not related to the transition. It has largely been applied against single firms, although the joint actions of firms could be addressed by the provision.

Article 92(1) declares that 'any aid granted by a Member State or through State resources in any form whatsoever which distorts or threatens to distort competition by favouring certain undertakings or the production of certain goods' is incompatible with a common market where it affects trade. However, the rest of the article outlines conditions where aid may be permitted, for example with regard to the promotion of economic development in poor regions, or areas where there has been an economic disruption, or for sectoral development.

The responsibility for administering these rules, which has been granted to the Commission by the Council in a series of regulations (most importantly the implementation of regulation 17 of 1962) lies with Directorate General Four (DG IV) and the Commissioner responsible for competition policy. The Directorate also carries out policy in areas related to competition policy, principally those relating to state trading monopolies, covered by Article 37 of the Treaty. The implementing regulation of 1962 provides the Commission with a number of powers to enforce its role. The most visible of these relate to the so-called 'dawn raids' powers. Although few such raids occur, the Commission does possess a number of key powers such as the right to examine the books, enter any premises and seek explanations. Moreover, the regulation provides the Commission to file infringements or failures to comply with these requirements.

As with all EU law, the competition rules prevail over national legislation. Where issues purely affect domestic markets, member state law applies. On issues affecting the Community, however, the Commission has exclusive competence. The Commission, however, is a very small bureaucracy to manage such a regulatory task. Accordingly, various techniques have been adopted to streamline the process of applying competition law, in particular to permit certain types of agreement and to provide clarification.

Applying competition rules has been a feature of EU policy making for the past forty years, particularly since the provision of implementing powers in the early 1960s. It would be naïve to think that the policy has been consistently and rigorously implemented, however. Quite apart from the cumulative nature of policy making and its interaction with Court decisions, the conduct of policy has often operated within political limits, of both the priorities of the Commissioner and the Commission and the politics of member states' attitudes. Thus some areas of policy have only emerged in recent years or have been subject to considerable delay in their development.

That these areas have come to view reflects the increased activism of the Community competition authorities. From being a largely reactive body, often unable to implement effectively the rules of competition, as was the case throughout the 1970s (Allen, 1983), DG IV has become a much more effective and visible part of the Commission. This is at least partly a result of the capabilities of Commissioners Sutherland and Brittan who were responsible for DG IV from the mid-1980s to the early 1990s; they took a much more pro-active approach to both monitoring behaviour and extending the scope of policy. However, the higher profile also parallelled the completion of the Single Market (in some cases, such as air and sea transport, it was a key mechanism for implementing the Single Market objectives) and there is a recognition that, in the wake of 1992, competition policy has an even more important role to play, preventing the re-emergence of national preference and European cartels (Montagnon, 1990b).

8.4 Current issues in EU competition policy

In this section I shall review some of the issues which EU competition policy addresses, both on the operation of Articles 85, 86 and 92 and on some recent initiatives to develop EU competition policy, primarily through the increased use of

Article 90 and the application of the Merger Regulation. As the scope of policy has extended, this has had implications for the relationship between EU policy and both national level anti-trust rules and the wider international environment.

8.4.1   Articles 85 and 86

The Commission's activities under Article 85 are at the very core of competition policy. Its treatment of cartels and other market arrangements has been a continuous feature of policy since the 1950s; given the breadth of the Article, it is not surprising that it has been the focus for most of the Commission's activities. The most spectacular cases concern those cartels discovered by the Commission during 'dawn raids' and subject to heavy fines, the arrangements which have prevailed in certain parts of the chemical industry being the most notorious.

The powers and to some extent the effectiveness of Commission actions have been one reason why firms have in many cases sought clarification of their own activities. Since Regulation 17 was introduced, various procedures have been put in place, for example, for 'negative clearance' of agreements (if the Commission does not object, the agreement is approved). Another mechanism has been the block exemption which allows certain classes of agreement to be approved. These have covered such issues as distribution agreements, patents, R&D, and arrangements in the shipping and air transport industries.

Pursuing cases under Article 86 has been easier said than done because of the criteria which have to be met. Under the provisions of the Article, both the relevant market and the nature of dominance have to be defined, while the fact of abuse also has to be established. The question of market definition has proved problematic because, while a firm may have a large market share inside the EU, this may be a reflection of the scale of operations which is necessary to compete internationally. There has been a long-running debate within the Community and the Commission on the size of European firms, particularly on the problem of ensuring both competition within the EC and international competitiveness (see below and Chapter 9). There may also be problems in identifying the nature of the market, especially as regards the availability of substitutes. The related task of determining dominance can embrace not only market share but also other factors, such as degree of vertical integration or the structure of the market. Moreover, the possession of such a dominant position may not be in itself illegal; the act of abuse also has to be identified.

Given these problems, it is perhaps not surprising that the mechanism has been used in relatively few cases (the first of which did not take place until 1971). However, a sufficiently large number of cases have been decided upon to indicate some aspects of the Commission's approach, such as use of fidelity arrangements, discriminatory pricing and access to technology. Moreover, in two recent cases, the Commission and the Court have extended the scope of their approach. The *Akzo* case of 1991 was notable for punishing predatory pricing behaviour while the *TetraPak* case of 1991 was notable for the scale of fining applied by the Commission (75 million ECU). While a part of a wider policy of tougher fining, it may also reflect the determination to stamp out such behaviour by an exemplary and deterrent fine. Since this case the Commission has pursued relatively few cases on an Article 86 basis, although it is expected that utility liberalization (and particularly the question of network access) is likely to prompt complaints and actions on this basis.

8.4.2 Article 92 and state aids

As noted earlier, an important dimension of EU competition policy is directed towards the actions of governments. The provisions of Article 92(1) set out a tough control on aids which distort or threaten to distort competition. However, this strongly worded prohibition is moderated by a series of provisions which permit aid to be given, although permission for such aid has to be given by the Commission: the power of derogation lies with the Commission, not the member states. This is achieved through the following mechanisms: a requirement that member states give the Commission prior notification of any plan to provide aid and that the Commission approval is needed; a system of review carried out by the Commission; a procedure whereby the Commission can modify or suppress an aid. Rather than scrutinize individual cases (although this can be and is done in particular cases) the Commission examines the overall framework for aid schemes, leaving member states to subsidize within those frameworks (Bellamy and Child, 1987).

For much of the EU's history, the Commission has largely approved aid schemes, perhaps reflecting the limited use of such mechanisms by governments. Even during the economic problems of the 1970s and early 1980s, subsidies were to some extent approved as part of a process of adjustment (Gilchrist and Deacon, 1990). More recently, a much tougher line on state aids has been apparent, particularly in the wake of the single market programme. The White Paper programme was largely aimed at removing various distortions, many of them the result of government policies, to create a single market; the continued and possibly increased use of another government measure – subsidies – would jeopardize the single market. Some have even warned that, without controls, the EU members might resort to a subsidy war to support national industries (Winters, 1988).

The Commission's tougher policy on subsidies was also enhanced by the Competition Commissioner, Sir Leon Brittan. Announcing his intention to 'make a bonfire of subsidies', he launched a more rigorous process of scrutinizing state aid in the EU (Brittan, 1989); since then five reports have been published monitoring the conduct of member states. These initially revealed a large, if gradually declining, level of aid: if Community support is excluded, aid has fallen from an average of approximately 100 billion ECU in the first half of the 1980s to just under 90 billion ECU in 1990, slightly less than 3% of EU GDP. However, in the last year for which figures are available – 1994 – the aid has stabilized, a worrying trend for the Commission (COM (97) 170). The aid is spread across all sectors (manufacturing, mining, services and agriculture) although the level and distribution of support vary markedly from country to country, with the countries such as Italy particularly generous. Much of the aid goes to three sectors (coal, railways and agriculture), but a significant proportion goes to industry.

Getting a better idea of how much aid national and local authorities grant is part of the process of improving transparency, one of the Commission's main objectives on state aids: in order to control them, it is necessary to know how much and in what form aid is being given. The other element in the Commission's policy is stricter and wider enforcement of the rules on aid. Thus the Commission has been seen to disallow aid or impose conditions in a number of specific instances (Renault, Rover, Sabena), and to broaden the scope of what it considers to be aid (Brittan, 1992). At the same time, however, it has shown flexibility, particularly as regards the provision of so-called horizontal aid, i.e. support for such activities as regional development, environmental protection and research. It is clear, however, that the Commission's task in controlling subsidies is extremely delicate. In the wake of its most recent review of subsidies, Commission attempts to extend its powers have been rejected by member states.

8.4.3 Article 90 and the treatment of public ownership and utility industries

One area where the Commission has been particularly active has been that of aids to publicly owned enterprises. However, the Treaty does not tackle the question of public ownership. More precisely, it addresses the issue of ownership by excluding itself from any opinion on the matter: Article 222 of the EEC Treaty states that the Treaty 'shall in no way prejudice the rules in Member States governing the system of property ownership' (and similar provisions are in place in the ECSC and Euratom Treaties). In principle, and as elaborated in various Court judgments, the EU is indifferent to whether or not a company is privately owned or is nationalized. There was, however, considerable debate in the period prior to the creation of the EEC and the years immediately afterwards about how far such enterprises could be reconciled with the model of the free market economy envisaged by the EEC Treaty of Rome (Deringer, 1964; Schindler, 1970; Marenco, 1983; Papaconstantinou, 1988). Moreover, certain provisions of the Treaty are addressed to state-owned firms, principally Articles 37 and 90. Questions of aid have arisen in the context of Article 90 which brings public enterprises under the competition rules.

While the provision of aids to public firms should have been addressed, little was done by the Commission until the late 1970s. The opposition of most governments to its efforts meant that concrete measures were adopted only slowly. Nonetheless, the Commission insisted on its powers to act in this area and although it stressed its indifference to ownership under Article 222, it nonetheless noted that,

> the undeniable liberty of a Member State to choose the system of property ownership it prefers does not diminish its responsibility to ensure that both its administration of the public sector and the market behaviour of its public undertakings are in accordance with Treaty rules. (CED, 1979e)

In 1980 the Commission adopted a directive on transparency of financial linkages between public enterprises and governments, utilizing its powers under Article 90.3 to impose the legislation in the face of member state opposition, the first time that the article had been employed (CEC, 1980d). This obliged member states to supply information to the Commission upon request on the nature and effect of their financial links with public undertakings, primarily in the manufacturing sector. The use of Article 90 to pursue this was opposed by a number of governments who took the Commission to the Court; the Court upheld the Commission's right to intervene. Governments, however, continued to resist the Commission's initiative (for example, by giving only partial responses to Commission requests for information on financial aid). The scope of the directive was extended in 1985 to cover the utility industries (CEC, 1985g) and in 1991 the Commission proposed to tighten its operation. In particular, the Commission has sought to define more strictly how governments grant aid to industry. A key element of this has been the rational investor principle, that any aid should be granted according to criteria equivalent to those applied when a private investor injects capital. In practice, however, it may be difficult for the Commission to use this provision to prohibit aid, although it may be able to use it to impose conditions on governments and firms.

The Commission's increased scrutiny of aid to the public sector has been paralleled by its activism towards utility or public service firms. These are the 'natural monopoly' industries which constitute the infrastructure of national economies, covering such activities as electricity and gas supply, postal and telephone services and certain categories of passenger transport. These sectors have evolved from local to national networks often in public hands, always with a franchise granted by government to operate monopolistically. Such a structure has been justified on many grounds and, until recently, was generally accepted as the norm.

As 'legitimate' monopolies operating primarily within national boundaries, these sectors have not been a primary target of EU policy or Commission attention. For the most part, national authorities and firms have sought to maintain their autonomy regarding the operation of these industries, not least because they perform a significant industrial policy role beyond that of infrastructure provision. The Commission's interest in this area has therefore lain dormant for most of the Community's history, as has a formal challenge of its competence. However, over the last ten years in particular, the basis of a Community policy has emerged. The reasons for this and the details of it for transport and energy utilities are covered in Chapters 12 and 13. Here we will focus on the role of competition policy and DG IV in the development of the EU role, touching on the case of telecommunications where the policy has arguably gone furthest and raised the most concern.

At the root of these initiatives is the use or the threat of Article 90, part of the EEC Treaty's competition provisions. The article applies to both public undertakings and those performing functions of general economic interest. The article was designed to ensure that competition rules could be waived for firms carrying out such functions, but only those. Where an undertaking is engaged in other activities, the competition rules would apply. Moreover, under Article 90.3 the Commission would be able to act directly in pursuit of this task.

The Article therefore provides not only the basis for ensuring that such firms comply with the EEC Treaty of Rome but also a mechanism for acting directly, by imposing decisions or directives without the approval of the Council of Ministers. However, in the competition provisions, in contrast to other provisions as noted the use of Article 90 has been quite limited. The failure to apply it may have been due to factors such as the rather imprecise language used in the Article, the lack of interest in tackling the sectors which were covered by it (primarily the utility industries) and the heavy workload of the Commission in developing the other aspects of competition policy. However, the failure to apply it may also have been due to the highly sensitive nature of the Article and its implications (Pappalardo, 1991; Hancher and von Slot, 1990).

In 1988, the Commission used its powers under Article 90.3 to force a degree of liberalization in the telecommunications sector. The telecommunications industry had been characterized by usually one PTT supplying all communications services, its monopoly extending into a range of other areas such as equipment provision. The issue was increasingly a sensitive one and in 1987 the Commission published a green paper on telecommunications designed to create a single market in telecom services by 1992 (CEC, 1987e). It sought to do this by a variety of mechanisms including harmonization and research support but an important weapon would be liberalization. It followed its report up by addressing a directive on the opening of supply arrangements for equipment at member states (later followed by similar moves on service provision). The action was challenged by a number of states, but the Commission's actions were upheld by the Court. Over the 1990s, moreover, the Commission has continued to use the Article as one means of liberalizing the telecommunications sector: full liberalization of the sector is on course for 1998 (notwithstanding limited delays for poorer member states) and attention has now switched to how competition policy can be used to regulate the European telecoms market (Centre for European Policy Studies, 1996).

Overall, however, the use of Article 90 remains controversial: the French and Belgian governments sought to have it amended in the Intergovernmental Conference of June 1997, partly because of the nature of the article but also because of wider concerns over the effects of liberalization *vis-à-vis* the traditional public policy roles of utility industries (universal service, uniform pricing etc.; see McGowan, 1995). Thus, although the attempt to amend the article was unsuccessful, the principle has found its way into the Amsterdam Treaty in a milder form (under Article 7) and the Commission has underlined its willingness to consider universal service considerations in all the utility industries (COM (96) 443).

8.4.4 Mergers

One of the most significant omissions from the EC's competition rules was an explicit control on mergers. Such a rule had been included in the Treaty of Paris covering the coal and steel industries. However, from the point of view of the 1950s, the omission is less remarkable (the rules in the ECSC treaty could be explained by the special nature of the industries covered and the conditions surrounding the decisions on competition rules, in particular the influence of the United States). No such provisions existed in member states' policies at that time; on the contrary, the policy in most countries was to encourage concentration in order to build up larger firms capable of competing in world markets. Commission policy into the 1960s followed a similar line, and indicated that mergers were preferable to cartels as market rationalization instruments (Frazer, 1992).

By the 1970s, although still positive towards most mergers, the Commission saw the need to control those concentrations which might be deemed anti-competitive. It proposed a regulation on merger control in 1973, but this was opposed by a number of member states. The Commission, to the extent it intervened on mergers, used its general powers under the Competition rules of the Treaty, both Articles 85 and 86, and supported by decisions of the Court of Justice. An intervention by the Commission forbidding a merger on the grounds of abuse of dominant position (the *Continental Can* case) was upheld by the Court. The circumstances of that decision were such that the Commission never repeated its decision (although it has been able to use it more informally to control some proposed mergers). Article 85 has been used primarily in merger-type arrangements such as joint ventures and minority shareholdings. With regard to the latter, the Court upheld another Commission action, the *Philip Morris* case (George and Jacquemin, 1990).

It was the prospect of the Commission intervening in a series of mergers on the strength of that judgment which prompted the Council to finally agree to a Mergers Regulation (Frazer, 1992). Member states recognized that a set of rules would be more predictable for national businesses than the Commission exercising its discretion. The fact of an agreement also owed something to wider developments in the Commission, not least to its increased activism on competition matters under Commissioners Sutherland and Brittan and the general dynamic of the Single Market programme.

The regulation entered into force in September 1990. It applies only to mergers where the global turnover is 5 billion ECUs and the EC turnover of each firm is 250 million ECU. Mergers which involve firms whose turnover is concentrated in a single member state are not covered by the regulation. The regulation also sets out a number of criteria which should be taken into account including market structure, consumer interests and technical and economic progress. A task force was established inside DG IV to apply the regulation.

The application of the regulation has been relatively uncontroversial, with most notified mergers being approved by the Commission. The main exception was the proposed merger between two aircraft manufacturers, de Havilland, Alenia and Aerospatiale. The Commission rejected this on the grounds that it would lead to too much concentration in the commuter aircraft market. The decision proved to be highly controversial, with considerable opposition from France and some other governments. Although the Commission held to its position, the case exposed the twin issues of how such politically sensitive cases would be handled and whether the Commission should have complete discretion in such cases. The row which the de

Havilland case provoked may have contributed to a certain wariness on the Commission's part ever since – of the 234 cases decided in 1995 and 1996, only five were rejected outright and six were accepted pending conditions – although generally the process is seen as effective and efficient.

Even so, the Commission feels that there are cases which have fallen out with its jurisdiction but where the 'European' dimension has been significant. On the grounds of subsidiarity and of efficiency – the 'one-stop shop' view – the Commission argued that it should deal with a wider range of such cases, lowering the threshold and covering multiple notifications. The proposals were opposed by some member states, notably the United Kingdom, which was reluctant to see any further centralization of competition powers at Brussels. A compromise agreement has focused the Commission's role on mergers involving three or more member states. In these cases, the Commission will have authority in cases where the combined global turnover of the firms involved was 2.5 billion ECU, where the EU turnover was 100 million ECU, and where in each member state involved at least two of the firms have a turnover of 25 million ECU. However, the overall thresholds remain unchanged.

8.4.5 EU Competition policy and national convergence

Although the merger regulation has been amended to expand the scope of EU responsibility, the burden of commitments upon the Commission is such that it is keen to see national competition authorities playing a more active role in applying EU rules. A draft notice published in 1996 argued that national agencies were better placed to monitor local developments and that the principle of subsidiarity therefore required that these agencies be more closely involved (CEU, 1997b). However it should be noted that the sharing of responsibilities is oriented around the effective application of EU competition policy with national approaches converging with that policy. A recent survey by the Commission showed that, of the 15 member states, seven administrative authorities directly apply Articles 85 and 86 whereas eight do not. Nonetheless the last few years have seen member states move to converge.

The German government recently announced proposals to update the country's cartel legislation which are partly aimed at bringing the law into line with EU rules. Although German and EU competition policy have much in common – after all the German law and the EEC Rome Treaty were both finalized in 1957 – the government has recognized the need to update and to align more closely national law. The changes – which are unlikely to find their way into law before 1999 – would forbid cartel agreements, impose fines on any abuse of dominant market position, regulate mergers before rather than after completion and open up access to key infrastructures such as ports and airports (although other network industries such as telecommunications and energy are being dealt with by separate legislation). Reform of British competition policy to align it with EU rules has been debated for some years, but no legislative changes were introduced. The new government has also indicated that it is keen to reform United Kingdom law, although recently some of the more radical measures – such as a requirement that firms demonstrate that mergers are in the public interest – have been dropped. Incorporation of EU competition policy – particularly fining principles and a tougher approach on predatory conduct – looks likely to remain a part of any new policy. There may, however, still be some doubts over when such reforms will be included in the new government's legislative timetable. The potential of adapting EU policy into domestic legislation has been demonstrated in Italian competition policy. Since legislation in 1990 incorporated EU principles and created an independent competition agency, the Italian economy has been subject to a much more rigorous regulation. As well as monitoring anti-competitive behaviour, the agency has been particularly active in tackling the Italian government's evolving programme of privatization where it has lobbied for structural changes of major state monopolies before they are sold. However, the Italian experience also demonstrates the continued limitations of policy – many of its interventions have been ignored or overturned and the retiring head of the Italian anti-trust agency has recently criticized the persistence of many rigidities in the country's economy.

8.4.6   EU competition policy and the rest of the world

The EU's competition policy constitutes the first example of an effective international competition policy. Its success contrasts with the failure of other multilateral attempts to develop such a regime, starting with United States-led efforts in the abortive International Trade Organisation, and continuing through the ECOSOC, WTO and UNCTAD over the next two decades. Some modest agreements have been reached (for example, the UNCTAD model rules and various declarations in the OECD) but these fall short of a regime equivalent to the EU rules in their coverage and enforcement procedures. The EU has been active in promoting international solutions to competition problems. Cooperation agreements have included provisions on anti-trust while both the European Economic Area and pre-accession negotiations for East Europe have incorporated aspects of EU policy. The EU itself has sought to conclude agreements with its major trading partners, most notably a bilateral cooperation arrangement with the United States.

However, the EU's greatest contribution may rest on its vanguard role in reviving the multilateral debate. In the wake of the last GATT Round, the question of the relationship between trade and competition policy has been re-opened. The Commission has been keen to be at the fore of this debate – in July 1995 a group of experts, mostly but not all Commission officials, published a set of recommendations on international competition policy, subsequently adopted by the Commission (COM (96) 284). This outlines a step-by-step process which could ultimately lead to the creation of some form of global anti-trust rules. The Commission's enthusiasm for the issue undoubtedly contributed to its being included on the post-Singapore agenda.

8.5 Problems of competition policy

EU competition policy is now at the forefront of the regulation of industrial conduct within the EU and arguably now serves as the guarantor of an economy without internal barriers. The commitment to that ideal, which has been rigorously pursued by DG IV, albeit with a fair degree of political sensitivity, has not always been appreciated by member states: competition officials have been criticized as 'Ayatollahs' for their pursuit of competition over national interests and Community 'competitiveness'. However, it is difficult to see how a more flexible approach would be possible without compromising the credibility of the Commission as an independent regulator. That credibility is arguably greater than is enjoyed by most national authorities: on this issue, the Commission has rarely been criticized as 'captured' by special interests (McGowan and Seabright, 1994).

There is, however, a more serious criticism of the Commission which to some extent derives from its autonomy in carrying out competition policy; that its policy is unpredictable and not founded on a consistent analytical approach. The Commission's actions are rarely spelt out or supported by rigorous analysis, in contrast to the ECJ and the opinions of some national competition authorities (Korah, 1990). There is accordingly a risk that the Commission may act in ways that are not always the result of a careful calculation of what is best for EU consumers. Moreover, such a system raises questions over the accountability of the Commission and leaves it with considerable scope for discretionary policy making, for example by using derogations and exemptions to make policy decisions without consultation. Whatever the merits of specific decisions made in this way (for example the 1990 agreement by the Energy and Competition Commissioners to permit the subsidizing and protection of a tranche of high-cost national energy resources on the grounds of 'supply security') there must be grounds for concern over such policy making by proxy.

The question of autonomy and the relationship with other policies has arisen in the light of discussions at the June 1997 Amsterdam Intergovernmental Conference. The German government was anxious to see the establishment of an independent European cartel office which would enjoy even more autonomy than the Commission and be insulated from political pressures. The scheme was rejected not only by governments less keen to see competition policy take on a more independent focus but also by the Commission itself. For van Miert himself there was a need for competition policy to be integrated into the whole range of EU policies (van Miert, 1996).

8.6 Conclusion

The ethos of competition policy inside the EU was crystallized in the Commission's first report in 1972: 'Competition is the best stimulant of economic activity since it guarantees the widest possible freedom of action to all. An active competition policy

... makes it easier for the supply and demand structures to adjust to technological development ... Competition policy is an essential means for satisfying the individual and collective needs of our society' (CEC, 1971b).

To a large extent the Commission has been able to follow a policy informed by such ideals. That it has done so is remarkable given the difficult conditions in which such a policy had to develop, most notably the ambivalence, and in some cases hostility, towards competition in many member states. There remains a tension in the EU between the traditional outlook in many countries and the Commission's approach, and that tension is exacerbated when the latter seeks to extend the scope of the policy or otherwise to limit the conduct of national governments. To the extent that national sovereignty in this area is restricted by the Commission's activism, it is inevitable that any deficiencies in the transparency of decision making and the accountability of decision makers will be set upon by disgruntled governments and firms. Such criticisms should not detract from the Commission's record of competence and, for the most part, consistency in applying the policy, but nor should that record of effectiveness prevent a real debate on how the Commission conducts itself and its relations with other Community institutions and national governments.

chapter nine

EU industrial policy

F. McGOWAN

For more than a quarter century, the debate on industrial policy has ebbed and flowed and, with it, the interest and commitment of governments. The mix of priorities and mechanisms identified by economists and politicians, in particular the balance between state intervention and market forces, has shifted. At the EU level, the twists and turns of policy of the sort witnessed in a single country have been compounded by both the divergent approaches of member states and their attitudes to an EU role in this area. Indeed, for the most part, the development of a formal EU industrial policy, although often proposed by the Commission, has not been enthusiastically endorsed by national authorities, even though the EU does play an important role in this area as demonstrated by the range of EC and EU initiatives and rules which impinge on the competitiveness of European industry. Moreover, despite a widespread reluctance to allow the Community an explicit industrial policy role, governments and firms are not averse to use the powers and the budget of the EU as a means of support or protection *vis-à-vis* the rest of the world.

This chapter looks at both the formal and informal aspects of industrial policy in the EU. It examines the development of proposals for an EU industrial policy and tracks their record of success or failure. It also discusses some of the other EU activities which operate as a *de facto* industrial policy or have significant implications for industrial competitiveness and member state strategies. However, in order to understand the record, it is necessary to examine three things: the nature of industrial policy and the international (US and Japanese as well as European) debate on it; the industrial position of Europe; the different approaches of the member states.

9.1 The industrial policy debate

Competitiveness has been at the centre of the debate on industrial policy, even though establishing the 'territory' of industrial policy in terms of a portfolio of policy techniques is almost as difficult as identifying what that policy should comprise (Grant and Sargent, 1987). The objective of enhancing competitiveness is, of course, a broad one: in principle almost any government economic policy (and some more besides) could be regarded as contributing to that goal (Grant, 1982).

Everything from educational policy to new rules on corporate tax allowances can be regarded as components of a national effort to promote competitiveness. By contrast, specific initiatives labelled 'industrial policies' occupy a relatively narrow policy scope literally targeting particular activities in industries or firms. Neither captures the flavour of the debate on industrial policy, either embracing or excluding too much. Is a compromise between these two positions available?

It is possible to identify a range of other government activities which have an industrial policy effect in addition to more narrowly defined and explicitly targeted initiatives. Policies such as those for regional development, training and research can be seen as playing a 'sponsorship' role. Another element consists of policies which ostensibly act as constraints on what can be done in the name of competitiveness and economic viability. However, while these 'regulatory' policies, primarily in the areas of trade liberalization and competition, theoretically set the limits of industrial policy, they can be stood on their head and employed to promote competitiveness. This manipulation can be seen when trade policy mechanisms are used to protect specific sectors or when competition rules are amended to permit certain forms of cooperation between firms. The configuration of these core policies has an important shaping effect on national (and EU) industrial policies. There are regular calls for a rebalancing of them to promote competitiveness, whenever changes to industrial policy are proposed. However, arguably the debate has focused on a more basic choice: whether to give a leading role to the state or to the market.

The debate on industrial policy can be regarded as involving protagonists across a spectrum of opinion. At one extreme are those in favour of a highly interventionist, state-led policy, even involving an ownership role in those activities where the market is seen to fail; such a role could be substantial given that this perspective identifies market failure as the rule rather than the exception (Cowling, 1989; Thomson, 1989). At the other extreme are those who view the market as, if not perfect, then the best available means of allocating resources in an economy. For them, government is almost inevitably going to interfere in the wrong place at the wrong time for the wrong reasons (Curzon Price, 1981; Hindley, 1984). In many cases, proponents of this view point to the tendency of the state either to pursue its own short-term political objectives or to be 'captured' by industrial interests intent on receiving public support or protection. In between these two extremes are a variety of opinions which allow for either minimal roles by the state or a somewhat larger presence to meet specific tasks for the general good (for example, infrastructure or skills development). Some critics point to the theoretical possibility of effective intervention, but caution that practical experience suggests less than successful outcomes (Kierzkowski, 1987; Buigues and Sapir, 1992).

This public versus private debate has raged in various forms for at least 25 years. At the level of practical policy, the high water mark of interventionist industrial policy was the period from the 1960s to the early 1980s. While never as extreme as some academic analyses of the era would have wished, policies in this era did embrace both intervention and public ownership as key tools in fostering industrial development (Shonfield, 1965). Subsequently, there was a swing away from such policies, in part as a reaction to what were seen as their indifferent or even disastrous results, towards a greater emphasis on market forces (Kay and Silbertson, 1984). In recent years the debate on industrial policy has moved on, or at least it appears to have done so. The dirigiste strategies of protectionism, planning and public ownership are still out of favour, but so too are policies of *laissez-faire* and the minimal state. At the levels of both theory and practice, a much wider range of policies is proposed. What sorts of ideas are now being put forward, and do they constitute a real shift in the debate?

One of the most important ideas revolves round the question of strategic industries. However, whereas in the past the definition of 'strategic' was one where the emphasis of industrial policy was on picking winners, either forcing firms together or creating new ones in the public sector, now the emphasis is on enabling such winners to emerge. One aspect of this facilitative approach is a renewed interest in 'knowledge', whether it be the training of a skilled workforce or supporting the university research base. Another important element of this policy is the preparedness to encourage cooperation among firms. Thus, the aim may be to foster pre-competitive research in particular 'generic' technologies or it may be the weakening of existing anti-trust rules to allow companies to create joint ventures or alliances in high-cost and normally high-technology sectors (Sharp and Shearman, 1987; Sawyer, 1992). The other element of this policy is a willingness to secure advantages *vis-à-vis* competitors. Premised on the notion of strategic trade policy, proponents argue that it is possible to intervene effectively to support national firms. Thus a characteristic of these new arrangements is the adoption of aggressive but selective trade policy stances (Tyson, 1992).

Another strand of new thinking on industrial policy is more diffuse in its impact. According to this perspective, the pattern of production of goods is changing as markets globalize, new technologies emerge and new production arrangements and processes are developed. In this environment, the critical determinants of success are not the lowest cost, but best quality at the right moment. This cooperative approach to adding value to products requires new relationships among firms, particularly between manufacturers and suppliers of components and subcontractors. Thus there is considerable interest in special relationships between buyers and suppliers in a particular sector, especially the potential advantages to be gained by encouraging such networks of firms. Such ideas have been particularly important in defining the regional aspects of industrial policy: by fostering technological collaboration in particular localities, it is hoped that spin-off effects would be felt in that economy (Thomson, 1989; Best, 1990).

A final strand of new thinking focuses on the need for a good 'infrastructure'. The importance of this has always been recognized by governments not least as a means of stimulating industrial activity through specific projects. However, the importance attached to it has, if anything, grown with an emphasis on new as well as old infrastructure (telecommunications as well as roads). Yet the focus is not purely on the benefits of the projects themselves, but also on the effects of the infrastructure being in place.

How 'new' are these strands of industrial policy thinking? A cynic might suggest that strategic and network policies seem to be nothing more than mercantilism in new clothing: protectionism and cartels. Equally, so is the refocusing of government roles. Much seems to be based on observing characteristics of successful economies, in particular Japan, and is attempting to emulate them (often at the same time as seeking to exclude them from local markets). What matters, however, is not whether the ideas are old or new but whether they are any likelier to translate into coherent and successful policies. The problems of getting the balance right and managing to implement it might lead one to wonder whether there is a need for an industrial policy in the EU.

Is the EU economy in need of treatment badly enough to embark on such a project? After all, the EU is often identified as one of the key economic powers in the global economy. There is no doubt of that as far as overall economic resources are concerned. However, in terms of its relative position there has been increasing concern. While claims of deindustrialization might appear rather apocalyptic, there is an increasing doubt as to whether its status as an industrial power is secure, particularly if one compares with other industrialized economies.

Perhaps the clearest evidence is seen in relation to the United States. The EC economy grew on average at 4.7% per year in the period from 1960 to 1973, compared with 3.9% in the US. The US economy grew slightly faster than the EC's in the period of 1973–90 and has consistently outpaced it since 1992. By 1995 a significant productivity gap has opened up between the two, with EU productivity being 80% of US levels in 1995. This is seen in the employment rate: whereas in 1960 the employment rate was 67% in the EU and 63% in the US by 1995 the EU employment rate was 60% compared with 72% in the US. Nor is it only in the labour market that the EU lags behind: R&D as a share of GDP is 1.9% in the EU compared with 2.5% in the US (industry R&D is 1% and 1.6% respectively). Overall industrial value added has risen on average by 2.4% in the EU over the last ten years compared with 3% in the US (CEU, 1997c).

Such figures raise the question of where the EU's industrial strength lies. A number of sectors have undergone severe restructuring over the last twenty years, but, as recent experience shows, those changes may not have been sufficient: the steel industry, despite considerable rationalization and investment, is experiencing severe difficulties. At the other end of the industrial spectrum, the EU record on high-technology industries is mixed, as the recourse to trade protection implies. Some sectors, however, remain strong, notably the chemical industry, a sector where the major EU firms have continued to invest and where efforts to enter the industry by NIEs have failed (Sharp and Pavitt, 1993).

Coping with these developments has been to a large extent the preserve of national governments. Each member state has had its own priorities and strategies in this regard. Germany's economic success over much of the post-war era has been premised on both its macroeconomic management and its industrial policy approach. The traditional view of German industrial policy is not dissimilar to that of economic management as a whole in that country: *laissez-faire*, with a minimal government role (Grant, 1982). Such a view has, however, always been a little simplistic. The Federal government has played a more important role than is generally recognized in setting a framework for industrial development. This policy relies on a variety of policy mechanisms, including that of extending even to subsidization. The *Land* governments are also active in this area, offering a range of incentives and supports to local industry and new investors. It is true, however, that, in contrast to other European countries, industrial policy has been carried out with a detailed system of administrative guidance and with a strong commitment to free trade (Hart, 1992). French industrial policy has been characterized as interventionist as French governments have repeatedly intervened to support national industries whether in decline or in development (Aujac, 1986). In the 1980s it could be argued that the consensus was tested. The socialist government of 1981 undertook a major nationalization programme and signalled a shake-up of the country's industrial system. What was by European standards already a rather interventionist policy was made more so: the government used its public ownership strategy to pursue a new programme of industrial development (Stoffaes, 1986; Gourevitch, 1986). While this policy was short lived the overall tenor of French industrial policy has persisted. UK industrial policy has been more variable over the post-war period. Since 1979 there has been an impression that industrial policy was dropped from the political agenda and that policies of privatization and deregulation had replaced them (Kay and Silbertson, 1984). While the latter did reflect an increased emphasis on market forces, they were not themselves key to improving competitiveness (aside from the privatization of major industrial companies). It is notable, however, that a change of government has not led to a redefinition of industrial policy; on the contrary, the principal tenets of the last two decades have remained in place.

9.2 The development of EU industrial policy

Although the Commission was active in many aspects of economic policies since its inception, the development of industrial policy did not take place until relatively late on. It was not until the mid-1960s that a directorate for industrial policy was established (Hodges, 1983). The Commission's first communication on industrial policy published in 1970 addressed a broad range of policies, recognizing that industrial policy was inextricably bound up with 'other aspects of economic policy and with other common policies' (CEC, 1970b). Some of these are worth noting both to compare ideals with outcomes and in considering the current debate. These include improving 'the conditions and the dignity of labour', encouraging 'active participation by workers', developing educational roles, protecting the environment and fostering 'a more even distribution of wealth throughout the world'. Whether or not the EU has had any success in these areas is debatable, but they have not been raised in an industrial policy context.

Even beyond the rhetoric, however, the paper set out an ambitious agenda. On the surface, the Commission strategy appears modest: 'the Commission is far from claiming to solve all the problems of industrial development', and is mindful that 'enterprise and competition are the primary and irreplaceable factors for expansion'. The Commission was particularly concerned to stress that it was not its intention to redistribute economic growth away from the most advanced member states. Notwithstanding these reassurances, the Commission laid out a set of policy initiatives, horizontal and sectoral. The report stressed the need for a single market and for rules to establish European companies, and, more controversially, measures to improve the European position in high-technology sectors.

The report was aimed at maintaining the EC's competitiveness by fostering European-scale firms in a European market. With its provision for significant intervention, the report encountered some opposition, particularly from Germany. Yet it received sufficient support for a deeper debate to be undertaken. Over the early and mid-1970s, however, there was relatively little in the way of concrete follow-up measures. The single market proposals scarcely progressed and related initiatives such as the Mergers Regulation were left undecided. Yet, at the same time, the economic climate deteriorated, particularly for heavy industry. The problems of adjustment both within the EC and with its trading partners meant the Commission became involved (Kirchner, 1982).

For much of the 1970s and 1980s, EC industrial policy focused on the task of simultaneously encouraging the restructuring of traditional manufacturing sectors and cushioning the impact of that process. This complex and sensitive task involved laborious negotiations among governments and between them and the Commission. It also entailed a juggling of regional, competition and trade policies in fostering an adjustment of industrial activity which could be compatible with the Treaty of Rome (EEC) and relations with other countries without imposing too high a social and political cost on Community member states. However, such a compromise has not always been achieved (Hager, 1982).

Both the successes and the shortcomings of that approach can be seen in the Community's policy towards the steel industry. Because of the provisions of the Paris Treaty, this was a sector where an EEC role was explicitly envisaged. Moreover, its central role in Community history owed a lot to the destructive powers of the period. The steel industry has been the backbone of industrial development in the EC and elsewhere: as a basic material in construction and manufacturing, it has been a significant part of most industrialized and industrializing economies. Given its centrality, however, it has been a highly cyclical industry, sensitive to trends in the economy as a whole and its own dynamics. Its importance and susceptibility to economic developments combined to give the sector a high political profile. That profile was never higher than inside the Community over the 1970s and 1980s, when the industry faced a major structural crisis. In contrast to previous periods of boom and bust, the steel industry faced a fundamental problem of adjustment. Not only was there an economic downturn, but higher energy prices and emerging industries in the developing world left the Community industry highly vulnerable (Dreyer, 1980). To compound the problem, the industry had been artificially supported to preserve and in some cases to expand capacity (Jones, 1983). In short, the sector had a chronic surplus capacity problem, and much of that capacity was outdated and inefficient.

Over the course of the late 1970s and early 1980s, the industry underwent a dramatic adjustment, with the Commission and its Industry Commissioner, Viscount Davignon, playing a major part. A variety of instruments were used – minimum prices, import restrictions and a controlled programme of subsidies – although the most important element was the declaration of 'manifest crisis', a device in the Paris Treaty which permitted the Commission to exercise a tougher policy, including quotas on production (Grant, 1982).

Similar cocktails of policies were devised in other traditional industrial sectors although, largely because of the more limited nature of its powers under the Rome Treaty, in most cases the Community dimension was less important, normally only reflecting the actions of member states rather than directing the process. The Community shipbuilding industry faced problems arguably more acute than those in the steel industry: the degree of subsidies was higher, reflecting even greater competitiveness problems. The Commission was able to secure an agreement on controlling subsidies and this has been revised on several occasions since. There has been a rapid reduction in shipbuilding capacity, reflecting perhaps the limited political influence of the European shipbuilding lobby (Strange and Tooze, 1981).

Restructuring old industries was not the only element of EC industrial policy: concerns over the competitiveness of the EC in high-technology industries led to a series of initiatives over the course of the 1970s and 1980s. Where these were directed to specific technologies, the results were rather poor, reflecting rivalry between governments and their reluctance to let the Commission play a leading role. However, a successful strategy was devised by Davignon. By bringing the heads of major European firms together he was able to trigger a range of new research collaborations among firms and researchers, focusing on pre-competitive projects in the electronics and telecommunications sectors (Cawson et al., 1990; Petersen, 1991).

The concerns of the recession and competitiveness affected member states. Another attempt to develop a common industrial policy was made in the wake of the recession, largely at the initiative of the French. Towards the end of 1983, they submitted a memorandum on a common industrial and research area to the Council. Drawing upon the debate within that country, and probably reflecting the problems which the French realized Community rules presented to such a strategy, the memorandum argued for a competence initial policy creating a single market but protected from external competition. Arguing that the EC was falling behind the United States and Japan, the French proposed a series of initiatives, including research cooperation and support for new infrastructure projects, reshaping of EC competition law to allow greater cooperation among leading industrial players and selective protection for both industries in decline and new high-technology sectors. However, although elements of the memorandum either were absorbed into specific policies or were already on the table, the overall orientation of the document was not incorporated into EC policy (Pearce and Sutton, 1986).

Instead, the Community embarked on a more liberal strategy: the completion of the Single Market. The relative success of that initiative and the amendments introduced in the Single European Act marked a high point in expectations of what Community policies could achieve. That process was not likely to satisfy everyone: the new thrust of policy imposed more constraints on member states' own industrial policies (Klodt, 1989). This tension was to be further explored in the debate on the Maastricht Treaty.

In 1990, the Commission presented a new communication on industrial policy to the Council (COM (90) 556). This set out a rather more liberal approach to the issue, reflecting the orientation of policy in the wake of the Single Market programme and the increased activism of competition policy as well as the priorities of the Industry Commissioner Martin Bangemann (Bangemann, 1992). The new report made it clear that policy was to operate in an open and competitive environment. It set out to promote structural adjustment of Community industry, to ensure coherence of EC policies in this area and to address industrial adjustment through 'horizontal' measures. This EC industrial policy aimed to promote the internal market and an open trading system. Sectoral policies were not excluded, but they were expected to promote adjustment, not to protect inefficient industry.

It was this perspective on industrial policy which found its way into the Maastricht Treaty. The debate on an industrial policy chapter in the Treaty was evidently heated, and different governments had different expectations of what it was supposed to encompass. It is clear, for example, that the French hoped such a provision could be used as a counterweight to the provisions of competition policy, justifying policies which would otherwise have been seen as contrary to those rules. However, the provisions which entered the Treaty would not have satisfied such hopes: the chapter explicitly states that it 'does not provide a basis for the introduction by the Community of any measures which may distort competition' (Bourgeois and Demaret, 1995).

The reorientation of Community policy efforts was confirmed by economic developments in the early 1990s. The recession – which was deeper than in the United States or Japan – was regarded by many as exposing structural problems, including a lagging productivity and employment record which suggested serious labour market rigidities. There were, as noted, increasing doubts over the competitiveness of European industry. The debate prompted the Commission to publish a White Paper on Growth Competitiveness and Employment. Its call for stable macroeconomic policies, active labour market policies and a structural adjustment policy consolidated the shift in Community industrial policy towards competitiveness. In 1994 the Commission published an industrial competitiveness policy for the EU (COM (94) 319) which stressed four objectives:

- promoting intangible investment (by giving priority to training in its investment support and by giving greater attention to near market research in its R&D programme);

- developing industrial cooperation (providing information and assistance to

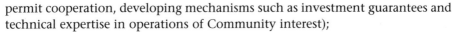

permit cooperation, developing mechanisms such as investment guarantees and technical expertise in operations of Community interest);

- ensuring fair competition (to reduce public subsidy and streamlining state aid monitoring, reconciling regional development with this, promoting trade liberalization after GATT's Uruguay Round, developing international rules on competition, combating fraud);

- modernizing the role of public authorities (reviewing legislation and administrative procedures and improve transparency, improving decision-making procedures).

An action programme to implement these objectives followed in 1995 (COM (95) 87) which stressed the Commission's role as one of facilitation and regulation. A Competitiveness Advisory Group was established to identify weaknesses in the EU economy, while the Commission itself has proposed a 'benchmarking' exercise designed to compare the performance of EU industry with competitors in terms of price quality and innovation (COM (96) 463). While financial programmes are still important (notably in TENS – where the Commission has pinpointed the importance of infrastructure for industrial development – and R&D but more recently in such areas as the promotion of small and medium enterprises (Oughton and Whittam, 1997). The Commission has, like most member states, pulled back from attempting to pick winners.

9.3 Issues in EU industrial policy

In this section I shall examine in more detail some of the strands of current EU policy towards industry, focusing on two areas: the Single Market initiative (see Chapter 7 for full discussion) and R&D.

9.3.1 The Single Market

The Single Market programme is often referred to as the completion of unfinished business in the Community: as noted earlier, the main strands of the '1992' initiative (standardization, liberalization of procurement, taxation) were the major objectives of the Commission's first communication on industrial policy. The liberalizing thrust of this initiative may seem at odds with the conventional view of industrial policy as heavily interventionist (rescuing lame ducks or picking winners). If, however, we consider industrial policy as a programme designed to enhance the competitiveness of domestic firms, the anomaly disappears.

Moreover, a closer look at the rationale for both the 1992 initiative and earlier Commission statements betrays that some traditional industrial policy concerns are at work, even if the means to achieving them are not the usual ones. The most important of these is, of course, the pursuit of scale. European firms have been seen as too small to be competitive in international markets. The pursuit of national champions has prevented the emergence of European champions and it has been preferential government purchasing arrangements and national standards systems which have been the main mechanisms.

The liberalization of procurement markets is therefore justified on the grounds that it will force a rationalization of national firms. Instead of a single supplier for each member state operating in a monopoly position, there would be a concentration of suppliers competing across the Community. Achieving greater economies of scale would lead to a more efficient allocation of resources within the Community, it is argued, and create companies better able to compete in global markets (Cecchini, 1988; Weiss, 1992).

However, to identify some of the problems of the Commission's approach and the debate on industrial policy more generally, it might be useful to explore the case of public procurement in a little detail. Governments have for many years exercised their purchasing power in ways which favour local suppliers, and often with the purpose of fostering technological innovation. There have been a number of studies which purport to show how effective procurement policies can be in developing competitive advantages in this sphere (Rothwell, 1982). The use of procurement is seen as more malleable than devices such as tax incentives for R&D (Geroski, 1990). Equally, however, procurement could be seen as a way of protecting inefficient suppliers from foreign competition, keeping prices higher than they otherwise would be (McGowan and Thomas, 1990).

For the most part, the Commission's point of view has been more aligned with the latter interpretation of public procurement. As we have seen, the Commission has sought to open up procurement relationships on the grounds that it would lower prices to the consumer sector and improve the performance of suppliers by both encouraging better productivity and rationalizing the sectors. Such a view has itself been criticized both for not taking account of higher transaction costs and for adopting a rather naïve view of how industries conduct their procurement. Harking back to our account of long-term relationships, these critics argue that industries such as the car industry do not 'shop around' for the cheapest source of supply, but maintain close links with component suppliers. However, at times, the Commission seems to adhere to the other rationale, except that European champions replace national champions. In the 1970s the Commission sought to encourage transborder alliances in such areas as power plant supply to compete in high-technology markets. To some extent, a similar motive shaped the inclusion in recent procurement rules of Community preference criteria (provoking in the process a bitter trade dispute). There is therefore a risk that the Commission's approach implies an attempt to create a frontierless industrial base behind a fortress of protection.

However, there may be a more fundamental problem with the Community's strategy in this area. In recent years, the pursuit of scale advocated by most proposals for industrial policy has begun to be questioned. There has, of course, always been a concern that too much scale creates market power, necessitating greater scrutiny by competition authorities. However, now the uncertainties are rather more fundamental and concern the trade-off between scale and diversity. Hitherto diversity was dismissed as an obstacle to the achievement of scale economies. Now, it is increasingly seen as a valuable aspect of economic life and of the European economies in particular. Such diversity is most marked in the range of final products available: a greater diversity is regarded as likely to satisfy consumer preferences more than a smaller range. However, diversity may be equally significant both in the types of technology chosen to produce a good or a service and in terms of the institutional structure in which both supply and demand choices take place (Geroski, 1989b; Matthews and McGowan, 1992).

With the achievement of the 1992 programme, the importance of the Single Market for EU industrial policy is increasingly concerned with two issues: completion of the market in new areas and enforcement of the market. On the former, particular importance has been given to utilities and infrastructure. Questions of energy, transport and telecommunication costs figure in both the Commission's action programme and the reports of the Competitiveness Advisory Group and the completion of the internal market in these sectors (and the development of better infrastructures through the TENs programmes) is seen as important for reducing the cost base of European industry. Increasingly, however, attention is focused on the implementation and enforcement of the Single Market, with competition policy of particular significance (see Chapter 8). Given that the Commission's own *post hoc* calculation of the benefits of the programme fell far short of what was envisaged in the Cecchini Report, it is clear that success depends as much on engaging with the spirit as well as the letter of the law (CEC, 1996a).

9.3.2 European technology policy

Fostering Europe's technological position has always been a part of the EU's agenda. The EEC Treaty was aimed as much at encouraging a Community presence in what was seen as the next big technology as at promoting new energy resources. Yet the treaties do not provide the Commission with the capability to act in this area (Sharp, 1991). The sorry history of Euratom shows how the Commission was unable to play a significant role in high-technology industries (Nau, 1974).

There was considerable debate in the 1960s over the European capabilities to develop in order to meet *le defi americain*. In a number of high-technology industries, European companies and governments sought to cooperate on new projects, almost all of them without success. The principal exception to this list of failures was Airbus, a project in which the Community played no role.

Given the problems which such large-scale ventures encountered, the Community adapted its strategy and sought to deal with high technology in a collaborative manner. In the late 1970s the then Industry Commissioner, Etienne Davignon, sought to foster cooperation amongst the leading European firms on pre-competitive research, laying the ground work for future technological advantage. After discussion with the major electronic and electrical engineering firms the Community launched a programme of R&D in Information Technology, ESPRIT. The programme involved not only major European firms, but also smaller companies and universities and parallelled similar initiatives at a national level.

ESPRIT became the model for a series of similar initiatives in other high-technology sectors. These were funded out of a core Community research budget – the Framework Programme. Although Community resources for R&D were in place for many years, it was only in the wake of the SEA, when research was incorporated as a key Community competence, that a coherent and relatively significant financial provision was made. However, the budget for this four year programme is a source of more or less continuous dispute between the Commission and the member states. The Fourth Framework Programme (1994–98) saw a significant expansion of the budget (COM (96) 437). Discussions have now begun on the structure of the fifth programme (COM (97) 47) and it is to be hoped that the fifth programme will take on board the recognition of Commission's own studies that more needs to be done in near market research and in developing the 'intangible' base (education and training, intellectual property, etc.). The Commission's own Green Paper and Action Programme on Innovation (COM (95) 688 and COM (96) 589) aim to promote an 'innovation culture' in the EU.

Although EU technology policy is primarily concerned with promoting the international competitiveness of member states' industries, there has been increased interest in using it to foster EU cohesion. There is considerable disparity between the levels of technological capabilities in different member states (Caballero Sanz and Catinat, 1992) and there is a widespread concern, especially in the poorer countries and regions, that the Single Market programme will have intensified those disparities. It is doubtful, however, whether Community R&D resources will be either appropriate or adequate means of addressing this problem; if anything there is a risk that they have widened the differences between member states (CEC, 1997a). More generally, there is still considerable scepticism of the added value of the EU's efforts – critics argue that national research programmes remain to the fore (Petersen, 1996).

9.4 Conclusion

The limited results of the single market initiative and the debatable effects of the framework programmes do not bode well for EU industrial policy. In both areas it could be argued that there was a relatively clear EU role (whether in rule setting or the strategic disbursement of significant financial resources), yet the results have so far been modest. It could be argued that both are essentially long-term 'investments' (in a more competitive market environment and the knowledge base of the European economy). Nonetheless, they do call into question the value of a specific Community industrial policy. Indeed, beyond these programmes the shape of European industrial policy is hard to pin down (in contrast to other areas of EU policy making such as trade, competition or agriculture).

It is true that the Commission has embraced 'competitiveness' as the guiding principle for its industrial policy efforts. However, the substance of such initiatives appears to be largely based on providing information and acting as a forum for the exchange of ideas. It is not obvious that there is any great advantage in conducting these activities at the EU rather than the national or even the local level. Moreover, as the Commission has itself recognized, competitiveness is fundamentally about firms rather than countries or regional blocs.

chapter ten

The Common Agricultural Policy

A. M. EL-AGRAA

Unlike the EFTA, the EU extends its free trade arrangements between member states to agriculture and agricultural products. The term 'agricultural products' is defined as 'the products of the soil, of stockfarming and of fisheries and products of first-state processing directly related to the foregoing' (Article 38), although fisheries has developed into a policy of its own – see Chapter 11. Moreover, the EC dictated that the operation and development of the common market for agricultural products should be accompanied by the establishment of a 'common agricultural policy' among member states (Article 38).

One could ask: why were the common market arrangements extended to agriculture? or why was agriculture (together with transport) singled out for special treatment? Such questions are to some extent irrelevant. According to the General Agreement on Tariffs and Trade (GATT, now WTO, the World Trade Organization – see appendix to Chapter 1 –

> a customs union shall be understood to mean the substitution of a single customs union territory for two or more territories, so that ... duties and other restrictive regulations of commerce are eliminated with respect to substantially all the trade between the constituent territories of the union. (Dam, 1970)

Since agricultural trade constituted a substantial part of the total trade of the founding members, especially so in the case of France, it is quite obvious that excluding agriculture from the EC arrangements would have been in direct contradiction of this requirement (see next section). In any case:

> a programme of economic integration which excluded agriculture stood no chance of success. It is important to appreciate that the Rome Treaty was a delicate balance of national interests of the contracting parties. Let us consider West Germany and France in terms of trade outlets. In the case of West Germany the prospect of free trade in industrial goods, and free access to the French market in particular, was extremely inviting. In the case of France the relative efficiency of her agriculture ... as compared with West Germany held out the prospect that in a free Community agricultural market she would make substantial inroads into the West German market ... Agriculture had therefore to be included. (Swann, 1973, p. 82)

The purpose of this chapter is to discuss the need for singling out agriculture as one of the earliest targets for a common policy; to specify the objectives of the Common Agricultural Policy (CAP); to explain the mechanisms of the CAP; to make an economic evaluation of its implications and to assess the performance of the policy in terms of its practical achievements (or lack of achievements) and in terms of its theoretical viability.

Before tackling these points, it is necessary to give some general background information about agriculture in the EU at the time of the formation of the EC and at a more recent date.

10.1 General background

The economic significance of agriculture in the economies of member staes can be demonstrated in terms of its share in the total labour force and in GNP. Table 10.1 gives this information. The most significant observations that can be made regarding this information are as follows:

1. At the time of the signing of the treaty many people in the original six were dependent on farming as their main source of income; indeed, 25% of the total labour force was employed in agriculture – the equivalent percentage for the United Kingdom was less than 5 and for Belgium was about 9.

2. The agricultural labour force was worse off than most people in the rest of the EC: for example, in France about 26% of the labour force was engaged in agriculture, but for the same year the contribution of this sector to French GDP was about 12%.[1]

3. A rapid fall in both the agricultural labour force and in the share of agriculture in GNP occurred between 1995 and 1975,[2] and this trend is being maintained, albeit at a slower pace.

It is also important to have some information about the area and size distribution of agricultural holdings. This is given in Table 10.2. The most significant factor to note is that in the original six, at the time of the formation of the EC, approximately two-thirds of farm holdings were between 1 and 10 hectares in size. At about the same time, the equivalent figure for the United Kingdom was about two-fifths. Since then there has been a steady increase in the percentage of larger size holdings.

A final piece of important background information that one needs to bear in mind is that, except for Italy and the United Kingdom, the EC farming system is an owner-occupier system rather than one of tenant farming.

10.2 The problems of agriculture

The agricultural sector has been declining in relative importance and those who have remained on the land have continued to receive incomes well below the

Table 10.1 ● Share of agriculture in total labour force and GDP (%).

		Belgium	France	Germany	Italy	Luxemburg	Netherlands	Denmark	Ireland	UK	Greece	Portugal	Spain	Austria	Finland	Sweden
Labour force	1955	9.3	25.9	18.9	39.5	25.0	13.7	25.4	38.8	4.8	–	–	–	–	–	–
	1970	4.1	12.7	5.6	13.1	11.0	5.8	9.0	25.7	2.7	–	–	–	–	–	–
	1975	3.4	10.9	7.1	15.5	6.1	6.5	9.3	23.8	2.7	33.2[b]	–	–	–	–	–
	1981	2.9	8.4	5.8	13.0	5.6	4.5	8.4	18.9[a]	2.8	30.3[a]	–	–	–	–	–
	1986	2.9	7.3	5.3	10.9	4.0	4.8	6.2	15.8	2.6	28.5	21.9	16.1	–	–	–
	1990	2.7	6.1	3.4	9.0	3.2	4.6	5.7	15.0	2.2	25.3	17.8	11.8	–	–	–
	1994	2.5	4.8	3.0	7.9	2.8	4.0	5.7	12.0	2.2	20.8	11.6	9.8	13.3	8.3	3.7
National output	1955	8.1	12.3	8.5	21.6	9.0	12.0	19.2	29.6	5.0	–	–	–	–	–	–
	1970	4.2	6.6	3.3	9.8	3.3	6.1	6.4	16.9	2.7	–	–	8.9	–	–	–
	1975	3.2	5.6	2.9	8.7	3.5	4.7	7.4	18.1	1.9	19.0	7.3	–	–	–	–
	1981	2.5	4.0	1.9	6.4	2.8	4.3	5.0	11.3[a]	2.1	16.3	–	–	–	–	–
	1986	2.0	4.0	2.0	5.0	–	4.0	6.0	14.0	2.0	17.0	10.0	6.0	–	–	–
	1989	2.4	3.3	1.7	4.0	2.4	4.6	4.2	10.5	1.5	16.5	5.5	4.7	–	–	–
	1994	1.6	2.0	0.8	2.6	0.9	3.2	2.5	5.4	0.9	7.5	2.0	2.7	2.2	1.8	1.0

[a] 1980.
[b] 1973.

Source The Agricultural Situation in the Community: 1995 Report, EC Commission, Brussels, and World Bank's World Development Report 1997.

Table 10.2 ● Size distribution of agricultural holdings (% of total).

Year	Hectares	Belgium	Denmark	France	Germany	Greece	Ireland	Italy	Luxemburg	Netherlands	Portugal	Spain	UK
1960	1–<5	48.5	18	26	45	–	20	68	32	38	–	–	29.5
	5–<10	26.5	28	21	25	–	24	19	18	27	–	–	13
	10–<20	18	28	27	21	–	30	8.5	26	23	–	–	16
	20–<50	6	23	21	8	–	21	3	22	11	–	–	22.5
	50+	1	3	5	1	–	5	1.5	2	1	–	–	19
1967	1–<5	37	13	24	40	–	21	69	24	35	–	–	30
	5–<10	27	23	20	23	–	22	18	16	24	–	–	13
	10–<20	24	31.5	26	24	–	30	8	25	27	–	–	15
	20–<50	10	27.5	24	12	–	22	3	32	13	–	–	22
	50+	2	5	6	1	–	5	2	3	1	–	–	20
1973	1–<5	31	12	22	36	72a	15b	68b	21	25	78c	56c	16
	5–<10	23	20	16	20	20.5	16.5	17.5	13	22	12.5	18	13
	10–<20	27	29	24	24	6	31	8.5	20	31	5	12	16
	20–<50	16	32	28	18	1.5	29	4	41	20	2.5	8.5	26
	50+	1	7	10	2	0.0	8.5	2	7	2	2	5.5	29
1980	1–<5	28.4	11.1	20.4	34.5	72	15.2	68.1	19.1	24.0	77.9	55.8	11.8
	5–<10	19.8	17.6	14.6	18.6	19.9	11.9	16.7	10.6	20.2	12.6	18.0	12.5
	10–<20	26.6	26.5	21.1	22.7	6.2	30.3	8.7	14.9	28.9	5.2	12.0	16.0
	20–<50	20.9	34.7	30.4	20.3	1.6	29.8	4.5	38.3	23.9	2.5	8.7	27.1
	50+	4.2	10.1	13.3	3.9	0.2	8.8	2.0	17.0	2.9	1.8	5.5	32.6
1987	1–<5	27.7	1.7	18.2	29.4	69.4	16.1	67.9	18.9	24.9	72.5	53.3	13.5
	5–<10	18.1	16.3	11.7	17.6	20.0	15.2	16.9	9.9	18.4	15.0	19.0	12.4
	10–<20	24.5	25.3	19.1	22.1	7.6	29.2	8.7	12.4	25.0	7.2	12.3	15.3
	20–<50	23.9	39.4	32.8	24.8	2.5	30.5	4.6	32.5	27.3	3.4	9.4	25.4
	50+	5.8	17.2	18.1	6.1	0.5	9.0	1.9	26.2	4.4	1.9	6.0	33.3
1993	1–<5	33.5	2.3	27.2	29.5	67.6	10.5	67.4	25.7	32.7	78.1	54.7	11.3
	5–<10	15.0	16.0	9.7	16.6	20.0	14.3	16.4	8.6	16.5	11.1	17.8	12.9
	10–<20	19.3	23.1	13.0	20.0	9.0	28.8	8.9	8.6	19.1	5.9	12.1	15.8
	20–<50	25.0	36.3	25.8	24.8	2.8	34.8	5.1	22.9	25.9	3.0	9.1	25.7
	50+	7.2	22.3	24.3	9.1	0.6	11.7	2.2	34.3	5.8	1.9	6.3	34.3

Data are not provided for Austria, Finland and Sweden since they are not relevant at this stage.
a Interpolation between the surveys of 1971 and 1977–8.
b 1975.
c 1979.

Source. Calculated from EC Commission, *The Agricultural Situation in The Community*, various reports, and from *Eurostat Review 1977–86*, but the figures have been adjusted to cater for mistakes in the totals.

national average. Governments of most developed countries have, therefore, always found it necessary to practise some sort of control over the market for agricultural commodities through price supports, subsidies to farmers, import levies, import quotas, etc. In this section I shall analyse the background to such practices.

It should be plain to all that the production of many agricultural commodities is subject to forces that lie beyond the direct control of the farmers concerned. Drought, floods, earthquakes and to some extent invasions of pests, for instance, would lead to an actual level of agricultural production far short of that *planned* by the farmers. On the other hand, exceptionally favourable conditions could result in *actual* production being far in excess of that *planned* by farmers. It is therefore necessary to have some theoretical notions about the effects of such deviations between planned and actual agricultural produce on farmers' prices and received incomes.

The predictions of economic theory can be illustrated by reference to a simple diagram. In Figure 10.1, SS represents the range of quantities that farmers plan to supply to the market at various prices in a particular period of time given a certain set of 'market circumstances', for example agricultural input prices, farmers' objectives for production, agricultural technology, etc. DD represents the various quantities that consumers of agricultural products plan to purchase at alternative prices in a specific period of time given a certain set of 'market circumstances', for example consumers' tastes for agricultural products, their incomes, population size and composition, etc. D_1D_1 and D_2D_2 represent two such demand curves, with D_2D_2 being less elastic than D_1D_1.

If consumers' plans and producers' plans actually materialize, P_3 will be the equi-

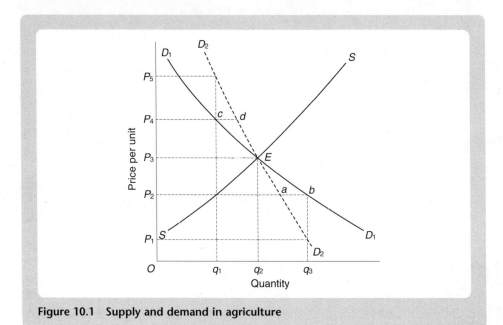

Figure 10.1 Supply and demand in agriculture

librium price which will clear the equilibrium output Oq_2 off the market. As long as this situation is maintained, agricultural prices (represented by P_3) will remain stable and agricultural incomes (represented by the area OP_3Eq_2) will also remain stable. However, actual agricultural production may fall short of, or exceed, the equilibrium planned production Oq_2 for any of the above-mentioned reasons. If a shortage occurs such that actual output is Oq_1, the price will rise above the equilibrium level to P_5 (for D_2D_2) or P_4 (for D_1D_1). In the case of an actual supply of Oq_3, the price will fall to P_1 or P_2 respectively. Therefore, when actual agricultural production deviates from the planned output, fluctuations in agricultural prices will result, such that an excess actual output reduces prices and a shortage in output increases prices. The extent of these price fluctuations is determined by the price elasticity of demand: the more (less) price inelastic the demand curve, the wider (narrower) the margin of price fluctuations.

Moreover, as long as the demand curve does not have a price elasticity of unity, agricultural incomes will fluctuate from the planned level OP_3Eq_2: with a price elastic (inelastic) demand curve, an actual shortage will result in a lower (higher) income for the farmers and an actual excess supply will lead to higher (lower) incomes.

At this point it is appropriate to mention two further characteristics of agriculture in advanced economies. Firstly, as people's incomes rise they tend to spend a smaller proportion of it on agricultural products: the income elasticity of demand is low. (People spend relatively less on food as their incomes rise, therefore they spend even less on agricultural products because a higher proportion of the expenditure on food goes on processing, packaging and presentation.) Hence poor (rich) nations tend to spend a large (small) proportion of their income on agricultural products.

Secondly, because of advances in technology and growth of factors of production, average incomes have been rising in developed economies. Agricultural economists would argue that, for the same reason, agricultural outputs tend to rise at least at the same rate as those of the non-agricultural sector. Once it is realized that consumers would want to spend relatively more on non-agricultural products as their living standards rise (the income elasticity of demand is high for these products), it is inevitable to conclude that there would be a relative tendency for a fall in the demand for farm products. Hence farm incomes would tend to lag behind the incomes of those engaged in the non-farm sector.

Furthermore, once one appreciates that the demand for most agricultural (non-agricultural) products has a low (high) price and income elasticity and that agriculture as an industry is becoming at least as efficient as the national average (because of technological progress in the agricultural sector, the supply curve is moving to the right all the time), then it is easy to understand that agricultural (non-agricultural) price levels and incomes have a tendency to relative decline (rise) with economic growth. This adds a new dimension to the problem, in that, if an 'agricultural stabilization policy' is to be introduced, its aim must not simply be one of stabilizing agricultural prices and incomes, but also of raising agricultural incomes to the national average – if only because policy dictates so.

However, the assumption that agricultural outputs tend to rise at at least the same rate as those of the non-agricultural sector does not stand up to close scrutiny. In the United Kingdom, according to the Cambridge Department of Applied Economics Programme for Growth 12, agricultural productivity grew at a rate of 1.6% per annum compound during the period 1948–68, as against 1.8% for manufacturing. In the United Kingdom, manufacturing productivity growth has been low and agricultural productivity growth, because of the form of policy, high. In the rest of Europe the disparity will be much greater. Since agriculture started as a low-productivity industry, the disparity has indeed worsened – the impact of science and technology on farming is less than on manufacturing for two reasons: firstly, agriculture is characterized by decreasing returns to scale while manufacturing is characterized at least by constant returns to scale; secondly, there are severe institutional constraints on increasing the size of farms, and therefore technology can make its impact only from specialization within the existing farm structure. Economies of specialization are limited within this constraint and furthermore there are offsetting losses of economies of joint production (from rotations, etc.) which are more pronounced in agriculture than elsewhere and are virtually lost from specialization. Hence the problem of agricultural incomes stems from declining agricultural productivity (in comparison with manufacturing productivity) rather than from inelastic demand for agricultural products. In any case, the elasticity has not been so low once population growth is taken into account. (For a forceful and detailed explanation of these points, see Bowers, 1972.)

This is a more convincing argument in that it suggests that the setting of reasonable agricultural prices, given the declining relative efficiency of agriculture, ensures declining agricultural incomes. Hence, the way to increasing agricultural productivity is to encourage the marginal agricultural labour to seek alternative employment. This view is consistent with the structural problem of the EC, where declining farm incomes are attributed to the fact that labour does not flow out of agriculture quickly enough (trapped resources with low salvage values).

The above suggests why most advanced mixed economies have been adopting some kind of agricultural support policies. Other arguably more important considerations include historical factors, strategic considerations and the strengths of the agricultural lobby; indeed, it is commonly accepted that the latter is the main determining factor of these apparently uneconomic policies.

10.3 Agricultural support policies

With the foregoing analysis and observations, we are in a position to attempt a specification of the necessary elements in an agricultural policy and to point out the difficulties associated with such a policy.

In most advanced mixed economies where living standards have been rising, agricultural policies were introduced with the aim of achieving the following:

1. As a minimum requirement, avoid impeding the *natural* process of transferring

resources from the agricultural sector to the non-agricultural sector of the economy, and if necessary promote this process.

2. Aim at protecting the incomes of those who are occupied in the agricultural sector. The definition of the farm sector raises a number of problems, for instance:

> should one's policy be devised to guarantee prosperity to any who might wish at some future date to enter agriculture – and moreover to assure a reasonable rate of return for any amount of capital that they may wish to invest in farming? Or should one's policy be geared to those already in the industry who have made resource allocation decisions based on expectations of the future which governments then feel under an obligation to realise? (Josling, 1969, p. 176)

3. Aim at some kind of price stability, since agriculture forms the basis of living costs and wages and is therefore the basis of industrial costs.

4. Make provision for an adequate agricultural sector since security of good supplies is essential for a nation.[3]

5. Ensure the maintenance of agriculture as a family business, and the maintenance of some population in rural villages.

Unfortunately these objectives are, to a large extent, mutually contradictory. Any policy which aims at providing adequate environmental conditions, secure food supplies and agricultural incomes equal to the national average interferes with the economy's natural development. Moreover, the provision of stable farm incomes, let alone rising farm incomes, is not compatible with the provision of stable agricultural prices. This point can be illustrated by reference to Figure 10.1.

Suppose that $D_1 D_1$ is a demand curve which has unit price elasticity along its entire range. In order to keep farmers' incomes constant it would be necessary to operate along this curve, keeping farmers' incomes equal to $OP_3 Eq_2$. If agricultural production deviates from Oq_2, the following will ensue:

1. When an output is equal to Oq_3, the authority in charge of the policy must purchase ab in order to make certain that the price level falls only to P_2 rather than P_1, therefore ensuring that farmers' incomes remain at the predetermined level.

2. When output is equal to Oq_1 the authority must sell cd in order to achieve the price level P_4 rather than P_5.

Hence a policy of income stability can be achieved only if the price level is allowed to fluctuate, even though the required level of fluctuation in this case is less than that dictated by the operation of the free market forces.

On the other hand, a policy of maintaining constant price levels (constant P_3) will give farmers higher incomes when output is Oq_3 (by $q_2 q_3 \times OP_3$) since the authority will have to purchase the excess supply at the guaranteed price, and lower incomes when output is Oq_1 (by $q_1 q_2 \times OP_3$). Therefore, a policy of price stability will guarantee income fluctuations in such a manner that higher (lower) agricultural outputs will result in higher (lower) farmers' incomes.

This throws light on another aspect of agricultural polices: if average farm prices are set at too high a level this will encourage farmers to increase production, since at the guaranteed price they can sell as much as they can produce. This, in effect, results in a perfectly elastic supply curve at price level P_3. Under such circumstances, an excess supply of these commodities could result. This is a point that has to be borne in mind when assessing the CAP.

10.4 EC member policies

Prior to the formation of the EC, member countries (except for the Netherlands) had adopted different practices in their agricultural stabilization policies. This is an appropriate point to turn to a discussion of these policies.

Agricultural policies in Western Europe as a whole since the Second World War have been rather complicated, but a substantial element of these policies had been the support of prices received by farmers for their produce. In this respect, a variety of methods have been practised:

1. *Deficiency payments schemes* (supplements to market-determined prices): these refer to policies of guaranteed farm prices which the government ensures by means of deficiency payments. These prices become the farmers' planning prices. This system was used in the United Kingdom before it joined the EC; however, the United Kingdom was moving away from this system for budgetary reasons, not as a preparation for joining the EC.

2. *Variable levies or import quota systems*: these systems are concerned with policies which effectively impose threshold prices and charge levies on imports equal to the difference between world prices and the threshold prices.

3. *Market control systems*: these aim at limiting the quantities of agricultural produce that actually reach the market. This can be achieved by ensuring that the produce is marketed by single private authorities (agencies) or by certain government departments. The quantity that is not allowed to reach the market can

    either be destroyed, stored (to be released when prices rise), exported, donated to low income countries or needy groups within the home economy, or converted into another product which does not compete directly with the original one. Examples of this last course of action are 'breaking' of eggs for use as egg powder and rendering some cereals and vegetables unfit for human consumption (usually by adding a dye or fish oil) but suitable for animal feed. (Ritson, 1973, p. 99)

    This system was widely used in the original Six.

4. *Direct income payments*: this term describes schemes whereby incomes are transferred to the farmers without these bearing any relationship to the level of output. The nearest to this system was the Swedish system.

5. *Non-price policies*: a miscellaneous set of policies such as import subsidies on both current and capital inputs, output increasing measures (R&D), export sub-

sidies and production quotas. Of course, input subsidies do add to the effective protection afforded to agriculture.

Let us now turn to an analytical consideration of these schemes. The analysis of (1), (2) and (4) is slightly different from that illustrated by Figure 10.1 in that one needs to deal with products which compete with imports. This is because most Western European countries, specially the original Six, were net importers of most agricultural products at the time of the inception of the EC; the nearest they came to self-sufficiency was in livestock.

Assume (unrealistically in the context of the EU, since Western Europe is a large consumer) that the level of imports does not influence the world prices of agricultural commodities and that, allowing for transport costs and quality differentials, the import price level is equal to the domestic price. Then consider the different support systems with reference to Figure 10.2.

In Figure 10.2, P_w is the world price, O_{q1} is the domestic production level and q_1q_4 is the level of imports given free trade conditions. When a deficiency payment scheme is in operation, P_d becomes the guaranteed farmer price. This leads to an increase in domestic production (from O_{q1} to O_{q2}) which guarantees the farmer a deficiency payment of P_wP_dbc (equal to $(P_d - P_w) \times O_{q2}$) and which results in foreign exchange savings of q_1acq_2. On the assumption that the supply curve is a reflection of the marginal social opportunity cost of resources used in production (for a detailed discussion of this see El-Agraa and Jones, 1981) it is possible to make some significant remarks regarding this new farm revenue.

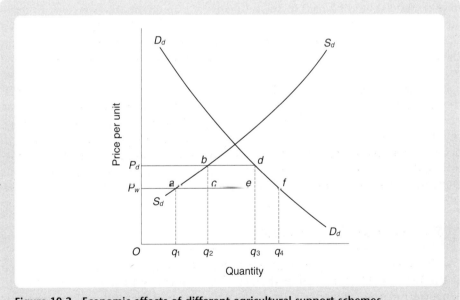

Figure 10.2 Economic effects of different agricultural support schemes

The area q_1abq_2, in an extremely simple analysis, approximates the value of the extra inputs attracted into agriculture by the deficiency payment policy. The area P_wP_dba represents the additional producer's surplus, or economic rent.[4] This can be thought of as an income transfer in favour of the farming sector.[5] Area abc represents the net loss to the society for adopting this policy; this is because the price for the consumer remains at P_w and therefore the level of imports is equal to cf.

When a variable levy scheme is in operation, the relevant farmer price equals the threshold price so that P_d becomes the price facing both farmers and consumers. Hence, the effects on the agricultural producing sector are exactly the same as in the previous case. However, the foreign exchange savings would now be equal to q_1acq_2 plus q_3ef_4 due to the fall in consumption by q_3q_4 (from O_{q4} to O_{q3}) – imports fall to bd. The loss of the policy is therefore equal to the areas abc and def. Area $bced$ (the revenue accruing from the levy) represents a transfer from the consumers to the government.

Under extremely restrictive assumptions, it can be demonstrated that the operation of a quota system equal to q_2q_3 produces the same result as a variable levy of the same equivalence.[6] There is another problem here relating to who gains the area $bced$, which in the variable levy system represents government revenue: if the government assumes responsibility or if the importers are well organized there is no problem, but if the foreign exporters are well organized they can absorb this area in the form of economic rent or excess profit – see El-Agraa (1989b).

In a purely static theoretical analysis, direct income subsidies have no economic costs (see Johnson, 1965a), particularly since they do not harm the consumer or the foreign supplier. However, for these subsidies to be strictly neutral in their economic impact, they should be paid in such a manner as to 'allow the recipients to leave farming without prejudice to their income from the payment scheme'.[7] Moreover, in the real world costs will be incurred in the process of dispersing the income, and there is also the question of where the money to finance the subsidies should come from.

From the foregoing analysis it is evident that the income transfer system, given the stated provisos, is the most efficient mechanism for farm support and that the variable levy or import quota system is the least efficient in this respect.[8] This is because the income subsidies and deficiency payment schemes allow the consumer to decide according to the cheapest international prices available, while the variable levy and import quota systems interfere with both producers and consumers. This comparison should be borne in mind when reading the conclusions of this chapter.

10.5 Objectives of the CAP

Owing to the variety of agricultural support policies that existed in Western Europe at the time of the formation of the EC, it was necessary to subject agriculture to equal treatment in all member states. Equal treatment of coal and steel (both necessary inputs for industry and therefore of the same significance as agriculture) was already under way through the ECSC and the importance of agriculture meant that equal treatment here was vital.

The objectives of the CAP are clearly defined in Article 39 of the Treaty. They are as follows:

1. 'To increase agricultural productivity by promoting technical progress and by ensuring the rational development of agricultural production and the optimum utilisation of all factors of production, in particular labour'.

2. To ensure thereby 'a fair standard of living for the agricultural community, in particular by increasing the individual earnings of persons engaged in agriculture'.

3. 'To stabilise markets'.

4. 'To provide certainty of supplies'.

5. 'To ensure supplies to consumers at reasonable prices'.

The Treaty also specifies that in:

> working out the Common Agricultural Policy, and any special methods which this may involve, account shall be taken of:
> (i)   the particular nature of agricultural activity, which results from agriculture's social structure and from structural and natural disparities between the various agricultural regions;
> (ii) the need to effect the appropriate adjustments by degrees;
> (iii) the fact that, in the member states, agriculture constitutes a sector closely linked with the economy as a whole.

The Treaty further specifies that in order to attain the objectives set out above a common organization of agricultural markets shall be formed:

> This organisation shall take one of the following forms depending on the product concerned:
> (a) common rules as regards competition;
> (b) compulsory co-ordination of the various national marketing organisations; or
> (c) a European organisation of the market.

Moreover, the common organization so established:

> may include all measures required to achieve the objectives set out … in particular price controls, subsidies for the production and distribution of the various products, stock-piling and carry-over systems and common arrangements for stabilisation of imports and exports.
>   The common organisation shall confine itself to pursuing the objectives set out … and shall exclude any discrimination between producers and consumers within the Community.
>   Any common policy shall be based on common criteria and uniform methods of calculation.

Finally, in order to enable the common organization to achieve its objectives, 'one or more agricultural orientation and guarantee funds may be set up'.

The remaining articles (41–47) deal with some detailed considerations relating to the objectives and the common organisation.

The true objectives of the CAP were established after the Stresa conference in 1958 which was convened in accordance with the Treaty. The objectives were in the spirit of the Treaty:

(i) to increase farm incomes not only by a system of transfers from the non-farm population through a price support policy, but also by the encouragement of rural industrialisation to give alternative opportunities to farm labour;

(ii) to contribute to overall economic growth by allowing specialisation within the Community and eliminating artificial market distortions;

(iii) preserving the family farm and ... ensuring that structural and price policies go hand in hand.

It can be seen, therefore, that the CAP was not preoccupied simply with the implementation of common prices and market supports; it also included a commitment to encourage the structural improvement of farming, particularly when the former measures did not show much success (see the later section on assessment). Regarding the latter point, the main driving force has been the Mansholt Plan of 1968.[9] Dr Sicco Mansholt, who was the Agricultural Commissioner at the time, emphasized that market supports by themselves would not solve the agricultural problem. The plan, which basically relates to the guidance aspects of the CAP, proposed the following principal measures:

(a) A first set of measures concerns the structure of agricultural production, and contains two main elements:

(i) One group of measures, varying widely in character, must be taken to bring about an appropriate reduction in the number of persons employed in agriculture. Older people will have to be offered a supplementary annual income allowance if they agree to retire and thereby release land; younger farmers should be enabled to change over to non-farming activities; the children of farmers, finally, should be given an education which enables them to choose an occupation other than farming, if they so desire. For the two latter categories, new jobs will have to be created in many regions. These efforts at reducing manpower should be brought to bear with particular force on one group of persons within agriculture, namely, those who own their farm businesses, inasmuch as the structural reform of farms themselves ... largely depends upon the withdrawal of a large number of these people from agriculture.

(ii) Secondly, far-reaching and co-ordinated measures should be taken with a view to the creation of agricultural (farming) enterprises of adequate economic dimensions.[10] If such enterprises are to be set up and kept running, the land they need will have to be made available to them on acceptable terms; this will require an active and appropriate agrarian policy.

(b) A second group of measures concerns markets, with the double purpose of improving the way they work and of adjusting supply more closely to demand:

(i) Here a major factor will be a cautious price policy, and this will be all the more effective as the enterprises react more sensitively to the points offered by the market.

(ii) A considerable reduction of the area of cultivated land will work in the same direction.

(iii) Better information will have to be made available to all market parties (products, manufacturers and dealers), producers will have to accept stricter discipline and there will have to be some concentration of supply. Product councils and groupings of product councils will have to be set up at European level to take over certain responsibilities in this field.

(c) In the case of farmers who are unable to benefit from the measures described, it may prove necessary to provide personal assistance not tied either to the volume of output or to the employment of factors of production. This assistance should be payable within specified limits defined in the light of regional factors and the age of the persons concerned.

After a lengthy discussion the Council issued three directives (72/159–72/161) in April 1972: Directive 72/159 allowed member nations to support their farmers' modernization through grants or subsidized interest rates on the condition that these farms were capable of generating income levels comparable with those of other local occupations; Directive 72/160 permitted member nations to extend lump-sum payments or annuities to farm workers aged between 55 and 65 years to lure them into leaving the industry; Directive 72/161 aimed at encouraging member countries to establish 'socio-economic guidance services' to entice farm workers to retrain and relocate. However, although the precise method of implementation, itself not mandatory, of these directives was left to the discretion of national governments, about a quarter of the necessary outlay (65% for Ireland and Italy) would be borne by the CAP guidance section. Thus, these directives were in the spirit of the Mansholt Plan.

Yet the EC expenditure on the structural aspects of the CAP remained very small. Indeed, the annual grants under all of the three directives over the 1975–84 decade averaged no more than about 100 million ECU (at 1986 prices) for about 4 million farms of less than 10 hectares in area in 1975. However, these directives were replaced by a new ten-year structural plan in 1985. The rationale for this was the realization by then that the surpluses generated at the time did not justify a policy of trying to solve the plight of small farms through increased output, and that the slower rates of economic growth being experienced then made it more difficult for farmers to find alternative employment. Thus the new plan shied away from fundamental changes in the farm structure and put emphasis on cost reductions and quality improvement, and at the same time the aim of achieving incomes for the sector comparable with those in non-agricultural occupations was abandoned altogether. In other words, the aim was no longer to transform small farms into larger ones to enable them to obtain higher incomes, but rather to make it possible for small farmers to survive with a reasonable quality of living. In support of the plan, an average of 420 million ECUs per annum was to be provided over the 1985–94 period and a further annual sum of 270 million ECUs was to be made available for schemes aimed at improving agricultural marketing and processing. However, total budgetary expenditure on guidance was 3.7 billion ECUs in 1996, or about 4.5% of the total budget and under 10% of total expenditure on the CAP.

10.6 The CAP price support mechanism

The original CAP machinery did not apply to every product and, in the cases where it did, it varied from one product to another – see Table 10.3. Although major changes have since been introduced (see below), the mechanism still applies to some products and sheds light on some of the disastrous consequences of the policy earlier on; hence it is instructive to give it some consideration.

The farmers' income support is guaranteed by regulating the market so as to reach a price high enough to achieve this objective. The domestic price is partly maintained by various protective devices. These prevent cheaper world imports from influencing the EC domestic price level. But, in addition, certain steps are taken for official support buying within the EC, so as to eliminate from the market any actual excess supply that might be stimulated by the guaranteed price level. These surpluses may be disposed of in the manner described in the section on the policies of the EC member nations.

More specifically, the basic features of the system can be represented by that originally devised for cereals, the first agricultural product for which a common policy was established.

A 'target' price is set on an annual basis and is maintained at a level which the product is expected to achieve on the market in the area where cereal is in shortest supply – Duisburg in the Ruhr Valley. The target price is not a producer price since it includes the costs of transport to dealers and storers. The target price is variable, in that it is allowed to increase on a monthly basis from August to July in order to allow for storage costs throughout the year.

The 'threshold price' is calculated in such a way that when transport costs incurred within the EC are added, cereals collected at Rotterdam (Europe's major port) should sell at Duisburg at a price equal to or slightly higher than the target price, the consequence being that adding the levy and transport costs to Duisburg would make it unprofitable to sell cereals anywhere in the EC at less than the target price. An import levy is calculated on a daily basis and is equal to the margin between the lowest priced consignment entering the EC on the day – allowing for transport costs to the major port (Rotterdam) – and the threshold price. This levy is then charged on all imports allowed into the EC on that day. All this information is illustrated in Figure 10.3.

It is quite obvious that, as long as the EC is experiencing excess demand for this product, the market price is held above the target price by the imposition of import levies. Moreover, import levies would be unnecessary if world prices happened to be above the threshold price since in this case the market price might exceed the target price.

If target prices result in an excess supply of the product in the EC (see Figure 10.3), the threshold price becomes ineffective in terms of the objective of a constant annual target price and support buying becomes necessary. A 'basic intervention price' is then introduced for this purpose. This is fixed for Duisburg at about 7% or 8% below the target price. Similar prices are then calculated for several locations

Table 10.3 ⬭ Price and market regimes for agricultural products.

Product	Target price	Guide price	Norm price	Basic price	Intervention price	Withdrawal price	Minimum price	Production aid	Deficiency payment	Threshold price	Sluice-gate price	Reference price	Variable levy	Supplementary levy	Customs duty	Export refund
Common wheat	x				x					x			x			x
Durum wheat	x				x			x[a]		x			x			x
Barley	x				x					x			x			x
Rye	x				x					x			x			x
Maize	x				x					x			x			x
Rice	x				x					x			x			x
Sugar: white	x				x					x			x			x
beet							x									
Oilseeds: colza	x				x			x								
rape	x				x			x								
sunflower	x				x			x								
soya beans		x						x								
linseed		x						x								
castor		x					x	x								
cotton								x								
Peas and field beans	x[b]						x	x								
Dried fodder								x	x							
Fiber flax and hemp								x								
Milk products:																
butter					x					x			x			x
smp					x					x			x			x
cheese[c]					x					x			x			x
Beef: live		x														
meat					x								x		x	x
Pigmeat				x	x						x			x		x
Eggs											x			x		x
Poultry											x			x		x
Fish		x			x[d]	x						x			x	x
Silkworms								x								
Fresh fruit and vegetables				x		x						x			x	x
Live plants															x	
Olive oil	x				x			x	x[e]	x		x				x
Wine		x			x[f]							x			x	x
Hops								x						x		
Seeds for sowing								x				x[g]				
Tobacco			x		x			x							x	x

[a] Certain regions only; [b] activating price; [c] Italy only; [d] sardines and anchovies only;
[e] olive oil consumer subsidy; [f] wine storage contracts and distillation; [g] hybrid maize only.
Source. Adapted from R. Fennel (1979), p. 106.

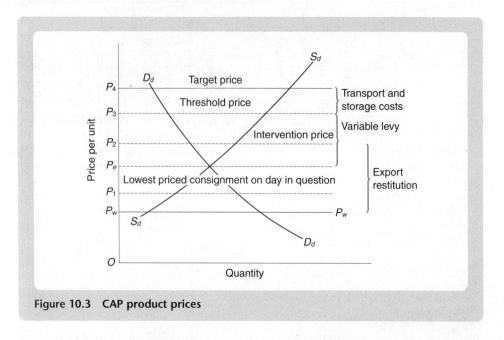

Figure 10.3   CAP product prices

within the EC on the basis of costs of transport to Duisburg. National intervention agencies are then compelled to buy whatever is offered to them (provided that it conforms to standard) of the 'proper' product at the relevant intervention price. The intervention price is therefore a minimum guaranteed price.

Moreover, an export subsidy or *restitution* is paid to EC exporters. This is determined by the officials and is influenced by several factors (world prices, amount of excess supply, expected trends) and is generally calculated as the difference between the EC intervention price (P_2) and the world price (P_w).

For the latest position on this mechanism and the new methods that the EC has introduced to tackle the problems of excess supply, see the section below on assessment.

10.7 The green money

The various agricultural support prices were fixed by the Council in units of account. For each member country there is a 'green rate' at which the support prices were translated into national prices. The unit of account originally had a gold content equal to a US dollar, but in 1973 was linked to the 'joint float'; since the introduction of the European Monetary System (EMS) in March 1979 it has been given a value equal to the European currency unit (ECU) called a 'green ECU'. This implies that if a member country devalues (revalues) its currency, its farm prices expressed in terms of the national currency rise (fall). It should also be noted that the scope for changing green currency rates (allowed because of the desire of member states to stabilize farm prices in the face of exchange rate fluctuations at the time) gives the member countries scope for altering internal farm prices *independently* of price changes determined at the annual review for the EC as a whole. In August 1969 the French franc was devalued by 11.11%, which obviously disturbed the common farm price arrangements in favour of the French farmers, and the rise in their price level would obviously have stimulated their farm production and aggravated the excess supply problem (see next section). Moreover, the devaluation of the unit of account would not have improved matters in such a situation, since it would have depressed the price level for the farmer in the rest of the EC, even though it would have nullified the effects of the devaluation of the French franc. Therefore, a more complicated policy was adopted: the French intervention price was reduced by the full amount of the devaluation so as to eliminate the unfair benefit to the French farmer; French imports from and exports to the rest of the EC were to be restored by asking France to give import subsidies and levy duties on its exports to compensate for the effects of the devaluation. The term 'monetary and compensatory amounts' (MCAs) was coined to describe this system of border taxes and subsidies. Since then, the MCA system has become general in application and more complicated with the changes in the rates of exchange of the currencies of other EC members.

Even though the EC persisted in announcing its intention to discontinue the MCA system, it has not completely succeeded in doing so. It did make an attempt through the introduction of the 'switchover mechanism' in 1984, which was meant, *inter alia*, to neutralize exchange rate changes by tying the common support price levels to the strongest EC currency, the German mark, starting from 1984, but this was to no avail. Also, although it did suspend the MCA system altogether in 1993 with the introduction of the single market, the widening of fluctuations within the Exchange Rate Mechanism to ±15 (see Chapters 5 and 16) has not helped. However, if everything goes according to plan, the introduction of a single currency by 1999 (or 1997) would ensure its demise. The system therefore warrants some further explanation. It should be remembered that one of the basic aims of the CAP is to establish a uniform set of agricultural prices for all the participating nations. Since these prices are expressed in units of account, when a member country decides to devalue its currency (i.e. its official rate), the prices of agricultural products will rise in terms of the domestic currency by the full percentage of devaluation (given a simple analysis). This increase in the domestic prices will distort trade between the member nations and its effect on intra-EC trade can be fully eliminated (again in a simple analysis) by imposing equivalent taxes on the export of these products and by granting equivalent subsidies to the imports of the products. This in effect amounts to operating a system of multiple exchange rates. On the other hand, when a member of the EC decides to revalue its currency, it will have to tax intra-EC imports and subsidize intra-EC exports to eliminate a fall in agricultural prices. Since the 'green rates' of exchange – known as 'representative rates' – are officially used for converting prices expressed in units of account into national currencies –

official rates – it follows that, when the 'green rate' deviates from the official rate, these taxes on, and subsidies to, intra-EC traded agricultural products are used to maintain uniform agricultural prices. This is the MCA system which, once adopted by a member of the EC, will remain until that country is able to restore its 'green rate' to that on the foreign exchange market.

The MCA system is therefore basically simple; it became complicated because of several factors. First, the French devaluation of 1969 was followed almost immediately by the German revaluation and the French and the Germans asked for the adoption of MCAs which were to be eliminated within periods of two and three years respectively. Secondly, the EC agreed to these arrangements and met part of the cost, hence increasing the financial burden of the CAP. Thirdly, the later weakness of the US dollar was used as a reason by the EC to introduce MCAs in order to protect its farmers from 'worldwide unfair competition – the EC claimed this was because the United States, being a net exporter of agricultural products, was able to determine the world price level for agricultural products and this was in spite of the fact that the unit of account was fixed in terms of dollars. Finally, the floating of the pound sterling in 1972 and the Italian lira in 1973, which led to the sinking of both, encouraged the use of MCAs to protect the stronger EC currencies from agricultural price increases.

The reader who is particularly interested in this area of the CAP is advised to read Irving and Fearne (1975), Josling and Harris (1976), Mackel (1978), Hu (1979), Fennell (1979) and Marsh and Swanney (1980, 1985).

10.8 Financing the CAP

Intervention, export restitution and the MCA system need to be financed. The finance is supplied by the EC central fund called FEOGA (Fonds Européen d'Orientation et de Garantie Agricole), in English the European Agricultural Guidance and Guarantee Fund (EAGGF), so named to incorporate the two basic elements of the CAP: support and guidance. At the time of inception of the CAP it was expected that the revenues collected from the imposition of extra area import levies would be sufficient to finance FEOGA. Since then, the rapid rise in agricultural output has led to a reduction in EC imports and therefore to a reduction in receipts from levies. Also, the cost of the support system has increased beyond expectation (see the McDougall Report (CEC, 1977c) and Chapter 15). Thus the EC deemed it necessary to make provision for direct budgetary contributions from national governments on the basis of a formula which is discussed in some detail in the McDougall Report. However, in 1970 the EC switched to a system of own resources, which became fully operative in 1980 – see Chapter 15.

In order to put the expenditures in their proper perspective, it should be noted that the general budget of the EU makes provision for the administrative expenses of the European Parliament, the Council of Ministers, the ECJ, the ECSC, and the European Development Fund (EDF), and for the administrative costs and the other operational expenditures of the Commission, which include the Agricultural Guarantee and Guidance Funds, the Social Fund, the Regional Development Fund and the structural funds. For the financial year 1996 the budget amounted to some 82 billion ECU or, roughly, $72 billion, of which agricultural expenditure accounted for about 54%. The revenue for agricultural levies is estimated at about 2 billion ECU, approximately 2.4% of the total budget – see Figure 10.4 for trends of EAGGF guidance expenditures and the 1995 commodity breakdown.

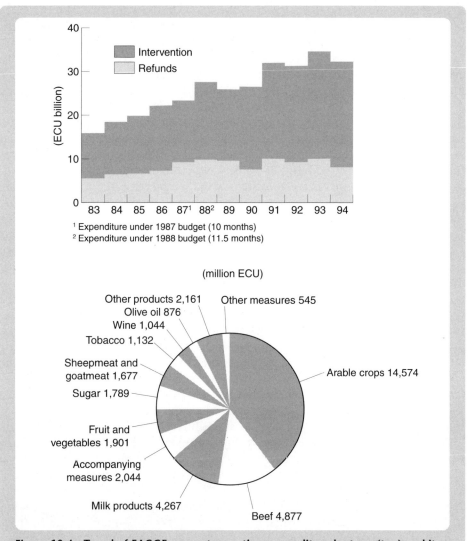

Figure 10.4 Trend of EAGGF guarantee section expenditure by type (top) and its sectoral breakdown by budget appropriations in 1995 (bottom)

10.9 Assessment

Judged in terms of its own objectives, the CAP would seem to have had several successes. Firstly, the various agricultural support systems that existed prior to the formation of the EC have been liquidated and a common, although highly complicated, system has been achieved. Secondly, to a qualified extent, intra-EU free trade in agricultural products has been accomplished through the removal of all intra-EU trade impediments. Thirdly, the EU as a whole has become more or less self-sufficient in farm products going to the final consumer (in 1993–94, the EU of fifteen members had self-sufficiency rates of 12%, 13% and 105% in, respectively, cereals, sugar and wine, while the EC of twelve had rates between 101% and 211% except for wine and sheep meat and goat meat, with, respectively, 97% and 87%) even though the Community still depends a great deal on imported agricultural raw materials, for example, fertilisers and animal feed. Fourthly, Directive 75/268, which deals with mountain and hill farming in certain disadvantaged areas, was adopted in 1975 and this amounted to a recognition of the fact that special provision would have to be made for these areas. Fifthly, it should be mentioned that agriculture has experienced a high rate of technical progress and increased productivity and that the CAP has resulted in stability of EU agricultural markets and in increasing self-supply; these achievements are consistent with the objectives set out in Article 39. Finally, it could be claimed that the CAP has achieved much progress in increasing the size of farm holdings and in reducing the number of farm businesses – see Table 10.2.

On the debit side, the CAP has failed to achieve any progress on the structural aspect of encouraging farmers to seek alternative occupations (even though the drift from land to industry is a natural process), that is the reason why this objective was finally abandoned. Moreover, the CAP has been the cause of embarrassing surpluses: the butter and beef mountains; the wine lakes; earlier on, the grain and sugar surpluses; more recently, the milk lake. However, it should be noted here that a 'co-responsibility levy' was introduced in 1977, the purpose of which was to hold the farmers partly responsible for the surpluses they had created. The CAP has had the effect of making the prosperous farmers richer, but has not helped the poorer farmers as it has retained them in the industry through high intervention price levels. Finally, the CAP has failed to provide reasonable and stable prices for the consumer; indeed, the initial prices were set at the high German level.

These successes and failures have to be examined more carefully. *Firstly*, most economists would agree that the embarrassing surpluses are caused by the high level of intervention prices. This of course has serious consequences for the financing of the policy.

However, it should be added here that the member nations of the EC agreed on 31 March 1984 on a package which reduced the EC's common farm prices by 0.5% and relied on a system of quotas to restrict milk production from 103 million tonnes in 1983 to 99.2 million and 98.4 million tonnes in 1984 and 1985 respectively; thereafter it was to be pegged for a further three years. Moreover, the quotas which had already been applied to sugar beet were extended to other surplus products such as cereals, oilseeds and processed tomatoes. In order to reduce wine production, new vine plantings were banned until 1990. Finally, various production and consumption subsidies to livestock, butter, fruit and vegetables were reduced, and the MCAs were to be phased out over four years. It should be added that the EC Council of February 1988 decided that the annual growth rate of EAGGF guarantee expenditure shall not exceed 70–80% (later specified as 74%) of the annual growth rate of EC GNP. New agricultural stabilisers are to be introduced. For example, the threshold for cereals was set at 155–160 million tonnes per year for the period 1988–91, and an additional co-responsibility levy of 3% was charged at the beginning of each marketing year to ensure that agricultural expenditure stays within specified limits. Similar quotas are set for oil seeds and protein products, existing stabilizers will continue for olive, oil and cotton, the quota system for milk will be extended for another three years, etc. What is significant, however, is that the Council agreed to adopt provisions to limit supply by withdrawing agricultural land from production. This 'set-aside' programme is devised to complement policy measures, and will be compulsory for member countries but optional for producers. The EU has therefore made very serious attempts to tackle the problems of surplus. (The reader should note that these developments and their implications are discussed more fully in Chapter 15.)

Moreover, the EU has recently reinforced this approach. In June 1992, a further package of reforms (known as the MacShary reform package; Ray MacShary of Ireland was the EC Commissioner in charge of agriculture at the time), the central element of which is the linking of price cuts for the main products to the withdrawal of land from production, was adopted:

1. Cereal prices will be reduced by 29% over three years starting in 1993–94. The reduction is expected to bring EU prices down to current world prices. However, a minimum import price would be set for cereals to maintain a margin of about 40% of EU preference. In addition, an agreed amount of arable land will be taken out of cereal production each year in line with forecast market needs; 15% in the first year – this does not apply to farmers with 20 hectares below the EU average.

   Farmers will receive full and direct compensation for loss of earnings resulting from price cuts, but the 15% reduction in land under cereals, oilseeds and protein crops is a precondition for the receipt of compensation. The payments will be in the form of direct income support and will be calculated on the basis of the average yields in each farming region. Compensation will also be paid on the same basis for land taken out of production. Small farmers qualify for full compensation without setting aside any land.

   Thus, the cereal sector will be subject to the same conditions set for oilseeds, processed vegetables, olive oil and tobacco.

2. Beef prices will be cut by 15% over three years. Farmers raising beef cattle on open grazing land will receive extra per capita premiums; the idea is to discour-

age intensive factory farming since premiums will not be available for farmers raising cattle in stalls, but they will be able to offset the drop in beef prices through the use of cheaper cereals as animal feed. Also, existing premiums paid for bulls, steers and suckling cows will be increased.

3. These measures will be accompanied by others aimed at developing more environmentally friendly types of agriculture (using less pesticides and fertilisers), financing afforestation programmes, and ensuring the management of land taken out of production.

4. The EU will also co-finance an improved early retirement scheme for farmers aged 55 years or over who make way for younger people.

Since these reforms were for a number of years, the prices for 1993–96 simply reinforced these aims. For example, for 1996–97 prices were frozen across the board at the 1995 level except for rice (fixed in December 1995) and fibre flax (pending restructuring of the common organization of its market).

The EU has claimed that these measures mark a watershed in the reform of the CAP not only because they apply the previous sensible reforms to the most important agricultural products but also because they come under the category of 'compulsory expenditures', i.e. payment for them comes first (see Chapters 2 and 15). One should add, however, that these reforms did not come entirely from within; indeed many analysts would argue that it has been the persistent pressure by the United States that has been the driving force: the United States had linked the successful conclusion of the on-going Uruguay round of GATT negotiations to a 50% cut in EC agricultural subsidies; the EC has so far offered a cut of 25%.

Secondly:

> low earnings in agriculture are the consequence of low alternative earnings arising from disparities in education levels in rural areas. But in these circumstances any price policy based on some concept of giving to farm resources the ability to achieve parity incomes with the non-farm population is doomed to failure. Higher prices are largely translated into the purchase of more inputs from the non-farm sector (fertilisers and machinery) and into the values of assets the supply of which [are] fixed (mainly land). Input suppliers and landlords gain, but the new entrants get no benefit. This accounts for the seemingly insatiable appetite of farm programmes for public money and the desire to hide the appropriations in the form of higher food costs even if the same transfer could be made more efficiently by direct payments. Agriculture adjusts in size to the level of support it is given; price support policies have never influenced long-run resources returns appreciably. The implication of this is that the only way to raise farm incomes is to control the inflow of resources into agriculture, or to increase the level of education in rural areas. (Josling, 1969, pp. 268–9)

Thirdly, the MCA system which most observers had thought was a temporary phenomenon became very well established in the mechanism of the CAP; indeed, the MCA system and the 'green money' came to be used in a very sophisticated way to enable farmers to accommodate their national interests within the CAP (Ritson and Tangermann, 1979). The MCA system seemed a positive deterrent to intra-EC trade – traders had great difficulty in predicting MCAs and presumably offset this by adding them to their margins. This had created unequal prices and justifiably led to the use of the term 'the uncommon market'. Although now close to its demise, the spirit of the system still lives – see above.

In global terms, the CAP has been seen as undermining the interests of the United States and the Third World. This point has two elements to it: firstly, by disposing of surpluses at subsidised prices to countries such as the former USSR, the EU is depriving the developing world of potential export earnings and the United States of real income (since EU sales are achieved at the cost of American exports); secondly, and most importantly, the EU, in protecting its own agriculture, is competing unfairly against imports from these same countries. Indeed, some economists would argue that under free international trade conditions, Western Europe would have no comparative advantage in agriculture and that the industry would virtually disappear under such circumstances. However, this is not entirely correct since it could be argued that even with perfectly free agricultural trade there would be a cost advantage in providing nearly all dairy products, much meat (grass based) and a good deal of cereals, fruit and vegetables within the EU.

A possible response to these claims is that 'it would be churlish to question such a goal of prosperous agriculture contributing to economic growth in the community' (Josling, 1969, p. 268), particularly in a world where agriculture is a highly protected industry, as is the case in the EU's most eminent competitors, the United States and Japan. Moreover, agriculture should be seen as an industry for which the EU has a sociopolitical preference (secure food supplies and pleasant environmental conditions?) in terms of output and employment; this is the case of a preference for a collective good discussed in detail elsewhere (see, for example, El-Agraa and Jones, 1981, and Chapter 4). Additionally, absolutely free trade in agriculture would have been detrimental to the interests of countries such as France and Italy, unless the argument for free trade was applied simultaneously to *all* industries. Finally, the EU does not produce the same range of agricultural products as does the developing world.

However, these responses have no solid foundation. It is difficult to see why it is churlish to question the goal of a prosperous agriculture, particularly when this goal can be achieved, if at all, only at the expense of alternative goals – it is a question of priorities. Moreover, the EU *does* compete with countries such as Argentina, Australia, Canada, New Zealand, the United States, and several developing countries, in terms of sugar, cereals, vegetables and beef; the self-sufficiency figures published by the Commission do not reflect this because they are a manifestation only of the protectionist nature of the CAP. It is nonsensical to compare the EU with the United States when the United States is a net exporter and the EU is basically (under free trade conditions) a net importer of agricultural products. Of course, this is not meant to suggest that the United States has a true comparative advantage in *all* the agricultural products (since the subsidies provided by the United States to some of its farmers may be the main reason for their exports), only in some of its exports. Finally, the argument for a social preference for employment in agriculture is not very appealing in the context of the EU, particularly since the world supplies are cheaper and the movement away from agricultural employment, which is what the CAP structural policies are trying to promote, is a 'natural' phenomenon.

The gist of this argument is that some agricultural economists seem preoccupied with the 'trade creation' elements of the CAP and seem to ignore completely the 'trade diversion' aspects of it. Because trade diversion has been ignored, the successes have been exaggerated and the failures have been underestimated.[11] The reader who is interested in a full survey of the actual cost estimates of the CAP should consult Chapter 12 of El-Agraa (1989a), Baldwin *et al.* (1988) and the references given there. To conclude this section, we shall concentrate on a summary of an estimate, which, although carried out about a decade ago, is still the most comprehensive in both coverage and scope.

Stoeckel (1985) and Breckling *et al.* (1987) made estimates using a simplified general-equilibrium approach. Since the Breckling *et al.* study was a more sophisticated version of the Stoeckel work, this section is devoted to this later attempt; Stoeckel himself was a joint author of the Breckling *et al.* study.

The study commenced by stressing the three major problems facing the EC:

1. The excessive surpluses created by the CAP in most (?) agricultural products necessitating huge restitution costs to enable their disposal on the international market.

2. The high level of unemployment which in 1987 reached about 11% of the total labour force.

3. The declining competitiveness of the EC manufacturing sector – the share of the EC in OECD exports of equipment goods having declined by more than 25% since 1964 and its imports share having risen by more than the same percentage; it is the traditional industries that have lagged behind while the new technology industries and products with high growth in demand are lacking.

The authors correctly believed that these problems were interrelated, hence their employment of a general-equilibrium approach. They conceded that the causes were numerous and complex but they were certain that the CAP 'has contributed significantly to the EC's relative economic malaise' (Breckling *et al.*, 1987, p. 2).

The model specified a general-equilibrium structure for each of the largest four EC economies and estimated the effects of protecting the agricultural and food processing sectors on the rest of the economies in terms of exports, factor markets and total unemployment. The four economies accounted in 1982 for 86% of the GDP of the EC; hence they were fairly representative of the EC as a whole. They were, in ranking order: West Germany (28%), France (23%), the United Kingdom (19%) and Italy (16%). The reason for concentrating on these four was simplicity.

Each of these countries had large *services* and *manufacturing* sectors, representing about 55% and 25% of their respective GDPs. Agriculture accounted for a small percentage of GDP, ranging from 2% in the United Kingdom and West Germany to 6% in Italy. The food processing sector (which was subject to CAP support) represented about 4–6% of the GDP of these countries. About 26% of the agricultural production of the EC came from France, about 21% from Italy, 17% from West Germany and about 12% from the United Kingdom.

A basic feature of EC agriculture was the coexistence of small- and large-scale farm enterprises. Within the EC of ten, large-scale farms represented about 10% of the total number of farm enterprises but accounted for 40% of the total agricultural output. The large-scale farms were mostly (in ranking order) in the United Kingdom, West Germany and France – see Table 10.2. It was always recognized that, *on the whole*, the large-scale farms tended to be more capital intensive relative to the small-scale ones.

The authors believed that the least controversial explanation for the high level of unemployment in the EC and its sharp rate of increase in the United Kingdom between 1975 and 1982 was rigidity of real wages. This belief was based on the study by Klau and Mittlestädt (1986) which showed the United Kingdom, France and Italy to have the highest real wage rigidities of all the members of the OECD. The same study showed West Germany to have a low level of real wage rigidity despite narrow wage differentials reflecting minimum wage legislation and cost-of-living adjustments.

The formal model incorporated all these features. It was based on a linearized Samuelson–Heckscher–Ohlin general-equilibrium framework first advanced by Woodland (1982) and adapted for the EC by Stoeckel (1985); the present study extended it to a multicountry representation of the EC.

As indicated before, the EC was represented by its four major producers. For each of these, four production sectors were distinguished, reflecting the authors' focus on the CAP: agriculture, being the supplier of the products and the main recipient of financial support; food processing, being an intensive user of agricultural inputs and the second major recipient of financial support; manufacturing, being representative of all other tradable goods; services, being the labour-intensive and mostly non-traded goods sector. The agricultural sector was disaggregated into small- and large-scale farm enterprises. The main instruments used in the approach to reflect CAP support were production subsidies, export restitutions, variable levies and the VAT tranche forming an own resource of the EC budget.

The authors felt that agriculture warranted special treatment, given the study's focus on it. A common agricultural sector, encompassing the four EC countries, was specified, and the agricultural products of these countries were treated as a single homogeneous product, which was exported, in aggregate, to the outside world. However, non-agricultural commodities produced in the EC were assumed to be exported not only to the rest of the world but also to other members of the EC. Except for the composite agricultural product, all EC commodities were distinguished by both country of origin and destination. All four countries were assumed to import both agricultural and non-agricultural commodities from the outside world. Each of the four countries was seen to be large enough to influence the world price of its traded goods.

Each industry was assumed to use domestic and imported intermediate imports as well as primary factors in the production process. The model incorporated four factors of production: capital, labour and land use in both the agricultural subsectors, and land specific to the large farmers. All factors other than labour were assumed to be fully employed, while labour could be either so or unemployed. Both capital and labour were assumed to be mobile domestically but immobile within the EC, in spite of the *economic union* nature of the EC.

All factor endowments were assumed to be determined exogenously, implying, for the capital stock, that sectoral investment could take place only through the reallocation of capital (other than large-scale land) amongst the sectors, i.e. at the margin, capital was 'malleable and ... usable' by all sectors. Another implication was that all commodities were used in current production and could not be reproduced.

The main behavioural assumptions were that producers minimize costs subject to technological constraints, with each sector producing a single product; there was a single consumer in each country maximizing utility subject to a budget constraint; perfect competition ensured that all factors, except labour, received their marginal product and were fully employed; *Walras's law* applied with results being independent of the choice of reference price – this being the consumer price index for each country – hence only 'real' changes took place with movements in real income acting as a welfare indicator.

The basic model was non-linear. The solution procedure involved first linearizing it using logarithmic differentiation. The resulting elasticity version was then solved by matrix inversion. The linear approximation is valid for the estimation of small changes in the endogenous variables from exogenous stimuli, but, because of the large exogenous changes in the export restitutions and import levies, the authors conceded that the linearization errors were substantial, particularly in the case of trade parameters.

Given the Samuelson–Heckscher–Ohlin nature of the methodology employed, the authors' (Breckling *et al.*, 1987, p. 11) expectation with regard to the CAP (agricultural protectionism) was that it would have adverse effects on the other traded goods sectors and the economy as a whole by the following:

1. Distorting the pattern of trade through agricultural import taxes (export taxes on non-agricultural goods) and agricultural export subsidies (import subsidies on non-agricultural goods).

2. Worsening the terms of trade for the EC, thus reducing EC welfare.

3. Increasing unemployment in the relatively labour-intensive industries, given the assumption of real wage rigidities.

4. Promoting research into and investment in relatively inefficient industries.

The aim of the study was to establish the magnitude of each of these expected effects. The results were obtained through simulation. 1979 was chosen as the base year for calculating the impact of CAP support, modelled as exogenous shocks, on member countries since it was the year when the own resources system for financing the EC budget was formally phased in. The full absorption time for such shocks was thought to be typically a five-year period; thus the authors interpreted the results as changes covering the period 1979–83.

The database was the *Standard Input–Output Tables of EEC Countries for Years around 1975* (UN, 1982) augmented by trade shares obtained from OECD trade tapes used in their *Interlink Model* (OECD, 1983). Unemployment figures were obtained from OECD country-specific statistics for 1979 (OECD, 1985). The ratio of unemployment benefit to employment wage was set at 0.5 in the four EC nations, and real wages were assumed to be fixed. The input–output shares of the agricultural subsector were derived from the *Farm Accountancy Data Network* (*Eurostat*, 1982) since their preliminary tables for 1986 suggested no change from their 1975 calculations.

Behavioural elasticities were taken from Whalley (1985), Stern *et al.* (1976) and Deaton and Muellbauer (1980b); these are given in Table 10.4. The authors claimed that, although the calculations may have varied considerably, 'a preliminary sensitivity analysis has indicated that, except on the trade side, the results are fairly robust and that the effect on the economy is negligible' (Breckling, *et al.*, 1987, p. 22).

Table 10.4 ⬤ **Behavioural elasticities.**

Description	Elasticity
Production and consumption substitution elasticities (CES)	
Between domestic and imported goods and primary factors for all countries	0.8
Between imported goods and domestic goods for all countries	2.0
Consumer income elasticities	
Agricultural products for all countries	0.2
Food processing products for all countries	0.4
Manufacturing products for all countries	0.8
Service sector products[a]	
West Germany	1.18
France	1.17
United Kingdom	1.17
Italy	1.23
Export price elasticities of demand by rest of world	
Agricultural and agrifood products for all countries	2.0
Manufacturing products for all countries	1.0
Service sector products for all countries	4.0
Import price elasticities of supply by rest of world	
Agricultural and agrifood products for all countries	2.0
Manufacturing products for all countries	4.0
Service sector products for all countries	5.0

[a] These settings ensure that the weighted sum of expenditure elasticities is unity in each country. Leisure demand (unemployment supply) elasticity for all countries was set to 1.0

Source Breckling *et al.* (1987), p. 23.

The CAP support was modelled by four exogenous shocks:

1. A 12.32% agricultural production subsidy.

2. Subsidies of 80% on all agricultural and food processing products exported to the rest of the world.

3. Import levies of 40% on all agricultural and food processing products imported from the rest of the world.

4. A 0.75% VAT tax on all consumer goods in the EC countries.

The sizes of these shocks were chosen by reference to the EAGGF accounts. All storage costs were rated as implicit export subsidies and production aids were regarded as implicit production subsidies. The precise value of the agricultural production subsidy was selected to guarantee that the EC budget constraint was met. Note that the measurement of these shocks assumed a distortion-free base in 1979, i.e. 1979 was the year of equilibrium.

On the expectation that CAP support may have promoted investment in agricultural research and development (by assumption, to the advantage of large, capital intensive farmers), two shocks were used to capture this effect:

1. A 5% increase in total factor productivity on large farms.

2. A 5% decrease in total factor productivity on small farms.

Finally, the simulations were carried out on the assumption that the MCAs and national government supports were held constant.

The simulation results, given in Table 10.5, indicated the following:

1. The agricultural production subsidy and the VAT necessary to finance agricultural support were more important instruments than the border measures.

2. EC agricultural production increased by 18%, mainly as a result of the production subsidy. Output grew fastest in the United Kingdom (about 54%), and least in Italy (about 7%) with West Germany's growing by about 20% and France's by about 12%. Since the average growth rate for the EC was just under 20%, the British and West German agricultural enterprises increased their share of total EC production.

3. The increase in agricultural production was associated with price rises for the factors used most intensively in agriculture, especially land. These increased land costs favoured the countries least intensive in the use of land, i.e. the United Kingdom and West Germany.

4. Given the assumptions made about technology, it was not surprising to discover that the large farms were the main beneficiaries. Indeed, output growth on small farms actually declined by about 35% in the United Kingdom and remained almost constant in the rest of the EC.

5. The food-processing sector expanded, on average, by about 10% throughout the EC. Most of this growth was attributed to the 80% export subsidy, since the

Table 10.5 Country-specific simulation results.[a]

Variable	West Germany (%)	France (%)	United Kingdom (%)	Italy (%)
Gross output				
Agriculture				
Small farms	−1.1	0.3	−35.4	−1.2
Large farms	51.2	27.0	98.5	29.3
Total	20.2	11.7	53.7	6.8
Food processing	8.0	13.7	15.9	5.1
Manufacturing	−1.4	−1.9	−2.5	−1.1
Services	−1.3	−0.6	−3.1	−0.7
Producer prices				
Agriculture	−2.6	−4.6	−3.8	−2.9
Food processing	0.2	−2.0	1.3	−0.9
Manufacturing	−0.5	−0.7	−0.4	−0.6
Services	−0.3	−0.2	0.3	−0.4
Domestic consumer demand				
Agriculture	11.1	6.0	7.8	3.2
Food processing	0.9	2.9	1.6	1.6
Manufacturing	−0.8	−0.2	−2.0	−0.1
Services	−0.6	0.4	−1.5	0.2
Primary factor returns				
Labour	0.0	0.0	0.0	0.0
Capital	−0.5	0.4	1.7	−0.3
General land	17.6	11.7	14.0	9.5
Large-scale land	72.5	40.2	130.4	44.8
Labour movement				
Employment	−0.9	−0.4	−1.8	−0.6
Unemployment	7.8	3.4	16.0	5.2
Exports to rest of world				
Food processing	149.9	150.2	145.3	151.5
Manufacturing	−4.4	−6.2	−5.7	−4.6
Services	−18.3	−26.7	25.4	−19.4
Imports from rest of world				
Agriculture	−32.1	−34.0	−26.8	−33.6
Food processing	−33.1	−32.4	−28.4	−33.3
Manufacturing	5.1	7.3	5.8	5.4
Services	6.2	9.0	0.0	6.0
Real income	−0.1	0.8	−0.6	0.4
Exchange rate	4.9	6.9	6.1	5.2
Terms of trade	−0.4	1.9	−0.5	0.2

[a] All price changes are relative to the consumer price index in each country.
Source Breckling *et al.* (1987), p. 14.

export sector accounted for 10% total demand. The differences in growth rates in the EC countries were attributed to their different export shares.

6. The manufacturing and service sectors contracted by about 1% in each country, except in France where manufacturing declined by about 2% and the United Kingdom where manufacturing declined by 2.5% and services by 3.1%. However, except for the United Kingdom, manufacturing was more adversely affected relative to the services sector, a situation which was to be expected since in this model agricultural protection resulted in an appreciation of the real exchange rates, which depressed exports; this was not so in the case of services since they were, by assumption, non-traded, but this left unexplained the UK reverse position.

7. As expected, unemployment increased throughout the EC, given the assumption of rigid real wages and the fact that the declining non-agricultural sectors were relatively intensive employers of labour. Calculations showed that the unemployment rate would become higher than in the absence of the CAP by 1.8% (450,000 fewer persons employed) in the United Kingdom, 0.9% (220,000 fewer persons employed) in West Germany, 0.6% (110,000 fewer persons employed) in Italy and 0.4% (80,000 fewer persons employed) in France. The rationale for greater job losses in the United Kingdom and West Germany was attributed to the lower contraction rate in the non-agricultural sectors of France and Italy, implying that jobs in the United Kingdom and West Germany were being lost in favour of France and Italy, reflecting the fact that labour was assumed to be immobile between members of the EC. It should not come as a surprise to learn that the relative effect of the CAP on unemployment followed an almost identical pattern to that in the non-agricultural sectors.

8. The CAP was found to create substantial changes in the pattern of consumer expenditure. For instance, consumer demand for locally produced manufactured goods declined in all four countries in the sample, particularly so in the case of the United Kingdom. The demand for services contracted in the United Kingdom (1.5%) and West Germany (0.6%), but marginally increased in France and Italy.

9. Exports of both processed and unprocessed products by the EC to the rest of the world rose by about 150% – see also Table 10.6. This largely reflected the size of the export subsidy, and the authors claimed that this result was consistent with 'the evidence of massive surplus production' (Breckling et al., 1987, p. 15). On the whole, the EC exports of manufactures and services declined by about 5% and 23% respectively. On average, intra-EC trade in processed agricultural products increased by about 7%. The terms of trade worsened for the United Kingdom and West Germany, were almost unchanged for Italy and improved for France by about 2%.

10. As Table 10.7 shows, the simulations suggested that France was the main beneficiary from EC budgetary transfers by 8% of its gross export income. The loss by the United Kingdom and West Germany is attributed to their relatively small agricultural sectors.

Table 10.6 ● Aggregate EC simulation results for agriculture.

Variable	Change (%)
Gross output	+18.3
Producer price	−2.3
Exports to rest of world	+155.4

Source Breckling *et al.* (1987), p. 15.

Table 10.7 ● Intra-EC transfers.

Variable	West Germany (%)	France (%)	United Kingdom (%)	Italy (%)
Value of exports	−1.9	−2.4	−0.4	−4.8
Value of imports	−1.0	+0.6	−0.8	−0.8
Consumption tax	3.3	4.1	3.2	3.8
Production subsidy	4.2	7.1	2.8	7.8
Import tariffs on agriculture	2.7	0.6	2.3	0.8
Import tariffs on food processing	2.3	2.0	4.3	2.6
Agricultural export subsidy	−1.0	4.2	0.0	0.3
Agrifood export subsidy	1.6	3.4	2.6	0.8
Net transfers	−3.5	8.0	−4.4	1.7

Source Breckling *et al.* (1987), p. 16.

This approach is to be applauded since economists should be interested in the total economy-wide effects of any projectionist policy. Moreover, the approach improves on the five areas identified by Stoeckel (1985) as requiring more attention: the need to incorporate an agricultural sector, to specify a multicountry framework, to model explicitly the transfers within and between countries, to model a heterogeneous agricultural sector where just over 10% of farms produce almost half the total output and to specify labour market rigidities in an acceptable model of unemployment.

However, both the model specification and some of the assumptions employed here leave a lot to be desired. Theoretically, the model is inappropriate for dealing with large changes, as is the case with the CAP. The authors concede this point and are working on an improvement of the solution procedure in order to remove the linearization error, but, until those errors are eliminated, one should not have much faith in their preliminary results.

This point is reinforced when one carefully examines the assumptions built into the model. First, factors of production are not allowed to move across the borders of the EC. Of course, factor mobility has not been enhanced to any substantial extent by the formation of the EC, but there is evidence to suggest that some labour mobility does take place, and substantial amounts of capital and technology do move about within the EC – see Chapter 20. Second, large farms are not only intensive in their use of capital but also have access to land not available to small farms, the implication being that *all* large farms are more efficient than small farms. There is much evidence to suggest that some small farms are more efficient than large farms, depending on the agricultural product under consideration. This takes one to the third point: because all agricultural products are counted as one aggregate, no such disaggregation is possible, and hence this reality is completely ignored in the calculations. Related to this is another point: in the EC, surpluses have been confined to certain products only, mainly milk and wine, and occasionally to other products, but because there is no room for disaggregation, the estimates of this model suggest surpluses all round. The authors, realizing this result, began by claiming that there have been surpluses in most agricultural products; there are no statistics to support such a claim. Also, and more importantly, a model which incorporates such assumptions is bound to produce the sort of results obtained, i.e. the model has been specified in such a manner as to produce these results; therefore both the formulation of the model and its application leave one unmoved. However, this does not diminish the need for a general-equilibrium approach.

10.10 Conclusions

Having explained the CAP, its mechanisms, financing, successes and failures, it is now possible to attempt some final conclusions.

Firstly, the structural problems and the embarrassing surpluses that bedevilled the CAP were due partly to the intervention prices being set at too high a level. The only justification for such high prices was that the authorities were not in a position to know the shapes of the relevant supply and demand curves for agricultural products, but, when the authorities erred consistently, it must have been because they wished to do so, i.e. they were under great pressure to accede to the wishes of the farming lobby.[12] A lower level of intervention prices should have disposed of the surpluses problem and should have encouraged people who are inefficiently engaged in the farm sector to seek alternative employment. As we have seen, the EU has recently attempted this, but it remains to be seen whether or not the end result will be success.

Secondly, the CAP has, for a long time, failed to adopt the most efficient method of implementing its own objectives. It was clearly demonstrated that direct subsidies and deficiency payments are, in that order, economically superior to the variable levy system. Presumably the reason for not using subsidies in the first place was the problem of finding sources of finance. But with the surpluses and the substantial requirements for supporting artificially high prices draining the finances of

EAGGF, a central budget finance system (more on this in the McDougall Report) which would make subsidies possible is inevitable. The recent reforms are a step in the right direction, but they are not stringent enough to approach the ideal mechanism.

Thirdly, the CAP has been a success for the EU in that one system has been adopted to replace the elaborate support systems that had existed before. (Some commentators have gone to the extent of stating that the only success of the CAP is that it exists.) However, the system is at present a dual one, incorporating the old and new regimes, leading to utter confusion in the case of the uninitiated. Moreover, it can be argued that the common system contains the worst features of all the others. It is arguably also more protective than any member state on its own would contemplate being; indeed the demands by the United States for the reform of the CAP are tantamount to this.

In fairness, it should be added that the Commission has been working very hard for a proper reform of the CAP; it would seem that the strength of the agricultural lobby has been the main deterrent. The latest package of reforms together with the substantial reduction in subsidies demanded by the United States may be cast in the same vein: the success of the French Conservatives in the March 1993 elections is arguably mainly due to their promise to force the EC to change its concessions to the United States regarding the reduction in subsidies.

Notes

1. A rough indication of average levels of income of people working in agriculture, relative to incomes of people in other occupations, can be obtained by comparing agriculture's share of the total workforce with its share of national output. Such a comparison suggests that, when the EEC was formed, average agricultural incomes in the three largest countries, France, Germany and Italy, were only about half those of other occupations. (Ritson, 1973, p. 96)

2. 'Agricultural incomes have risen, but in France, Germany and Italy there is little evidence that the gap in incomes between agriculture and other occupations has diminished' (Ritson, 1973, p. 69).

3. It is argued by some that the provision of an adequate agricultural sector incidentally helps to ensure a pleasant environment for the nation's inhabitants. However, there is considerable argument that intensive agriculture is detrimental to the environment, e.g. removal of hedges, odours from intensive livestock, etc. (see Bowers, 1972).

4. 'This does not, however, accrue to farmers alone: in fact it represents increased return to fixed factors in both farming and in the purchased input industries' (Josling, 1969, p. 296).

5. It is possible to derive expressions for the average cost (in terms of extra resources or budget payments) of achieving a unit of objective in this case income transfer. Such calculations are meaningful if comparing the policy with a free market. More relevant

in the case of a policy where the level of guaranteed price can be changed from year to year is the marginal cost of gaining an additional unit of objective. (Josling, 1969, p. 272)

6. Bhagwati (1965) demonstrates that tariffs and quotas can be equivalent in their effects only if it is assumed that free competition exists in both the importing countries and in the industry under consideration – see El-Agraa (1983b, chapters 8–10, and 1989b, chapters 8–10).

7. Josling (1969), p. 277. For a more detailed discussion of distortions, the reader should consult Johnson (1965a) and Chapter 4.

8. For an estimate of the average and marginal costs of some of these policies the reader should consult Josling (1969), pp. 278–80.

9. This refers to a series of six documents which were submitted to the Council in December 1968. The first of these was called 'Memorandum on the Reform of Agriculture in the European Community', in *Bulletin of the European Community*, 1969, Supplement. The series is available in one volume as *Le Plan Mansholt*, Brussels, July 1969 – see Fennell (1979) for details.

10. The average size of holding in the United Kingdom in 1970–71 was in excess of three times that in the original Six – if one were to include farms of less than one hectare, the difference would be more extreme.

11. Using 1953–69 annual observations, Thorbecke and Pagoulatos (1975, p. 322) reached the conclusions that 'the formation of the CAP has affected the pattern of international trade flows by inducing a shift from extra-EEC producers to partner countries or domestic sources of supply for nine out of . . . fourteen individual commodity groups'; and that 'agricultural protectionism in the Community has slowed down the rate of labour out-migration'.

12. Mr Roy Jenkins, when he was President of the EC Commission, was unable to clarify this position.

> I mentioned a minute ago the question of surpluses. *They are not always a bad thing. It is better for the consumer to have a small surplus than a small shortage.* But that is not the same with European milk production. One-sixth of milk output is already surplus to requirements, while total consumption of milk products is declining. We shall not be able to persuade Europe's taxpayers and consumers to support that indefinitely. We cannot expect importers and other exporters of milk outside Europe to relieve us of that burden, even though we can dispose of some part outside the Community. (In *Bulletin of the European Community*, September 1978, p. 9. The emphasis is not in the original text.)

chapter eleven

The Common Fisheries Policy

A. M. EL-AGRAA

It was stated in the previous chapter that in the Treaty of Rome fisheries were included in the definition of agricultural products; but in 1966 an effort was made by the EC Commission for the establishment of a Common Fisheries Policy (CFP – in its *Report on the Situation of the Fisheries Sector in the Member States of the EEC and the Basic Principles for a Common Policy*, 1966); prior to that, many fish stocks in what are now EU waters were controlled by the NE Atlantic Fisheries Commission (NEAFC). However, agreement on the CFP was not reached until 1983, after six years of negotiations and hard bargaining. The purpose of this chapter is to examine briefly the background to these developments and to explain the nature and implications of the CFP. The reader who is interested in a detailed account of the developments leading to the creation of this policy together with its geographical and political implications is advised to read Wise (1984).

However, before tackling the main body of this chapter, a few points are in order. The first is about the inclusion of fisheries in agriculture. This is not altogether illogical since the two industries have a lot in common: both are subject to price instability (owing to the highly specialized human and physical capital in the fisheries industry, making its short-term supply highly inelastic, and to fish having a rather low price elasticity); both have low income elasticity for their products; both are prone to random shocks owing to natural causes over which they have no control; both have large numbers of small, self-employed producers. The second concerns the need for a common policy. Many analysts would argue that a common policy for fisheries makes more sense than one for agriculture since most fishing activity is conducted across and beyond national territorial waters, and fish takes no notice of national frontiers (for example, about 90% of the North Sea codfish spends its first year in waters off the coasts of Denmark, Germany and Holland, but by the time it is three years old and ripe for catching, most of it will have migrated to British territorial waters). However, others would counter by stressing that even when activities ancillary to fishing are added (such as processing, transport and ship maintenance), the total industry involved no more than 1% of the entire EC of the early 1970s (1.2 million), but the response would be that the industry, like agriculture, had political clout due mainly to its concentrated nature, involving whole communities in remote areas with no prospects for alternative employment, and that being a risky industry, it draws a lot of sympathy, especially when disaster strikes. The third is that during the 1960s there was agreement at the time that any vessel can fish anywhere barring a twelve-mile coastal zone reserved for vessels belonging to the country in consideration, exception being granted to vessels from other nations that had traditionally fished there, i.e. those that had traditional rights. However, prompted by a unilateral action by Iceland, claiming exclusive fishing rights within 50 miles of its coast, in 1970 the United Nations decided two years later that any country could establish an Exclusive Economic Zone (EEZ) in waters up to 200 miles from its coastline, appropriate consideration being allowed for overlapping zones. Needless to add, this had drastic implications for most EC nations, given their traditional fishing areas. Finally, because of advances in vessel technology fish catches were beginning to outstrip existing stocks, and hence something had to be done to stop biological disaster.

11.1 Background

It could be argued that what prompted the emergence of a CFP was the situation in 1966. Then, production in the original Six began to stagnate, the attitude of non-member nations regarding their twelve-mile limits became increasingly restrictive and there was a sharp decline in the Community's self-sufficiency rates for the major fish species. As a consequence of this, proposals were advanced in June 1968 which amounted to a set of basic ingredients for a CFP, and the basic foundations were agreed at the end of June 1970, on the day before membership negotiations were due to commence with the new applicants. These proposals were adopted by the Council in October 1970 (Regulation 70/2141 on conservation rules and Regulation 70/2142 on the establishment of a common marketing organization with an intervention price system to be run by recognized producer organizations in each member state; hence the mechanism resembles that for the CAP) and came into force in February 1971.

The striking feature of this policy was the recognition by all six member states of the principle of 'equal access' for all EC fishermen to the territorial waters of the EC together with a free EC market for fish. This was opportune, given the fact that the waters of the three imminent member countries of the EC (as well as those of Norway, which finally decided not to join the EC, arguably because of this very issue) were rich in fish: the total catch of the original Six was half that of the three imminent partners. Hence, the negotiation of 'access' was vital if the CFP were to become a reality.

It should be added that the agreements reached between the original Six and the three new member nations included arrangements for fisheries which entitled the fishermen of coast countries (those countries highly dependent on fishing for their livelihood) to a general and exclusive six-mile zone and to a twelve-mile exclusive zone in some areas with the proviso that these zones would become EC waters after 1982 if no review of the CFP took place in the meantime. However, the three nations did not view this as a permanent solution since they felt that they were losing more than they expected to gain. Thus an atmosphere ripe for conflict was created.

However, during the period 1974–76, the United Nations Convention on the Law of the Sea (UNCLOS III) was in session and one of the points which occupied a large part of its deliberations was the issue regarding the extension of national fishing zones to 200 miles. The nine member nations of the EC were actually about to implement such an exclusive zone limit, but preferred to await the outcome of the conference. In the end, UNCLOS III failed to reach agreement on this issue, and when Canada, Norway and the United States announced their intention of adopting a 200-mile zone, the EC decided (in The Hague in October 1976) to follow suit and to implement what it had already intended, especially since the United Kingdom was threatening to do so unilaterally. In The Hague meeting, it was also decided to ask the EC Commission to proceed with negotiations with third countries. Obviously, without specific agreements, the 200-mile zone limit was bound to exclude countries which had in the past fished in what came to be known as the 'Community pond'. It should be clear that whether or not these countries should be allowed access to the EC pond would depend on the size of catch granted and the extent of reciprocity extended to the EC in terms of EC fishermen having access to the waters of such countries. Not surprisingly, the EC Commission, for this purpose, classified third countries into three categories.

1. Possible reciprocators such as Iceland and Norway.
2. Countries like Canada and the United States which have no interest in the EC pond but which might have surpluses in their waters to which the EC fishermen might want to gain access.
3. Countries which would like access to the EC pond but could not reciprocate, such as the nations of Eastern Europe.

By 1976 the same old questions began to surface again. Were the member nations to have completely free access to the EC pond or would they be granted exclusive zones on a permanent basis? Would the EC go for a maximum catch, partly determined with conservation in mind, which would be shared out between the member states on a percentage basis? Would the EC perhaps opt for both these possibilities? What compensation would Ireland and the United Kingdom receive, in terms of access to the EC pond, for losing some of their own waters to countries like Iceland because of the common 200-mile zone?

The position of the United Kingdom was that the 12-mile limit was unacceptable, and the British government started by demanding a 100-mile exclusive zone, but later dropped this limit by 50%. During the negotiations that followed, more emphasis was laid on a limit on the total catch to be divided into national quotas and less on exclusive zones. Late in 1977, the EC Commission proposed possible national quotas, giving about 30% to the United Kingdom; but this was only two-thirds of what the United Kingdom had hoped for.

The first detailed proposals of a CFP went to the Council in September 1976. These comprised measures for 'conserving fishery resources (total allowable catches – TACs – and quotas), for safeguarding, as far as possible, employment and incomes in coastal regions, and for adjusting fleet size in the light of the catch available' (*Bulletin of the European Communities*, no. 1, 1983, p. 1). It should be emphasized that TACs are determined by biological, not economic, criteria; they are calculated in terms of the maximum number of fish to be caught without reducing the total fish population to a level at which it would not be capable of maintaining itself. Therefore, they would naturally vary from year to year in accordance with variations in the size of the fish stocks. In October 1976 the Six agreed to extend their fishing limits to 200 nautical miles as from 1 January 1977 (North Sea and North Atlantic). It should therefore not be surprising to learn that the negotiations were very tense and difficult since it was not just that the question of access had to be solved but also that TACs had to be fixed and then allocated to each member country of the EC on a quota basis at a time when there was evidence of over-fishing. Indeed, final resolution of the matter was not reached until 25 January 1983 when the ministers in charge of fisheries in the ten member nations of the EC agreed on the new CFP. This was based on the proposals that the EC Commission had itself initiated. The relief expressed by the EC Commission on reaching an agreement, after six years of hard bargaining, should not be underestimated.

11.2 The policy

The delight of the EC Commission with the new CFP can be clearly captured from their statement that a Blue Europe had been born (CEC, 1983c, p. 193).

In that report, the EC Commission states that the following ground rules were laid down for EC fishery activities:

1. 'Equality of access to resources in Community waters except, by way of derogation and for a renewable period of 10 years, for the preferential arrangements for in-shore fishermen within the 12-mile limit'.

2. 'Compliance with a common policy for the conservation of resources, including both technical measures concerning the different fisheries and such stock management measures as the fixing of total allowable catches . . . and annual quotas'.

3. 'The scope of agreements with non-Community countries to be reinforced and extended so as to safeguard fishing possibilities in their waters'.

4. 'Market support by implementation from 1 January 1983 of a common organisation of the market, with the changes decided upon on 29 December 1981'.

5. 'Modernization of development of the fishery and aquaculture sector, through measures financed by a Community budget of 250 million ECU over three years'.

The Report added that in 1983, the Blue Europe was experiencing some difficulties in settling down with the new ground rules. To cater for this, 'structural rules' were introduced on 4 October and TACs and catch quotas for 1983 were determined on 20 December of the same year, thus reinforcing the agreement.

In short, the new CFP covers four aspects. Firstly, the policy has a 'system' for the conservation of sea resources within the EU. Secondly, the policy has a common organization of the market. Thirdly, the policy includes 'structural' measures. Finally, the policy asks for fisheries agreements with non-EU countries and for formal consultations between EU nations so that they can act in concert in the context of international agreements.

With regard to the conservation of resources, the Council has adopted a regulation which establishes an EU system which provides for measures to curtail fishing activities, sets rules for utilizing resources and makes special provisions for coastal fishing. More specifically, a conservation box has been established around the Orkney and Shetland Islands and the number of licences offered to EU fishermen over-fishing endangered species has been made more limited. Hence both 'access' and TACs are aspects of crucial importance here.

Table 11.1 provides information on the 1984 and 1985 TACs and the individual country quotas together with the TACs for 1982, 1986 and 1997 (the latest year for which announced TACs are available). I have provided fuller data for 1984–85 simply for ease of exposition. This is because the Council decided that fishing during the first few months of 1983 should have been conducted on the basis of the 1982 TACs and quotas (due allowance being given to normal seasonal fluctuations), thus making the 1982 figures provisional in nature. Moreover, the levels for 1984 can easily be compared with those of 1983: the 1984 figures were slightly lower for cod, haddock and whiting and slightly higher for mackerel, place and saithe, with the TAC for redfish remaining unchanged at 70,500 tonnes. For 1997, the TACs have declined for all categories except for herring, but new categories have been included. Thus there is enough information to compare the TACs in the three years, but such a comparison is too obvious to warrant specification. However, attention should be drawn to the fact that although the TAC for cod has declined over the period 1983–85, Denmark has absorbed more than the total decline since all the countries in the table have increased their share, with Ireland maintaining its quota. A more drastic situation also applies to Denmark with regard to haddock, plaice and whiting since the TACs have increased relative to 1984. The reader who is interested in following the detailed yearly changes in the TACs and their allocation between the member nations of the EU is advised to consult the *Official Journal of the European Communities*; these yearly comparisons will not be pursued here simply because the variations in them are not determined just by the bargaining position of the individual nations: as already indicated, changes in conservation criteria and in the natural catch environments are crucial.

The market organization covers fresh fish and frozen and preserved products and its main objective is to apply common-marketing standards and to facilitate trading between the member nations of the EU. More precisely, however, it should be stated that the objectives of the marketing aspect are to guarantee an adequate income to

Table 11.1 ⬭ Allocations for 1984 and 1985 catch quotas in EU waters and in water managed in cooperation with non-member countries and TACs for 1982, 1983–86 and 1997 (tonnes).

	Cod	Haddock	Saithe	Whiting	Plaice	Redfish	Mackerel	Herring[a]
Belgium								
1984	8,230	1,670	80	3,680	12,030	0	100	0
1985	9,030	1,830	90	3,970	12,990	0	400	8,920
Denmark								
1984	234,350	18,615	7,550	34,190	46,110	4,890	7,400	43,770
1985	166,420	11,690	8,390	15,870	42,100	0	8,000	90,260
France								
1984	36,390	19,340	69,850	37,510	7,250	2,410	17,100	1,930
1985	39,540	20,270	95,020	41,400	7,500	4,410	14,930	35,430
West Germany								
1984	84,380	7,110	21,110	3,900	9,860	62,820	25,600	22,180
1985	87,840	7,530	25,260	4,330	10,780	62,535	22,190	65,760
Ireland								
1984	11,520	4,370	3,060	17,800	3,070	0	85,300	27,170
1985	11,520	3,820	3,730	22,700	3,730	0	72,640	31,900
Netherlands								
1984	23,230	1,120	190	8,630	66,890	0	37,300	7,850
1985	25,950	1,270	210	9,290	71,810	0	32,180	82,900
United Kingdom								
1984	117,910	140,840	20,860	79,480	53,710	380	234,700	38,800
1985	129,550	151,540	27,400	92,890	59,570	375	200,160	98,180
EC[b]								
1982	524,700	201,700	101,760	208,120	159,960	70,500	375,000	219,400
1984	516,010	193,065	122,700	185,190	198,920	70,500	407,500	141,700
1985	469,350	197,950	160,100	191,450	208,480	65,320	350,500	413,350
1986	377,470	245,630	157,000	176,200	212,690	0	349,000	514,415
1997[c]	321,662	155,000	139,000	146,340	109,240	0	343,855	801,770
EU share								
	310,592	146,900	79,200	122,960	106,130	0	295,885	727,330

[a] The herring quotas excluded provisional North Sea allocations to six of these countries – Belgium (1,570), Denmark (6,920), West Germany (4,350), France (4,520), Netherlands (9,030) and the United Kingdom (7,910).

[b] Both Greece and Italy are not involved in the TACs simply because they conduct all their fishing in the Mediterranean.

[c] There are now also TACs for (the first figure is the total TAC while the second is the EU share) anchovy (45,000; same), anglerfish (55,900; same), atlantic salmon (1,204,750; same), blue whiting (522,500; 205,500), capelin (0; 0), deep water prawn (10,500; 5,610), hake (69,130; same), horse mackerel (422,000; 430,000), megrim (35,840; same), Norway lobster (65,980; same), Norway pout (36,505; same), 'Panaeus' prawn (4,108; 4,000), pollock (22,100; same), sole (36,505; same) and sprat (401,540; 370,540).

Source Calculated from the various issues of the *Bulletin of the European Communities*, no. 1, vol. 17, 1984, p. 37.

the producers, to enhance rational marketing, to alter supply in accordance with market requirements, to ensue that consumer prices are reasonable and to promote common marketing standards – see Cunningham and Young (1983, p. 2).

The structural measures can be described more precisely by stating their aims. The main objectives are to ensure that the resources of the sea are rationally utilized, to ensure that the fishermen of the different member nations of the EU are treated on an equal basis and to conserve resources or to reduce overcapitalization (Cunningham and Young, 1983, p. 3). With regard to these aspects, the Council agreed on 25 January 1983 to activate, within six months, special EC measures which were designed to 'adjust capacity and improve productivity of fishing and aquaculture'. These measures consisted largely of proposals put forward by the EC Commission between 1977 and 1980 and included 'aids for laying up, temporarily or permanently, certain fishing vessels so that capacity can be adjusted in the light of the conservation needs', 'aids for exploratory fishing and cooperation with certain non-member countries in the context of joint ventures in order to encourage the redeployment of the Community's fishing activity' and 'aids for the construction and modernisation of certain fishing vessels and aquaculture facilities and for the installation of artificial structures to facilitate restocking and develop the fishing industry generally' (*Bulletin of the European Communities*, no. 1, 1983, p. 2). As stated above, these measures were to apply for three years and were to qualify for EC financing to the total of 250 million ECU: 76 million ECU for capacity adjustment; 18 million ECU for exploratory fishing and joint ventures; 156 million ECU for restructuring, i.e. for encouraging investment in the fishing industry (see Table 11.2 for details). It should be added, however, that the EU's financial contribution to any approved project is generally limited to 50% of its total cost, and that these are EU monies for which EU citizens can apply irrespective of the nationality. With regard to the latter point, Wise (1984, p. 244) argues that since a large percentage of these funds was 'designed to help fleets adjust to nearer-water fishing following the loss of rights in far-off grounds, Britain could expect to continue as a major recipient of [EC] structural aid following a pattern established over the previous 10 years'. The United Kingdom received about 40.8 million ECU during 1973–82 for the construction and modernization of vessels from EAGGF; this amounted to 35.8% of total EAGGF expenditures on this item over the specified period – see below.

Finally, with regard to agreements with non-EU countries, framework fisheries agreements were signed with the Faeroe Islands, Guinea, Guinea-Bissau, Norway, Spain, Sweden and the United States. In 1991, new protocols were concluded with Senegal, Morocco, Mauritania and São Tomé and Príncipe. The Council also decided on the provisional application of the protocol with Morocco, Guinea-Bissau, the Comros, Mozambique and Guinea and adopted two decisions on extension and amendment of agreements with the United States and the extension of the agreement with South Africa. The EU Commission was also authorized to negotiate fisheries agreements with the Caribbean countries of Antigua, Dominica, Saint Lucia and Suriname, all of which have been concluded. It was also authorized to negotiate agreement with Ecuador and Venezuela. Multilateral agreements were concluded

Table 11.2 ⬤ EC funds to assist the fisheries sector. 1983–86.

Proposed measures	Total expenditure (million ECU)
1. Directive on adjusting capacity	
(a) temporary withdrawal	44
(b) permanent withdrawal	32
2. Regulation on exploratory fishing and joint ventures	
(a) exploratory fishing	11
(b) joint ventures	7
3. Regulation on a common measure for restructuring, etc.	
(a) construction and modernisation of fishing vessels	118
(b) aquaculture	34
(c) artificial structures intended for restocking	4
Total expenditure over three years	250

Source Official Journal of the European Communities, 26, C28, 3 February, 1983, 1.

with a view to the Community's participation in international agreements covering the north-east and north-west Atlantic, the Antarctic and salmon in the north Atlantic, and talks were in progress with regard to the EU's participation in international agreements on tuna and whaling and to its joining the organizations that control fishing in the Baltic, and in the central and south-east Atlantic.

One could continue along these lines by adding the annual changes that have been introduced, but such developments are easy to follow by reading the appropriate sections of various EU publications. Thus all that needs adding is to state that the major external events in this sector in 1996 were the signing on 26 February of a new four-year agreement on cooperation in the sea fisheries sector between the EU and Morocco, the work carried out in various international organizations, especially the signing of the agreement on the implementation of UNCLOS regarding the conservation and management of straddling stocks and highly migratory species, and the EU's accession, within the framework of FAO, to the agreement to promote compliance with international conservation and management measures by fishing vessels on the high seas. Within the EU, the Commission adopted a proposal for a decision on the objectives of and rules for restructuring the EU's fishing industry for 1997–2002, with a view to achieving a sustainable balance between resources and their exploitation.

11.3 Developments in the CFP

The progress of the CFP has been almost along the expected lines, especially when two years after the inauguration of the CFP, the EU began to take decisions on TACs and their country allocation in December so as to inform the EC fishermen of their expected catches well before they started fishing. Although later agreements on the TACs and individual country quotas took longer to reach than expected, the delays were mainly for technical reasons and took no longer than two or three months, which is natural, given the bargaining nature of the situation.

With regard to the promised assistance for the restructuring of the fishing industry, Table 11.3 gives some indication of the progress made in this regard. The table shows that for the period 1983–86 the EC intended to extend aid totalling about 219 million ECU, but for the first three years the total was only about 174 million ECU. Thus it would seem that the aid for the restructuring of the fisheries industry fell short of the promised of 250 million ECU for the first three years of the CFP. If, however, one were to include aid amounting to about 68 million ECU granted under Regulation (EEC) 355/77, which was adopted on 15 February 1977 and which

Table 11.3 ⬤ Aid granted under the common measures for the restructuring, modernizing and developing of the fisheries industry and for developing aquaculture under Regulation (EEC) 2908/83 (million ECU).

Appropriations	1983	1984	1985	1986	1987	1988
Belgium	0.35	3.95	2.41	2.38	0.41	0.10
Denmark	2.71	4.60	4.09	7.69	1.21	3.29
France	6.07	12.80	5.86	13.78	12.42	4.74
West Germany	3.13	3.18	1.12	4.92	4.41	1.39
Greece	6.70	2.44	3.95	9.51	6.37	5.41
Ireland	5.91	3.07	1.45	3.50	1.84	4.99
Italy	10.68	22.11	11.22	18.99	16.12	11.40
Netherlands	1.87	2.06	0.46	2.68	0.66	0.57
Portugal	–	–	–	–	11.22	2.85
Spain	–	–	–	–	32.30	18.11
United Kingdom	7.39	9.90	5.04	11.07	7.23	7.50
Total	44.81	64.11	35.60	74.52	94.09	60.35

Source Calculated from various issues of the Bulletin of the European Communities.

comes under the EAGGF structural fund, then the latter sum is only about 8 million ECU short of the target.

Another way of looking at the finances provided by the EC to support the restructuring of the fisheries industry is simply to quote the figures from the EC General Budget which come under the heading of fisheries (chapters 40–47). These are given in Table 11.4. It does not matter which three years cover the appropriate sum mentioned in the CFP since it is evident that the total of 250 million ECU was exceeded between 1983 and 1986. The comparison is made even more difficult by the EC's decision to inject a further 850 million ECU for restructuring over the five-year period 1988–92: if one took the 1988 figure as the starting point, the EC would be on target, and the drastic fall since 1993 corroborates this.

It should be added that the projects covered by the 1983 regulation amounted to 4,271 while those covered by the 1977 regulation added a further 299 to this total. Moreover, a large number of new projects is being added each year, for example, in 1991 alone, 591 projects were approved for the modernization of vessel capacity. Also, Wise's expectation of the United Kingdom getting about 36% of the total aid is way off target since the average received by the United Kingdom between 1983 and 1986 was about 15% – see above.

These figures also point to the most significant development in the CFP: the accession of Portugal and Spain. These countries were expected to increase the number of EC fishermen by 90%, the fishing capacity by 80% and fish consumption

Table 11.4 ⬤ Allocations from the EC General Budget for the restructuring of the fisheries industry.

Year	Million ECU
1983	107.24
1984	112.35
1985	111.73
1986	189.62
1987	197.29
1988	325.89
1989	348.24
1990	431.57
1991	530.80
1992	594.90
1993	25.00
1994	25.64
1995	28.20
1996	35.50
1997[a]	45.95

[a] Provisional figure.

by EC citizens by about 50%. The changes in these totals reflect this reality. It should be added that as a result of the Iberian enlargement the EU has become the third largest fishing area in the world, and this position is further consolidated with the addition of Finland and Sweden.

Finally, as already indicated, the EU continues to negotiate agreements with third countries.

Before bringing this section to an end, it should be mentioned that the EU Commission has decided that the measures that have been introduced have not succeeded in halting the danger to fish stocks, owing to excessive mortality, particularly in the case of juveniles, and over-capacity of the fishing fleet. It has, therefore, recommended that the CFP should be amended, with special attention given to the following:

1. Distribution of responsibility in accordance with the 'subsidiarity' principle, conferring responsibility on the parties concerned, especially fishing organizations.

2. More stringent regulation of access of resources by a system of licences to cut back excess capacity.

3. A new classification of fishing activities (multiannual, multispecies and analytical TACs, as appropriate).

4. More stringent control mechanisms, by improving in particular the monitoring of vessel movements.

5. Enforcement of rules which are in the common interest, through suitable economic incentives and, where appropriate, the use of deterrent sanctions.

6. Greater synergy between management of internal and external resources.

7. Maintenance of certain principles established, notably the principle of relative stability with regard to fishing activities, the derogation from the principle of freedom of access within the twelve-mile limit and the present arrangement for the Shetland area (possibly extending this to other regions).

8. Stronger structural management, mainly by the inclusion of structural measures under the reform of the structural funds.

9. Introduction of appropriate social accompanying measures, in accordance with the principle of cohesion, with particular emphasis on the concentration of EU resources and instruments in support of those regions least developed and most dependent on fisheries.

Thus, at least in the Commission's opinion, the recent developments in the CFP should galvanize all concerned into undertaking appropriate action.

11.4 Reservations

Although the agreement on the CFP has been much applauded, a great deal of caution should be exercised. Firstly, the use of such words as 'rational' and 'fair' immediately reminds one of the problems of the CAP where similar terminology came to mean self-sufficiency and an income to farmers much closer to, if not in excess of, the national average. Indeed, one aspect of the CFP is that, when the price of fish falls, the fishermen can withdraw their excess stocks from the market in return for the receipt of financial assistance from the funds designated for the purpose. Secondly, there is the apparent conflict between the structural aspects and the market organization, since the structure seeks conservation, while the market organization encourages larger catches by giving price supports which are directly related to the size of the catch. Thirdly, it is inevitable that TACs will be negotiated annually; hence a tense bargaining atmosphere is likely to be generated over quota allocations. This reminds one of the classical case where it is desirable for oligopolists to pursue a policy of joint profit maximization, but where the outcome is for each oligopolist to try to maximize his or her share of the profit. Fourthly, as Cunningham and Young (1983, p. 3) rightly state, even if the structural measures could be achieved

> almost complete reliance is placed on management methods which might be termed 'biological' in that, while they generally improve the condition of the fish stock itself, they will not result in any long-term improvement in the economic health of the [fishing industry]. Typical of such biological techniques are net mesh size restrictions, closed seasons, closed areas and limitations on the use of certain efficient methods of capture.

11.5 Conclusion

Although the CFP is about a decade old and the accession of Portugal and Spain has gone smoothly and no problems are envisaged regarding the membership of Finland and Sweden (Austria has no concerns here), it is still too early to make firm predictions about the appropriateness or otherwise of this policy. This is because the points mentioned in the previous section do indicate that there are potential problems which the EU Commission must keep constantly in mind if the situation is not to be potentially explosive. Moreover, as we have seen the Commission feels that the CFP has been facing severe problems; hence its proposals for further drastic action. That stated, one must conclude by sharing in the applause for the reaching of agreement in 1983 after negotiations which took six years of hard bargaining and mackerel wars with Denmark, and for the smooth incorporation of the Iberian countries into the agreement, finalized through the adoption of Regulation 2027/95, relating to the establishment of a system for the management of fishing activities in certain EU fishing areas and resources which started to apply from 1 January 1996. One must also add that since the CFP puts emphasis on restrictions on output and sets prices which bear some relationship to actual market prices, it would seem that the excesses and absurdities of the CAP will not be repeated here.

chapter twelve

EU transport policy

F. McGOWAN

Transport is one of the few areas where a Common Policy was explicitly provided for in the original Treaties forming the Community. However, the substance of the Common Transport Policy (CTP) has always lagged behind the ambitions of both the original intention and the Commission's efforts. Although the 1990s have seen the Commission more active than ever – and with more successes than in the past – the objective of a CTP remains elusive. To understand why efforts towards such a policy have had such limited results is to understand something of the priorities of national policy making, of the scope for a Community role, and of the interaction between the Commission and other member states towards establish a division of labour.

Given the dynamics of policy making in this area, the chapter takes a broad view of the transport policy debate in the Community. It considers the nature of the debate at a national level, particularly the policy implications of the links between national transport industries and governments, as well as the broader trends in both the transport industries and in policies towards them. The chapter touches upon the role of other Community policies (such as environment and competition policy which have provided opportunities for Commission action). The focus is, however, on the development of transport policy, both in terms of the effort to create a Common Transport Policy and the specific initiatives in different sectors.

12.1 The transport sector and transport policy

To understand what transport policies comprise, it might be useful to ask why transport policies are needed: what are the characteristics of the transport industries that require government intervention? The structural characteristics of the sectors necessitate that transport policy has included a significant regulatory dimension: the control of monopolies (most notably in railways, although with some manifestations in other transport sectors) and of 'excessive' competition (in industries such as road haulage, urban transport, shipping and air transport); and the management of externalities such as pollution, safety and congestion. Other characteristics point to a more interventionist or 'managerial' dimension: public goods issues, infrastructure provision and coordination of services. Finally, there may be general questions of economic policy which are acutely manifest in the transport sector: the provision of services to the needy or those in remote locations; and the use of transport for macroeconomic purposes such as controlling inflation through price controls, or pump-priming. Transport policy is therefore driven by a range of concerns, and is implemented by a variety of mechanisms: direct provision and ownership; legal controls and licenses; taxes and subsidies; information provision and research. There is a high degree of overlap between policy techniques in practice; public ownership may be a means of tackling both monopoly and equity issues. Equally, however, often the objectives to be served by measures will not be met or may have unintended consequences (Button, 1982).

The orientations of national transport policies vary across borders and over time, emphasizing different priorities and techniques. Thus, in the United Kingdom, the balance of policy has swung away from government intervention through public ownership and control of market access towards much greater reliance on market forces as evidenced by policies of privatization and liberalization. In Denmark, Germany and the Netherlands, transport policy is increasingly driven by environmental concerns. In France, there has been (and to some extent continues to be) a strong attachment to techniques of planning and central control. In the less developed member states, transport policy may be geared towards infrastructure development, on the basis of regional policy concerns. Interestingly, the potential contribution of improved networks to economic growth has also been rediscovered in more affluent member states (Gramlich, 1994; Roy, 1994).

Yet, despite these differences, certain broad characteristics of transport policy can be identified. In practice, national transport policies have been dominated by supplier interests, fostered by the close links between governments and industries in many sectors and countries: in most countries mass passenger transport (buses, railways, airlines) and some elements of freight transport, have been in public hands (OECD, 1992). Moreover, for the most part, policy making was characterized by an engineering philosophy where it often seemed that the primary objective was to maximize output rather than to distribute resources efficiently. In a sense, policy was orientated around the need to ensure sufficient supply to meet demand, but in practice this objective was self-serving as increased capacity often fostered increase in demand. Other concerns, such as environment, quality of life and efficiency in both the allocative and the technical senses, were often subordinated to this goal. The predominance of supplier interests was also reflected in the ways in which transport industries were regulated. For the most part systems of controlling prices and access served the interests of the incumbents in most industries. Many sectors were structured as cartels or monopolies, ostensibly on the grounds of managing co-ordination, but in practice to protect the industries as much as the consumers.

More recently, it appears that a wider range of interests, beyond those of the producer firms, is being accommodated within transport policy; in particular, consumer and environmental movements have gained a higher profile and their concerns are reflected in transport policy much more than was the case in the past. This has been reflected in a shift in policy which some regard as 'decentralization' or 'deregulation' (van Gent and Nijkamp, 1991). For a variety of reasons, partly ideological and partly as a result of increasing constraints in public budgets, there has been a move towards more market-based mechanisms in transport provision such as increased reliance on user charges or greater competition. Such changes cannot be viewed as irreversible but they have shifted the debate in many member states (Nijkamp *et al.*, 1990). As in other sectors (see Chapter 13), this increased emphasis on market mechanisms has an ambivalent relationship with environmental priorities; in some cases the two complement each other (as in the efforts to allocate the costs of externalities such as congestion, but in others there is a clear tension, for example, between the *laissez-faire* approach to meeting consumer needs and a more interventionist tendency in most environmental programmes – see Button, 1993).

The nature of national debate has been reflected at the Community level, although here the scope of interests addressed has probably been wider and the balance of policy has, on paper at least, been more liberal than in most member states.

12.2 The development of EU transport policy

Why was there a need for a common transport policy? Much of the justification focuses on the fact that transport is an essential element of economic activity. While the EU transport sector is important in its own right, accounting for about 4% of GDP employing over 4.5 million people and accounting for 28% of final energy consumption, its real importance stems from its infrastructural role. A Community approach it has been argued could improve coordination and produce cost savings in the provision of transport services. Although for most products transport charges account for a very small element of costs, their persuasiveness would mean that any savings would have an across the board effect, as well as a more substantial effect on the costs of those bulk commodities where transport is a larger component of total expenses. A common transport policy would be necessary to achieve these savings. For member states, the importance of transport was reflected in the high degree of government regulation and control of transport services and charges. There was a risk that such national arrangements would lead to differences in treatment, and even active discrimination, towards firms from other member states. A Community dimension to transport policy would, it was suggested, limit the extent of any such distortions to transport markets. Moreover, by tackling barriers to entry and facilitating a single system of rules governing transport, a Community dimension could contribute to a common market for goods as well as for transport services.

Such considerations, along with the political desirability of including it as part of the 'bargain' cast in the Rome Treaty negotiations (primarily to satisfy the Dutch who sought to take advantage of their location (Swann, 1992), meant that the drafters of the Rome Treaty included a whole chapter on the question of transport. The chapter focused on inland transportation and the carriage of goods by road, rail and river. It outlined a number of obligations upon member states to create a policy which would bring a European transport system into being. However, having attached such importance to transport policy in the Treaty, there were a number of omissions which reflected the failure of member states to agree on the priorities of a common policy. The most important was the exclusion of maritime (as opposed to inland) shipping and air transport. These sectors were excluded for political reasons, the desire of most states to maintain existing systems particularly of self-regulation in those sectors. The other, and more immediately problematic, omission was the lack of detail on how a policy for those sectors covered by the Treaty would be instituted and what it should address.

The Commission took the first steps in a memorandum published in 1961 and an Action Programme published in 1962. It indicted that such a policy should be designed to create competition in the transport sectors, reducing obstacles to trade, and to integrate Community transport systems by harmonizing fiscal, social and technical conditions and encouraging closer investment coordination. Yet, as noted, transport was a highly regulated, even protected, sector, with prices and production controlled through tariff systems and licenses and quotas. In its original proposals to liberalize these controls, the Commission took a gradualist approach, not seeking the complete removal of existing measures, but increasing the scope for competition. Indeed, the emphasis initially was arguably on harmonization rather than liberalization of national approaches to transport regulation. Even so, progress in agreeing to even modest reforms was limited and there were few achievements beyond a few regulations, for example requiring that member states consult with the Commission on national legislation and some weak rules on quotas, tariffs and investment. After a gap in activities caused by the French boycott of Community activities, the Commission presented further proposals for a common transport policy and received a limited response from the Council: agreement was reached on applying competition law to inland transport services, as well as some harmonization measures and rules on defining public service obligations (Degli Abbati, 1987). However, agreement on major reforms and a framework for determining them remained elusive.

Over the 1970s, the pace if anything slowed, as new member states and new policy shocks (such as energy crises and environmental concerns) had to be absorbed (Molle, 1990). Following the accession of Denmark, Ireland and the United Kingdom in 1973, the balance of opinion on transport issues shifted slightly; the United Kingdom was even then pursuing a relatively more liberal transport policy than that pursued in most other member states. In practice, however, the differences between member states and their reluctance to accept a major role for the Community prevailed. In 1973, the Commission presented new proposals on a common policy, reflecting the wider concerns of such a policy (regional development, energy and environment, etc.). However, the priority remained one of harmonization to establish a Community transport system (Erdmenger, 1983). The Commission scaled down its proposals on a policy but to little avail. Some initiatives on transport were taken but they were disparate and did not in any sense constitute a common transport policy.

Such was the lack of progress in agreeing Community policies for the transport sector that in 1983 the European Parliament took the Council to Court on the grounds that it had failed to act (a move supported by the Commission and the Dutch government). The Court's judgment obliged the Council to move more substantially on a common policy, particularly in those areas where transport services needed to be opened up to intra-Community competition (other areas were seen as non-obligatory). The measures needed to bring about such a market were absorbed into the 1992 programme.

The White Paper identified services as a key area for completion of the internal market, with transport a particularly important target. Drawing on the Court's decision, the Commission outlined a range of initiatives designed to open up transport services: ending quotas on transport of goods by road, permitting freedom of services for road passenger transport, cabotage rights in freight transport by road and inland waterway, and liberalization of sea and air transport services. In addition, it sought to liberalize frontier controls to permit freer flow of transport and a harmonization of indirect taxation regimes which impinged on the transport industries. The Commission established a timetable for these objectives and threatened that failure to make progress would mean the use of competition rules to open up the transport sector (CEC, 1985g). Although the Commission stressed that these measures formed only one part of a common transport policy, they were to dominate transport discussions over the following years. While the timetables for achieving progress originally laid out were not kept to, by the end of 1992, almost all of the measures planned had been agreed. As the Single Market provisions pushed forward the liberalizing aspect of transport policy, other elements began to gain a higher profile, in particular infrastructural questions and the impact of transport on the environment.

Infrastructure has been part of the Community's transport policy agenda since the 1960s. The balance of policy proposals has focused on two elements: the allocation of costs to users of infrastructure and the coordination of development of and investment in transport systems (Whitelegg, 1988). Attempts to allocate the costs of infrastructure and charge for their use have long been discussed, but have failed to be developed at a Community level; to the extent that different approaches in member states led to differential treatment, a Community role was needed. However, possibly because of the sensitivity of national policies, member states continued to pursue their own policies in this area. It is possible, however, that growing interest in the environment, which has extended the debate on cost allocation to questions of internalizing the external costs of transport in terms of pollution and congestion, might bring this issue back on the agenda.

Infrastructure coordination has been discussed since the 1960s; indeed a procedure for consultation was one of the very few achievements of that period. However, even after amendments in 1978, this measure proved to be rather ineffective, not least because it was without any supporting budget. Such a budget was provided in the early 1980s, but the policy has mainly focused on infrastructure within rather than between member states, largely for regional development purposes.

Over the 1980s, however, spurred on by pressures from European industry for a greater level of investment to plug the 'missing links' in the European transport network, and a series of initiatives in member states (such as the high-speed train and the Channel Tunnel), the idea of a better transborder infrastructure has taken off (Vickerman, 1995; European Round Table, 1985). Indeed, transport infrastructure has been the most important component of the 'Trans-European Networks' initiative which has become embodied in the Maastricht Treaty (McGowan, 1993a).

Environmental protection has also played a role in transport policy deliberations, at least since the 1970s. However, it was not until the 1980s, when the issue's political salience had grown, that it had a significant impact in its own right. Part of this impact was seen in the inclusion of environment in the SEA, a development which permitted a much more activist approach by the Commission. In the transport sector, this activism culminated in 1992 with the publication of a green paper on the impact of transport on the environment. This put forward the concept of 'sustainable mobility', identifying the need for action, taking into account the manifold impacts on the environment (COM (92) 80).

Spurred on by the success of the Single Market programme in securing a number of agreements on specific transport industries, the Commission returned to the development of a coherent common transport policy. In its report, 'The Future Development of the Common Transport Policy', the Commission identified 1992 as a turning point in transport policy: no longer would the Community's role in the sector be challenged, while in most aspects an open transport market would be in place. With the Treaty on European Union, the Community would be able to develop the transport infrastructure, and use the sector to contribute to cohesion and competitiveness. In a sense, the focus of attention would shift from 'negative' policies, removing obstacles to a single market, towards a much more positive and comprehensive policy (COM (92) 494).

The Community's Common Transport Policy has therefore shifted its emphasis towards pro-active policies. Older concerns have not disappeared but in many cases the task facing the Community in those areas is now one of regulation and implementation rather than negotiating what should be done. According to the Commission, the policy priorities now cover five main themes: the development and integration of the Community transport system; safety in transport; environmental protection; social protection; external relations.

The development and integration of the Community transport system covers a wide range of objectives. There is a regulatory dimension which covers issues of infrastructure and externalities charging, the removal of the remaining barriers to a common transport market and the control of state aids. There is also a technical and research aspect to this work which covers such issues as the standardization of networks and control systems and an R&D programme. These activities also contribute to the Community's role in network development, in particular the use of telematics in such activities as road traffic management.

Safety, environmental and social aspects indicate the broadening-out of the Common Transport Policy; while aspects of these issues have been present in

Community programmes in the past, the priority on competition and internal market issues – and the difficulties in reaching agreement – meant that little was done in these other areas. Safety controls will cover such issues as carriage of dangerous goods, accident investigations and road safety. Environmental protection initiatives will embrace the concept of 'sustainable mobility' and cover the encouragement of public transport, the development of rules to control noise and gas emissions and waste management. The application of social protection will cover rules on qualifications, training and working conditions, particularly working hours.

A further broadening of policy is apparent in the Commission's plans for Community roles in relations with third countries. One aspect of the special nature of transport has been its international nature. Some arrangements date back to the 19th century and it has been an uphill battle for the Commission to play a role. The new document aims at establishing a Community mandate for the negotiations of agreements with non-EU states. However, the Commission's plans also include the participation in international agreements and the provision of aid and assistance, particularly to Eastern Europe and the CIS.

These objectives were synthesized in the 1995 Commission's Action Programme for a Common Transport Policy – which outlined the Commission's work programme until the end of the century – which set three objectives: quality improvement, the Single Market and external policy (CEC, 1995j). Quality improvement refers to the overall improvement of the transport system including the integration of transport modes, new technologies and particularly alternatives to private road transport. This objective includes initiatives from the Trans-European Transport Network Programme through the Short Sea Shipping initiative to the so-called 'Citizens' Network'. The proposals for furthering the Single Market address questions of market access (through greater competition policy and liberalization and tackling overcapacity), pricing techniques and the social dimension (mainly working conditions). The proposals on external relations are mainly concerned with the development of closer links with neighbouring states to the south and the east of the Union.

12.3 Transport policy and other EU policies

Community policies towards the transport sector encompass a wider range of concerns than those contained in the official sectoral policy statements: in addition to the issue of environmental policy discussed earlier, elements of competition, industrial and regional policy impinge on decisions taken by firms and governments.

Competition policy is an area where the Commission has taken a careful approach. The problems facing the Commission in developing a transport policy were for many years compounded by the difficulties which it faced in applying competition law to the different sectors of the transport industry. Regulation 17/62, the general enabling rules for the competition provisions, was disapplied from the transport sector under Regulation 141/62 (Maltby, 1993). It was not until 1988 that the rules were applied to inland transport, 1986 to maritime transport and 1987 to air transport. There is certainly a balance to be struck in the Community's use of competition rules in the transport industries. As noted, many sectors operate in monopolistic and cartel-like ways, contrary to the Treaty of Rome. Yet many of the reasons for such arrangements (time-tabling, scheduling, etc.) can have positive effects. The problem has been how to maintain such advantages without permitting the more questionable practices associated with such arrangements (price setting): can competition rules be applied to prevent the disadvantages of cut-throat competition and monopoly (Erdmenger, 1983)?

Industrial policy impacts focus primarily on the interaction between the transport providers and their suppliers, and are concentrated in technological innovation initiatives (although some sectors are also covered by the Community's procurement regime; see Chapter 9). As part of the Community's research and development Framework Programme, new developments in materials and information technology with implications for the transport sector are supported. There are also specific initiatives, notably DRIVE, which aims to develop guided transport systems, and similar programmes in the maritime and aerospace sectors. Regional policy concerns have largely been manifested in the very substantial funds devoted by the Community to developing infrastructure in less developed regions. It is likely that such a regional approach will be intensified under the Trans-European Networks Initiative which seeks to improve transport links between member states, especially in the areas of roads, high-speed rail systems and air traffic control.

12.4 EU policy towards transport sectors

As noted, the main focus of transport policy for much of the Community's history has been the inland carriage of goods by road, rail and river, and some effort to apply a common regime to all of them was made, at least initially. In practice, however, policies have diverged and concentrated on discrete characteristics of each sector. Policies as other transport activities have also been driven by the nature of the sectors and the national and industrial interests involved. In order to understand how much or how little has been achieved, therefore, it is necessary to examine how policy has developed in each sector.

12.4.1 Road transport

Community policy in this area has focused primarily on the carriage of goods, although some initiatives on both coach travel and car transport have also been discussed. Goods transportation has been tightly regulated in most member states in a way that was protectionist in its outcomes (OECD, 1990). That protection extended to a reluctance to open up services when proposals from the Commission were made to liberalize prices and capacity controls and to harmonize other aspects of national policy which might be regarded as affecting competition.

Community policy on pricing aimed at a relaxation of the controls which had prevailed in most markets through the introduction of a rate bracket system which specified maximum and minimum rates within which carriers and consignors would be free to negotiate. While the policy was largely a pragmatic one, intended as an interim measure given the opposition of many members to total liberalization, it also accorded with transitional transport policy views that price controls were needed to prevent both monopolistic pricing and destructive competition. Policy on capacity has aimed to open up the systems of licensing and quotas for international services both of which were primarily based on bilateral agreements among member states, and eventually to remove restrictions on national markets, permitting cabotage. The existing system led to a highly inefficient use of resources since trucks would often have to travel long distances without any cargo. Although gradual progress was made in this area – primarily through the development of a Community 'quota' for each member state's industry – the effects were limited, often because the Commission's initial proposals would be watered down before approval was given by the Council: the Community quota was intended to replace bilateral arrangements but remained 'experimental' and was confined to a small proportion of the market for many years. National traffic was left untouched by Community policy for many years (Degli Abbati, 1987).

The lack of progress in this area was one of the reasons why the 1992 project focused on transport. Even within that programme, the rate of progress on securing agreement remained slow. It was not until the summer of 1993 that the Council agreed to the final measures of road haulage liberalization, a system of cabotage. The agreement draws together a number of strands of road transport policy, primarily that of road charging, and phases in cabotage over the period until 1998.

The other element of road haulage policy, harmonization, has scarcely fared any better. Over the years, the Commission has tackled a range of policy areas which it felt required harmonization: social policy (hours of working), technical standards (weights and dimensions of trucks), infrastructure changing and fiscal regimes (excise duty and road taxation). Each aspect has provoked more controversy than might have been expected (the 1970s tachograph dispute when the UK opposed plans for a device to monitor driving patterns being the most bizarre). Again, the Single Market initiative has brought some aspects of the harmonization problem closer to resolution, such as road charges.

Community policies on road passenger transport are rather less developed perhaps because cross-border, mass road transportation has been relatively limited. A series of measures on coach and bus services was introduced in the 1970s but with little effect. Community policy on individual passenger transport by car has been largely indirect. Community policy has impinged on support for national vehicle manufacturers, on trade in vehicles, on relations between suppliers and distributors of cars, on energy taxes, on emissions and on new technologies for guided transport, but not on car transport directly. This is perhaps unsurprising, given the nature of such transport which is generally seen as a matter of personal liberty. What may prompt a more visible Community role in policy on cars is the increasingly intractable problems of pollution and congestion, although again the impact may be indirect, supporting the development of rail services or encouraging infrastructure charges or environmental taxes. The Commission's recent initiatives on road pricing and the 'citizens' network' (COM (95) 601, COM (95) 691) are indicative of this concern (although the main outcomes are likely to be modest financial support since EU controls in this area are likely to face opposition and legal challenge).

12.4.2 Rail transport

Community policy on rail transport has had to address a series of problems. For many decades the railway sector in the Community has been stuck as a loss-making industry, requiring massive government subsidy. In terms of both freight and passenger services, traffic has been in decline for most of the period (as rail lost out to motor transport for short-distance and air transport for longer-distance travel), while the costs of maintaining services have been increasing. While many of the problems facing the industry are a result of productivity problems within the industry, it is also clear that in some respects the industry is in an unfair position. The railways have to bear the costs of their infrastructure in a way which other transport modes are not required to do. They are also obliged to support public service obligations, often without direct compensation.

In its policy towards the industry, the Commission has sought to rationalize the operations of national railways by encouraging a clearer allocation of costs between different aspects of the industry's operations. While it has been able to secure some agreements from member states, the practical effects of these reforms have up until recently been rather limited.

While the Community's policy originally focused on freight transport by rail (where the issues have been similar to those arising in road haulage), it has also been involved in overall railway issues, encompassing passenger services as well. The main issues to be addressed by the Commission have been relationships between railways and national governments. In a series of regulations dating from the 1960s, the Commission's aim has been to render these relationships more transparent, in accounting terms, and to ensure that social objectives are directly supported by governments. This effort was consolidated in the 1970s when the Commission sought to improve the railway industry's financial position, by separating out the different functions of railway service provision.

For the most part these efforts came to nothing, with member states at best conforming with the letter but not the spirit of Community requirements. Policy in this area appeared moribund. However, the revival of rail transport in some member states, largely thanks to the development of high-speed train services, has also affected Community involvement, reinforced by the growing influence of environmental and competition concerns within the Commission.

The interest in high-speed rail transport has been a focus for rivalry between European states for many years. However, it was only with the determination of the French government and state railway to make a reality of the idea of a high-speed network that the issue returned to the political agenda. The Paris–Lyon route, opened in 1981, proved a dramatic success, gaining market share at the expense of road and particularly air transport. Over the 1980s the government and SNCF extended the network. Other countries also sought to repeat the success of the TGV, though generally without devoting the same resources (for example, seeking to run on existing tracks rather than building new ones as was done in France). The Channel Tunnel also helped. In 1988, the Community of European Railways launched a plan for a high-speed network across the Community, justifying it on environmental as well as economic grounds (CER, 1988).

These developments interested the Commission. It sought to develop the idea of a high-speed network across the Community, granting some funds for developing such routes in member states, and relaunched its policy for the railway sector, drawing on ideas first considered in the 1970s, but not implemented since. In its Communication on Community Rail Policy, the Commission spelt out its plans to increase transparency in the industry by separating out the different functions of rail transport (track and services). This would allow both subsidies to those elements which required it and competition on those elements where it was possible. The Commission felt that, while rail had lost out to other transport forms partly through unfair treatment (policies favouring road use in particular), much of the industry's problems stemmed from its own inefficiencies engendered as a result of closed national markets. If these were opened up, not only would the industry benefit from competition where possible (particularly on a new network of high-speed services), but social and regional objectives could be pursued in a more efficient way (Henry, 1993). A 1996 White Paper on rail policy sought to extend liberalization beyond the international freight and passenger markets, whether through direct competition between railway companies or through competitive franchises for less attractive routes (CEC, 1996k).

The proposals on reorganization have met with considerable opposition from some member states and national railways. Their arguments have been similar to the attitudes of other public utilities insofar as they have seen European rail policy as working against the various social and regional policy objectives. In other states (notably the Netherlands and Sweden) the momentum of policy has gone beyond that envisaged in current EU proposals (although in one country – the UK – the reform stopped short of a radical restructuring).

As for the high-speed network, there appears to be a sustained momentum, boosted by the aforementioned Trans-European Networks initiative. A number of countries have developed HST services between major cities and there are moves to link across borders (notably the Paris–Brussels–Amsterdam–Cologne route). There is, however, a question over how different national systems can be harmonized in time (voltages, loadings, etc.) while the benefits of such a system seem likely to focus upon the core of the Community and wealthier groups in society (Community of European Railways, 1995; Whitelegg, 1992).

12.4.3 Shipping

In addressing the shipping sector, the Community has been developing two rather distinct regimes: one dating back to the early years of the Community, on inland transportation and one, dating largely from the late 1970s, for maritime transportation.

Community policy towards inland waterways has followed many of the priorities of harmonization and liberalization encountered in other inland freight markets although, as in those sectors, progress has for the most part been very slow. Over the years policies on price and other activities have been agreed. In recent years, however, there has been more effort to address liberalization and to tackle the problems of over-capacity in the sector. Proposals to move away from the rotation scheme of cargo allocation towards a more competitive regime were made in the early 1990s while a programme to encourage scrapping of excess capacity – whereby owners are given financial incentives to scrap vessels and no new vessel can be constructed without an equivalent reduction in tonnage – was agreed in the same period (COM (95) 199). While policy has been concerned largely with the immediate problems of over-capacity in the sector, there is a recognition that the contribution of the sector could be much greater and considerable efforts are being made to improve its prospects. This is driven by the view that (as with rail) the sector could take some of the strain off congested roads and interface more effectively with other modes of transport. As a result a programme for a Trans-European Inland Water-Way Network has been proposed (CEC, 1995a).

While progress on developing policy for inland waterway transport has been slow, at least it was seen as a legitimate area of policy; the principle of a policy for sea transport was not even generally accepted until the 1970s. The problem with securing agreement on a policy in this area lay in the wording of Article 84, paragraph 2, the final section of the Title on Transport within the Treaty of Rome. This states that 'The Council may, acting unanimously, decide whether, to what extent and by what procedure appropriate provisions may be laid down for sea and air transport'. The wording is ambiguous – did the drafters of the Treaty intend that these sectors be excluded from the Treaty as a whole or just the Transport Title? It appears that the intention of the Dutch in pushing for this provision was to keep the sector away from Community scrutiny, in line with their own *laissez-faire* approach to the sector (Bredimas and Tzoannos, 1983). Certainly that was the result as with other elements of the Treaty, ambiguity effectively exempted the industry.

It is understandable why those in favour of the status quo would have wanted exemption. A substantial element of the industry was hardly structured competitively. The non-bulk shipping services were organized as cartels within the 'conference' system: agreements among shipowners which allocated cargoes, fixed prices, capacity and schedules (Sturmey, 1962). The system, which has its roots in the last century, was supported by most governments as necessary to avoid what they believed to be destructive competition. At face value, however, such a system was not compatible with the Treaty of Rome and its provisions on competition (Bohme, 1983).

The conference system has dominated the Community debate on a common maritime policy. An important factor leading to the development of Community policy was the agreement within the United Nations Conference on Trade and Development on a code of conduct for liner conferences, adopted in 1974. The code, which was intended to protect and promote developing country shipping industries through various market sharing devices, was at odds with EC law. A number of member states ratified the Treaty on the strength of a regulation which reconciled the spirit of the code with Community law (as well as committing the Commission to develop a regulation on applying competition law in the sector – see House of Lords, 1986).

The pace of debate on a common maritime policy quickened in the 1980s, largely motived by the need to bring the industry into line with Community competition rules and to respond to policies of other states to protect their own industries. In 1985, the Commission presented a package of measures which tackled these issues: the Council agreed to them by the end of 1986. The package consisted of four regulations which covered the application of competition rules to maritime transport, the principle of freedom to provide services within the Community and between the Community and third countries, measures to tackle unfair pricing and measures to safeguard access to cargoes. Of these measures, the regulation on competition has probably been the most important.

The competition regulation is intended to reconcile the practices within liner shipping (principally conferences) with the provision of Articles 85 and 86. At the core of the regulation is a block exemption, which unlike other such provisions is not limited in time. Indeed, it is generally agreed that the regulation applies a rather liberal set of rules to the conference system, albeit providing the Commission with the scope to intervene (Kreis, 1992). A further extension of competition law to other forms of market sharing (such as consortia) was agreed in 1992. Equally, however, the Commission has been prepared to use its powers when arrangements between companies overstep the mark. The Commission applied the competition rules for the first time in 1992, when it fined a number of liner companies operating services to West and Central Africa (Maltby, 1993).

One of the issues which they have tried to tackle has been the decline in the shipping industry within the Community. A relative decline in the importance of the fleet has been under way for many decades. However, over the 1980s the decline accelerated as the absolute size of the fleet halved. The decline reflects not only a smaller industry but the move by many operators to flag out. This process has been driven by a need to cut costs by registering shipping in countries where lower standards of social protection and wages, tax advantages and (allegedly) less exacting technical standards are in place. A number of member states have attempted to tackle the problem by offering special treatment to local fleets, for example by setting up offshore fleets.

The problem has also been tackled at a Community level. At the time of the agreement on the 1986 package, the Council recognized the need to maintain and develop the industry. In 1989 the commission forwarded proposals. In its analysis, the Commission argued on grounds which resembled those familiar in other cases of protection (strategic importance, both economic and military, employment and training considerations, and balance of payments). However, the proposals stopped short of those used in other industries, perhaps reflecting the international nature of the industry and the need to maintain a broadly open market for shipping services. The Commission's solution focused on the development of a European registry (along with other measures and a clarification of conditions under which fiscal and financial support could be given to the industry – see CEC, 1989b), but the measures do not seem to have arrested the decline of the sector, as the most recent Commission initiative recognized (CEC, 1992h). However, while this communication covered the range of maritime affairs (from aquaculture to research and development) and aimed to foster a revival of the sector, its only substantial initiative was the establishment of a forum for debating the industry's fortunes.

Given the near impossibility of the traditional policy of promoting–protecting the sector, the last few years have seen a significant reorientation of Community policy with the emphasis less on the 'producers' (shipowners) and more on the 'users' (shippers). The emphasis is now on efforts to liberalize European shipping markets (where possible), to improve the viability of the European fleet, to increase the efficiency of shipping operations, to promote new shipping markets (as in the initiative on promoting short sea shipping as an alternative to road haulage – see COM (95)) and to protect the workforce and the environment (CEC, 1992h, CEC, 1996i).

12.4.4 Air transport

The European air industry has been dominated by government-owned carriers for most of its history. These airlines are responsible for the bulk of scheduled air transport, both internationally and internally. While private companies did exist (such as British Caledonian and many of the operators in the charter market), they were for the most past second-order carriers. Needless to say, the public operators have been protected by governments in the international regulatory framework; like most international air transport, European civil aviation is regulated by a combination of bilateral treaties and airlines. The bilateral agreement covers the range of terms and conditions of air services between countries, in particular issues of market entry, tariffs, routes and capacity (McGowan and Trengove, 1986).

The EC countries have traditionally conducted air transport regulation individually with each country negotiating a set of bilateral agreements. The Community was not involved in the sector, despite the identification of air transport as a *'sector d'urgence'* by the Spaak Committee which laid the blueprint for the Treaty of Rome (Comité intergouvernemental créé par la conférence de Messina, 1956). It has only been in the late 1980s that a specifically Community regime for the industry emerged. Like the marine transport sector, air transport was exempted from coverage by the Treaty's broader principles until an agreement on a specific policy was achieved.

The first serious efforts to formulate an aviation policy were made in the early 1970s and were largely unsuccessful, despite the previously mentioned ECJ decision of 1974, which found that the general rules of the Treaty did apply to the air transport (as well as the sea) sectors. A few years later, the Commission published its first formal memorandum on air transport policy with the aim of suggesting measures to bring more 'flexibility' to the European air transport market (CEC, 1979c). It recommended limited liberalization in the areas of access, state aids and competition policy. It was effectively ignored by member states and their airlines, and only a few limited measures were adopted in its wake (on regional services and on pricing).

A more comprehensive and committed effort at reform was made in 1984 with the publication of the Second Memorandum on Air Transport (CEC, 1984d). Although it established a wide-ranging agenda, it was aimed at gradual reform. The Memorandum stated at the outset that a US-style deregulation was not desirable and couched its proposals for change very much within the context of the existing regulatory framework: 'There is scope for introducing more flexibility and competition into the existing system without destroying it or losing the benefits it has brought about.'

The initial proposals in the package were the removal from bilateral agreements of any obligations, placed on airlines by governments, to participate in arrangements (such as revenue pooling) potentially inconstant with the Treaty's competition rules and a relaxation of most of the conditions found in bilaterals (on capacity, fare setting). In addition, however, the proposals also provided a limited exception of various fare-setting, capacity-sharing and revenue-pooling activities from the competition rules for a fixed period (seven years). However, although the reforms were relatively modest in their impact, the bulk of governments and airlines remained opposed to reform (the United Kingdom was the main exception). For the most part they sought to obtain exemption from competition rules without offering concessions on greater flexibility and access.

The Commission was helped in securing an agreement by the publication of a judgement from the ECJ in the *Nouvelles Frontieres* case which concerned a French court action against a discount travel agent which was accused of offering tickets at below approved levels. The French court took the case to Europe to establish whether or not the competition rules applied in the case. The Court found the competition rules did apply to the sector, but left it to the Commission and the national governments to apply them in the wake of an aviation policy. The Commission was able to use the judgment to threaten legal action against national airlines and, in the process, to use the ruling as a bargaining counter with which to secure an agreement with member states on a package of reforms (McGowan and Seabright, 1989).

By mid-1987, the Council had agreed on such a package, which effectively built on the Second Memorandum proposals (final agreement was postponed until the end of that year owing to an Anglo-Spanish dispute over the status of Gibraltar airport). At the same time, the rules of competition policy were applied to the sector (initially only international air transport within the Community). Two regulations were agreed which provided the Commission with the framework for reconciling the operations of the industry with the principles of the Treaty. The first regulation identified a number of areas of agreement between airlines on what might be called technical issues (such as standards, training, etc.) and excluded them from the purview of the provisions of Article 85 (1). The second regulation granted the principle of block exemptions under Article 85 (3) in areas such as fare setting, capacity planning, revenue sharing, slot allocations and CRS systems, even though they were recognized as infringements of article 85 (1) (Argyris, 1989).

The Commission also made clear its commitment to regulating the EC air transport industry in a number of other initiatives. Aside from attempting to develop a Community policy in areas such as air traffic control, the main thrust of policy was in the area of enforcing competition. Its most important action was its intervention in the BA–BCal merger in 1987–88. After the takeover was finally agreed at the UK level, the Commissions' Competition directorate indicated that it considered the merger a potential abuse of dominant position and sought further concessions by BA on limiting its operations from Gatwick within Europe (successfully). Further indications of the Commission exercising a regulatory role, checking abuses of market power and restrictions on access, followed. In 1988 it fined the Belgian airline Sabena 100,000 ECU for denying another carrier (London European Airways) access to its CRS system. It also developed a general regulation on CRS systems establishing a Code of Conduct which specified the terms of access, ranking, data processing and charges. It reviewed a number of proposals for joint ventures where airlines proposed to operate common services (with programmes and timetables determined jointly and costs and revenues shared).

By the beginning of 1989, therefore, the Commission had demonstrated its commitment to regulating the conduct of air transport. It was helped in its task by another ECJ ruling, in the *Ahmed Saeed* case, involving the right of a German travel agent to offer discount tickets purchased in other countries to German tourists, which confirmed that competition rules did apply to the sector, including domestic services and services involving non-Community countries. Moreover, there was an increased preparedness by carriers to take their complaints to the Commission. Second-order carriers such as Air Europe and UTA complained over the behaviour of flag operators and governments.

These actions gave added ammunition to the Commission's efforts to liberalize the industry. In the summer of 1989 the Commission published its next package of proposals while extending and developing the application of competition policy to the sector. Although the measures increased the scope for airlines to enter markets and to price competitively, their content was rather less ambitious than many had expected. Full deregulation of the Community air transport industry was only achieved with a third package of reforms agreed to in 1992 and implemented in 1993.

The third package covered the issues of carrier licensing, market access and fare setting. The conditions on carrier licensing are designed to ensure minimum standards of operation, particularly regarding financial liquidity and Community ownership. The effect of the rules was not only protective; it also established rules for (and therefore permits) companies establishing airlines anywhere within the Community. The importance of this factor depends in part on how effective the Commission's other proposals for route licensing are. In effect, these should permit full fifth freedom rights to operators, subject to some controls for very small routes, and extend cabotage to Community carriers by 1997. The fare-setting procedures will be set according to double disapproval, although again there will be some constraints for routes operated on a public service basis. These measures came into force at the beginning of 1993.

Although there is now a situation akin to complete deregulation, it is not at all clear how far they will have the effects seen in countries such as the United States, where deregulation was implemented much more swiftly. Moreover, the reforms were introduced at a time when the industry, both in the EC and beyond, was in crisis (triggered initially by the Gulf War and then by recession). Even in the more buoyant market of the mid-1990s the effect of the liberalization measures has been modest. According to the Commission's own research, the impact of reform on prices has been confined to those trunk routes where more than two carriers operate, while there are signs that, on other routes, fully flexible fares have actually increased (even though average fares continue a long trend of reduction). Although there has been an increase in the number of airlines and the number of routes the position of the incumbent flag carriers remains largely untouched (CEC, 1996c).

Indeed, these operators present the Commission with its greatest challenge, seeking out alliances and aid to cope with the pressures of a more competitive market. The Commission's response to joint ventures and mergers has been ambivalent. In cases such as *BA/Sabena*, the Commission's conditions contributed to the collapse of deals; in others such as Air France takeover of UTA, the takeovers of Dutch carriers by KLM, and the wave of strategic alliances between Community airlines and carriers from other regions, the Commission has approved details with only weak conditions being attached. On aid, the Commission has for the most part approved the package subject to conditions (including the requirement that no further support be given to operators).

The major consequence of these changes is that a number of private and independent operators have disappeared, either bankrupted or taken over by flag carriers. This development casts doubt over the overall impact of liberalization, unless of course the rewards of competition and the strength of the Commission are sufficient to encourage the major airlines to start competing more vigorously against each other.

Some of the ambivalence in the Commission's approach to these issues arises from the different stances of different parts of the Commission: the Directorate General for Competition favours an opening of markets, while the Directorate General for Transport appears to take the interests of the industry (and particularly the flag carriers) as its main concern.

In spite of these divergences, the Commission itself remains very active on air transport issues, suggesting that a Community presence in the industry is now well established. At the time of the Gulf War, the Commission approved a number of emergency measures to allow airlines to cooperate in limiting services. The Commission has also been active in developing codes of conduct for opening up access to slot allocation procedures, introducing proposals for regulating the charter market and proposing that it take on the role of negotiating agreements on air transport with non-EU states. The resistance of member states to this last proposal, however, suggests that there may be limits to the Community role.

12.5 Conclusions

With the completion of the 'internal market' agenda for transport and the growing importance of competition and environment law in transport activities, it might appear that, for the first time in over forty years, there is now a significant Community dimension to transport policy. Certainly, the Commission appears to think this is so, as its proposals for a redefined Common Transport Policy demonstrate. However, while the last five years have seen the pace of change on transport matters accelerate, there are grounds for caution in appraising how significant the Community dimension to transport policy is and how far a common transport policy is achievable.

The significance of Community roles in the transport sector will only emerge once we have seen those rules in operation. In the air transport industry, for example, Community policies brought about a near-open air transport market from the beginning of 1993, but so far the results have been rather limited. It is, to be sure, early days but there are reasons for believing that the new regime may not lead to dramatic changes (at least for the consumer). The incremental nature of change in the sector (the first proposals made in 1979, the first major reforms in 1988, the final reforms in 1993 but not complete until 1997) allows the major operators plenty of time to adjust to, and in some cases to pre-empt, the potential for competition. The shortage of certain key resources and the inadequate nature of Community solutions have also neutered the effects of reform. The most important factor, however, is the extent to which much of the implementation and enforcement of air transport policy will remain in the hands of member states. Since many of these governments have opposed reform, a fact not unconnected with their continued ownership stakes in national carriers, leaving them in charge of applying the policy may not have been the best way of guaranteeing change.

There is therefore a credibility gap between the agreements on reforms and their implementation. It might of course be argued that the vigorous application of competition or some other element of Community law would bring member states and their transport industries into line. While this may be so, the limited resources at the Community level, the politicized and 'bargaining' nature of policy making in the Commission and the existence of conflicts in policy objectives make such rigorous enforcement difficult in practice.

The constraint of conflicting objectives, of course, is the best rationale for developing a Common Policy. By agreeing to an overall strategy within which different objectives can be balanced and integrated, it is argued, member states and transport industries can be guided by a coherent policy. Again, however, achieving such perfect harmony is easier said than done. To the extent that this is possible, it probably requires a substantial pooling of sovereignty, leaving Community institutions to arbitrate, determine and decide. It is not, however, clear that member states are prepared to surrender their scope to define national policies. As we noted earlier, while there are some common orientations to the policies of member states, substantial differences persist. Are national authorities prepared to see their room for manoeuvre further constrained by a policy which takes little account of their domestic policy priorities and interests?

chapter thirteen

EU energy policy

F. McGOWAN

The idea of a Common Energy Policy (CEP) for the EU is almost as old as the Community itself. In the years since the European Community was founded, numerous policy proposals have been made by the Commission or its predecessor, though they have been marked by a shifting balance of priorities and a range of proposed mechanisms, depending on the conditions in the energy markets and the influence of the Commission. For the most part, these attempts have come to nothing, with member states variously rejecting or ignoring them. Since the 1980s the Commission has again been active in the energy sector, as the momentum of the 'Single Market' debate has gathered pace and environmental concerns have intensified. However, although there has in recent years been an increased Community profile in this sector, a CEP remains elusive, as demonstrated by the failure to incorporate an energy chapter into either the Maastricht or Amsterdam Treaties.

This chapter seeks to consider the Community's role in energy policy. It notes past attempts to create a CEP, assesses the factors behind their failure and examines why the Community has been able to influence national policies more successfully in the last few years or so. After discussing the current policy proposals and the context to them, the chapter reviews the situation in the different energy industries of the EU, noting their main characteristics and the balance of past and present EU policy towards them. Finally it assesses some of the difficulties the Commission faces both in developing a credible energy policy and in addressing the energy industries without such a framework.

13.1 Past attempts and present successes

13.1.1 The treaties and energy

That the EC attached great importance to the energy sector is demonstrated by the fact that two of the three treaties on which the EC is based are specifically concerned with energy: the European Coal and Steel Community (ECSC) and Euratom Treaties were devoted to the coal and nuclear sectors. The details of these treaties (and their rationale) are covered elsewhere, but their significance for energy policy is clear enough. The 1951 ECSC treaty reflected the dominance of coal in the energy balance of member states (as well as its role in the steel industry); by tackling coal, most EC energy supply and demand issues were addressed. The 1957 Euratom treaty sought to foster cooperation in the development of civil nuclear power, then perceived as the main source of future energy requirements (Lucas, 1977). Both treaties, moreover, were in principle geared towards the creation of free and integrated markets in these sectors: the ECSC sought to abolish all barriers to trade between member states while controlling subsidies and cartel-like behaviour amongst producers; Euratom also paid lip service to the idea of a common market in nuclear products.

A common market for other energy sectors was addressed in the Rome Treaty. While the EEC was orientated towards more or less competitively structured sectors, it was also intended to cover the more oligopolistic or monopolistic sectors such as oil, gas and electricity. Accordingly, in addition to being subject to the EEC Treaty's general provisions on opening up markets, these energy industries' special characteristics were covered by the Treaty's provisions on state enterprises and their conduct.

13.1.2 Policy efforts 1951–73

The gap between intentions expressed in the Treaties and the outcomes, however, has been a large one for energy, more so than for most other parts of the economy. The Commission's attempts to develop an energy policy of any sort, let alone one reflecting the ideals of the treaties, have proved to be only of limited success.

From the 1950s on, the Commission or its equivalents sought to develop a policy first for coal and then for energy more broadly. On coal, the High Authority was unable to impose the spirit of the Paris Treaty on national industries; it was mainly involved in tackling the crises which beset the European coal industry from the mid-1950s on (Lindberg and Scheingold, 1970). In the sphere of energy more generally, initial efforts were made as the negotiations for the EEC were progressing. The Messina conference recommended that the potential for coordinated energy policy be considered, but the Spaak Committee determined that this would not be necessary (von Geusau, 1975).

Following the establishment of the new Communities, there was a renewed attempt to develop a CEP. The formation of an interexecutive Committee on energy in 1959 sought to develop a policy focusing on the creation of a common energy market. The main concerns of the Committee were with the effect of energy prices on industrial competitiveness and, to a lesser extent, security of energy supply (PEP, 1963). However, governments largely rejected the Committee's attempts to gain access to energy policy; instead they exercised benign neglect towards the energy sector. This inertia on energy policy reflected the largely untroubled energy markets of the period. However, when there was concern over supply in the 1950s and 1960s (such as in the wake of the Suez crisis), governments were keen to retain their autonomy.

The merger of the Communities in 1968 saw the Commission renew its efforts to develop a CEP. In its document 'First Guidelines Towards a EC Energy Policy' (CEC, 1968), the Commission noted that barriers to trade in energy persisted and stressed the necessity of a common energy market. Such a market, based on the needs of consumers and competitive pressures would help obtain security of energy supplies at the lowest cost. To this end the Commission suggested three broad objectives: a plan for the sector involving data collection and forecasting as a means of influencing members' investment strategies; measures to bring about a common energy market (tackling issues such as tax harmonization, technical barriers, state monopolies, etc); measures to ensure security of supply at lowest cost.

The proposals proved difficult to put into practice partly because of the scale of objectives and the contradictions between the substance of different goals, but mainly because of the resistance of member states to the goals. Even though the Council approved the strategy, it ignored most of the Commission's subsequent attempts to enact the proposals. The principal measures adopted in the wake of the Commission's proposals concerned oil stocks (following OECD initiatives) and some requirements for energy investment notification. These actions owed more to growing concern about security of supply than to the creation of a common energy market, and presaged a wider shift in Commission and member state perceptions of the priorities of energy policy. The reaction to the 1973–74 oil crisis confirmed the change in orientation of energy policy proposals away from markets and towards security.

13.1.3 Energy crises 1973–86

The backdrop for the new emphasis on security of supply was the development of the Community's energy balances and the changes in global energy markets generally. Since the 1950s, the member states had become less reliant upon domestically produced coal and more on imported resources, primarily oil. This shift in demand reflected the growth in energy demand overall, but also a gradual but absolute decline in energy resources among the then member states. By 1970 over 60% of the EC's needs were imported, leaving it highly vulnerable to the supply disruptions and price increases of 1973–74 (see Table 13.1).

In the midst of the first oil shock, the EC attempted a crisis management role but failed even to provide a united front *vis-à-vis* OAPEC over their oil embargo of the Netherlands (Daintith and Hancher, 1986). Member states pursued their own policies or worked through the International Energy Agency (IEA). Formed in 1974, the IEA overshadowed the EC both in breadth of membership (covering all the OECD countries except France) and in terms of its powers on oil sharing in a new crisis (van der Linde and Lefeber, 1988).

Even so, the shock of oil price increases reinforced the reassessment of energy policies in member states and the Commission. The Commission attempted to develop a more strategic approach to the management of energy supply and demand. The 'New Strategy' (*Bulletin of the European Communities Supplement 4/1974*) which

Table 13.1 ● EU energy balances (million tonnes oil equivalent).

	Energy production	Net imports	Supply[a]
1960	360.3	206.2	551.4
1970	410.6	651.0	1017.9
1980	583.0	688.3	1217.6
1990	700.9	651.2	1318.9
1994	727.5	644.2	1348.6

Figures for all years are for EU-15.
[a] Includes adjustments for stocks.
Source International Energy Agency.

was only agreed to after much wrangling and dilution (a proposal for a European energy agency was abandoned after member state opposition – see Lucas, 1977) envisaged a number of targets to be met by 1985 (COM (74) 1960). These included the reduction of oil imports, the development of domestic energy capabilities (notably nuclear power) and the rational use of energy (see Table 13.2). The policy, while only indicative, mobilized resources for R&D and promotional programmes on energy, covering conventional and nuclear technologies but also (albeit to a limited extent) renewables and energy efficiency technologies. The new strategy also provided the basis for a handful of directives designed to restrict the use of oil and gas.

The policy clearly entailed a change in emphasis for energy policy and the goal of a common energy market was demoted, although it was alluded to in areas such as pricing policies and some measures directed at the oil sector (see below). Overall, policy was concerned with changing the structure of energy balances rather than the structure of energy markets. The condition of energy markets (notably after the second oil shock) and concern over energy prices and security in the early 1980s was such that the policy was sustained into the decade. Further rounds of energy policy objectives were agreed in 1979 (to be met by 1990) and 1986 (for 1995). The 1995 objectives included a number of 'horizontal' objectives, aimed at more general energy policy concerns, such as its relationship with other EC policies. Each round sought to build on the previous one, and although in general the goals appeared to be on target, in some cases they reflected a degree of failure either across the EC or in certain member states, and subsequent rounds would adopt a rather less ambitious agenda (COM (84) 88 and COM (88) 174). The objectives approach has reappeared as part of current EU energy strategy (COM (96) 431).

By the mid-1980s, therefore, the Commission had succeeded in establishing a

Table 13.2 ⬤ **The EU's energy objectives for 1985, 1990, 1995 and 2010.**

1985 objectives

To increase nuclear power capacity to 200 GW.
To increase Community production of oil and natural gas to 180 million tonnes oil equivalent.
To maintain production of coal in the Community at 180 million tonnes oil equivalent.
To keep imports to no more than 40% of consumption.
To reduce projected demand for 1985 by 15%.
To raise electricity contribution to final energy consumption to 35%.

1990 objectives

To reduce to 0.7 or less the average ratio between the rate of growth in gross primary energy demand and the rate of growth of gross domestic product.
To reduce oil consumption to a level of 40% of primary energy consumption.
To cover 70–75% of primary energy requirements for electricity production by means of solid fuels and nuclear energy.
To encourage the use of renewable energy sources so as to increase their contribution to the Community's energy supplies.
To pursue energy pricing policies geared to attaining the energy objectives.

1995 objectives

To improve the efficiency of final energy demand by 20%.
To maintain oil consumption at around 40% of energy consumption and to maintain net oil imports at less than $\frac{1}{3}$ of total energy consumption.
To maintain the share of natural gas in the energy balance on the basis of a policy aimed at ensuring stable and diversified supplies.
To increase the share of solid fuels in energy consumption.
To pursue efforts to promote consumption of solid fuels and to improve the competitiveness of their production capacities in the Community.
To reduce the proportion of electricity generated by hydrocarbons to less than 15%.
To increase the share of renewables in energy balances.
To ensure more secure conditions of supply and to reduce risks of energy price fluctuations.
To apply Community price formation principles to all sectors.
To balance energy and environmental concerns through the use of best available technologies.
To implement measures to improve energy balance in less-developed regions of the Community.
To develop a single energy market.
To coordinate external relations in energy sector.

2010 objectives

To meet Treaty objectives notably market integration, sustainable development, environmental protection and supply security.
To integrate energy and environmental objectives and to incorporate the full cost of energy in the price.
To strengthen security of supply through improved diversification and flexibility of domestic and imported supplies on the one hand and by ensuring flexible responses to supply emergencies on the other.
To develop a coordinated approach to external energy relations to ensure free and open trade and to secure investment framework.
To promote renewable energy resources with the aim of achieving a significant share of primary energy production by 2010.
To improve energy efficiency by 2010 through better coordination of both national and Community measures.

place in energy policy making, but it was far from being central to member states' energy policy agendas, let alone one being sufficiently influential to dictate the development of a common energy market. Instead, its role consisted of information gathering, target setting and enabling activities (the latter had a substantial budget for energy R&D and promotion). While these measures ensured that the Commission had an influence on policy, they were not without problems – some of the objectives were showing few signs of achievement while aspects of the Commission's funding strategies were also open to criticism (Cruickshank and Walker, 1981). Moreover, aside from a few legislative measures, the Commission's policy had few teeth. The locus of power remained with national governments which generally chose to follow their own energy policies, resisting too strong a Commission role.

13.1.4 The new energy policy agenda: competition and the environment

In the course of the 1980s, however, the agenda for energy policy began to change. Developments in energy markets, the attitudes of governments towards the energy industries and the overall position of the Commission in policy making contributed to a turnaround in the concerns of EC energy policy. The new agenda rests on two broader objectives: the creation of a competition-oriented single energy market and the pursuit of environmental protection.

A key factor in the changed regime was the shift in energy markets. Prices stabilized and faltered in the early 1980s and continued to weaken until the 1986 oil price collapse. The reasons for this were more fundamental than the rows within OPEC which precipitated the fall in prices. The price increases of the early 1980s had had the effect of boosting output in OPEC countries, as well as fostering exploration and production in the rest of world. Furthermore, many countries had sought to improve energy efficiency and diversify sources of energy (if not to the levels sought by the Commission). The economic recession of the 1980s also dampened demand. The combined effect of these factors was a massive over-capacity in supply and minimal demand growth (see Table 13.1) which forced down prices. The effects were not only confined to oil: gas and coal were in equally plentiful supply, while the consequences of past over-investment in electricity capacity also boosted the energy surplus.

The combined effect of these developments was to weaken the scarcity culture which had prevailed among suppliers, consumers, governments and the Commission. As prices fell and markets appeared well supplied so the concerns of policy focused less on energy supply *per se* and more on the price of supply and existence of obstacles to the lowest price.

This change in market conditions made many energy policies, especially those fostering conservation or diversification from high-price fuels, hard to sustain or justify. In any case, in some countries, governments were abandoning traditional approaches to energy policy. The United Kingdom was the most notable example, making an explicit move to rely on market forces for determining supply and demand. A major plank of that policy was deregulation, with attempts to introduce competition to gas and power, and privatization, with the sale of oil interests and then the gas and electricity industries (Helm *et al.*, 1989). Shifts in policies were under review in other parts of the EC (Helm and McGowan, 1989), although these were often conceived at a less ambitious level or pursued for rather different reasons.

The deregulatory thrust was not confined to the energy sector – indeed it was probably more widely spread initially in other areas of the economy. It was, for example, to the fore in the Commission's plans for the Single European Market (SEM) as covered in the White Paper (CEC, 1985a). Partly as a reflection of past energy policy failures, the Commission did not include energy in the initial agenda for the SEM. However, areas where energy was affected indirectly by more general SEM measures (such as indirect taxation and procurement policies) meant that the sector was not untouched by the proposals.

Indeed, there were already some signs of a different policy towards energy. The issue of price transparency was extended across the energy industries with attempts to agree a directive on the issue. While the moves failed, they indicated a greater interest in the issue by the Commission. The Commission was also taking a greater interest in energy subsidies (as in the case of Dutch support to its horticultural industry through the provision of cheap gas). Other indications of change included moves to tackle state oil monopolies and the types of support given to the coal industry in a number of member states.

The potential for more radical action was indicated by a number of moves taken by the Competition Directorate of the Commission towards other 'utility' industries. It sought the introduction of more competitive arrangements in the civil aviation industry and was able to threaten use of legal powers to this end. In the field of telecommunications, it sought to open access for equipment and service sales, using powers under Article 90 to do so (see Chapter 9). These moves demonstrated not only a willingness to act but also a range of mechanisms which could be used in other sectors. The further the policy went in one industry the more likely it would be applied to others.

This changing agenda meant that the idea of an internal energy market (IEM) was once again an issue for the EC. While the 1995 goals were largely flavoured by energy security concerns, one of the 'horizontal' objectives was the creation of an IEM. As the prospect of a SEM became realizable with the '1992' campaign the idea of extending it to energy took root, and in 1987 Energy Commissioner Mosar announced a study of the barriers to an IEM.

The Commission's thinking was revealed in 'The Internal Energy Market' (COM (88) 238), a review which set out the potential benefits of an IEM and the obstacles that faced it. The IEM would cut costs to consumers (particularly to energy-intensive industries), thereby making European industry as a whole more competitive; it would increase security of supply by improving integration of the energy industries; it would rationalize the structure of the energy industries and allow for greater complementarity among the different supply and demand profiles of member states. The benefits would stem from a mixture of cost-reducing competition and the achievement of scale economies in a number of industries. Taken together these would more than recover the 0.5% of EC GDP which the Commission claimed was the 'cost of non-Europe' in the energy sector (although, as noted, energy was not part of the original SEM debate nor of the 'cost of non-Europe' exercise which assessed the benefits of the SEM – see Cecchini (1988) and Emerson *et al.* (1988)).

According to the Commission, the obstacles to the IEM were to be found in the structures and practices of the energy industries. These ranged from different taxation and financial regimes to restrictive measures which protected energy industries in particular countries and conditions which prevented full coordination of supplies at the most efficient level (the latter applying to the gas and electricity industries). However, as the Commission admitted, the effects of particular practices were difficult to assess given the special nature of the energy industries. Indeed, in certain cases, the Commission appeared hesitant over the extent of the IEM. Nonetheless, the document demonstrated that the Commission was committed to implement an IEM and would examine all barriers to its development. It has followed up on that commitment with measures to implement the White Paper proposals (on taxation and procurement) and to apply EC law to the sector.

In the period since the IEM document was published, the Commission has completed the programme of measures liberalizing the energy industries' procurement practices, but has been unable to achieve an effective harmonization of indirect taxation. It has also made some progress on liberalizing the electricity and gas supply markets and the offshore exploration industry but very little has been achieved by way of coal industry reform. To the extent that the policy has been successful, it has been aided not only by changes in EC decision-making procedures, notably the majority voting conditions allowed under the Single European Act (SEA), but also by the prospect of the Commission using its powers to investigate the energy sector from a Treaty of Rome perspective. However, there remain many aspects of the policy to be implemented, where the Commission will have to overcome the opposition of member states.

Since 1988, the IEM has played a major role in Commission proposals on energy policy. It has, for all its problems, shifted the emphasis in Community policy towards the energy sector. Over the same period, however another element has also gained a higher profile in deliberations on the sector: the environment.

The Commission's interest in environmental issues is not new. The formal commitment of the EC to environmental policy dates from early 1972 when, in the wake of the Stockholm conference, the Council agreed a programme of action, while some measures on environmental problems predated even this initiative (Haigh, 1987). While the Commission's concerns on environment are very wide ranging (see Chapter 9) covering issues such as chemical wastes, water quality, and noise pollution, the consequences of energy choices are a major part of the policy.

The importance of EC environmental policy for the energy sector has paralleled the ascent of the issue up the political agenda in an increasing number of member states, particularly as the Greens have become a political force. In those cases where governments have been obliged to introduce new controls on pollution, they have sought to have them generalized across the EC so as not to lose competitiveness. The best example has been the acid rain debate where the German government, forced to introduce major controls on domestic emissions from industrial and electricity plants, has pressured for similar controls in all member states (Boehmer-Christiansen and Skea, 1990). These were agreed in 1988, setting targets for emission reduction into the next century.

The emergence of the environment has given the Commission a higher profile in energy matters and another, more robust, lever on energy policy (Owens and Hope, 1989). The importance of the issue to energy policy was demonstrated in the 1995 objectives where environmental concerns were identified as a major consideration in policy. The status of environmental issues overall was confirmed in the SEA where it was given its own provisions (allowing it to enforce decisions on a majority vote). The SEM proposals also identify the need for high standards of environmental protection in the EC and this has impacted on the IEM debate.

Integrating environment and energy has not been easy for the Commission; a document on the issue was apparently the focus for considerable dispute within the Commission because of the different perspectives of the Directorates for Energy and for Environment (COM (89) 369). However, the issue which has both brought the environment to the centre of Community energy policy making and exposed the tensions between the two policies most starkly has been the greenhouse effect.

The Commission has sought to coordinate a common European response to the threat of global warming. In 1991 the member states, with the exception of the United Kingdom, agreed to stabilize emissions of CO_2 by the year 2000. In the following year it produced proposals for decreasing emissions of greenhouse gases, particularly CO_2 (COM(92) 246). These comprised four elements: programmes to encourage the development of renewable energy sources (which have zero or very low carbon dioxide emissions) and of energy efficiency, a monitoring system and a carbon-energy tax to discourage use of fossil fuels.

While much has been achieved by the Commission in incorporating conservation and renewables into a strategy for tackling global warming, the carbon tax has all but been abandoned. The proposed tax consists of two elements, one related to the energy used and the other to the carbon emitted by the fuel in question. The tax therefore penalizes coal use most strongly but not as much as if it were a pure carbon tax. Small renewable-based energy sources are not covered by the proposal. More importantly, large industrial consumers are also exempt from it and the proposal will not be put into effect unless equivalent steps are taken by other industrialized countries (Pearson and Smith, 1991). Despite these conditions, which were included after considerable lobbying of the Commission, the proposal has drawn a good deal of criticism from industries and governments, and, although modifications have been made, the chances of an agreement in the Council appear slim. Subsequent attempts to use taxation as an instrument of environmental policy in the energy sector have also been opposed (Finon and Surrey, 1996).

Although the Single Market and environment dominate energy policy, the

Commission continues to pursue a variety of other energy policy objectives. It continues with its support for energy efficiency and renewables through research budgets and other measures designed to encourage their use (such as recommendations for preferential terms for renewable sources of supply). It has developed policies for supporting energy infrastructures primarily in less-developed areas of the Community, although this goal has been broadened in the light of attempts to increase integration of gas and electricity supply, through the initiative on fostering 'trans-EC networks' (McGowan, 1993b).

The Commission has even sought to develop a role in the traditionally difficult area of security of supply. The policy it has proposed addresses two aspects of the problem: the development of indigenous energy resources and the management of Community activities in the event of supply disruption. The first element, which was developed in response to the British government's desire to protect the nuclear industry after privatization, allows authorities to subsidize up to 20% of its energy requirements on the grounds that, while it may infringe the Treaty's free market provisions, it also supports the Community's own energy resources (Brittan, 1992). The second element of the policy comprises a variety of measures designed to establish a clearer role for the Commission in energy crisis management and diplomacy.

It is largely for securing supplies that an increasingly important part of the Community's energy policy activities is the links with the rest of the world. These are focused on immediate neighbours to the north, east and south of the Community. The principal element of these links has been its efforts to draw Eastern Europe into secure energy links through the European Energy Charter ((COM (91) 36). This was the initiative of the Dutch Prime Minister Lubbers who sought to use an agreement on energy, symbolically echoing the ECSC in ending the cold war, and, more importantly, acting as a framework for closer energy links between the Community and the East. An agreement on a basic charter was reached at the end of 1991 and an Energy Charter Treaty signed at the end of 1994. The Treaty sets out the basic conditions for investment in markets but important related questions such as energy transit and the application of competition rules have been incorporated in only the most limited manner. Ratification of the Treaty has been completed by a number of member states as well as by some East European and former Soviet Union states and the entry into force of the Treaty is expected this year (Waeterloos, 1992; Dore and de Bauw, 1995).

13.1.5 The prospects for a common energy policy

Such a variety of activities, along with the increased recourse to the Community institutions by member states and pressure groups on energy matters, would suggest that the Commission anticipated the Community finally taking responsibility for energy policy. However, attempts to formalize its role in the Maastricht Treaty were unsuccessful. While the Commission was able to insert a relatively weak commitment to a Community role which was kept in the draft Treaty up to the very last negotiations, a number of member states indicated their objections to it and obtained its removal at the last stage in the negotiations. The Commission subsequently embarked on an extensive consultation exercise in order to clarify its role in energy policy making. A green paper was published at the end of 1994 with a White Paper following at the end of 1995. Both documents stressed the importance of energy matters by drawing attention to the prospect of increased energy dependence: Commission forecasts suggested that imported energy would account for as much as 70% of energy needs by 2020 (CEC, 1995c). The documents reiterated the need for a Community energy policy on the basis of reconciling the objectives of supply security, environmental protection and an internal market; a Community dimension was justified on the basis of existing treaty powers (particularly in competition policy and the internal market), the international nature of energy markets and problems and existing policy and budgetary commitments (CEC, 1995c). The White Paper established an Energy Consultative Committee to ensure transparency and set out an extensive work programme for the Community in the energy sphere (although interestingly the Commission has also been willing to review, and where necessary to discard, existing policies): since the White Paper the Commission has conducted two reviews of energy legislation and recommended the rescinding of some measures (including those affecting oil and gas use in such sectors as power generation).

Despite its ambitious scale, the While Paper did not seek to justify the inclusion of energy in the next round of Treaty negotiations. However, the Maastricht Treaty had included a condition that the status of energy – along with some other policies – be reviewed as part of those discussions. In its report the Commission, while being careful not to call explicitly for a chapter on energy, indicated that inclusion was desirable given the various goals of Community energy policy and the need to rationalize the coverage of the energy sectors across the Treaties. The Commission followed this up in the latter part of 1996 and early 1997 with documents designed to justify a Community role: although these documents spelt out a range of recommendations (including a new set of energy policy objectives) they were clearly designed to strengthen the case for a formal CEP (COM (96) 431). The 1997 Treaty makes no new mention of energy, let alone a new chapter (though it has been suggested that provisions could be added if the proposed rationalization of Treaty texts takes place).

13.2 The EU and the energy industries

13.2.1 Coal

The coal industry in the EU has undergone a major restructuring since the 1950s when it was the mainstay of the industrial European economy. Indigenous production of hard coal has been in more or less constant decline (lignite and peat have actually shown a slight increase but they are relatively unimportant owing to their low thermal value). In 1960, coal production accounted for 85% of energy production and 55% of energy supply in the countries which now make up the Community. By 1994 production accounted for only 20% of energy produced and just over 10% of energy supply. This decline reflected a restructuring of demand away from domestic and industrial markets towards power generation and away from local production towards imports: in 1960 net imports accounted for just over 5% of coal requirements; by 1994 they constituted 36% of coal supply (see Table 13.3).

Imports might account for an even greater amount of coal consumed were it not for the barriers to entry in a number of member states which maintain a domestic industry. The restructuring of the sector has seen some countries close down the industry, while some have maintained capacity, often on a large scale. The competitiveness of these industries varies considerably, depending on developments in world coal prices, although some are clearly only maintained by a mixture of direct subsidy and government-backed agreements with electricity utilities (IEA, 1988a, 1988b). In a number of countries these measures have come under increasing criticism – primarily from the consumers who have to bear the higher cost of electricity production – and the pressures for reform have intensified.

Considering the major restructuring under way in the industry and its position in the EU's treaties and institutions, the role of the Commission in coal policy has been limited. As noted, many of the attempts to develop policy from the 1950s on came to little as a result initially of a series of crises (which were largely dealt with at a national level) and subsequent concerns over the EC's vulnerability to imported sources of energy (concerns which worked to the advantage of indigenously produced coal).

Table 13.3 ⬤ EU coal balances (million tonnes oil equivalent).

	Coal production	Net imports	Supply[a]
1960	304.6	18.4	331.7
1970	281.7	36.3	326.0
1980	250.9	63.8	304.7
1990	209.3	87.9	300.1
1994	137.4	87.7	244.1

Figures for all years are for EU-15.
[a] Includes adjustments for stocks.
Source International Energy Agency.

The relative impotence of the Commission is demonstrated by its failure to control national subsidies. The Paris Treaty all but prohibited the provision of state aids to the industry, yet such support was endemic across the Community. The Commission sought to rectify this conflict by making its approval of aid subject to conditions and ultimate phasing out (Lucas, 1977). However, national support largely continued without much Commission interference for much of the first thirty years of the ECSC.

The Commission attempted to adopt a tougher policy towards the sector in the 1980s. In 1985, the Commission proposed a much more stringent set of controls of government policies including a major reduction in the level of subsidy to the industry. As the Commission noted, whereas the old rules were dominated by supply concerns, the new ones would emphasize 'the need to achieve viability ... and reduce the volume of aid even if this means substantial reductions in uneconomic capacity' (CEC, 1985a, p. 130). The proposals were opposed by most coal-producing countries and the Commission was obliged to accept a less ambitious policy. This policy set a framework for continuing aid until 1993 on the basis of three criteria: to improve the industry's competitiveness; to create new economically viable capacity; to solve the social and regional problems related to developments in the coal industry. In addition, the Commission developed a more detailed procedure for approving those aids and for reviewing progress made on improving the industry's financial and economic position and for bringing into line the different forms of aid offered by member states.

The effect of the Commission's scrutiny policy has been difficult to assess since many countries were already pushing their own rationalization policies. In its most recent review, the Commission noted that, after some years of decline, the level of aid had increased in 1994 although this was largely a function of the closure of relatively low cost capacity in the United Kingdom (CEC, 1996e). The process of rationalization in the high-cost industries of Germany and Spain has been much less dramatic (largely because of the greater political sensitivities surrounding the issue in those countries). These two governments opposed a Commission initiative to reduce subsidies through a 'reference price' (*International Coal Report*, 1992). Under this proposal member states would have been able to subsidize their coal industries to the level of the average production costs within the Community (the two plus the United Kingdom). However, since both industries' cost structures exceed the proposed price level they would have been obliged to shut down capacity much more rapidly than was politically feasible. Instead it has been left to each state to determine the pace of rationalization (and ironically it has been the United Kingdom, which has the cheapest coal resources in the Community, which has cut capacity most dramatically (see McGowan *et al.*, 1993)).

If anything, the Community's effect on the coal sector has been primarily felt on the demand side, where environmental policies have been to the fore. The area of Community policy which is most damaging to the coal industry's survival is, however, the environment. Attempts to combat the problems of acid rain and global warming have targeted coal as the main culprit. The principal initiative for controlling emissions causing acid rain has been the Large Combustion Plants Directive, which, by restricting national emission levels of the principal gases, effectively requires the installation of capital intensive equipment on power stations, or the use of low-sulphur fuels or alternatives such as natural gas. In some countries, the effect of the directive has been to accelerate the reduction in the domestic coal industry (Boehmer-Christiansen and Skea, 1990).

However, whereas the control of acid rain can be reconciled with the use of coal (whether from the Community or elsewhere), such a bargain is much harder with regard to the control of emissions of carbon dioxide. Although all fossil fuels emit CO_2, coal emits the most. Consequently, most strategies for controlling or reducing emissions seek to restrict the use of coal: the Commission's plans for a carbon tax would penalize coal more than other fossil fuels. If the momentum behind the greenhouse effect debate continues, coal is likely to play an ever shrinking role in Community energy balances. The Commission has indicated that it is keen to encourage the clean use of coal (its research programme has subsidized various 'clean coal' technologies) but the willingness of member states to follow suit is far from clear (Cleutinx, 1996).

13.2.2 Oil

As in the rest of the world, the importance of oil in EU energy balances has increased dramatically since the 1950s, even allowing for the levelling off which has occurred since the 1980s. By 1960 oil accounted for 25% of energy requirements in the original six countries which now constitute the EU. By the early 1970s, it had risen to over 60% before gradually declining and stabilizing at just over 45% in the mid-1980s. The bulk of these requirements was met by imports since EC production was limited until the mid-1970s. It was then that North Sea oil began to come on stream: output increased from 14.5 million tonnes in 1970 to nearly 160 million tonnes in the mid-1990s, up from 8% to 28% of oil requirements (see Table 13.4).

The major factors controlling demand have been the oil shocks of the 1970s which demonstrated the EC's vulnerability to supply disruptions and price increases. In response, member states shifted policies (at different intensities), with some attaining major reductions in oil dependence (for example, Denmark cut its reliance on oil from nearly 90% of energy requirements in 1973 to 57% in 1986). However, oil remains the largest single element of primary fuel requirement.

The structure of the industry is quite diverse, reflecting in part the existence or otherwise of indigenous reserves. Where a production capability emerged (either at home or in colonies or dependencies), there has been a strong domestic element – often publicly owned – involved in the industry. In others, the multinationals have dominated through their subsidiaries and have played a part in the development of almost every industry (although for many years state companies enjoyed near monopolies in imports, refining and distribution – see Osborne and Robinson, 1989).

Given this diversity, and particularly the influence of international companies

Table 13.4 ⬤ **EU oil balances (million tonnes).**

	Oil production	Net imports	Supply[a]
1960	14.5	187.4	178.4
1970	17.7	611.8	578.5
1980	97.7	595.2	629.8
1990	120.8	468.3	555.4

Figures for all years are for EU-15.
[a] Includes adjustments for stocks.
Source International Energy Agency.

and markets, the industry is apparently more competitive than other energy industries. There is not the same natural monopoly element in distribution and marketing found in other sectors, while production and refining is notionally competitive. However, the close-knit structure of the international industry has prompted fears of collusion, while the dominance of state firms in some countries also raised fears of unfair trade practices.

As noted, much of EU policy effort on energy has been focused on the oil sector with policies aimed at reducing vulnerability and maintaining security of supply. The objectives set in the 1970s and 1980s have been supplemented with actions to restrict use of oil in power stations and encouraging stockpiling arrangements. Another aspect has been the encouragement of oil exploration in the EC and supervising the restructuring of the refinery industry which underwent severe overcapacity when demand turned down in the 1970s and 1980s (COM (88) 491). Finally, policy has sought to maintain a diversified source of supply and to continue a dialogue with major supply countries. More ambitious policies such as the attempts to develop a minimum support price have largely failed (Wyman Jones, 1986). The Commission has sought to increase the transparency of oil industry pricing. It also sought to tackle the practices of state oil monopolies in a number of member states (notably the new Mediterranean members).

In applying the IEM to oil, the Commission has sought to maintain these two aspects of past policy, but with the emphasis on market conduct. While accepting that the oil industry was structured more competitively than other energy industries, the Commission noted the persistence of a number of barriers, including exploration and production monopolies, exploration and production licensing procedures, oil field development conditions, taxation of oil production, landing obligation, restrictions on imports of oil and its byproducts, flag protection for shipments of oil, restrictions on refining and marketing rights, differences in technical norms and rules, pricing systems, and indirect taxation conditions.

The Commission's initial target was the implementation of the White Paper goals on taxation (harmonizing excise duties and VAT and abolishing other taxes – see Chapter 14), standards (uniform standards on product quality and equipment) and procurement (opening up markets for offshore exploration equipment). Its efforts have met with limited success: although the procurement rules are now in place, most national offshore industries have successfully obtained exemption from the procedures which the Commission wanted to apply. Nonetheless, the Commission has pushed ahead with further proposals to open up the market, primarily on the producer and exploration sides. The Commission's aim has been the harmonization of access conditions for these activities and it has managed to overcome the opposition of some member states.

More problematic have been efforts to tackle the demand side of the oil market. Aside from the limited progress on taxation issues, the Commission has also experienced considerable opposition to its attempts to address the environmental aspects of oil use, particularly in the transport sector. The 'Auto-Oil' programme is an initiative to improve environmental standards in both the quality of fuels and the efficiency and effectiveness of fuel use in new vehicles. So far the initiative has had little impact despite (or perhaps because of) the intervention of the petroleum and automobile industries (COM (96) 143).

The Commission has been keen not to ignore the traditional importance of supply security issues in the oil sector. However, national authorities also have maintained their reluctance to see the Community play the leading role in energy crisis management. The Commission attempted to revive this issue at the time of the Gulf War, with measures to coordinate member states' actions. Although the issue remains unresolved, it is unlikely that the Commission will be any more successful in this area than in the past. Nonetheless the Community dimension to dialogue with oil producers (notably in the cooperation programme with the Gulf Cooperation Council) continues to develop.

13.2.3 Natural gas

The EU gas industry has seen dramatic growth in the last twenty years, considering that the industry was rooted in town gas for most of its history and seemed in definite decline. The discovery of natural gas, first in Gronlngen after the Second World War and then in the North Sea, indicated its potential to supply Europe with energy. Production in the countries which constitute the EU today has risen from just over 10 million tonnes of oil equivalent in 1960 to just under 160 million tonnes of oil equivalent by the mid-1990s. Demand has outpaced supply and imports have met a steadily rising proportion of consumption (currently approximately 37%) (see Table 13.5). While natural gas accounted for 3% of energy requirements for the EU in 1960, it had risen to just under 20% by 1994.

The gas industry shares the characteristics of the exploratory production indus-

Table 13.5 ⬭ EU gas balances (million tonnes oil equivalent).

	Gas production	Net imports	Supply
1960	10.2	0	10.2
1970	61.3	1.5	62.8
1980	135.5	47.3	182.8
1990	132.7	89.9	222.6
1994	159.6	94.2	253.8

Figures for all years are for EU-15.
Source International Energy Agency.

tries such as oil and the network utility industries such as electricity. On balance the industry is dominated not so much by production companies but by the transmission companies which import and carry gas. Production is widespread (with the Netherlands and United Kingdom predominant) and is carried out by oil exploration companies. Transmission and imports are normally carried out by national monopolies (Germany is the exception where the monopolies are organized regionally). Distribution is also a monopoly and is generally carried out by local companies. Ownership is largely public with the exception of Germany and the United Kingdom. The extent to which monopoly or oligopoly prevails is reinforced by the substantial degree of vertical integration in the industry thanks to long-run contracts between the suppliers and transmission companies and between the transmission companies and the distributors. Some attempts have been made to introduce competition into the industry, with the United Kingdom the most advanced, but they are not widespread in the EU (Stern, 1989).

The EU's past policy towards the gas industry was mainly concerned with supply security (limiting gas use in power stations) and price discrimination (investigating prices charged to large consumers in the Netherlands). The first signs of a wider agenda for gas came with the publication of the Commission's review of the natural gas industry in the EC (COM (86) 518). This indicated not only that the prospects for supply and demand appeared healthy (and underscored the fuel's relatively benign environmental effects), but that the industry should move towards a European structure with as much competition as possible in the system. The IEM objectives for the gas market straddle the two components of the industry. To the extent that the gas is produced in the EC, then considerations related to oil production and barriers to that market would also apply to the gas industry (as discussed in the previous section). To the extent that the gas industry at the distribution level approximates the natural monopolies such as electricity, it is subject to similar proposals on extending grid integration, encouraging competition and determining regulation (see the next section).

One of the Commission's main objectives is to see the creation of an EU-wide gas network. While applauding the widespread integration of the system of continental Europe and the joint ventures created, the Commission has sought to integrate the whole of the Community into the gas market and to improve links with neighbouring states. Community funds have been used to bring gas to Greece and Portugal while the TransEuropean Networks initiative has sought to strengthen the network across the continent (in the latter case, however, financial support is limited to supporting feasibility studies and facilitating other sources of funding).

While there has been general support for extending the network, the issue of competition in the gas market is much more controversial. Although some member states already permit consumers to buy direct from gas suppliers using the network as a common carrier, the idea is not supported by the industry as a whole or by many governments. Attempts to introduce rules for the transit of gas between utilities were opposed by a number of member states and the Commission's proposals were eventually passed by majority vote. At the time of writing, measures to liberalize the market have yet to be agreed. Opponents of reform argue that such a system (by introducing competition) would not provide the certainty required for the long-run investments needed in the sector and would jeopardize existing contractual arrangements. Progress in liberalizing the European electricity market (see below) rekindled the prospects for a similar arrangement in the gas sector but so far the Council has failed to resolve the differences between member states.

Whatever the outcome of this debate, however, it is unlikely to stem the growing share of gas in Community energy balances. The Commission has accordingly placed great importance on ensuring stable supplies of gas, particularly from the former Soviet Union. The European Energy Charter covers all fuels but there is no doubt that ensuring gas supplies to the Community is the primary concern (Stern, 1992).

13.2.4 Electricity

Electricity has seen the most rapid growth in the post-war period. Electricity demand and production in the EC rose rapidly for many years (in the 1950s and 1960s by an average of 8% annually). Although the mix of production technologies has changed over the years for many decades (with a decline in the role of coal and the rise of nuclear power), the industry has benefited from a virtuous circle of improving supply technologies reducing costs and prices on the one hand and increasing demand on the other (see Table 13.6). In the last decade the electricity sector has seen slower growth rates for demand and greater investment in gas and renewable-based capacity at the expense of coal and nuclear.

The electricity supply industry (ESI) retains a wide diversity of institutional forms,

Table 13.6 ⬭ **EU electricity generation by fuel.**

	Electricity total production (TWh)	Coal (%)	Oil (%)	Gas (%)	Nuclear (%)	Hydro (%)
1960	511.9	55.6	8.5	1.5	0.4	33.2
1970	1104.3	45.3	24.1	4.9	3.9	20.7
1980	1672.7	42.0	20.4	7.6	12.6	16.6
1990	2140.7	37.4	9.1	6.9	33.6	12.1
1994	2250.5	32.3	8.6	9.2	35.2	13.1

Figures for all years are for EU-15.
Source International Energy Agency.

with differing levels of public and private participation and/or centralized or decentralized organisation (Hughes, 1983; McGowan and Thomas, 1992). The diversity owes much to the origins of the industry in each country, whether in rural cooperatives, municipal companies or industrial firms selling surplus power. The determining factor in shaping the development of the ESI, however, has been the political–economic structure of the country; much of the way in which industries have evolved can be attributed to the balance of power between public authority and private enterprise in the economy and between central and local government in the political realm (Hughes, 1983).

The shared position of the utilities has extended to international contacts. Despite the different structures and practices of the industry, for the most part they share a common perception of their obligations and future options, and are organized within a common pressure group for international issues. Cooperation has also extended to operational aspects – most EU utilities are linked into common despatch systems for optimizing the use of peak and reserve capacity (Bruppacher, 1988).

In more recent years, the pattern of steady improvement and the status of the utility have faltered. Technological improvements turned out to be harder to obtain and (in scale economies) self-defeating, demand faltered, and costs and prices rose. The industry's record on environmental affairs also came under criticism in the 1970s and 1980s. However, the most important factor in change was in the relationship between the utilities and the consumers (particularly the largest industrial users).

In the 1980s, a number of large consumers sought to gain access to the national systems in various member states (either to buy from private producers or from exporters), but without success. In this environment, tensions between utilities also increased, and in the face of irreconcilable positions a number of consumers (primarily large German industrial users seeking to purchase cheap nuclear surplus power from France) threatened the use of the Rome treaty to support their goals (Lippert, 1987).

As noted the idea of a European component to the ESI pre-dates the EEC, and figured in the debate on the development of the EC at some stages. However, an EC role was rejected in the 1950s and most moves on integrating systems have occurred outside the EC framework. Commission interest has intermittently focused on the EC (such as on investment notification and rules for equipment procurement), but mostly these interventions have been unsuccessful or have reinforced the autonomy of member states and of the utilities.

Certainly there has been little in EC policy on electricity prior to the IEM which would indicate such a transformation. While the Commission indicated that an integration and liberalization of the ESI was desirable, the idea did not receive any serious consideration. Policy has for the most part been developed in the 1970s and was largely informed by the need to diversify fuel types in power production by discouraging and encouraging various forms of power generation. The use of gas and oil was limited in 1975 (although it was a measure that was largely honoured in the breach), while incentives for coal, nuclear and renewables were also devised.

The Commission's view of how the IEM should affect electricity has sought to balance the special characteristics of the sector with the drive to integrate and liberalize its structure. Integration of the electricity market is the Commission's principal objective. The Commission believed the development of international interconnection in Europe to be very limited by comparison with the potential of an EC-wide electricity pool. The system of interconnection was balkanized between different groupings of countries; none of these had any executive power. Within each grouping, moreover, trade was conducted on a bilateral basis on terms agreed by the utilities. The Commission viewed the structure of the system as a major constraint in the emergence of more competitive pressures in electricity production, failing not only to take advantage of the potential downward pressure on costs which a more competitive market might provide, but also, and more importantly, to exploit the comparative advantages of a mix of supply sources and the economies of a fully integrated system.

The Commission's view implicitly criticized the dominance of national systems in the ESI by identifying a number of distortions and barriers to trade within and between these systems. According to the Commission, these differences in treatment of the industry between countries were key obstacles to an economically efficient ESI: divergences proliferated in such areas as fiscal and financial treatment, planning procedures and standards. In terms of the industry's operation, the critical factor which has distorted the emergence of a market has been the influence of governments on utility purchasing, affecting the purchase of new power plant and the options available in fuel supply.

According to the Commission, the main obstacle to these developments has been the organizational structure of the ESI in most member states. The close organizational links between production on the one hand and transmission and distribution on the other have tended to favour national supply solutions for electricity. A change in the relationship between these constituent parts of the ESI would help to foster the development of trade in power. The Commission hinted at a radical transformation of the industry when it suggested that 'a change in the operational (as distinct from the ownership) system would be conducive to further opening of the internal market' (CEC, 1988b, p. 72). Although the Commission was aware of technical and security of supply issues associated with the development of open access or common carriage, it chose to push for such policies on the basis of what it believes to be the benefits to be derived from opening the market up to both large consumers and co-generators.

In 1989, the Commission took the first steps to creating a single electricity market. The first element of this was a revival of its pricing policy proposals aimed at increasing the transparency of electricity prices. In a review of transparency in the energy sector (CEC, 1989a), it considered the lack of publishable information on prices to large consumers as unacceptable. It sought to devise reference tariffs against which consumers across the EC can assess and compare their own prices. The measure was accompanied by moves to increase the scope for trade (or transit) and to foster investment coordination between the utilities. After nearly two years of negotiations, the Council agreed to the transparency and transit directives but not to the Commission's plans for investment coordination, committing themselves to a better use of existing agreements in this area.

The Commission's next step was to consult with governments and industry on the feasibility of greater competition. After an inconclusive series of reports, which would probably have rejected the idea of competition were it not for the support of the British government and electricity industry, a prolonged debate within the Commission took place, the result of which was a set of limited proposals for reform. These called for an extension of market access to independent power producers, distribution companies and large consumers, with the possibility of a complete market opening some time in the future. The directive was, however, drawn up as a proposal to the Council; the Commission did not use Article 90 to force the proposals through (although it had been debated). Moreover, the directive itself was framed in a way that emphasized gradual implementation, concessions to supply security and maximum national autonomy in applying the directives (COM (91) 548; Argyris, 1993).

An agreement to liberalize the electricity market was eventually reached in 1996 after further watering down of the original proposal: competition will only be introduced for the largest consumers with a gradual opening of the market over nine years. Countries will be able to opt for either 'negotiated third party access' or a 'single buyer' system (the latter preserving to some extent the position of the single vertically integrated utilities which enjoy a near monopoly in some member states), although in both cases the different components of the market (production, transmission and distribution) will have to be 'unbundled' (a separation of accounts for each component – see Klom, 1996). While the agreed reforms fall short of outright deregulation, it is clear that many member states are considering (and some such as the UK and Sweden have already implemented) more radical reforms.

13.2.5 Non-fossil sources: nuclear, renewables, conservation

Growing concern over supply security and latterly the environment has fuelled an interest in non-fossil fuel sources of energy in many member states. In the 1970s and early 1980s nuclear power was the main focus of interest. More recently, however, the potential of renewables and energy conservation measures has been recognized.

The growth of nuclear power in the EU has been rapid but not dramatically so. Its contribution to electricity input in the EU has risen from almost zero in 1960 to just over one-third in the mid-1990s. The position varies widely from country to country, reflecting the different political climates within which the industry has developed: some such as France obtain 80% of electricity from nuclear power while others such as Denmark have none. The industry has been badly shaken by scandal (Transnuklear) and crisis (Chernobyl) and characterized by highly variable operating record and cost levels (Thomas, 1988). Now nuclear power is promoted less for its economic than for its environmental benefits (since it does not emit greenhouse gases). Nonetheless, not even its proponents stick to the optimistic forecasts made in the 1950s and which persisted into the early 1980s.

The EU nuclear industry is broadly composed of utilities, national authorities and fuel agencies. In almost every case the industry is predominantly publicly owned. Advanced nuclear technologies (such as the fast breeder reactor and fusion) are even more the preserve of the public sector. As part of the ESI, and given its special characteristics, the industry has not been subject to competitive pressures. Commission policy on the sector has never lived up to the expectations of the Euratom treaty. Too many countries have endeavoured to maintain autonomy over the industry. Yet the Commission has sought to sustain the industry as much for its industrial policy implications as for energy concerns (CEC, 1970b). Considerable resources have gone into promoting nuclear power and particularly joint ventures on advanced technologies: of the 1,200 million ECUs proposed for energy research in the third Framework Programme, over 75% was allocated to the nuclear sector.

The Commission's treatment of nuclear power and the IEM is separate to that of electricity, and as a result focuses less on the economics of nuclear power as a source of electricity than on the characteristics of nuclear fuel, plant and services. As in the case of coal, the Commission notes the wide disparities in policy and practice across the EC and the relative weakness of Euratom, the Treaty guiding the sector's development and the obstacles facing the development of a European and competitive market for nuclear fuels and equipment. In the first case, the long-term nature of contracts for enrichment and reprocessing means that any moves towards an internal market will have to wait for their expiry (CEC, 1988e).

Aside from very significant levels of research support, the Commission has scarcely addressed the nuclear issue since the mid-1980s, confining itself to reviews of the current status of the industry. The divisions between member states have persisted, effectively preventing any Community policy to emerge (though the inertia which grants almost all Community energy R&D funds to nuclear persists). There have been four developments which may allow a policy to develop in future, however. The first is the greenhouse debate. For many in the nuclear industry, the fears surrounding global warming may rekindle interest in nuclear investments although it has not so far led to a formal declaration of Community support. The second issue is industrial policy: supporters of the sector in member states and the Commission have stressed the importance of the sector as a 'high technology' sector. A related issue is the potential for rebuilding the nuclear industry in the former socialist bloc: poor safety and performance records in East Europe and the former Soviet Union have presented the European nuclear industry with new opportunities for investment and maintaining industrial capabilities (Defrennes, 1997). The final issue is market liberalization. As part of its attempts to apply the competition rules to the energy sector, the the Commission scrutinized British attempts to protect the nuclear industry during the privatization of the electricity industry. In this case, the Commission was able to limit the level and duration of support given by the British government, justifying the exception on the grounds of supply security. If the development of an internal energy market exposed more market distortions relating to nuclear energy, this mechanism could be used again.

It may be, however, that the uncertain economics and the controversial politics of nuclear power will continue to rule it out in future EU energy strategy. In that context more and more attention and resources will have to be given to the other non-fossil options: renewables and conservation.

The most established renewable energy industry is hydroelectric power which accounts for a sizable proportion of electricity (most major sites are in use and new developments face considerable opposition). The 'new' renewables such as minihydro, solar, wind and wave have largely developed in the aftermath of energy crises and growing environmental concerns. While still small in terms of power contribution, they are a fixture in many utilities and their role is set to grow in most, as their reliability and competitiveness improve. The sector industries largely consist of joint ventures between governments, utilities and manufacturers.

The importance and structure of conservation industries are even harder to discern. While advisory, architectural and control systems companies (each offering ways to reduce energy consumption) proliferate, their impact is difficult to assess (given that they are aiming to help consumers to forgo energy usage). The overall improvement in energy efficiency must be partly due to these companies but also to other factors such as economic restructuring and price effects. Largely private, these companies have received varying degrees of support from governments while the energy industries have for the most part been lukewarm, perceiving it as a threat to growth of their market. More recently, however, some large energy companies have adopted a higher profile on conservation issues as a means of developing their market and diversifying.

Policy initiatives have also intensified largely as a result of the pressure of environmental concerns. On renewables, the Commission announced in 1988 a recommendation to allow favourable access for such supplies (on the basis of their environmental benefits) to public grid systems. Further measures were proposed in the wake of the Commission's greenhouse strategy. A four-part initiative – ALTENER – was tabled in 1992, involving the promotion of a market for renewables, fiscal and economic measures, training and information (Tiberi and Cardoso, 1992) while more recently the Commission published a green paper on renewables and set the objective of doubling the share of renewables in the Community's energy balances (COM (96) 576). On conservation, the Commission has developed a number of programmes, the most recent of which – SAVE – sets out a variety of measures including labelling of appliances, third party finance, audits and inspections (Fee, 1992). Given parallel interests in member states, it may be that these options will be taken more seriously in the future than they were in previous energy strategies. However, an attempt to overcome the regulatory barriers to the development of these options looks unlikely to be accepted. In recent years the Commission has sought a new approach to energy investment – so-called integrated resource planning is designed to factor in 'externalities' (most importantly, impact upon the environment) to investment choices. Such techniques have been used in the US and some member states to support renewable and conservation options. The measure is opposed by the larger utilities across the Community as well as by a number of governments.

13.3 Conclusion

It is more than 40 years since the first Community initiatives on energy policy were proposed, yet a coherent policy remains elusive. As is clear, each of the energy sub-sectors has been affected by Community policies, largely invoked on the back of the internal market and environmental protection. While not all policy proposals are agreed to or implemented successfully, there is no longer any doubt that what the Commission proposes should be taken seriously by member states and the energy industries. In a sense, however, its relative success with certain initiatives has meant that the Community has many policies for the energy sector, but no overall policy.

The absence of such a policy means that there is a danger of conflicting objectives. This is not a new problem. From 1951 to 1973, energy policy efforts tried to balance the goal of a single and open energy market with the need to maintain security of supply. For the next ten years, the security goal predominated. Now the balance of policy is even less clear. The tone of many debates and the nature of proposals suggest that the IEM agenda is in the ascendant, with a corresponding emphasis of policy towards free markets. At the same time, however, the growth of the environment as a policy concern highlights rather different priorities, casting doubt on a purely market-driven approach. Nor has the 'old' agenda of supply security disappeared, and the temptation to use the energy sector for industrial, regional and social policy objectives also persists. The problems of such a multi-dimensional 'policy' would be considerable if any institution had the task of coordinating them. Given that there is no remit for such a role to be played, how much greater are the risks of contradictory signals to governments, energy suppliers and consumers and how much more difficult are the intra-Commission disputes (i.e. those between different directorates)?

It may be that the pressures of different policy objectives and the need both to reconcile these and to rationalize and regulate derogations from them will push the Community towards a *de facto* energy policy. This, however, raises a number of questions about accountability and democracy which are all too apparent in a range of EU policy areas. The irony is that such problems as do arise from the absence of energy policy or an *ad hoc* approach will be the result of a failure by member states to consider and debate a coherent and common energy policy for the Community.

chapter fourteen

Tax harmonization

A. M. EL-AGRAA*

Tax harmonization has turned out to be a very thorny issue for the EU: witness the vehement utterances during 1988–89 by Baroness Thatcher when she was British Prime Minister (see Chapter 25), and by both German Chancellor Helmut Kohl and Jacques Delors when he was President of the EU Commission (Commission, hereafter), when she flatly declared that tax harmonization was not EU business only to hear the other two announce that it was indispensable for EU integration. Nevertheless, tax harmonization still remains an area where new EU legislation requires unanimity; hence a single EU member nation can frustrate any new initiatives within this domain. The purpose of this chapter is to clarify what tax harmonization means before going on to assess the progress the EU has achieved in this field.

14.1 Tax harmonization in the context of fiscal policy

Very widely interpreted, fiscal policy comprises a whole corpus of 'public finance' issues: the relative size of the public sector, taxation and expenditure, and the allocation of public sector responsibilities between the different tiers of government (Prest, 1979). Hence fiscal policy is concerned with a far wider area than that commonly, but arguably, associated with it, namely, the aggregate management of the economy in terms of controlling inflation and employment–unemployment levels.

Experts in the field of public finance (Musgrave and Musgrave (1976) rightly stress that 'public finance' is a misleading term, since the subject also deals with 'real' problems) have identified a number of problems associated with these fiscal policy issues. For instance, the relative size of the public sector raises questions regarding the definition and measurement of government revenue and expenditure (Prest, 1972), and the attempts at understanding and explaining revenue and expenditure have produced more than one theoretical model (Musgrave and Musgrave, 1976; Peacock and Wiseman, 1967). The division of public sector responsibilities raises the

* I am grateful to my colleague, Professor Kenji Iwata, and my graduate student, Sagar Sharma, for their assistance with data collection and verification.

delicate question of which fiscal aspects should be dealt with at the central government level and which aspects should be tackled at the local level. Finally, the area of taxation and expenditure criteria has resulted in general agreement about the basic criteria of *allocation* (the process by which the utilization of resources is split between private and social goods and by which the 'basket' of social goods is chosen), *equity* (the use of the budget for achieving a 'fair' distribution of income), *stabilization* (the use of the budget as an instrument for achieving and maintaining a 'reasonable' level of employment, acceptable inflation and economic growth rates and for achieving equilibrium and stability in the balance of payments), and *administration* (the practical possibilities of implementing a particular tax system and the cost to the society of operating such a system). However, a number of very tricky problems are involved in a consideration of these criteria. In discussing the efficiency of resource allocation, the choice between, for example, work and leisure, or between private and public goods, is an important and controversial one. With regard to the equity of distribution, there is the problem of what is meant by equity: is it personal, class or regional equity? In a discussion of the stabilization of the economy, despite the controversy between 'Kenyesians' and 'monetarists', there still exists the perennial problem of controlling unemployment and inflation and, in spite of the relative demise of 'Phillips curve', the trade-off between them. A consideration of administration must take into account the problem of efficiency versus practicality. Finally, there is the obvious conflict between the four criteria in that the achievement of one aim is usually at the expense of another; for example, what is most efficient in terms of collection may prove less (or more) equitable than what is considered to be socially desirable.

These complex considerations cannot be tackled here, given the level of generality of this chapter. The interested reader is, therefore, advised to consult the very extensive literature on public finance.

The above relates to a discussion of the problems of fiscal policy in very broad national terms. When considering EU fiscal policy, there are certain elements of the international dimension that need spelling out and there are also some inter-regional (intra-EU) elements that have to be introduced.

Very briefly, internationally, it has always been recognized that taxes (and equivalent instruments) have similar effects to tariffs on the international flow of goods and services – non-tariff distortions of international trade (generally referred to as non-tariff trade barriers, NTBs – see Baldwin, 1971). Other elements have also been recognized as operating similar distortions on the international flow of factors of production (Bhagwati, 1969; Johnson, 1965a, 1973).

In the particular context of the EU, it should be remembered that its formation, at least from the economic viewpoint, was meant to facilitate the free and unimpeded flow of goods, services and factors (and the other elements discussed in Chapter 1) between the member nations. Since tariffs are not the only distorting factor in this respect, the proper establishment of intra-EU free trade necessitates the removal of all non-tariff distortions that have an equivalent effect. Hence, the removal of tariffs may give the impression of establishing free trade inside the EU, but this is by no means automatically guaranteed, since the existence of sales taxes, excise duties, corporation taxes, income taxes, etc., may impede this freedom. Indeed, this is precisely what happened in the EC: the removal of tariffs in the 1960s immediately highlighted the significance of NTBs. This is also the reason why the EU Commission was able to persuade the member nations to adopt the Single European Act (SEA) to enable the creation of one internal market free of such distortions from the end of 1992 – see below and Chapter 7. The moral is that not only tariffs, but all equivalent distortions, must be eliminated or harmonized.

At this juncture it becomes necessary to emphasize that there are at least two basic elements to fiscal policy: the instruments available to the government for fiscal policy purposes (i.e. the total tax structure) and the overall impact of the joint manoeuvring of these instruments (i.e. the role played by the budget). The aim of this chapter is to discuss the meaning of and the need for tax harmonization, and to assess the progress made by the EU in this respect. The other element of fiscal policy, the general budget of the EU, is discussed in the following chapter. Hence, the two chapters complement each other in that, taken together, they cover the two basic elements of EU fiscal policy.

14.2 The EU tax structure and its implications

In case it is not obvious why taxes should give rise to trade distortion (Swann, 1978), it may be useful to examine the nature of taxes before the inception of the EU (see

Table 14.1 ⬤ Percentage composition of tax receipts and tax burdens in the EC, 1955.

	Income and property taxes	Turnover taxes	Consumption taxes	Tax receipts as % of GNP
Belgium	50.7	26.5	22.8	17.1
France	38.4	41.5	20.1	19.6
West Germany	52.4	26.9	20.7	21.9
Italy	32.3	21.1	46.6	22.9
Luxemburg	66.4	15.4	18.2	23.6
Netherlands	60.0	20.1	19.9	26.6

Source Balassa (1961)

Table 14.1), as well as to consider the treatment given at the time to indirect taxation on internationally traded commodities.

Before considering these aspects, however, it may be useful to remind the reader that there are two basic types of taxation: direct and indirect. Direct taxes, such as income and corporation taxes, come into operation at the end of the process of personal and industrial activities. They are levied on wages and salaries when activities have been performed and payment has been met (income taxes), or on the profits of industrial or professional businesses at the end of annual activity (corporation taxes). Direct taxes are not intended to play any significant role in the pricing of commodities or professional services. Indirect taxes are levied specifically on consumption and are, therefore, in a simplistic model, very significant in determining the pricing of commodities, given their real costs of production.

Historically speaking, in the EU there existed four types of sales, or turnover, taxes (Dosser, 1973; Paxton, 1976): the *cumulative multistage cascade system* (operated in West Germany until the end of 1967, in Luxemburg until the end of 1969 and in the Netherlands until the end of 1968) in which the tax was levied on the gross value of the commodity in question at each and every stage of production without any rebate on taxes paid at earlier stages; *value-added tax* (VAT), which has operated in France since 1954 where it is known as TVA – *Taxe sur la Valeur Ajoutée* – which is basically a non-cumulative multistage system; the *mixed systems* (operated in Belgium and Italy) which were cumulative multistage systems that were applied down to the wholesale stage, but incorporated taxes which were applied at a single point for certain products; finally, *purchase tax* (operated in the United Kingdom) which was a single-stage tax normally charged at the wholesale stage by registered manufacturers or wholesalers, which meant that manufacturers could trade with each other without paying tax.

Although all these tax systems had the common characteristic that no tax was paid on exports, so that each country levied its tax at the point of entry, one should still consider the need for harmonizing them.

A variety of taxes also existed in the form of excise duties, the main purpose of which is to raise revenue for the governments. The number of commodities subjected to these duties ranged from the usual (or 'classical') five of manufactured tobacco products, hydrocarbon oils, beer, wine and spirits, to an extensive number including coffee, sugar, salt, matches, etc. (in Italy). The means by which the government collected its revenues from excise duties ranged from government-controlled manufacturing, e.g. tobacco goods in France and Italy, to fiscal imports based on value, weight, strength, quality, etc. (Dosser, 1973, p. 2).

As far as corporation tax is concerned, three basic schemes existed, and still exist in a slightly disguised form, but not in any single country at all times. The first is the *separate* system which was used in the United Kingdom – the system calls for the complete separation of corporation tax from personal income tax and was usually referred to as the 'classical' system. The second is the *two-rate* or *split-rate* system which was the German practice and was recommended as an alternative system for the United Kingdom in the Green Paper of 1971 (HMSO, Cmnd 4630). The third is the *credit* or *imputation* system which give shareholders credit for tax paid by the company, and this credit may be used to offset their income tax liability on dividends; part of the company's tax liability is 'imputed' to the shareholders and regarded as a prepayment of their income tax on dividends – this was the French system and was proposed for the United Kingdom in the White Paper of 1972 (HMSO, Cmnd 4955) and adopted in 1973 – see Kay and King (1983) for a full explanation of how the system works within the United Kingdom context; in the appendix to this chapter, a bare skeleton of the system is provided.

Generally speaking, corporation tax varied from being totally indistinguishable from other systems (Italy) to being quite separate from personal income tax with a single or a split rate which varied between 'distributed' and 'undistributed' profits, to being partially integrated with the personal income tax systems, so that part of the corporation tax paid on distributed profits could be credited against a shareholder's income tax liability (Dosser, 1973, p. 2).

The personal income tax system itself was differentiated in very many aspects among the original six, as regards not just rates and allowances, but also administration procedures, compliance and enforcement.

Finally, the variety in the para-tax system relating to social security arrangements was even more striking. The balance between sickness, industrial injury, unemployment and pensions was very different indeed, and the methods of financing these benefits were even more so – see Chapter 18.

In concluding this section, it is useful to discuss certain problems regarding these taxes. Since VAT is the EU's turnover tax (see the section below on EU progress on tax harmonization), I shall illustrate the problems of turnover taxes in the cotext of VAT.

The first relates to the point at which the tax should be imposed. Here, two basic principles have been recognized and a choice between them has to be made: the 'destination' and 'origin' principles. Taxation under the destination principle specifies that commodities going to the same destination must bear the same tax load irrespective of their origin. For example, if the United Kingdom levies a general sales tax at 8% and France a similar tax at 16%, a commodity exported from the United Kingdom to France would be exempt from the United Kingdom's 8% tax but would be subjected to France's 16% tax. Hence, the United Kingdom's export commodity would compete on equal terms with French commodities sold in the French market. Taxation under the origin principle specifies that commodities with the same origin must pay exactly the same tax, irrespective of their destination. Hence, a commodity exported by the United Kingdom to France would pay the United Kingdom tax (8%) and would be exempt from the French tax (16%). Therefore, the commodity that originated from the United Kingdom would compete unfairly against a similar French commodity.

The choice between the destination and origin principles raises a number of technical issues which cannot be tackled here. Those interested should consult the voluminous literature on the subject (Shoup, 1966, 1972; Dosser, 1973; Paxton, 1976; Pinder, 1971).

The second problem relates to the range of coverage of the tax. If some member countries are allowed to include certain stages, e.g. the retail stage, and others made allowances for certain fixed capital expenditures and raw materials, the tax base will not be the same. This point is very important, because one has to be clear about whether the tax base should be consumption or net national income. To illustrate, in a 'closed' economy:

$$Y = W + P = C + I$$

where Y = gross national product (GNP), W = wages and salaries, P = gross profits, C = consumption and I = gross capital expenditure. If value-added is defined as $W + P - I$ (i.e. GNP minus gross capital expenditure), then consumption will form the tax base. If instead of gross capital expenditure one deducts only capital consumption (depreciation), then net national product will become the tax base. Obviously, the argument holds true in an 'open' economy. It is therefore important that members of a union should have a common base – see Table 14.2 for variations in the percentage of GDP devoted to domestic investment in the EU member states.

The third problem relates to exemptions that may defeat the aim of VAT being a tax on consumption. For example, in a three-stage production process, exempting the first stage does not create any problem, since the tax levies on the second and third stage together will be equivalent to a tax levied at all three stages. Exempting the third stage will obviously reduce the tax collection, provided of course that the rates levied at all three stages were the same. If the second stage is exempt, the tax base will be in excess of that where no exemptions are allowed for, since the tax on the first stage cannot be transferred as an input tax on the second stage, and the third stage will be unable to claim any input tax from items bought from the second stage. The outcome will be a tax based on the total sum of the turnover of stages one and three only, rather than a tax levied on the total sum of the value-added at all three stages.

With regard to corporation tax, a proper evaluation of any system raises national as well as interregional (intra-EU) questions. The national questions relate to the standard criteria by which a tax system can be judged: its effect on budget revenue and aggregate effective demand, on income distribution, on the balance of payments, on the rate of economic growth, on regional differences and on price levels. It is obvious that what is very efficient for one purpose need not be so for the other purposes.

The intra-EU questions relate to the treatment of investment, since, if capital mobility within the EU is to be free from restrictions as guaranteed by the Maastricht Treaty and encouraged by the Treaty of Rome (EEC) before that, investors must receive equal treatment irrespective of their native country (region). Here, Dosser highly recommends the separate system since it is 'neutral' in its tax treatment between domestic investment at home and abroad, and between domestic and foreign investment at home, provided that both member countries practise the same system (Dosser, 1973, p. 95). Prest (1979, pp. 85–6) argues that even though a separate system does not discriminate against partner (foreign) investment, it does

Table 14.2 EU gross domestic investment as a percentage of GDP.

	1960	1970	1982	1992	1995
Austria	28	30	22	25	27
Belgium[a]	19	24	16	20	18
Denmark	23	26	16	15	16
Finland	30	30	25	17	16
France	24	27	20	20	18
Germany[b]	27	28	21	21	21
Greece	19	28	22	20	19
Ireland	16	24	23	16	13
Italy	24	27	17	19	18
Netherlands	27	30	18	21	22
Portugal	19	26	29	na	28
Spain	21	27	25	23	21
Sweden	25	25	17	17	14
United Kingdom	19	20	17	15	16

[a] Includes Luxemburg.
[b] The figures refer to only the Federal Republic.
Sources Collected from various Eurostat publications and issues of the World Bank's World Development Report

discriminate between 'distributed' and 'undistributed' profits, and that the imputation system, even though it is neutral between 'distributed' and 'undistributed' profits, actually discriminates against partner (foreign) investment. Prest therefore claims that neither system can be given 'full marks'.

Again, at this level of generality, one cannot go into all the complications raised by such questions. The interested reader is therefore advised to consult Dosser (1966, 1971, 1973, 1975), Dosser and Han (1968), Paxton (1976) and Pinder (1971), or the vast and growing literature on this subject.

As already mentioned, excise duties are intended basically for revenue-raising purposes. For example, in the United Kingdom excise duties on tobacco products, petroleum and alcoholic drinks account for about a third of central government revenue (Kay and King, 1996). The issues raised by the harmonization of these taxes are specifically those relating to the function of these taxes as raisers of revenue and to the equity, as opposed to the efficiency, of these methods.

Finally, the income tax structure has a lot to do with the freedom of labour mobility. Ideally, one would expect equality of treatment in every single tax that is covered within this structure, but it is apparent that, since there is more than one rate, the harmonization of a 'package' of rates might achieve the specified objective.

14.3 The meaning of tax harmonization

Having discussed the problems associated with taxes in the context of economic integration, it is now appropriate to say something about the precise meaning of tax harmonization.

In earlier years, tax harmonization was defined as tax coordination (Dosser, 1973). Ideally, in a fully integrated EU, it could be defined as the identical unification of both base and rates, given the same tax system and assuming that everything else is also unified. Prest (1979, p. 76) rightly argues that 'coordination' is tantamount to a low-level meaning of tax harmonization, since it could be 'interpreted to be some process of consultation between member countries or, possibly, loose agreements between them to levy tax on a similar sort of base *or* at similar sorts of rates'. It is therefore not surprising that tax harmonization has, in practice, come to mean a compromise between the low level of coordination (the EU is much more than a low level of integration – see Chapter 1) and the ideal level of standardization (even if the Maastricht Treaty is fully implemented and without the opt-out protocols, the EU will come close to but will not become a complete political entity – see Chapter 2). However, the SEA asks for the creation of one internal market, and this has been interpreted to mean a market without fiscal frontiers which the Commission insists must be one where taxes are near equal – see below. The Maastricht and Amsterdam treaties have reinforced this decision.

14.4 The EU's experience with tax harmonization

To discuss the experience of the EU with tax harmonization meaningfully, it is sensible to consider the developments before the adoption of the SEA separately from those after it.

14.4.1 The period leading to the SEA

During this period, the main driving force was Article 99 of the Treaty of Rome, which specifically calls for the harmonization of indirect taxes, mainly turnover taxes and excise duties. Harmonization here was seen as vital, particularly since the removal of tariffs would have left taxes as the main source of intra-EU trade distortion. However, given the preoccupation of the EU with the process of unification, the Treaty seemed to put very little stress on the harmonization of its initial tax diversity. Moreover, the Treaty is rather vague about what it means by 'harmonization': for example, in Article 100 it does not specify more than that laws 'should be approximated' with regard to direct taxation. The whole development of tax harmonization during this period was influenced by the work of special committees, informal discussions, etc., i.e. the procedure detailed in Chapter 2. This, however, should not be interpreted as a criticism of those who drafted the Treaty. On the contrary, given the very complex nature of the subject and its closeness to the question of political unification, it would have been short-sighted to have done otherwise.

Given this general background, it is now appropriate to describe the progress made by the EU with respect to tax harmonization during this period.

In the area of indirect taxation, most of the developments were in terms of VAT, which the EU adopted as its turnover tax following the recommendations of the Neumark Committee in 1963, which was in turn based on the Tinbergen study of 1953 (CEC, 1953) – particularly since it was realized that the removal of intra-EU tariffs left taxes on traded goods as the main impediment to the establishment of complete free trade inside the EU. Between 1967 and 1977, six directives were issued with the aim of achieving conformity between the different practices of the member countries. These related, apart from the adoption of VAT as the EU sales tax, to three major considerations: the inclusion of the retail stage in the coverage of VAT; the use of VAT levies for the EU general budget (see the following chapter); the achievement of greater uniformity in VAT structure. These directives were later supplemented by several minor ones and by a series of draft directives.[1]

What, then, was the state of play? (See Table 14.3 for information covering this period). Having adopted the VAT system and having accepted a unified method of calculating it, the EU also acceded to the destination principle which, as we have seen, is consistent with free intra-EU trade. It was agreed by all the member states that the coverage of VAT should be the same and should include the retail stage (now the normal practice), that crude raw materials, bought-in elements and similar components were to be deductible from the tax computation, and that investment stock and inventories should be given similar treatment by all member nations. There was agreement about the general principle of VAT exemptions, but the precise nature of these seemed to vary from one member country to another, thus giving rise to the problems concerning the tax base discussed earlier.

On the other hand, this similarity of principles was, in practice, contradicted by a number of differences. The tax coverage differed from one member country to another, since most of them had different kinds, as well as different levels, of exemptions. For example, the United Kingdom applied zero rating for foodstuffs and children's clothing (zero rating is different from exemptions, since zero rating means not only tax exemption from the process, but also the receipt of rebates on taxes paid at the preceding stage – see Dosser, 1975; Paxton, 1976; Prest, 1979). There was a wide difference in rate structure.

Table 14.3 ● Taxes and actual social contributions, VAT and corporation tax.

	Taxes and actual social contributions (% of total), 1980				Effective rates of VAT (%), 1982[c,d]			Corporation tax[e,f]		
	Taxes linked to production and imports	Current taxes on income and wealth	Capital taxes	Actual social contributions	Standard	Reduced	Increased	Rate (%)	System	Imputation credit (%)
Belgium	27.1	41.8	0.8	30.3	17.0	6.0	25.00	48.00	Imputation	49.8
Denmark	41.5	56.3	0.4	1.8	22.0	–	–	37.00	Imputation	25.5
France	35.5	20.4	0.6	43.6	18.6	5.5/7.0	33.30	50.00	Imputation	50.0
West Germany	32.0	32.7	0.2	35.1	13.0	6.5	–	56.36	Imputation	100.0
Ireland[a]	49.1	35.6	0.4	14.9	30.0	0.0/18.0	–	45.00	Imputation	52.4
Italy[b]	30.9	32.3	0.2	36.6	15.0	2.0/8.0	18.35	36.25	Imputation	58.6
Luxemburg	27.2	43.5	0.2	29.1	10.0	2.0/5.0	–	40.00	Separate	None
Netherlands	25.6	34.5	0.5	39.5	18.0	4.0	–	45.00	Separate	None
United Kingdom	43.6	38.5	0.5	17.6	15.0	0.0	–	52.00	Imputation	39.6

[a]1979, [b]1978, [c]1978, the effective VAT rate is that on the price net of tax, [d]Greece was still to introduce VAT, [e]proposals were made in August 1982 for increasing Italy's to 35–38%, and [f]the West German system is a two-rate one.

Source Eurostat, 1982 (various publications) and *Bulletin of the European Communities*, Supplement 1/80.

With respect to corporation tax, the Neumark Report of 1963 (CEC, 1963) recommended a split-rate system, the van den Tempel Report of 1970 (CEC, 1970c) preferred the adoption of the separate or classical system, and the draft directive of 1975 went for the imputation system. Moreover, the method of tax harmonization which was accepted was not the ideal one of a single EU corporation tax and a single tax pattern, but rather a unified EU corporation tax accompanied by freedom of tax patterns. Hence, all systems were entertained at some time or another and all that can be categorically stated is that by 1986 the EU limited its choice to the separate and imputation systems – see Table 14.4.

Table 14.4 ⬭ **Corporation tax structure and rates, 1986.**

	System	Corporation tax rate (%)	Imputation credit (%)
Belgium	Imputation	45.0[a]	40.87
Denmark	Imputation	50.00	25.00
France	Imputation	45.00	61.11
West Germany	Imputation	56.00/36.00[b]	100.00
Greece	Imputation[c]	34.00 to 47.20	100.00
Ireland	Imputation	50.00[a]	53.85
Italy	Imputation	46.368[d]	100.00
Luxemburg	Separate	40.0[a]	0.00
Netherlands	Separate	42.00	0.00
Portugal	Imputation[c]	42.20 to 47.20	100.00
Spain	Imputation	35.00	18.57
United Kingdom	Imputation	35.0[a]	75.81

[a] Reduced rates are applied to low income.
[b] The 36% is levied on distributed profits.
[c] Greece and Portugal have no corporation tax on distributed profits – this is tantamount to a 100% imputation credit.
[d] This is the sum of both central and local taxes.
Source various publications by the Commission and national sources.

As far as excise duties were concerned, progress was rather slow, and this can be partially attributed to the large extent of the differences between the rates on the commodities under consideration in the different member countries – see Tables 14.5 and 14.6 for information during this period. This is a partial explanation, however, because, as was pointed out earlier, these taxes are important for government revenue purposes and it would have been naïve to have suggested that rate uniformity could have been achieved without giving consideration to the political implications of such a move.

The greatest progress was achieved in tobacco, where a new harmonized system was adopted in January 1978. The essential elements of this system were the abolition of any duties on raw tobacco leaf and the adoption of a new sales tax at the manufacturing level, combined with a specific tax per cigarette and VAT. Prest (1979) argues that the overall effect of this would have been to push up the relative prices of the cheaper brands of cigarettes.

It has been suggested (Prest, 1979) that the harmonization of tax rates here is misguided, since the destination principle automatically guarantees fair competition. This is a misleading criticism, however, since the harmonization of the tax structure

Table 14.5 ⬤ Excise duty application in each member state as a percentage of EU average (July 1979 = 100).

	Cigarettes	Spirits	Wine	Beer	Petrol (high grade)	Gas–oil
Belgium	86	62	69	46	99	85
Denmark	299	289	240	272	132	51
France	42	89	4	7	127	156
West Germany	118	63	0	29	92	203
Ireland	74	147	218	289	76	72
Italy	57	18	0	34	140	27
Luxemburg	54	34	34	33	74	44
Netherlands	77	62	69	46	91	82
United Kingdom	92	136	265	144	68	180

Source Bulletin of the European Communities, supplement 1/80.

Table 14.6 ● Excise duties, proposed and current in 1985 (ECU).

Excisable goods	Proposed rate	EU average		1985 rates in the member states[a]											
		Arithmetic	Weighted	B	D	WG	F	Gr	Ir	It	L	N	P	S	UK
Alcoholic beverages															
Pure alcohol (1 hl)	1,271.0	1,271.0		1,252	3,499	1,174	1,149	48	2,722	230	842	1,298	248	309	2,483
Intermediate products (1 hl)	85.0	103.0		61	292	70	6	2	404	0	41	63	0	0	286
Wines (1 hl)	17.0[b]	58.0		33	157	20	3	0	279	0	13	33	0	0	154
Beers (1 hl)	17.0	22.5		10	57	7	3	10	81	17	5	20	7	3	49
Mineral oils															
Petrol, leaded (1,000 l)	340.0	340.0	336	261	473	256	369	349	362	557	209	340	352	254	271
Diesel (1,000 l)	177.0	153.0	177	123	236	213	190	106	279	178	100	109	162	124	229
Heating gas/oil (1,000 l)	50.0	62.0	50	0	236	8	53	109	48	178	0	44	23	38	15
Heavy fuel oil (1,000 kg)	17.0	26.0	17	0	266	7	25	93	10	7	2	15	11	1	11
LPG (1,000 l)	85.0	85.0	61	0	163	160	138	40	222	96	21	0	17	27	1,353
Cigarettes															
Specific excise (per 1,000)	19.5	19.5		2	77	27	1	1	49	2	2	26	2	1	43
Ad valorem duty + VAT (%)[c]	52–4.0	53.0		66	39	44	71	60	34	69	64	36	65	52	34
Other manufactured tobacco[c]															
Cigars (%)	34–6.0	35.0		22	40	26	50	31	56	39–63	23	20	40	21	50
Cigarillos (%)	34–6.0	35.0		27	40	29	54	31	56	39–63	23	25	40	21	50
Smoking tobacco (%)	54–6.0	55.0		37	58–83	36–54	65	63	70	71	38	56	26	31	65–70
Other (%)	41–3.0	42.0		37	41–57	20	37–59	64	20–70	42	38	56	30	36	13–50

[a] Rates are as on 1 April 1987, in ECU.
[b] Sparkling wines: 30 ECU/hl.
[c] Ad valorem duty + VAT, as a % of the retail price.

Source EU Commission's *Europe Without Frontiers* (*Information* 1987, p. 51); COM (87) 325–8.

should be seen in the context of the drive in the EU for monetary integration (see Chapter 5) and political unification (see Chapter 2), processes which become increasingly difficult without tax harmonization – see next section.

Some progress was achieved with regard to stamp duties. Harmonization here was necessary for promoting the freedom of intra-EU capital flows. The 1976 draft directive recommended a compromise between the systems existing in the member countries. This recommendation was accepted, with the proviso that time would be allowed for adjustment to the new system.

Nothing was attempted in the area of personal income taxation and very slight progress was achieved in social security payments, unemployment benefits, etc.; the only exception was the draft directive of 1979 which dealt with equity in the taxation of migrant workers, but this did not have any serious impact. These issues are discussed in some detail in Chapter 18.

14.4.2 The period beginning with the SEA

The SEA was to have transformed the EC into a single internal market by the end of 1992, i.e. the EC should have become 'an area without internal frontiers in which the free movement of goods, persons, services and capital is ensured' (see Chapter 7); thus, the SEA reiterates the original objectives of the Treaty of Rome, but is more explicit on NTBs. The Commission emphasizes the 'Europe without frontiers' since it is convinced that frontiers are the clearest symbol of divisions within the EU. It is adamant that, if frontiers persist, they will be used as convenient locations for practising some protectionist measure or another.

The most significant feature of frontiers is the customs posts, and, as we have seen, these crucially relate to taxes. Of course, as Baroness Thatcher has persistently claimed, and both her successors (Major and Blair) have reiterated, they may be very important for controlling the movement of terrorists and drug trafficking; but our concern here is with the free movement of 'licit' goods and factors of production. As our earlier discussion has demonstrated, customs controls protect the indirect taxes of one EU member country from relative tax bargains which are obtainable elsewhere within the EU. Moreover, customs controls guarantee that governments can collect the VAT that belongs to them. A frontier-free EU would undermine these factors unless the rates of indirect taxation within the EU were brought much closer to each other. They do not have to be equalized, not only because of the 'package' nature mentioned above, but also because the experience of the United States indicates that contiguous states can maintain differentials in sales taxes of up to about 5 percentage points without the tax leakage becoming unbearable. The Commission would ideally like to see an equalization of the rates, but given the United States' experience and the subsidiarity principle (see Chapter 2), it has decided to aim for a position similar to that of the United States.

Given the brevity of this chapter, it is unjustifiable to devote space to the development of the position that the Commission would have liked the member nations to have adopted. Those interested in a full description and some analysis of this development are advised to consult Guieu and Bonnet (1987), Bos and Nelson (1988) and Smith (1988). Here we shall concentrate on the position adopted by the Commission in 1985.

In the 1985 White Paper, the Commission reached the conclusion that, to treat EC transactions crossing frontiers within the EC in exactly the same manner as transactions within an EC member state, certain measures would have to be adopted with regard to VAT and excise duties. For VAT, these were as follows:

1. The replacement of the system of refunding tax on exportation and collecting it on importation by a system of tax collection by the country of origin.

2. The introduction of an EC clearing mechanism to ensure that revenues would continue to accrue to the EU member nation where consumption took place so that the destination principle would remain intact.

3. The narrowing of the differentials in national VAT rates so as to lessen the risks of fraud, tax evasion and distortions in competition.

With regard to excise duties, three conditions were deemed necessary:

1. An interlinkage of the bonded warehouse system (created to defer the payment of duty since, as long as the goods remain in these warehouses, duties on them do not have to be paid; recall that excise duties are levied only once on manufacture or importation).

2. Upholding the destination principle.

3. An approximation of the national excise duty rates and regimes.

The initial recommendations advanced by the Commission regarding how to achieve these requirements were examined by an *ad hoc* group invited by the Council of Ministers for Foreign Affairs (ECOFIN). The group reported (Council of the European Communities, 1986) that some of its members did not endorse the need for abolishing fiscal frontiers. However, they felt that, if frontiers had to be removed, the proposals put forward by the Commission were necessary, but inadequate: the group advanced a number of serious problems with respect to the clearing mechanism and the system of interlinked bonded warehouses.

The Commission responded in August 1987 (CEC, 1987b) by mainly elaborating on the proposals put forward in the White Paper and by advancing different recommendations concerning the VAT clearing mechanism and the approximation of excise duties; thus, it responded in precisely the way it had been instructed. These recommendations were as follows:

1. The creation of a central account, in ECUs, to be administered by the Commission and to which net exporting member nations would contribute on a monthly basis and from which net importing member countries would receive payment.

2. The settlement of accounts on the basis of statements made by each member state about its net position (the balance of its VAT on intra-EU input and output).

The new clearing mechanism differed from the one suggested by the *ad hoc* group in that, apart from the proposal that the Commission should administer it, it asked for a clearing of net VAT flows, not a clearing of claims based entirely on input VAT data. The Commission justified this new proposal by stating that it is soundly based; guarantees each member nation its correct VAT allocation; minimizes the extra burden on traders; ensures the system's compatibility with the existing VAT administrative structure; bases clearance on data on individual transactions; and ensures that the mechanism is self-financing.

The Commission was also of the opinion that the removal of fiscal frontiers was impossible unless the approximation of VAT rates was achieved first. It therefore put forward proposals for both the number and level of rates and the allocation of products to the rates. Being well aware that the SEA did not extend the system of majority voting to taxation (see Chapter 1), owing to the obsession with national sovereignty, the Commission stuck closely to the prevailing system: it suggested a dual-rate structure consisting of a standard (normal) and a reduced rate. The reduced rate was to cover basic necessities such as foodstuffs, energy products for heating and lighting, water supplies, pharmaceuticals, books, newspapers, periodicals and passenger transport. To discourage excessive tax-induced distortions on competition, it proposed a six-point band for the standard rate (14–20%) and a five-point band for the reduced rate (4–9%) – see Figure 14.1.

Precise rates were also proposed by the Commission for excise duties. These rates were fixed amounts, specified in ECUs, for the various excises (on alcoholic beverages, mineral oils and tobacco products). Only for the sum of the *ad valorem* elements of excise duty and VAT (on tobacco products) was an optional margin allowed, the impact of which on retail prices would equal the VAT band for non-excisable products – see Table 14.6. The approximation of excise duties was tantamount to an equalization of rates which the Commission deemed to be necessary because VAT was also charged on excisable products, and the combined effect of differentials in excise and VAT rates might otherwise result in unreasonably high tax-induced differences in prices.

Of course, as mentioned above, some of these developments were not necessary if all that was being sought was an internal market. For example, the factors that influence prices are both numerous and diverse, and differentials in tax rates are only one such factor. That is why some authorities argue that it is only when frontiers are abolished, without prior harmonization of tax rates, that the distortions arising primarily from fiscal factors can be measured. We have also seen that, even in a federation as strong as the United States, the equalization of tax rates has not been necessary. Moreover, in the case of excise duties, the system prevailing in post-1986 ensured that duties were charged where the goods were sold since exports were duty free; thus, for those dutiable goods mainly purchased by consumers, such as alcoholic drinks and tobacco products, that system provided fiscal neutrality with respect to the location of production, even though the member states applied very different levels of duty (Smith, 1988, p. 154). Be that as it may, the relevant criterion for judging the position of the Commission is the dynamic one concerning where

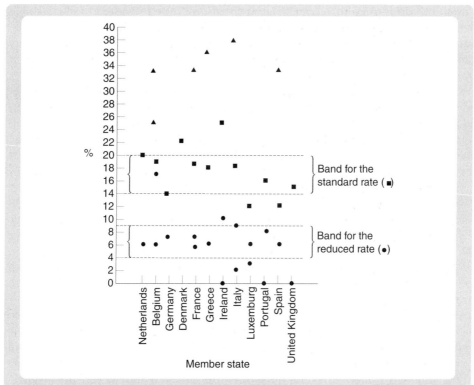

Figure 14.1 VAT in the EC – bands proposed by the European Commission and current rates in the member states (1987): ■, standard rate; ●, reduced rate; ▲. increased rate. (*Source* CEC, *Europe Without Frontiers* (Information 1987, p. 51); COM (87) 325–8)

the EC wanted to go after 1992, and the EU has since then adopted the Maastricht Treaty which is supposed to lead to, *inter alia*, an EMU, a common defence policy and closer political cooperation, but the Amsterdam Treaty of June 1997, although it confirms EMU, says nothing specific on the last two (see Chapter 2). Thus it was perfectly in order for the Commission to have asked for an approximation of rates. The piecemeal analyses carried out by most economists seem to centre around what is happening at a particular moment in time, but the Commission in entrusted with introducing measures consistent with EU policies as well as with initiating efforts for the further integration of the EU, even though this role has formally been taken over by the European Council; hence its perspective is, rightly, much wider and goes further into the future: reaching the summit requires looking out for the precipices.

Given this background, one needs to ask about what has actually been happening. It would be both tedious and unnecessary to provide here every single directive or communication that has been passed by the EU in this respect. Therefore, all that

I intend to do is to go through the latest situation; those interested in every single detail can do so by simply following the appropriate directives by glancing at the latest issue of the *Bulletin of the European Union*, the *Official Journal of the European Union* and the *Annual General Report of the Activities of the European Union*, and then tracing back to the year in question.

Since the late 1980s, the EU has made considerable progress with tax harmonization. With regard to VAT, on 19 October 1992, the Council (Council, hereafter) adopted a directive (92/77/EEC) on the approximation of rates, which is a follow-up to an earlier directive (91/680/EEC) supplementing the common system, setting the standard rate of VAT at no less than 15% and the optional and reduced rates at not less than 5%, and abolishing the increased rates. Provision has also been made for certain zero and extra-low rates to be retained for a transitional period.

As to turnover taxes, on 2 July 1992, the Commission adopted a proposal for a directive designed to abolish certain derogations in Article 1(1) of Directive 77/388/EEC of 1977 and the second subparagraph of Article 1(1) of Directive 89/465/EEC of 1989. The aim of this proposal for amending the sixth directive on VAT is to revise and generally to limit the derogations from the common system granted to the member countries in respect of the basis of assessment in order to move closer to a uniform basis of assessment.

In the case of excise duties and other indirect taxes, major progress was also achieved. On 25 February 1992, the Council adopted a directive (92/12/EEC) on the general arrangements for products subject to excise duty and on the holding and movement of such products, which lays down the rules for movement within the EU of products subject to excise duty (fuel, tobacco and spirits) and the arrangements for the collection of excise duties once border controls have been abolished. As regards trade, the new arrangements are based in particular on the movement of products via tax warehouses established throughout the EU. Under the directive, from 1 January 1993, individuals should have been able to purchase in other member countries dutiable products for their personal use at the rates obtaining there. In contrast to the harmonized VAT system, these general arrangements are definitive. On 14 December 1992, the Council adopted a directive (92/108/EEC) designed to clarify the previous one, but without altering its content or substance.

On 19 October 1992, the Council also adopted directives (92/78/EEC to 92/84/EEC) on the harmonization of excise duty structures and on the approximation of excise duty rates on cigarettes and other manufactured tobacco, on mineral oils and on spirits and other alcoholic beverages, together with a decision (92/510/EEC) authorizing member countries to continue to apply to certain mineral oils, when used for specific purposes, existing reduced rates of excise duty or exemptions from them.

On 19 February 1992, the Commission adopted a proposal for a directive on the excise duty rates applicable to motor fuels from agricultural sources (biofuels) with a view to bringing about an EU-wide reduction in the rates applied to such products. The proposal is based on the principle that biofuels can help to improve the EU's security of energy supplies, that they are more environmentally friendly than other fuels and that they will encourage the growing of non-food crops on land subject to compulsory set-aside in line with the reform of the CAP initiated by the MacShary package (see Chapter 10).

In the case of corporation taxes, the Commission submitted a communication on guidelines on 24 June 1992 (CEC, 1992l). This was based on the report by the Committee of Independent Experts on Company Taxation, chaired by ex-Finance Minister of Denmark Onno Ruding, which was submitted on 18 March, and which endorsed the Commission's own position as indicated in its April 1990 report. Those guidelines were approved by the Council on 23 November and by the Economic and Social Committee on 24 November. The gist of these guidelines is that priority should be given to the abolition of double taxation of cross-border flows as a means of eliminating the competitive distortions stemming from tax disparities between the member countries.

In addition to the recommendation for eliminating double taxation, the Commission examined the Ruding Committee's proposals relating to the rates, the base and the systems of corporation tax. Although the Commission felt that some of these suggestions went beyond what is strictly necessary at the EU level (the subsidiarity principle suggests that there is no need to harmonize the system itself), it agreed that the idea of a minimum EU rate of 30% for corporation tax is worth thorough examination. It felt that the same sentiment applied to their recommendations regarding the tax base for company profits and tax incentives for promoting research and environmental protection.

Since 1992, there have been no fundamental or major changes; the very latest developments are in the nature of refinements, adjustments, adaptations or fine-tuning. These can be followed in the manner suggested above. However, Table 14.7 gives the latest picture with regard to corporation tax and VAT rates and Table 14.8 somewhat duplicates the corporation tax rates for 1996, but demonstrates their real complexity; there have been very minor variations in excise duties relative to those given in Table 14.6, so all one needs here is a specification of the EU minimum standards, i.e. a member nation's excise duty may not be lower than this rate:

1. *Cigarettes and other manufactured tobacco products*. The overall minimum duty (specific duty plus *ad valorem* duty excluding VAT) is fixed at 57% of the retail selling price, inclusive of all taxes for cigarettes in the most popular price category, while the specific duty (per unit of product) must be between 5% and 55% of the total tax burden (total excise duty plus VAT) on cigarettes in the most popular price category.

   The rates fixed for cigars and cigarillos and for smoking tobacco may be *ad valorem*, specific or composite rates. The overall excise duty inclusive of all taxes, expressed as a percentage or for a given number of items, may not be lower than:

   - 5% of the retail selling price, or 7 Ecus per 1,000 items or per kilogram (kg), for cigars and cigarillos;
   - 30% of the retail selling price, or 20 Ecus per kg, for fine cut smoking tobacco intended for the rolling cigarettes;

Table 14.7 ⬭ EU corporation tax and VAT rates, 1996.

	Corporation tax (%)	VAT (%) Standard	Reduced
Austria	34	20	10
Belgium	39	21	12/6
Denmark	34	25	0
Finland	28	22	6/12/17
France	36⅔	20.6	5.5/2.1
Germany	45,30	15	7
Greece	35	18	4/8
Ireland	38	21	0.25/12.5
Italy	37	19	4/10/16
Luxemburg	33	15	3/6/12
Netherlands	35	12.5	6
Portugal	36	16	5
Spain	35	16	7/4
Sweden	28	25	0
United Kingdom	33,35,25	17.5	8

Source Various publications and issues by the EU.

- 20% of the retail selling price, or 15 Ecus per kg, for other smoking tobaccos (pipe tobacco).
2. *Alcohol and alcoholic beverages.* The minimum rates of duty are:
   - 0.748 Ecu per hl/degree Plato or 1.87 Ecu per hl/degree of alcohol for beer;
   - 0 Ecu per hl for still and sparkling wine;
   - 45 Ecu per hl for intermediate products;
   - 550 Ecu per hl of pure alcohol and alcohol contained in other beverages.

However, member nations which apply to the last category of products a rate exceeding 1,000 Ecu per hl of pure alcohol may not reduce their national rate. In addition, member states which apply to those products a rate exceeding 1,000 Ecu per hl of pure alcohol may not reduce their national rate below 1,000 Ecu.

3. *Mineral oils.* The minimum rates are:

- 337 Ecu per 1,000 litres on leaded petrol;
- 287 Ecu per 1,000 litres on unleaded petrol;
- 245 Ecu per 1,000 litres on gas oil used as a propellant;
- 18 Ecu per 1,000 litres on gas oil used for other purposes;
- 18 Ecu per 1,000 litres on heating gas oil;
- 13 Ecu per 1,000 kg on heavy fuel oil;
- 100 Ecu per 1,000 kg on LPG and methane used as a propellant;
- 36 Ecu per 1,000 kg on LPG and methane used for other purposes;
- 0 Ecu per 1,000 kg on LPG and methane used for heating purposes;
- 245 Ecu per 1,000 litres on kerosene used as a propellant;
- 18 Ecu per 1,000 litres on kerosene used for other purposes;
- 0 Ecu per 1,000 litres on kerosene used for heating purposes.

14.5 Conclusion

In conclusion, it should be emphasized that the lack of fundamental progress with tax harmonization in the EU, especially during the period prior to the adoption of the SEA, should not come as a surprise. There are three basic reasons for this. First, lest it be forgotten, the EU stands for the harmonized integration of some of the oldest countries in the world, with very diverse and extremely complicated economic systems, and this diversity and complexity is increasing with the enlargement (and potential enlargement) of the EU. Second, tax harmonization is intimately connected with the role played by the government in controlling the economy (a role subject to great debate and controversy, with the neo-Keynesians and monetarists standing poles apart; the latter not only completely dismissing the importance of the government's role in this respect, but also claiming that it is actually detrimental) and, since this role depends on a complicated package of taxes, it should be apparent that the separate harmonizing of the different components of the package is not only extremely difficult, but is also misguided. Finally, and more importantly, tax harmonization, or at least the complex and sensitive elements within it, is very closely linked with the question of monetary integration and political unification – see Chapter 5 for a technical argument on the inseparability of these issues. It would therefore be naïve to expect substantial progress in tax harmonization, without similar progress in these other fields. The full implementation of the Maastricht Treaty on *European Union*, leading to the adoption of economic

Table 14.8 ● EU taxes on company earnings in 1996 (%).

CT system / Member state	CT (on retained profits)[a]	Dividend relief Particulars	Dividend relief As a percentage of classical tax burden[b]	Ordinary top PT[a]	CT + PT on distributed profits[c]	Top PT on interest[d]	Top PT on capital gains[e,f] Ordinary shares	Top PT on capital gains[e,f] Substantial holdings
		Tax credit as a fraction of net dividend						
Imputation system								
Finland	28	7/18	100	57.5	28	28**	28	28
France	36⅔	½ (basic CT)	91	60.2	61.5	19.4*	19.4	19.4
Germany	56[g]	⅜ (CG/CT)	59	57	64.4	57*	–	π[h]
Ireland[l]	38 (10)	23/77 (⅛s)	49	48	58.1 (50.6)	42*	40	40[i]
Italy	53.2	37/63 (CG/CT)	66	51	58.7	12.5**	15	25
UK	33	¼	51	40	49.8	40*	40	40
Tax credit method		*Tax credit*						
Portugal	39.6	60% of CT[k]	91	40	42.2	20**	–[m]	–
Spain	36	40% of net div.[l]	71	56	60.6	56*	π[m]	π[m]
Special PT rate		*PT rate*						
Austria[n]	34	22	109	50	48.5	22**	–	Half of PT
Belgium[n]	40.2	25[o]	135	60.6	55.1	15**[o]	40	40
Denmark	34	40[p]	105	61	60.4	61	40	40
Greece	35	0	152	45	35	15**	–	25.6
Luxemburg[n]	40.3	Half of PT	62	51.3	55.6	51.3	–	–
Sweden	28	30	152	56	49.6	30	30	30
Classical system		*No relief*						
Netherlands	35	–[q]	0	60	74	60	–	20

Abbreviations have the following meaning: CT = company income tax; PT = personal income tax; CG = central government; π = reduced rate.

Some information may be incomplete or out of date.

Percentages have been rounced to one decimal place.

[a] Rates include surcharges, su·taxes or profit (income) taxes levied by local governments (if different, an average or representative rate has been chosen). Net wealth or capital taxes – levied in Germany, Italy and Luxemburg – are not included.

[b] Measured against the combined CT+PT under the classical system, according to the formula

$$\text{Dividend relief} = \frac{CT+PT \text{ without relief } - \text{ Actual } CT+PT}{CT+PT \text{ without relief } - CT+PT \text{ with full relief}}$$

[c] Calculated as CT + [(1 − CT)PT] *minus* any tax credit, if available. Under the dual income tax in Finland, the top PT rate on capital income equals the CT rate of 28%. In countries with special PT rates on dividend income, obviously the special PT rate is taken as the top PT rate in calculating the CT+PT on distributions. Dividend payments to residents are subject to withholding tax in Austria (22%), Belgium (25%), Denmark (25%), Germany (25%), Italy (12.5%), Luxemburg (25%), the Netherlands (25%), Portugal (12.5%) and Spain (25%).

[d] An asterisk (*) denotes that interest payments are subject to a withholding tax; a double asterisk (**) means that the withholding tax is final. Generally, royalty payments to residents are not subject to withholding tax, except in France (15%) and the UK (25%).

[e] Usually, capital gains realized by companies are subject to CT at the normal rate; generally, the tax is deferred if the gain is re-invested.

[f] Capital gains are adjusted for inflation in Ireland, Italy, Luxemburg and the UK. Alternatively, short-term and long-term gains are taxed at different (effective) rates in Denmark, France and Spain as well as in Ireland. PT rates shown are for long-term capital gains. Various countries exempt small amounts of capital gains.

[g] A lower rate of 30% applies to distributed profits. This rate is 42% if the 7.5% surcharge and the 17% tax-exclusive, deductible, local tax, are included. This form of partial dividend relief at company level is called the split-rate system. Overall, however, imputation is the dominant feature of Germany's CT/PT system.

[h] Capital gains up to DM 30 million on substantial holdings (more than 25% of the share capital) are taxed at reduced rates.

[i] The rates/fractions given in parentheses apply to profits/tax credits of qualifying manufacturing and processing companies.

[j] In Ireland, the capital gains tax rate is 27% on the disposal of shares in unquoted trading companies held for at least five years.

[k] In Portugal, 60% of the underlying CT is creditable against the PT without gross-up. Alternatively, a special (final) PT rate of 12.5% applies to net dividend income. This provides dividend relief at 70%, distributions being taxed at a CT+PT rate of 47.2%.

[l] In Spain, 40% of the net dividend is grossed up and credited against the PT. However, there is no compensatory tax on distributions out of profits not subject to CT.

[m] Reduced rates are related to the length of the holding period and the amount of other income.

[n] Austria, Belgium and Luxemburg permit a (limited) deduction from personal income of expenditures on the purchase of new shares.

[o] In Belgium, the PT rate is 15% on dividends paid on shares issued after 1 January 1994 and 25% on interest paid on bonds issued before 1 March 1990.

[p] Share income not exceeding Dkr 33,800 (Dkr 67,600 for married couples) is taxed at 25%.

[q] Df 1,000 dividend income is exempt from PT (Df 2,000 for married couples).

Source International Bureau of Fiscal Documentation, *European Taxation* (Amsterdam: loose-leaf).

and monetary union (EMU), with a single currency by 1999 for the member coun-tries able to pass the criteria (set in the Maastricht Treaty and affirmed in the Amsterdam Treaty of June 1997 – Chapter 5), one common EU defence policy and closer political cooperation will bring the EU closer to becoming a 'United States of Europe'. As we have seen, this process hastened the need for fiscal harmonization, but not necessarily for tax-rate equalization, something that does not exist, and need not prevail, even in the United States.

Note

1. The first (67/227/EEC – this is the official notation where '67' refers to the year, '227' to the number, and 'EEC' to the legislating authority, but in this note I shall provide only the number) and second (228) VAT directives (all the directives mentioned in this note are issued by the Council) were issued on 11 April 1967; they are related to the harmonization of legislation in the EU member states – see *Official Journal of the European Communities* (*Union* from the end of 1993; here-after, *OJ*), no. L 71, 14 April 1967. The sixth (388) VAT directive of 17 May 1977 was also concerned with harmonization in the member states (*OJ* Nos. L 145, 13 June 1977 and L 149, 17 June 1977).

   The minor directives include the eighth (1072), of 6 December 1979 which is concerned with foreign taxable persons (*OJ*, no. L 331, 27 December 1979) and the tenth (386), of 31 July 1984 concerning the application of VAT to the hiring out of movable tangible property (*OJ*, no. L 208, 3 August 1984).

   The latest act of draft directives is rather complex, and thus the following is just a sample:

   - Proposal (referred to as 'COM' for communication) for a twelfth VAT direc-tive concerning a common system of VAT, expenditure on which tax is not deductible (professional and private usage), COM (82) 870, 25 January 1983 and COM (84) 84, 16 February 1984 – *OJ*, no. C 37 of 10 February 1983 and no. C 56 of 29 February 1984.

   - Proposal for a thirteenth VAT directive relating to the refund of VAT to tax-able persons not established in EU territory (in parallel to the eighth VAT di-rective), COM (82) 443 of 15 July 1982 and COM (83) 413 of 24 June 1983 – see *OJ*, no. C 223, 27 August 1982 and no. C 196, 23 July 1983.

   - Proposal for a seventh VAT directive concerning a common system of VAT for used goods, COM (78) 735 of 6 January 1978 and COM (79) 249 of 4 May 1979 – see *OJ*, no. C 26, 1 February 1978 and no. C 136, 31 May 1979.

   - Proposal for a sixteenth VAT directive concerning the implementation at the EU level of the ruling by the EU Court of Justice regarding the avoidance of double taxation and of used goods imported by a consumer in one EU member nation from a consumer in another, COM (84) 318 of.18 July 1984 and COM (86) 163 of 25 March 1986 – see *OJ*, no. C 226, 28 August 1984 and no. C 96, 24 April 1986.

- The eighteenth VAT directive concerning the abolition of certain derogations, which are still authorized within the framework of the sixth VAT directive, by 1 January 1992 at the very latest, COM (84) 649 of 30 November 1984 – see *OJ*, no. C 347, 29 December 1984.

- Proposal for a nineteenth VAT directive regarding clarifications to the sixth directive, COM (84) 648 of 22 November 1984 and 6 December 1984 – see *OJ*, no. C 347, 29 December 1984.

Appendix: An illustration of the imputation system

To illustrate how the system works, consider a shareholder who has received a cheque for £100 as his/her annual dividend. With a corporation tax rate of 52%, the company has had to use £208 of pre-tax profits to pay this dividend, with the balance of £108 (52% of £208) going to the United Kingdom's Department of Inland Revenue (UKDIR) in corporation tax. Part of this corporation tax bill is in fact prepayment of income tax at the basic rate on dividends which is deducted at source, and this component is paid to the UKDIR when dividends are distributed. Since this is usually before the date when the companies are called upon to pay corporation tax on the year's profits, this element of tax is called 'advanced corporation tax' (ACT), but in fact it is more properly regarded not as a company tax but as deduction at source of standard rate income tax on dividends. The remaining tax payments to the UKDIR are described as 'mainstream' corporation tax. It is these payments which constitute the effective corporate tax burden, since the amounts which are described as ACT would be paid, as income tax, even if corporation tax were completely abolished.

The essence of the imputation system is that when the shareholder receives his/her dividend cheque for £100 (s)he is deemed to have already paid income tax at the basic rate on the dividend. If all shareholders paid income tax at the basic rate that would be the end of the matter. However, some shareholders have higher marginal tax rates, and others lower, and this complicates matters somewhat because one has to calculate the amount of extra tax, or of refund, which is due. To do this, one should ask the question: what dividend before tax would I need in order to finish up with £100 after payment of the basic rate of income tax? Suppose the basic rate of income tax is 33⅓%. Then to end up with £100 after tax, one would need £150 before tax. This is the notional pre-tax dividend which the shareholder receives, the 'grossed-up' dividend, and £50 is the notional tax which one has paid.

If all this seems rather abstract to the shareholder, then (s)he should think again, for with the dividend cheque for £100 will come a piece of paper representing tax credit of £50 exactly equal to the notional tax that has just been described. On the tax form, the shareholder must enter the notional pre-tax dividend of £150 (which is equivalent to the value of the dividend of £100 plus the tax credit of £50) which will then be added to the shareholder's other income to calculate his/her total income tax bill. But since (s)he is deemed to have already paid the notional tax, (s)he can use the credit as an offset against his/her income tax liability. If our shareholder pays tax at the basic rate, the credit eliminates his/her liability and (s)he can forget about the imputation system of corporation tax. If the shareholder's marginal income tax rate is 60%, then his/her tax liability on the dividend is £90 minus the tax credit of £50. The shareholder will have to send a cheque for the balance of £40 to the UKDIR. However, if the recipient of the dividend cheque were a charity or pension fund, and hence not liable to tax, the boot would be on the other foot and the UKDIR would have to refund the tax credit of £50 to the shareholder. Of the pre-tax profit of £208, a basic rate taxpayer would receive £100, an effective rate of 52%, a charity would receive £150, a tax rate of 28%, and an individual with an income tax rate of 60% would receive £60, an effective tax rate of 71.2%.

chapter fifteen

The General Budget

A. M. EL-AGRAA

As stated in the previous chapter, the General Budget of the European Union (EU, or EC, Budget hereafter) forms an integral and very important part of the EU's fiscal policy. Recall that, very widely interpreted, fiscal policy comprises a whole corpus of public finance issues, and that there are at least two basic elements to fiscal policy: the instruments available to the government for fiscal policy purposes (the total tax structure) and the overall impact of the joint manoeuvring of the instruments (the role played by the budget). The former was tackled in the previous chapter; the purpose of this chapter is to explain briefly the nature of the EU Budget, to discuss recent developments concerning it, to demonstrate why it has been inequitable and to suggest ways in which it could be made less so.

15.1 Expenditures

The EU Budget expenditures are grouped into two categories: compulsory and non-compulsory. The former is the expenditure emanating essentially from commitments in the treaties (such as the price support provided by the European Agricultural Guarantee and Guidance Fund – EAGGF – and certain types of foreign aid to third countries), while the latter arises from the operational areas of the EU Budget (such as some of the expenditures of the European Regional Development Fund – ERDF – and the European Social Fund – ESF). Compulsory expenditures have a priority claim, which is why the EU Budget is necessarily 'functional', i.e. the EU has been endowed with revenues to discharge certain specific functions arising from well-defined activities it was required to undertake either in the original treaty or as subsequently agreed by the EU Council, including, of course, any financial commitments arising from the adoption of the SEA and the Maastricht Treaty.

It should also be pointed out that the EU Budget expenditures are classified into two other types: payment appropriations and commitment appropriations. Payment appropriations define expenditure to be actually incurred during the financial year under consideration. Part of the payment may be in settlement of commitments made previously. Commitment appropriations define the ceiling on resources to be pledged in the current financial year. Part of the payment of commitment appropriations may be spread over subsequent years. As one would expect, the 'commitments' have always been in excess of the actual 'payments'. Note that the distinction originated in the Euratom Treaty (Article 176), but was not applied to other areas of expenditure until Regulation 76/919/ECSC, EEC, Euratom of 21 December 1976 was approved. Even then it was agreed as applicable only in some areas of expenditure, with many other areas dependent on a single set of 'undifferentiated' appropriations for payment during the year under consideration. In addition, special exemptions from the payment rules apply, for example, to EAGGF guarantee section in case of difficulties in disbursing actual payments within the financial year.

The EU Budget provides for two types of expenditure. First, there are the administrative expenses (staff salaries, costs of providing and disbursing information, etc.) of the institutions of the EU: the Commission, the Council, the European Parliament, the Court of Justice, the European Coal and Steel Community (ECSC), the ESF, the ERDF, etc. (see Chapter 2). Second, there are the operational expenditures of the EU Commission, such as the intervention and guidance expenses of EAGGF, ERDF support grants and 'food aid'. The EU Budget also provides for a miscellaneous collection of 'minor' expenditures.

In 1985, when the White Paper introducing the internal market was issued, the EC Budget amounted to about 28.4 billion ECU (see Table 15.1), which was roughly equivalent to 18 billion pounds sterling (then, 1 ECU = £0.567748) or $21 billion (then, 1 ECU = $0.734949) or ¥5,206 billion (then, 1 ECU = ¥183.113). The total for 1986 was 31.8 billion ECU for the EC of nine and 35 billion ECU for the EC of twelve, with the expenditure on the EAGGF guarantee section of the CAP falling to 62.9%; the 59.7% for 1982 was by then the smallest ever expenditure on this section of EAGGF. Note that the figures are in current, not constant, prices, but this does not matter since no analysis of growth rates is being considered here, especially since the total actual EU Budget is less than 1.2% of EU GDP (see below), its growth rate in nominal terms has been low and the number of member countries over the relevant period covered in the table has increased from nine to twelve (1986) to fifteen (1995). If one is particularly interested in data at constant prices, one can be informed that, for example, the figure for total appropriations for 1988 (45.3 billion ECU) would have increased to only 52.8 billion ECU in 1992 instead of the nominal figure of 66.1 billion ECU. However, some pertinent points, such as the accumulation of commitments which had to be paid and some disturbing developments in the EC Budget itself are considered in detail in section 15.6.

The total size of the EU Budget in 1997 is of the same order of magnitude as that of a large UK department such as Education and Science. In US terms, it is equivalent to about 90% of state and local expenditure on higher education in 1993 (latest year for which data are available). In terms of Japan, it is equal to about 80% of the expenditure by the Ministry of Posts and Telecommunications in 1995 (latest year). The allegations regarding a very powerful EU Commission are thus ill-founded. Moreover, the suggestion that the EU has a large bureaucracy is also incorrect since

Table 15.1 ⬤ The EU Budget, 1986–97.

Year	Total appropriations (million ECU)	Total payments (million ECU)	EAGGF guarantee (% of payments)
1986	36,052	35,174	62.9
1987	37,415	36,313	63.2
1988	45,344	43,820	62.8
1989	47,268	45,690	56.2
1990	49,047	46,790	53.6
1991	59,370	56,085	56.3
1992	66,118	62,827	49.7
1993	69,058	65,523	52.0
1994	73,444	70,013	52.1
1995	80,892	76,527	49.6
1996	86,525	81,888	49.9
1997	89,137	82,366	49.5

Sources Various issues of the *General Report of the Activities of the European Communities* and *General Report of the Activities of the European Union* supplemented by data from various Eurostat publications.

only about 5% of the EU Budget is expenditure on administration and the EU Budget itself is limited to a maximum of 1.27% of EU GDP in 1999 (the maximum was 1.2%, but the Edinburgh European Council of 11/12 December 1992 decided to raise this gradually, starting in 1993 and reaching the limit by 1999 – more on this below). However, one should add that this is not a justification for the vast number of translators and interpreters employed by the EU to assist with its official publications and meetings; it is high time the EU decided to reduce its official languages to a sensible number instead of the present system of using all the main EU languages.

Table 15.2 ● Revenues of the EU General Budget, 1982–96 (%).

Revenue	1982	1983	1984	1985	1986	1987	1988	1989	1990	1991	1992	1993	1994	1995	1996
Agricultural and sugar levies	12.2	11.7	9.1	7.4	6.8	8.6	6.0	5.5	4.5	4.9	3.8	3.3	3.5	2.9	2.5
Customs duties	31.6	34.6	30.1	30.2	24.3	24.7	21.4	23.3	24.7	22.7	21.1	18.7	18.9	18.5	16.1
VAT	54.6	52.0	55.2	54.4	66.1	64.7	55.1	59.5	59.3	54.0	58.1	54.3	55.2	52.9	43.9
Financial contributions	0.9	0.8	–	–	0.6	0.6	0.5	–	–	–	–	–	–	–	–
GNP based own resources	–	–	–	–	–	–	14.0	6.5	0.2	13.2	14.0	25.3	28.1	19.3	26.0
Miscellaneous revenue	0.7	0.9	1.8[a]	1.0	0.9	1.1	0.9	0.8	0.9	0.8	0.8	0.8	0.9	0.8	0.9
Advances from member states	–	–	3.8	7.0	–	–	1.2	–	–	–	–	0.0	0.0	0.0	0.0
Balance of VAT and GNP-based own resources from previous years					1.3	0.3	0.9	1.8	3.7	2.1	0.1	–1.7	–5.9	–1.1	1.0
Budget balance from previous year								2.6	9.6	5.1	4.6	1.5	1.5	8.8	11.4
Own resources collection costs									–2.9	–2.8	–2.5	–2.2	–2.2	–2.1	–1.8
Total	100.0	100.0	100.0	100.0	100.0	100.0	100.0	100.0	100.0	100.0	100.0	100.0	100.0	100.0	100.0

[a] The figure includes the surplus from 1983 (307.1 million ECU) and VAT/GNP balances corrections (−111.7 million ECU).
Sources *Bulletin of the European Union*, various issues; *General Report on the Activities of the European Union*, various issues; and various Eurostat publications.

15.2 Revenues

Turning to the financing side, the EU Budget revenues come from gross contributions termed 'own resources', i.e. the EU has its own independent and clearly defined revenue sources such that the EU member nations pay to it what actually belongs to it. This principle of 'own resources' was adopted after the Council Decision of 21 April 1970, and in 1980 fully replaced the previous system which was entirely based on national contributions determined largely in accordance with the member nations' relative economic strength.

Before the introduction of more radical changes in the EC Budget in 1987 (see section 15.5), there were three basic categories of own resources:

1. Agricultural and sugar levies.
2. Customs duties, i.e. the proceeds from industrial tariffs on imports from third countries.
3. Until 1984, up to 1% of the common VAT base yield (see Table 15.2).

If more than 1% of the VAT base yield is required, further legislation ratified by all the member nations becomes necessary – see below.

15.3 Net contributions

Table 15.3 gives gross contributions and gross receipts in 1980, together with net receipts for the period 1979–81, broken down by member nation; the choice of this period is to highlight the reasons for the budgetary battles during the early 1980s (later developments are considered below). It should be clear from the table that the United Kingdom and West Germany provided the largest share of gross contributions with regard to all three categories of the EC Budget revenues; the levies and tariffs categories are easily explained in terms of the two countries' large extra-EC trade. The table also shows Germany and the United Kingdom to have been the only net losers with regard to net receipts; this was the main reason for the UK budgetary battles with the EC, particularly since the United Kingdom was the second largest net contributor when its position in the league of EC GDP was third from the bottom. This anomaly arose simply because a large percentage of the EC Budget expenditures falls on agriculture when the size of the agricultural sector is not strictly related to GDP (Denmark with a large agricultural sector had the highest per capita income within the EC) and because VAT contributions, which are to a large extent related to GDP (see the previous chapter and Nevin, 1988), form only just over half of the total EC Budget revenues.

Finally, although the EU Budget is meant to be balanced, it is not true that gross contributions and expenditures always sum to zero; earlier on, there was a small increase in cash balances held by the EC 'which exercises a small deflationary effect' on the EC (Godley, 1980b, p. 76). However, in later years the EC became short of

Table 15.3 ● EC Budget, 1980.

	Gross contributions, 1980 (% share)	Gross contributions by source, 1980			Gross receipts 1980 (% share)	Net receipts (million ECU)		
		Agricultural levies	Industrial tariffs	VAT		1979	1980[a]	1981[a]
Belgium and Luxemburg	6.1	11.0	7	5	11.9	+394	+250	+351
Denmark	2.4	2.0	2	3	4.4	+246	+174	+157
France	20.0	13.0	15	24	20.0	−50	+41	+102
West Germany	30.1	20.0	30	31	23.5	−924	−1,177	−1,260
Ireland	0.9	0.5	1	1	3.8	+352	+372	+340
Italy	11.5	20.5	9	14	16.8	+345	+329	+215
Netherlands	8.4	15.0	9	6	10.5	+186	+215	+81
United Kingdom	20.5	19.0	27	16	8.7	−549	−203	−56

[a] The 1980 and 1981 'Net receipts' allow for refunds to the United Kingdom (see Table 13.4 for further details).
Source Wallace (1980), and various publications by the EC Commission.

funds and had to seek special financing arrangements from the member nations in order to pay for overdue expenditures on the CAP – see Table 15.2. Does this mean that inflationary pressure was being exerted on the economies of the EC? The answer depends on how these deviations from a balanced EC Budget were financed and on whether or not one was a 'Keynesian' or 'monetarist'; but this is not the place to discuss this issue.

15.4 Budgetary transfers

If the EU Budget is to be regarded as the 'embryo centre of a federal system' (Brown, in the first two editions of this book), its size relative to EU GDP (just over 1%) means that it is at a very early stage in its development – more on this below. However, because the EU Budget expenditures are still dominated by agricultural spending, it does play a significant role in the transfer of resources between the member nations; hence the British budgetary quarrels with the rest of the EC during the early 1980s. Discussion of this aspect has been very disappointing indeed; it concentrated on the CAP when a 'proper' evaluation of the extent of transfers should have included a similar treatment of industrial products. For example, if a member nation ceases to import a manufactured product from outside the EU and replaces it with imports from a partner nation, that country will contribute less to the EU Budget revenues (reduced proceeds from industrial tariffs); but since this act is one of 'trade diversion' (see Chapter 4), the country will pay more per unit of that product in comparison with the pre-membership situation. This element of transfer of resources must surely be included in any proper evaluation – simply to allege that, on balance, this element is 'mutually advantageous' to all the member nations (*Cambridge Economic Policy Review*, no. 5, April 1979) and hence that it is appropriate to ignore it, is to bypass the intricate issues raised with regard to the elimination of such effects – see El-Agraa (1989a), Mayes (1982) and Chapter 6. In short, in order to assess the budgetary effects of the transfer of resources between the member nations, one needs to take into account *all* the elements that enter into such calculations.

15.5 Developments prior to the SEA

The inequity of the EC Budget was the main reason for the heated quarrels between the United Kingdom and the rest of the EC during the early 1980s. Through protracted discussions and compromises, the United Kingdom managed to reduce its net contribution (see Table 15.4) – note that 2.0 billion ECU was equivalent to £1.1 billion, $1.5 billion or ¥366 billion. The 24–25 June 1984 Fontainebleau settlement, which asked for the raising of VAT to 1.4% in 1986, included paying the United

Table 15.4 ⬤ UK net contribution to the EC Budget before compensation, compensation and net contribution after compensation, 1980–83 (million ECU).

Year	Net contribution before compensation	Compensation	Net contribution after compensation
1980	1,512	1,175	337
1981	1,419	1,410	9
1982	2,036	1,079	957
1983	1,900[a]	750	1,150[a]

[a]These figures were approximate.
Source Kindly supplied by Commissioner Christopher Tugendhat.

Kingdom 1.0 billion ECU in 1984 and 66% of the *difference* between its VAT contribution and the EC Budget expenditures in the United Kingdom in subsequent years. This was later interpreted to mean rebates of 1.0 billion ECU for 1985 and 1.4 billion ECU for 1986. These provisions were conditional on agreement regarding some changes in the CAP. First, the agriculture ministers agreed on 31 March 1984 on a package which reduced the EC's common farm prices by 0.5% and relied on a system of quotas to restrict milk production from 103 million tonnes in 1983 to 99.2 million and 98.4 million tonnes in 1984 and 1985 respectively; thereafter it was to be pegged for a further three years. Ireland, whose dairy production was equivalent to 9% of its GNP, was awarded a special dispensation in that its quota was actually increased (see Table 15.5); Greece (which was undergoing transition at the time) was the poorest EC member nation and was awarded treatment better than that of Ireland. Moreover, the quotas which already applied to sugar beet were extended to other surplus products such as cereals, oilseeds and processed tomatoes. In order to reduce wine production, new vines were banned until 1990. Finally, various production and consumption subsidies to livestock, butter, fruit and vegetables were reduced and the MCAs were to be phased out over four years (see Chapter 10).

The EC Commission felt that for 1985 the prices for most agricultural products should be kept unchanged, or, if they were to change, that the changes should be modest and not exceed 2%. For certain items, the Commission proposed significant reductions in prices, particularly for products where the guarantee threshold was exceeded. Indeed, the agreed package for 1985–86 included reductions in the prices of butter, beef/veal, sheepmeat and olive oil, with the target price for milk kept at the 1984–85 level.

These changes affected countries such as Germany, the Netherlands and the United Kingdom by the full impact of the price cuts since they had positive MCAs.

Table 15.5 ⬤ EC changes in milk production, 1984 (%).

	Milk quota
Belgium	−3.0
Denmark	−5.7
France	−2.0
West Germany	−6.7
Greece	+7.2
Ireland	+4.6
Italy	0.0
Luxemburg	+3.5
Netherlands	−6.2
United Kingdom	−6.5

Source CEC (1984a).

Countries with weak currencies found that the price cuts actually led to price rises ranging from 1.5% for Denmark to 17.6% for Greece (see Table 15.6). According to *The Economist* (7–13 April 1984), the outcome of the MCA changes 'is to turn the apparent 0.5 per cent cut in the ECUs into an average rise of 3.2 per cent in national currencies, which are the ones farmers get paid in'. Note that in all EC countries farmers experienced a fall in their real earnings when the 1984 inflation rates were taken into consideration; British farmers suffered the largest fall (5.9%) and French farmers the smallest (2.1%).

It may come as a surprise to learn that the agreed package did not reduce costs but actually raised them in 1984 and 1985. The package cost about 0.9 billion ECU in 1984 and about 1.4 billion ECU in 1985. However, in the longer term, relative costs are bound to decline, provided other things remained the same (the fall in the percentage of the EU Budget expenditure on EAGGAF guarantee since then could be advanced in support, but that would be overstretching the point).

All these changes were formally adopted and ratified by the European Parliament and the EC member nations. The British government was pleased with them since a tightening of expenditures on the CAP was necessarily beneficial to countries like

Table 15.6 ⬭ Price changes for the 1984–85 farm year.

	Change in ECU (%)	Change in national currency (%)	1985 inflation forecast
Belgium	−0.6	+ 2.7	+5.8
Denmark	−0.7	+1.5	+4.9
France	−0.6	+5.0	+7.1
West Germany	−0.6	−0.6	+2.8
Greece	+0.4	+17.6	+19.8
Ireland	−0.6	+2.7	+7.8
Italy	−0.4	+6.4	+11.0
Luxemburg	−0.5	+2.8	+7.4
Netherlands	−0.5	−0.5	+2.0
United Kingdom	−0.6	−0.6	+5.3

Source CEC (1984a).

the United Kingdom. Moreover, as pointed out in Chapter 10, these reforms in the CAP were being continuously pursued by the EU, the MacShary package on which has been described as marking a watershed in the reform of the CAP. However, as we shall see in the final section, there is no reason for elation over this matter.

15.6 Most recent developments

15.6.1 The 1988 Council decision

The most recent developments in this area are to be found in the decisions reached in the 11–12 February 1988 Council meeting. In order to appreciate them fully, it is necessary to have some background information first. This background is set out fully in the Commission's submission to the Council and Parliament on 28 February 1987 (COM (87) 101 final).

In that report, the Commission drew attention to some disturbing developments concerning the EC Budget. Firstly, although the own-resource system was meant to provide financial stability so as to enable the Commission to concentrate on policy decisions, it had failed to do so, owing to the following:

1. The erosion in the traditional own resources (customs duties and agricultural levies) because of tariff reductions and increasing self-sufficiency in the EC.
2. The VAT base growing at a slower rate than economic activity because of the reduction in the share of consumption in total GNP.
3. The Fontainebleau mechanism actually decreasing the resources available insofar as the ceiling on VAT rates applied to the individual member nations which financed the abatement, not to the EC as such.

Secondly, as a consequence of the reluctance to provide additional finance to the EC, budgetary practices had arisen which disguised the real impact of expenditure decisions. These practices had to continue because new own resources were insufficient even by the time they were finally adopted. Thus, for the 1984 and 1985 EC Budgets, intergovernmental advances were needed to cover legal expenditure obligations, equivalent to an increase in the VAT rate of 0.14% and 0.23% respectively. For 1986 and 1987, underbudgeting of expenditure took place owing to the exhaustion of the own resources then available, equivalent to 0.10% and 0.23% respectively. For all the years under consideration, the EC failed to provide a proper financial depreciation of agricultural stocks. The Commission argued that these, and similar, developments led to a heavy burden weighing on the own resources in future years. Thirdly, apart from the above, the system had not been adapted to more fundamental developments in the EC. This was because at best, VAT revenue produced little, if any, redistributive effect in relation to the relative prosperity of the member nations; the system as such provided no buffer for a structural decline in one of the components once the VAT ceiling had been reached – several types (not just two) of own resources are required to make the system sufficiently flexible; and VAT own resources were not in reality own resources of the EC, rather contributions by the member states – as such, EC expenditure was not subject to direct taxpayer control; the Commission argued that had the actual collection of VAT in member states been made on the harmonized VAT base, it would have been impossible for taxpayers to identify the EC share, and taxpayers would have been able to react similarly to other directly collected revenue by the EC.

The detailed analyses supporting these considerations cannot be tackled here, but it should be stressed that the Commission strongly argued that agricultural stocks represented a considerable potential liability on the EC Budget. Moreover, it pointed out an additional liability consisting of what had come to be known as the 'cost of the past'. This concerned in particular the EC's structural funds, but also related to development aid. Because of the marked increase in structural expenditure in recent years, mainly due to the two enlargements, the volume of outstanding commitments had risen rapidly. Indeed, the rapid build-up of commitment appropriations had been stated policy as reflected in the annual EC Budget procedure. However, given the regulations and management practices, the scale of the rise had created some problems. Firstly, the underestimation of the time needed to complete the political, administrative and technical aspects of the operation had meant that commitments had translated into payments at a slower rate than had been expected. There had also been a tendency to inflate annual commitment appropriations to levels beyond the Commission's management capacity and the absorption capacity of the potential beneficiaries. Secondly, the failure to keep sufficient watch on the progress of operations had meant that a certain volume of commitments no longer had any real equivalent in terms of projects. These commitments should have been cancelled; but this was not always possible under the existing rules.

In short, one has to agree with the Commission's conclusion that to contain the growth of the 'cost of the past' and to return to proper EC Budget management, including its enactment in good time before the beginning of the fiscal year, the payment appropriations provided should flow from the commitments decided. Therefore, it was appropriate to apply budgetary discipline only to commitment appropriations and to do this only with due respect given to the political undertaking by the competent authority in the EC prior to the annual EC Budgetary process.

Given this background, the Commission put forward its own proposals for new EC own resources. These were largely endorsed by the Brussels Council of 29–30 June 1987. However, the finer details were left to the Copenhagen Council which met later in December; but since that Council ended in disagreement, the final decisions were left to the February 1988 Council. However, this is not the place to discuss the actual differences between the proposals suggested by the Commission and the final Council decisions.

The Council decided (Council, 1986) that there would be both an overall ceiling on own resources and annual ceilings for the period 1988–92. This would be done by laying down a ceiling for commitment appropriations in 1992 and determining an orderly evolution for them, maintaining a strict relationship between commitment appropriations and payment appropriations to ensure their compatibility and to enable the achievement of the ceilings for subsequent years as expressed in payment appropriations.

It also decided that the annual growth rate of EAGGF guarantee expenditure should not exceed 70–80% of the annual growth rate of EC GNP. The expenditure on EAGGF guarantee was defined as that chargeable to Section III, Part B, Titles 1 and 2 (EAGGF Guarantee) of the EC Budget, less amounts corresponding to the disposal of ACP (the Afro-Caribbean–Pacific group – see Chapter 22) sugar, food aid refunds, sugar and isoglucose levy payments by producers and any other revenue raised from the agricultural sector in future years. For the financial years 1988–92, systematic depreciation costs for newly created agricultural stocks, commencing at their time of establishment, were to be financed from these allocations. The Council was to enter each year in its draft EC Budget the necessary appropriations to finance the costs of stock depreciation. Moreover, Council Regulation 1883/78 was to be modified so as to create a legal obligation to proceed to stock depreciation over the specified period in order to arrive at a normal stock situation by 1992.

The costs connected with the depreciation of existing agricultural stocks will be kept outside the guideline; 1.2 billion ECU will be inscribed in Title 8 of the EC Budget for this purpose for 1988, and 1.4 billion ECU per year, at 1988 prices, for the period 1989–92. Spain and Portugal will be treated in this respect as if their depreciation had been entirely financed by the EC in 1987; an appropriate restitution will be entered in Title 8 of the EC Budget for this purpose.

The reference basis for the definition of the annual allocations for EAGGF guarantee expenditure will be the 1988 figure of 27.5 billion ECU, at 1988 prices, adjusted in accordance with the points specified above regarding sugar, food aid, etc. The annual maximum allocation for any year after 1988 will be this figure multiplied by 70–80% of the growth rate of EC GNP between 1988 and the year in question, again, given the above proviso.

In addition to this, new agricultural 'stabilizers' will be introduced. For example, the threshold for cereals will be set at 155–160 million tonnes per year for the period 1988–91, and an additional co-responsibility levy of 3% will be provisionally charged at the beginning of each marketing year to ensure that agricultural expenditure stays within the specified limits. Similar quotas are set for oilseeds and protein products, existing stabilizers will continue for olive oil and cotton, the quota system for milk will be extended for another three years, etc. What is significant, however, is that the Council agreed to adopt provisions to limit supply by withdrawing agricultural land from production. This 'set-aside' programme is devised to complement market policy measures, and will be compulsory for member countries but optional for producers. Exceptions to compulsory application will be possible for certain regions 'in which natural conditions or the danger of depopulation militates against a reduction in production'. In the case of Spain, the exceptions may also relate, on the basis of objective criteria, to 'specific socio-economic circumstances, pursuant to the relevant' EC procedure. In the case of Portugal, the set-aside arrangements will be optional during the transition period. The set-aside period is a minimum of five years, but farmers may be allowed to terminate it after three years. The area involved must be at least 20% of arable land used for cultivating products covered by the common market organization, and the premium should cover the income lost by the farmer, the minimum level being 100 ECU/ha and the maximum 600 ECU/ha, rising to 700 ECU/ha in exceptional circumstances to be determined by the Commission. Farmers opting to set aside 30% of their equivalent land will also be exempted from the basic and additional co-responsibility levy for 20 tonnes of cereals marketed. The EU contribution to the premiums will be 70% of the first 200 ECU, 25% for ECU between 200 and 400, and 15% for ECU between 400 and 600. The member states may grant farmers the possibility of using the land set aside for fallow grazing by means of extensive cattle farming or for producing lentils, chick peas and vegetables, but the conditions for these are still to be determined. The essential point, however, is that the EU undertakes to be responsible for only 50% of the amount granted, with its contribution being 70% for the first 100 ECU, 25% of the next 100 ECU and 15% of the third 100 ECU; hence, the responsibility rests with farmers and the EU as well as the member nations. The EU contribution will be 50% financed from the EAGGF guarantee section and conversion will be introduced on a trial basis for three years; after that the Commission is asked to report to the Council and to submit appropriate proposals. In addition, the Council agreed to introduce optional EU arrangements for promoting the cessation of farming (early retirement). As we saw in Chapter 10, special incentives have been provided for this in the latest package of CAP reforms.

In order to promote efficient budgetary management, the Council decided that EAGGF expenditure should be controlled by operating an efficient 'early warning' system for the development of the individual EAGGF expenditure chapters. Before the start of each budget year, the Commission is asked to define expenditure profiles for each budget chapter based on a comparison of monthly expenditure with the profile of the expenditure over the three preceding years. The Commission will then submit monthly reports on the development of actual expenditure against profiles. Given this early warning system, if the Commission finds that the rate of development of real expenditure is exceeding the forecast profile, or risks doing so, it will be entitled to use the management measures at its disposal, including those which it has under the stabilization measures, to remedy the situation. If these measures prove insufficient, the Commission is asked to examine the functioning of the stabilizers in the relevant sector and, if necessary, to present proposals to the Council calculated to strengthen their action. The Council is then required to act within a period of two months in order to remedy the situation.

To enable the Council and the Commission to apply the above rules, it was agreed that measures shall be taken to accelerate the transmission and treatment of data supplied by the member countries on agricultural expenditure within each marketing organization in order to ensure that the rate at which appropriations in each chapter are used is known with precision one month after the expenditure has occurred. Existing agricultural legislation will be adapted to ensure this. The special provisions concerning the financing of the CAP decided for 1987 will continue to apply. However, the delay of the advances by the Commission to member states shall be extended from two to two and a half months. The existing system for payment of interest will be continued, but payment of EC advances is made conditional on member states complying with their obligation to make available to the Commission the information given above justifying EC payment.

The above decisions, together with the statement that the agricultural price proposals should be consistent with the specified limits and the provision of a 'monetary service' of 1 billion ECU to cater for movements in the ECU/US dollar rate, can be broadly described as decisions consistent with the Commission proposals for 1987, as are the latest proposals in this area.

With regard to non-compulsory expenditure, the Council reaffirmed its 1987 Brussels decision that budgetary discipline must be applied to all EC expenditure, both to payment appropriations and to commitment appropriations, and this must be binding on all the institutions which will be associated with the implementation. The Council, for its part, decided to apply the provisions of Article 203(9) of the Treaty in such a way as to ensure that two guidelines will be respected:

1. Progression of the non-compulsory expenditures which have been the subject of a multi-annual financing decision by the Council for the period 1988–92 (structural funds, IMP – integrated Mediterranean programme – and research) ensuring that such decisions will be honoured.

2. Progression of non-compulsory expenditures other than that referred to in (1) equal to the maximum rate of increase communicated by the Commission.

The results of these guidelines should be considered as a maximum by the member states during all the budget procedure.

It was also decided that, in the interest of better budgetary management, carry-overs of differentiated appropriations shall no longer be automatic. However, it was also decided that the size of any future negative reserves in the EC Budget should be limited to 200 million ECU.

As to the structural funds, it was agreed that the member states shared the broad outlines of the Commission's general approach on the reform of the funds: they confirmed the conclusions of the Brussels Council concerning renationalization of the funds' objectives, concentration of their measures in accordance with EC criteria, due account being taken of the relative underdevelopment of certain regions or of regions in industrial decline and recourse to the programme method. It was re-iterated that the EC operations under these funds, the EIB (European Investment Bank) and the other financial instruments should support the achievement of the general objectives set out in Articles 130(A) and 130(C) of the Treaty by contributing to the achievement of five priority objectives:

1. Promoting the development and structural adjustment of the less-developed regions.

2. Converting the regions, border regions or part regions (including employment areas and urban communities) seriously affected by industrial decline.

3. Combating long-term unemployment.

4. Facilitating the integration of young people.

5. Speeding up the adjustment of agricultural structures and promoting the development of rural areas, all within the context of reforming the CAP.

The funds' finances are to be increased in a manner consistent with these objectives. The details of these increases are too elaborate to state here.

As to own resources, a limit of 1.25–1.30% of EC GDP was adopted but, before the end of 1991, the Commission was asked to report on the operation of the system and the application of the budgetary discipline. It was also affirmed that the EDF will continue to be financed outside the EC Budget. It was further agreed that the correction of budgetary imbalances would be carried out in such a way that the amount of own resources available for EC policies was not affected.

With regard to the details of own resources, the Council has decided to continue to use the agricultural levies and sugar and isoglucose duties as a source, together with the addition of ECSC duties, but has refused the Commission's suggestion regarding the elimination of the 10% refund for collection costs in both cases – it can be seen from Table 15.2 that these have been close to 5% of revenues but were 3.8% in 1992. The Council also offered the Commission two options for remaining sources. The first option includes:

1. The application of a rate of 1.4%, valid for all member states, to the assessment basis for VAT which is determined in a uniform manner for member states according to the EC rules.

2. The application of a rate to be determined under the budgetary procedure in the light of the total of all other revenue, but not exceeding 1.4%, to an additional base representing the difference between the sum of GNP at market prices and the sum of the bases for VAT as stated in (1) of all member states. It was added that for each member state this additional base may not exceed 55% of GNP at market prices.

The second option included:

1. As in first option, but with the specific rate being 1.4% in 1988, 1.3% in 1989, 1.2% in 1990 and 1.1% in both 1991 and 1992, and the assessment basis for VAT may not exceed 60% of GNP at market prices for each member state.

2. The application of a rate to be determined under the budgetary procedure in the light of the total of all other revenue to an additional base representing the sum of GNP at market prices.

No logical explanation has been provided to justify these formulae. Note that Table 15.2 provides all the information that is needed for a comparison of what the EU has been doing in order to meet these commitments. The table does not include the facts that the 1989–92 budget outlays amounted to between 1.01% and 1.08% of EC GDP; the commitments were for 1.17–1.12%.

As to the compensation mechanism for the United Kingdom, it was decided to continue with the Fontainebleau mechanism.

15.6.2 Delors II package

With regard to the latest position, on 11 February 1992 the Commission adopted a communication entitled 'From the Single Act to Maastricht and beyond: the means to match our ambitions', the aim of which was to give shape to the policies arising from the Maastricht Treaty, either by adjusting old policies or by creating new ones. As we have seen, especially in Chapters 2 and 5, these include the following:

1. The creation of a Cohesion Fund by 31 December 1993 to help the poorer nations of the EU (defined as those with a per capita GDP of less than 90% of the EU average, i.e. Greece, Ireland, Portugal and Spain).

2. The adoption of a new approach to competition policy.

3. The introduction of a common industrial policy.

4. The promotion of research and technological development.

5. The taking of steps to strengthen social policy and to promote vocational training.

6. The developing of infrastructure networks.

In short, the communication contains a package (called the Delors II package, the first being the one just discussed) that concentrates on three major aspects: expanding external action in a manner consistent with the EU's new responsibilities in world affairs, which has been interpreted to mean promoting balanced economic and political relations with the rest of the world and assisting people faced with exceptional situations; strengthening economic and social cohesion, which was an essential condition for the acceptance of the Maastricht Treaty, and which the Commission believes is an essential basis for political union; the creation of an environment conducive to improving the competitiveness of EU business, not by helping EU companies directly, but by anticipating and cushioning change.

One should emphasize that the package is based on the two fundamental principles now governing EU activities. The first is that of subsidiarity which, as we have seen, has been defined to mean that action at the EU level should be limited to areas where the EU is most effective, i.e. do not do at the EU level what can best be done at the individual member country level. The second is that of solidarity which is reflected in the objective of promoting economic and social cohesion.

With the above in mind, the Commission proposed a doubling, between 1992 and 1997, of the financial resources allocated to external action. It also proposed increasing by two-thirds the funds allocated to the structural funds for the poorer EU nations, while other funds are to be increased by 50%. These, together with the funds needed to meet the third objective, amount to a raising of the ceiling on EU own resources from 1.20% to 1.37% of Community GDP between 1992 and 1997. This would represent an annual growth in the EU budget of about 5% in real terms.

However, the Edinburgh Council, which extended the period by two years (1992–99), reached agreement on different figures. It was decided that the ceiling on own resources will gradually rise from 1.20% of Community GDP in 1993 to 1.27% in 1999. Payment appropriations will rise from 65.9 billion ECU in 1993 to 80.1 billion ECU in 1999. The proportion of these amounts devoted to the poorer regions will increase by 72%, and a further 15.15 billion ECU is allocated to the Cohesion Fund which will double the commitments made to the four poorer nations of the EU to date. Expenditure on external action will increase to 5.6 billion ECU in 1999 from 3.9 billion ECU in 1993, while that on internal policies will rise from 3.64 billion ECU in 1993 to 5.1 billion ECU in 1999, and this is despite the fact that the Commission had argued strongly in favour of the provision of adequate resources to cover the cost of internal priorities, such as research and trans-EU networks.

It should therefore be clear that the EU Commission continues to put forward proposals consistent with the policies adopted by the EU member countries, while the member nations continue to shy away from providing the full resources needed to carry out what they commit themselves to.

15.7 A proper budget?

Before concluding this chapter, it is interesting to ask whether the EU Budget can be made to perform proper fiscal policy functions, i.e. can it be used to reduce income disparities between the member nations? Can it perform stabilizing functions? Even with the new and increased own resources, the budget will not do much in this respect, given the recommendation of the McDougall Report (CEC, 1977c) for a minimum budget of about 2.5% as a necessary precondition for EC monetary integration. However, even the MacDougall recommendations are in the nature of a compromise since a proper system must necessarily incorporate progressivity (rather than the somewhat arbitrary structural fund allocations) in order to ensure a narrowing of income disparities between the member nations and an equitable distribution of any possible gains and losses. In El-Agraa and Majocchi (1983) it was demonstrated how a progressive income tax method can gradually be introduced in such a way that the EU Budget eventually approximates to the ideal. This section is devoted to a brief consideration of this vital issue.

To describe the nature of the proposed mechanisms, an exercise can be developed with regard to fiscal year 1980 when the principle of own resources (a decision on which was taken on 21 April 1970) was fully operational – see above and Wallace (1980, pp. 54–8). 1980 is a convenient year since then Greece, Portugal and Spain were not parties to the inequity issue. However, the original figure given for that year (24.8 billion ECU) has in reality come closer to the 1983 payment appropriations. The main hypothesis is that the size of the EC Budget is to be made equal to 2.5% of EC GDP, in accordance with the recommendations of the MacDougall Report. EC Budget expenditures are, therefore, to increase to 49.6875 billion ECU. These expenditures are to be financed by the traditional resources plus an income tax. The first two sources of revenue (agricultural levies and customs duties) are provided according to the factors determining them. The differences between these receipts and payments appropriations is covered by VAT and the income tax.

The burden of income taxation must fall among the member states in a progressive way. To achieve this, the EC establishes at the beginning a proportional rate that can be fixed, say 50% of the share of EC expenditures in EC GDP. The total yield of the proportional income tax is, therefore, 24.8438 billion ECU (see Table 15.7). The yield for each country is obtained by multiplying the common rate (1.25%) by the national GDP and is equal, as a share of the total yield, to the proportion of each country's GDP in EC GDP (see Table 15.8, columns 1 and 2).

The parameter chosen for a progressive distribution of income taxation among EC countries is per capita income. Column 3 of Table 15.8 shows the ratio between each country's per capita income and the EC average. The amount of income tax attributed to each country under a progressive scale is determined in two stages. First, multiply the proportional yield for each country (column 1) by its per capita income relative to the EC average (column 3). This is given in column 4. Then divide each country's relative per capita income (column 3) by the sum of column 4.[1] Thus, the new share for each country of the total yield is established (column 5). By multi-

Table 15.7 ⬤ Financing an EC budget equal to 2.5% of the EC GDP in 1980.

	Million ECU	% of total
Agricultural levies	1,535.4	3.09
Sugar levy	466.9	0.94
Customs duties	5,905.7	11.89
VAT	16,324.1	32.85
Miscellaneous	611.6	1.23
Indirect taxation	24,843.7	50.00
Income taxation	24,843.8	50.00
Total	49,687.5	100.00

Source *Fourteenth General Report of the Activities of the European Communities* (Brussels, 1981), p. 57.

plying such a share by the total yield to be provided, the amount of income tax is determined for each EC nation (column 6). The per capita burden of income taxation is thus different in each country and a scale of rates follows ranging from 0.58 for Ireland to 1.49 for West Germany (column 7). The effective rate for each country equals the proportional rate multiplied by a progressivity coefficient (column 8), represented by the ratio between the effective share of each country in total yield (column 5) and the share of each country in EC GDP (column 2).

If the chosen size of the EC Budget is different, the effective rate for each country can be established by multiplying the proportional rate, fixed with regard to the level of expenditure to be covered by income taxation, by the progressivity coefficient of column 8.

The degree of progressivity, as measured by the elasticity of the yield with regard to the change in income, is very high and near 2%. The implicit tax function, estimated by normal cross-section regression, has in fact the following exponential shape:

$$\log T/N = -13.407 + 2.004 \log Y/N$$
$$(0.04463) \quad (0.00501)$$

where the values in parentheses are the standard errors of coefficients.

The distribution among the member states of the burden of income taxation is

Table 15.8 ⬤ National distribution of income tax burden.

	1[a]	2[b]	3[c]	4 (= 1 × 3)	5[d]	6[e]	7[f]	8[g]
Belgium	1,048.4	4.22	1.1188	1,172.95	4.47	1,110.5	1.32	1.059
Denmark	598.8	2.41	1.2260	734.13	2.80	695.6	1.45	1.162
France	5,868.1	23.62	1.1489	6,741.86	25.71	6,387.4	1.36	1.088
West Germany	7,373.6	29.68	1.2597	9,288.52	35.42	8,799.7	1.49	1.193
Ireland	159.0	0.64	0.4915	78.15	0.30	74.5	0.58	0.469
Italy	3,547.7	14.28	0.6536	2,318.77	8.85	2,198.7	0.78	0.620
Luxemburg	42.2	0.17	1.1903	50.23	0.19	47.2	1.43	1.145
Netherlands	1,508.0	6.07	1.1219	1,691.83	6.45	1,602.4	1.33	1.063
United Kingdom	4,698.0	18.91	0.8824	4,145.52	15.81	3,927.8	1.04	0.836
Total	24,843.8	100.0		26,221.96	100.00	24,843.8		

[a] $T_i = t_a Y_i$ with $\sum_{i=1}^{9} T_i = T = t_a Y$, $t_a = 0.0125$.

[b] $Y_i/Y = T_i/T = y_i$.

[c] $k_i = (Y_i/N_i)/(Y/N)$.

[d] $t_i = (k_i T_i)/(\sum_i k_i T_i)$.

[e] $T_i^* = t_i T$.

[f] $t_{ai}^* = t_a(t_i/y_i) = (T_i^*/Y_i)$.

[g] t_i/y_i

Y is GDP, t the tax rate, and T the total tax yield.

thus defined, and the target (of a progressivity hitting the richer countries more heavily than the poorer) is attained. The second step is the distribution within each country among its own citizens. In the proposed scheme, this is left for each country to determine in accordance with its income-tax progressivity scale. The distributive formula among the citizens is therefore considered to be beyond the boundaries of EC competence: what is important, from an EC viewpoint, is only the levelling of economic conditions for the member states such that a true economic and monetary union can be realized.

The gap between the amount of payments appropriations and the revenue accruing from income taxation, agricultural levies and customs duties is filled by VAT collections; hence VAT plays a residual role. The expected yield is divided by the VAT base to determine its rate.

The distribution of the total burden of financing an EC Budget equal to 2.5% of EC GDP among the member nations is represented in Table 15.9. The share computed for each country by the Commission for fiscal year 1980 is adopted with respect to agricultural levies, customs duties and VAT. The values for the income taxation are taken from Table 15.8.

The result is shown in column 1, where the global share for each country of the total yield from the proposed scheme can be compared with the effective share in fiscal year 1980 (according to the Commission calculations) – column 2 – and with the share of each country's GDP in EC GDP – column 3. From the revenue side, a redistribution-oriented budget emerges, which should support a more balanced growth of the EC economy.

Table 15.9 ⬤ **National distribution of the total income tax burden.**

	Agricultural levies, etc.	VAT	Income tax	Total	1	2	3
Belgium	660.2	723.2	1,110.5	2,494.0	5.02	6.00	4.22
Denmark	168.7	419.5	695.6	1,283.8	2.58	2.40	2.41
France	1,238.7	3,943.9	6,387.4	11,570.0	23.29	20.00	23.62
West Germany	2,319.9	5,259.7	8,799.6	16,379.2	32.96	30.10	29.68
Ireland	81.8	140.4	74.5	296.7	0.60	0.90	0.64
Italy	1,153.6	1,905.0	2,198.7	5,257.3	10.58	11.60	14.28
Luxemburg	5.1	34.4	47.2	86.6	0.17	0.10	0.17
Netherlands	874.1	1,025.2	1,602.4	3,501.7	7.05	8.40	6.07
United Kingdom	2,017.4	2,873.0	3,927.8	8,818.2	17.75	20.50	18.91
Total	8,519.6	16,324.1	24,843.8	49,687.5	100.00	100.00	100.00

Source Eurostat Review, 1971–80.

One should ask at least two questions about the proposed scheme. Is it a just and efficient one? Is it a feasible one? From the point of view of justice, it seems difficult, at first sight, to accept that the per capita burden of income taxation differs in the member states according to the level of average income in each state. It is important to recall here that the national income-taxation quota is distributed among the citizens according to the progressivity scale applied in domestic taxation. It is therefore unlikely that the poor in a richer country will pay more than the rich in a poorer country. In any case, the difference in the burden of income taxation can be justified if one also takes into account the fact that the poor citizens of a richer member state can exploit many opportunities and enjoy benefits that are unavailable to those of a poorer member nation.

With regard to efficiency, this type of taxation introduces a strong fiscal incentive to reduce disequilibria within the EC. In particular, the stronger countries take an interest in the growth of per capita income in the weaker member nations insofar as, if convergence ensues, their own burden of income taxation is reduced. Indeed, if a perfect equalization of per capita incomes is attained, the coefficient of progressivity will become one for all the member nations, and the distribution of income taxation among them will become proportional. Meanwhile, the weaker member nations have no incentive to slacken their efforts in reducing disparities in the level of income since, with a progressive income taxation, the elasticity of disposable income is less than unity, but considerably larger than zero.

Concerning the political feasibility of the proposal, it is important to stress the need to clearly define an overall strategy relating to the growth of the budget. A plan for economic and monetary union involves a whole series of coordinated decisions spread over a long period of time. Since such decisions have to be taken at different times by more than one decision-making body, they are unlikely to be effective if there is no stated general frame of reference. If the Maastricht Treaty is fully implemented so that the EC will introduce a common central bank and one currency before the end of this century, this proposal will have to be discussed seriously and immediately; the introduction of a cohesion fund, though to be applauded, will not take care of this problem.

15.8 Conclusion

It should be apparent from the foregoing that a proper analysis of the future prospects for the EU Budget cannot be confined to its present structure. The EU Budget must be seen not only in its proper context of public finance, but also in the wider context of the ultimate objectives of the Community as a whole. Given its existing structure and the present stage reached in the EU integrative process, an equitable EU Budget, in the absence of a more *fundamental* reform of the CAP, must aim at increasing the non-compulsory expenditures (regional, social and industrial aspects including employment generation, not just the so-called structural expenditures). This would require more than the mere strengthening of the recent changes in the EU Budget (as agreed in the Edinburgh summit in December 1992) since the introduction of a progressive income tax facility for revenue-raising purposes (recall that VAT, which is still prominent in the new EU Budget structure, is regressive), especially now that the EU has agreed to introduce an EMU – see Chapter 5. The proposal put forward in El-Agraa and Majocchi (1983) is a practical one with very clear guidelines, since it has a well-defined framework for reference. Moreover, it is not beyond the reach of the EU, given the Maastricht Treaty and re-calling that before the own resource system was introduced in 1970, the EC Budget was financed by national contributions determined according to each member nation's relative prosperity within the EC.

Note

1. With the introduction of the progressivity coefficient, the yield of income taxation does not change unless:

$$[t_a \sum_{i=1}^{6} Y_i(Y_iN/N_iY) + t_a \sum_{j=1}^{3} Y_j(Y_jN/N_jY)] - [t_a \sum_{i=1}^{6} Y_i + t_a \sum_{j=1}^{3} Y_j] = 0$$

where countries i have an above EC average per capita income, and countries j a per capita income lower than the EC average. Rearranging the terms, the condition can be expressed as:

$$\sum_{i=1}^{6} Y_i(Y_iN/N_iY - 1) - \sum_{j=1}^{3} Y_j(1Y_jN/N_jY) = 0$$

Thus, the condition shows that the yield increases if a progressivity coefficient larger than 1 is applied to countries i with a large (in absolute terms) cumulative national income and a progressivity coefficient lower than 1 to countries j with a small cumulative national income, the final result depending also on the values of the progressivity coefficients. This is what is happening in the numerical example in Table 15.8.

chapter sixteen

The European Monetary System

D. G. MAYES*

Most interest at present focuses on economic and monetary union (EMU) rather than on the European Monetary System (EMS). However, this chapter focuses on the EMS while Chapter 5 deals with the issue of EMU. The two are, of course, intertwined and as the member states move into EMU so the role of the EMS declines. Ultimately there would be no internal exchange rates if all member states have adopted the single currency. This chapter therefore explores the EMS, its history and how it is likely to evolve over coming years.

16.1 Founding and inception of the System[1]

With the current focus on the prospects for economic and monetary union (EMU) in the EU, the European Monetary System (EMS) is sometimes presented as if it was from the outset intended as the route to EMU. Although some undoubtedly hold that view, its original aims were more limited, and part of the difficulties over recent years stem from the way it has evolved or more accurately failed to evolve. The EMS began operation on 13 March 1979 following a decision of the Council of Ministers meeting in Brussels in December 1978. The short delay between the Council's favourable decision and the actual inception of the EMS accommodated the negotiation of additional assistance to Italy and Ireland, both of which were thought likely to encounter some difficulties in adjusting to the EMS. The initiative for the establishment of the EMS came, not from the EC Commission, but from the prime ministers of Germany and France, Helmut Schmidt and Giscard d'Estaing. Their decision was in turn guided by a perception that the United States was not capable at the time of exercising a responsible leadership in global monetary affairs and the proximate aim of the EMS was to create a zone of monetary stability in Europe – see Chapter 5. This aim accorded well with the strong, historically based aversion to inflation which governed German economic policy and the German interest in shielding its currency from the effects of irregular speculation against the US dollar

---

*A previous edition of this chapter was written by Michael Artis. His text has been updated and extended in subsequent editions.

together with the long-standing desire of successive French governments to break away from the global dominance of the United States in monetary affairs. The initiative also filled what had been perceived as a disturbing deceleration in the momentum of political development of the EC and corresponded closely to a call made by the Commission's President in his speech at Florence in October 1977 for a corrective initiative along just these lines.

Preparations for the establishment of the EMS involved extensive discussions among the potential members from the moment when the idea was first floated in the Council of Ministers meeting at Copenhagen in April 1978 and in these the United Kingdom played a full role, although it was clear from the start that the British side had substantial reservations about the idea. (Ludlow, 1982, gives a very ample account of the negotiations involved.) When the time for decision came, the EMS, although involving all the other members of the EC at the time, was launched without the full participation of the United Kingdom.

16.2 Provisions of the EMS

The most significant provisions of the EMS relate to the so-called parity grid of bilateral exchange rates or what is called the 'exchange-rate mechanism' (ERM). This is the vital aspect of the operation of the EMS and is the part to which the United Kingdom decided not to adhere on inception of the system. Although the United Kingdom 'shadowed' the ERM for a period in the mid-1980s, it did not join until October 1990. Even so, its membership was short lived since it left in September 1992 when market pressures pushed sterling out of the grid.

Under the provisions of the parity grid, member countries – aside from Portugal, Spain and the United Kingdom – undertook to maintain their exchange rates with each other within $\pm 2\frac{1}{4}\%$ of a central rate of exchange.[2] Italy and Ireland negotiated a wider $\pm 6\%$ band for its currency to enable it to achieve a smoother transition from outside the previous snake arrangement, and in June 1989 Spain followed the Italian precedent, joining the ERM with a similar $\pm 6\%$ band. Portugal and the United Kingdom also entered with these wide bands while Italy moved to the $\pm 2\frac{1}{4}\%$ band in 1990 (although it too left the ERM in the September 1992 collapse). When the EU was expanded in January 1995, Austria immediately joined the ERM. Finland joined in October 1996 and Italy rejoined the following month.

Central rates of exchange are denominated for convenience in terms of a composite currency, the European currency unit (ECU), and may be changed by collective decision in a formal 'realignment'.[3] Table 16.1 shows the composition of the ECU which, as can be seen, comprises literally so many French francs, so many deutschmarks, so many pounds sterling, etc. These components were selected so as to provide a weighting of currencies in the ECU in accord with relative GNP and trade and were subject to review every five years. It may be noted that representation of a country's currency in the ECU and its participation in the ERM are *not* coterminous, as, for example, neither the pound sterling nor the drachma belongs

Table 16.1 ● Composition and weighting of the ECU.

Country (currency)	Composition of the ECU (units of national currency) 13 March 1979–14 September 1984	17 September 1984–18 September 1989	From 21 September 1989	Percentage weight from 25 February 1993	Percentage weight from 31 December 1996
Belgium–Luxemburg (franc)	3.80	3.85	3.431	8.61	8.64
Denmark (krone)	0.217	0.219	0.1976	2.70	2.69
France (franc)	1.15	1.31	1.332	20.26	20.62
Germany (mark)	0.828	0.719	0.6242	32.24	32.41
Greece (drachma)	–	1.15	1.44	0.60	0.49
Ireland (punt)	0.00759	0.00871	0.008552	1.10	1.07
Italy (lira)	109.000	140.00	151.8	8.09	7.96
Netherlands (guilder)	0.286	0.256	0.2198	10.10	10.13
Spain (peseta)	–	–	6.885	4.94	4.20
Portugal (escudo)	–	–	1.393	0.78	0.71
United Kingdom (pound sterling)	0.0885	0.0878	0.08784	10.58	11.08

Source: Bank of Finland, *Financial Times*.

to the ERM. Until September 1989 the Spanish peseta and the Portuguese escudo were not included in the ECU. Since the last revision in September 1989 the weights have remained fixed and will continue to be fixed until the *Euro* comes into operation. When the EU was expanded to include Austria, Finland and Sweden in January 1995 the definition of the ECU was not changed and hence these countries' currencies are not included in the weights.

The use of a composite currency in which to denominate the central rate is not strictly necessary to the operation of the parity grid – participants in the ERM could simply have announced their adherence to a consistent set of bilateral central rates and bands. But the use of the ECU has useful symbolic connotations and may be felt to give the EMS an identity over and above that which would be commanded by a mere agreement to stabilize exchange rates – the identity, in fact, of a potential monetary union. EU transactions are denominated in ECU, as are the debts acquired by central banks intervening to support their currencies in the framework of the EMS.

In addition, the ECU did provide a necessary basis for what appeared at the time to be the most innovative technical feature of the EMS, that of the 'divergence indicator' (DI). The essential role that the DI was designed to perform was that of enforcing timely and symmetrical adjustment. The idea of the indicator was that it should be designed so as to signal when a currency was becoming out of line with the rest of the system. Coupled with the injunction that the 'flashing' of the indicator gave 'a presumption' of corrective policy action on behalf of the country whose currency was singled out in this way, the DI would – it was hoped – enforce adjustment equally on a strong-currency country or on a weak-currency country, provided that the currency in question stood out from the pack. Combining this role with that of providing an early warning, the DI was to be triggered when a currency crossed a threshold set at 75% of its permitted ± 2¼% movement against all other currencies in the EMS. Because each currency is itself a component of the ECU, the DI threshold in terms of the ECU is less than $\pm(0.75 \times 2.25 = 1.6875\%)$ of the currency's central rate by an amount which is larger the larger is that currency's weight in the ECU.

Flanking these exchange-rate provisions, with the obligation to intervene at the bilateral limits and the 'presumption of action' created by a triggering of the DI threshold, the EMS also provided for credit mechanisms to enable weak-currency countries to borrow in order to defend their currencies. The principal of such a mechanism, called the VSTF (very-short-term financing facility), provides for the extension of credit from one central bank to another, repayable over a term initially of forty-five days; at the bilateral limits one central bank can call on another for credit in the partner's currency without prospect of a refusal, the amount being repaid under this mechanism. In the extensions to the EMS negotiated in Nyborg in September 1987 (frequently referred to as the Basle–Nyborg agreement), the term of repayment under the VSTF was increased to sixty days and, more important, the provision for 'automatic' borrowing for intervention at the limits was extended to cover intervention *within* the limits (so-called intramarginal intervention). In association with its credit mechanisms the founding of the EMS called for the central banks concerned to pool 20% of their gold and dollar reserves in exchange for ECUs in a central fund, the EMCF (European Monetary Cooperation Fund).

16.3 Precursors of the EMS

The provisions and aspirations of the EMS reflected in part lessons felt to have been learnt from past endeavours among EC members to stabilize their currencies.[4] The recurrent failures marking these endeavours contributed to the absence of high aspirations to European monetary union (EMU) in the stated objectives of the EMS: by contrast, the Werner Report of 1972 had projected the achievement of EMU by 1980 – for a fuller discussion of this, see Chapter 5. Recent practical experience embodied in the failure of the so-called snake also contributed to the design of the DI and to a greater degree of self-consciousness about the need for multilateral decision making on such issues as realignments.

The snake took shape in April 1972 as a response to the acceptance by the EC of the Werner Committee's optimistic goal setting, and more immediately as a response to the Smithsonian Agreement of the previous December. That Agreement sought to extend the life of the Bretton Woods system by re-instating a global system of fixed but adjustable exchange rates on the basis of wider bands than had prevailed during previous decades; the dollar, although undergoing a discrete devaluation of its price in terms of gold, remained the numeraire key currency of the new system. Since the exchange rates of individual European currencies against the dollar were to be confined under the Smithsonian to $\pm2\frac{1}{4}\%$, this implied that European currencies could move against each other by $\pm4\frac{1}{2}\%$. The European countries sought to correct this and the snake agreement, which involved all six of the founding members, joined shortly after its inception by the United Kingdom, Ireland, Denmark and Norway (all countries which at that time expected to become members of the EC), simply suggested that exchange rates between participating countries should also be limited to $\pm2\frac{1}{4}\%$ bands of fluctuation. It was from this period that the system earned the sobriquet 'snake in the tunnel', in that while the snake currencies were pegged within the Smithsonian margins against the dollar (the 'tunnel'), their variation against each other was more tightly constrained by the provisions of the snake agreement. The provisions of the snake continued to be pursued even after generalized floating against the dollar took place (in 1973), whereupon it became known as the 'snake outside the tunnel'. Just the same analogy can be applied to the EMS as the system as a whole floats against third currencies such as the US dollar.

The snake agreement was a failure. Sterling left it as early as June 1972 and the lira left in February 1973. The French franc left the snake, rejoined it and left again. There were several other changes. It ended as a collection of smaller currencies heavily dominated by the deutschmark and including some non-EC currencies – a 'worm' or small deutschmark zone – and even within this grouping there were

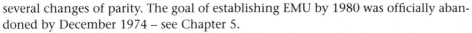

several changes of parity. The goal of establishing EMU by 1980 was officially abandoned by December 1974 – see Chapter 5.

One reason diagnosed for the calamity of the snake was that German dominance of the system was excessive and the invention of the DI was in part a result of this apprehension. Another was that decision making was unilateral (as it had been in the Bretton Woods system), so countries could change their parity agreement without feeling any restraining influence from other members of the system.

The EMS benefited from lessons learnt from this period to emerge as a better-founded arrangement with more modest immediate objectives than its predecessor. Nevertheless, when it was launched, scepticism was widespread that the EMS could succeed where its precursors had failed. It was not difficult to greet the inauguration of the EMS as yet further evidence of the triumph of hope over experience.

16.4 The System in operation: the overall balance sheet in summary

The survival of the EMS has belied this early scepticism and although there are reasons for expressing renewed scepticism (see below) there is little dispute that the EMS has so far been something of a success. This success can be seen as embodied in three principal achievements.

First, despite occasional realignments and fluctuations of currencies within their pre-set bands, it seems that the EMS has succeeded in its proximate objective of stabilizing exchange rates – not in the absolute sense but in the relevant and realistic sense of appearing to have brought about more stability than would have been enjoyed without it. Moreover, up till 1992 this was done without provoking periodic speculative crises such as marred the demise of the Bretton Woods system.

Second, the claim is made for the EMS that it has provided a framework within which member countries have been able to pursue counterinflationary policies at a lesser cost in terms of unemployment and lost output than would have been possible otherwise.

Third, while it is claimed that nominal exchange-rate stability has been secured, it is also argued that the operation of the EMS has prevented drastic changes in *real* exchange rates (or 'competitiveness'). This is contrasted with the damaging experience in this respect of both the United Kingdom and the United States over the same period.

Finally, while not an immediate objective of the EMS as such, it is well worth mentioning that the ECU has become established as a significant currency of denomination of bond issues, which can be viewed as some testimony to the credibility of the EMS and the successful projection of its identity.

These achievements – which we detail and examine below – have not been without some qualifications. The DI mechanism does not appear to have withstood the test of time, for example, while sceptics would charge that the counterinflationary achievements of the EMS in fact amount to little more than a bias against growth and expansion.

The enforced changes to parities in and after September 1992 have considerably reduced the credibility of the system and called into question the validity of the idea of approaching monetary union through increasingly fixed exchange rates while having no controls over capital flows. Although the widening of the bands to ±15% in August 1993 appeared to remove much of the effective distinction between the ERM and freely floating exchange rates, the practice has been for very considerable convergence and for a system which takes only limited advantage of the flexibility that has been offered.

What we have seen since 1993 has effectively been pressure on member states through the convergence criteria for EMU (see Chapter 5). The requirement to keep inflation close to that of the least inflationary member states, the need to follow a prudent fiscal policy and the requirement for longer-term interest rates to coverage will also tend to lead towards exchange rate stability.

16.5 Exchange-rate stability

As the EMS allows for realignments and for fluctuations of its currencies within the bands, absolute exchange-rate stability has not been achieved. However, realignments have been few in number, have not always involved the major currencies, have usually been small and have grown less frequent with the passage of time. Table 16.2 details all the realignments that have taken place, from which the support for these contentions is obvious. A particular feature of the realignment process is that, until the second half of 1992, it was largely free from speculation. When the speculative crises which dogged the end of the Bretton Woods system are recalled, this is a remarkable achievement. An innovation of the EMS in this regard is the practice of carrying out a realignment in such a way that the central rate and bands are changed without disturbing the market rate. This device was introduced to rob the market of the opportunity to make a one-way bet. The difference is illustrated in Figure 16.1. The one-way bet realignment is sketched in Figure 16.1(b): the discrete disturbance of the market rate, if correctly anticipated, affords huge gains to speculators.[5] For example, if a currency is allowed to drift to the bottom of its band so that it can only be expected to be devalued by, say, 5%, the gross gains from correctly anticipating the day on which this takes place substantially exceed, in annual interest rate terms, a rate of 1,500% (5% × 365). Speculators could take advantage of this situation by borrowing the weak currency to buy the strong one in anticipation of the devaluation, thereafter redeeming the loan in cheaper currency: clearly interest rates in the weak-currency country would have to be very high indeed to challenge the huge gains in prospect. The EMS technique of changing the central rate and thus the bands *around* the current market rate in a 'timely' realignment (Figure 16.1(a)) robs the speculator of the incentive of such large gains. In practice, EMS realignments have not always been 'timely' – Kenen (1988) estimates the pro-

Table 16.2 ● Realignments of EMS currencies (% changes).

Dates	Belgian–Luxemburg franc	Danish krone	DM	Drachma[a]	Escudo	French franc	Dutch guilder	Punt	Lira[c]	Peseta	£[c]
24 September 79	–	−3.00	+2.00	–	–	–	–	–	–	–	–
30 November 79	–	−5.00	–	–	–	–	–	–	–	–	–
23 March 81	–	–	–	–	–	–	–	–	–	–	–
05 October 81	–	–	+5.50	–	–	−3.00	+5.50	–	−6.00	–	–
22 February 82	−8.50	−3.00	–	–	–	–	–	–	−3.00	–	–
14 June 82	–	–	+4.25	–	–	−5.75	+4.25	–	–	–	–
21 March 83	+1.50	+2.50	+5.50	–	–	−2.50	+3.50	−3.50	−2.75	–	–
18 May 83[b]	−1.90	−1.90	−1.90	–	–	−1.90	−1.90	−1.90	−2.50	–	–
17 September 84	–	–	–	–	–	–	–	–	−1.90	–	–
22 July 85	+2.00	+2.00	+2.00	–	–	+2.00	+2.00	+2.00	−6.00	–	–
07 April 86	+1.00	+1.00	+3.00	–	–	−3.00	+3.00	–	–	–	–
04 August 86	–	–	–	–	–	–	–	−8.00	–	–	–
12 January 87	−2.00	–	+3.00	–	–	–	+3.00	–	–	–	–
08 January 90	–	–	–	–	–	–	–	–	−3.68	–	–
14 September 92	+3.50	+3.50	+3.50	–	+3.50	+3.50	+3.50	+3.50	−3.50	+3.50	+3.50
17 September 92	–	–	–	–	–	–	–	–	–	−5.00	–
23 November 92	–	–	–	–	−6.00	–	–	–	–	−6.00	–
30 January 1993	Devaluation of the Irish punt (10%)										
13 May 1993	Devaluation of peseta and escudo (8% and 6.5%)										
06 March 1995	Devaluation of peseta and escudo (7% and 3.5%)										

a Not participating in ERM
b Technical realignment of £
c Suspended participation in ERM 17 September 1992
Source Eurostat, The Economist, Banco de Espana Economic Bulletin.

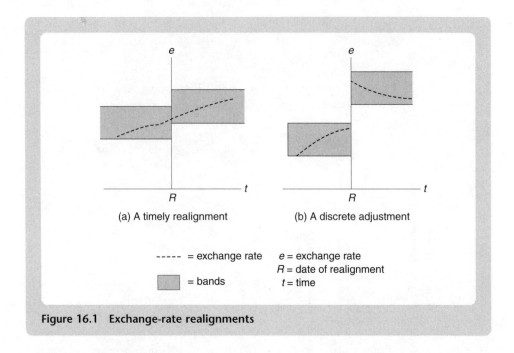

Figure 16.1 Exchange-rate realignments

portion to be just over 70% – and exchange controls have also played a role in deterring speculation. The demise of these controls will put a higher premium on the exercise of the non-provocative realignment procedure described; a premium which turned out to be too high to bear in autumn of 1992.

Given that realignments have taken place and that currencies have fluctuated within the permitted bands, it cannot be assumed that the EMS has necessarily imparted stability to nominal exchange rates. This question can, however, be examined statistically. Investigators who have done this have taken to assuming as a counterfactual (or *anti-monde*) that, in the absence of the EMS, exchange-rate stability would have evolved in the same way for the EMS currencies as it did for non-EMS currencies. Thus the examination proceeds by comparing a measure of exchange-rate stability for the EMS currencies with a similar measure for non-EMS currencies before, and after, the EMS period itself. By varying the precise measure of the exchange rate used (bilateral or effective; (log) level or (log) change), the data frequency (weekly, monthly, quarterly), and the precise measure of stability employed, this basic counterfactual assumption has supported a variety of estimates. From them, however, a strong consensus has emerged that the EMS has exerted a stabilizing influence on the bilateral nominal exchange rates of its members and on their effective nominal rates.

An authoritative example of this kind of approach is provided in a study for the IMF by Ungerer *et al.* (1986), an excerpt from which is shown in Table 16.3. The results quoted in this table are for nominal bilateral exchange rates against ERM cur-

Table 16.3 ⬤ **Exchange-rate variability against ERM currencies, 1974–85.[a]**

| | Period means | | | |
| | Levels | | Log changes | |
	1974–78	1979–85	1974–79	1979–85
France	31.6	15.9	16.8	7.6
West Germany	29.2	16.3	14.7	7.0
Italy	36.0	19.3	19.3	8.8
Average ERM[b]	28.4	15.1	14.8	7.3
Japan	44.5	48.1	21.1	21.7
United Kingdom	32.7	37.8	16.8	20.9
United States	34.7	55.7	18.8	27.4
Average non-ERM[c]	34.5	35.9	17.2	17.9

[a] Weighted average of variability of bilateral nominal exchange rates against ERM currencies (their log change), monthly data, IMF MERM weights. Variability is measured by the coefficient of variation for levels, and by the standard deviation for log changes (in both cases × 1000). Period means are unweighted.
[b] Including all ERM countries.
[c] Includes Japan, United Kingdom, United States, Australia, Canada, Norway, Sweden and Switzerland.
Source H. Ungerer *et al.* (1986), table 7, p. 35.

rencies, the exchange rates being weighed together according to the pattern of weights implied by the IMF's multilateral exchange-rate model (MERM), which is standard for this type of application. Two concepts of stability are then explored – stability of the actual level and stability of the (log) change. The latter thus allows for some regular change as the norm against which variability is to be assessed. For levels, the authors use the coefficient of variation (the standard deviation divided by the mean) and for log change the standard deviation itself (both scaled by 1,000) as a measure of month-to-month variability. As can be seen, for both levels and log changes, the index of variability rises for the three main non-ERM countries and falls for the three main ERM countries. Including in addition the smaller ERM countries in the coverage and a set of other developed countries in the non-ERM average, the conclusion remains the same: where volatility falls sharply for the ERM countries between the pre-EMS and the EMS period, it rises for the non-participant countries. Weber (1991) extends this analysis to 1988.

16.6 A framework for counterinflationary policy

The inception of the EMS coincided with the second oil shock. Following a meeting in December 1978, the OPEC countries raised oil prices in several stages through 1979 by some 130%. On the fact of it, such a shock, coming so soon after the founding of the EMS, might have been supposed to ensure its early demise. After all, the failure of the snake in the 1970s followed the disruption created by the first oil shock in 1973–74, in the aftermath of which countries followed different adjustment policies incompatible with maintaining fixed exchange rates between themselves. It could well have been apprehended that the second oil shock would expose the EMS to similar strains. In fact, the EMS not only survived the shock but, in the eyes of some observers, proved to have some added advantages in providing for its members a framework within which to prosecute efficient counterinflationary policies.

The first advantage the EMS proved to have over the snake was the provision for realignment. As Table 16.2 shows, the realignments at the beginning of the life of the EMS were quite frequent. It was important for the survival of the EMS that it should have been able to accommodate exchange-rate realignments at this stage and still to continue as a system. This contrasted with the snake, where countries changing their exchange rates were deemed to 'leave' the snake. In the early period, then, as countries accommodated the inflationary shock of the oil price rise in different ways, the EMS displayed sufficient flexibility to survive. Later on, countries in the EMS converged in their attitudes towards the inflationary problem, tending – in common with developments in other countries outside the system – to give first priority in their economic policy objectives to the defeat of inflation.

The claim is made for the EMS that it provided a particularly advantageous framework in this respect. The analysis of that claim is based on the modern theory of the value of reputation in economic policy and the important role played by expectations in the inflationary process. Both features are to an extent controversial and the empirical value of the claim made for the EMS is a matter of controversy. To take the two elements in the claim in reverse order: it is well known from work in the late 1960s by Phelps and Friedman that inflationary processes are capable of being sustained by self-fulfilling expectations. One of the things that a government intent on reducing inflation has to do is to break the climate of inflationary expectations. One way of doing this, of course, is to reduce demand so drastically that, despite the impetus given by strong expectations of inflation, actual inflation winds down and, as it does so, so also does the expectation of inflation. Such a process is potentially very costly in terms of the output which will be lost and the unemployment which will be created by the deflationary demand policy. The more stubborn the expectations are, the higher these costs will be. Another way of breaking the climate of inflationary expectations is for a government to find a direct means of persuading agents that inflation really will fall. In the 1960s and 1970s the device of incomes policies had been popular for this purpose but these policies fell out of favour and in the 1980s the principal counterinflationary policy commitment was provided by the publication of targets for the reduction of the rate of growth of the money supply.

At this point we must take account of the theory of 'reputational' policies. This theory points out that the credibility of a government's commitment cannot just be taken for granted. For electoral and other reasons a government may be led to cheat on commitments it makes; if the apprehension of cheating is sufficiently widespread the commitment will be distrusted. If a government's announcements about its counterinflationary intentions and policies are distrusted, perhaps because of a poor reputation acquired by past behaviour or simply because the electorate considers this to be the way of governments, the government will be unable to influence expectations directly. Inflation can then be brought down only by the costly route of demand deflation. But a government may be able to secure greater credibility in various ways: in particular, by committing to policies which are easy to monitor and by raising the visible costs to itself of cheating. The policies must, of course, be plausibly related to the goal. Membership of the EMS offers three important advantages in these respects for the control of inflation. First, the dominant economy in the EMS is Germany, which has a very secure and well-known record of low inflation; targeting exchange rates in the EMS involves targeting against the deutschmark and to the extent that exchange rates reflect relative inflation, a stable deutschmark exchange rate must imply low, German-like, rates of inflation. Second, an exchange-rate commitment is exceptionally easy to monitor; exchange rates are quoted every minute of the day and it is clear what an exchange rate is. Third, by committing itself to the EMS, a government puts its credibility on the line, not only with its own electorate but also with foreign governments; the commitment is the more credible for this reason.[6]

This is the theory. What are the qualifications and what is the evidence? An immediate qualification is that the argument takes for granted that EMS membership puts a heavy premium on exchange-rate fixity: yet, as we saw earlier, realignments are a part of the EMS and were not infrequently used in the early years. How do agents know that the rules have changed from permissiveness to a more disciplined approach and how can they be sure that their government will not go back to the earlier ways of the system?

The evidence does not really help to give a decisive verdict on the claim. It is not, of course, true that the EMS countries alone have brought inflation down; as Table 16.4 shows, inflation has fallen in the United States and the United Kingdom as well even though the United Kingdom was outside the ERM for much of the period. The claim that the EMS provides a superior counterinflationary framework does not deny that other countries could bring inflation down – only that the costs of doing so are higher for them. A 'quick' indicator of the costs of disinflating is the ratio of the cumulative rise in unemployment to the reduction in inflation – the so-called sacrifice ratio.[7] Table 16.4 gives estimates at four intervals for this ratio. It can be

Table 16.4 ⬭ Inflation and the 'sacrifice ratio'.

| | Consumer prices − inflation (% pa) | | | | |
	United States	West Germany	France	United Kingdom	Italy
1980	13.5	5.4	13.6	18	21.2
1981	10.3	6.3	13.4	11.9	19.3
1982	6.1	5.2	11.8	8.6	16.4
1983	3.2	3.3	9.6	4.6	14.9
1984	4.3	2.4	7.4	5	10.6
1985	3.5	2.1	5.8	6.1	8.6
1986	1.9	−0.1	2.7	3.4	6.1
1987	3.7	0.2	3.1	4.1	4.6
1988	4.1	1.3	2.7	4.9	5
1989	4.8	2.8	3.6	7.8	6.6
1990	5.4	2.7	3.4	9.5	6.1
1991	4.2	3.6	3.2	5.9	6.5
1992	3	5.1	2.4	3.7	5.3
1993	3	4.5	2.1	1.6	4.2
1994	2.6	2.7	1.7	2.5	3.9
1995	2.8	1.8	1.7	3.4	5.4
	Sacrifice ratios[a]				
1980–84	0.64	4.43	1.40	1.51	0.42
1980–86	0.51	3.82	1.55	2.00	0.63
1980–88	0.36	6.73	2.29	2.69	1.01
1980–92	0.05	117.33	3.41	2.99	1.76
1980–95	−0.20	14.7	4.64	3.58	2.47

[a] The ratio of the cumulative increase in unemployment to the difference between inflation in 1980 and inflation in the terminal year (1984, 1986, 1988, 1992, 1995).
Source OECD Economic Outlook, December 1996.

seen from this that Germany has the highest sacrifice ratio of all. However, this is not necessarily inconsistent with the hypothesis at issue in as much as it is the non-German members which are supposed to reap the benefit of Germany's extreme inflation aversion by targeting the deutschmark. Indeed, it can be seen that the sacrifice ratios for France and Italy were lower than those for the United Kingdom, consistent with the hypothesis. More recently, the ratio for France has risen. It is the United States, on the other hand, which seems to do best of all (there was no cumulative rise in unemployment by 1992). While this might be treated as a special case, it is obvious that the evidence is far from unambiguous. At the moment, a position on the agnostic side of the question is probably the safest.

Whatever the position on the differential advantage of using the EMS as a counterinflationary framework, it must certainly be acknowledged that it has, in fact, been used as such. The DI has been an inevitable casualty of this, for a simple reason. Whereas the DI was designed, as explained above, with the purpose in mind of inducing symmetry of adjustment – and, in particular, of inducing adjustment by Germany – the counterinflationary policies of the period ran counter to this conception. It was not desirable to induce Germany to raise its inflation to the EMS average (even supposing this could have been done); rather, the point was to bring the average down to the German level.[8]

16.7 Competitiveness

The *real* rate of exchange, the nominal rate corrected for relative prices, provides an index of competitiveness. Although the formal provisions of the EMS focus on nominal exchange-range agreement, in a customs union exchange-rate arrangements must ensure a degree of stability in real rates of exchange. The reason is that because the real rate of exchange governs an economy's competitiveness, a sharp change – say a large appreciation in the real rate producing a large fall in competitiveness – will arouse protectionist pressures and thus threaten the reversal of the customs union's achievements in removing internal tariff barriers. Other, non-tariff barriers may be promoted and progress slowed on the removal of these and other obstacles to intraunion trade. Whether reflecting this 'inner logic' or not, the evidence does confirm that whereas the real rates of exchange of both the United Kingdom and the United States have undergone large changes in the 1980s, changes in competitiveness of the EMS economies have been more muted. Thus it appears that among the achievements of the EMS might be included that of reducing the extent of exchange rate 'misalignment', deviations of real rates of exchange from equilibrium levels.

A qualification must be entered at this stage. It is one thing for the real exchange rates of EMS countries to show less evidence of misalignment than those of some key non-EMS (or non-ERM in the case of the United Kingdom) countries. It is another thing to be sure that the record of the EMS in stabilizing real rates of exchange is adequate. A reason why it might not be adequate is the fact that, as argued above, countries have used the EMS as a counterinflationary framework. Among other things, this has meant that realignments, although always changing central rates in the direction indicated by relative inflation, have been deliberately tardy and niggardly in doing so. The object has been to ensure that realignments do not accommodate and encourage inflation. A consequence of this is that an economy which persistently inflates above the EMS average rate will undergo prolonged pressure not to adjust its exchange rate to accommodate this and so will gradually lose its competitive edge. Because of the 'inner logic' of real rate stabilization referred to earlier, such a situation could not be regarded as sustainable. The position of the United Kingdom and to a lesser extent Italy shows this clearly. In 1992 the system broke down and these currencies were forced to devalue.

16.8 The popularity of the ECU

As described above, the ECU is simply a 'composite currency', with no necessary role in the critical parity grid of the EMS. It has no central bank of issue and even its role as the foundation for the DI mechanism seems unimportant in light of the proven weakness of that mechanism.

Nevertheless, the ECU has proven quite popular as a currency of denomination of international bond issues; in 1985 it became the fifth most used currency of denomination of such issues outside the US dollar, its share rising to nearly 11.5% (see Table 16.5).[9] While the official transactions of the EC itself are denominated in ECU, the ECU is barely used as a means of payment by the private sector.[10] Its attraction is that of a 'currency cocktail', in that it offers some 'hedging' properties that agents find worth while. Thus, a trading company whose activities are concentrated in, say, three different markets may find that the best way of hedging its liabilities, if it needs to borrow, is to issue bonds which are denominated in a cocktail of the three different currencies used in those markets. The alternative of issuing bonds in one currency only (one of the three used in the markets where it trades or a fourth outside currency) inevitably involves the company in taking on the risk associated with changes in the exchange rates between the currency of denomination of the bond and the currencies used in the markets it operates in. While the risk, in itself, is as much a risk of gain as of loss, the trading company may not be interested in, or able to afford, to speculate in this way. For this reason, a demand for currency-cocktail borrowing arises from traders who are averse to risk. ECU-denominated bond issues appeal to businesses whose activities are concentrated in the EC for this reason. In a similar fashion, a demand for assets of this denomination arises from firms and institutions whose liabilities are of a similar nature. In fact, most of the bond issues have been made by EC organizations and national governments, although more recently corporate ECU borrowings have become significant. Both the Italian government (since 1987) and the British government (since 1988) have issued short-dated ECU-denominated debt instruments, helping to correct a deficiency in the market for short-term ECU assets. In addition to the ECU bond market there has also been a development of bank lending and borrowing in ECU.[11]

The apparent success of the ECU depends on something more than its currency-cocktail quality, however, since modern financial procedures readily allow cocktail mixing to take place and it does not seem difficult to imagine that for many purposes cocktails containing slightly different mixes of EC currencies (and perhaps including the Swiss franc, for example) would be preferable. Two main points should be mentioned.

One is that ECU borrowing can be seen in some countries of the EMS (France and Italy) as a reflection of exchange control. Certainly, the largest sources of ECU borrowing have been Italy and France, where the special status accorded to the ECU has permitted residents, in effect, to borrow from overseas in a way that would not be allowed if the borrowing was done in a single currency or, indeed, any other currency cocktail. At the same time, the comparatively high interest rates available on

Table 16.5 ⬤ Non-dollar international bond issues by currency of denomination (%).

	1981	1983	1985	1987	1990	1995
Swiss francs	44.7	42.7	23.0	21.2	18.5	10.0
Sterling	7.3	8.8	10.1	13.2	9.2	7.1
Deutschmark	13.4	19.6	17.4	13.2	7.7	22.9
Yen	16.2	12.4	18.9	22.0	23.1	30.3
ECU	1.3	4.9	11.4	6.5	13.8	3.0
Others	17.1	11.7	19.2	23.8	27.7	26.8

Sources Computed from data shown in Walton (1988) and from the *Bank of England Quarterly Bulletin*.

ECU-denominated loans have made these loans quite attractive to residents of some low interest rate countries. Viewed in this light, the prevalence of ECU-denominated borrowing and lending is a rather ambiguous advertisement for the EMS. However, it does seem clear that the volume of private sector ECU issues is well above what can be attributed solely to such features and in itself this counts as a highly positive declaration of the credibility established by the EMS. So the second point to make is that the fact that the ECU is chosen rather than some other cocktail testifies to a perception of the credibility of the EMS and would have paved the way, if other conditions permitted, for the ECU to become a genuine EC currency. This makes the collapse of September 1992 all the more unfortunate as it disturbs not just the prevailing transactions but longer-run trends as well. This may help explain why the new European currency is to be labelled the Euro and not the ECU as was widely expected.

16.9 The position of the United Kingdom

The United Kingdom declined to participate in the operation of the EMS, to begin with, out of a belief that the system would be operated in a rigid way which would threaten the United Kingdom, with its high 'propensity to inflate', with a decline in its competitiveness, especially *vis-à-vis* Germany. This concern for the United Kingdom's freedom to determine or preserve its competitiveness still marks one strand of oppositional thinking on the question of British membership of EMU today. The problems of September 1992 in many ways served to reinforce the views that had led to the initial reluctance to join the ERM and hence were not wholly uncongenial.

While opposition to full membership of the EMS was voiced on these grounds by the Labour government of Mr Callaghan, opposition on different grounds was voiced by the incoming Conservative government headed by Mrs Thatcher. The Thatcher government wished to run an experiment in monetary policy in order to bring inflation down and reasoned, correctly, that if the instruments of monetary policy (principally interest rates) were to be directed at reducing the rate of growth of the money supply, they could not simultaneously be used to target the exchange rate. Technically, this dilemma could be avoided by maintaining a suitably strong set of exchange controls; such controls would allow a government some freedom to maintain two different targets for monetary policy but the Thatcher government was keen to remove these controls in any case and did so not long after taking office.

Events were to turn out somewhat paradoxically. The first phase of the Conservative government's monetary experiment was associated with a very marked *appreciation* of the exchange rate – so competitiveness would have been *better* preserved inside the EMS – and the deep recession that soon set in was attributed by many observers to this cause. The view took root that while the Thatcher government was correct to say that membership of the EMS was incompatible with pursuit of an independent monetary policy and would involve a loss of sovereignty in this respect, better results would nevertheless be attained by adhering to the EMS. In particular, the exchange rate would be steadier and competitiveness more assured, while inflation would be dragged towards the modest German level (we have already described the claims made for the EMS as a counterinflationary framework).

This view gained momentum as official British policy towards the exchange rate as a target changed and as it became clear that monetary policy was no longer aimed in single-minded fashion solely at controlling the supply of money. In fact, with practice preceding the public statement, the Chancellor of the Exchequer made this very clear in his 1983 budget speech. A House of Lords report on the question of entry into the EMS, published a little later in the same year, favoured 'early, though not necessarily immediate' entry into the system.

That report referred to four problems that the United Kingdom had had in relation to the EMS and noted that in each case events had moved in a favourable fashion. The first problem was the apprehension that the EMS would prove rigid and inflexible: the committee noted that the EMS had allowed a number of realignments. The second problem was that the United Kingdom had wanted to put the control of the money supply ahead of the goal of stabilizing the exchange rate – where, as described, policy had already retreated somewhat. The third problem was related to the UK position as an oil exporter, with sterling subject to quite a different response from the EMS currencies to oil price shocks. The committee saw this as less problematic as the oil market had become less disturbed. The fourth problem arose from sterling's still persistent role as a vehicle currency, i.e. one widely held by agents other than those solely concerned with UK trade. The committee acknowledged that this might mean that it would not be so easy to stabilize sterling in the ERM.

The viewpoint of the House of Lords report appears to have been representative of a wide range of opinion. Although the later report of a subcommittee of the House of Commons Select Committee on the Treasury and Civil Service revived some of the earlier arguments against entry, the general climate of opinion had changed markedly in a favourable direction by the early 1980s. With the passage of time the lingering reservations over the exposure of sterling to oil shocks and over the problem of speculation diminished still further, while the case for exchange-rate management became more widely and firmly accepted. The initiative launched by the United States in 1985 to secure the coordinated actions of its major partners to bring the dollar down substantially reinforced the latter process.

In September 1986, at the meetings of the International Monetary Fund, the Chancellor of the Exchequer advertised the non-speculative realignment process of the EMS and not long afterwards followed this up with a policy of 'shadowing the EMS', keeping the sterling exchange rate closely in line with the deutschmark. This policy initiative lasted for just over a year; by the end of February 1988, following a well-publicized exchange of views between the Chancellor and the Prime Minister, sterling was uncapped. Higher interest rates, invoked as a means of dampening monetary growth and in response to forecasts of inflation, caused the exchange rate to appreciate through its previous working ceiling. The incident underlined the inconsistency between an independent monetary policy and an exchange-rate policy and at the same time served to confirm that sterling was unlikely to participate in the ERM during the prime ministership of Mrs Thatcher. Even when sterling ultimately went into the ERM in October 1990 it appeared to be with considerable reluctance.

16.10 The challenge of the Single Market

Full participation in the EMS is not a requirement of membership of the EC nor is it implied in the original Rome Treaty. The SEA, however, does add a section to the Treaty calling for member countries to take steps to ensure the convergence of economic and monetary policy, prefiguring the emergence of monetary union from the EMS and the ECU. However, the provisions of the Single Market which are of immediate consequence to the EMS are those that require the dismantling of exchange controls. The consequences of this for the functioning of the EMS are profound and for its future, some sceptics suggest, possibly fatal as was demonstrated during the last part of 1992.

Exchange controls of the type maintained by Italy and France throughout the first ten years of the life of the EMS have as their immediate object the prevention of the short-run export of capital. Controls of this type therefore forbid the direct export of financial capital, restricting or forbidding portfolio investment overseas, the holding of foreign-currency-denominated bank deposits and lending (and borrowing) overseas. These restrictions are not watertight but they are effective. They have two important effects. First, they prevent or slow down speculation. Agents anticipating a devaluation of a currency cannot, if they are residents of the country concerned, simply sell the currency for foreign exchange in the expectation of making a quick gain when buying it back after the devaluation; nor can they lend the currency to non-residents who could carry out the same speculative raid. Secondly, the controls break the link that holds currencies together when there are no obstacles to perfect arbitrage. The interest parity link states that the interest differential between two currencies is equal to the expected rate of change in the exchange rate between them. Thus, taking two countries, say France (F) and Germany (G), interest parity would have $r_F = r_G + d_{F/G}$ where r_F, r_G are interest rates on similar-maturity, similar-risk instruments denominated respectively in the French and German currencies and $d_{F/G}$ is the expected rate of depreciation of the French franc against the German mark.

The removal of exchange controls therefore poses two problems for the EMS. First, a protection against speculation is lost. Second, because interest parity is no longer prevented, interest rates everywhere are tightly linked as the amount of expected depreciation is confined by the bands of permissible fluctuations of the currencies against one another. Because Germany is by far the largest economy in the EMS, this means that interest rates, and hence monetary policy, everywhere in the system will be dominated by Germany. Unless Germany in turn tempers its monetary policy by concern for the economic situation in other countries this can turn out to be an unacceptable state of affairs.

These problems have been realized and various solutions proposed. First, as regards the problem of speculation the mechanisms of the EMS have been improved by measures to accommodate automatic lending by a strong-currency country to a weak-currency country in the event of need; whereas previously this automaticity applied only when intervention was taking place at the edge of the band it has, since the deliberations of the EMS finance ministers in Nyborg in September 1987, applied also to so-called 'intramarginal' intervention, i.e. foreign exchange operations taking place to support a currency before it has reached its limit. These new provisions were tested by a speculative run on the French franc in the autumn of 1987 and proved successful; the Bundesbank lent heavily to the Banque de France but the lending was rapidly repaid once the speculation subsided and confidence returned. The second problem – that of excessive German dominance – has yet to be as well resolved. The Nyborg provisions called for much closer monetary cooperation, implying more continuous exchange of information, and interest rate movements within the EMS have since that time displayed a high degree of synchronization. However, the cooperation called for also seems to imply a degree of common decision making going beyond simply following a German lead in a prompt and well-prepared way. Progress on this front is less evident. The anxiety of France on this score has, however, led to important initiatives. First, France has called upon Germany to discuss economic policy on a regular basis and an economic council has been set up for this purpose. Second, it was on French initiatives that the EC was led to call for an investigation into the requirements of full monetary union, an investigation subsequently carried out by the Delors Committee, the recommendations of whose Report were endorsed by all twelve nations of the EC in June 1989, leading to the Maastricht Treaty on European Union.

The path which the EMS participants agreed to follow thus calls for increasing intervention resources and other devices to combat the threat of speculation and for increased economic and monetary cooperation between member countries, eventually leading to the creation of a European Central Bank. But we should note that there are alternative short-run solutions. Thus, one way in which countries could recover a greater measure of independence from the dominant power would be to enlarge the bands of exchange-rate fluctuation; another would be to compromise on 1992 by retaining a measure of exchange control. Either device has obvious counterspeculative advantages too. If maintained over the long term, these alternative solutions would be in effect a defeat for the higher aspirations of the EMS. But either one could, in principle, be adopted on a purely monetary basis until such time as the political prerequisites for greater cooperation were met.

The removal of exchange controls undoubtedly poses problems for the future of the EMS. Following the delicate path to which the member countries have agreed exposes the system to the hazards of speculation and poses political problems relating to the acceptance of German dominance in monetary affairs. The alternative short-run solutions have the disadvantage of taking the pressure off the search for a solution to the political problem, or perpetuating an obstacle to the integration of the European financial area.

The forecast threat to the system duly occurred in September 1992 and in some respects is yet to be resolved. Uncertainty about the outcome of the French referendum on the Maastricht Treaty contributed to speculation against the weakest currencies in the ERM, sterling and the lira. Both were unable to resist the pressure despite substantial increases in interest rates. By the summer of 1993 not even the French franc could survive the pressure and the bands had to be widened to allow it to devalue.

Other currencies have also come under pressure such as the Irish punt and the Swedish krone, which was shadowing the ERM, being forced to devalue (see Table 16.2). There was considerable pressure on the French franc in September 1992 but it survived, aided by substantial intervention by the Bundesbank on its behalf. It is arguable that all the currencies which were devalued were in some sense overvalued in terms of their long-term sustainable values. (One interpretation of this is the Fundamental Equilibrium Exchange Rate, FEER, the rate at which the balance of payments is sustainable in the long run.) However, the problem was not merely one of great domestic inflation by the devaluing countries but of the special problems of the dominant German economy leading to a divergence from the domestic objectives of the other countries.[12] German interest rates were driven up by the need to finance unification over and above the willingness to raise taxes. With the tight linkage of EMS interest rates other states also had to have rates that were high in real terms.

In the case of the United Kingdom it was clearly a relief that the constraints of the ERM could be broken. Interest rates had already been progressively cut to the point that sterling was close to its lower bound. A domestic recession was being exacerbated by the inability to use monetary policy to alleviate it. Interest rates have since been lowered by four percentage points in virtually as many months. There is no immediate prospect of sterling re-entering the ERM and indeed its fall of over 15% is no larger than that suggested by the FEER and its subsequent rise as the economy recovered was predictable.

The EMS has suffered considerably through being unable to organize an orderly realignment of exchange rates. The mechanisms existed but political pressures meant that the member states could not agree among themselves. Blame has been placed in a number of quarters – on the Bundesbank for not taking greater account of the impact of its policy on other countries and on the United Kingdom for not being sincere in trying to maintain parity within the bounds – but the basic weakness of the system remains: that trying to have narrow bands without exchange controls is really not sustainable when there are substantial shocks to the system. This has now been admitted in practice by widening the bands.

16.11 Experience since 1992 and prospects

The EMS has taken a back seat since the devaluations of September 1992 and the widening of the band to ±15% in August 1993. However, the system has remained intact and has slowly been regaining credibility. Despite three devaluations of the peseta and the escudo between November 1992 and March 1995 the participating currencies have been moving back into closer alignment. At the end of 1996 all bar the Irish punt were within the 2.25% band. Although sterling and the drachma have remained outside the ERM and the Swedish krone has not yet joined, Italy rejoined in November 1996 and Finland (October 1996) and Austria (January 1995) have also become participants.

Assuming that EMU does take place as planned then the EMS as it currently stands will come to an end. However, since it is unlikely that all the member states will be participating in Stage 3 of EMU from the outset there will be a successor system based on the Euro. The intention is to have central rates with respect to the Euro for EU member states that are not in Stage 3. The range of permitted divergence is yet to be agreed but the principles remain the same. Competitive devaluation is to be avoided, and convergence so that membership of Stage 3 becomes possible encouraged. This represents a return to a clearly one-sided system where those not in Stage 3 have to make the adjustments to converge. Convergence will be assisted by the restraints on fiscal policy imposed by the surveillance of the European Commission on all of the member states.

Although this is a transitory mechanism, it could remain in a state of transition for some time if the EU is progressively expanded to include central, eastern and other European states. These may very well not be in a position to move straight to full participation in EMU directly, in which case they will become part of the successor to the current EMS.

The combination of the single market and no exchange controls has clearly added to the risk from speculative pressures for the EMS. It is not surprising therefore that there has been the very strong pressure to move to Stage 3 of EMU despite the costs of transition.

Notes

1. The final steps towards stage 3 of EMU are scheduled over the coming months. Both this process and significant deviations from, could outdate some of the content of this chapter.

2. As from 2 August 1993, this became ±15% for all participating countries, although the Netherlands is maintaining a ±2.25% fluctuation limit with respect to the deutschmark.

3. Realignments in the EMS have only gradually become collective decisions (see Padoa-Schioppa, 1985).

4. The reader should refer to Swann (1988) for a useful summary and to Kruse (1980) for a detailed account of these past endeavours.

5. This is excellently illustrated by the huge gains reported for speculators against sterling in September 1992.

6. The title of the paper by Giavazzi and Pagano (1986) on this issue is indicative. However, the deutschmark itself has experienced problems since the unification of Germany and cannot, for the time being at any rate, be regarded as the least inflationary country in the ERM.

7. The sacrifice ratio is normally computed on a cyclical basis (see Mayes and Chapple, 1995, for example). The fall in inflation is thus contrasted with the rise in unemployment over the period up to the point that the economy gets back to its trend growth. However, other factors also affect unemployment both positively and negatively over the period and it has been argued that there has also been a strong secular upward movement in unemployment in Europe over the period.

8. Thus a strong currency country should in these circumstances revalue, not inflate. This is very clear in the European Commission's evidence to the House of Lords (1983). This is precisely what Germany did not do in the immediate aftermath to unification in the early 1990s. Here the obvious response would have been a revaluation but suitable changes were only achieved by devaluation of many of the other currencies outside the process of agreed realignment within the ERM.

9. The crisis of September 1992 brought new issues in the ECU market to a grind-

ing halt, and as yet it has not regained its popularity. The focus has turned back towards the deutschmark.

10. Walton (1988) notes that ECU invoicing accounts for 1% of all foreign trade in Italy and France, where it is most popular.

11. The reader is referred to Bank for International Settlements (1989) for a detailed account.

12. Cobham (1996) provides a helpful exposition of the different possible explanations of the crisis.

chapter seventeen

EU regional policy

H. W. ARMSTRONG

Member states of the European Community are anxious to ensure their harmonious development by reducing the differences existing between the various regions and the backwardness of the less favoured regions (Preamble to the Treaty of Rome, 1958).

In order to promote its overall harmonious development, the Community shall develop and pursue its actions leading to the strengthening of its economic and social cohesion.

In particular the Community shall aim at reducing disparities between the various regions and the backwardness of the least favoured regions, including rural areas (Article 130a, Single European Act, 1986; reaffirmed as Article 130a of the Maastricht Treaty, 1992).

These two quotations, written more than thirty years apart, illustrate the strength of the EU's commitment to regional policy. The commitment to regional policy is, at first-sight, a curious one. The EU has aspirations to become a federal system. Regional policy of the type we know in Europe is, however, rarely found in long-established federal countries such as the United States, Canada and Australia. To understand EU regional policy requires an understanding of the uniqueness of the European situation, with a patchwork of independent nation states seeking to move step-by-step towards closer economic, social and political relationships.

This chapter examines EU regional policy at a pivotal moment in the step-by-step process of European integration. The Single European Market (SEM) legislation set in train between 1986 and 1992 combined with the Maastricht Treaty of 1992 paving the way towards economic and monetary union (EMU) carry with them immense implications for EU regional policy.

This chapter begins with an examination of the case for having an EU regional policy running alongside the regional policies operated by each of the member state governments. This is followed by an overview of the ways in which economic integration can affect regional disparities. Attention will subsequently be concentrated on the EU regional policy which emerged in 1989 in the aftermath of the decision to create the SEM. Finally, the key issues which confront EU regional policy in the late 1990s and the new millennium will be considered.

17.1 The case for an EU regional policy

Regional policy has always been controversial. It is undeniably interventionist. Those who distrust the competence of governments fear that regional policy penalizes successful businesses in prosperous regions while simultaneously encouraging unsuitable economic activities in the depressed regions. To those who hold this opinion, regional disparities are the inevitable outcome of the market system – something to be tolerated until market forces such as labour migration, capital investment and expanding trade combine to revitalize low-wage depressed regions automatically.

Supporters of regional policy are much more sceptical of the ability of market forces to solve long-standing regional problems. An array of arguments is marshalled in support of an active government-led regional policy. The main arguments are as follows:

1. *Equity and 'fairness'.* Regional policy is seen as a way of ensuring that all parts of society can share in the benefits of a modern, growing economy.

2. *Extra income and production.* Regional policy is portrayed as being essential if underutilized resources – particularly unemployed labour – are to be drawn into productive use.

3. *Lower inflation and faster growth.* The concentration of economic activity in a few already-prosperous regions means that during periods of economic upturn markets in regions such as South East England quickly tend to 'overheat'. The resulting surge in wage levels, house prices, rents, etc., sends a wave of inflationary pressure rippling across the remainder of the economy and also results in a rise in imports to meet the growing demand, thus worsening the balance of payments position. Regional policy, by spreading economic activity, eases bottlenecks in the market economy. This is turn allows the economy to enjoy lower inflation and more sustained growth over time, to the benefit of all.

4. *Fewer urban problems.* Economic activity in Europe is heavily concentrated in the big metropolitan areas and capital cities of the member states. The quality of life in these cities is a cause of great concern. Traffic congestion, pollution, crime and overcrowding are serious problems. Regional policy offers a way of easing the pressures on the big cities by diverting part of the economic activity elsewhere.

These are powerful arguments and most are as valid now as they ever were. They do not in themselves, however, constitute a case for an *EU regional policy*. In the past they have been used to justify individual member state regional policies. In the United Kingdom, for example, the national government has had its own regional policy since 1928, a policy which has survived a succession of governments of widely different ideologies (Armstrong, 1994; Armstrong and Taylor, 1993). The crucial question from an EU point of view is why a separate EU regional policy is required *in addition to* the regional policies of the individual member states. The individual regional policies of the member states have continued alongside EU regional policy over the years since 1975 (when the European Regional Development Fund was established). There is no suggestion that they should be laid down in favour of a single EU regional policy.

Several distinct arguments can be advanced in support of a regional policy operated at EU level. Each argument will be considered in turn.

17.1.1 The 'vested interest' argument

The nation states of Europe are becoming increasingly integrated economies. Rapidly expanding trade links, together with much freer capital mobility and more slowly growing cross-border labour migration, are being stimulated by EU initiatives such as the SEM. Increasingly, the economic well-being of citizens of one member state depends on the prosperity of the economies of other member states. The presence of disadvantaged regions experiencing low incomes and high unemployment is in the interests of no one. Put another way, the citizens of one member state have a *vested interest* in ensuring that the regional problems in *other* member states are reduced. An EU regional policy can therefore be justified as a mechanism which allows one member state to become involved in policies which stimulate economic activity in regions of other member states.

Why do citizens in a prosperous member state such as Germany have a vested interest in helping to solve regional problems in, say, Greece or Spain? They have a vested interest because the solution of regional problems elsewhere generates *spillover benefits* – benefits which spread across member state boundaries. The more integrated the EU becomes, the bigger are the spillover effects of one member state on another. At present they are significant, but still relatively small, and comprise the following:

1. Equity spillovers.
2. Efficiency spillovers.
3. Spillover of non-economic benefits.

Equity spillovers arise because there is a widely held view in the EU that the benefits of integration should be 'fairly' distributed across regions and member states. Residents in more prosperous EU member states derive utility gains from helping citizens of poorer regions and member states to improve their economic status.

In addition to the pervading desire for 'fairness', reducing regional problems in the EU also generates *efficiency spillover* gains in already-prosperous regions and member states. Lower unemployment increases income and production for the EU as a whole, and also stimulates tax receipts (e.g. VAT) for the EU while simultaneously reducing the pressure on EU spending programmes such as social policy. An EU regional policy also has the potential to create gains for everyone in the form of lower *overall* EU inflation and easing the urban problems in the big cities at the heart of the EU.

Some of the benefits of EU regional policy are in the form of *non-economic spillover gains*. Reduced regional disparities can help in achieving greater social and political 'cohesion' in Europe. Areas that feel 'left out' of the benefits of integration are unlikely to cooperate or to embrace the concept of a more united Europe fully. Some would go further and argue that a strong EU regional policy is vital if the EU is to survive and to progress towards a fully fledged federal system. If this is true, the citizens of already-prosperous regions will support an EU regional policy as a means of protecting and extending the existing EU. In doing so they may also reap additional non-economic benefits in the form of extra security, the preservation of local languages and cultures and the extraordinary sociocultural diversity for which Europe is famous.

17.1.2 The 'financial targeting' argument

The second main argument in support of an EU regional policy is concerned with the effectiveness with which regional policy is operated in Europe. Regional policies are expensive to operate and resources must be found from public sector budgets. The disadvantaged regions of the EU are not evenly distributed among the member states of the EU. Some member states carry such a burden of depressed regions that they constitute depressed regions in their own right. This is particularly the case with some of the member states in the Mediterranean south of the EU.

Given the inevitable pressure on public sector budgets, it is not surprising to find that it is precisely those member states with the most severe burden of regional problems that have the greatest difficulty in financing an active regional policy. Leaving regional policy wholly to the member states is not therefore effective from an EU perspective. Member states such as France and Germany (prior to unification), with fewer regional problems, can best afford an active regional policy. Those with the most severe regional problems such as Greece and Portugal already have severe budget deficits and find it difficult to fund their domestic regional policies adequately. This is clearly revealed by Figure 17.1. The four most seriously disadvantaged countries (Greece, Ireland, Portugal and Spain) are shown on the left of the graph. Their per capita *domestic* regional policy expenditures are surprisingly low relative to other member states such as Germany which have less severe regional problems.

The difficulties faced by member states in ensuring that the most disadvantaged EU regions receive the greatest volume of assistance represents a powerful case for an EU regional policy. Member states on their own are simply unable to target regional policy funds on the most disadvantaged regions. Only the EU, it can be argued, is capable of drawing resources from more prosperous parts of the EU and ensuring that they are allocated to the most heavily disadvantaged regions.

17.1.3 The coordination argument

The third argument which can be made in support of an EU regional policy concerns the advantages of a coordinated approach. The EU has immense potential to

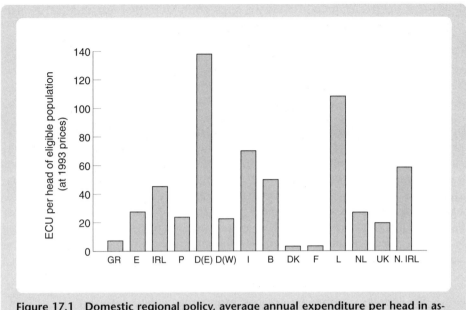

Figure 17.1 Domestic regional policy, average annual expenditure per head in assisted areas, 1989–93. (*Source* CEU (1996a), Graph 22)

improve the effectiveness of the regional policy effort by acting as a supranational coordinating agency. Regional development initiatives within the member states are offered by a bewildering array of organizations. As well as the member state governments, typically also involved are regional governments, local councils, non-elected development agencies and, increasingly, private-sector organizations and joint-venture schemes between private and governmental bodies.

Lack of coordination can be very wasteful. Firms seeking assistance in the disadvantaged regions may be bewildered and deterred by the complexity of the types of help on offer. Different regions may compete, using regional policy subsidies as a weapon, for one another's firms or for inward investment projects of Japanese or US firms. In addition, valuable development opportunities (e.g. cross-border transport links) may not be implemented as a result of coordination failures. The potential coordination role for an EU regional policy is clearly a wide one.

In exercising its supranational coordination role the EU must simultaneously attempt to link together the following:

1. EU regional policy with *other EU policies* (e.g. agriculture, social).

2. EU regional policy activities within a given member state with the regional policy of the member state government.

3. Member state regional policies one with another, particularly where the member states share a common border.

4. EU regional policy, member state regional policy and the initiatives being operated by regional and local level organizations.

This is an enormous and difficult task, but one which only the EU has the potential to perform.

17.1.4 The 'effects of integration' argument

This is the most controversial of the arguments advanced in support of an EU regional policy. EU involvement in regional policy, it is argued, is necessary to overcome the adverse regional impact of the integration process. This argument rests upon two suppositions. The first is that economic integration tends to cause a worsening ('divergence') of regional disparities. The second is that it is the EU, rather than the member states, which is best placed to tackle the regional problems that develop as integration proceeds. Both suppositions have been the subject of fierce debate. The effects of integration on regional disparities is an issue of immense importance and will be considered further in section 17.2.

17.1.5 The 'effects of other EU policies' argument

A further argument frequently advanced in support of EU regional policy is that it is needed to help to mitigate the adverse regional effects of other EU policies. A number of EU policies are known to have particularly severe effects on the disadvantaged regions. Value-added tax, for example, a major source of EU revenues, has long been known to be a regionally regressive tax (CEC, 1977c). Other EU policies also have their own distinctive patterns of regional effects (Franzmeyer *et al.*, 1991). The adverse regional effects of EU agriculture price guarantee policy – a major item in the EU budget – have been a source of particular concern. The concentration of EU agriculture policy help on products such as cereals, milk, oilseed and beef (products of the more prosperous northern EU farming regions) means that '70% of guaranteed expenditures, or fully 40% of the entire Community's budget, is in effect working against the Community's regional policy objectives' (Franzmeyer *et al.*, 1991, p. 52). Powerful further evidence of the adverse regional impact of the agricultural policy has recently been presented in the *First Cohesion Report* (CEU, 1996a).

The ideal solution, of course, to policies with adverse regional impacts such as EU agriculture policy would be to alter the nature of the policies themselves. This is, however, only occasionally possible and may not, in any case, be desirable. The EU, therefore, has adopted a twofold approach as part of its regional policy effort. Firstly, regular regional impact assessment studies of major EU policies are conducted to identify, and where possible to rectify, policies with adverse regional effects. Secondly, the results of regional impact studies are used to guide EU regional policy initiatives designed to mitigate adverse regional effects of other EU policies.

17.1.6 The 'further integration' argument

This argument centres upon the incomplete nature of the EU integration process. An EU regional policy, it is argued, is necessary to ensure that the benefits of integration are more fairly spread. Only if this is done will all member states be willing to countenance further steps towards full integration. This argument too is a controversial one. Even if one accepts, post-Maastricht, that economic and political union is an acceptable goal, there is little hard evidence that *regional* disparities prevent *member states* from agreeing to further integration.

The list of arguments in favour of a separate EU regional policy is a long one. The case is a strong one too. It should be noted, however, that there is no case for a *complete* transfer of regional policy powers from member states to the EU. The EU's own commitment to 'subsidiarity' – the maximum devolution of powers – requires that member states and regional and local authorities all have a role. Many regional policy initiatives (e.g. advice to firms, training policies) also require an active local input to be effective. The remoteness of Brussels from many of the problem regions, the lack of specialist local knowledge and experience, and the virtue of allowing variety and experimentation in regional policy all suggest that partnership, not dominance, is the appropriate EU role.

17.2 The effects of integration on EU regional disparities

The implications of economic integration for EU regional disparities are very poorly understood. The economic processes at work are extremely complex and long-lasting. The regional effects of the creation of the original customs union have not yet been fully experienced; the regional implications of the '1992' SEM process are, in reality, only just beginning; and the regional ramifications of EMU, should it ever be achieved, will take decades to manifest themselves.

An examination of the existing pattern of regional disparities in the EU reveals an array of problems which are formidable by comparison with other parts of the world such as the United States. Figure 17.2 shows regional GDP per capita for the EU in 1993. The most affluent ten regions in the EU have GDP per capita values more than three times higher than the bottom ten. These GDP per capita disparities are two and a half times as great as those found in the United States (Armstrong, 1995a; CEC, 1991a), and over three times as great as those found in Australia. Figure 17.3 shows the extent of EU regional disparities using another popular indicator, the regional unemployment rate. In 1995, the ten worst affected regions had an average employment rate of over 2.6%, while the ten least affected had an average rate of under 4% (CEU, 1996b).

The regional problems confronting the EU are extremely diverse as well as being severe. The EU itself identifies four main types of problem regions. These are Lagging Regions (or 'Objective 1' regions), whose GDP per capita fall well below the EU average, Declining Industrial Areas (or 'Objective 2' regions), certain Rural

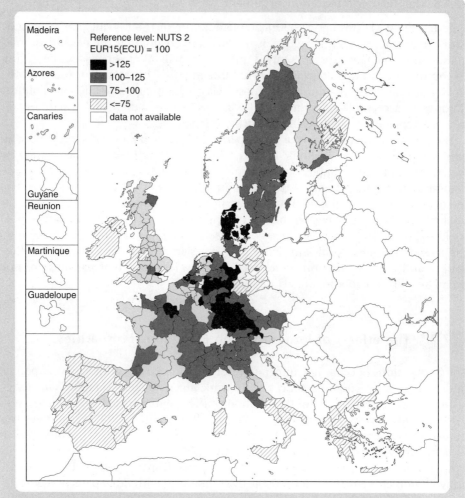

**Figure 17.2 Gross domestic product (GDP) per capita, 1993. (*Source* Eurostat,
Statistics in Focus: Regions, 1996(1). Luxemburg)**

Regions (or 'Objective 5b' regions) and areas with very low population densities
('Objective 6' regions). The Objectives referred to here are those laid down for the
EU's regional development fund in a set of reforms introduced in 1989, and sub-
sequently, amended in 1995 when Austria, Finland and Sweden joined the EU.

These broad categories of disadvantaged regions hide within them an extraordinary array of different types of problem region. Some are rural in nature, others
urban. Some regions are suffering from problems arising from their geographical isolation from the main EU markets. Yet others suffer from economic dislocation
caused by the removal of internal frontiers (disrupting their traditional trade pat-

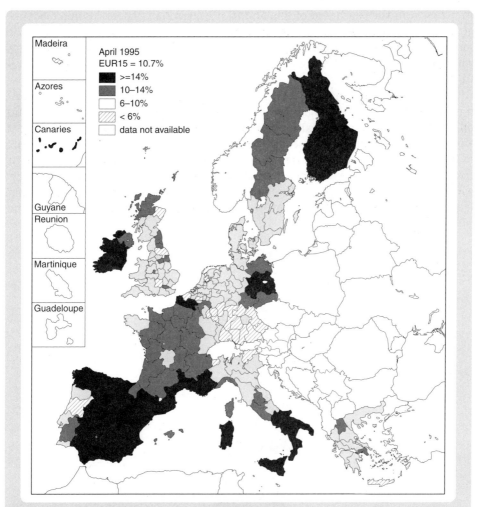

Figure 17.3   Unemployment rates, total (*Source* Eurostat, *Statistics in Focus: Regions*, 1996(2), Luxemburg)

terns) or because they lie along the external borders of the EU. Another distinctive category of problem region is represented by the large number of island economies, many in very isolated locations indeed.

Despite the great variety of EU regional problems, the overwhelming impression which one obtains from statistics such as those presented in Figure 17.2 is that there appears to be a well-established 'core–periphery' pattern to EU regional disparities. Most of the more prosperous regions lie at the geographical centre of the EU, while the most disadvantaged regions lie on the periphery, particularly, but by no means wholly, in the Mediterranean 'south'. The traditional prosperous core of the EU stretches from the south-east of England to northern Italy. There is some evidence of the possible emergence of a new growth belt from northern Italy through the south of France and into north-east Spain, as Figure 17.4 shows (CEC, 1991b). This will not, however, alter the overall conclusion that a 'core–periphery' situation prevails in the EU.

The 'core–periphery' nature of EU regional problems has existed for many years. It is the outcome of economic processes which pre-date the existence of the EU, and others that have come into existence as a result of the EU. Economic integration is a process which is progressing continuously on a world-wide scale. Improvements in transport infrastructure and transport technology have gradually reduced freight cost barriers to trade. So too have general improvements in production technology, which have had the effect of reducing the transport inputs required to assemble materials and to distribute the output of manufacturing industry. Moreover, in the

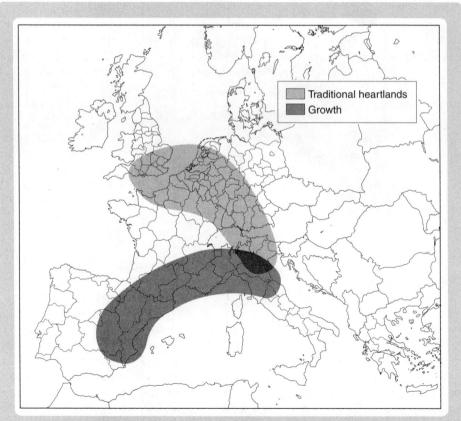

Figure 17.4   The traditional heartlands and current growth regions of the EU
(*Source* CEC (1991b))

period since the Second World War there has been a consensus in favour of freer trade which has led to successive international steps (e.g. GATT agreements) designed to reduce the barriers to trade. The member states of the EU have participated in these world-wide processes of integration, and the pattern of regional disparities which we observe today has been affected by them. Many of these processes predate the creation of the EU in 1958. In addition to these broad integration processes common to all countries, the EU has acted to trigger its own distinctive 'accelerated' integration programme. The current map of regional disparities (Figure 17.2) will have been affected by this too. The regional effects of the SEM process have not yet really been experienced and will take decades to be felt, while EMU is very much something for the future. Existing regional disparities, however, will have been affected by the creation of the EU customs union and by the successive widening of the customs union to include new member states in 1973 (Denmark, the United Kingdom and Ireland), 1981 (Greece), 1986 (Spain and Portugal) and 1995 (Austria, Finland and Sweden).

No two 'rounds' of economic integration ever have an identical effect on regional disparities. Each round in the integration process can be thought as having two groups of effects: a unique regional imprint or pattern of effects, combined with a 'core–periphery' effect in common with other rounds. The creation of the original customs union, for example, involved the removal of tariffs which had previously provided most protection to *manufacturing* industries. The most severe effects of this act of integration were therefore experienced in regions most heavily dependent on manufacturing industries. The creation of the Single Market between 1989 and 1992 has involved the removal of an array of non-tariff barriers. It is thought that a distinctive group of some forty manufacturing sectors will be most affected by the SEM, along with certain types of services such as banking and finance (CEC, 1990b; Quévit, 1992; Begg, 1992). Some regions are clearly more at risk than others, giving rise to a distinctive regional imprint (PA Cambridge Economic Consultants, 1989).

While it is obvious that each round in the integration process has its own distinctive regional impact, why integration in the EU should exhibit systematic core–periphery effects as well is less clear. Evidence to date suggests that integration tends to favour the central core regions of the EU. In practice, this 'centralizing' tendency is probably the outcome of two sets of countervailing forces: one set tends to cause regional *convergence* while the other tends to bring about regional *divergence*. Which set of forces will predominate in the years to come is an issue of prime importance to the EU.

The forces which tend to bring about *convergence* of regional disparities within the EU are predominantly a series of automatic equilibrating processes which occur whenever a system of freely functioning markets is in operation. Free trade in goods and services will, it is argued, lead to regions specializing in the production and export of goods and services in which they have a comparative advantage. Under traditional trade theory such as the Heckscher–Ohlin–Samuelson model all regions benefit from this process and regional differences in wage rates and capital rentals are also eliminated (Armstrong and Taylor, 1993). The convergence effects of freer trade are reinforced by the effects of freer factor mobility. Where wage rates differ significantly between regions, there is an incentive for labour to migrate from low-wage to high-wage regions, a process which reduces regional wage inequalities. Capital investment in the meanwhile is attracted to the disadvantaged regions by the low wages and excellent labour supply available there. This too reduces regional inequalities. The combination of freer trade and large-scale factor mobility offers real hope for the convergence of regional disparities in the EU. It is thought, however, that these processes operate only very slowly and that decades will be required before their full effects are felt. Moreover, there are forces leading to divergence of regional disparities. It is to these which we now turn.

At the heart of the economic integration process set in motion by the EU has been a desire to achieve free trade and the free movement of labour and capital. In order to enjoy the benefits of integration (Emerson *et al.*, 1988; CEC, 1988h, 1990c), it is essential that major restructuring of industry should occur. The various static and dynamic gains from integration require regions to switch production and concentrate on the production of those goods and services for which there is a comparative advantage. The greater the integration envisaged, the greater are the potential benefits, but the greater too are the restructuring implications. Painful though the restructuring process is for those involved, in principle it should be experienced by all regions. The crucial question, therefore, is why integration seems in the EU to be associated with systematic core–periphery effects. A series of different divergence forces are thought to accompany the integration process:

1. *Economies of scale.* These represent a potent source of benefit from integration. The concentration of production at larger plants can lead to great efficiency gains. Firms seeking to exploit economies of scale are likely to be attracted to regions at the core of the EU. Input assembly costs are lower, and access to the whole EU market is much easier from central locations. Moreover, the core regions are already the most prosperous regions and therefore represent the strongest markets.

2. *Localization and agglomeration economies.* Localization economies arise when firms in the same industry locate close to one another (e.g. access to labour with appropriate skills, information flows, ability to subcontract work). Agglomeration economies occur when firms from many different industries locate close to one another (e.g. transport facilities, financial facilities). These external economies of scale effects tend to favour the core regions of the EU. Firms are drawn towards existing successful agglomerations of economic activity. The core regions of the EU contain almost all of the main financial, industrial and capital cities and are a potent magnet for new activity.

3. *Intra-industry trade and dominant market positions.* Modern trade theory is increasingly sceptical of the ability of all regions to share equally in the growth associated with freer trade. There is evidence that intra-industry trade in similar products has shown the most rapid growth among the more prosperous core regions and member states of the EU (Neven, 1990). Regions in the

Mediterranean south of the EU have fallen behind in the participation in this important and fast-growing type of trade. Similarly, much trade in manufactured goods in the EU is now dominated by large multinational enterprises. These firms are already concentrated in the core regions of the EU and it is thought that they may exploit their ability to dominate markets in ways that disadvantage peripheral regions. Opening up peripheral regions to competition from large multinational firms could have serious effects for the smaller and less powerful firms more frequently found there.

4. *Lack of competitiveness in peripheral regions.* Research commissioned by the EU (IFO, 1990) has provided powerful evidence that many of the EU's peripheral region firms face severe problems in meeting the competitive challenges posed by integration. The lack of competitiveness is based on a combination of factors largely outside of the control of the firms themselves. These, as Table 17.1 shows, include poor location, weak infrastructure facilities (e.g. transport, telecommunications), low-skill labour forces, and local tax and financial sector problems.

5. *Selective labour migration.* The peripheral regions are also weakened, as integration proceeds, by the loss of migrants. The freeing of labour mobility stimulates migration from peripheral to core regions. Migration is highly selective. It is the young, the skilled and the economically active who migrate. Their loss is a severe blow to peripheral regions seeking to compete in an integrated EU.

6. *The loss of macropolicy powers in peripheral member states.* This is a particular problem with the next stage of integration – EMU. Member states have already lost a substantial degree of control over their exchange rates as a result of the adoption of EMS, despite the problems resulting from recent turmoil in EU exchange markets. Full EMU will mean the complete loss of powers to try to protect a weak local economy by way of a currency devaluation. With interest rates tending to equalize across the EU and with a single currency the member states will have lost the power to use monetary policy to stimulate a weak local economy. Even fiscal policy will be constrained under EMU. Peripheral member states face a future of very limited macropolicy power. This will limit their ability to protect their local economies.

The divergence forces set out above seem convincing and strong. There has been considerable discussion of the possibility that such forces may interact and reinforce one another in such a way that *cumulative causation* occurs. This is where the loss of firms and a continuous outflow of migrants so weakens a peripheral economy that it can no longer attract new economic activities and hence goes into a downward spiral of decline. This is by no means a theoretical possibility. A number of rural regions of the EU (e.g. the west of Ireland, parts of southern Italy) have experienced depopulation on a large scale.

The evidence that is available suggests that cumulative causation has not occurred, nor is it likely to occur in the EU. Prior to the mid-1970s regional disparities in the EC had experienced quite a long period of narrowing. This was followed by

Table 17.1 ⬭ The priorities of firms for the improvement of regional competitiveness[a].

Determinants of competitiveness	Lagging regions	Regions in industrial decline	Favoured regions
Financial markets			
1. Cost of credit	1	6	6
2. Income/corporate taxes	2	5	3
3. Exchange rates	10	8	8
4. Availability of risk capital	20	19	23
Educational system			
5. Supply of qualified labour	3	1	2
6. School facilities	15	26	26
7. Proximity of training facilities	28	33	33
8. Supply of unskilled labour	30	15	11
9. Proximity of third-level education	34	33	29
Labour market			
10. Indirect labour costs	4	1	1
11. Regulation of the labour market	5	8	6
12. Wages and salaries	13	4	5
Macroeconomic outlook			
13. Rate of economic growth	5	3	4
14. Sector medium-term outlook	12	10	9
Infrastructure			
15. Transport network	7	11	10
16. Supply and cost of energy	8	12	18
17. Industrial sites	14	17	25
18. Communication system	17	23	14
19. Supply and cost of waste disposal	26	21	14
National policies and institutions			
20. Industrial policy	9	18	12
21. Administrative procedures	16	25	20
22. Other national determinants	25	28	32
23. Legal regulations	29	22	19
Regional policies and institutions			
24. Regional policy incentives	11	14	20
25. Cooperation of local authorities	24	20	24
26. Other regional determinants	31	32	31
27. Local taxes	33	7	12
Regional economic structure			
28. Servicing machinery	18	31	27
29. Proximity of suppliers	19	23	28
30. Proximity of customers	21	15	22
31. Banks, insurance, lawyers	22	30	33
32. Business culture	26	26	30
33. Advertising and consulting	36	36	35
Social facilities			
34. Social climate	23	12	17
35. Cost of housing	31	29	16
36. Cultural and social facilities	35	35	36
37. Leisure facilities	37	37	37

[a] Ranking according to the frequency of company replies in response to the request to list the three determinants of competitiveness with the highest priority for improvement.
Source CEC (1991a).

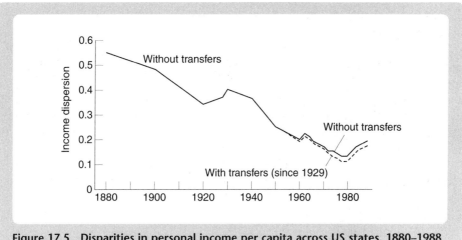

Figure 17.5 Disparities in personal income per capita across US states, 1880–1988 (*Source* Barro and Sala-i-Martin (1991))

periods of widening of disparities in the late 1970s and early 1980s. The EU's regional disparities now seem to have stabilized (CEC, 1991a; Armstrong, 1995b). Evidence from other countries with a long history of being fully economically integrated, such as the United States, also suggests that in the long term integration is associated with convergence of regional disparities rather than divergence, as Figure 17.5 shows for the United States (Barro and Sala-i-Martin, 1991). This evidence implies that the convergence forces at work eventually come to predominate over the divergence forces. The resulting balance of forces results in a process of convergence which is slow (2% per annum in the United States), but is also sustained over a long period (Sala-i-Martin, 1996).

17.3 Current EU regional policy

EU regional policy traces its origins to the decision in 1975 to create a European Regional Development Fund (ERDF). The policy subsequently underwent significant reform in 1979 and 1984 (Armstrong, 1978, 1985). The current EU regional policy, however, owes most of its distinctive features to the major reform of the EU's structural funds which took place in 1989. This reform was specifically designed to accompany the SEM process. The policy underwent further 'fine tuning' in 1993 ahead of the current 1994–99 budget period for the EU. Further major reform is expected in 1999. The EU's structural funds comprise the ERDF, together with the European Social Fund (ESF), the Guidance Section of the European Agricultural Guidance and Guarantee Fund (EAGGF) and the Financial Instrument for Fisheries Guidance (FIFG).

17.3.1 The ERDF and the 1989 and 1993 Reforms of the Structural Funds

The introduction of the SEM was phased in over the period from the SEA in 1986 to the end of 1992, by which time most of the many directives and regulations implementing the SEM were finally put in place. The SEM represented a major step towards integration in the EU and one which is gradually bringing about massive structural changes in the economies of the member states and their constituent regions. During 1988 and early 1989 a series of EU regulations were introduced which, taken together, represented a significant turning point in EU regional policy (see CEC, 1989e, for a summary of the reforms). The 1989 reforms established the ERDF as an integral part of the EU's policy for dealing with the effects of structural changes which inevitably accompany integration. The reformed policy was designed not only to accompany the SEM process, but also to form the basis of further reforms to EU regional policy to accompany further integration such as the process of EMU envisaged in the Maastricht Treaty, and the subsequent Fourth Enlargement which brought Austria, Sweden and Finland into the EU in 1995. In practice, the subsequent reform package introduced in 1993 to accompany the Maastricht Treaty essentially comprised only a 'fine tuning' of the system established by the 1989 reforms (see CEU, 1996b, for a summary). It was, however, accompanied by a major new infusion of funds for the ERDF and the other structural funds for the budget period 1994–99. The Fourth Enlargement in 1995 also triggered a series of small amendments to the ERDF and the other structural funds, the most notable of which being the designation of a new type of region to be eligible for assistance – regions with very low population densities in the sub-Arctic north of Sweden and Finland.

The outcome of the 1989 reforms and the subsequent amendments in the 1990s has been to create a comprehensive and coordinated delivery system for regional policy in the EU, and one which is very well funded by Brussels. By 1999 the structural funds' share of the full EU budget will have risen to 36%. The four structural funds (ERDF, ESF, the Guidance Section of the EAGGF, and the Financial Instrument for Fisheries Guidance – FIFG) have been given the task of attempting collectively to attain six priority objectives. These priority objectives are as follows, with the EU funds involved in each objective shown in parentheses:

1. Development and structural adjustment of the regions whose development is *lagging behind*, defined as having GDP per capita under 75% of the EU average (ERDF, ESF, and EAGGF).

2. The conversion of regions in *industrial decline* (ERDF and ESF).

3. Combating long-term unemployment (more than 12 months) and facilitating the integration into working life of young people (under 25 years of age) and of persons exposed to exclusion from the labour market. This is a 'non-regional' objective (ESF only).

4. Facilitating the adaptation of workers of either sex to industrial changes and to changes in production systems. This too is a 'non-regional' objective (ESF only).

5. Promoting rural development by:

   (a) speeding up the adjustment of agricultural structures in the framework of the reform of the common agricultural policy (a 'non-regional' objective relying on EAGGF and FIFG); and

   (b) facilitating the development and structural adjustment of rural areas (ERDF, ESF and EAGGF).

6. Promoting the development and structural adjustment of regions with an extremely low population density (ERDF, ESF and EAGGF).

As can be seen, the four objectives of particular importance to EU *regional* policy are (1), (2), (5b) and (6). It must be borne in mind, however, that the disadvantaged regions of the EU contain disproportionate numbers of long-term unemployed and unemployed young people and therefore also benefit substantially from the activities of the ESF which alone has responsibility for objectives (3) and (4). Indeed, the 1989 reforms attempted to strengthen further the deliberate regional bias built into the way in which the ESF operates. The structural funds are also reinforced by the activities of the Cohesion Fund, introduced along with the Maastricht Treaty, to help Greece, Spain, Portugal and Ireland to cope with EMU.

The 1989 reforms (and their subsequent fine-tuning in the 1990s) represent a clear break with the past in that for the first time in 1989 the EU drew up its own map of areas eligible for assistance. Prior to 1989 the ERDF had, in allocating help, simply relied upon the areas designated as eligible for regional policy assistance by the member states (as part of their own domestic regional policies). The current map of EU-assisted areas (for the 'regional' objectives (1), (2), (5b) and (6)) is shown as Figure 17.6. Detailed quantitative criteria are used to identify eligible assisted areas under each of the four regional objectives. The Objective 1 regions are by far the most important of the four categories of assisted areas and they cover 25.0% of the combined population of the 15 members of the EU. As can be seen from Figure 17.6, the main Objective 1 areas are in the Mediterranean (Greece, Portugal, Spain and southern Italy), Ireland and the former Eastern Germany. Objective 2 assisted areas are based upon smaller regional units, but still encompass 16.4% of the EU's population. They are scattered widely throughout the EU as Figure 17.6 shows. Objective 5(b) regions form a category of assisted areas much less important than the first two. They encompass 8.8% of the EU's population, while the specific Objective 6 (targeted on the remoter northern areas of Sweden and Finland) encompasses a mere 0.4% of the combined EU population. In total, the four types of assisted areas cover no less than 50.6% of the EU population. The map of assisted areas will be reviewed again in 1999 and it is expected that the accession of a number of very poor Eastern and Central European countries will force very large changes in the pattern of assisted areas.

The EU has deliberately concentrated the bulk of its financial assistance on the very poorest areas; in practice the Objective 1 regions. During the budget period 1994–99 the allocations for the four structural funds, by objective, are as follows (all at 1994 prices):

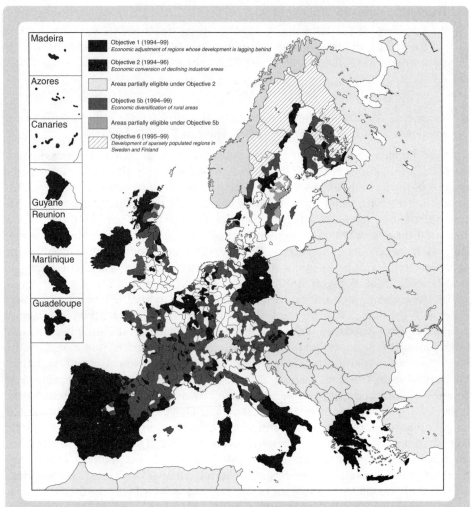

Figure 17.6 Areas eligible under the regional Objectives of the Structural Funds (1994–99)

Objective 1	93.972 billion ECU
Objective 2	15.360 billion ECU
Objectives 3 and 4 (non-regional)	15.180 billion ECU
Objective 5(a) (non-regional)	6.916 billion ECU
Objective 5(b)	6.862 billion ECU
Objective 6	0.697 billion ECU

In addition, some 14.051 billion ECU has been set aside for the 1994–99 period for

Community Initiatives (CIs). These are initiatives designed to tackle specific cross-country and pan-EC problems. The CIs are wide-ranging and include such initiatives as RECHAR (for coal mining areas), RESIDER (for iron and steel areas), PESCA (for fishing communities), INTERREG (for cross-border initiatives), and STRIDE (for research and technology). Objective 1 is scheduled to obtain 67.6% of the total structural funds' budget for 1994–99, while Objective 2 regions should obtain 11.1% of the total.

Objective 5(b) regions (with 4.9%) and objective 6 regions (0.5%) are relatively minor, although it should be borne in mind that their low populations mean that on a per capita basis the help given there by the structural funds is effectively very large. There has been a doubling in the real value of the structural funds between 1989 and 1993, followed by a further doubling again between 1994 and 1999. Accession of Eastern and Central European countries after 1999 is likely to mean that a further round of new expansion of the structural funds will be needed since these in-coming countries are so poor relative to the existing 15 member states.

The ERDF, as one of the four structural funds, has, of course, shared in this large increase in the funds' operations. The ERDF is directing the vast bulk of its operations towards the Objective 1 regions, with most of the remainder being allocated to Objective 2 regions. Similar comments apply to the other three structural funds. Table 17.2 shows how the structural funds are being targeted by member state and by regional Objective. The overwhelming size of the funds directed towards the Objective 1 regions and Objective 2 regions can be clearly seen.

The four structural funds of the EU are *grant-awarding* instruments, as is the Cohesion Fund. ERDF grants are essentially designed to assist industrial and infrastructure development. ESF grants are targeted on labour market initiatives such as training and mobility policies. The Guidance Section of the EAGGF and the FIFG assist a range of initiatives designed to facilitate the restructuring of the agriculture and fisheries sectors and the economic regeneration of the communities experiencing structural change. The post-1989 delivery system also encourages a close co-ordination of the structural funds with *loan-awarding* EU instruments. Most important of these are the European Investment Bank (EIB), together with the European Coal and Steel Community (ECSC). Both the EIB and the ECSC are long-established EU instruments and have always operated with a deliberate bias towards the disadvantaged regions. The EIB makes loans (often on advantageous terms) right across the EU, but makes a special effort to help the disadvantaged regions. In 1996, for example, 70% of the EIB's loans were made in the EU's assisted areas for regional development purposes. The ECSC, by concentrating on the coal and steel industries, is inevitably active in some of the most disadvantaged parts of the EU. The ECSC makes direct loans to the coal and steel industries themselves, but also helps other types of industries to set up in the coal and steel areas in order to create new jobs and to diversify the local economies. The ECSC also give grants to help with re-training and mobility of workers in the coal and steel areas. The EIB and ECSC have, since 1989, worked very closely with the structural funds.

Table 17.2 ● ERDF allocations, 1994–99 (1994–96 for Objective 2 regions) (millions ECUs at 1994 prices).

Member state	Objective 1 Lagging regions	Objective 2 Industrial areas	Objective 5(b) Rural areas	Objective 6 Low population density areas
Belgium	730	342	195	0
Germany	13,640	1,566	1,227	0
Greece	13,980	0	0	0
Spain	26,300	2,416	664	0
France	2,190	3,774	2,238	0
Ireland	5,620	0	0	0
Italy	14,860	1,463	901	0
Portugal	13,980	0	0	0
United Kingdom	2,360	4,581	817	0
Denmark	0	119	54	0
Luxemburg	0	15	6	0
Netherlands	150	650	150	0
Austria	162	99	403	0
Finland	0	179	190	450
Sweden	0	157	135	247
Total	93,972	15,360	6,862	697

17.3.2 Strategic planning, programming, partnership and additionality

As well as the commitment to a closer coordination of the activities of the EU's financial instruments, the 1989 reforms and subsequent amendments placed great emphasis on four further principles – the desire for a strategic planning approach to regional policy, an emphasis on the multiannual programming of assistance, the need for close partnership between all those involved in regional policy, and a desire that EU money should be a genuine supplement to regional policy spending by member states ('additionality'). None of these principles was new to the 1989 reforms. Strenuous efforts to implement them had been made prior to 1989 during earlier reforms. The 1989 reforms, however, represented a comprehensive attempt to create a system that would allow the principles to be achieved.

The system of medium-term (five year) *strategic planning* of regional policy set up by the 1989 reforms relies upon the drawing up of Single Programme Documents (SPDs). The regional SPDs are drawn up by regional teams in the member states. Their intention is to allow the member states to identify the regional policy expenditure requirements of their own disadvantaged regions. This is important – it is the member states which have the most detailed knowledge and experience of their own regional problems. Moreover, the EU is committed to 'subsidiarity', the retention of power wherever possible by the lowest tiers of government. Giving member states the initiative in formulating regional plans respects the concept of subsidiarity. The SPDs are meant to contain a detailed analysis of the problems faced, together with a development strategy and an analysis of how it is to be financed (with EU funds being only one part of the total). Despite some difficulties, the initial sets of SPDs following the 1989 reforms have allowed the strategic planning process to proceed (CEC, 1992a).

SPDs are approved by the Commission after regional plans have been submitted and after consultation with the member states. The SPDs are 'the Commission's response to the needs spelt out in the plans' (CEC, 1989e, p. 30). The SPDs are designed to set out the priorities to be followed for the period covered by the SPD, together with an outline of how these priorities are to be achieved and an indicative financing plan incorporating all three structural funds as well as the EIB, ECSC and member state roles. All subsequent requests for EU help fall within the SPD and should be justified by reference to it.

The whole medium-term planning process is supplemented by research and analysis of regional problems at the EU level. The 1989 reforms have continued the pre-existing system of regular *Periodic Reports* which analyze regional problems from an EU perspective (see CEC, 1991a, for the fourth of these reports, and CEU, 1995 for the fifth). Extensive research on EU regional problems is also conducted in house by the EU or commissioned from outside researchers. This work included regional impact assessment designed to identify the regional effects of EU policies (e.g. agriculture policy).

A key element in the 1989 and subsequent reforms was the emphasis placed on *multiannual programmes* as the method of attacking regional problems. The original ERDF set up in 1975 awarded grants on a project-by-project basis. Many member states (e.g. the United Kingdom) have long used this type of approach. From 1979 onwards, however, the EU began to experiment with a small number of programme-based initiatives. The 1984 reforms gave a further boost to the programme approach at the expense of project assistance. As well as being multiannual, programmes are essentially collaborative ventures between the EU and member states which encompass a variety of projects and initiatives designed to tackle a specific problem. The intention of the programme approach is to replace the *ad hoc* and piecemeal method of project assistance with a coordinated attack on specific problems within the medium-term planning process set up by the 1989 reforms. As we have seen, a distinctive category of programmes are the Community Initiatives (CIs). These are programmes which span the member states and are designed to tackle common problems. As their name suggests, they are initiated by the EU rather than the member states.

The 1989 and subsequent reforms contain a powerful new commitment to two long-held principles of EU regional policy – partnership and additionality. The concept of *partnership* is essential in an EU committed to the maximum devolution of power (subsidiarity). The reforms embody procedures designed to ensure that EU regional policy involves a continual dialogue between the Commission, member state governments and, increasingly, regional and local governments and development organizations. The SPDs, as well as the formal procedures for monitoring and evaluation of the policy, all include a requirement for close consultation. *Additionality* has proved to be a thorny issue in the EU's relationship with the member state governments. Some member states have been accused of responding to increases in EU regional policy expenditures by cutting back on their own domestic regional policy budgets. The 1989 and subsequent reforms envisaged that increases in EU spending would be at least matched by member state spending, and the SPD system was designed to try to ensure that this occurs. The issue continues to be a difficult one, as shown by the blocking by the Commission in April 1991 of £100 million of RECHAR money for the United Kingdom amid charges that the money was not clearly being used in an 'additional' manner.

17.4 Some key issues for the late 1990s and the new millennium

EU regional policy has shown itself to be capable of evolution and change over the years since its introduction in 1975. Some of the key issues which EU regional policy must confront in the 1990s and beyond are legacies of the past (e.g. additionality and the underfunding of the policy). Others such as the response of the policy to EMU, the Maastricht Treaty and Eastern enlargement are wholly new issues (Hall and Van Der Wee, 1992). Each will be considered in turn.

17.4.1 EU regional policy and EMU

The Maastricht Summit in 1991 stimulated a debate on what the appropriate EU regional policy response should be to the prospect of full EMU. Should the Treaty be implemented and the member states succeed in attaining the 'convergence conditions' necessary, EMU will occur, and a further round in the process of integration will be instituted. As with previous rounds such as the customs union and the SEM,

EMU will result in a distinctive regional imprint combined with some general 'core–periphery' effects. Moreover, all regions will experience structural change as the full implications of EMU work their way through the economic system (CEC, 1990c).

The Maastricht Treaty has proved controversial, and considerable uncertainty exists regarding its future. Initial Commission thinking in the aftermath of the Treaty (CEC, 1992b) led to a further significant boost to EU regional policy. This was because reducing economic disparities within the EU (between regions and member states) was regarded as vital if the key Maastricht Treaty goal of economic and social cohesion is to be attained. A new round of reforms in 1993 (CEC, 1992b, 1992c) led to the following:

1. That the basic principles of the 1989 reform to the structural funds (concentration of aid on lagging regions, programming, partnership and additionality) should continue to form the basis of EU regional policy in the 1990s.

2. Some fine-tuning of the procedures introduced in 1989, in the light of experience gained in the years since then, occurred. These changes included simplification of decision-making procedures, clearer definitions of responsibilities in the partnership process and more decentralization of detailed definition of projects and programme implementation, and an enhanced role for evaluation of regional policy initiatives.

3. Greater flexibility and the extension of assistance to education and health schemes in Objective 1 regions.

4. A bigger role for Community Initiatives.

5. The creation of a new Cohesion Fund in 1994. Although this is not strictly a regional policy fund (since it is designed for poorer *member states* – Greece, Ireland, Portugal and Spain), these countries contain many of the most depressed regions of the EU and benefited accordingly.

The Edinburgh Summit of EU Heads of State on 11–12 December 1992 began the process of implementing these proposals. Table 17.3 sets out the main regional policy decisions made at the Edinburgh Summit. The total structural funds budget was scheduled to be increased from 19.8 billion ECU in 1993 to 27.4 billion ECU in 1999 (both at 1992 prices). In addition, the Cohesion Fund was allocated a budget of 1.5 billion ECU in 1993, rising to 2.6 billion ECU in 1999.

Whether the reforms brought in at the time of the Maastricht Treaty will be adequate to meet the demands placed on it by EMU and the Single Market remains to be seen.

17.4.2 The issue of underfunding

Despite the increases in EU budget resources devoted to the structural funds, there is a lingering concern that the EU regional policy remains seriously underfunded for the tasks which it has set itself. This issue is a difficult one to examine since no one

Table 17.3 ⬤ **Principal decisions of the 1992 Edinburgh Summit concerning EU regional policy.**

1. Budget for structural actions, 1993–99

Year	Structural funds Total	Structural funds Objective 1	Cohesion Fund	Total
1993	19,777	12,328	1,500	21,277
1994	20,135	13,220	1,750	21,885
1995	21,480	14,300	2,000	23,480
1996	22,740	15,330	2,250	24,990
1997	24,026	16,396	2,500	26,526
1998	25,690	17,820	2,550	28,240
1999	27,400	19,280	2,600	30,000

Figures are in million ECU at constant 1992 prices. The sums represent cumulatively 176 billion ECU over the full period. They represent on average 25 billion ECU per year compared with 13 billion ECU per year 1988–92 (all at 1992 prices).

2. The cohesion fund

This was an entirely new fund. Member states are eligible if their per capita GDP is under 90% of the EU average. Currently eligible: Ireland, Spain, Portugal and Greece. The fund is designated for environmental projects and transport infrastructure projects. Initial allocations:

    Spain 52–58%
    Greece 16–20%
    Portugal 16–20%
    Ireland 7–10%

Source 'Conclusions of the Presidency', Final Communiqué of the European Council in Edinburgh, 11 and 12 December, 1992.

knows how much would need to be spent and over what time period for EU regional problems to be eliminated. The 1994–99 structural funds represent some 1.2% of EU GNP. While this is higher for countries with a lot of Objective 1 regions (3.4% of GNP for Greece, 2.1% for Ireland, 3.2% for Portugal and 2.2% for Spain) these are still not very large figures. The corresponding figures for Objective 2 and 5(b) regions are much smaller. The experience of the United Kingdom in the 1960s, where the member state government operated a regional policy with better funding (relative to GNP) than the current EU regional policy and still failed to eliminate relatively narrow regional disparities, suggests that EU regional policy is still significantly underfunded. The additional funds following the Maastricht Treaty will not help much since they will be needed to meet the *new* regional problems which EMU will create.

The underfunding issue is made more serious in the EU compared with federal systems elsewhere (e.g. the United States) by the inadequacies of the EU's system of *interpersonal* and *intergovernmental* fiscal transfers. On average, the four federal countries of Australia, Canada, Switzerland and the United States, for example, have redistributive transfer systems which eliminate some 40% of regional income differentials (O'Donnell, 1992). Such transfers are extremely weak within the EU and there would be considerable resistance by member states to a major expansion of them.

17.4.3 Equalization of disparities or equality of opportunity?

Although the current EU regional policy has taken great care in defining its priority objectives (in terms of the *types* of regions to be helped – lagging, industrial decline, rural, areas with low population densities), there remains the issue of what the final overall objective of EU regional policy should be. The complete elimination of regional disparities within the EU is unattainable – particularly in view of the underfunding problem. In recent years there has been considerable discussion of the possible goal of 'equality of opportunity' for the disadvantaged regions (National Institute for Economic and Social Research, 1991). This goal would imply that the disadvantaged regions would be given regional policy help such that their infrastructure, labour force skills and financial markets were of roughly equal quality to those found in the prosperous regions. Regional policy, it is argued, would thus be transformed from a policy designed to prop up depressed areas, to a policy designed to allow the depressed areas to compete on a level footing with other regions in the open trading system of the 1990s. Such a policy would need to have an explicit social welfare aspect (e.g. help for education, health and direct transfers to poor families) to provide a safety net for those who lose out in such a competitive environment.

17.4.4 Additionality

Despite the new initiatives in the 1989 reforms, it is clear that additionality remains a serious problem for EU regional policy, as the 1991 controversy over the UK government's use of RECHAR funds has shown. Member states faced with domestic public sector budget problems will always be tempted to cut their local regional policy efforts as EU regional policy is expanded.

17.4.5 New entrants in the 1990s and beyond

The prospect of a widening of the EU alongside the 'deepening' associated with EMU raises further serious issues for EU regional policy. The 1986 expansion to include Spain and Portugal resulted in a massive increase in the number of seriously disadvantaged regions within the EU. As a result, the disadvantaged regions of countries such as the United Kingdom and France have not received the kind of expansion of help that they could otherwise have looked forward to. The nature of the next phase of EU expansion is therefore a crucial issue for EU regional policy. The entry of Austria, Finland and Sweden in 1995 was beneficial since these are prosperous countries with minor regional problems. The looming entry of up to ten Eastern and Central European countries from 2004 onwards is causing serious concern. Given their present poverty, even the entry of the least poor of these states (e.g. the Czech Republic, Hungary and Poland) will pose a massive burden for the structural funds. On current regulations, the structural funds will be simply unable to cope (Baldwin, 1994). This will be a key issue in the upcoming 1999 review of the structural funds.

17.4.6 The final division of policy powers

Perhaps the most fundamental issue facing EU regional policy in the 1990s is the division of regional policy responsibilities among the different levels of government involved. The commitment of the EU to 'subsidiarity' is useful, but does not answer the crucial question of what the final assignment of powers is to be. What is to be the role of the EU? What are to be the roles of the member states, regional–local governments and unelected regional development agencies? Until this is decided, the EU will continue to find itself in a series of conflicts with the other partners in the regional policy effort.

chapter eighteen

EU social policies

C. D. E. COLLINS

18.1 Introduction

The central core of Community social policy is to be found in questions relating to employment, industrial health, the social costs of industry, labour mobility and the role of social spending in social affairs. In the early years of the EC, broader issues of social welfare seemed of little relevance but the subsequent growth of its social competences has been remarkable. Social affairs now form a large component of national public policy which, in turn, has to be fitted into a European framework and more problems have a transnational element. Community policies have also matured and as they reach into detailed areas of life, as in the equal opportunities policy, so they become more visible. In consequence, many people and organizations now recognize that their interests may be best served by lobbying in Brussels just as much as in the national capitals. The history of the EC also shows that the Commission, normally backed up by the European Parliament, has always believed it should play an active and positive role in social affairs and, particularly during the 1980s, it stepped up the social momentum as part of the drive to strengthen the political legitimacy of the EC in the move towards European union. It is hardly surprising that the Commission has clashed with national governments who still wish to claim credit with their citizens for their work to improve the conditions of life. Differences of view have surfaced, notably over the 'social dimension' of the single market. Here the biggest single issue has been whether the Community needs a common framework of employment law and certain rules relating to working conditions in order that the single market may work effectively. Since the most recent drive towards political union, the argument from Brussels has been that the EU must become 'closer to its citizens', a view which encourages an ever more important social role. The result of these pressures is that social policy now covers a wide range of individual policies with no less than five Commissioners and their Directorates having direct responsibilities for the items covered by this chapter.

The legal foundations for social policies are to be found in the Treaties of Rome (EEC), Paris (ECSC) and Rome (Euratom) as modified by subsequent developments. The Single European Act brought changes thought necessary because of the move to the single market while the Maastricht Treaty both widened responsibilities and sharpened up existing ones. While some treaty provisions are clear cut, others are of a very general nature and do not require legislation so much as political programmes with the result that at any moment there is a wide variety of social activities which demand different commitments from member states. One consequence is the growing overlap of interest with that of national authorities which leads to both cooperation and conflict. Although national governments remain primarily in charge in matters such as mainstream education, personal health care, the value of social security benefits and housing provision and national sources of finance are overwhelmingly important, it is routine for ministers to attend specialist Council meetings to agree both Community policy initiatives and joint activities in these matters. It is important, however, to retain a sense of perspective. Community interest is often marginal to the main body of work carried out nationally because it derives from economic objectives rather than a full-blown responsibility for social needs.

18.2 The Treaty of Rome

EU policy is shaped by two factors, the legal responsibilities of the treaties and subsequently agreed policies. Although it was usual to argue that the Treaty of Rome, setting up the EEC, was weak on the social side it was sufficient to allow much development. Firstly, it had general objectives of a broadly social character, such as a high level of employment and social protection and a raised standard of living. Secondly, Article 117 contained a recognition by member states of the need to improve living and working conditions and of their expectation that social policies would gradually align under the impact of the new system. There was agreement to collaborate in specific fields such as labour legislation, working conditions, vocational training, social security, industrial health and welfare and trade union and collective bargaining matters. Here the Commission was given the responsibility of promoting collaboration. In this way, scope for joint action was left open should the evolution of the EC require it but it was not considered inevitable that common policies would be required.

Thirdly, the question of the effect of social costs on competition was raised in 1957. The sensitivity of French industry on this point led directly to the principle of equal pay for men and women (Article 119). This has proved the basis for some significant policy developments. Fourthly, the belief that manpower was ineffectively utilized led to the setting up of the European Social Fund (ESF) whose aim was to help both occupational and geographical mobility. In addition, the treaty included an agreement to establish the common principles of vocational training.

The fifth item of great social significance was the adoption of the principle of the free movement of wage earners, along with rules to give it practical effect and to ensure the equal treatment of such migrants with indigenous workers. It was agreed, also, that rules would be necessary to allow the free establishment of the self-employed and for services to be provided across frontiers. These clauses gave rise to programmes of great complexity.

The free movement policy, together with its supporting policies of employment exchange collaboration, maintenance of social security rights and protection of equal working rights for migrants, was a major EC success although it owed much to the buoyant economic conditions of the time. Subsequent attempts to move the policy into the much more difficult area of social integration and social equality and to evolve a policy towards migrants from outside have been far harder to accomplish.

Sixthly, special protective measures, which derive from the appropriate treaties, were set up in the coal, steel and nuclear sectors. Not only is there a special concern for health and safety matters but, in coal and steel, pioneering work was done to operate a system of cash benefits and services for workers losing their jobs as the industries lost their pre-eminence in the economy.

18.3 The Single European Act and the Social Charter

The prime social aim of the SEA was to develop the provisions made necessary by the internal market although there were disagreements as to what these were. It also began the process of widening the concept of social policy. It made an important statement of principle in its preamble affirming the fundamental civil, political and social rights of citizens, drawing on the work of the Council of Europe for this. By doing so, it strengthened the EC's moral base and thus the hands of those who wished to see the EC play a more positive social role. A special section of the SEA supplemented the Rome Treaty. Article 118A agreed to pay special attention to better health and safety standards at work and to harmonizing standards while maintaining existing high ones. It reflected the fear that firms would be tempted to cut standards as they entered a more competitive situation. Minimum standards were to be introduced gradually by directives and passed by QMV in the Council of Ministers. At the same time, a cautious note was sounded by stressing that the conditions in member states must be taken into account and the needs of small businesses considered. Article 118B made the Commission responsible for encouraging a dialogue between management and labour at the EC level, which might, in turn, lead to formal agreements between the two sides of industry.

Certain reservations about the use of qualified majority voting continued. In the social field, unanimity was still required for free movement rules, for the rights and interests of employed persons and for the passing of directives which would require alteration in the methods of training for, and practice in, some professions. Article 100A referred to the need for the Commission to use high standards when regulating health, safety and environmental issues and when dealing with consumer protection.

Underlying these legislative provisions were considerable uncertainties. Some member states feared that, by having EC standards imposed upon them, their goods would be unable to compete, others feared pressure to lower their standards to meet competition from members with lower labour costs, and yet others feared the import of goods, livestock and plants that would introduce new forms of disease. Denmark added a special declaration to the SEA designed to ensure that it could continue with its own high standards. The United Kingdom was anxious to prevent the imposition of labour regulation which would damage the upsurge of small businesses and thought the social dialogue provisions would encourage the revitalization of trade union power which the Conservative government had been attacking at home. No solutions were found to these conflicts of interest but the SEA, by introducing clauses to satisfy everyone, made future conflict inevitable. This soon began to occur.

A new subsection introduced the concept of economic and social cohesion. Primarily concerned with regional policy and the support of the most backward Community members, it affected the use to be made of the ESF. Environmental issues were also brought under the EC umbrella for the first time.

The SEA gave a boost to the development of social policy. New initiatives to encourage language teaching, student exchanges, better vocational training and to establish health and safety norms soon began to appear and were broadly acceptable to member governments. However, the Commission was less successful in mobilizing support for proposals relating to working conditions. The opposition was led by the United Kingdom whose government disliked such formal controls over business and was suspicious of the opportunity offered by some of the proposals for the growth of trade union power but it also objected to what it considered a misuse of treaty powers in that directives were being proposed under cover of the implementation of the single market when they were not really necessary for this purpose. In consequence, they could be passed by QMV. The matter received great publicity when the Commission produced a Charter on the Fundamental Social Rights for Workers (Social Charter) setting out the proposed actions thought necessary in consequence of the single market. There were 47 initiatives in all, many of them non-controversial and some already agreed but others moved onto contested ground. In December 1989, the Social Charter was accepted by all governments other than the British and it became, not a legally binding document, but a statement of proposed action which the commission subsequently used as a document to organize its work.

18.4 The growth of social policy

Given the rather incoherent guidance of the early years, it is not surprising that the development of social policy was patchy. The first decade saw the major steps taken to implement the policy on labour movement, a formal adoption of the equal pay policy, a narrow exploitation of the ESF and considerable discussion of, study and research into labour questions but there was a sense of social policy hanging fire. However, a new impetus can be detected by the end of the 1960s when hopes in western Europe were high for social improvements and the EC benefited from this optimism. A widespread unease existed over environmental pollution, the problems of the disadvantaged, social inequalities and the increasing distance between the citizen and the services run by big bureaucracies originally developed to help the ordinary man and woman. There was a certain vacuum in social policy which enabled the EC to establish a role. The Hague conference in December 1969 agreed that the EC needed to go further in the pursuit of common economic and political goals in which a 'concerted social policy' would have a part. This line was continued by the Paris summit of 1972 which asserted the importance member states attached to vigorous action in the social field. Specifically, it referred to the need to widen participation in decision making and action to lessen inequalities and to improve the quality of life. The political momentum thus established led to the first social action programme (SAP). Its hopes were, however, quickly dashed by the onset of recession and the burden of large-scale unemployment and it was this that began to dominate social concerns as the EC experienced structural changes in employment patterns, including a rapid growth in part-time and shift work, together with formidable problems of long-term and youth unemployment. A major preoccupation for the EC became the need to analyze unemployment issues, to encourage cooperative action by member states, and to support programmes to help to overcome specific problems such as lack of training.

By the 1980s, a new momentum in the EC can be discerned, in which social policy had an important role. In 1981, the newly elected French socialist government had proposed a programme for a 'social space' for the EC and the following year the European Parliament called for a reform of the treaties and the achievement of a European union which would require a new policy for society. The entry of Greece, Portugal and Spain added another dimension by turning attention away from the urban problems of the more developed North to the importance of devoting resources to the characteristic problems of agricultural inefficiency, disguised unemployment in rural areas and lack of training for industrial work. The later entry of Austria, Sweden and Finland maintained the interest in social policy and brought the strong Scandinavian welfare tradition into the counsels of the EU.

The urge to establish the single market and the insistence that this must be accompanied by some steps towards cementing European union drove the Community towards a fresh consideration of citizen's rights. The European Council accepted two reports from the *ad hoc* Adonnino committee in 1985 which included a host of recommendations for building 'The People's Europe'. Some were new, others asked for current policies to be pursued more rigorously. Although some were implemented, others ran into difficulties.

18.5 The Treaty of Union

Subsequent to the passing of the SEA, controversy in social matters revolved round questions raised by the single market and, in particular, over possible extensions of European employment law. The Maastricht negotiations led to a totally unexpected result. Amended Articles 2 and 3 reiterated the social goals of the Treaty of Rome but in a broader, often more explicit, form. They now include respect for the environment, a high level of employment and social protection and the raising of the standard of living and the quality of life. Subsequent purposes include the free movement of people, measures concerning the entry of people, a continuation of the ESF and the policy of cohesion, a contribution to a high level of health protection, to education and training and to the flowering of culture as well as to consumer protection and to measures in the sphere of tourism.

Most importantly, the treaty establishes the legal concept of Union citizenship 'to strengthen the protection of the rights and interests of the nationals of the Member States'. Citizens have the right to move and reside freely, to vote and stand as a candidate in municipal and European parliamentary elections in all member states on the same terms as nationals (each right being subject to certain limitations). Citizens, when outside the Community, have the right to diplomatic protection from the services of any member state. They may petition both the European Parliament and the European Ombudsman. Directives are now in place to give effect to these political rights and the Ombudsman appointed. In the future, states may be penalized for violating these rights.

The novelty was that eleven (subsequently fourteen) states, excluding the United Kingdom, signed an attached Protocol and Agreement, popularly known as the Social Chapter (but see below). This affirmed their wish to continue with the Social Charter and clarified the goals contained in Articles 117–122. Article 1 of the Agreement reformulated social goals to include 'the promotion of employment, improved living and working conditions, proper social protection, dialogue between management and labour, the development and the combating of exclusion'. The Agreement made explicit that the Community is competent to act in the fields of the working environment, working conditions, equality of men and women concerning opportunities and treatment at work, the social integration of excluded groups and with regard to the information and consultation of workers. It established the right of the Council to pass directives on minimum standards by the use of qualified majority voting for matters of health and safety, working conditions, information and consultation, equality at work and the integration of those outside the labour market. The Council may also act, by unanimity, on social security and protection, protection of redundant workers, the defence and representation of workers' and employers' interests, employment conditions for third-country nationals, and financing of measures for employment and job creation (not the use of the ESF which is in the main treaty). Pay, the right of association and the right to strike and impose lock-outs are specifically excluded, while states may continue to provide specific advantages for women in order to equalize their working opportunities.

The Agreement strengthened the corporatist element in decision making through a stronger role for management and unions. Firstly, member states may delegate to the social partners the task of implementing directives relating to the above goals, secondly the Commission must consult them before submitting any formal social policy proposals and, thirdly, the Agreement recognizes that the social partners may be in a position to agree on actions for themselves. In addition, they can agree to ask for the formal structures to implement agreements they have reached. Some analysts see the clauses relating to the social dialogue and the role of the social partners as very significant, arguing that they signal a new way of applying doctrines of partnership, consultation and openness and of implementing the principle of subsidiarity. Although the United Kingdom opted out, its employer and union organizations are represented in the European umbrella organizations and so its voice is not entirely unrepresented and this is important as the consultation procedures are in constant use. The protocol was concerned with the use of the Community's institutions by the signatories to the Agreement.

The treatment of workers in flexible and part-time work and a change in the burden of proof in sex discrimination cases have both been referred for consultation under these procedures and other matters are pending but little actual legislation has been brought forward under the Agreement. This has dealt with matters left over from previous programmes where agreement could not be reached. In 1997, the new British government announced that it was now ready to accept the social Agreement which will thus be brought within the scope of the Treaty of Amsterdam and temporary arrangements will ensure full British participation in the work until the treaty is in force.

The Union treaty also brought changes regarding the entry of migrants. Most member states are under pressure from nationals of third countries at present and, in consequence, immigration and asylum policies are being re-examined. A new Article 100C gave the Council of Ministers the duty to determine the third countries whose nationals must be in possession of a visa, at first by unanimity but, from January 1996, by qualified majority. Emergency arrangements may be made to deal with a sudden inflow of people. Other aspects of migration are referred to in the provisions on cooperation in the fields of justice and home affairs (see section 18.16 below).

All in all, the Union treaty gave the EU more standing in social affairs, tidied up existing policies and made explicit where the Community had arrived in the execution of its work. This, in itself, helped to avoid future arguments about the legal basis of proposals with the one exception of the United Kingdom whose objections centred on some provisions of employment law and which have now been removed. The more significant developments are to be found in the broadened objectives and enhanced role of the social partners.

This chapter now turns to examine individual policies in more detail, reflecting the fact that unemployment is the major preoccupation of the moment. Since policies are run by the European Community but citizenship is a matter for the European Union, the terms EC and EU are used as appropriate.

18.6 European citizenship

It is logical to begin with the notion of European citizenship, introduced with the Maastricht Treaty. Its meaning is a mixture of ideas about the provision of legal rights and the development of policies to improve well-being. The reasoning behind the move was that political union requires an assumption of responsibility for the social condition of the people who are unlikely to support a Union which appears disinterested in their needs. The argument appeared justified when the unpopularity of the European project surfaced during the debates on ratification of the Maastricht Treaty. This heightened the belief that the EU must not only do more for the general public but must be seen to be doing so. A greater transparency of action, more efforts to inform the public of what was happening, taking decisions closer to the people and involving them more in decision making became aims to be met through greater publicity, closer relations with voluntary organizations and the use of procedures under the social Agreement. Of course, if the social dialogue is to be a means of reaching out to the citizen and to be a channel of influence on broader issues than at present then it, in turn, requires to broaden its membership. This remains for the future but it is worth noting that, in 1996, the Commission argued that the social dialogue could well be promoted at sectoral level leaving the European discussions to concentrate on strategic priorities. The more broadly these are defined, the stronger becomes the case for admitting representatives of voluntary organizations, the churches and local authorities to membership.

Political rights having being covered in the treaty, discussion has moved on to human and social rights. Despite the commitment in Article F to respect the European Convention on Human Rights and Fundamental Freedoms, the question is still raised whether the EU should formally subscribe to it. The ECJ has studied it more than once, concluding that, to do so, would require a full-scale treaty revision (Opinion 2/94 28.3.96). There are already a number of references to the importance of human rights in the treaties. Article F of the TEU refers to their importance in internal affairs while the provisions on a common foreign and security policy assert their significance for external matters. One of the objectives is to develop respect for human rights and fundamental freedoms abroad (Article J1(2)) while in their cooperation in judicial and home affairs members have agreed to abide by the European Convention. The Commission has set out its views on the protection of human rights within the EU and the priorities for action in 'The European Union and human rights: from Rome to Maastricht and beyond' (COM (95) 567). The Treaty of Amsterdam allows for the suspension of voting rights if a member fails to respect these principles. It is also usual to find that contractual ties with third countries make 'respect for democratic and human rights' an essential part of the text and the Commission is particularly watchful in the case of aspiring Union entrants and the recipients of development aid.

A closely associated view is that social rights should also be brought into the main treaty. When the social Agreement is incorporated this, in itself, will strengthen the social commitment. A 1996 forum discussion, with wide representation and sponsored by the Commission, was in favour of a charter of social and civil rights to be inserted in any new treaty and protected by the ECJ. A first list of eight rights would cover equality before the law, a ban on discrimination in fields of race, sex and religion, equality between men and women, free movement within the EU, the right to choose an occupation or profession, to choose to use any Union educational system and the rights of association, collective bargaining and collective action. Other rights were envisaged for the future as they involve costs and raise questions of resource allocation. They include the right to education, social security, work and a minimum income for all. These rights bear a close resemblance to those already adumbrated in the European Social Charter of the Council of Europe but would obtain greater force if part of the EU treaty system and the 1997 treaty has emphasized the importance of social rights. It also intends that the Council of Ministers should be able to act unanimously to combat discrimination based on sex, racial or ethnic origin, religion or belief, disability, age or sexual orientation.

The judicial cooperation procedures have led to a number of agreements which impact on the idea of European citizenship. Extradition can be difficult in the absence of common definitions for example of alleged political offences or membership of a proscribed organization and if the conditions are tighter when a state is asked to extradite its own nationals. Simplified procedures were agreed in 1995. Proceedings and sentences in criminal matters may require greater harmonization across the Union if they are not to create anomalies. Control over entrants to the EU and the extent of their ability to move freely within the Union were identified at Maastricht as requiring common rules. The 1997 conference agreed to strengthen judicial cooperation in civil matters and in the combating of crime and to establish common rules for the control of external frontiers. As many items are brought under the EC pillar so the control by the European institutions will strengthen at the expense of national ones.

At the Dublin summit meeting in December 1996, a programme to fight organized crime, terrorism and the drugs trade was agreed and moves were taken to curtail drug production and addiction. A European Drugs Unit, set up under Article K3 of the TEU, has joined Europol, the police agency created under Article K1. The latter has extended its remit to cover trafficking in human beings while common definitions of paedophile crime have been agreed. Although a single travel area for citizens has not yet been achieved, the Schengen agreement has been accepted by all but two members and will be incorporated into the EU. Although it will be some time before these agreements become fully operative they will begin to mould the concept of European citizenship in a meaningful way, clarifying the rights of qualifying individuals.

18.7 Free movement

An essential element of citizenship is the ability to move freely through the territory to which one belongs but, although great strides have been made, this does not apply fully in the EU and it seems generally accepted that it will be a long time before it does. The policy reflects the original economic objectives by growing out of the need to establish the free movement of workers. Piecemeal extensions have

been made which have brought in more categories of people but it is not yet possible to say that free movement of persons can be taken for granted.

The 1957 provisions were primarily concerned with the mobility of unskilled
labour and, in practice, were mainly of benefit to Italy. Today, matters look different. Movement within the EU takes place for many reasons. It may be a way of
escaping local unemployment, of filling skill shortages, of temporary posting from
one branch of a company to another or of a firm fulfilling a contract elsewhere in
the EU.

The essential structure to ensure free movement of wage earners within the EC of
six members was in place by 1968 or settled not long afterwards. The rules protected
the right to move for work and to remain in a country subsequently, gave entry
rights to families and elaborated a complex system for the maintenance of social
security rights. They also confirmed the right to join a trade union and to stand for
office, the right of access to vocational training and the right to use the employment
services. In this way, the principles of equal treatment and of ensuring non-
discrimination were accepted. Broadly speaking, these rules were applied without
undue difficulty. Individual cases of discrimination continue to find their way to the
ECJ, eligibility to social security benefits being a particularly complex area, but,
gradually, the rules have become better understood and observed.

It is necessary, of course, constantly to develop the rules as gaps are found or as
the nature of migration changes. Social security for the self-employed as possibilities for movement were opened up, rules concerning the right of families to move
and to receive certain benefits soon required attention. In later years, the movement
of skilled persons, managerial staff and professional people became more important.
These groups can be more affected by occupational benefits than by statutory social
security systems, especially for pension entitlement, or by the quality of housing,
availability of schools and leisure facilities and, although the EU has not become involved in all these matters, questions of transferability of occupational pension
schemes, the incidence of taxation on the transfer of monies and variations in taxation methods are all ones in which it has expressed interest.

Bringing vacancies and workers together was recognized as a necessity from the
start but proved a tremendously difficult project. It is much affected by the
efficiency of national employment services and by the existing procedures for job
descriptions, methods of achieving qualifications and the content of skills expected
by such qualifications. Great efforts have been made by the EC to bring some uniformity into these matters so that expectations on both sides match reasonably well.
Gradually, agreed European norms are being introduced into national qualifications
and into job descriptions without bringing standardization. The latest attempt at a
mechanism for matching up jobs and applicants was launched in 1994 (EURES)
while handling the exchange of information between social security systems has
been greatly developed (TESS).

The original principle applied only to the movement of workers and their families but this came to seem anomalous with the growing number of retired people
who might wish to move elsewhere and of students wishing to study in another

member state. Indeed, mobility in higher education is actively encouraged by the EU. The principle of a right of residence was seen to complement the introduction of the single market and, as is usual, is being implemented in stages. Three directives form the basis of extension. Directive 90/366/EEC covers students and their families for the period of education, Directive 90/365/EEC gives employees and self-employed people the right to remain and Directive 90/364/EEC covers all other groups. In all cases, the right is subject to the possession of adequate financial resources.

There are, however, still problems to overcome to ensure that workers benefit as they should from EU policies. Problems are still reported, for example concerning access to training or the application of the principle of equal opportunity while in the host country (COM (90) 108 final). In practice, the right to obtain work in the public sector is often restricted, for example by applying a nationality rule to areas of work which are unconnected with the exercise of public authority in any way. The tax treatment of those who live in one country and work in another or the workings of an early retirement scheme may penalize a migrant while there is a general need for coordination between the rules for occupational and supplementary pension schemes, especially now that these are becoming more important. Technical formalities are often formidable but there are plans for a standardized EU Resident card for the automatic renewal of a residence permit, including for those whose work is interrupted by unemployment or ill-health.

Free movement of the self-employed and the ability to supply services across frontiers were both written into the original treaty but were very hard to apply owing to differences of standards of training, in its content and in the way services are provided in different states. Sometimes the right to supply services has been qualified by rules concerning nationality, place of origin or where qualifications were obtained and dismantling such barriers without damage to standards is a highly technical matter. The application of rules to ensure conformity of national qualifications can take many years and in the meantime other barriers can be used to avoid letting non-nationals practice. Disputes, such as that of non-French ski instructors barred from access to work on French ski slopes, can rumble on for years.

The EU has, therefore, always been interested in the comparability, and mutual recognition, of qualifications as a necessary precondition for the mobility of labour and of the self-employed. In 1985 the Council of Ministers agreed that the mutual recognition of qualifications must be speeded up and directions were provided on how to establish comparability (OJC, 264/83; OJC, 208/84). A ruling from the ECJ made it clear that many university courses could be considered as vocational training and that students from all member states must be admitted on the same terms as nationals (*The Times*, Law Report, 4 April 1988) and this also helped to open up the issue of the content of professional courses. It is generally accepted, however, that it is a field of great complexity and there is a long way to go before a full transparency and understanding of qualifications is obtained.

The health sector saw some of the early work since basic training could be harmonized to a degree to allow for movement for some doctors, nurses, dentists, veterinarians, midwives and pharmacists. Other professions followed but it became necessary to adopt a general directive for the recognition of professional standards of university level and above, other than those already recognized by existing sectoral directives (Directive 89/48/EEC). This established a general right to practise, subject to the right of the state to apply limited tests to ensure competence. This was complemented by a second directive (Directive 92/51/EEC OJL 209/92) designed to cover a wide range of education and training courses, including on the job training in some instances, but where specific qualifications are not laid down (Commission *Opening up the Internal Market* 1991).

18.8 Employment

There have been striking changes in the labour force of the EU since 1957 (see the latest issues of Eurostat *Review* and EC *Employment in Europe* Annual). It is very much bigger as the population of working age has grown, women have come into the workplace and the EC has enlarged to become the EU. Further increases in membership are foreseen. At the same time, the employment structure has altered. One of the most dramatic changes has been in the growth of information and communications technology both as a new industry and as a business tool. Often, however, the new growth is not geographically well placed to absorb redundant workers who, in any case, would need new skills, while the jobs it offers are frequently part-time or temporary, taken by women rather than men. Overall, the EU does not generate new jobs at a rate comparable with that of the USA and Japan and the European rate is inadequate to absorb the larger labour force. It is always hoped that the major economic policies of the Union, such as the single market and economic and monetary union either directly or indirectly will create jobs but, often, taking advantage of developments means that workers must be more mobile and more highly trained than heretofore. It is obvious that there are great linguistic and cultural barriers in the EU to worker mobility and, meanwhile, there is a serious mismatch of jobs and workers which implies high unemployment rates. Within the overall picture, there are higher than average rates of unemployment among young people and, in most countries, women and a seemingly intractable problem of long-term unemployment. A great deal of time is devoted to these questions by European policy makers.

It has proved hard for states to grapple with the new situation and particularly difficult for the EU to find a positive role since it operates at one remove. Nevertheless, employment is so central to the work and significance of the EU that it has found ways of developing a wide range of policies to deal with particular employment issues. In 1957, the Treaty of Rome referred to the promotion of a high level of employment and at a time of prosperity the Community could devote itself to specific tasks, such as the free movement and equal pay policies. As the pace of change accelerated and unemployment seemed composed of a number of difficult subissues, doubts were expressed as to whether western Europe would ever again experience very low unemployment rates. Voices were heard suggesting that the treaty required a new goal with a definite commitment to promote employment and in 1997 it was agreed to give employment a higher treaty profile. A new employment chapter asks the Community to promote high employment through a coordinated strategy which includes training a more highly skilled workforce, guidelines for member states to follow, encouragement to best practice and annual assessment of the situation. Employment considerations should, in the future, influence new policy decisions. A limited financial support will be given to experimental initiatives and the EIB asked to encourage small and medium-sized businesses and new technological activities which are the main job creators. An employment summit will be held in 1997, a new employment committee created and a resolution on growth and employment is to buttress the stability pact accompanying the policy for economic and monetary union.

During the 1990s a number of documents set out the agreed positions and what might be done by members and by the EU to help with the supply of jobs and to assist individuals to obtain the necessary training and qualifications to fill them. Among them the White Paper on Growth, Competitiveness and Employment of 1993 (COM (93) 700 final) was something of a turning point, helping to elevate employment to a place in the highest EU counsels. It referred to a necessary re-orientation of labour market policies to meet new competitive requirements and stressed the significance of the arrival of a knowledge-based information society and the new jobs it was bringing. Subsequently, the Essen Council meeting of December 1994 agreed major policy lines which have been kept going by later summit meetings. A marked policy shift moved away from the traditional approach of income support for the unemployed as the main service available to the belief that far more had to be done to match people's qualifications to the jobs of today and tomorrow. It stressed that individuals must be actively encouraged to enter, or to return to, the labour market.

At the Essen meeting states agreed on the need for more investment in education and vocational training, the importance of increasing the employment intensity of growth, notably through the re-organization of working time, moderate growth in wages and opening up new areas of employment. They accepted the need to reduce indirect labour costs, to increase the efficiency of labour market policy by moving towards active measures and by targeting services onto specific groups of job seekers.

Studies show that, even today, the so-called passive benefits cost states more than the active, individualized measures. Nevertheless, the European effort is put into the support of schemes for the unemployed which encourage job seekers to (re)train, to look actively for work, to persist in job applications and to help to make themselves more attractive to employers. Traditional employment services need to change themselves if they are to provide these new types of assistance.

If growth itself does not provide a sufficiency of jobs, then governments have to consider what they can do to support more labour-intensive work. Society has a significant demand for service jobs, notably in environmental improvement, child care and social services, while it may be necessary for some time to come to ensure that some vacancies remain for unskilled workers. Since it is small and medium-sized firms that have the better record in job creation it is worthwhile considering how to help them to prosper. A main theme for the Commission has been to encourage local initiatives, employment intensive growth, to help with training and extra costs and to help firms to overcome legal obstacles which face firms who wish to take on someone who has been unemployed for some time.

Subsequent summits have continued to stress the importance of job creation and effective measures to help the unemployed. By 1996, the Commission had devised 'Action for Employment. A Confidence Pact' as a way of ensuring that states keep these questions at the top of their domestic agendas. It discussed ways to help small and medium-sized businesses and to support local initiatives, still seen as the most useful areas for job creation, and backed the idea of pilot projects. The overall approach was of an employment-friendly strategy, primarily based on investment in physical and human resources, in knowledge and skills and in ensuring an entrepreneurial environment quite different from earlier objectives relevant to previous working patterns.

The EU supports a number of institutional structures designed to keep the question of employment under review and to ensure that interested parties remain committed to the task of job creation. A long-standing Employment committee is still the main forum for bringing the views of the Council, Commission and social partners together on an employment strategy although the social dialogue under the Agreement is also relevant here. A newer Employment and Labour Market Committee aims to monitor employment trends and to keep the Social Affairs Council up to date with developments (OJL 6/97). The Employment Observatory links national organizations together in a mutual support structure and provides regular information on employment trends and on developments in national strategies.

18.9 The European Social Fund

The principal weapon which the EU possesses to combat unemployment directly is the ESF which operates through grant aid to approved schemes of vocational training and employment support. It has undergone several reforms and extensions and today is part of a more coordinated effort to fight unemployment. Its work is primarily concentrated in poorer regions and countries as part of a targeted effort by all the structural funds which are increasingly considered together. Nevertheless, a reference to the past may help in understanding the complicated arrangements.

The ESF started in a limited way and primarily assisted migrants from the Italian south to move north into the industrial areas but a subsequent reform, in 1971, created a larger and more flexible fund which could be used to help with training and which gave special attention to the needs of particular groups of workers or regions. By the 1980s it was felt that the fund needed further adaptation. It began to concentrate upon work to promote the employment and training of young people under 25 years of age and, subsequently, of the long-term unemployed. By 1985, grants were also available to members of both groups wishing to set up in self-employment. Grants to special groups such as the handicapped, women workers and migrants continued, as they still do, but were no longer earmarked. Employment in small and medium-sized businesses was encouraged and special grants were introduced to aid vocational guidance and placement. The most deprived regions continued to receive special aid but otherwise the fund directed its efforts to areas of persistently high unemployment and where large reconstruction projects were required.

Much of this work was formalized following the SEA. Perhaps the most important effect was the recognition of the need to pursue economic and social cohesion as a goal which would offset the possible disadvantageous effects of the single market in some areas. A master regulation was agreed (EEC/2052/88) which established that the European Regional Development Fund, the European Agricultural Guidance and Guarantee Fund (Guidance section) and the ESF, now known jointly as the structural funds, should coordinate their work and should work closely with the European Investment Bank as well. Objectives applicable to all funds were laid down and these, with some modifications, remain in force. The first two relate to work in the lagging regions, frontier regions and those in severe industrial decline. Objective 5a concentrates on the agricultural and fishing industries and 5b on the economies of vulnerable areas. Objective 6 was recently created for sparsely populated outer regions as in Finland and Sweden. In addition, the ESF has two goals specific to itself in Objectives 3 and 4. The former is directed to the long-term unemployed and opportunities for young people. Priorities for 1997–99 are to help to create pathways to work for people aged 25 years and over, to help young people to get a good start, to provide equal opportunities for men and women in the labour market, to provide assistance to the Community development schemes and to support the most disadvantaged groups. Objective 4 grants are to help workers who need to adapt to industrial change by giving aid to training for workers threatened by unemployment so that they may adapt to structural changes as well as by aiding companies to enable them to train their workers so that they may increase their competitiveness, improve the qualifications of their staff and develop new jobs within the company, thus staving off unemployment. The objective is particularly innovative for the ESF as it allows assistance for retraining for workers who are still in work although in danger of losing it. In practice, the work of the ESF is concentrated in the vulnerable regions under Community support frameworks owing to the pressure on the budget.

10% of ESF monies is handled directly by the Commission and used to support cross-frontier schemes and innovative experiments in job creation.

The emphasis for the ESF is very much on training which is linked more closely to employment vacancies than was once the case. Indeed the White Paper on European Social Policy (COM (94) 333 final) listed three priorities for its work. The first was to help to improve the quality of education and initial training and to facilitate access by target groups to vocational training. The second was to help to increase competitiveness and to prevent unemployment through the adaptation of the workforce. This has led to an emphasis on continuous training and to the concept of lifelong learning. The third is to improve job prospects for those threatened by long-term unemployment and socioexclusion for whom the concept of the 'pathway of re-integration' has been coined. Throughout, special attention is given to the provision of equal opportunities for men and women with a degree of special training for women.

The post-1988 system also brought important changes in administration. The ESF had always been criticized for being slow and cumbersome and there has been a shift towards making schemes find their place in an overall national plan which can then be approved in Brussels. The emphasis is on partnership between the Commission, member governments, local authorities and other representatives who should together formulate multiannual programmes to their mutual satisfaction and which should give a necessary stability of finance to individual schemes. The Commission, instead of being involved in the minutiae of scheme approval, is expected to develop its monitoring, control and evaluative functions. This arrangement has put far more control into the hands of the central national agency, usually the Department for Employment or its equivalent, which acts as a channel for the submission of applications and disbursement of grants. Administratively, this arrangement works much more smoothly than when the Commission was involved in the detail of schemes and it can, of course, be argued that national authorities know their own needs best but one obvious danger is that the Commission is less able to impose its views on how grant aid should be used. Since it tends to be forward looking with an interest in the spread of new skills and in grasping the opportunities of technological change it may clash with national representatives who are often under pressure to maintain jobs in declining industries or to support new schemes of job creation as an immediate method of reducing unemployment irrespective of long-term viability. Such clashes of priorities will clearly continue.

A further difficulty facing the Commission is to ensure the principle of additionality. The intention has always been that, by insisting upon matching grants from member states, more work is actually done than otherwise would have been the case but whether this is truly so often remains a mystery.

The ESF has become a significant part of the EU structure especially now that its mandate has broadened to enable it to play a role in delivering a highly skilled and adaptable workforce. It has begun, in a small way, to reach out beyond the immediate confines of work by recognizing social factors which inhibit potential workers from coming forward and thus it is beginning to play a part in the prevention of social exclusion and to reflect the view that disadvantaged people must be helped to become self-supporting. It is, however, a long way from becoming a true social, as opposed to a work-related, fund (COM (96) 502 final for 7th *Annual Report on the Structural Funds*).

18.10 Education and vocational training

From the start, the EEC had certain responsibilities in the field of vocational training and these have led to its gradual move into educational work. The dividing line between training and education is increasingly hard to draw since it is now believed that, in the past, educational systems were too divorced from economic reality so that many young people left school ill-prepared for the world of work. A further impetus has come from the need to reconsider the content of training in order to equip the labour force with the higher skills that industry requires. The Community, no less than member states, is in the process of adapting to these new requirements and trying to make its services appropriate for the needs of the day. At the same time, more attention to education and training provides an opportunity to encourage greater awareness of the EU and its objectives among the rising generation (see COM (95) 590 final) *Teaching and Learning: Towards the Learning Society* and COM (96) 389 final *Living and Working in the Information Society: People First*).

The Maastricht Treaty revitalized the legal base for action in the fields of education and vocational training (Articles 126, 127). It refers to the Community's role being to contribute to quality education while fully respecting the responsibilities of member states for educational services and their cultural and linguistic diversity. Educational action is aimed to develop a 'European dimension' through helping to improve language skills, to increase mobility and exchanges among students and staff, through work to ensure the recognition of qualifications, to promote cooperation between educational establishments and long-distance education. Similar phraseology surrounds the vocational training policy which is designed to support and supplement national efforts through encouraging adaptation to industrial changes, improved training and retraining and facilitating access to it, greater mobility and cooperation between instructors, training establishments and trainees.

A new drive on education and vocational training policy was symbolized by the White Paper on *Education and Training: Towards the Learning Society* (COM (95) 590). Its themes are linked to the need for a better quality of education, a spread of qualifications throughout the population and work to make national systems more comparable. Since states themselves are actively engaged in recasting educational and training systems, the Commission's role is to act as a stimulus, to help to set up schemes and to encourage their development in ways which help to cement the EU. A special interest is to foster innovation and effective use of technology through the encouragement it can give to young people, the learning of new skills and the transfer of knowledge.

Following the White Paper the Commission regrouped the many programmes it was running into three main groups. Its *Youth for Europe* scheme continues in an expanded form. This arranges youth exchange schemes, short visits and voluntary participation in common projects in order to increase European awareness. *Leonardo da Vinci* is concerned with vocational training. Like Youth for Europe it includes Norway, Iceland and Liechtenstein and will extend to cover Central and Eastern Europe, Cyprus and Malta. Placement and exchange schemes enable those in training or on university courses to obtain work placements in another member state with the aim of improving vocational training and promoting language skills. A particular interest is for placements in the use of information technology.

It was as early as the 1970s that the Commission became aware of the problem of young people leaving school inadequately prepared for work and it began to encourage schemes to provide better pre-training preparation for them. At the same time, it established the European Centre for the Development of Vocational Training (CEDEFOP), now in Thessaloniki, to encourage greater awareness of training needs and learning opportunities and to act as an information and resource centre. The Centre has a series of agreements with other European states to ensure a basic compatibility between all training developments. In similar vein, a European Foundation for Training, in Turin, maintains links with CEDEFOP and acts as a channel offering similar support to the countries of Central and Eastern Europe, the ex-Soviet states and Mongolia. One particular problem is that some states need to prepare their training systems for the hoped-for closer association with the EU and this aim requires considerable change and a great deal of effort to improve fluency in at least one EU language.

Thirdly, the *Socrates* programme, which again includes Norway, Iceland and Liechtenstein, has responsibilities in higher education. Student exchanges figure prominently with a special interest in language studies, joint courses and teacher exchanges. The aim is still to have 10% of the student population spending some time abroad so as to create a growing pool of graduates with EU experience for the future but this target has not yet been reached. A newer venture is to support university courses which wish to introduce a European element into courses which are not formally joint or exchange schemes but which will, nevertheless, include a measure of joint cooperation. A system of Course Credit Transfer is being developed which should make student mobility easier over time and this, in turn, may well lead to a greater uniformity in course content with the benefit of making it easier for courses followed to be recognized.

The main innovation recently has been the *Comenius* programme covering the secondary school years. Here the aims are very similar, being based on the development of partnerships between schools which may cooperate in language and other subject teaching; this is made easier by the growth of computer networks and fast communications. Children of migrants and itinerants have been able to benefit for many years from language and introductory courses which have been grant aided through the ESF and these are now operated within the *Comenius* scheme.

Language teaching at all levels is today supported more strongly than ever with the aim of seeking proficiency in three Community languages for younger generations. This depends critically on being able to offer opportunities in other member states for language teachers and teachers in training. Improved teaching material is to be offered and the use of open learning techniques encouraged. Support for courses in European studies in adult education is beginning.

The *Eurydice* network to provide information and the exchange of experience continues as do other informative services. A new office for education statistics has been created and the *Iris* network for the exchange of information on women's education is maintained.

A particular effort is being made towards Central and Eastern Europe, including the ex-Soviet states and Mongolia, to aid the reform of higher education. For the relevant states, this is believed to be a necessary preliminary to membership of, or association with, the EU. The projects are becoming more varied as different national needs are identified but it is considered important that universities, in general, should open up to outside influences. A rough division can be made between the group of states from the ex-Soviet area and Mongolia, the group preparing for membership of the EU or at least some form of pre-membership for whom the need for change in educational and training systems is in known, specific ways, and a third group. Their membership is a very long way off but their geographical position demands sympathy for their aspirations such as the states of ex-Yugoslavia (other than Slovenia which falls into the second group) and Albania. Contacts with the universities of western Europe, the provision of teaching materials and an increased mobility for students and staff are all important.

A clause in the TEU decreed that the Community should contribute to the flowering of the cultures of the members. Its particular tasks are to concentrate upon encouraging cooperation between member states, improving knowledge about European culture and history and conserving the cultural heritage of European significance. As a result, the Commission has a range of initiatives relating in particular to the last-mentioned goal (*Raphael*) and to promoting knowledge of European literature (*Ariane*). The work programme includes designating European cities of culture. One of the most contentious issues has been the use of television and, with the increase in the number of channels, whether transmission should give some priority to European programmes. Despite efforts to make it mandatory to devote half viewing time to European productions it appears likely that the EU will persevere with voluntary quota systems.

18.11 Consumer policy

The Maastricht Treaty gave consumer protection the status of a full policy (Article 129) which the Amsterdam Treaty will strengthen. The single market raised the problem that consumers simply would not know how to judge the quality of goods bought unless minimum standards were applied, would have difficulty in obtaining redress for faulty goods, would not understand what was being offered by a service and so on. Much depends on making sure that the public has full information about goods and services on offer but recent worries over food safety (bovine spongiform encephalopathy) and the lack of information provided through food labelling (genetically modified maize) suggest that a good deal more has to be done. The Consumer Committee gives direct access to the Commission for national consumer organizations but consumer representation is poorly developed in the southern states and in central and eastern Europe. The Commission has recently created a new food safety division in DG XXIV in response to the beef scandal.

A directive and recommendation on direct selling and an improved directive on misleading advertising are slowly moving through the EC procedures. A time share directive was adopted in 1994 and the general product safety directive of 1992 is now in the hands of states to implement. A database on home and leisure accidents has been extended until the end of 1997 and some protection is given on the use of computer-held personal data (*Consumer Protection in the EU – Progress and Priorities for the Future*, Backgroumd Report ISEC/B12/96).

18.12 Working conditions and industrial relations

Collective bargaining remains a matter handled within member states and it is only gradually that industrial relations acquired a European dimension which the Commission has welcomed although some of its initiatives have met with fierce opposition. From the Community's point of view, three themes stand out which, in day-to-day affairs, are often tangled together. There are the beliefs, firstly, that it is important to involve employers' associations and unions in the operation of the EC, secondly, that consultation, or even cross-Community negotiation, may be essential in particular cases and, thirdly, that an integrated market may require some changes in traditional national arrangements.

The Paris and Rome Treaties established certain formal structures, notably the ECSC Consultative Committee and the EEC Economic and Social Committee to associate representatives of employers and labour (and other groups) with EC affairs. Subsequently, various advisory committees, such as that for the ESF, were constituted with joint representation: many joint committees meet to consider the problems of a particular industry as required (and see references to institutional structures in section 18.8 above). Another route has been through a Tripartite Conference which tried to establish a dialogue between finance, social affairs ministers and the social partners. However, none of these methods proved entirely satisfactory and the dialogue became more tense as unemployment grew and both sides became more defensive in their attitudes. The Commission President, Jacques Delors, was a prime mover in attempts to give the 'social dialogue' more prominence, seeing it as one way in which trade union and business opinion can be mobilized behind the process of European integration.

The theme of consensus between the social partners, leading to agreed policies to improve working conditions and social security benefits, is a long-standing one in some Continental systems of industrial relations but is alien to others. The British government, in particular, during the 1980s, disliked both any attempt to give the social dialogue a formal place in Community affairs and the greater legal regulation of industrial matters to which it can give rise. Nevertheless, the UK agreed to a new Article 118B in the SEA which gave the Commission the duty to develop the dialogue between management and labour at European level. The treaty recognized that this could, if both sides agreed, lead to formal arrangements between them. Later pressure to take this further was resisted by the United Kingdom. Hence the new provisions on the social dialogue under the Maastricht Social Agreement (see section 18.5), which carry the promise of a bigger role for the social partners, were a major stumbling block for the United Kingdom, now removed.

A recent addition to the machinery is the European Industrial Relations Observatory set up in 1997 primarily to study questions of the workplace, to establish a database and to keep national centres in touch with developments across the Union.

How far regulation of working conditions by the Community is made necessary on moral grounds, on economic grounds to ensure competitive fairness or simply on political grounds to meet demands from powerful interests has never been resolved. Although in recent years it has been a major bone of contention, there now exists a body of European legislation which is in the process of being bedded down. It is not expected to grow a great deal during the next few years. Some of this is extremely precise and detailed but some is more of an outline which member states are expected to apply themselves. This is particularly true in health and safety measures.

In the early 1970s, a particular form of job loss came through a spate of takeovers and mergers, often connected with the growth of multinational companies. Here the EC felt it could claim a particular interest and successfully passed directives on the procedures to be followed in the case of collective dismissals (Directive 75/129/EEC), the maintenance of employee rights when companies merged (Directive 77/187/EEC) and the protection of rights when a firm became insolvent. Revision of the first one has been agreed (COM (91) 292 final) and the second one replaced (COM (94) 300). However, some judgments of the ECJ have thrown the rules on the maintenance of rights when the ownership of a firm is transferred into serious confusion (see *Financial Times* 12 March 1997). Subsequent attempts by the Commission to pursue higher standards of employment law proved less successful and a succession of proposals relating to worker participation in decisions and disclosure of information to the workforce, to parental leave and to leave for family reasons were either dropped or postponed. However, more recently, there have been signs of agreement on a number of regulatory matters. Limits on working time were the subject of a proposed directive in 1990, being agreed in principle by the Council of Ministers in 1992 and finally adopted in November 1993 (Directive 93/104/EC OJL 307/93). An objection by the UK that the directive should not have been presented as a matter of health and safety but under Article 235 in which the Council of Ministers must act unanimously was rejected by the ECJ in 1996. The directive ensures a weekly rest period of one complete day, rules for annual holidays which must be a minimum of four weeks by 1999, the need for a break after six hours work, a maximum working day of eleven hours and night shifts whose average maximum is eight hours. Already revisions are under discussion to try to limit the large number of exempted posts. These include workers in transport, sea fishing and doctors in training. Managers may be exempt apart from the annual holiday clauses and governments can find ways of shielding some industries, including the media, agriculture and the utilities. Collective agreements may be used to modify the rules. Workers can volunteer to work for longer hours (at least until 2003) and some flexibility exists in working out the 48 hours by averaging out the hours worked over a period from four months to one year. The impact is expected to be variable and the rules are so elaborate that to get round them will probably not be difficult. It is thought that small firms will be the most disadvantaged (*Economist* 16 November 1996, *Financial Times* 2 November 1996).

A proposal on the protection of pregnant women at work became law as Directive 92/85/EC (OJL 348/92). A directive on the provision of proof of an employment contract (Directive 91/533) was agreed but a proposal to safeguard the conditions of workers temporarily posted elsewhere in the Community dragged on until 1996 (Directive 96/71/EC OJL 21.1.97). It applies to firms which post workers to another member state and to temporary employment agencies engaged in hiring out labour in another member. Its aim is to allow workers to benefit from the working conditions operative in the state to which they are posted subject to certain exemptions. States have until February 1999 to implement it.

A long-drawn-out project has been to ensure the information and consultation of workers in Europe-wide firms through the setting up of Works Councils or their equivalent. Apart from disagreements about the substance of the proposals there have been practical difficulties about how to implement them. Real differences of national practice and interest appeared involved as well as a clash between the conception of a single market as one of deregulation and free enterprise or one in which the future requires the prior agreement of the social partners and a framework of European employment law. The quarrel led to the first directive under the social Agreement (Directive 94/45/EC OJL 254/94) which became operative in December 1996. It covers firms with at least 1000 employees, operating across borders and with at least 150 employees in each of two countries or more. It aims to give employees a degree of information about, and influence on, operations. British companies with staff elsewhere in the EU had to comply if they fell within the rules as did non-EU firms. Some affected British companies included their British staff as it was simply more convenient to do so and most companies which believe in consulting their workforce do so in ways which conform to the rules so that signing the Agreement is unlikely to have much effect. Existing arrangements registered by 22 September 1996 were acceptable and many British firms met this deadline; 140 agreements had been registered by July. An advantage of a voluntary agreement is that the details can be more varied but, in the last resort, eligible firms may have the form of agreement imposed upon them. British companies subject to the directive include BT, Coats-Viyella, Pilkington, GKN and NatWest. The directive seems to have been accepted without much difficulty and employer hostility fell away when it became clear that voluntary agreements, which many firms had anyway, were acceptable.

The present Commissioner (Mr Flynn) has proposed that similar consultative procedures should be applied to all companies, excluding only those with but a handful of employees. The current proposal comes in a very flexible form with a list of minimum requirements. In addition, provisions for consultation which will be suitable for inclusion in the suggested statute for a European company and which have been discussed for a quarter of a century are now being revived and have a chance of acceptance.

A directive on parental leave (Directive 96/34/EC OJL 148/96) also demonstrates the Social Agreement at work. A framework agreement was produced by UNICE, CEEP and the ETUC and subsequently submitted to the Commission to be put up to the Council of Ministers for adoption in June 1996. Men and women are entitled to three months unpaid leave to be taken before the child's eighth birthday and to time off for urgent family reasons. It sets out minimum standards only and stresses the importance of not using the directive to level down or to indulge in discriminatory practices, makes states responsible for compliance and allows them to fix penalties for infringement. It will apply in the United Kingdom in due course.

The encouragement of employee asset holding and profit sharing was done through a recommendation (COM (91) 259 final) and a directive to give better health and safety protection for part-timers (COM (90) 22811 final) was adopted in June 1991.

Employment difficulties are acute for the disabled and handicapped. The Council passed a recommendation in 1986 stressing the importance of providing fair opportunities for training and employment and setting out a model code of action. A proposed directive (COM (90) 588 final) lays down rules to assist workers with motor disabilities with travel to and from work in employer-provided and public transport (see also section 18.15).

Another long-standing issue is the question of whether European controls are needed over the conditions of part-timers and those on temporary contracts. The Commission has long held the view that they should be employed on the same terms as full-timers on a *pro rata* basis including the same chances of promotion and access to the same range of benefits. The social partners have been negotiating on flexible working time and worker safety, looking at the many new forms of work now offered. This in itself is a more modern and flexible approach to a difficult subject which accepts that atypical employment has become the norm for many people and can, if handled carefully, even produce a better balanced lifestyle as long as it can be developed without exploitation. Agreement on contractual rights for part-timers (whether on permanent, temporary or fixed contracts but not casual workers) has now been reached but awaits adoption. It covers occupational pension rights, paid occupational sick leave, staff discounts and paid holidays.

18.13 Health and safety

The protection of industrial health and safety stretches back to 1951 when the ECSC established a programme of research and standard setting. Special Commissions were created for the steel industry and for mining, the latter including offshore oil wells, and a large number of recommendations have been issued. The Euratom treaty gave the Commission power to establish precise standards of protection in the nuclear industry while monitoring of the amount of radioactivity in the environment is carried out under Article 36. Industrial health and safety was included in the Treaty of Rome as one of the matters on which the Commission might encourage collaboration and it developed an active programme of research and recommendation as a result.

Over the years, EC interest broadened. Its span extended to include environmental pollution and issues of protection and conservation. Meanwhile, the EC edged towards a clearer role in community health with an emphasis on preventive programmes, interesting itself in questions such as the effect of modern industrial lifestyles on human welfare, the social costs of night work, the incidence of alcoholism and drug abuse and of social scourges such as cancer and AIDS. The ever-increasing cost of social security, of which health care forms a large part, pushed the EC into taking a greater interest in the specific question of the costs of personal health care.

Much of the work reflected the fact that there are many problems which can no longer be dealt with in a national context. Thus basic standards to protect both the general public and workers against ionizing radiation were published in 1980 and updated following the Chernobyl accident. An outline directive on the protection of workers against the use of dangerous substances was agreed the same year and was followed by one concerned to protect against the hazards of a major accident, this following the chemical disaster at Soveso, Italy. This directive is being replaced by an updated version, Directive 96/82/EC OJL 10/97, which must be fully operative by February 1999. All such factors meant that health ministers found it advantageous to meet together and to set up cooperative and joint programmes.

The drive to the internal market renewed interest in industrial health and safety standards if only because of their possible effect upon the new policy. The act took the path of agreeing to minimum standards, to avoid placing an excessive burden on small and medium-sized businesses, and accepted that no state should be forced to lower its existing standards. A framework directive was passed to cover all main sectors of activity and setting out the duties of employer and employees. This provided the context for more specialized directives dealing with particular industries. However, it remained a difficult field in which industrial change required a faster momentum of work in order to keep pace, control and monitoring had to be made effective and the growing number of public complaints handled. It became clear, too, that interpretations differed as to what subjects should be included in terms such as 'the working environment' and 'health and safety'. The Maastricht Treaty made it explicit that the Community has a duty to contribute towards ensuring a high level of health protection (Articles 3(0), 129) and singles out disease prevention, including drug dependence, as a main field of interest by encouraging research and information and educational programmes. However, these can lead to awkwardness. It is often pointed out, for example, that support of research into the ill-effects of nicotine and the drive to discourage consumption sit ill with subsidies to tobacco growing under the CAP.

Community health problems are constantly changing and the EU, by virtue of its responsibilities in both health and the free flow of goods, necessarily takes on new subjects as demonstrated by the question of the import of American products containing genetically modified maize and of British beef exports once BSE had been identified. The need for better data and informational programmes seems set to grow and a five year programme for health action was established despite arguments over its financing (see COM (95) 282 final *Medium Term Action Programme for Health and Safety at Work 1996–2000*).

Although some enthusiasts would like to see minimum standards of health care established, the EU does not have a responsibility for personal health care but it does have an effect on service provision. The free movement policies have meant the need to establish the mutual recognition of the qualifications of health professionals some of whom now have the right to practise anywhere while others still do not. EU citizens who trained outside the EU are not normally covered although bilateral arrangements may overcome this problem. In practice, movement is on a small scale because administrative barriers abound, hidden discrimination is reported and linguistic difficulties are genuine.

The free movement of citizens may have a greater impact on the patients than the staff should they begin to move to obtain treatment. For some years people have been entitled to treatment if they fall ill when visiting another member state, special schemes cover some groups of workers, for example transport workers or students, and cross-frontier services have become acceptable although in a controlled way. There is, as yet, no explicit right for people to travel to seek help but it can be arranged while there are examples of cross-frontier agreements with hospitals to supply surgery where there is pressure on beds. There are other interesting questions looming, for example whether the growth of private health insurance should develop to cover care in another member state and whether a prescription issued in one country should be honoured in another. Although the legal basis for action is limited, there are considerable pressures towards seeing EU health policy expand in the future and the Amsterdam Treaty has inserted a new chapter on public health to encourage Community action.

18.14 Equal treatment of men and women

Work to improve the position of women, both socially and economically, has proved one of the most positive policies. Starting from a limited legal base, the EC was able to exploit the absence of effective national policies and to become an important influence on their development. Unusually in social affairs it had a relatively clear field which allowed it to adopt a leadership role for which its position makes it well suited.

An equal pay policy was written into the Treaty of Rome at French insistence.

France already had a legal requirement for equal pay and its industrial costs were assumed to be generally high. There remained, however, a noticeable lack of enthusiasm about the enforcement of the treaty until the 1970s. Some publicity had been attracted to Article 119 by the problem of a Sabena air hostess who had lodged a complaint in Belgium concerning the inequality in her conditions of service. The question of her pay led ultimately to a consideration by the European Court of Justice which made clear its view that Article 119 was meant to be taken seriously and properly applied. One result was to spur the Commission to produce a directive on equal pay in 1975 (Directive 75/117/EEC OJL 45/75). This included a definition of equal pay, to include both identical work and work of equal value, established certain controls and required an effective appeals system. It therefore provided a much·stricter framework within which member states had to apply the policy.

It soon became clear, however, that by itself this was a reform of limited value if women were to achieve equality at work. Apart from the need to clarify the concept of equal pay, which is gradually being done through court judgments, men and women had very different social security coverage and Directive 79/7/EEC (OJL 6/79) required the progressive implementation of the principle of equal treatment over a six year period. There were still certain exclusions to the rules, notably for family and survivors' benefits and member states could still continue some differences if they wished. The most important was the right to continue with different ages for retirement pensions although, in practice, this difference is slowly disappearing. In 1986, the principle of equal treatment was extended to cover occupational schemes and provision for the self-employed (Directive 86/378/EEC OJL 225/86 and 283/86). This directive was intended to ensure equal rights in the private sector by 1993 subject to some latitude allowed for differences in life expectancy. An important ECJ judgment in 1990 (Case C–262/88) held that occupational pensions are to be considered as part of pay and, therefore, that the rules of Article 119 apply. Different ages for eligibility for such pensions cannot be used although the judgment is not retrospective to the date of the case. Employers appear to be reacting by raising the age for women's eligibility rather than reducing that for men.

The Commission has been anxious, for some time, to see a new directive on social security to include benefits still outside the scope of EU directives, notably to include equal treatment for the sexes in retirement and in claiming benefits for dependents. It would also like to move the legal basis for entitlement to that of an individual's rights rather than deriving rights from the concept of dependency and this would put many women workers in a very different position from the one they hold today. Progress on these two moves is slow.

Underlying questions of pay and social security is the whole question of women's position in the labour force which is still less favourable than that of men. Women in practice earn less, often because they are concentrated in low-skilled and low-paid work, much of it part-time and in industries particularly vulnerable to unemployment. These factors may result in an indirect discrimination which is much more difficult to remedy through Court rulings.

Recognition of the lack of equal opportunities to obtain work and of equality of treatment at work opened the way to a variety of EC support programmes. These have ranged from a consideration of the types of education offered to girls to the importance of effective support for the working mother through more flexible hours and the development of child care facilities and the need to encourage men to take on more household chores. Thus EC policy has, for some years, followed twin paths. On the one hand have been measures to ensure legally enforceable rights and, on the other, programmes to encourage a fuller social and working role for women. Equality of treatment for men and women in the labour market and the need to pay more attention to the balance between employment and family responsibilities received a modest priority in the first Social Action Programme and resulted in a directive to establish equal opportunity with regard to employment, job recruitment, promotion and training (Directive 76/207/EEC OJL 39/76). In 1995, the so-called Kalanke judgment by the ECJ (Case C–450/93 Preliminary Ruling 17 October 1995) raised fears that affirmative action was illegal if two candidates, a man and a woman both equally qualified, applied for the same post in a sector in which women are underrepresented. The Commission, believing that it was the idea of automatic preference being given to such a woman candidate to the neglect of other relevant factors such as individual circumstances, proposed an amendment to the directive to specify the kinds of positive action that are permitted but the Council has, so far, been unwilling to accept it. Equal treatment in self-employment has been begun by Directive 86/613/EEC (OJC 113/84).

Attempts to strengthen, and equalize, the position of workers taking parental leave, or leave for family reasons, were persistently blocked but they are a useful reminder that an equal treatment policy may sometimes require more rights to be given to men (see section 18.12 above). A Council recommendation on the need to develop child care facilities for working parents and for those taking courses was passed in 1992 (OJL 123/92).

The ESF has always been interested in grant-aiding schemes which help women at work and these have been important in raising the level of understanding about women's needs. Upgrading work through better education and more appropriate training have been encouraged through the NOW programme. Grant aid has been given to help women return to work after child rearing, to enter posts normally filled by men, to train for work using new technologies and to finance child care facilities and to give help to the female entrepreneur. The fourth Community Action programme on equal opportunities for men and women (COM (95) 381 final) runs from 1996 to 2000 and sets out current ambitions.

The Commission has submitted a draft directive on the provision of the burden of proof in sex discrimination cases before industrial tribunals. No longer, it argues, should the complainant have to carry the entire responsibility to prove a case but should be required to submit strong evidence of discrimination which the employer would then be expected to rebut. It is also working on a code of practice to encourage the wider spread of equal pay and intends to submit proposals for a Council recommendation to speed up the entry of women into decision-making positions. A guide to the prevention of sexual harassment at work was agreed some years ago (OJC 157/90) and the possibility of further action leading to a binding measure is being studied as well as the need for a help and advisory service. Further work is necessary on the individualization of social security rights and on taxation assessments.

The Commission is attempting to set an example in recruiting women to posts of greater responsibility, hoping that states will follow suit in their public sectors. Targets have been set for directors, heads of units and administrators in the Commission staff. Finally, the commitment to promoting equality between men and women has been stressed in the Treaty of Amsterdam and agreement reached on the importance of eliminating inequalities.

18.15 Social exclusion

The limited social responsibility of the early treaties and the emphasis upon economic integration left the EC open to the charge of weakness in social policy. Criticism mounted in the 1960s as the darker side of affluence was exposed. The marginalization of many groups including the inhabitants of the inner cities, migrants, elderly and disabled people made it clear that the EC itself had small scope for action to ameliorate the conditions of the most disadvantaged although it pursued active policies of encouragement to member states. Special mention of disability has been made in the Treaty of Amsterdam.

An important factor in clarifying the role of the EC arose through the strain put upon social security policies as unemployment rose, the number of retired people grew rapidly, pressures on health care mounted and governments attempted to restrict social security expenditure. At the same time, schemes needed to adapt to the growth of part-time and flexible working, to the changing position of women and to new health needs. A considerable study programme was launched by the Commission which included consideration of the argument that the single market would require an alignment of social security costs and benefits. Although this is not accepted as a necessary goal, the EC has accepted a recommendation (COM (91) 228 final) on the ultimate convergence of objectives and policies in view of the similarity of many of the social problems now faced by member states. At present, these include the funding of long-term care, early retirement and sustaining pension commitments. It continues to report on the trends in social security and is anxious to maintain the debate on the wider subject of social protection (COM (95) 457; COM (95) 466).

There has been some interest in the proposition that the EC should seek to establish a basic minimum resource level but this has, so far, proved impossible to define and is far from being politically acceptable. The Council of Ministers did, however, accept a recommendation in 1992 that states should provide a guarantee of basic assistance with effective administrative measures (Recommendation 92/442/EEC OJL 245/92).

An anti-poverty programme was included in the first SAP as a result of an Irish in-itiative. This gave rise to interesting experiments and drew attention to the need for, and difficulties of, cross-national research. Grant aid for projects helping groups in poverty concentrated on new, and sometimes unorthodox, procedures and drew the Commission into close, direct contact with social reform movements and local authorities and associations. Programmes, however, have not been continued owing to political objections of an ideological and financial nature. Some elements such as the networks and the research projects are continuing and there is a degree of com-pensation through the projects funded through the ESF. This requires greater preci-sion in the use of grants through a focus on urban projects and on vulnerable groups. Some of the activities of the anti-poverty schemes, such as its concern with housing, health or mobility programmes and which were not directly concerned with (re)insertion in the labour market, are more difficult to replicate. The encour-agement of a multidimensional approach, the use of partnerships to ensure effective cooperation between local actors and active participation of excluded groups them-selves are not aims which always fit comfortably with the ESF whose competences are not broad enough to encompass all the aims of the anti-poverty approach (COM (93) 435 final).

For some years, disabled people have been a group eligible for aid from the ESF for training and, in addition, the third action programme (*Helios II* 1992–96) had a budget of 46.3 million ECUs (COM (91) 350 final). This meant that grants were available for tasks such as access to creative activities, sport and tourism, integration in nursery schools and functional rehabilitation. An emphasis was placed on the use of new technology as an aid to integration, independent living, and education and training. The programme was recently refreshed by a new disability strategy in-tended to place activities within the broader goal of equal opportunities and full participation in social life for all. The Commission has suggested that member states should commit themselves to a resolution on equal opportunities for disabled people through the use of the structural funds, mobilizing the work of non-governmental organizations (NGOs), improving access to employment oppor-tunities and using information technology to pursue equal opportunities (COM (96) 406).

Elderly people, too, have become a group in which the Community is interested. They are, of course, affected by many general EC policies, notably the extension of the free movement policy to allow retired people to spend their later years anywhere in the Community or rules to control atypical work. Problems connected with aging have figured in the health research programmes and a small action programme (1991–93) was set up to exchange knowledge, ideas and experience. At present, the Commission is very involved in setting up networks and encouraging a dialogue be-tween itself, NGOs and independent experts. A new support programme has been submitted to the Council for a decision (COM (95) 53 OJC 115/95) but has run into problems similar to those facing the anti-poverty programme.

18.16 Migration and Asylum

The creation of the EEC, and more particularly the passing of the SEA and the Maastricht Treaty, progressively distinguished people entering the EU as migrants from EU nationals moving across national frontiers and from people moving from one area to another within one state. Yet the reasons for movement are often similar, being rooted in employment, and may present similar problems of family reunion, new working patterns, finding adequate housing and schooling as well as language difficulties. The scale of migration, from whatever source, during the 1960s brought anxieties about social integration but member states were wary about allowing the EC a competence in some of the more sensitive areas of domestic policy. As migrants came from further afield, cultural gaps became more evident and pressures on local services increased in congested urban areas.

By the late 1970s, the Commission had begun to question the value of large-scale, uncontrolled migration. The situation became further confused as unemployment grew, member states began to ban the entry of non-EC nationals, work permits expired and many third-country migrants decided to stay in the EC illegally rather than risk the possibility they would not be allowed back when conditions improved again.

EC policy made uncertain progress at this time with the Commission limited to encouraging states to extend to all the improvements resulting from the free movement policy. It made all migrants eligible for grants from the ESF and tried to improve the education of children through grants for induction courses, language teaching and special training for teachers. These attempts remained on a small scale and it was anyway difficult to see the lines of an effective policy when settlement policies were so different, ranging from that of the United Kingdom which received migrants from the Commonwealth expecting to stay for permanent settlement to Germany with a great influx from Turkey whose workers were expected only for a short while and for whom issues of family settlement were, at first, of less importance.

Current estimates suggest that there are between twelve and fourteen million legally resident 'third-country nationals' in the EU. By no means all of them are in a vulnerable position; their legal rights will vary from state to state and according to country of origin. It is clear, nevertheless, that many of them are still not fully part of the society in which they now live and that problems are being inherited by the second and third generations. The Netherlands has recently announced that it will be trying a more forceful type of assimilation policy through a plan to make attendance at induction and language courses compulsory for long-term migrants although exemptions apply to EU nationals, foreign businessmen, academics and those on short-term contracts (*Times* 30 November 1996).

A European Migrants Forum now exists to lobby in the EU while the Council of Ministers has set up a Consultative Committee to monitor the expression of racism and xenophobia which has seen a disturbing rise in recent years. The European Parliament, in particular, has urged the EU to take a stand against such phenomena and a number of declarations have been issued. 1997 has been designated as the Year against Racism, Xenophobia and Anti-Semitism, a Monitoring Centre is to be set up, the Commission is supporting projects designed to promote good relations and a move exists to insert an anti-discrimination clause into any revised treaty. The Commission is also urging all states to provide legal protection against the various forms of discrimination which exist. Meanwhile the Justice and Internal Affairs Council, meeting in March 1996, reached agreement on legal cooperation in order to prevent infringements of national rules against public incitement and the circulation of racist literature and the Amsterdam Treaty should ultimately lead to greater protection.

New immigration on a large scale is no longer thought of as desirable and the Commission's view is that emigration needs to be controlled through cooperation with sending countries and will lessen if the EU helps to create jobs at home (Background Report ISEC/B6/1992). It is still likely, however, to attract better-qualified migrants, people who wish to set up in business, students in training and, no doubt, other special groups and the question remains of what EU action is necessary. Members have accepted that immigration is a matter of common interest so the way is open for more agreed policies. In particular, it has been realized that, with the abolition of internal frontiers, travel for non-EU citizens becomes much easier. The only satisfactory final outcome is for residents' permits and visas to conform to general principles and to become valid for the whole of the EU. A start has been made with a Council resolution in 1996 which dealt with the factors, such as income and health, to be considered when states authorize long-term residence. It has been suggested that such residents, not holding EU citizenship, should have preference over third-country nationals when it comes to recruitment and the EP argues that such populations should have the same rights as EU citizens.

Recent moves towards common rules have also been seen in asylum policy. These have become acceptable not just because of the very large number of recent applications whose claims are often confused but with the realization that the existence of a single market means that all states are affected by the policies of the receiving state. Sudden large influxes of refugees have thrown great burdens on services in receiving states but also mean that states are now more reluctant to grant refugee status while the long delays in processing asylum applications have led to distress and difficulty. The 1990 Dublin Convention, which should be ratified by all EU members by the end of 1997, made a single state responsible for examining an application for asylum on the basis of objective criteria (subject to the rights of other states if they are particularly affected) and allows for the exchange of information on asylum activities. In 1995 the Council agreed on a harmonized definition of a refugee, minimum guarantees for asylum procedures and a resolution on burden sharing to help with temporary problems. In 1997, it was agreed that decisions on immigration and asylum policy should pass to the Community although decisions will continue to be subject to unanimous vote for at least five years.

The abolition of internal border controls raises the question of the effective policing of the external frontier and no subject has required more soul searching in recent years. If the state of first entry is lax then criminal elements, terrorists and unwanted migrants gain easy access and can pass anywhere within the EU. As a fore-runner of a single system, a group of neighbouring states signed the Schengen agreement in 1985, outside the EU treaties. This has now been signed by thirteen members and is operative in seven, creating a frontier-free zone within which people can move freely. The 1997 IGC agreed to incorporate the agreement into the Treaty of Amsterdam so that it will be part of the EU arrangements in which decisions on immigration and asylum will be taken by unanimous vote for at least five years (see Chapter 2, section 2.6). A proposed directive is designed to ensure that controls on people crossing frontiers are eliminated.

18.17 An overall view

The range of topics discussed here shows how diverse the social concerns of the EU now are. At first sight, they can appear as a miscellany rather than a single coherent policy but this is inevitable given the range of modern social policy. A hard core of matters relating to employment is the bedrock of Community social policy. Although there is agreement that some minimum standards are necessary to support the single market policy, there is strong suspicion that some proposals are covert measures to protect national markets from the competition that the single market is designed to bring and it is unlikely that there will be a swift resolution of this difference of view.

One difficulty in standard setting is that precision is often impossible and all that can be achieved is agreement on a general principle which then must be interpreted and applied in a host of different circumstances and it is undoubtedly difficult to ensure that such agreements are effectively applied and do, in fact, achieve a comparable result. Often it is a case of changing attitudes, encouraging developments in similar directions and explaining current best practice and the Commission is in a favourable position to carry out such tasks. A further noticeable feature is the support that it gives to research, investigations and pilot schemes which normally have cross-national elements and attempt fresh approaches to old problems.

During the 1970s, it was agreed to set up three European institutes for study and research. In 1977, CEDEFOP began work to give new impetus to a common policy of training through the harmonization of national systems and to promote new initiatives. In 1975, a Foundation for the Improvement of Living and Working Conditions was set up in Dublin. Finally, the Council agreed to support a project of the European Trades Union Confederation to set up a European Trades Union Institute for the study of union affairs. A more recent development has been to set up Observatories to monitor and analyze social policies and to encourage mutual understanding of national policies and cross-national networks. Observatories exist, for example, for family policies, aging and older people, policies to combat social exclusion and employment. A recent addition is the Industrial Relations Observatory to work closely with the Dublin Foundation.

Many of these activities may be classified as educational and promotional. For the specialist circles that are involved they play an important part in enhancing mutual understanding. Grant aid in the social field may still be small compared with the scale of national spending but for some of the poorer countries it is very significant, for example the ESF grants for training. Even in countries where it is less important in amount, it is, nevertheless, money that governments like to have and, however grudgingly, they do adapt their activities to conform to EU ideas.

Social policy has developed in the shadow of economic policies. At the time of the SEA it was described as a flanking policy to the introduction of the single market and the obvious need to deal with the social consequences of intended action provides a strong argument for the development of social standards. However, some argue for the establishment of a 'European Social Policy' rather than a social policy of the single market and this is linked with the demand for a full European citizenship based on fundamental and social rights. The Social Agreement appears to strengthen the right to pursue goals of social justice and makes it clear that directives may be used in relation to some of them. The incorporation of the Agreement into the Amsterdam Treaty, together with a new stress on social goals, should further strengthen social policy. Whatever happens, and such changes are dependent upon the political evolution of the EU, a glance back to the early days of the ECSC shows how far social policy has come and that there is now a European dimension in health, social security, equal pay, working conditions and many more social fields. There is no reason to suppose that this process will come to a halt.

Supranational social responsibilities are constantly clarified through the activities of the EU. It is in an excellent position to identify the processes of economic and social change occurring in western Europe and to suggest responses to them. Often such changes require similar national reactions but these do not always have to be standardized. Insofar as major economic policies bring adverse social consequences for some people, it seems only fair that the EU should shoulder the responsibility of mitigating them. However, arguments are as lively as ever as to how far its actions need to go, whether EU legislation is necessary and what should be left to national governments.

A fruitful source of disagreement over appropriate functions seems inevitable as the Commission works out its ideas of subsidiarity, participation and partnership since it is evident that, in many social matters, both national governments and the EU have valid concerns. The Commission needs to be in touch with local and regional authorities, voluntary organizations and citizens' groups and may easily tread on national sensitivities as central governments try to hold on to their position as the conduit through which relations with the Community are handled.

The growth of an international society is also affecting the methods of handling social policy. The 1996 version of the Council of Europe's Social Charter embodies ideas also to be found in ILO conventions and bears a strong resemblance to the moves towards equal opportunities, more information for workers, greater participation in relevant decisions and protection for the elderly which are so much of the EU's current interests. Contacts with central and eastern Europe bring awareness of other social priorities and methods of approach while developing countries often find it helpful to discuss with the Commission their plans for social security and educational development. The recent discussions in the World Trade Organization show that social standards have reached an international scale. Multilateral and bilateral cooperation are now widely practised but have grown in an *ad hoc* way which might now benefit from systematization.

It is clear that the EU does not have a social policy whose *raison d'etre* is large-scale resource redistribution but one that depends on many relatively small-scale programmes, framework agreements, legal rules and a multiplicity of efforts to align attitudes, to share experiences and generally to encourage social progress. A broader question remains to be fought over. It becomes increasingly difficult to envisage an EU which has developed politically without a stronger commitment to ensure citizens a place in society, in which human rights are protected and institutions effectively democratized. The 1994 White Paper on Social Policy pinpoints the values which are shared between members and which are at the basis of the EU's social policy as democracy, individual rights, free collective bargaining, the market economy, equality of opportunity, welfare and solidarity. It is still struggling to determine what, in practical terms, it needs to do in order to promote them on the grounds that member states are no longer fully competent to do so alone.

chapter nineteen

EU environmental policy

A. MARIN

19.1 Background

For a long time it was not clear whether there was any legitimate basis at all for an EC policy on the environment. In the 1950s there was no influential generalized concern for the environment. Occasionally, a specific particularly harmful episode of pollution would give rise to remedial action to deal with the specific problem, but no more. For example, in the winter of 1952–53 there was an even denser than usual smog in London, leading to a dramatic increase in mortality among the elderly and bronchitic. As a result, following an inquiry, new laws were introduced to allow the control of domestic coal fires. But the episode did not lead to a more widespread concern with air pollution generally. The same attitude was prevalent in other countries at that time. Hence, the Treaty of Rome made no provision for any joint EU policy on controlling pollution, let alone more general environmental conservation.

By the end of the 1960s, however, a new attitude which led to demands for new policies had become widespread. Although, perhaps, not initially as strong as in the United States, noticeable numbers of people in western Europe had begun to express concern over degradation of the environment. There were various strands, not always compatible, within the burgeoning 'environmentalist' movement, both in terms of the issues of concern and of the political outlooks of those most prominent.

There were various organized groups who had an effect on EC environmental policy, especially where they gave a stronger crusading force to the aspects of environmental concern which had most influence on policy. Some were the groups who stressed ecology and preservation. It is not simply that they have eventually succeeded in getting enough votes to have some 'Green Party' members in the European Parliament (MEPs), as well as representatives at national and lower levels; some national governments have felt obliged to be seen to be responsive to public opinion on environmental issues, in order to try to keep the Greens from gaining enough seats to be a threat to the government majorities. These governments, initially primarily the German and Dutch, have an extra incentive to support EU environmental policies.

The areas which seem to be of general concern to the wider public (and where the Green movements have sometimes provided the impetus) are partly the preservation of natural amenity and wildlife, and, more importantly for EU policy, pollution. The change from 1957 is that pollution is seen to be a general, ongoing, problem. Concern may be heightened by particularly harmful and/or well-publicized cases, for example the disposal of toxic waste from Seveso, but it is now considered that action should not be limited to reacting to such cases but should be introduced to control harm before blatantly dangerous situations occur.

As a result of the changes in attitudes just outlined, in October 1972 the heads of government (prompted by a report from the Commission earlier that year) called for an EC environmental programme, which led to approval in November 1973 of the *1st Environmental Programme 1973–78*.[1] This has been followed by subsequent programmes up to the *4th Programme 1987–92*. The 5th Programme has no formal concluding date, but is supposed to cover the period up to 2000.

Despite the agreement of the heads of government to an EC programme, and thus to a commitment to joint policies, for some years there was doubt as to whether there really was a legal basis for issuing directives in this area. The doubts were particularly strongly expressed within the United Kingdom.[2] On several issues (as will be detailed later), the UK approach to pollution control differed sharply (or so it seemed in public statements) from the majority view among the other member states. There were some who proposed a challenge to the legality of the directives – although a recourse to the ECJ was never, in fact, pursued.

The official basis for actions that were clearly not foreseen in the Treaty of Rome was twofold. Firstly, a few of the types of pollution dealt with could result from the use of goods, for example, noise and exhaust emissions from vehicles, or packaging and labelling of solvents. In these cases, joint EC standards could clearly be justified as part of product harmonization to prevent different national standards acting as a non-tariff barrier to interstate trade.[3] However, many of the directives concerned types of pollution and environmental standards that could not constitute a hindrance to interstate trade on any reasonable criterion, such as the quality of bathing (i.e. swimming) water or the hunting of wild birds.

The second basis claimed for EC environmental policies would justify joint policies on all types of environmental concern, even where trade is unaffected. Article 2 of the Treaty of Rome stated that 'The Community shall ... promote throughout the Community a harmonious development of economic activities, a continuous and balanced expansion ... an accelerated raising of the standard to living.' It was claimed that measures to protect the environment could be considered to further a balanced expansion and raised standard of living, given the importance now attached to the environment by public opinion and the extent to which people's sense of well-being was threatened by pollution and environmental degradation.[4]

No legal challenge was ever mounted to the Community's right to make decisions on the environment; the matter is now beyond dispute. In 1986, Articles 130R–130T were inserted into the Treaty by the SEA. These Articles are explicitly devoted to the environment; see Chapter 18 for more on this and other developments.

Furthermore, according to Article 100A, actions taken to further the 'completion of the internal market' are supposed to take as their base a high level of environmental protection. In addition, allowance is made for individual member states to set higher environmental standards, provided that these do not constitute barriers to trade – this allowance and the proviso may require further decisions by the ECJ to define the acceptable boundaries. Conflicts can also arise over whether particular directives should be treated as relating to production harmonization (therefore falling under Article 100A concerning the internal market) and thus subject to majority voting or as environmental protection (therefore falling under Article 130S) and requiring unanimous agreement. Decisions by the ECJ in several disputes about the correct Article to use seem to be somewhat contradictory. The amendment of Article 130S at Maastricht further extended majority voting to some aspects of environmental policy, but still left room for ambiguity over whether Article 100A or 130S should be used in some cases.

The SEA, Maastricht and, especially, Amsterdam Treaties increased the power of the European Parliament. This can also lead to stronger EU policies on the environment and the adoption of stricter standards. The European Parliament is generally considered to be more concerned about environmental issues than the Council. This is partly due to the Green MEPs, but seems to affect MEPs of other parties as well. There has been one case where pressure from Parliament clearly helped to push the Council to take stronger action: Parliament's amendment in April 1989 of the Council's proposal on exhaust emissions resulted in more stringent limits which could be met only by using catalytic converters on all cars. Given the general movement towards environmental consciousness in the preceding year, the previous opponents of stringent limits (especially the United Kingdom) were not prepared to face the odium of no action at all as a result of rejecting the Parliament's amendment.

Whatever the legality according to the unamended Treaty of Rome of EC directives on issues affecting the environment, there still remains the question of why the governments of the member states wanted a *joint* environmental policy at all, on those aspects where individual national policies would not be a barrier to trade and where transfrontier flows of pollution were not a problem. (As already indicated, the small group which could lead to barriers could be dealt with under the procedures on product harmonization.) It is never possible to be completely sure what is in people's minds, but discussions at the time and subsequently suggest two primary motivations.

Firstly, statements by EC leaders often stressed that it was felt to be important that, if there were to be public support for the European ideal, the EC should be identified in the minds of the public with issues with which they were concerned. It should not be thought to be limited to 'boring' technical issues, whether product standard harmonization or the minutiae of calculating transports costs between Rotterdam and Duisberg. Joint EC policies on an issue which had recently become the focus of much media discussion and campaigning would help to convince the public that the Community was relevant to them and responsive to their worries.

Secondly, it was clear to governments in member states that they would have to respond to public pressures over pollution and environmental preservation. This was especially true of the German and Dutch governments among the original six, but the others were not immune either. Many of the measures which would be required were likely to raise production costs. For example, firms would have to install new equipment rather than just pouring noxious waste into rivers or sewers, or would have to buy the more expensive low-sulphur fuels to limit emissions of sulphur dioxide. If some countries were to have tighter standards than others, then their firms would face 'unfair competition' from firms that had lower production costs just because they were located in countries that had laxer requirements on pollution abatement.[5] Uniform emission standards (referred to as UES in the literature) would prevent this threat to competitiveness. Hence the desire of governments for joint EC environmental policies which would affect all member states equally.

19.2 Economic (or economists') assessment of environmental policies

In order to judge the appropriateness of EU environmental policies, it is necessary to have criteria. The criteria used elsewhere in this book are primarily (although not exclusively) those of standard neoclassical welfare economics.

For the policies examined in this chapter, equity – at least in terms of income distribution – has not been a major consideration.[6] However, it is worth noting that one difference between the approach of many environmentalists and that of many economists is related to the standard assumptions of welfare economics. Economists tend to judge policies and institutions by their effects on the welfare of individuals.[7] Environmentalists, however, often feel that some things are worthwhile even if no humans are affected. They place a value on the diversity of natural habitats and the continuation of species, even where there is no benefit to humans. By their training, many (although not all) economists are resistant to such a view.[8]

There have been few EU policies which deal with protection of species *per se*. One exception is the 1979 directive on the conservation of wild birds, augmented by a directive on habitat protection. Some have argued that the directives on water quality for rivers and estuaries containing fish or shellfish are not just to protect human health but also to protect the fish *per se*. Another, limited, exception is the 1985 directive requiring an environmental impact assessment before certain large development projects are undertaken. This exception is limited, both because the types of project requiring the assessment are largely left to national governments and because, once the assessment has been made, there is no requirement for any weighting to be given to adverse environmental effects in deciding whether the project should proceed. There are also EC directives concerning other endangered species (seals and whales), but, although motivated by environmental concerns (and the repugnance at the methods of killing seal pups), these formally deal with trade in the products of the species.

Most of the EC environmental polices have concerned pollution in some form.

For economists, pollution is a problem that cannot be solved by the market mechanism because it is an externality. Indeed, most textbooks on microeconomics use pollution as the classic example of an externality. One way of viewing externalities is that they are cases where the actions taken by one economic agent (individual or firm) affect others, but where there is no feedback mechanism leading the agent to take correct account of the effects on others. It is not the existence of an effect on others that constitutes an externality, but the lack of incentive to take full account of it. Every economic action may affect others, but in a well-functioning system the price mechanism provides incentives to take account of the effects.

For example, when deciding whether to drive my car to the shops or walk, in reaching my decision I use my car only if the benefit is greater than the price I have to pay for the petrol. If the price equals the marginal cost (the usual criterion for Pareto optimality), then I will use my car only if the benefit is greater than the cost to society of the scarce resources used up in providing me with the petrol. Hence the price system provides me with the correct incentive to take account of the effects of my action (driving my car) on others (using up scarce resources, which are therefore not available to provide somebody else with that petrol). However, if the use of my car pollutes the air and causes annoyance, or more serious harm, to others, there is no incentive for me to allow for this. I could be said to be using up another scarce resource (quiet and clean air), but I do not have to pay for it. Hence, there will be times when I use my car even though the benefit to me is less than the true cost to society, i.e. the sum of the costs of which I take account (the petrol) plus those of which I do not (the pollution); the result is therefore not optimal. Thus another, exactly equivalent, way of expressing an externality is to define it as when the marginal private cost is not equal to the marginal social cost.[9]

There are two diagrams which are often used to analyze the problem of pollution and to indicate possible policy solutions.[10] The first one concentrates on the divergence between social and private cost, usually in the context of a competitive industry which causes pollution during the production of some good. In Figure 19.1 the supply curve of the industry is, as always, equal to the sum of the marginal (private) costs of the firms. Given the demand curve, Q_0 is produced and sold at a price of P_0. This is not optimal. If the pollution emitted during production is allowed for, the true sum of marginal social costs for the firms is given by MSC, and the optimal output is where $P = MSC$, i.e. at Q_1 and P_1.

Figure 19.1 has the advantage of stressing that part of the result of pollution in production is that the price to consumers is too low and therefore consumption is too high. Conversely, any policy to achieve efficiency will involve a higher price and less output and consumption. It is therefore not surprising that both employers and trade unions in the industries affected are sometimes among those opposing particular EU policies to control pollution. Nor is it surprising that, in some countries of the EU (possibly in contrast to the United States), the importance attached to environmental policies declined in the second half of the 1970s and early 1980s. The rise in unemployment led to more stress on the reduction in output that might result from pollution control measures,[11] an example of the more general point that

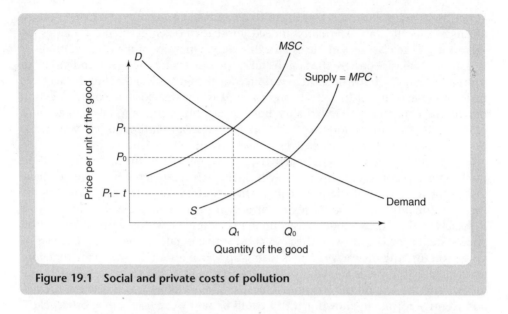

Figure 19.1 Social and private costs of pollution

if displaced workers are not confident of finding alternative jobs easily, then employment becomes an aim in its own right and policies are not judged solely by the total consumption of goods (even allowing for the 'consumption' of 'bads' involved in pollution).[12]

As a means of analyzing policies to control pollution, Figure 19.1 has the disadvantage of neither explicitly showing what happens to pollution nor showing whether pollution can be reduced by means other than a drop in production of the final output of the industry. For these reasons, an alternative diagram is now often used, which draws attention to these aspects, although it has the disadvantage that the implications of Figure 19.1 to which we have drawn attention are left implicit, and may therefore be inadvertently downplayed.

In Figure 19.2, the pollution is measured explicitly. For convenience, we have drawn the diagram with the abscissa measuring pollution abatement from the level that would occur with no policy controls. Some authors use pollution emissions instead. This is equivalent to Figure 19.2 working leftwards from the 100% abatement (zero remaining pollution) point. The diagram shows the abatement of some particular form of pollution for some particular industry. The marginal benefits (MB) of pollution abatement are the avoidance of the external costs placed on others – health, annoyance at noise, loss of amenity, etc. The marginal costs (MC) of pollution abatement to the firms in the industry are the costs associated with various abatement techniques, such as the treatment plant for noxious effluents in our earlier example, as well as the loss of profits if emissions are reduced by cutting back on the level of output of the final product sold. The approach in Figure 19.2 draws explicit attention to the possibilities of using other resources (labour, capital) to

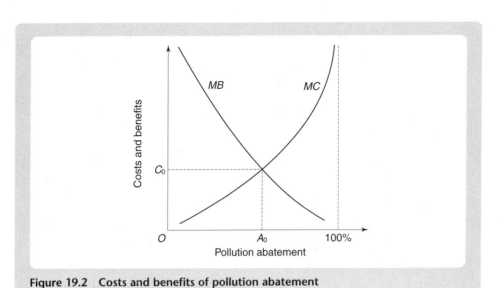

Figure 19.2   Costs and benefits of pollution abatement

reduce emissions (unlike Figure 19.1 which is usually drawn on the assumption that the externalities associated with each level of output are fixed).

The shapes of the marginal benefit and cost curves in Figure 19.2 follow from what is known for many types of pollution – some abatement is often easy but, when 95% of potential emissions have already been removed, removal of the remaining 5% is usually much more expensive. On the benefit side, the marginal curve is usually drawn downward sloping, although the justification is less well founded and there may be some forms of pollution (especially affecting amenity) where the downward slope is not correct; for example, once a line of pylons has been put over a previously unspoiled mountain range, any further developments do less marginal harm. However, most of the EU pollution policies deal with worries about effects of pollution on human health, and for this the downward MB curve is usually reasonable (as it is for the policies on sulphur dioxide and some car exhaust emissions where the motivation is also partly human, partly the effects on forests).

In some cases it is suspected that there may be thresholds of pollution below which the body can cope, but above which harm may start. In these cases, the MB curve may have the shape in Figure 19.3.

Returning to the more general case of Figure 19.2, one important policy implication of this way of analyzing pollution is that there is an optimum level of pollution. Except in very special cases, it is not optimal to aim for the complete elimination of pollution.[13] Less than 100% abatement is desirable. The optimum level, which maximizes welfare, is where the marginal costs of further abatement just equal the marginal benefits, level A_0 in Figure 19.2. This is an implication of the economists' approach which is uncongenial to some in the Green movement.

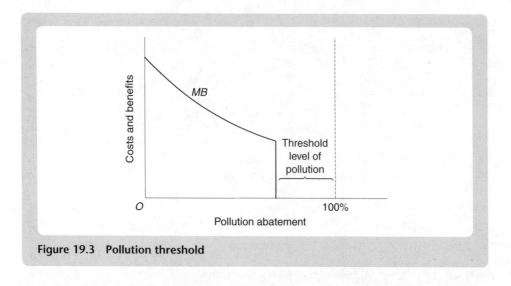

Figure 19.3   Pollution threshold

EU policies have followed the economists' approach on the whole. In the early years of EC action there were some clashes between member states. The United Kingdom, in particular, advocated its traditional policies, summed up in such expressions as 'best *practicable* means' of pollution control. The notion of 'practicable' involves a weighing up of costs and benefits – although this balancing seems always to be implicit rather than explicit and to rely on the intuition of the relevant inspectorates. The United Kingdom feared that at times the other member states were proposing the approach of best *available* technology, i.e. pushing as far as technically feasible towards 100% abatement, irrespective of costs. Ultimately, although some directives still mentioned that best available technology should be adopted, there was no time limit set for adoption, or else the phrase was qualified by saying that the adoption should be provided if it did not entail 'excessive cost' – which reduces it to practicable – or else some other let-out was included. It is actually doubtful that the other states were completely unconcerned with costs. In reality, the apparent disagreements seem to have been rather over how much abatement was desirable, with the other countries saying in some cases that the United Kingdom tended to overestimate the costs of abatement, to underestimate the benefits and urgency of reductions in pollution, and often to claim that more evidence was needed before action should be taken. One example is the UK position on sulphur dioxide, where for a long time the United Kingdom delayed reductions, partly because of claims that the evidence failed to show that UK emissions contributed significantly to forest damage elsewhere in West Europe. The new 'Environment' title inserted by the SEA specifically refers to the need to take account of 'the potential benefits and costs of action or lack of action' (Article 130R, 3). From the other side, in an attempt to appear to bridge the gap, at least superficially, UK legislation has now adopted the principle of 'BATNEEC', which stands for 'best available technology not entailing excessive cost'. But the 'NEEC' implies that there has been no real change in the approach.

If the problem is that of externality, the 'obvious' solution might seem to be to 'internalize the externality'. It is often suggested that an implication of the economists' analysis is that polluters should have to pay a tax equal to the external costs imposed on others. In terms of Figure 19.2, if a tax equal to C_0 were levied for each unit of pollution emitted, firms would abate up to level A_0. At abatement levels less than A_0, it is less costly for them to abate than to pay a tax of C_0. From A_0 onwards, the marginal cost of further abatement is higher than the tax, and hence it will be more profitable to continue to pollute and pay the tax. A tax will therefore achieve the optimum. The idea of controlling pollution by taxation rather than by quantitative regulations imposed on firms also seems to fit economists' predilection for relying on price (here the 'price' of using up clean air, etc.) rather than quantitative controls. The latter are supposed to require information rarely possessed by the central authorities.

Despite the common view that analyses such as Figure 19.2 show the desirability of controlling pollution by taxes, and that all (respectable?) economists agree, there is a serious flaw in the argument.[14] To achieve the optimum level of pollution, a government needs to know the size of the correct tax, C_0. But to know C_0 requires knowing the marginal costs and benefits of abatement and where the curves intersect. But this information is the same as required to know, and directly to impose, A_0. Hence a government which can achieve optimality via taxes can achieve it via regulation as well.

Although it is easy to draw diagrams for hypothetical cases of unspecified pollutants and industries, to estimate reliable MB and MC curves quantitatively in real-life cases is much more difficult. Very often the MB curves are little more than guesses. There is a two-stage problem:

1. Working out the physical relationship between varying levels of the pollutant and the harm caused (the dose–response relationship).

2. Putting a monetary valuation on the harm.

It is not just the economic problem of the latter stage – although that is often contentious enough – but that scientists usually have only sketchy and controversial evidence on the first stage, i.e. the way that the damage changes with different levels of the pollutant. The experts sometimes disagree over whether a substance is harmful at all, and often disagree over whether there is a safe threshold or whether even the minutest dose has some small chance of doing some harm to somebody; for example, whether there are any safe levels of lead absorption or nuclear radiation.

As a result, the level of pollution aimed at – often called the 'standard' in the EC literature – is often at best a very rough guess. However, perhaps surprisingly, once it is accepted that the aim is not an optimal level of pollution, there is then a strong argument for achieving the fairly arbitrary standard by the use of taxes, rather than by simply telling all firms contributing to the pollution to abate by some particular percentage, or telling all firms that they can each emit only some particular amount of pollution. The reason is that typically some polluters have lower abatement costs than others. To minimize the costs of achieving any given arbitrary level of aggregate abatement, more of the abatement should be done by firms who can abate more cheaply. Normally, the abatement should be spread between firms in such a way that the *marginal* cost of abatement is equal for each firm. But the argument given above as to how firms will react to a pollution tax shows that, in response to a given tax, each firm will abate up to the point where the tax equals its marginal cost of abatement. Since each firm faces the same tax, they will all end up where they have equal marginal costs of abatement. Hence taxes will minimize the cost of abatement.

Despite this cost-minimization argument, until recently pollution taxes have hardly been used in most EU countries, and are still rare (Sweden is probably the EU country with most use).[15] Among the minor exceptions is the reduced tax in some countries on lead-free petrol as compared with leaded petrol, during the period when both are available. In terms of Figure 19.1, a tax differential equal to t has been imposed on petrol containing lead.[16] Ironically, however (in the year preceding the final Council agreement of 1989), the Commission – at the urging of the French and UK governments – had been threatening to take the Dutch to the ECJ for offering tax concessions to purchasers of cars fitted with catalytic converters which reduce exhaust pollution. This was said to be a distortion of trade – the British and French car makers not having moved as fast as the Germans and some others in adapting their production towards cars which can be easily fitted with converters.

However, the EU itself is now taking pollution taxes more seriously. In 1989 the Council of Environmental Ministers requested the Commission to draft proposals on environmental taxation. Specific proposals by the Commission emerged with the debate on global warming, and the need to reduce emissions of carbon dioxide.[17]

In 1991 the Commission proposed an energy tax in two parts: one part related to the carbon content of fossil fuels and the other part on all non-renewable energy. Thus, for example, nuclear power might be taxed at a rate which would be about half that levied on electricity from oil-burning power stations. The proposal also allowed for possible exemptions for some industries which are particularly energy intensive, such as steel, in order to preserve international competitiveness – such exemptions could be removed if other competitor countries agreed to tax such industries in a similar way.

The proposals aroused considerable opposition, especially from fuel producers and many industrial groups. The result was that the Commission effectively agreed to make implementation contingent on the acceptance of carbon taxes in the major competitors, especially Japan and the United States. At the Earth Summit in Rio de Janeiro in June 1992, US opposition ensured that no binding international agreement was reached on controlling carbon dioxide emissions (the US government claimed that lack of evidence on carbon dioxide emissions and global warming meant that the costs of controlling the emissions were unjustified). As a result, the Commission did not push its energy tax proposal with much urgency, and the

Council could not come to an agreement on the tax. Eventually, UK refusal to agree to directives which could be seen as giving the EU power over member states' taxation forced the abandonment of any EU-wide carbon tax, irrespective of its other merits or drawbacks. Currently, EU directives merely 'encourage' member states to use environmental taxes.

Some interesting economic issues are raised by the episode as it developed. One is the justification for the non-carbon part of the energy tax. The Commission mentioned encouragement of energy efficiency. This is only justifiable if there are other externalities which are due to the use of energy, which are not fuel specific and which cannot be taxed directly; but the case has not been made. It is probable that the aim was really to avoid substitution to nuclear power, because of its own risks, but that it was considered politically more acceptable to achieve this as part of a new tax ostensibly aimed at global warming rather than as a control of nuclear power in its own right. The general economic issue is the interrelatedness of environmental impacts – as with any other aspect of resource allocation, affecting one input or output will have repercussions on others, and an overly partial analysis will miss these interconnections. The EU is now explicitly attempting to deal with such interrelatedness by its 1996 Directive 96/61/EC on integrated pollution prevention and control, which will be applicable to some heavily polluting installations.

Another issue raised by the EU energy tax proposals is that of international competitiveness and distortion of trade, as exemplified both by the initial exemptions on energy-intensive industries and by the reluctance to impose carbon-content taxes unless competitor nations do the same. From an economic efficiency perspective, it is precisely the most energy-intensive industries that should either be induced to substitute other inputs for energy usage or else raise their prices and cut back production the most, as they are the heavy users of a resource with what is now considered to be a high social cost. As seen in Figure 19.1, the relative prices of their products should rise and their outputs should therefore fall. Furthermore, if there are any possibilities for a move away from energy use in production, then the cost-minimization argument implies that they should not be exempt from the tax, at least at the margin.[18]

The reluctance to impose any carbon-related tax unless other countries do, confuses a valid and an invalid argument. Since the benefits of any reduction in carbon dioxide emissions in the EU would accrue globally, it is reasonable to argue that the EU should not abate at all unless other countries do the same – it is a classic free-rider problem, since the pollution is a public bad at the global level. However, if other countries were to agree to cut back their emissions, but decide to do so by means other than economic incentives, this should not affect the EU's decision on using taxes. For any cut-back that the EU wishes to achieve, it will be better off if it achieves that cut-back at the minimum cost – precisely the argument in favour of pollution taxes that has been outlined above. As always in arguments over international trade, there is a conflict between the employment impacts of changes that alter the pattern of production, and the efficient allocation once employment has adjusted to the new pattern.[19]

Despite the cost-minimization argument discussed in this section, as stated above, pollution taxes are currently rare in the EU. Nevertheless, the theory outlined here does have important implications for some other controversies over EU environmental policies.

19.3 Further implications for EU policies

In the course of the above discussion of the standard economic analysis of pollution control, we have noted in passing a few of the implications for EU policies. There are other important aspects of the policies which can also be usefully examined in the light of the analysis.

19.3.1 Polluter pays principle (PPP)

The EU has followed the rest of the OECD in accepting this principle (now incorporated in Article 130R, 2 by the Maastricht Treaty). At first, many commentators mistakenly thought that the PPP was an acceptance of the taxation approach ascribed to economists, in which polluters pay taxes on unabated pollution. However, this was not the meaning of the PPP. It was instead an agreement that governments should not subsidize firms for the costs imposed upon them by anti-pollution regulations. The PPP is satisfied if the polluters bear the cost of achieving the prescribed standards.

The PPP is thus a way of making firms 'internalize the externality'. If the standards they have to meet are correctly chosen, then, given the constraints placed on them, individual firms' own choices of abatement techniques and of output will be correct from a social standpoint.

It might also be noted that from the point of view of the first-order conditions for achieving efficiency, a subsidy per unit abated would achieve the same result as a tax per unit emitted (though in the long run the size of the industry might differ because of the different profitability). The opportunity cost to the firm of continuing to pollute would include subsidy forgone. Thus the rationale for PPP is not to enforce efficiency, but rather fears of 'unfair competition', as discussed above.

Within the EU, although PPP (as well as the general limits to state aids in Articles 92 and 93 of the Treaty of Rome; see Chapter 8) has meant that subsidies for pollution abatement are generally forbidden, this has been applied very strictly only for the higher running costs associated with operating equipment to reduce emissions. Transitional costs may be subsidized. Its new guidelines also allow some temporary operating cost relief to avoid harming international competitiveness when new environmental taxes are first introduced.

At times the Commission has allowed some help with initial investment costs to install abatement equipment in order to adapt to new mandatory standards, to speed the implementation of agreed standards prior to the final compliance date or to encourage firms to go beyond the mandatory standard. In the latter case the maximum limits are higher at 30%, as compared with 15% for the adaptation to new standards (40% compared with 25% for SMEs).[20]

19.3.2 Thresholds and standards

As stated above, it is very difficult to get convincing evidence about the dose–response relationships of pollutants. The problems of obtaining evidence make the techniques used much closer to those of econometricians rather than those of laboratory-based science testing.[21] Where human health is concerned, it is simply unethical to laboratory test; for example, taking very young babies and giving them feeds containing different levels of nitrates to observe the level which causes serious damage. Most EU policies are concerned with potential health effects. But even where only amenity is at stake, the number of possible interactions and natural variations in them still make it difficult to gather conclusive evidence. The arguments over the cause of forest die-back are a case in point. There are various possible pollutants which may interact in causing damage, damage may depend on soil and weather, and the route taken between emissions of sulphur dioxide and nitrogen oxides on the one hand and the precipitation of acid rain on the other is difficult to forecast.

One result of this is that it is important to try to obtain reliable data on a range of pollutants, over many years and at a sufficient number of locations, so as to enable statistical studies relating various aspects of health to pollution to be based on enough observations to be significant (in a statistical sense). One of the focuses of EU environmental policy has been to require monitoring of pollutants. The earliest requirements were for smoke and sulphur dioxide (from 1975 onwards), water pollution (from 1977 onwards) and, more recently (from 1987), there has been an attempt to gather systematic data on damage to trees. The European Environment Agency, established by the EU in 1993, is similarly concerned with collecting and assessing data.

More fundamentally, the lack of definitive knowledge on the damage caused by different levels of pollution means that any standards adopted are done so largely by a political process disguised as a scientific one. Different groups put pressure on governments to be more or less lax, and the governments then take stands in the Council according to the balance of their feelings; often, possibly the position they have previously taken domestically is then taken with respect to EU policy. Each government will claim scientific backing for its stand, usually refusing to admit the uncertainty. Those pushing for the laxest standard will tend to claim that there is no conclusive evidence of harm, while not admitting that there is no conclusive evidence of lack of harm either; the UK position on sulphur dioxide mentioned above is one example. Others will mention the studies which suggest that there could well be serious damage caused by the current levels of pollution. As part of the process, there is the temptation to look for a threshold, as in Figure 19.3, even where there are no strong grounds for expecting one. If a threshold did exist, it would often make sense to adopt it as the standard – the MC curve would have to cut the MB curve to the left of the threshold to justify less abatement (higher pollution).

A large number of medical scientists are doubtful that overall thresholds exist for many pollutants. The levels of a pollutant, such as smoke, that may be harmless to a healthy person may be deleterious to somebody already vulnerable, such as a bronchitic old-age pensioner living in a damp flat. Thus, a threshold which would be applicable to all might well be at so low a level of pollution as to be useless for policy.

Once a standard has been decided upon, by whatever process of bargaining based on whatever motives and justifications, it is then too often treated as though the agreed standard were really a well-defined threshold. On the one hand, governments may use the fact that an EU standard exists to try to allay public anxiety over the potential harm from some pollutant and to claim that because levels are below the accepted standard there is nothing at all to worry about – even if new evidence has since emerged to suggest that low levels are more harmful than was thought before. On the other hand, environmentalists and other pressure groups may use the breach of a standard as an indication that the health of the public is being seriously damaged and argue that pollution must be immediately reduced to the standard, whatever the cost.

In most cases, the EU has laid down that member states must notify the Commission if they cannot reach the agreed standard by the required date. The Commission then has to decide whether the failure can be condoned or not. At this stage, the pressures mentioned in the previous paragraph come into play again: is the standard just a rough guess at the level at which marginal costs equal marginal benefits, so that less abatement is justified if a particular country can plausibly claim that its costs are especially high, or is it a well-defined threshold of pollution above which completely unacceptable harm is caused? The decision is complicated by the worry that, if some member states are granted exemptions too readily, others will in future not comply because fears of 'unfair competition' from those given exemptions.

19.3.3 Emission versus ambient standards

In the diagrams above we followed most of the literature in simply linking pollution to damage. However, on closer examination it becomes apparent that there are various stages of pollution. There is the initial emission at the point where the pollution is produced, such as the factory chimney or waste pipe outlet. The pollution may then flow through various media, for example, it may be carried by wind through air, then deposited on plants, then eaten by animals which are then slaughtered. During the processes, the pollution from any one source is added to by pollution from other sources and simultaneously diluted by fresh air, water, etc., mixing with the carrying medium, and much of the substance may be deposited where it does no harm. The ultimate stage to be considered is where the pollution finally directly affects humans.

From the economist's, anthropocentric, viewpoint, the pollution that matters is when it affects human beings. Typically, therefore, we are concerned with the ambient levels of pollution – i.e. the concentration in the medium which affects health, such as micrograms per cubic metre of lead particles in the air or milligrams per litre of nitrates in drinking water.

In setting standards for pollution, a standard could be applied at any of the stages of the process. At the final stage, one could set standards of acceptable levels of absorption of pollution by people; for example, there was at one time a Commission proposal to set a maximum limit for the level of lead in people's blood. Obviously one would hardly fine or imprison people with more lead in their blood than the standard. Instead, the idea was that if tests showed that anybody was above the limit, then the government of their country should take agreed action to reduce their lead intake. In fact, governments do use monitoring of human exposure or absorption as a trigger for action, and occasionally set standards in this form, such as radiation exposure limits for workers. In the EC case, partly as a result of UK pressure, the directive on blood lead levels was watered down somewhat and became one for an EC-wide screening programme, primarily for information gathering and with a member state required to take only such actions as the government itself thought were appropriate measures if too many people were above the specified values.[22]

The next stage back is that mentioned above, i.e. the concentration in the medium that directly affects people. In the EU standards defined for this stage are sometimes called 'exposure standards' or 'primary protection standards'. Another example, in addition to those for drinking water or air, would be the bacteria content of bathing water.

Sometimes the standards are somewhat further back in the process, but still concern ambient levels. These are often called 'environmental quality standards'. The standards applying to water, in rivers or lakes, which could be taken for drinking, or those applying to water with shellfish, are examples.

Standards may also be set at the initial emission stage. These are usually called 'emission standards'. A similar stage is when the pollution is caused by the use of products which are sold, such as car exhaust pollution or noise from lawnmowers. A somewhat similar stage is where the EC mandates labelling or other aspects of products to avoid *potential* danger from misuse, for example, the controls on the shipment of toxic waste.

As already stated, from an economist's viewpoint it would seem that the relevant standard should be as far down the chain as is technically possible – exposure standards where possible or at least environmental quality standards. The only cases for EU standards on emissions would be either where they were also product standards (to allow unhindered trade) or where there was some reason why even environmental quality standards were not feasible. Otherwise, it should be up to the relevant government inspectorate/agency to find the least-cost way of achieving the environmental quality or exposure standard. If pollution taxes were not used, then the requirement for pollution abatement should be shared between the various sources of emissions in the most efficient way possible.[23] As explained earlier, the aim would be (subject to information/enforcement limitations) to require abatement by each polluter up to the point where the marginal cost of abatement was equal.

In the 1970s there was a heated controversy over whether the EC should define its policies by environmental quality standards (EQSs) or UESs, with the latter defined as maximum 'limit values' so that member states could have stricter emission limits if they wished. The issue arose over a linked series of directives on water quality aimed at rivers and estuaries – there was a framework directive, finally passed in 1976, on the approach to 'Dangerous substances discharged into the aquatic environment', followed by subsequent directives on specific pollutants/industries.[24] The contestants were the United Kingdom on the side of EQS and the other member states, plus the Commission, on the side of UES.

The reasons for the attachment of the Commission and other member states to UES were partly explicable in terms of one of the motivations for having a joint EC policy at all: the fear of 'unfair competition' if different countries had different emission standards for a set of pollutants which were primarily industrial effluents. Countries such as the United Kingdom, which has a long coastline with relatively fast-flowing estuaries and rivers, would be able to achieve any given EQS with much higher emissions than their trade partners (rivals?). In addition, countries which shared river systems (as along the Rhine) would find it difficult to allocate individual polluters' emission levels to achieve an EQS: upstream countries would have little incentive to impose severe cutbacks on their industries. The issue of transfrontier pollution is of less importance for the United Kingdom, which is not only primarily an island (ignoring Northern Ireland and its border) but has the fortune to be mainly upwind of its nearest neighbours. The other member states felt that the cooperation which should underlie the Community ought to lead to policies in a form which would help, not hinder, the solution of joint problems, including transfrontier pollution.

On the other side of the debate, the United Kingdom put views which are close to part of the approach taken by most economists and outlined above. Since it is the damage to humans which is the problem, an EQS is what matters, not emissions *per se*. Emissions need only be limited to the extent that they lead to unacceptable damage. In terms of a traditional British statement: 'There are no harmful substances, only harmful concentrations.' On the question of unfair competition, the UK government said that it was no more unfair that the United Kingdom should benefit from its coastline and estuaries than that Italy could benefit from its sunshine: it would be absurd to require the Italians to grow tomatoes in greenhouses just to stop them having an 'unfair' advantage over the Dutch. Although not stated in those terms, this was an application of the theory of comparative advantage, applied to polluting industries.

In the end, a typical EC compromise was reached. Countries could choose *either* to accept UES in the form of limit values *or* to establish EQS, provided that they could show the Commission that the quality standard was being met. Only the United Kingdom chose the latter. The subsequent directives for particular dangerous and persistent pollutants followed the same compromise of a choice of either approach, although within the EQS approach it is odd that separate directives should be issued for separate industries.[25]

Despite the strong disagreements over UES or EQS, it could be argued that neither side was really consistent. The United Kingdom, despite the type of statement mentioned above, had in many cases applied UESs to whole industries (in some cases only to new pollutants, but the EC also made a similar distinction). For example, the old Alkali Inspectorate typically applied its notion of best practicable means to the whole of an industry it supervised and the same applies to the newer Pollution Inspectorate (now part of the British Environment Agency) and BATNEEC. Conversely, other EU policies set EQSs without any fuss from the member states, for example the air quality standards for nitrogen dioxide, sulphur dioxide and particulates. It could also be argued that the dispute forced the United Kingdom to be much more rigorous about the EQSs that were needed.

19.3.4 Damage and designated areas

One last issue in EU environmental policy that we shall examine is also linked to the economic analysis. The stress on the costs and benefits of abatement implies that it is not merely the dumping itself of something into water, air or earth that matters, but the harm done relative to the benefits from the activity. The harm done will depend on the potential use by people (directly or indirectly) of the medium. It therefore makes sense to vary the desired standard of pollution according to its use. Water used for drinking could well require stricter standards on its nitrate concentration than water used only for boating. The EU has followed such a policy.

In some cases the use of the medium is obvious; in other cases, less so. In the latter cases there may be some decentralization so that countries are allowed to designate particular areas for the application of particular standards. For example, the standards for bathing water apply to stretches of water where bathing is traditionally practised by large numbers of people. Similarly, member states can designate areas where water standards need to be set to protect shellfish.

Although the approach seems sensible, the application has not always been so. In particular, insofar as governments have discretion over the areas designated, they can use this as a way of avoiding the effective implementation of EU policies that they feel are unnecessary. This has indeed happened. In the case of standards for water supporting different sorts of freshwater fish, and for the shellfish case already mentioned, some member states simply did not designate any waters at all. Similarly, those readers who are familiar with English seaside resorts might be interested to know that the UK government originally used its discretion over how to assess where 'large numbers' traditionally bathed to exclude both Blackpool and Brighton. At that time the UK government was worried about public expenditure, and any improvement in water quality of beaches would require new sewerage works. Later on though, in 1987, in response to threats from the Commission over infringement, as well as strongly adverse comments from the Royal Commission on

Environmental Pollution (and the beginning of a changed attitude by the UK government to its poor reputation on environmental issues), many more beaches were added to the list.

A final example is a 1975 directive on the sulphur contents of gas–diesel oil, which is a medium-grade oil used for heating of commercial, light industrial and domestic buildings, as well as for diesel fuel for vehicles. The directive is interesting partly because it was a mixture of UES and EQS, although it is also concerned with product harmonization. It set two limits on the sulphur content of the oil, and the higher sulphur type could be used only in areas designated by member states. The aim was that the higher sulphur oil should only be used where air pollution from sulphur dioxide was not a problem. In the event, the UK government decided that the whole of the United Kingdom was to be designated for the use of the higher sulphur content oil *except for roads*. The road network would therefore be designated for the lower sulphur oil – since diesel for vehicles was already low sulphur compared with other gas/diesel oil.[26]

19.4 Conclusions

In some ways the EU policies on the environment can be counted as a success story. Despite the fact that it may not be clear that common policies are required at all in many cases, nevertheless a set of policies has emerged. Furthermore, despite some of the problems mentioned above and despite the failure to move quickly on some other policies because of the conflicting interests of the member states, as compared with other common policies (such as for transport or agriculture), progress has been fairly steady and not too divisive, acrimonious or blatantly inefficient.

In the 1990s there has been a revival of public interest in the environment, even in those member states where interest waned in the decade after 1974. Those in favour of stronger environmental policies may well feel divided about EU actions. Those who live in those member states where Green pressures are strong will feel that they are held back, as compared with what their governments could achieve (or be pressured into achieving) without the requirement to carry other member countries with them. Conversely, environmentalists who live in those countries whose governments tend only to move on these issues when really compelled can be grateful both for the more stringent standards set by EU policies and for the possibility that the Commission will enforce compliance.[27]

In the second half of 1992, during the British Presidency, it seemed as though EC environmental policy might be put into reverse. Following the problems in summer 1992 with ratification of the Maastricht Agreements, the United Kingdom (especially) stressed the notion of subsidiary that had been incorporated into the proposed Treaty amendments. To various extents, the other member states, and even the chastened Commission, also said that subsidiarity should be taken seriously, and that EC policies should be scrutinized to see whether joint action was really necessary. As indicated at various points in this chapter, the justification of EU level environmental policies is often debatable. It was possible, therefore, that the movement on subsidiarity might lead to the reconsideration of some existing EU environmental directives.

However, subsidiarity has not made a major difference as far as existing policies are concerned. It is difficult to judge whether new EU level joint actions on the environment have been as readily adopted as previously, even where there is no strong reason for an EU, rather than a national, policy. My own subjective judgement is that any diminution has been minimal or even non-existent, and I do not expect this to change despite the new Articles on subsidiarity in the Amsterdam Treaty. Not only do they include transnational problems as a reason for joint actions, but they also include the correction of 'distorted competition'. As explained above, however misguided it may be from an economist's viewpoint, the standard interpretation of 'distorted competition' has always been a prime reason for EU level environmental policy.

Notes

1. For earlier years, references to the Official Journals for the environmental programmes and various directives can be found in the Economic and Social Committee (1987) outline, Haigh (1989), or Press and Taylor (1990). The 5th Programme has been published separately by the Commission under the title *Towards Sustainability* (CEC, 1993) with a progress report on it in COM (95) 624. The annual *Reports* and *Monthly Bulletins* by the Commission have brief sections on the Environment. A useful summary is in the semi-annual series of UK Government Reports *Recent Developments in the EU*.

2. Including reports during 1977–80 by the House of Lords Select Committee on the European Communities.

3. Some of these directives predate the proposal for an EC Environmental Programme.

4. Once it was accepted that environmental policy could be fitted in as an objective of the Community, Article 235 then gave legal power for binding actions.

5. As in other applications of this notion of 'unfair competition', or 'distortion of competition' as it is often called in EU documents, it contains implicit assumptions about the fixity of wages, prices and exchange rates. These assumptions are often not realized and their validity may or may not be dubious. This point will also be relevant to controversies discussed later in this chapter.

6. Although some of those opposed to action on the environment have alleged that concern about environmental issues is a middle-class luxury, which is not shared by the working class or the poorer members of society.

7. Formally, the arguments in the social welfare function are the individual welfares or utilities, even if the functional form (weighting of individual welfares) may reflect egalitarianism or some other values.

8. Theoretically, in formal treatments, there would be no obstacle to putting concern for endangered species into somebody's utility function, even where the person does not know of the existence of some of the species. Conversely, environmentalists sometimes appeal to the possible future uses to man of endangered species of plants, which would be forgone if the species were destroyed before the discovery of their uses.

9. An externality also occurs when marginal private benefit is not equal to marginal social benefit. Pollution is a negative externality, i.e. private cost is less than social cost. Some older microeconomic textbooks sometimes use the term 'social cost' to refer only to the *excess* cost imposed on others, which is a different usage from that followed here.

10. For further detailed discussion, there is now a wide range of textbooks on the economics of pollution control, e.g. Baumol and Oates (1988).

11. According to the *Financial Times* (4 December 1996) even Germany, previously viewed as an EU pace-setter in environmental protection laws, has reacted to its recent rise in unemployment by a reluctance to introduce new anti-pollution measures which might raise costs. There are even moves to reduce existing measures as part of the drive to deregulation.

12. Another way of putting the same point is to say that the MPC curve in Figure 19.1 is too high because the true opportunity cost of labour is below the wage rate. Hence the MSC, which should measure the cost of resources by the value of their alternative use, includes some components which make it lower than the MPC – see Chapter 4. Note also that if the industry is not perfectly competitive, the output may be too low for the usual reasons, despite the externality – it depends on the balance between the strength of the externality (output too high) and the imperfection (output too low).

13. A possible exception is the case of pollutants which are cumulative (non-degradable) and highly toxic – see Pearce (1976).

14. A more detailed discussion of this and other problems of using pollution taxes is in Marin (1979). Also see Kelman (1981) for a study of some other reasons for the hostility of non-economists to the idea of pollution taxes.

15. A summary of pollution charges can be found in OECD (1995).

16. This case is suitable for Figure 19.1, as once the leaded petrol has been put into the fuel tank, the motorist has no realistic options for varying the total emissions of lead for each gallon bought. The same applies to the carbon content fuel tax discussed below.

17. A brief account and assessment of the Commission's proposals can be found in Pearson and Smith (1991). More detailed analyses are in the papers in Carraco and Sinisalco (1993). The EC had already agreed to aim at stabilizing CO_2 emissions at the 1990 level by the year 2000.

18. If we concentrate on the cost minimization argument only, and (for the reasons already discussed) ignore overall optimality, imposing the pollution tax but

giving lump-sum subsidies to these industries (to avoid a large rise in their average costs) might be acceptable.

19. The argument here is made within a framework which assumes perfect competition inside countries. To what extent it still holds within the framework of the 'New Trade Theory' of oligopolistic competition is currently the subject of research.

20. The Commission's original position is briefly restated in CEC (1991c), paragraph 284, and given in greater detail in CEC (1987d), paragraph 159. The new guidelines were published in OJC 72, 10.3.94 and summarized in the 25th Report on Competition Policy (CEU, 1996e).

21. The examples in this and the following paragraphs are taken from EC environmental policies.

22. The debates over this directive (77/312) illustrate not only the monitoring function of the EC mentioned above, but also the sensitivity to thresholds. Part of the objection to the original proposal was that it would suggest that the standard was a threshold which, if exceeded by anybody, would mean they were in danger.

23. Whether pollution taxes or quantitative regulations are used to apportion the necessary abatement between emitters, allowance should be made for the different contributions of emissions in difference places to the pollution measured as environmental quality, e.g. because of prevailing wind or tide patterns. Unlike the United States, the EU has not used tradeble pollution permits – which should similarly allow for differential contributions.

24. An excellent detailed account of the controversies is given in Guruswamy *et al.* (1983). As pointed out in this article, although originally the term 'environmental quality objective' meant something else, the EQS is now sometimes referred to as 'quality objective'.

25. Mercury from the chloralkali industry. The directive for the titanium dioxide industry had already been foreshadowed in the First Environmental Action Programme, together with controls for the pulp and paper industries (the latter has never been enacted).

26. In 1992 the Council agreed on a new directive setting a uniform limit on the sulphur content of all gas–oils.

27. A politically important example in the United Kingdom was the Commission's threat to prosecute over the failure to meet the standards for nitrates in water (other countries besides the United Kingdom were also threatened). In the absence of these threats, especially given UK official scepticism over the levels of the EQS actually laid down in the directive, there would have been an even greater lack of urgency over an issue which was so adverse for the privatization process. (In 1992 both the United Kingdom and Germany were found by the ECJ to be in breach of the directive.)

chapter twenty

Factor mobility

D. G. MAYES

Although the freedom of mobility of labour and capital were objectives enshrined in the Treaty of Rome itself, only fairly limited progress had been made by the early 1980s in turning this into a reality. Most countries had capital controls of one form or another and labour faced considerable constraints on movement through lack of recognition of qualifications and other problems over establishment. The slow progress stemmed from two sources. In the case of capital, member states were worried that having free movements would lead to destabilizing flows which would disturb the running of the domestic economy. The main fear was a capital outflow which would depreciate the currency, drive up the rate of inflation and require monetary and fiscal contraction to offset it. Labour controls, on the other hand, were more concerned with inflows. Employees in the domestic economy feared that an inflow from other countries would lose them their jobs – countries would export their unemployment. Much of this was dressed up as a need to have certain skills, standards and local knowledge for the protection of consumers. A closer examination reveals that only some of this was necessary. However, much of the fear stemmed from ignorance of what others' qualifications meant and overcoming this required a long and tedious process of determination and negotiation.

The 1985 White Paper on completing the internal market and the 1986 Single European Act (SEA) signalled the determination to break through this complex of restrictions and move to a much more open market, with freedom of movement of capital and labour being two of four basic 'freedoms' set out as the objective of the market (the other two being freedom of movement of goods and services). In the case of capital, this was to be achieved by 1 July 1990. This target was largely not met for EC(9) and Portugal and Spain managed to participate in 1992 only for the ERM crisis of September 1992 (see Chapter 16) to require some controls to be re-introduced by member states in the hope of stabilizing their exchange rates. However, the Maastricht Treaty has confirmed the intention to move to a situation where, for wholesale markets at any rate, the free movement of capital will be a reality. For smaller firms and households local relationships and networks are still likely to dominate.

The legislative programme for the Single Market measures was intended to be complete by the end of 1992. While this was largely achieved, some of the labour mobility measures are still to have their full effect. The Maastricht Treaty also covers labour through the 'Social Protocol'. However, the fact that the UK was not prepared to participate and the fact that the other eleven member states felt it necessary to introduce further requirements for minimum standards at work suggest that the actual exercise of labour mobility, and indeed capital mobility if it has consequences for employment, is still feared within the EU rather than being viewed an ambiguous benefit.

The logic behind achieving a 'free movement' of capital and labour is elementary if the full opportunity for exploiting efficiency gains within the EU is to be achieved. The practice in the case of capital movements was that those countries frightened of an uncontrollable outflow realized that with the increasing ease of international capital transactions they were both making their own firms pay a higher price for capital and making themselves a less attractive location for mobile investment. The increasing stability of the EMS may also have acted as an incentive, although this provides somewhat of an irony as the removal of capital controls has itself served to destabilize the EMS (see Chapter 16).

In the case of labour there were also two main factors involved in easing the decision to remove barriers. The first is simply that with the exception of Greece, Portugal and Spain there were no great pressures for major destabilizing labour flows; hence their removal would not have major consequences. Secondly, in the professions and more skilled jobs it is proving possible to find a way round the impasse and to move forward much more rapidly by countries accepting mutual recognition of each others' qualifications, rather than attempting the extremely difficult task of agreeing a common standard. However, it still remains to be seen in practice how well such recognition will work (Brazier et al., 1993). Even in highly internationalized professions such as the academic one, employment of foreigners tends to be more on the basis of work they have published than by qualification alone. Furthermore, the EU is now finding itself threatened by migration problems, not from within, but from Eastern Europe and North Africa.

20.1 The historical perspective

As illustrated by the North Atlantic Free Trade Area (NAFTA), most of the emphasis and interest in negotiations and assessments concerning integration tends to concentrate on products rather than inputs. However, freedom of movement of products within the EU does not necessarily entail the absence of protection or completely free competition if there are still constraints on inputs; this was recognized by the single market programme. In the case of imported produced inputs, intermediate goods and services, the subject has been extensively explored with the measurement of effective protection. The differences between nominal rates and effective rates can be quite striking. If the EU's Common External Tariff (CET) was 5% on a particular product, while the CET on the main produced inputs (which form 50% of the production costs) was zero, then the effective rate of protection would be double the nominal rate (all other influences such as differential transport costs for the finished and intermediate products being ignored). Effective protection is thus the rate of protection of the value-added in the production of the final product – see El-Agraa (1989b).

Similar considerations apply to the non-produced inputs of labour and capital in the productive process. If there are restraints on the mobility of labour, then differences in the price of labour can exist between countries in the same way that differences between product prices can exist when the mobility of products is restricted. Thus, for products with a high labour content, considerable competitive advantages could accrue to the country with the lower wage levels even if trade in the products were completely free. This separation of labour markets is not, of course, just an international phenomenon. It occurs widely within individual countries and hence a range of wages is to be expected.

It might be possible to get round some of the problems of immobility of labour if capital were mobile. Thus, instead of labour moving to take up opportunities elsewhere, firms could set up new plants and hence remove much of the differential in wages. Where capital mobility is also restricted, differences can persist across the EU.

It is important to recall that if a firm in one country wishes to sell a product to a consumer in a second country, there are three ways in which it can go about it (assuming there is just one step in the productive process). It can export the finished product, it can set up a manufacturing plant in the second country or it can set up a manufacturing plant in a third country. The first of these thus involves trade flows, the second capital flows and the third both. The development of trade patterns will be crucially affected by the degree of factor mobility. *Ceteris paribus*, the greater the factor mobility, the smaller trade needs to be for any particular pattern of consumption.

Although the Single Market programme will remove many of the remaining restrictions on factor movements, it is unlikely that capital, let alone labour, will be as mobile as it is within individual member countries. Factors reducing mobility include differences in tastes and customs, and variations in risk. Having a single currency will be an important step in removing one source of risk and reducing transition costs.

The 1992 programme enables integration; it does not compel it. Thus, in the same way that the idealized total specialization of trade in economic theory is rarely realized, we would not expect total perfection in capital markets and nothing like it in labour markets where many other factors lead to continuing segmentation. To quite some extent this is affected by the nature and treatment of the services in which the labour is embodied which have national diversity in the same way as there is diversity in the demand for goods.

If factors and goods can move between countries freely, then, neglecting any transport or transfer costs, the whole trading area can be treated as a single market with a uniform reward right across the area to each factor, and uniform product prices. However, such a system is not only very far from a description of the reality of the EU after 1992, but is also indeterminate and does not tell us the extent to which the good rather than the factors move – a typical problem of underidentifi-cation (see Mayes, 1988). The imperfections of the real world, however, are actually an aid in this case as they increase the chance of being able to identify the deter-minants of the various movements.

Although there are some differences in the way in which labour can move from one country to another, particularly when countries have common land frontiers, the movement of labour usually involves the person concerned moving to and living in the new country. However, in some cases it may be possible to commute across the border and to work in a foreign country while continuing to be resident in the home country. Movements can be long or short term and the worker may or may not bring his or her family along too. Nevertheless, there is fairly straight-forward behaviour involved in most movement of labour.

Capital, on the other hand, can be moved in a variety of ways. While the basic distinction lies between direct investment, which involves the setting up or acqui-sition of a 'subsidiary' in a foreign country, and portfolio investment, involving the purchase of shares and bonds or the making of other forms of loan to a company in a foreign country, other, more complicated, arrangements exist which involve the effective transfer of capital between countries even if this is not recorded as such in the statistics on capital movements. 'Back-to-back' loans are a simple example whereby exchange control can be evaded. In such a case, although the parent company can use only domestic currency while wanting to invest in foreign cur-rency in the foreign country, it can make the domestic funds available to a foreign borrower who is essentially in the same position – his or her funds are in his or her own currency while he or she wishes to use foreign currency. The exact matching process may be much more complicated than this simple one-to-one swap. (The problem is more complicated if the investment abroad is financed solely by a loan raised abroad. In such a case, there is not really any international movement of cap-ital.) In a single capital market, a firm can raise debt or equity anywhere in the market by having access to all financial services on the same basis as all other bor-rowers. In the same way, of course, providers of capital would have equal oppor-tunity to offer services. Simple removal of exchange controls also does not necessarily achieve this.

In the case of labour movement, individuals physically move from one country to another and then provide their labour services in the second country. Capital, on the other hand, in the sense usually considered, involves the transfer of claims through a financial transaction and not the transfer of capital goods themselves in the form of plant, machinery and vehicles. If existing physical capital is exported, then the financial transfer is lowered. If new physical capital is purchased from the home country, there is an additional export but the net inflow of physical capital is smaller. The net flow is largest when the new physical capital is all produced in the country where the new plant is set up.

Some of the distinctions between types of capital movement may not be very important from the point of view of actual output and trade patterns. Portfolio in-vestment resulting in control of the foreign enterprise may be largely indistinguishable from direct investment, for example. However, the major distinction normally lies in the type of investor.[1] Direct investment is undertaken by firms on their own behalf (or by governments). Portfolio investment, on the other hand, is more usually undertaken by financial companies of one form or another, although cross-share holdings by commercial companies are common in some parts of the EU. Much of this latter investment may therefore not seem particularly relevant to the problem in hand as it relates to a change in the ownership of existing assets rather than the direct financing of the creation of new physical assets used for the production of goods and services. However, this is mistaken from two points of view: direct investment may also be purely a change in ownership, this time involving control; secondly, we need to inquire what subsequent use the funds released to the seller were put to. The ability to exchange domestic debt for foreign equity can affect the range of options open to a firm. Moreover, even if the purpose of capital inflows into a country is to 'enable' the foreign government to run a deficit which cannot be financed fully by its private domestic sector, such lending may permit a higher level of investment in physical capital in that country than would otherwise be the case.

Clearly, the latter form of capital flow is of more than passing interest in a group of countries which are attempting some coordination of their economic actions. When exchange rates are relatively fixed between member countries through the snake or the European Monetary System (EMS), balance of payments surpluses/ deficits on current account may open up rather wider than would otherwise be the case. Insofar as these imbalances are not met by official movements (or reserves), they must be eliminated by countervailing capital movements, encouraged in the main by differences in covered interest rates.[2,3] With freely floating exchange rates, the exchange rate can take rather more of the burden of adjustment between countries and capital flows rather less. Coordination of fiscal or monetary policies between countries will also affect the ways in which capital flows have to balance the remaining transactions.[4]

These considerations raise many issues which lie outside the scope of this chapter; but it must be borne in mind that capital transfers take place between countries for reasons that are not necessarily related to the essentially microeconomic decisions of the individual firm. To invert the argument, wider issues influence the values of the macroeconomic variables which affect firms' decisions over their overseas investment and these wider issues themselves form part of the way in which the members of the EC choose to conduct the handling of economic policy, both jointly and independently. Since direct investment abroad and borrowing of foreign funds by enterprises in foreign countries may both involve not just the same size capital inflow but also the same increase in capital formation within the country, it is not possible to set aside either long-term or short-term portfolio investment as being irrelevant to the purpose in hand.

As is clear from Table 20.1, portfolio investment from abroad had usually been much less important for the United Kingdom than direct investment until the mid-1980s.[5] The lifting of exchange controls in 1979 resulted in a similar switch in the

Table 20.1 ● Inward and outward investment in the United Kingdom, 1972–94 (£ million).[a]

	1972	1976	1980	1982	1984	1986	1988	1990	1992	1994
Overseas investment in UK										
Direct investment	408	799	2,541	1,137	−181	5,837	12,006	18,514	9,184	6,823
Investment by oil companies[b]	78	819	1,714	1,770	–	–	–	–	–	–
Portfolio investment	290	438	1,499	−11	–	12,181	15,564	11,763	24,616	32,609
Miscellaneous investment[b]	−4	35	100	120	1,288	–	–	–	–	–
Total	772	2,091	5,854	3,016	1,107	18,018	27,570	30,277	33,800	39,432
Private investment overseas										
Direct investment	−737	−2,145	−3,371	−2,123	−6,036	−11,678	−20,944	−10,490	−10,850	−18,363
Investment by oil companies and miscellaneous investment[b]	−61	−214	−1,495	−1,968	–	–	–	–	–	–
Portfolio investment	−604	90	−3,150	−7,565	−9,753	−22,777	−11,239	−17,206	−27,346	17,968
Total	−1,402	−2,269	−8,016	−11,656	−15,789	−33,955	−32,183	−27,696	−38,196	−395

[a] Assets and liabilities are shown from the point of view of the United Kingdom: increases (decreases) in assets +(−), increases (decreases) in liabilities −(+), both net of investment.
[b] After 1983 included in direct investment.
Source UK Balance of Payments.

composition of the outflow of capital, with portfolio investment replacing direct investment as the most important category. The issue is complicated by the activities of oil companies which are separately covered in the table. Fortunately, the more detailed statistics (available in *Business Monitor MA4*) also distinguish non-oil investment, and in the discussion which follows we shall also try to omit oil investment as the movements of capital are largely unaffected by any considerations relating to the EC. The other EC countries do not exhibit these distortions to the pattern of capital flows in a manner which confuses their changes in response to the formation and development of the EC to the same extent as those of the United Kingdom. As the 1994 figures make clear, there can be striking readjustments in the portfolio.

20.2　Capital movements

Exchange controls were eliminated in the United Kingdom in October 1979, but the reasons for that move had little to do with membership of the EC. At that stage, the remaining Community countries all had restrictions on capital flows, although these varied in their degree of tightness. Since the start of the single market programme, these restrictions have been steadily removed and there is now effective freedom of capital movements and, with the exception of the new members, freedom throughout the Community was in place by July 1990, the start of stage I of the EMU. In most cases there was a distinction between controls applied to residents and non-residents, with the restrictions being lighter in the latter case. However, interestingly enough, such restrictions as did apply to non-residents usually applied equally to all such non-residents, regardless of whether they were residents of another EC country or of a third country. There is thus no counterpart to the preference system applied to trade through differential tariffs as far as capital movements are concerned, nor, it seems, was there any intention of taking the opportunity of introducing discrimination against third countries by making this freedom of movement only in respect of fellow members.[6] To a large extent this is a practical matter, because it is difficult to control some transactions when others do not have to be vetted. However, 'reciprocity' is an argument which is being used in other parts of the single market programme in order to obtain concessions for the EC in third-country markets. In one sense, therefore, this simplifies the analysis as one potential source of substitution, and encouragement of capital flows does not in the main exist. However, the restrictions which matter are not in the capital movements themselves but in how those funds can be used to purchase physical assets. Constraints, or indeed incentives, apply to inward investment, to mergers and acquisitions and to the operation of multinational companies. Thus, freedom of capital movements is to some extent a myth if there are further constraints on how the funds can be used. Nevertheless, it is clear that restrictions are being progressively eliminated.

Of the other EU countries, Germany has probably had the most liberal capital controls. The controls in the Netherlands were also mainly intended to facilitate the inflow and outflow of capital (which was largely free) in the short run. There were, for example, restrictions on deposits from non-residents during the period 1972–75 to ease the pressure from high capital inflows. The Netherlands has been a net capital exporter in most recent years.

The situation in Belgium and Luxemburg, which can for the most part be treated as a single unit, has been complicated by a two-tier exchange-rate system. This comprised a 'free' capital market and a controlled market for current transactions. The net effect, however, was not restrictive and the two categories are normally referred to as the 'financial franc' and the 'convertible franc'. It is in France and Italy that the greatest controls have been found, although in the French case direct investment was one of the two main exceptions to the tight controls on the export of capital. As is to be expected, inflows by non-residents were less controlled than outflows by residents. However, inwards direct investment has been subject to control by the French government when the foreign control of the companies entailed has been thought unsuitable. In Italy also, restrictions related to flows other than direct investment, although, since import and export financing were exempted, it has been possible to get round many of the regulations.

The general direction of changes in controls on capital movements over the period has, of course, been for reduction with final elimination for all but Spain, Portugal and Greece taking place in July 1990. Thus, as for trade flows, we would expect to observe a more rapid increase in direct investment abroad than in GDP itself. This duly occurred in the second half of the 1980s, but was not confined to the EU. However, the distribution of that investment by country of investor is unlikely to have been affected by any changes relative to the EU as such because liberalization has almost entirely been non-discriminatory. The influence of the EU on capital flows is as a result likely to be in changes in discrimination in the traded goods and services market. Increased trade flows are likely to involve changes in capital flows – to set up distribution networks and to establish local production as market penetration increases – although the direction of the change is still problematic as we cannot tell *a priori* the extent to which trade and direct investment might be substitutes rather than complements.

20.3 The determinants of direct investment

Investment flows between countries cannot really be treated in the same manner as investment within the economy because, although total investment can be explained through well-known relationships, the split between home and foreign expenditure, on an economy-wide basis, is not so clear. In the first place, magnitudes are sufficiently small for a limited number of decisions by individual companies to have a noticeable effect on the final outcome. Secondly, we are concerned in this case not just with what resources firms are prepared to put into capital for future production, but where they are going to site it. Most consideration, therefore, has been devoted to the problem at the level of the firm itself rather than through modelling of the components of the capital account of the balance of payments. Even within the confines of aggregate explanation there has been a tendency to avoid modelling direct investment flows directly, modelling them indirectly through the determination of the exchange rate as a sort of reduced-growth approach. (See Cuthbertson *et al.* (1980) for a discussion of this work.)

Such an approach may be appropriate for the explanation of portfolio investment, particularly since much short-term portfolio investment is usually described as speculative in nature, but it is much less useful for direct investment because of the degree of permanence embodied in the existence of physical capital held abroad. Such capital will tend to generate profits, which themselves form direct investment if they are not remitted to the investing country. Furthermore, such productive facilities have costs of closure and require a continuing stream of new investment to remain profitable, thus reflecting rather different considerations from those that might be thought appropriate to portfolio investment decisions and allocations.[7]

Perhaps the easiest route into the problem is to consider what the position of a supplier of a good on a world-wide scale would be. Other things being equal, sales to any particular foreign market would be affected by market size. Divergences from this simple position would occur as costs between the supplier and its competitors varied and according to the tastes in the particular market. Thus, in the case of the EU, one would expect greater trade between partner countries, first because of the discriminatory tariff and second because the countries tend to be near neighbours. Elaborating this to consider the problem from the point of view of the country rather than the firm, shares in markets will tend to be affected by the economic size of the supplying country as well. Such an approach leads to the sort of gravity models of trade put forward by Linnemann (1966) and Bluet and Systermanns (1968), and discussed in the context of the EU by Aitken (1973) and Mayes (1978). Here trade flows are primarily determined by the size of the supplying country, the size of the destination country, the transport cost between them and any special factors discriminating against or in favour of that specific flow. In these models the effects of the EU on trade flows can be measured as the *ex post* discrepancy between trade patterns observed for the EU and patterns seen for the rest of the world (allowing for distortions from other trading areas).[8]

The pattern of direct investment might be revealed by the other side of this same relation, namely, the trade model can show what desired trade is in a non-discriminatory world. The extent of the barriers and the degree to which actual trade diverges from this 'desired' level might then give an indication of the market which could be reached by production inside the trade barriers of the foreign country, hence giving the demand for direct investment abroad to set up the facilities to achieve the desired output. The distance between countries, since it contributes to transport costs, would also lead to direct investment rather than trade.

By this simple model, direct investment abroad among the EU countries would decrease as their tariffs on mutual trade fell, but that from (and in) third countries would increase: it would become increasingly difficult for these third countries to compete through trade as the costs of their partner competitors were reduced by the size of the tariff cut (although producers might choose to offset all or part of the gain). From this simple point of view, direct investment 'creation' and 'diversion' as a result of the lowering of tariff barriers on mutual trade by the EC would be of opposite sign to that of the corresponding trade creation and trade diversion. However, as with the two trading concepts, direct investment creation and diversion would be static effects lasting for a transitional period only.[9]

There is, moreover, a major distinction between investment and trade which would blur the relation which has just been outlined even if it were correctly identified. Previous direct investment results in the accumulation of capital in the form of a foreign subsidiary or associated company. Although, like all domestic companies in the foreign country, it will face increased competition for its products from companies in the other EC countries as tariffs are removed, the subsidiary may continue to make profits and to invest. Although no transfer of funds takes place with the parent company, any increase in assets of this form will be classified as direct investment according to the definition we have outlined. The foreign subsidiary is thus operating like any other domestic firm and it will participate in market growth like the other firms, thus continuing the upward path of direct foreign investment.

The behaviour of multinational companies is a reflection of variations in costs of inputs in various locations as well as the structure of markets they wish to serve. The pressure for the European Single Market came just as strongly from European multinationals as it did from political sources. Wisse Dekker, then head of Philips and the European Round Table of major companies, put forward a plan in January 1985 to achieve a single market in five years, i.e. by 1990, thus anticipating the White Paper. This globalization of markets reflects the nature of technology and the pace of change. New products have to be exploited quickly round the world rather than by tackling individual country markets one at a time.

These technical changes are complex, as, with just-in-time manufacturing and other improvements to reduce inventory costs and improve quality, links between companies have to be closer and quicker to execute. One facet of this is to cut down on the number of suppliers. This may actually lead to a concentration of production, disturbing some of the simpler trends of direct investment.

However, the simple model disguises a further facet of investment abroad. The development of foreign sales will normally follow an evolutionary pattern which starts with trading (unless the barriers are insurmountable) and is only followed by direct investment once the potential market looks worth while. Initial investment is more likely to be in distribution rather than manufacturing, as an agency is replaced by a more direct arrangement. Once the market is adequately covered, then production in the local market may follow.

Since there are economies of scale in production in many industries, the number of overseas subsidiaries may be strictly limited on a regional basis. Thus, US and Japanese firms may wish to invest in only one EU country and supply the rest of the EU from that base. Similarly, for the multinational company, it may be advantageous to split various parts of the manufacturing operation to take advantage of particular resources which are available in different countries – raw materials, cheap hydroelectricity, etc.

While there were technical, customs and other barriers between the member states, there was an incentive to invest in several member states rather than to concentrate in a single location. This pressure is weakened in the Single Market and there is some incentive to reorganize. However, it appears that in practice countries not only want to get inward investment for themselves but they show reluctance to treat investment in others on an equal basis by demanding local content rules – as in the case of French resistance to Nissan cars built in the United Kingdom.

This multinational structure of production and pressures to expand it have consequences for trade. The existence of subsidiaries rather than purely domestic firms tends to create trade between various parts of the multinational company. In 1980, 30% of exports covered by the Department of Trade enquiry across a sample of over 7,000 enterprises went to related enterprises abroad.[10] While this trade would not be zero if there were no related enterprises, one would expect it to be much smaller. Unfortunately, the statistics do not refer to related imports, so we cannot build up a symmetric picture. It is possible to break down the percentage by the main industrial categories and by whether they are US controlled, controlled by other foreign companies, or are UK companies as shown in Table 20.2. But the number of firms in the sample is very small in some cases, so the results should be treated with care. Nevertheless, two figures stand out from the table. The first shows that almost two-thirds of motor vehicle exports went to related enterprises and the second that US-controlled UK enterprises had over half their exports going to related enterprises. On any basis, it is clear that the level of related exports is considerable when direct investment has taken place. The consequences for the structure of trade are therefore complex.

Most early empirical work on direct investment flows in the EU concentrated on inflows from the United States, partly because of the quality of data available. However, attention has turned towards Japan, whose direct investment has increased dramatically in the second half of the 1980s (see Table 20.3). In the United Kingdom, for example, there are approximately 100 Japanese subsidiaries; two-thirds of these have been set up since 1985. Japan has replaced the United States as an investment 'threat', with a heavier political overtone, as the US economy has always been fairly open to return investments and acquisitions. Indeed, the level of recent direct investment in the United States has been so great that concern is being expressed, while Japan is a much more difficult economy to enter either through export or investment. Traditionally, US investment in Europe has had a strong element of takeover of existing enterprises. Japanese investment, on the other hand, tends to be greenfield. Arrangements with existing European firms tend to be joint ventures without Japanese majority control. This generates worries about technology transfer, the greenfield sites often being assembly operations of established products, while the joint ventures are sometimes accused of being more effective in transferring technology to Japan.

Table 20.2 ⬤ **Percentage of direct exports from the United Kingdom going to related enterprises in 1980.[a]**

Industry	US-controlled UK enterprises	Other foreign-controlled UK enterprises	UK associates of foreign enterprises	UK enterprises with overseas affiliates	Total[b]
Food, drink and tobacco	45	19	–	28	26 (112)
Chemical and allied industries	40	49	10	45	41 (166)
Metal manufacture and engineering	53	46	20	23	32 (555)
Shipbuilding and vehicles not elsewhere specified	55	27	38	21	21 (32)
Motor vehicles	77	31	–	56	64 (32)
Other manufacturing industries	27	40	18	19	20 (609)
Other activities	35	21	20	25	16 (568)
Total	52 (375)	38 (378)	19 (59)	28 (622)	31 (2074)

[a] The number of enterprises is indicated by the figures in parentheses.
[b] Includes UK enterprises with no overseas affiliates.
Source Business Monitor MA4, 1980.

It is noticeable that most modelling of inward investment relates to flows into the EU from outside, not to the flows within the EU itself. Yet it is these internal flows which should be of prime interest in the case of the Single Market. The studies of external flows suggest that there are three basic mechanisms at work. First, investment tends to increase with sales to the EU, i.e. supporting trade rather than substituting for it (Scaperlanda and Balough, 1983). Barrell and Pain (1993) suggest, following Vernon (1966), that there is an initial level of exports which is required

Table 20.3 ⬤ Japanese direct investment flows, 1982–95 ($ million).

Year	United Kingdom–Ireland	Spain–Greece–Portugal	France	Germany–Denmark	Italy	Benelux	United States
1982	176	19	102	194	19	264	2,738
1985	456	127	37	173	32	997	5,395
1988	3,998	169	463	411	108	3,180	21,702
1991	3,690	388	817	1,115	322	2,448	18,026
1994[a]	2,562	192	430	746	179	910	17,668
1995[a]	3,906	48	1,659	563	126	485	23,220

[a] Updated using annual average exchange rates to convert yen to US$.
Source Financial Statistics of Japan, Barrell and Pain (1993).

before it becomes worthwhile setting up dealer networks and other downstream services. Secondly, investment takes place to overcome trade barriers (Culem, 1988; Heitger and Stehn, 1990) or anti-dumping duties (Barrell and Pain, 1993). However, overseas investors having a choice of locations and flows are also affected by relative costs and relative barriers. Thus, when anti-dumping actions were at their height in the United States in the mid-1980s, this acted as a spur to Japanese investment there. Finally, investment flows are crucially affected by the availability of funds in the investing country. The recent slowdown in Japan and fall in stock market prices has resulted in a major fall in direct investment in the EU (Table 20.3).

We can approach the problem of the effect of changes in relative trade barriers by examining the development of direct investment flows into and out of the EC over the period of UK accession. These flows are shown in aggregate in Table 20.4, from which it is immediately clear that the patterns of outward and inward flows for the United Kingdom are very different. In the period before accession to the EC, around two-thirds of direct investment in the United Kingdom came from the United States; but over the same period, UK investment in the United States varied between only one-tenth and one-quarter of total outward investment. However, outward investment itself was more than twice as large as inward investment, and thus simple proportionate comparisons give little idea of bilateral balances. The United Kingdom has invested widely abroad in both the developed and the developing world whereas, not surprisingly, it is mainly the developed world which has invested in the United Kingdom. (As countries gain increasing maturity they tend to

Table 20.4 ● Direct outward and inward investment in the United Kingdom, 1970–85 (£ million).

	1970	1972	1974	1976	1978	1980	1982	1985
Outward								
Total	546	737	1,576	2,145	2,740	3,492	2,122	8,994
United States	134	105	401	378	969	1,784	1,414	3,187
% share	24.5	14.2	25.4	17.6	35.4	51.1	66.4	35.4
EU	88	256	367	497	579	482	−173	2,553
% share	16.1	34.7	23.3	23.2	21.1	13.8	−8.2	28.4
Belgium and Luxemburg	13	31	49	85	37	19	−5	295
Denmark	2	9	25	5	15	23	3	15
France	27	62	74	79	69	109	45	248
West Germany	20	64	109	176	113	376	47	290
Ireland	14	12	49	40	169	93	34	245
Italy	8	24	26	39	47	32	23	120
Netherlands	10	42	35	73	130	−168	−321	1,340
Inward								
Total	354	405	854	799	1,292	2,576	1,137	4,331
United States	223	266	410	550	807	1,678	372	2,323
% share	63.0	65.7	48.0	68.8	62.5	65.1	32.7	53.6
EU[a]	51	38	76	177	310	153	167	1,313
% share	14.4	9.6	8.9	22.2	24.0	5.9	14.7	30.3
Belgium and Luxemburg	6	3	6	22	42	15	13	81
Denmark	0	0	2	19	15	13	28	7
France	1	17	25	85	155	48	21	226
West Germany	15	5	34	34	69	34	58	44
Ireland	0	1	−7	37	23	24	20	6
Italy	4	8	6	11	−4	−16	6	73
Netherlands	25	6	11	−31	9	35	20	856

[a] Includes all eight countries shown throughout, although Denmark and Ireland were not members until 1973.

move through a number of phases of direct investment flows. Initially they have difficulty in absorbing investment, then the ability to absorb inward investment increases while outward investment is negligible. Eventually, although the ability to absorb inward investment increases, outward investment exceeds inward investment as overseas locations of production offer increasing advantages and sales networks are expanded. See Chapter 3 of El-Agraa (1988a) for a fuller explanation.)

As is clear from Tables 20.4 and 20.5, the United Kingdom has been the largest investor overseas in the EU and is the second largest in the world after the United States.[11] Only the Netherlands among other EU countries has been a net direct capital exporter over the last ten years, although West Germany had substantial net exports between 1975 and 1990. There was a clear surge in inward investment in the EU in 1973 and 1974, and more strikingly so in West Germany over the longer period of 1971–74. It was only in those four years that investment in Germany was greater than that in the United Kingdom. Investment in France, however, shows a strikingly different pattern, with France attracting the highest investment of all the EC countries in 1975 and 1981, and the second highest after the United Kingdom for the period 1977–80. At the other end of the scale is the very low level of direct investment in Italy. Thus, despite any attractiveness which may have existed from surplus and cheaper labour in Italy, this factor advantage has been met by labour outflow rather than capital inflow. Italy similarly has a low level of direct investment abroad, although it is still sufficiently large to show net capital exports over the last four years.

There is little of uniform pattern of investment flows among the EU countries. However, what is clear in general is that outward direct investment has been rising considerably faster than in the United States, while inward investment has risen more slowly. Thus, while in 1981 and 1982 the Unites States was a net capital importer, the EU was a substantial exporter. Much of EU direct investment must therefore be directed outside the EU rather than to other EU countries, as is clearly the case for the United Kingdom.

Direct investment abroad, like domestic investment, is substantially affected by trade cycles. Thus the peak in 1973–74 coincided with the peak of a cycle and the sharp fall in 1975 with the consequence of the first oil crisis. Of course, 1980 is an exception, for although there was a sharp downturn in UK activity (preceding that of the world in general), it coincided with the removal of exchange controls, whose effect we have already discussed. Accession to the EC may thus have its effects obscured by the trade cycle, as total direct investment could have been expected to increase at the same time as the transition period, purely because of the trade cycle. Looking at proportions may help to reduce this confusion. The most striking facets are, first, that there is no proportionate surge of investment by the other EU countries in the United Kingdom immediately following accession. There is some increase in 1976–78, but it is by no means clear that this represents any particular change in behaviour as wide year-to-year fluctuations have been observed earlier.

Outward investment by the United Kingdom in the EU, on the other hand, shows a very considerable surge *before* accession, in 1971–72, a process which is ended by

Table 20.5 ● Direct investment flows of EU countries 1984–93 (ECU million).

	1984			1987			1990			1993		
	Intra	Extra	Total	Intra	Extra	Total	Intra	Extra	Total	Intra	Extra	Total
Outward												
BLEU	-635	60	-575	-1,655	-545	-2,200	-3,077	-1,175	-4,252	-2,698	-1,469	-4,167
Denmark	-122	-222	-344	-278	-219	-497	-649	-415	-1,064	15	-1,234	-1,219
Germany	-1,168	-2,978	-4,146	-1,610	-5,266	-6,876	-9,577	-5,369	-14,946	-8,869	-4,440	-13,309
Greece	-9	-48	-57	-1	-9	-10	-16	-3	-19	-3	-4	-7
Spain	-827	-1,747	-2,574	-270	-227	-497	-1,023	-733	-1,756	-836	-796	-1,632
France	-25	-100	-125	-3,639	-3,483	-7,122	-11,409	-6,864	-18,373	-4,575	-4,644	-9,219
Irish Republic				-65	-86	-151	-548	-22	-570	-353	32	-321
Italy	-642	-1,512	-2,154	-998	-495	-1,493	-3,250	-1,031	-4,281	-3,316	-1,530	-4,846
Netherlands	-1,262	-1,011	-2,273	-1,998	-3,607	-5,605	-6,459	-4,497	-10,956	-4,118	-3,155	-7,273
Portugal	-3	-11	-14	8	-6	2	-83	-26	-109	-151	-3	-154
UK	554	-9,627	-9,073	-1,730	-16,728	-18,458	-3,100	-392	-3,492	-5,935	-4,609	-10,544
EU12	-4,213	-17,407	-21,620	-12,344	-30,670	-43,014	-39,295	-20,527	-59,822	-30,844	-21,854	-52,698
Inward												
BLEU	749	64	813	1,265	693	1,958	6,454	1,355	7,809	5,749	3,343	9,092
Denmark	-8	32	24	-127	151	24	269	567	836	308	911	1,219
Germany	694	115	809	250	215	465	4,235	2,187	6,422	2,181	1,410	3,591
Greece	15	-27	-12	102	87	189	229	79	308	300	60	360
Spain	1,316	1,387	2,703	1,976	1,338	3,314	6,062	2,956	9,018	4,028	1,846	5,874
France	141	-30	111	1,654	2,056	3,710	4,009	3,365	7,374	5,652	2,929	8,581
Irish Republic	867	927	1,794	160	327	487	2,233	964	3,197	1,804	1,291	3,095
Italy				1,310	1,745	3,055	2,085	3,020	5,105	2,266	1,410	3,676
Netherlands	-1,098	139	-959	1,315	664	1,979	4,542	3,013	7,555	4,977	809	5,786
Portugal	99	135	234	230	97	327	1,135	586	1,721	758	284	1,042
UK	559	1,996	2,555	4,085	5,619	9,704	8,327	14,661	22,988	2,825	7,260	10,085
EU12	3,334	6,512	10,365	12,344	12,991	25,335	39,295	32,753	72,048	30,844	21,090	51,934

'Intra' refers to flows to–from other EU countries, 'Extra' to flows to–from the rest of the world.

Source Eurostat, European Union Direct Investment, 1984–93.

1974. Since the benefits from investment are usually not immediate, some antici-patory investment might have been expected to take full advantage of membership when it occurred. There is thus some change which could be viewed as evidence of an initial investment effect of membership in this one respect. Since we are dealing with proportions, changes in one area necessarily entail relative changes elsewhere. In the case of outward investment, the short-run decline was taken by the residual (non-EC, non-US) category – the same category that absorbed much of the surge in UK investment in the United States after 1977.

It is also not realistic to treat the EU as a largely homogeneous unit from the point of view of direct investment. For example, direct investment flows between the United Kingdom and the Netherlands were far larger than relative economic size would suggest both before and after accession to the EU. This presumably reflects, among other things, the number of Anglo-Dutch multinational companies. How-ever, the nature of the relation is not clear as the major sectors of disinvestment in 1977, 1979 and 1980 were different (the disaggregate tables – tables 3.3 and 4.3 in *Business Monitor MA4*, 1980 – are rather difficult to interpret, as the sum of the parts is very different from the total, despite the existence of 'other' categories in both manufacturing and non-manufacturing industry).

Other differences between EU countries can readily be observed. Although Germany is economically larger than France and the United Kingdom, outward in-vestment has followed that relation and inward investment has followed a different pattern, with French investment tending to be the larger. However, in both cases UK investment has been larger than the reverse flow. Irish investment in the United Kingdom, which was negligible before accession to the EU, has picked up substan-tially since. This is perhaps more difficult to explain than geographical nearness might imply, as the easy movement of funds was possible prior to accession. The total picture is thus rather confused, but it suggests that there has been no dramatic switch in the nature of direct investment in the United Kingdom as a result of its accession to the EU.

As noted earlier, between one-half and three-quarters of net investment abroad by the United Kingdom is composed of profits by overseas subsidiaries and associated companies which are not remitted to the United Kingdom. Net acquisition of over-seas companies' share and loan capital is, partly by consequence, around one-sixth to one-third of the total, except for the two years 1970 and 1980 when it was about half. Unfortunately, these same figures are only available for EC countries for the period 1975–80, so we cannot make any contrast of the position 'before' and 'after' accession to the EU. Nevertheless, for that period, taking the EU as a whole, un-remitted profits were as shown in Table 20.6.

The scale of net inward investment has meant that over the period 1973–79 there has been a steady increase in foreign ownership of UK firms, from 15% to 20% of net output in manufacturing. Not surprisingly, direct investment tends to be con-centrated on larger firms, for reasons of information if for no other, and this 20% of output was produced by 2.5% of the total number of establishments in the United Kingdom. These firms also have a below average labour intensity (14% of total em-

Table 20.6 ⬤ Unremitted profits as a percentage of total net outward investment by the United Kingdom.

	1975	1977	1979	1980	1982	1984	1985
In EU	74	55	112	40	40	a	122
In all countries	40	63	71	33	80	82	55

[a] Net outward investment negative.
Source Business Monitor.

ployment) and about average investment flow (21.5% of the total). This, however, gives us little indication about the nature of changes in investment flows which could be expected, although it does suggest that foreign-owned firms make an important contribution to productivity and investment for future growth, thus emphasizing the role that freedom of capital movement can play in increasing EU competitiveness.

It seems likely, therefore, that if we were to apply the same form of analysis as Scaperlanda and Balough (1983) to other flows of direct investment among the EU countries which involve the United Kingdom, we would not find any strong effect from changes in relative trade restrictions. Thus, while there may be some short-run effects, it does not appear likely that there are major changes in capital movements in the EU which involve the United Kingdom as there have been in trade patterns, as shown in Mayes (1983a), for example.

As mentioned earlier, figures on US direct investment are rather more detailed and hence we can get some idea of whether the United States changed either the extent of its investment in the EC relative to other areas, after the expansion of the EU in 1973, or the pattern of it among the member countries.

Prior to accession, the United Kingdom had a much larger proportion of US direct investment (Table 20.7) than its economic size alone would suggest. In the first few years after accession, although investment was still large in comparative terms, it was sufficiently lower to allow the United Kingdom's share of the existing stock of US investment in the EU to fall by nearly 4%. However, since 1977 the share of investment has been running ahead of the stock share again: hence the stock share has recovered half its previous loss. The shares of other EU countries in the total stock have also changed little. This is partly because of the scale of the change in the flow (investment) required to make any substantial change in the capital stock over a period as short as seven years, but also because of limited shift in the investment flows themselves. Changes are nothing like as striking as for trade flows. Again, it must be remembered that this evidence is very limited in itself, but it contributes to the overall picture.

Now that the 1992 programme is well developed, one might have expected to see

Table 20.7 ⬭ **US direct investment in the EU[a] 1973–95.**

	1973	1977	1980	1984	1987	1993	1995
Total stock ($ million)	18,501	27,747	41,476	69,500	118,614	564,283	711,621
% of total stock in individual countries							
United Kingdom	35.7	31.9	33.9	41.2	38.0	45.42	39.95
Belgium and Luxemburg	8.1	9.4	8.6	7.2	6.6	7.20	8.47
Denmark	0.4	0.5	0.5	1.7	0.9	0.72	0.75
France	15.9	14.9	14.3	9.3	9.8	10.11	10.87
West Germany	24.0	25.3	23.3	21.4	20.8	15.31	14.32
Greece	–	–	–	–	–	0.17	0.15
Ireland	1.7	3.4	3.9	4.2	4.7	3.75	3.65
Italy	7.6	7.1	8.0	6.6	7.2	5.30	5.57
Netherlands	6.5	7.4	7.5	8.4	12.0	8.70	12.46
Portugal	–	–	–	–	–	0.53	0.57
Spain	–	–	–	–	–	2.78	3.23
US investment in the EC as % of total US direct investment abroad	39.2	38.3	51.7	0.0	46.1	42.61	42.91
US investment in United Kingdom as % of US investment in the EC	29.7	39.2	58.5	[b]	17.6	42.62	42.92

[a] EC (9).
[b] Total investment in EC $8 million, investment in United Kingdom $891 million.
Source US Department of Commerce, *Survey of Current Business*, Department of Industry.

a change in behaviour but the position is largely unchanged. There has been no major diversion of US foreign direct investment to the EC. In fact, the share has remained remarkably stable. Expansion of the EC(9) to EC(12) shows little impact and investment is still flowing to traditional destinations.

Some of the most interesting evidence for a change in behaviour comes from the 1990 Special Edition of *European Economy* which explores the impact of the Single Market by industrial sector. Table 20.8 shows that there was a marked increase in mergers and acquisitions in the late 1980s in the EU. Of these, the proportion emanating within the EU but across the borders of the member states increased sharply in the final year.

The picture is weakened somewhat by the fact that this was part of a world-wide merger boom, but it is interesting that while joint ventures and minority investments also rose over the period it was on the whole nothing like the same scale.

Table 20.8 ● Mergers and acquisitions.

Year	Total (no.)	National (%)	EC (%)	International (%)
1983–84	155	65	19	16
1984–85	208	70	21	9
1985–86	227	64	23	13
1986–87	303	70	25	5
1987–88	383	56	29	18
1988–89	492	47	40	13

Source European Economy.

There has certainly been an increase in the cross-border movement of capital since the start of the 1992 programme. However, not all is due to that programme. Research by Molle and Morsink (1990) shows that foreign direct investment does respond to exchange rate changes, while the dramatic fall in share prices in Japan has led to a substantial reduction in the pace of their investment throughout the world including the EU. The pattern of this investment still strongly reflects the traditional pattern of ease of entry. It is by no means clear that entry by acquisition has become particularly harmonized or, indeed, greatly eased thus far. The market for capital has thus become freer, but linkages between commercial firms and the providers of capital remain which are little affected by the Single Market regulatory changes.

20.4 Labour movements

Although in the abstract economists tend to talk about the two main factors, capital and labour, in one breath, the differences in their behaviour from a practical point of view in the EC are enormous. At a simple level, it was noticeable that the total direct investment statistics for the United Kingdom in any one year were substantially affected by the behaviour of a single company. (For flows between any particular pair of countries, a single company can dominate the total effect.) Labour flows, on the other hand, are the result of the decisions of a large number of independent households (although actions by companies and communities can have a strong influence on these decisions). With some limited exceptions involving transient staff and actions in border areas, movement of labour simply involves a person shifting his residence from one country to another to take up a job in the second country. There is not the same range of possible variations as in the case of capital movements. There is also the great simplification that there is no equivalent problem of the relation between the financial flows (or retained earnings) and the physical capital stock. The number of foreign nationals employed will be the sum of the net inflows, without any revaluation problems and only a relatively limited difficulty for retirements (through age, naturalisation, etc.).

A major incentive to move is an income differential in real terms. However, it is not merely that the same job will be better paid in the second country; it may mean that the person moving will be able to get a 'better' job in the second country (in the sense of a different job with higher pay). There are severe empirical problems in establishing what relative real incomes are, not just in the simple sense of purchasing-power parities, but in trying to assess how much one can change one's tastes to adapt to the new country's customs and price patterns and what extra costs would be involved if, for example, the household had to be divided, and so on. This is difficult to measure, not just in precise terms for the outside observer, but even in rough terms for the individual involved. This sort of uncertainty for the individual is typical of the large range of barriers that impede the movement of labour, in addition to the wide range of official barriers that inhibit movement. Ignorance of job opportunities abroad, living conditions, costs, ease of overcoming language difficulties, how to deal with regulations, etc., is reduced as more people move from one country to another and are able to exchange experiences. Firms can reduce the level of misinformation by recruiting directly in foreign countries.

Even if it were possible to sort out what the official barriers are and to establish the relative real terms, there would still be a multitude of factors which could not be quantified but perhaps be given some implicit costs. These other factors involve differences in language, differences in customs, problems of transferring assets (both physical and financial), disruptions to family life, changing of schooling, loss of friends, etc. Of course, some of these factors could work in a favourable direction: it might be easier to find accommodation abroad, and setting up a new household and finding new friends might be an attractive prospect. All this suggests that margins in labour rewards between countries may be considerable in practice, even if free movement of labour is theoretically permitted. It should thus be no surprise to find that many differences in labour rewards exist among the EC countries. However, it would also be a mistake to think that there are no barriers in practice to employment in other EC countries. In the first edition of this book, El-Agraa and Goodrich (1980) set out the barriers which existed for one particular group: accountants. Skills and methods of working vary among the EC countries. There is a natural reluctance to accept those with different qualifications and experience, and considerable effort has gone into trying to make movement easier between countries.

Bourguignon *et al.* (1977) identify two other main determinants of the ease of movement in addition to the income differential (which they interpret in the narrow terms of monetary difference), namely, age and the attitude to risk. Their model, however, relates to the nature of the people who move: younger people, with less responsibility, who are willing to take risks. This is not very useful in the current context, where we wish to deal with the flows among the EC countries and the flows from non-members in aggregate. In our case, we need to consider variables which are of a similar aggregate nature: average per capita income, distance between countries, language differences, common land boundaries, etc. These factors, like those influencing capital movements, can be classified into three general groups which we could label 'push' factors, 'pull' factors and impediments. 'Push' factors relate to the tendency to emigrate – from poor living conditions, etc. – without regard to the destination; 'pull' factors correspondingly relate to the features attracting immigrants – availability of jobs, etc. – without regard to origin. The impediments are both general – applying to all migrants (both to exit, as in the East European countries before 1989, and to entry) – and specific: lifting of restrictions on members of other EC countries, for example.

It is clearly much more difficult to set out a model of labour flows when many of the restraints are not on a price basis (like a tariff), nor on a simple quantitative basis (like a quota). If, as appears to be the case for many non-member countries, there is excess supply of willing migrants at the prevailing income differentials and associated social difficulties of movement, we merely need to examine what determines demand (assuming, that is, that 'workers' cannot move without a work permit and that work permits are issued only in respect of specific jobs). In most cases this will be a combination of the wishes of firms as employers and governments as regulators. The British experience of regulation of inflows from the new Commonwealth is one example of the operation of the quantitative restrictions. However, movements of nationals of member states are not so readily determined. It may very well be that there is still excess supply in that flows take place when there is a job to go to. (Returning home, however, does not necessarily occur immediately a job is lost as some unemployment benefits will probably have accrued.) However, excluding the new members, Greece, Portugal and Spain, and with the possible exception of Italy, it is not likely that this is the case. If the market for within-EC migrants were demand constrained, then easing the restrictions could be expected to lead to rapid inflows from other member countries. Otherwise, the response would be more muted. Indeed, if the barriers did not result in any effective restriction, their removal would be without consequence.

20.5 Labour flows in the EU

The official position in the EU is straightforward. Freedom of movement of labour was part of the framework of the Treaty of Rome itself. However, the original six EU member nations had to start from a position of considerable restrictions of labour movement, and it was not until 1968 that work permits were abolished and preferences for home country workers no longer permitted. The Single Market programme has involved a range of measures to try to eliminate those fiscal barriers, not just for the worker but for the accompanying family as well. However, even within member states, changing jobs and location results in the loss of privileges: the number of days leave may increase with length of service, golf clubs may have waiting lists, etc. However, merely permitting labour mobility does not in itself either facilitate or encourage it. It is readily possible to make mobility difficult through measures relating to taxes and benefits which make a period of previous residence or contribution necessary for benefit.

The actual path of labour migration is heavily affected by overall circumstances. If an economy is growing and able to maintain 'full employment', it is likely to attract more labour from abroad for two reasons: firstly, because there are more job opportunities; and secondly, because there is less domestic opposition to immigration. In the period after the first oil crisis, when unemployment rose sharply and the EU economies moved into recession, there was much more resistance to the flow of labour between countries and an encouragement to reverse the flow. Although the position improved somewhat in the second half of the 1980s, unemployment is still a major problem and is likely to remain so for some time to come. The fall in the numbers of young people has eased the overall problem. Indeed, the problem for the future is the increasing dependency ratio as people live longer. Thus, there are simultaneous pressures to retire early in response to unemployment and higher real incomes, and to work longer as accumulated pension rights and wealth need to sustain a longer period of retirement.

There are several examples – Finland and Sweden, and Australia and New Zealand, for instance – where regular ebbs and flows in labour migration have been observed. Ebbs and flows in the EC seem to be less common to all countries with the possible exception of Ireland, where emigration has been common both to the United Kingdom and to the United States. While, as might be expected, the number of foreign workers fell after 1974 with the economic cycle in West Germany and the Netherlands, it rose in Belgium and Denmark. (There was little change in Italy and Luxemburg; suitable statistics on the same basis were not available from the Statistical Office of the EU for the remaining countries.)

The clearest feature of the development of the permitted mobility of labour among the EU countries was that restrictions were lifted on workers from other member countries rather than non-members. Nevertheless, as is clear from Table 20.9, only Belgium and Luxemburg have had a higher proportion of their foreign workers coming from within the EU than from outside it. The position has changed relatively little in recent years (see Table 20.10) with the exception of Germany, where there has been a small rise, and Luxemburg, where there has been a small fall in the number of non-nationals in the workforce. Looking at it from the point of view of country of origin, Table 20.11 shows that in all cases except Ireland only a very small percentage of the labour force has moved to other countries. (Those who have moved and changed their nationality will be excluded, but that is unlikely to make more than a marginal difference to the total.) With the exception of Denmark and Italy, it appears that size and percentage of working population abroad have an inverse relation. Looking at the same figures from a different point of view, with the exception of Luxemburg it is the EU countries with the lowest incomes that have

Table 20.9 ● Foreign employees by nationality (thousands).

	West Germany			France		Netherlands			Belgium			Luxemburg			United Kingdom		
	1974	1981[a]	1986	1975	1986	1974	1981	1986	1974	1979	1986	1974	1979	1986	1975	1981	1986
Total member countries[b]	718	558	498	305	590	51	76	76	130	181	187	31	32	52	323	313	398
of which:																	
Belgium	na	na	7	na	12	22	26	22	–	–	–	na	na	9	na	na	3
West Germany	–	–	–	na	15	na	na	16	na	na	6	na	na	6	na	na	18
Italy	341	292	188	230	85	na	na	7	83	na	61	11	11	8	na	na	57
Ireland	na	na	1	na	1	na	na	1	na	na	1	na	na	0	232	228	268
Total non-member countries[b]	1,613	1,364	1,048	1,595	583	66	149	92	77	141	46	17	18	3	468	447	423
of which:																	
Algeria	na	na	2	440	190	na	na	0	na	na	2	na	na	0	na	na	0
Morocco	na	na	14	130	132	9	34	25	na	na	17	na	na	0	na	na	4
Portugal	82	56	35	475	351	3	5	3	3	6	4	13	13	0	3	8	2
Spain	159	83	65	265	111	11	12	7	16	31	15	2	2	1	21	15	15
Tunisia	na	na	8	70	47	na	na	1	18	35	2	na	na	0	na	na	1
Turkey	618	576	499	25	23	22	49	36	11	21	10	na	na	0	4	6	7
Yugoslavia (the former)	473	340	283	na	31	na	na	5	na	na	2	1	1	1	na	na	4
Total	2,331	1,922	1,547	1,900	1,173	117	226	169	207	322	187	48	50	55	791	760	821
As % of employees	9.0	7.5	6.9	9.2	6.4	2.5	4.6	3.6	5.4	8.6	6.2	31.2	31.6	37.4	3.2	3.2	3.8

[a] At the end of January 1973 there were 268,000 Greeks employed in West Germany, 15,000 Moroccans and 11,000 Tunisians. By the end of June 1980 the number of Greeks had fallen to 133,000 but no comparable figures for Moroccans and Tunisians are available.

[b] In 1986 Spain and Portugal are included as members and not as non-members.

Source: Eurostat, OECD, Labour Force Statistics, 1970–81; [a] Owen-Smith (1983), p. 160.

Table 20.10 ◯ Labour force by nationality in EU member states, 1990 and 1995 (% share).

	National		Other EU		Non-EU	
	1990	1995	1990	1995	1990	1995
Belgium	94.6	92.2	5.2	5.4	0.2	2.5
Denmark	98.0	98.1	0.5	0.8	1.5	1.1
Germany	91.5	91.0	2.8	2.8	5.7	6.2
Greece	99.3	98.3	0.2	0.2	0.5	1.5
Spain	99.8	99.2	0.1	0.3	0.1	0.5
France	93.5	93.7	3.0	2.5	3.5	3.7
Ireland	97.4	97.0	2.1	2.4	0.5	0.6
Italy	na	99.6	na	0.1	na	0.4
Luxemburg	66.6	61.0	31.5	36.2	1.9	2.8
Netherlands	96.3	96.1	1.4	1.7	2.3	2.2
Portugal	99.4	99.6	0.1	0.2	0.5	0.2
United Kingdom	96.6	96.4	1.6	1.6	1.8	2.0
Austria	–	90.4	–	1.1	–	8.5
Finland	–	99.3	–	0.2	–	0.5
Sweden	–	95.9	–	2.0	–	2.1
EU	95.2	95.3	2.0	1.7	2.8	2.9

Source Labour Force Survey, 1991, 1995.

Table 20.11 ⬤ Foreign employees in the EC, 1976 (thousands).

	Nationals working in other member states	Domestic working population	(1) as a percentage of (2)
	1	2	3
Belgium	68	3,713	1.8
Denmark	7	2,293	0.2
West Germany	137	24,556	0.5
France	114	20,838	0.5
Ireland	455	1,021	44.6
Italy	694	18,930	3.6
Luxemburg	6	148	4.1
Netherlands	83	4,542	1.8
United Kingdom	61	24,425	0.2
Total EC	1,625	100,464	1.6
Spain	447	12,535	3.5
Greece	239	3,230	7.4
Portugal	569	3,279	17.4
Turkey	587	14,710	4.0
Yugoslavia	458		
Algeria	447		
Morocco	183		
Tunisia	85		
Others	1,392		
Total non-EC	4,407		
Total	6,032		

Source Emerson (1979).

the highest outward mobility. Greece, Spain and Portugal alter the picture fairly considerably. They all had above average numbers of people working elsewhere in the EC even before they joined, particularly Portugal. Thus, it might be expected that as restrictions are removed there will be some expansion in movement. However, despite high levels of unemployment, there are no obvious signs of this.

Turning to inward flows, the picture is a little more complex. Luxemburg stands out with around a third of the working population coming from foreign countries. France, Germany and Belgium form a second group with a little less than 10% of their workforce from abroad; and the remaining countries have smaller proportions, down to negligible numbers in the case of Italy. Since Italy is a major exporter of labour to West Germany, France and Belgium, it is not surprising to find that it is a negligible importer since these flows do not represent an exchange of *special* skills, but a movement of workers with *some* skills towards countries with greater manu-facturing employment opportunities.

As only principal flows are shown in Table 20.9, it is difficult to make any gener-alizations across the whole range of behaviour. Some special relationships are ap-parent which relate to previous history rather than the EC as a determinant of the pattern of flows: former colonies in the case of France and the United Kingdom and, to a lesser extent, in the case of Belgium and the Netherlands; and the relationship between the United Kingdom and Ireland. The West German policy of encouraging foreign workers is clearly shown with the large numbers coming from Turkey and (the former) Yugoslavia. What is perhaps surprising is that despite the recruitment ban on countries outside the EU in 1973 the shares of member and non-member countries in number of foreign nationals employed in West Germany was approxi-mately the same in 1974 and in 1981. The more recent data, provided in Table 20.10, show a fall in foreign labour in most countries by 1990 and stabilization thereafter. However, the switch is much larger for those from non-member states than from the other members.

At first glance it appears that labour, in proportionate terms, is rather less mobile than capital, particularly if one takes the United Kingdom as an example. The bal-ance of labour and capital flows tends to be in opposite directions according to the development of the various economies. However, there are many specific factors overriding this general relation. The wealthier countries have attracted labour and invested overseas at the same time, thus helping to equilibrate the system from both directions. However, there is little evidence inside the EU that there are large labour movements purely as a result of the existence of the EU. Some movement between contiguous countries is to be expected, especially where they are small, and also movements from those countries with considerable differences in income, primar-ily Greece, Italy, Ireland, Portugal and, to a lesser extent, Spain. However, the major movements have been the inflow of workers from outside the EU, primarily into Germany and France. Thus, despite discrimination in favour of nationals of member countries, the relative benefits to employers (the ability to offer worse conditions, readier dismissal, lower benefits, etc.) and to employees (the size of the income gain and the improvement in living standards for their families) makes flows from the lower income countries more attractive to both parties.

Worries about competitive exploitation of employees through reducing social pro-tection (known colloquially as 'social dumping') have led the Community to de-velop the social dimension of the Single Market programme, expressed through the Charter of Fundamental Rights for Workers and the action programme for its im-plementation (see Chapter 18). The measures are specifically designed to ensure a 'single market' for labour in the EC. This does not necessarily mean that labour will be more mobile or labour markets more flexible as a consequence. Indeed, the UK government has argued forcefully that these actions may make it more difficult to eliminate pockets of unemployment and hence harm some of these workers whom it is designed to protect. As a consequence, the United Kingdom did not signed the Social Charter and would not accept the Social Chapter proposed for the Maastricht

Treaty. As a result this chapter has been appended as a protocol to the treaty signed by the other eleven members. It remains to be seen whether in practice the United Kingdom will gain any increased mobility of labour *and capital* as a result of this difference. Thus far, measures have been agreed by the twelve so there is as yet no differential impact.

It should be no surprise that international mobility is limited when one sees the extent of reluctance to respond to economic stimuli for movement within countries. The existence of sharply different regional unemployment levels and regional wage differentials reveals the reluctance. In the United Kingdom the system of public sector housing is thought to aid labour rigidity. Possession of a council house in one district does not give any entitlement to one elsewhere. However, even for private sector house owners, negative equity and the very considerable transaction costs of sale and purchase act as a substantial restriction on mobility. Many of the social restraints also apply: disruption of the education of children, loss of friends, for example. The differentials in rewards or other incentives to move, therefore, have to be very considerable to induce international movement once a person has a family and a home. Mobility in the United States, on the other hand, is much greater, showing that the level of EU mobility is a facet of European society, not a necessary part of economic behaviour. Indeed, if movement had been more common it is unlikely that the member states would have been willing to permit a free flow under the 1992 programme.

20.6 Capital and labour movements combined

As was noted at the outset, factor movements cannot legitimately be examined without looking at the behaviour of the markets for internationally traded goods and services at the same time. Nor are the two factor markets independent. While the capital market has little of the characteristics of discrimination in favour of fellow members of the EU that form the basis of trading relationships between the countries, the decision over whether to invest abroad or at home is related to decisions over whether or not to export from the domestic market. Other things being equal, investment at home will generate more domestic employment, and indeed it may encourage an inflow of labour from abroad. Investment abroad, on the other hand, will tend to encourage employment in that country and a transfer of labour abroad as well.

The final outcome will depend very much upon whether there is full employment. When there is a shortage of skilled employees, or indeed a shortage of unskilled employees, at wages consistent with successful international competition, investment abroad, especially where costs are lower, may be a preferable substitute for labour-saving investment at home.

Clearly, within the EU there is less incentive to invest abroad where product prices are not subject to tariffs and hence no big gains in competitiveness can be made. Indeed, one would expect investment from non-members to increase because of the increased size of the common market. Thus, capital flows could be expected to change in the opposite direction to trade flows, with both an investment-reducing equivalent of trade creation and an investment-increasing switch from third countries as an equivalent to trade diversion. Controls on labour movements have been removed in a manner that favours inflows from EU members rather than non-members.

Running across these considerations are two other factors. Labour can be expected to move from where rewards are lower to where they are substantially higher (to cover the costs of moving), as is evidenced by the outflow from Italy. Secondly, capital investment could be expected to move to areas where labour costs are much lower, but this movement has been much less marked. Instead, capital movements have tended to follow sales opportunities and other locational advantages rather than just labour cost. Insofar as labour and capital movements do not take place, factor price differentials will continue to persist, assuming they are not eliminated by trade flows, and the allocation of resources among the EU countries, and indeed between them and non-members, will be inefficient.

Until the downturn in the European economy, this inefficiency would have been expected to take the form of insufficiently capital-sensitive investment, with a labour inflow being used to avoid restructuring. This would shift some more labour-intensive processes abroad to more labour-intensive EU members, or even outside the EU. Limits on labour mobility decrease this tendency, but with high levels of unemployment currently, and for much of the foreseeable future in the EU, it seems unlikely that any further encouragement to move will take place. Indeed, the pressures are the other way round. There is a danger that the new protectionism will apply not just to goods but to factor movements as well. Insofar as the EU continues its path towards increasing ease of factor mobility as set out in the 1992 programme, it may be able to maintain a competitive advantage over others who resort to this from of protection. It is not surprising, therefore, that third countries have been keen to operate inside the EU and are using just that freedom of capital movement to achieve it.

The experience with migration from central and eastern Europe since 1989 has greatly increased the caution over opening up the labour market more widely. It reinforces the suspicion that labour movement has been widely regarded as a key ingredient of European union largely because it has not occurred on a substantial scale.

Notes

1. Indeed, it is the concept of control which distinguishes direct from portfolio investment. The technical definition adopted by the IMF (*Balance of Payments Manual*, fourth edition, 1977) is 'Direct Investment refers to investment that adds to, deducts from or acquires a lasting interest in an enterprise operating in an economy other than that of the investor, the investor's purpose being to

have an effective voice in the management of the enterprise'. Clearly, this distinction can be made only by asking companies themselves about their overseas investment – by the Department of Trade, the Bank of England and the British Insurance Association, in the case of the United Kingdom.

2. 'Covered' in the sense that the forward exchange rate premium or discount is taken into account in the computation of the difference in interest rates between countries.

3. This description of capital flows 'balancing' trade flows could equally be phrased as trade flows 'balancing' capital flows. They are two sides of the same coin. If there is a differential in rates of return capital will be attracted into a country, this will raise the exchange rate thereby tending to encourage imports and lower exports and hence balancing the capital movement.

4. As was pointed out by Padoa-Schioppa *et al.* (1987), it is not possible to run a stable system with fixed exchange rates, free capital movements, free trade and independent fiscal policies. One or other of these must be constrained (the last in the case of an integrated single market).

5. In each case the transactions shown are the *net* transactions of the particular category of investor. Thus, outflows are net investments by UK firms abroad or by UK residents in foreign securities, and inflows are net investments by foreign companies in UK companies, etc. A positive value for net portfolio investment overseas from the United Kingdom thus means that the portfolio of foreign assets has been run down (net disinvestment).

6. There are, of course, differential restraints on the activities of financial institutions depending upon whether or not they are registered within the EU.

7. The data on capital flows (and stocks) are notoriously unreliable, which inhibits empirical work. For example, the distinction between debt and equity can sometimes be blurred when there are tax advantages in following one form of finance rather than another.

8. The analysis would be more effective if the nature of the barriers to trade and the size of the distortion through preferential tariffs could actually be inserted in the equations as well.

9. The analogy between trade diversion and creation, and investment diversion and creation should not be pushed too far as the trade concepts are welfare changes, not just changes in trade patterns.

10. *Business Monitor MA4* (1980), table 6.3 (oil and diamond companies are excluded). The equivalent figure in the 1976 survey was almost identical.

11: On an annual basis, the United Kingdom has been overtaken by Japan, but the United Kingdom's outstanding stock of foreign direct investment is still larger.

....

chapter twenty-one

EU external trade policy

M. BRÜLHART AND D. McALEESE*

The external trade policy of the EU impinges on fully one-fifth of world trade. Hence, an understanding of the principles and practice of the Union's trade policy, the Common Commercial Policy (CCP), is of vital importance to any student of the global trade environment. Research on the subject has grown significantly in recent years. The World Trade Organization's *Trade Policy Review of the EU* (WTO, 1995) provides a particularly valuable insight into how trade specialists view the EU and, no less important, how the EU sees its own role. Numerous academic studies of the EU's external trade policy have been published in recent years, addressing both broad themes and detailed aspects of the policy (Heidensohn, 1995; McAleese, 1993; Molle, 1994; Pelkmans and Carzaniga, 1996; Schuknecht, 1992; and Winters, 1994a, b).

Some special features of the CCP should be mentioned at the outset. Firstly, trade policy touches on an ever wider range of economic issues. In the early years of the CCP, discussions concentrated almost uniquely on the level and structure of the common external tariff (CET). These questions could be analyzed within the established framework of trade theory. As tariffs were reduced in successive GATT (General Agreement on Tariffs and Trade, predecessor of the WTO) rounds to near insignificance, other policy areas have become increasingly relevant to international trade: non-tariff barriers, taxation, industrial policy, exchange rates, competition policy, labour standards, consumer protection and environmental policy, to mention but a few. Most of these issues cannot be analyzed through manipulation of the standard trade models, and it is no longer possible, therefore, to provide a unified theoretical background to the discussion of the CCP.

Secondly, the CCP is inherently complex, being the outcome of different national legacies and numerous compromises at Council and Commission level. The Union is still in the process of defining its identity and forging solidarity among its members. Change in the CCP involves hard bargaining not just between the EU and non-member states, but between member states as well. The Union's approach to trade matters can therefore appear piecemeal, and its untidy collection of regional and

*The authors are grateful for valuable comments from Marc Auboin, Sam Laird and Alan Matthews. Excellent research assistance was provided by Sylvia Charmant.

national trade agreements makes generalization difficult. For example, traditional ties with former colonies go far towards explaining the complex series of preferential trade arrangements with African and Mediterranean countries.

Thirdly, EU policy makers frequently remain more concerned with the interests of their particular member state than with those of the Union as a whole. Hence, a unique feature of the EU's trade policy is that the impact of trade on the constituent national economies and regions weighs more heavily than in a unitary system. For example, in the United States, an employee who moves to San Francisco after being made redundant in Dallas enters the national statistics as a happy example of internal mobility. An Italian who moves to Munich after losing a job in Milan is seen in a different light. To the Italian government, emigration would have overtones of domestic policy failure and, to the German government, the inflow of Italian workers might be seen as exacerbating Germany's unemployment problem. Any analysis of the EU's trade regime therefore has to take account of the particular political priorities and sensitivities prevailing in the Union.

The background to EU trade policy is different in many respects to the trade policy of other major trading groups. For this reason alone, it constitutes a worthwhile subject of study. The evolving nature of the EU in a context of continuous globalization of the economy makes such a study even more challenging and important. In recent years, the CCP has been subject to far-reaching changes, induced both by initiatives within the EU, mainly in the context of the Single Market, and by initiatives on a multilateral stage, primarily related to the completion of the Uruguay Round in 1995. A stock-taking exercise on the EU's trade policy thus appears particularly timely.

This chapter is divided into five sections. The first presents an overview of the principles and policy instruments of the CCP. The second describes the pattern of trade between the EU and the outside world. The third considers EU trade policy specifically towards the main trading partners. The fourth contains an analysis of new trade policy issues, which are coming to the forefront in ongoing trade negotiations. The concluding section considers the future development of the CCP.

21.1 The CCP

The EU is an association of states with a particular legal character. It is regarded as a community in international law, not as a nation, although it possesses some features of 'nationality'. Many EU laws and regulations are enforceable in member states without requiring ratification by national parliaments. These transferred sovereign powers include foreign trade and the right to conclude trade agreements with different countries (Pelkmans, 1984; and Chapters 1 and 2).

A common trade policy for the EU is *necessary*, because in its absence the purpose of a common market will be frustrated. For instance, if member states had different tariffs, third countries would export to the member state with the lowest tariff. Once inside the union, the goods would then enjoy free passage to states with higher tariffs. High-tariff member states would of course object and would be tempted to impose restrictions on imports from the low-tariff member state. But such barriers would frustrate the whole concept of a single market. Hence, a common market needs to be complemented by a single commercial policy. A common trade policy, moreover, can be *desirable* insofar as it strengthens the bargaining power of the Union in negotiating with its trading partners. Small member states in particular benefit from this: on their own they would be more vulnerable to pressure from larger countries.

21.1.1 EU decision-making procedures and WTO constraints

The key provisions of the CCP are contained in Articles 110–116 of the Treaty of Rome. Article 110 contains the well-known aspiration:

> By establishing a customs union between themselves member states aim to contribute, in the common interest, to the harmonious development of world trade, the progressive abolition of restrictions on international trade and the lowering of customs barriers.

The cornerstone of the CCP is Article 113. It sets out the important rule that:

> the CCP shall be based on uniform principles, particularly in regard to changes in tariff rates, the conclusion of tariff and trade agreements, the achievement of uniformity in measures towards the liberalisation of export policy and in measures to protect trade such as those to be taken in the case of dumping or subsidies.

Article 113 functions on the basis of qualified majority voting in the Council (see Chapter 2). Subject to the Council's approval, the Commission is empowered to conduct negotiations in consultation with a special committee appointed by the Council for this purpose, the 'Article 113 Committee', and within the framework of such directives as the Council may issue to it. Association agreements concluded with third countries must also be ratified by the European Parliament. The EU has observer status at both FAO and the United Nations and negotiates on behalf of member states at the WTO.

The evolution of the CCP has been marked by continuing efforts by the Commission to centralize power over external relations policy in Brussels and, by so doing, to make the conduct of the CCP easier to adjust, quicker to implement and more efficient overall. In 1994, the European Court of Justice confirmed that the CCP fully covers international negotiations on trade in goods, thereby attributing exclusive competence in this area to the Union institutions.

The European Commission, however, does not have a completely free rein in determining trade policy. Under the 1994 Court ruling, the Union shares competence with the member states in negotiations related to services and intellectual property, and unanimity is therefore required for decisions in these areas. This division of competencies was confirmed by the Amsterdam summit in 1997. Furthermore, much discretion over trade policy has been voluntarily surrendered under the terms of successive multilateral GATT trade negotiations, the most recent of which, the

Uruguay Round, came into force in 1995. Under the terms of this agreement, the EU is committed to specific trade liberalizing measures and to an extensive range of obligations, which are monitored and enforced by the newly established WTO. The three main trade liberalizing measures are:

- an average 38% tariff reduction on imported manufactures,
- the conversion of variable levies and other import barriers on agricultural goods into equivalent tariffs, and the gradual reduction of these agricultural tariffs by 36%,
- the phasing out of quantitative restrictions on textile and clothing imports.

The EU has also participated in the liberalization of trade in services and has subscribed to internationally agreed codes of conduct relating to intellectual property and specific economic sectors. These issues are taken up later in this chapter.

The Commission is legally obliged to defend the commercial interests of the EU. Under the Trade Barriers Regulation, adopted by the Council in 1994, any EU firm, industry or member state can request the Commission to conduct an investigation against third countries which are believed to be in breach of WTO rules, and, if necessary, to initiate a dispute settlement procedure at the WTO. The Commission also plays a pro-active role, seeking to prise open foreign markets beyond the concessions already agreed. Its 'Market Access Strategy', launched in 1996, invites EU businesses to submit information on trade barriers in non-EU countries and assembles all the information in a market access database, made publicly available on the Internet.

21.1.2 Instruments of the CCP

The principles of the CCP are put into effect by means of *trade policy instruments* and *trade agreements*. First, we survey the main instruments of EU trade policy, while trade agreements with non-EU countries are discussed in section 21.1.3.

We can distinguish four main policy instruments which the Commission can employ to influence external trade: (i) tariffs, (ii) quotas, (iii) voluntary export restraints (VERs) and (iv) anti-dumping measures (Table 21.1). This list is by no means exhaustive. For example, in addition to import restrictions, the CCP also encompasses some measures to promote exports – although this domain is still dominated by national policies (WTO, 1995b). Even more important, the boundary between trade measures and other economic policies has become increasingly blurred over time. Restrictions on imports, therefore, constitute only part, albeit a highly visible and significant one, of the EU's policies influencing external trade.

(i) Tariffs

The most visible element of EU trade policy is the *CET*. In 1995, the overall average EU tariff rate stood at 9.6% of import values (WTO, 1995b). Tariffs are high on

Table 21.1 ⬤ Major instruments of EU trade policy.

Trade policy instruments	EU policy	WTO regime
Tariffs	• *overall* average: 9.6% of import value in 1995 • average for *industrial goods*: 6% of import value in 1995, 3.7% in 2000 • 40% of industrial imports free of tariffs; highest rate on trucks (22%), rates in excess of 10% on certain textiles, clothing, cars, microprocessors, radio and TV sets • average for *agricultural goods*: 26% of import value in 1995, 18.4% in 2000 • peaks on meat, dairy products and cereals in excess of 50% of import values • tariffs on computer and telecom related goods phased out by 2000	• non-discrimination (equal tariffs for all WTO members, except for regional integration agreements and preferences granted to developing countries) • tariff binding (commitment to tariff ceilings; EU to reduce average tariffs on manufactures by 38% in 2000 and average tariffs on agricultural goods by 36% in 2001)
Quotas	• no national quotas since Single Market • Multi-Fibre Agreement: quota restrictions on clothing and textiles phased out between 1995 and 2005 • remaining quotas on bananas, tuna and sardines, iron and steel from former Soviet Union, various manufactures from China	• banned in principle under WTO rules (Article XI) • exceptions for agricultural goods and balance-of-payments considerations • lax enforcement
Voluntary export restraints	• car imports from Japan (to expire in 1999) • VERs with Japan and South-East Asian countries on several other products	• banned under WTO rules if negotiated or enforced by governments • rarely challenged • to be phased out with fixed timetables under Uruguay Agreement
Anti-dumping measures	• imposed by the EU Commission if dumping margin and material injury to domestic industry are detected • 156 measures in force in 1994 • measures concentrated in chemicals, metals, non-electrical machinery and electric–electronic equipment	• allowed under Article VI of the GATT

Source: WTO (1995b).

agricultural imports (26% on average) but low on most manufactured imports (6% on average). These average rates will have been reduced by over a third by the year 2000, under the terms of the Uruguay Round. The revenues from import duties flow into the general EU budget, after a 10% deduction retained to cover the costs of customs administration by the importing country (see Chapter 15).

Tariff averages mask substantial variation of tariff levels across commodities. For example, about 40% of EU industrial imports enter the EU market free of tariffs, consisting mostly of intermediate products such as construction materials, steel, agricultural equipment, paper products and medical equipment. Under an agreement on information technology products signed in March 1997, the EU will phase out all remaining tariffs on computer and telecom related goods by 2000.

At the other extreme, so-called 'sensitive' imports, such as trucks, cars, clothing and footwear attract high tariffs, in excess of 10% *ad valorem*. The peaks are even more pronounced in the agricultural sector: tariffs on meat, dairy products and cereals were greater than 50% of import values in 1995. Tariffs on food products are exceptionally high because they have been raised as a replacement for variable levies, which were reduced under the Uruguay agreement. Many agricultural tariffs are not levied as a constant fraction of product values, but as a fixed import tax by weight or units ('specific tariffs') or with seasonal variations (see Laird, 1997). The effect of specific tariffs on exporters' margins is particularly severe in times of low prices, hence exacerbating the difficulties for agricultural producers outside the EU when prices are depressed. The agricultural tariff cuts by one-third agreed in the Uruguay Round and phased in between 1995 and 2000 do not promise much in the way of a more liberal EU regime in this sector. It has been argued that the conversion of variable levies into tariffs was calculated by the EU in a manner which maximizes tariff levels, mainly by choosing a reference period with an unusually wide differential between CAP target and world market prices (see Chapter 10). Pelkmans and Carzaniga (1996) conclude that, even after implementation of the EU's agricultural tariff commitments, 'tariff equivalents in many commodities will be higher than recent levels and higher than the level of protection of the last fifteen years'.

A frequently debated issue in the structuring of the CET is the degree of tariff escalation. A tariff structure is escalated when tariffs on imports of raw materials and intermediate products are lower than those on finished goods. Such escalation affords downstream activities higher effective protection than the nominal rates suggest. Under the Uruguay Round, tariff cuts were generally larger on high tariffs, so that the degree of escalation was reduced substantially. Nevertheless, significant escalation remains in textiles and clothing as well as in food products, where EU tariffs on fully processed imports exceed those on raw materials by a factor of nine and three respectively (WTO, 1995b).

(ii) Quotas

Theory teaches us that import quotas give rise to particularly severe welfare costs. Yet, the EU still applies quotas to products such as textiles and clothing, bananas, canned sardines and tuna, and some iron and steel imports. The Single Market project has forced EU members to replace national quotas by Union-wide restrictions, since monitoring of national quotas was no longer possible after intra-EU border controls were wound down. This has led to a considerable streamlining and easing of quantitative restrictions (Pelkmans and Carzaniga, 1996).

The most important quotas are imposed on imports of clothing and textiles, under the Multifibre Agreements (MFA, 'Agreement on Textiles and Clothing' since 1995), which have effectively exempted this sector from GATT disciplines since 1974 (Hoekman and Kostecki, 1995). However, the EU has committed itself in the Uruguay Round to phase out all MFA quotas between 1995 and 2005. Import quotas for the EU's eastern neighbours which have signed Europe Agreements will be eliminated by 1998. However, significant quotas remain in place for imports of certain types of textile-related and other basic manufactures from China and for steel products from Russia, Ukraine and Kazakhstan. The easing of these restrictions will depend primarily on the success of those countries' negotiations to join the WTO.

(iii) VERs

A VER refers to an agreement between an exporter and importer whereby the former 'voluntarily' undertakes to limit the quantity of goods consigned to the importing country. Such agreement can be obtained through political pressure from the importing country (e.g. with the threat of initiating anti-dumping procedures), or it can be genuinely voluntary, when import demand is sufficiently inelastic to increase the exporter's profits after a reduction in the quantity of exports (Tharakan, 1995). Although VERs negotiated or enforced by government are illegal under WTO law, no case has yet been brought before the WTO dispute-settlement panel (Hoekman and Kostecki, 1995). Perhaps this is because VERs, by allowing an increase in price, create rents which the two key players, exporters and import-competing domestic producers, can both enjoy at the expense of consumers. A point often made in trade policy discussion is that the interests of the consumer are difficult to organize and therefore tend to be underrepresented in international trade fora.

The most prominent VER currently in force is a 'consensus' on EU car imports reached with Japan in 1991 (WTO, 1995b). Under this regime, ceilings for Japanese car exports are set annually, based on 'supply forecasts' and on the principle that Japanese exports may account for no more than two thirds of market growth or for no less than two thirds of any market shrinkage. This VER will expire at the end of 1999. Other VER-type agreements exist with Japan on products such as video recorders, cotton fabrics and forklift trucks (see WTO, 1995b, and El-Agraa, 1995).

(iv) Anti-dumping measures

As visible and targeted trade barriers are being dismantled, new instruments have been applied to restrict imports in 'sensitive' sectors. One such instrument is anti-dumping policy. Dumping is defined as the selling in export markets below some 'normal' price. The imposition of countervailing measures is permitted under Article VI of the GATT, if dumping 'causes or threatens material injury to an established industry ... or materially retards the establishment of a domestic industry'. The 'normal' price of a good, which underlies the calculation of the 'dumping margin', is defined under EU rules as the price prevailing in the exporter's home market. Complex pricing policies and adjustment for indirect cost factors leave a degree of arbitrariness in the calculation of dumping margins and 'material injury'.

According to the WTO (1995b), to which anti-dumping actions have to be notified, the EU is one of the most frequent users of such procedures. Over the period 1988–94, the number of anti-dumping measures in force fluctuated between 139 and 158. Anti-dumping actions take one of two forms: anti-dumping duties equivalent to the dumping margin; or price undertakings, where exporting countries have to commit not to sell to the EU below an agreed price. Messerlin and Reed (1995) found a high success rate for anti-dumping cases lodged in the EU: 75% of cases initiated between 1979 and 1989 led to countervailing measures being taken. The industry with the largest share of cases initiated is chemicals, which accounted for a full 40% of cases over the same time period. Metals, non-electrical machinery and electrical equipment made up another 32% of initiated cases. When it comes to duties actually imposed, the sectoral and geographical distribution is far more concentrated: 83% of all imports subject to anti-dumping duties came from Japan in 1991, and 86% of all imports subject to such measures were in the electronics sector (European Parliament, 1993).

Probably the most high-profile anti-dumping actions currently in force are minimum prices imposed on semiconductor memory chips from Japan and South Korea, after the Commission had found that by selling chips at often below-cost prices, Japan had increased its market share in the EU from 25% in 1983 to over 70% in 1990 (*Financial Times*, 1 April 1997). Defenders of EU anti-dumping practice point out that the number of actions taken has remained roughly stable over the last decade (GATT, 1993), and that these measures affected a mere 0.46% of imports to the EU in 1995 (Laurent, 1996). They further point out that the EU is the only major trading partner with a 'lesser duty' rule, meaning that the Commission will impose a duty covering only the injury margin (which is generally lower than the total dumping margin) even though WTO rules permit duties covering the full dumping margin (Pelkmans and Carzaniga, 1996). Critics, however, have accused the Commission of bending the figures in favour of anti-dumping complaints (see Hindley, 1992; Tharakan and Waelbroeck, 1994). They argue, moreover, that the mere threat of anti-dumping procedures can act as a deterrent to exporters. Frequent investigations, even if they result in no definitive measures, can amount to a form of harassment of exporters, because they create uncertainty and costs, sometimes referred to as a 'trade chilling' effect (Tharakan, 1995). These effects cannot be quantified, but it is undeniable that anti-dumping policy contains at least the potential for protectionist abuse and should therefore be submitted to strict rules and scrupulous administration.

In addition to the four principal instruments of trade policy, several other measures with direct effects on the EU's external trading regime may be mentioned. Since the usage and overall economic impact of these measures are relatively limited, we provide only a summary listing (for a discussion see Hoekman and Kostecki, 1995):

- Based on the decisions taken in the United Nations Security Council, the EU has imposed trade *sanctions* on several countries for political reasons.

- If there is evidence of export subsidies in third countries, the EU can impose *countervailing duties*.

- *Safeguard clauses* under WTO provisions allow signatories to withdraw, or cease to apply their normal obligations in order to protect certain overriding interests.

- *Rules of origin* determine the proportion of the value of a product that must be added locally for a product to qualify as originating from a particular country. Such rules are important in the context of preferential trade agreements. The higher the required local content, the lower is the degree of preference granted to an exporting country.

21.1.3 The restrictiveness of the CCP

Traditionally, there are two methods of estimating the restrictive effects of trade policy. One way is by measuring the trade barriers in terms of their direct effects on prices. In the case of tariffs we estimate average tariff levels; in the case of non-tariff barriers we estimate the share of imports subjected to such barriers. This offers a crude indicator of the restrictiveness of a particular trade regime (see Chapter 6). A study by the OECD (1996b), for instance, shows that the 1993 import-weighted tariff average was 6.2% in the EU (which is lower than the 1995 average reported in Table 21.1, because it does not incorporate most agricultural pre-Uruguay border levies). This compares with 4% in the United States, 6.7% in Canada and 3.6% in Japan. Although there are methodological difficulties in quantifying the effects of NTBs, the OECD experts find that, weighted by production, the EU's NTBs have declined between 1988 and 1993 (the latest year for which calculations are available) and are less restrictive on average than those of other major traders. Weighting by trade, it is found that 7.7% of manufactured imports into the EU were affected by NTBs in 1988, as against 6.0% in 1993. Comparable 1993 figures were 17.9% for the United States, 6.8% for Canada and 3.2% for Japan. Therefore, the EU seems to be relatively open in terms of explicit import restrictions, and higher NTBs do not appear to have replaced falling tariffs.

Another, more sophisticated, method is to supplement information on direct prices by an analysis of quantity effects, based on elasticity estimates. This also permits calculations of welfare effects. Such estimates of the effects of the Uruguay Round indicate that the EU will enjoy considerable real income gains. According to simulations carried out by economists of the GATT (1994), EU income in 2005 will be higher by US$164 billion in 1990 prices, as a result of the liberalization agreed to in the Uruguay Agreement. This figure compares to an estimated total world gain of US$510 billion, hence fully one-third of the global gains will be reaped by the EU. Clearly the EU is a major beneficiary.

21.1.4 Trade agreements: a hierarchy of preferences

The EU has developed an elaborate web of preferential trade agreements, mainly with neighbouring countries and former colonies. WTO rules allow the formation of customs unions and free-trade areas as long as trade barriers on average do not rise after integration, tariffs and NTBs are eliminated within the area on 'substantially all' intra-regional trade, and the project is notified to the WTO in time for it to determine whether these conditions are satisfied. The GATT–WTO has never blocked such an arrangement notified to it (see WTO, 1995a).

Messerlin (1997) has argued that the institutional set-up of the EU results in a bias of trade policy towards bilateral or regional agreements rather than multilateral liberalization. Two reasons stand out. First, the EU authorities have no competence to conduct foreign policy, hence trade agreements tend to be used as a anchor for foreign relations of the EU. Second, the organization of the Commission also favours bilateral trade deals. The Commission lacks a unit of 'finance and economics' strong enough to defend multilateralism against the power of trade Commissioners, and the breakdown of the trade portfolio along geographical lines provides incentives for each Commissioner to sign specific agreements with 'his' countries.

The hierarchy of preferences among the EU's trade partners is summarized in Table 21.2. It is apparent that the EU trade regime is far from non-discriminatory: while the EEA countries enjoy full membership of the Single Market, the GSP beneficiaries depend on non-contractual discretionary concessions granted by the EU on a temporary basis. Note, however, that all the trading partners listed in Table 21.2 are granted preferential access. Further down in this hierarchy are countries which are members of the WTO but not of the GSP (such as the United States and Japan), while the EU's markets are least accessible to countries which are members in none of these groups (such as China and Russia).

21.2 EU trade and specialization patterns

21.2.1 The geographical structure of EU trade

The EU, comprising 15 industrialized countries and 372 million people, constitutes the largest trading bloc in the world. Excluding intra-EU trade, exports of the Union accounted for 21% of world exports in 1995. The corresponding United States and Japanese shares are 16% and 12% respectively (Table 21.3).

External trade has increased faster than EU GDP for most of the period since the 1960s. This was particularly evident during the 1990s. While EU GDP

Table 21.2 ⬭ **The EU's preferential trade system in 1997.**

Trading partners	EU preferences
Turkey	Customs union for industrial products since 1996; concessionary access for some agricultural products
European Economic Area, EEA (Norway, Iceland, Liechtenstein)	Extension of most aspects of the Single Market since 1994; free trade area (rules of origin necessitating some continuation of customs checks)
Europe Agreement Countries (Bulgaria, Czech Republic, Estonia, Hungary, Latvia, Lithuania, Poland, Romania, Slovak Republic, Slovenia)	Abolition of tariffs and quotas on most industrial products since 1995–96 (main exceptions: steel, textiles, clothing; to be removed by 1998); concessionary access for some agricultural products; creation of bilateral free-trade areas
Switzerland	Reciprocal abolition of tariffs and quotas on industrial products since 1973; bilateral negotiations on (*inter alia*) liberalization of transport markets, agricultural trade, public procurement and labour markets started in 1994
Israel	Reciprocal abolition of tariffs and quotas on industrial products since 1975; free-trade area with Mediterranean countries envisaged for 2001
Cyprus and Malta	Partial abolition of tariffs and quotas on industrial products since 1973 and 1970 respectively; customs union envisaged for 2001
Mediterranean countries (Algeria, Egypt, Jordan, Lebanon, Morocco, Palestine, Syria, Tunisia)	Non-reciprocal free access for most industrial products, raw materials and 'traditional' agricultural exports; free-trade area envisaged by 2010
African, Caribbean and Pacfic (ACP) countries (70 countries covered by Lomé Convention)	Non-reciprocal free access for industrial products and agricultural goods not covered by CAP; preferential access for agricultural goods covered by CAP
Generalized System of Preferences (GSP) beneficiaries (145 developing countries)	Autonomous temporary preferences (renewed multiannually); reduced tariff rates depending on the 'sensitivity' or products, subject to safeguard clause; tariff-free access for industrial and some agricultural goods from 45 'least developed countries'; GSP preferences withdrawn when beneficiary's exports exceed 25% of EU imports in certain sectors, or in the case of forced labour, prison labour or drug trafficking

Sources WTO (1995b), Pelkmans and Brenton (1997).

Table 21.3 ● The EU in world trade, 1996.

Exports from	Value ($bn)	%
World[a]	5,100	100.0
Western Europe[a]	929	24.7
European Union (15)[a]	788	21.0
Transition Economies	171	4.6
Central and Eastern Europe	81	2.2
North America	826	22.0
Asia	1,310	34.9
Japan	413	11.0
China	151	4.0
Six 'Asian Tigers'[b]	531	14.1
Africa	113	3.0
Latin America	250	6.7
Middle East	160	4.3

[a] Excluding intra-EU trade.
[b] Hong Kong, South Korea, Malaysia, Singapore, Taiwan, Thailand.
Source WTO Press Release 71, April 1997.

growth averaged 1.3% from 1990 to 1995, exports of goods and services grew by 4.3% on average and corresponding imports expanded by an annual 3.5% (WTO, 1996).

About 45% of extra-EU trade is directed towards *developed countries*. Within the developed countries group, the United States is the largest trading partner, followed by Japan and Switzerland (Table 21.4). If intra-EU trade were added to extra-EU trade with developed countries, we find that 80% of the Union's trade is with countries of broadly similar income levels. *Developing countries* (LDCs) account for 15% of

Table 21.4 ⬭ EU trade by area, 1995.

	Imports		Exports	
	$bn	%	$bn	%
World	2,012.3	100.0	2,027.5	100.0
Intra-EU(15)	1,276.7	63.4	1,275.0	62.9
Extra-EU(15)	735.6	36.6	752.5	37.1
Developed countries[a]	352.8	17.5	315.3	15.5
of which:				
United States	124.1	6.2	116.1	5.7
Japan	79.8	4.0	42.4	2.1
	49.2	2.4	56.9	2.8
Switzerland				
Norway	25.6	1.2	14.8	0.7
Other	74.1	3.7	85.1	4.2
LDCs[b]	285.1	14.1	312.3	15.4
of which:				
Africa	60.5	3.0	58.2	2.8
Latin America	42.7	2.1	50.4	2.5
Middle East	30.1	1.5	52.4	2.6
Asia	151.8	7.5	151.3	7.5
Central and Eastern Europe[c]	86.7	4.3	89.0	4.4
Other	11.0	0.6	35.9	1.8

[a] Western Europe, North America and Japan.
[b] Africa, Latin America, Middle East and Asia (excluding Japan).
[c] Central and Eastern Europe, Baltic States, Commonwealth of Independent States.
Source Computed from Table A10 in WTO *Annual Report*, vol. II, Geneva, 1996.

total EU trade and for 40% of extra-EU trade. EU trade with the south-east Asian countries has been expanding very rapidly. The combined share in EU trade of Hong Kong, Malaysia, Singapore, South Korea, Taiwan and Thailand increased from 14% to 22% in just two years, between 1993 and 1995 (Eurostat, 1997).

The share of *intra-EU trade* in total EU trade has risen steadily and for many years it has been the most dynamic element in total EU trade. As integration among EU members outpaced liberalization with the rest of the world, this relative expansion of intra-EU trade is perfectly in line with the predictions of customs union theory (see Chapter 4). Both trade creation and trade diversion show up in trade statistics as an increase in the share of intra-union trade flows. However, this share increase was accompanied by a rapid absolute growth of extra-EU trade also, indicating a preponderance of trade creation over trade diversion. With the exception of agricultural trade, the rise in intra-EU trade has not been at the expense of non-EU countries. Over a long period of thirty years, Lloyd (1992) found only weak evidence that regional trade groups such as the EU give rise to an increased share of intra-group trade in total trade of the group.

Fears of increasing trade diversion were raised in the late 1980s by the implementation of the Single Market. Some commentators warned against a *'Fortress Europe'*, expecting that the EU's efforts towards internal liberalization would divert energies away from liberalizing external trade and give EU firms an additional competitive edge over third-country exporters. However, contrary to these expectations, EU manufactured imports from non-members rose faster than intra-EU trade in the 1980s (Baneth, 1993). A more sophisticated *ex post* evaluation by Sapir (1996) further allays 'Fortress Europe' fears. During the period 1986–92 the share of domestic production in consumption of EU countries fell continuously, which is an indicator of trade creation. While import volumes were growing fast, the share of extra-EU imports remained roughly constant at 40% of total imports. The EU Commission's review of the Single Market (CEU, 1996c) found that extra-EU manufacturing imports had increased their share of consumption over the period 1980–93 from 12% to 14%. Looking specifically at LDC exporters, Buigues and Martínez (1997) have found that between 1989 and 1995 their share of EU imports has increased both in absolute terms and in comparison with the United States, and that this increase was particularly pronounced in the sectors most affected by the Single Market programme. The early evidence therefore suggests that the Single Market has not hurt imports from outside the EU.

The overall *balance on extra-EU trade* has traditionally exhibited small deficits, but it has swung into surplus since 1994 (WTO, 1996). The value of the EU's trade surplus in 1995 corresponded to 0.2% of GDP. In comparison, the United States recorded a deficit equivalent to 2.6% of GDP and Japan ran a surplus accounting for 2.4% of its GDP. Nevertheless, bilateral trade imbalances have been perceived as troublesome; in particular, the persistent deficit with Japan (equivalent to 0.3% of EU GDP in 1995). Furthermore, some EU member states have persistent trade imbalances. Greece, Spain and the United Kingdom typically record trade deficits, and Ireland switched from deficits to large surpluses in the mid-1980s.

The balances discussed here refer to merchandise trade only. Services trade and other current-account transactions often offset merchandise trade imbalance. Unified Germany, for instance, has been running current account deficits in spite of its positive merchandise trade balance. Of course, care must be taken not to succumb to the mercantilist fallacy of interpreting a trade surplus/deficit as a good/bad situation in itself. Examination of the EU's trade and current account indicates that any trade problems third countries experience with the EU do not originate from an intrinsic structural problem in the EU's trade balance.

21.2.2 The product composition of EU trade

The commodity structure of EU trade varies greatly among geographical areas (Table 21.5). Over 82% of the Union's trade with developed countries consists of trade in *manufactured goods*. A contrasting pattern is evident in trade with LDCs. As one

Table 21.5 ⬭ Commodity composition of EU trade with major trading groups (% shares).

	Food and primary products (SITC 0, 1, 2, 4)		Fuels (SITC 3)		Manufactures (SITC 5–8)	
	Exports	Imports	Exports	Imports	Exports	Imports
Developed countries[a]						
1980	15.1	18.7	9.1	9.0	75.8	72.3
1995	9.6	12.0	3.3	6.1	85.4	79.6
LDCS[b]						
1980	11.5	22.3	3.0	59.2	85.5	18.5
1995	12.5	22.3	1.2	16.1	86.2	57.5
Eastern Europe[c]						
1980	18.0	14.8	1.6	49.6	80.4	35.6
1995	15.1	22.4	1.8	20.4	81.9	54.5

Three categories do not always add up to 100%, owing to the omission of SITC Section 9.
[a] Western Europe (excluding intra-EU trade), North America and Japan.
[b] Latin America, Africa, Middle East and Asia (except Japan).
[c] Central and Eastern Europe, Baltic States, Commonwealth of Independent States.
Source WTO (1996).

would expect, fuels (9%) and food and other primary products (17%) are more heavily represented, although the share of manufactured goods in total imports from the LDCs has grown dramatically in recent decades (up from 18% in 1980 to 57% in 1995).

Trade in *services*, comprising travel, transport and, in particular, investment-related payments, has become an increasingly important component of European trade. For instance, annual growth rates averaged 9.2% in 1986–92, and the value of services trade corresponded to roughly one-third of the value of merchandise trade in 1992 (WTO, 1995b).

Much academic interest has focused on the composition of international exchanges in terms of intra- and interindustry trade. *Intraindustry trade* (IIT) refers to the mutual exchange among countries of similar goods. This type of trade runs against the predictions of neoclassical trade theory, according to which countries would export one set of products – those in which they have a comparative advantage – while importing an entirely different set of products – those for which the comparative advantage is enjoyed by other countries. IIT is based not on country-specific advantages, but on determinants such as consumers' taste for variety, increasing returns in production and the international dispersion of various stages in the production process of advanced industrial goods. IIT therefore typically dominates trade among diversified high-income economies.

Trade within the EU exhibits generally high shares of IIT. Brülhart and Elliott (1998) show that, on average, the IIT share of trade among EU countries rose from 48% to 64% over the 1961–92 period. Given that the definition of an 'industry' in that study is very narrow (SITC 5-digit), this is strong evidence that intra-EU trade, which has been growing more rapidly than trade with non-EU countries, is driven by factors other than comparative advantage. Evidence on the level of IIT in trade between member states and countries outside the EU is reported in Table 21.6. The data suggest that countries with the largest and most diversified industrial bases, Germany, France and the United Kingdom, have the highest levels of IIT with third countries. Greek and Portuguese extra-EU trade relations are still predominantly *interindustry*. The proportion of IIT in the EU's trade with developed countries such as the United States is high, as one would expect, and with developing countries it is low. IIT with Japan, however, is surprisingly low, a fact often interpreted as a symptom of the impenetrability of the Japanese market for advanced foreign exports (Lincoln, 1990). The EU's trade with Central and Eastern European countries (CEEC's) also displays comparatively low IIT values, but for different reasons to Japan. Hoekman and Djankov (1996) show that IIT with the CEECs has been increasing, albeit from a low level. Low IIT levels could imply that further trade liberalization with these countries might involve substantial structural adjustment costs for the EU (see Brülhart, 1994). This may explain in part the relatively cautious approach to the integration of Eastern applicants.

21.2.3 External trade and economic specialization: high-tech industries and low-skill workers

The changes in the EU's trade structure and trade policy regime detailed above would have been expected to stimulate corresponding changes in the production structure of the member states. A major transformation in the EU's pattern of specialization has indeed been observed. Thus, the share of agricultural employment in EU15 total employment has fallen from 12% in 1970 to 5% in 1994, and the share of industrial jobs has fallen from 41% to 31% in the same time period (OECD, 1996a). Some industrial sectors were particularly hard hit. Employment in the EU12 coal industry, for instance, has declined by 65% (329,000 jobs) between 1984 and

Table 21.6 ⬭ Intraindustry trade of EU countries in 1991.[1]

	OECD Europe	United States	Japan	CEECs and former USSR	NICs and China[2]	World
Austria	72	37	16	40	22	63
Belgium–Luxemburg	73	49	23	30	37	68
Denmark	66	41	17	27	19	57
Finland	53	24	15	27	16	43
France	81	57	22	34	30	68
Germany	81	58	45	38	28	68
Greece	23	8	0	18	3	21
Ireland	55	57	28	19	28	52
Italy	63	46	27	33	40	55
Netherlands	78	50	18	34	23	69
Portugal	42	22	2	13	18	39
Spain	64	31	9	30	21	55
Sweden	70	53	35	33	21	60
United Kingdom	80	69	29	32	32	68
EU15[3]	64	43	20	29	24	56

[1] IIT defined as unadjusted Grubel–Lloyd index, calculated from SITC 3-digit trade values.
[2] Excluding South Korea.
[3] Unweighted averages.
Source OECD (1994).

1993 (Eurostat, 1995). In the same period, employment also shrank significantly in iron and steel (less 31% or 140,000 jobs), in textiles (less 32% or 562,000 jobs) and in clothing (less 23% or 308,000 jobs).

Of course, specialization pressures induced by external trade are not the only force that shaped the observed changes in the EU's production structure. Even if the EU had existed in autarky, changes in technology, incomes, tastes and demography would have led to structural adjustment. For this reason, it is difficult to isolate and quantify the impact of external trade liberalization on observed specialization trends. However, some valuable insights into the processes at work have been yielded by recent empirical analysis. We concentrate here on two sectors, for which the role of extra-EU trade has been subject to particularly intensive debate and substantial research: *high-technology* industries and *low-skill intensive* industries. Both have been identified as losers from the EU's trade liberalization; the former because of insufficient R&D efforts in the EU, the latter because of the inexorable law of comparative advantage.

Trade performance in *high-tech products* has been a source of concern to the EU for many years. The EU's high-tech exports to third countries increased by only 2% per annum during the period 1982–90, compared with world export growth of 7.7% per annum in these products (McAleese, 1994). Further evidence based on a comparison of the share of EU's high-tech exports in total manufacturing exports in 1993 with the ratio in the United States and Japan shows the EU lagging seriously behind (*The Economist*, 23 November 1996). Some improvement in the position may have occurred during the 1990s. Thus, while the trade balance for high-tech industries such as machinery and transport equipment had worsened markedly and the balance on chemicals trade had improved slightly during the 1980s, Table 21.7 indicates a significant improvement in the performance of both sectors in the 1990s. Yet there are still grounds for concern: note, for example, the pronounced deterioration of the trade balance for office and telecom equipment, a sector with great potential for continued expansion, and capable of generating substantial technological externalities. Another example is semiconductor chips, where 80% of EU sales are imported from Japan and South Korea. Such sectors are often seen as 'strategic', in the sense that they produce economic rents for the host country (see Krugman, 1986). Policy makers are not indifferent to an apparent shift in comparative advantage in this industry, and 'strategic' considerations certainly play a part, for example, in the EU's continuing anti-dumping measures against Japanese and Korean semiconductor chips manufacturers.

The problem of high-tech industries relates to strategic positioning of the EU economy. The problem of low-skill intensive industries relates to a different type of concern. In the latter case, it is generally accepted that the EU will lose market share in these activities to third countries. What is at issue is the pace of change and its effects on the incomes of *low-skill workers*, particularly against the backdrop of the EU's high *unemployment*. Has the law of comparative advantage been working to the detriment of European blue-collar workers and, in an unholy combination with institutional labour-market rigidities, fuelled unemployment?

Table 21.7 ⬤ Extra-EU trade in selected products, 1980 and 1995 ($billion).

		Exports	Imports	Trade balance	Change in balance 1980–95
Chemicals	1980	35.7	17.2	+18.5	
	1995	94.3	57.4	+36.9	+18.4
Machinery and transport equipment	1980	115.9	58.0	+57.9	
	1995	328.5	242.1	+86.4	+28.5
of which: Non-electrical machinery	1980	43.1	13.6	+29.5	
	1995	111.3	38.0	+73.3	+43.8
Electrical machinery	1980	11.9	5.7	+ 6.2	
	1995	37.5	33.2	+ 4.3	−1.9
Office and telecom equipment	1980	11.3	17.2	− 5.9	
	1995	57.1	104.8	−47.7	−41.8
Automotive products	1980	27.5	8.2	+19.3	
	1995	68.6	30.7	+37.9	+18.6

Source: Computed from Table A10 WTO *Annual Report 1996*, vol. II, Geneva, 1996.

Trade economists have conducted numerous analyses with the aim of isolating trade-related determinants of structural change. Two concepts of structural change have been mainly employed: changes in wage differentials across industries and changes in unemployment rates. The starting hypothesis is that liberalization of trade *vis-à-vis* labour-abundant developing countries, particularly the south-east Asian 'tiger economies', has depressed demand for unskilled labour in industrialized countries. Trade liberalization therefore contributes either (a) to the widening gap between skilled and unskilled wages, as in the United States, or (b) to rising unemployment of unskilled workers in the EU, where union power and labour legislation impede United-States-style flexibility of wages. The precise question raised, therefore, is whether increased imports from low-wage countries have exacerbated the EU's unemployment problem.

Most available studies cover the United States or the entire OECD, rather than just the EU, and a number of different methodologies are used. Some studies estimate average factor contents of imports and exports, and infer net effects on domestic factor demands (see, for instance, Sachs and Shatz, 1994, for the United States).

Other studies regress changes in factor demands over various determinants including import penetration (see, for instance, Larre, 1995, for the OECD). A majority of analyses find that trade liberalization accounts for some of the fall in demand for blue-collar workers in developed countries, but that the contribution of trade is small and by far the bigger culprit is trade-independent technological change.

Wood (1994, 1995), however, has argued that import penetration from the LDCs is a major cause of falling demand for low-skill labour in the OECD. He refined the standard factor-content analysis and found empirical evidence that manufactured imports of OECD countries tend to have higher low-skill labour contents than similar goods produced locally, and that imports thereby crowd out low-skill jobs in developed countries. Furthermore, he detected a tendency for OECD industry to engage in 'defensive innovation', substituting capital for low-skill labour in order to survive competition from low-wage exporters, and he pointed to the (poorly documented and therefore often ignored) surge in service exports from those countries. Thus, he produced a summary estimate that trade lowered the economy-wide relative demand for unskilled labour in OECD countries by about 20% in 1990, compared with a hypothetical *anti-monde* assuming prohibitive barriers on trade with the LDCs.

The re-assessment of the trade–employment link initiated by Wood (1994) has led to an upward revision of the consensus estimate of trade effects (see Freeman, 1995). Furthermore, the pressures for trade-induced specialization are likely to intensify over time, as the EU continues to reduce its external trade barriers under WTO commitments, and as the exporting capacity of developing countries increases. It must be noted, however, that the emerging *empirical* consensus about the significance of trade liberalization for EU labour-market adjustment is superseded by even stronger *normative* agreement that a return to protectionism would be detrimental (see Wood, 1995; and Sachs and Shatz, 1996). Even though trade liberalization is acknowledged to produce losers, gainers are still in the majority. The appropriate policy response, therefore, is not to re-impose trade barriers to non-EU imports, but to deregulate EU labour markets, to subsidize employment of low-skill workers (in the short term), and to invest in education (in the long term).

21.3 Trade relations with the main partners

21.3.1 The LDCs

In spite of their relative economic weaknesses, the LDCs are a key trade partner for the EU (Table 21.5). Among them, the EU's *Mediterranean* neighbours are in the process of receiving the strongest trade preferences. Through the 1995 Barcelona Declaration, the EU and 11 Mediterranean countries have agreed to form a free trade area by the year 2010. Also contained in this programme are pledges to abolish NTBs, agricultural barriers and obstacles to trade in services on a reciprocal basis.

The Barcelona Declaration builds on a policy developed since 1972, whereby the EU granted duty-free access to industrial goods from the Mediterranean basin and some preferences to exports of agricultural products in which the EU was not self-sufficient. Up to now, however, the Mediterranean countries have not been able to benefit significantly from the EU's trade concessions on industrial goods. Their industrial base is generally small, and some of their most important export goods, such as clothing and textiles, have been subject to quantitative restrictions (Heidensohn, 1995).

Prior to the Barcelona programme, the *Lomé Convention* was the EU's most preferential agreement with LDCs (see Chapter 22). Signed in 1975, and renewed at regular intervals thereafter, it gives a group of African, Caribbean, and Pacific (ACP) countries free access to EU markets for manufactures and a substantial range of primary goods (70 such countries were included in the latest agreement, in force for the 1990–99 period). The Lomé accords encompass more than tariff reductions. They include the relaxation of NTBs, more flexible application of safeguard clauses, rules of origin and MFA restrictions. Trade concessions are supplemented by special aid and technical cooperation arrangements. In spite of the preferential access, the share of EU imports from ACP countries has been declining in most of the post-war period and accounted for only 3.4% of EU imports in 1995 (2.7% if oil is excluded). By contrast, the EU market still accounts on average for more than 40% of ACP sales. It must also be noted that the erosion of ACP import shares has been considerably less pronounced in the EU than in other markets (Auboin and Laird, 1997). The EU Commission (CEU, 1996d) has nevertheless concluded that the impact of trade preferences has been 'disappointing by and large'. Preferential arrangements, especially the protocols on specific products, have certainly contributed significantly to the commercial success of some countries (e.g. Côte d'Ivoire, Jamaica, Mauritius and Zimbabwe). But the bulk of ACP countries have lacked the economic policies and the domestic conditions needed to develop trade.

For most non-ACP developing countries the *Generalized System of Preferences* (GSP) dictates the degree of preferential access for their exports to the EU. Initiated in 1971 by UNCTAD, the purpose of the GSP was to help LDCs to industrialize through exports to the developed world. Most developed countries have adopted some version of the GSP, in the case of the USA and the United Kingdom not without some initial reluctance (MacBean and Snowden, 1981), and some 145 Third World countries receive preferences. The GSP provides substantially weaker trade preferences than the Lomé Convention. Under the GSP, the EU autonomously determines and regularly revises its trade concessions, whereas the Lomé Conventions are binding contracts among all signatories.

Prior to 1995, the GSP provided duty-free access for industrial products, subject to ceilings, classified by country of origin and member state of destination. This regime has been replaced by a 'modulation mechanism' which assigns trade concessions according to the 'sensitivity' of import goods without quantity ceilings (WTO, 1995b). The list ranges from 'very sensitive' products (textiles, clothing and ferro alloys), which are subject to 85% of the regular tariff, to 'non-sensitive' products, which benefit from duty-free treatment. This modulation system is complemented by a 'graduation' mechanism under which preferential treatment is gradually reduced once GSP countries have reached a certain level of economic development. The EU Commission has argued that the graduation mechanism strengthens 'the GSP as a development tool' (WTO, 1995b), given its automatic targeting of preferences to the least advanced economies. However, it could also be interpreted as a somewhat perverse mechanism whereby exporters are punished for their own success, and EU consumers are denied the full benefit of competitive imports from countries at intermediate stages of development. Only a few of the 45 least-developed countries which qualify for complete exemption from EU tariffs on industrial and certain agricultural products actually benefit from this clause, since most are ACP countries (non-ACP beneficiaries include Afghanistan, Bangladesh, Cambodia and Yemen).

The EU's multiplicity of agreements and special arrangements may appear more favourable to LDCs than is in fact the case. First, as *tariffs* have been reduced under the GATT rounds, the practical usefulness of tariff preferences has diminished. This holds despite the qualification that nominal tariffs are still high on some product groups of interest to LDCs, and that effective tariffs on these products, the best measure of the protective effect, are much higher than nominal tariffs. Second, *NTBs* in the form of VERs, quotas and anti-dumping measures remain an important barrier to exports from LDCs to the EU market. NTBs are imposed not only on food products but also on many 'sensitive' manufactured goods such as steel, TV sets, video cassettes, cutlery, footwear, textiles, clothing. Third, the EU's system of preferences is complex and uncertain in its application, even after its revision in 1995. Successful exporters to the EU complain that their very success leads to the imposition of new restrictions on their products.

21.3.2 The United States

The United States is the EU's largest single trade partner, accounting for 16% of combined extra-EU imports and exports (see Table 21.4). Although trade with industrial countries is in principle governed by the rules of the WTO, this has not prevented controversy arising on many specific issues.

EU economic relations with the United States have been based on strong political and cultural ties as well as common economic interests. Yet, at times, it appears as if the two partners are locked into a state of perpetual crisis. In the past, trade wars have threatened to erupt because of disputes over steel, pasta, citrus fruit, agricultural exports to Egypt and the Mediterranean enlargement. More recently, hormones in beef, subsidies to Airbus, public procurement and agriculture have taken centre stage. The EU has complained about 'Buy American' restrictions, unilateralism in United States trade legislation, discriminatory tax, public procurement and restrictions on non-nationals in the services industries. In April 1997, the EU refrained at the last minute from submitting a complaint to the WTO after President Clinton signed the Helms–Burton Act in March 1996, which penalizes individuals who trade in property 'confiscated' by Cuba from United States nationals. This Act is perceived by the EU as an infringement by the United States of its trade policy. The EU's restraint was won by a suspension of the most contentious parts of the Act, and the controversy has therefore been resolved only temporarily. On the other hand, the United States feared a protectionist 'Fortress Europe' arising from the Single Market programme and objects to EU protection in high-technology goods and services. The most acute and enduring cause of friction, however, has been trade in agricultural products. The erosion of the United States surplus in food trade with the EU has been ascribed to the domestic price support given by the CAP. The United States has further objected that growing EU food surpluses are being sold at subsidized prices on third markets, thereby creating difficulties for United States exporters to these markets. The EU retorts, with some justification, that agricultural subsidies are applied on both sides of the Atlantic. This illustrates the problems that arise when all countries try to subsidize the same product.

Although full-scale trade wars have threatened to break out on many occasions in the past, the strong mutuality of interests between the United States and the EU has, on each occasion thus far, saved them from the brink. Trade relations are characterized by constant levels of minor friction rather than deeply set divergence of interest. Certainly, a tit-for-tat series of retaliations would leave both Europe and the United States worse off, a fact which both sides appreciate. Indeed, there have been suggestions for a bold leap forwards towards a Transatlantic Free Trade Agreement (TAFTA; see Stokes, 1996), and it was agreed at a joint EU–United States summit in Madrid 1995 that a 'New Transatlantic Marketplace' would be constructed by progressively reducing or eliminating barriers that hinder the flow of goods, services and capital between the two blocs. However, the establishment of a TAFTA currently looks as remote as the eruption of a transatlantic trade war.

21.3.3 Japan

Trade policy towards Japan has been marked by resistance to what is perceived as excessively rapid import penetration in a narrow range of product markets. It is also notoriously marked by internal disunity within the EU (see O'Donnell and Murphy, 1994). Some member states, such as the United Kingdom and Ireland, have become important hosts to Japanese investment. Sales of Japanese firms are therefore viewed in a different light by these countries compared to EU members with a small presence of Japanese-owned production facilities. Furthermore, there is a difference between countries which have industries competing with Japanese exports and those for whom Japanese sales only compete with other imports. The figures are telling: in 1993, the market share of passenger cars imported from Japan was 43% in Ireland, 34% in Denmark, but only 5% in Italy and 4% in France (WTO, 1995b).

The EU's trade deficit (US$37bn in 1995) with Japan is attributed to the combined effects of the strong competitive performance of Japanese firms, of Japan's high savings rate and, controversially, of Japan's reluctance to open its market to EU exporters. In 1995, 11% of total extra-EU imports came from Japan, while Japan was the destination for only 6% of EU exports. The trade deficit with Japan amounted to under 0.5% of EU GDP. The Japanese trade surplus is the subject of contention mainly because it is concentrated in technology-intensive sectors perceived to be 'strategic' (see section 21.2.3).

On the basis of visible, explicit barriers to trade, the Japanese market appears relatively open. Japan has committed itself in the Uruguay Round to a trade-weighted tariff average on industrial goods of 1.7%. This is the second lowest average of all countries (surpassed only by Switzerland), and it compares favourably with the EU's average tariff of 3.7% (GATT, 1994). However, it is frequently argued that Japan's commitment to free trade is 'more apparent than real' (Heidensohn, 1995). Restrictions on access to the Japanese market arise from two main sources. First, regulatory obstacles impose effective barriers to foreign exporters in a variety of areas, from the specification of technical standards for electrical appliances to participation in the financial services market. Japanese non-acceptance of international standards and European certification procedures hampers trade in areas such as the agro-food sector, pharmaceuticals and construction. Second, certain structural features of the Japanese economy act as effective barriers to import penetration. The existence of tightly connected business groups ('keiretsu'), built upon interconnected manufacturers and distributors, makes it particularly difficult for European firms to sell to Japan.

The EU has exerted pressure on Japan to liberalize access to its market, but it has adopted a less confrontational strategy than the United States. Consultation is the keyword in EU trade diplomacy with Japan: annual summit meetings have been held between the Japanese Prime Minister, the President of the European Council and the President of the Commission since 1991, and a permanent dialogue was established in 1993 between MITI, the Japanese ministry for international trade and industry, and the corresponding Commission Directorate. In addition, export-enhancing schemes such as assistance for marketing in Japan and special visit and study programmes have been initiated to facilitate access to the Japanese market for European business. Notable successes in EU–Japanese trade diplomacy include the 1991 'consensus' to impose VERs on Japanese car exports until 1999, and Japan's agreement in February 1997 to end discriminatory taxation of imported spirits.

Partly as a means to circumvent European VERs and anti-dumping action, Japanese firms have invested heavily in production facilities within the EU (see Dent, 1997). Britain has attracted a large share of Japanese investment in Europe, and this investment has been eagerly sought by the less developed regions of the Union. Policy towards such investment has, however, been ambivalent. Direct investment is, on the one hand, seen as an effective counter to the accusation that Japanese imports are 'destroying' jobs in the EU, but, on the other hand, competition from Japanese subsidiaries is seen as a threat to established industry. (Never mind that 'established' industry includes subsidiaries of non-EU firms such as Ford whose only claim to preferment is that they got into the EU market first.)

Drawing sustenance from modern theories of strategic trade policy (Krugman,

1986), the EU has often insisted that its technological position must not be undermined, and that reciprocity must be the key concern in industrial sectors characterized by small numbers of producers and extensive R&D externalities. Clearly, a strategy of increasing EU exports to Japan would be much superior to protectionism. Also the EU consumer has gained enormously both from access to Japanese goods, and from the efficiency improvements forced on European industry by exposure to Japanese competition.

21.3.4 The CEECs

The political upheaval and ensuing economic reforms in Central and Eastern Europe have raised formerly isolated neighbours to the top the EU's list of candidates for trade integration. The EU has concluded Association Agreements with 10 former Soviet-bloc countries, and accession negotiations are scheduled to start in 1998. Most CEECs have been granted duty-free access for industrial products since 1 January 1995. Removal of remaining obstacles on sensitive sectors such as steel and textiles was agreed for 1998, and some concessions were granted for CEEC exports of agricultural goods. One important precondition imposed by the EU for further integration of the CEECs is that they adopt effective competition policies, aiming in particular at a reduction of state subsidies, in order to minimize competitive distortions in a liberalized European market.

The effects on trade policy of closer economic relations with the CEECs are difficult to predict. The starting point is one of low trade volumes. In 1989, EU trade with these countries, including the Soviet Union, accounted for some 6% of total EU trade on industrial products with third countries. Their lack of hard currency made the CEECs poor markets for EU exports, while many of their own goods carried little attraction in western markets. At the bottom of the EU's preferential ranking up to the late 1980s, and with even the small amount of trade riddled with interventions on both sides, past trade trends are an unreliable guide to the future. Yet, research based on gravity models suggests the potential for a dramatic (sixfold) increase in trade between the EU and the CEECs (Baldwin *et al.*, 1992).

Evidence on trade changes in the 1990s points towards a gradual process of trade re-orientation by the CEECs towards the EU. Increases in trade flows to the EU seem to consist of new products rather than a diversion of products previously exported to the Soviet bloc. Hoekman and Djankov (1996) have estimated that at most 20% of increased CEEC–EU exports were 'diverted' flows. The bulk of additional exports has been spearheaded by foreign subsidiaries or by outward contracting by EU firms. Firms have pursued a strategy of upgrading and differentiating 'traditional' exports, relying upon EU firms for new machinery, components and know-how.

The EU's barriers to imports of 'traditional' CEEC goods also explain the changing composition of trade. However, it is exceptionally difficult to predict what specialization pattern will emerge between the EU and the CEECs once the remaining obstacles are fully removed. Pressure will undoubtedly be placed on the EU's protected agriculture, steel, textiles, clothing and footwear industries and other

semiskilled activities. However, given the CEECs relatively high educational standards, they are unlikely to specialize in low-skill, low-tech sectors in the long run.
Intraindustry trade in advanced manufactured products and services is likely to
increase. Furthermore, the need for capital and intermediate goods in the reconstruction of many CEEC industries is set to provide opportunities for a thriving
export market for EU suppliers. However, the direct beneficiaries of Eastern Europe's
increased demand for imports are likely to be contiguous, and better-off, areas of
Europe (Germany, Austria, North Italy). Integration with the CEECs is therefore
poised to create redistributive tensions among existing EU members.

21.4 New issues in a globalizing world

Expanding volumes of international trade are the clearest indicator of the much discussed phenomenon of economic globalization. A manufacturing firm located in
one country, sourcing all its inputs domestically and exporting part of its output is
becoming more and more of a rarity. The typical firm in the globalized economy
shifts production among subsidiaries in several countries, switches among subcontractors and suppliers in many others, deals in intangible assets, engages in intrafirm
trade among subsidiaries, and competes with its rivals not in segmented national
economies, but in regional or even global markets.

The changing face of the international economy has both heightened the importance of trade policy and broadened its scope. Expanding international trade
flows imply that trade measures impact on an ever-larger part of economic activity,
and the growing complexity of international economic relations dictates a widening of the remit for trade policy. Negotiations on the two major recent liberalization
projects, the EU's Single Market and the Uruguay Round, have brought into focus a
whole list of new issues with relevance to trade policy, such as:

- rules regulating cross-border provision of services,
- international protection of intellectual property rights,
- linkages between trade and environmental policy,
- linkages between trade and labour standards,
- rules relating to foreign direct investment,
- international competition policy,
- harmonization of product standards, and
- the opening of public procurement to foreign suppliers.

Many of these issues have been addressed internally in the EU during the negotiations to implement the Single Market. The experience of EU integration therefore
can carry valuable lessons for liberalization at the global stage (see Pelkmans and
Carzaniga, 1996).

This chapter concentrates on the first four of the new issues listed above. These topics featured prominently at WTO negotiations and are likely to remain the focus of intensive debate in coming years.

21.4.1 Services

So far, this chapter has dealt primarily with merchandise trade. An increasingly significant part of international trade flows is not in goods, but in services. Services have traditionally been perceived as quintessentially non-traded. However, technological improvements and policy liberalization have led many service providers to compete on foreign markets. Considering that services account for over 60% of GDP in OECD countries, there seems to be enormous potential for trade expansion in this sector.

Unfortunately, data on trade in services are notoriously weak, since this trade is difficult both to define theoretically and to measure empirically. Services differ from merchandise, because they are intangible and cannot be stored. Some service trade (e.g. information sold by telecommunication) can occur across borders, just like merchandise trade. Most services, however, involve the movement of the provider to the consumer (e.g. transport, consulting) or vice versa (e.g. tourism, education). When it comes to trade liberalization in the service sector, a distinction is made between granting foreign companies a *right to do business* and granting them a *right to establish* (Jones and Ruane, 1990). All these transactions involve exchanges between the resident of one country and the resident of another and are therefore classified as international trade in balance-of-payments conventions (see Sapir and Winters, 1994).

Extra-EU services trade amounted to 36% of the value of merchandise trade in 1992 (WTO, 1995b). Travel was by far the largest sector, accounting for 28% of services trade. Service trade grew by 9% annually in the 1986–92 period; and the fastest growing sectors were banking (31% p.a.), travel (12% p.a.) and business services (11% p.a.), while only one sector displayed negative trade growth rates (sea freight: −0.1% p.a.). The EU has traditionally held a strong competitive position in services, and runs a surplus in service trade overall as well as in most subcategories.

Internal liberalization of trade in services has progressed considerably less than liberalization of visible trade in the EU. Even though liberalization of services is a cornerstone of the 1992 Single Market, many obstacles remain. Progress in the liberalization of intra-EU services trade has been hampered by delays in enacting Single Market rules into national law as well as by loopholes in the Single Market rules themselves, particularly in financial services (CEU, 1996c). Because of this, the share of extra-EU imports in total imports is higher in services trade (51% in 1992) than in merchandise trade (41%) (WTO, 1996b).

Extra-EU services trade has received a multilateral legal base through the General Agreement on Trade in Services (GATS), which was negotiated during the Uruguay Round. The scope of this agreement encompasses both the right to do business across countries and the right to establish, since it also applies to services provided by foreign affiliates of multinational firms. GATS extends the non-discrimination rule to all service sectors, except those listed in the Annex to the agreement by each signatory (the 'negative list'). *National treatment* (i.e. equivalent treatment to that given to domestic suppliers of a service) is granted to foreign suppliers in the sectors listed in each signatory's schedule of commitments (the 'positive list').

The EU's position in GATS negotiations was complicated by the European Court ruling whereby competence to conclude the GATS was shared between the Union and the member states. As a consequence, some sectors are not covered by the CCP (e.g. air transport), while a common stance was found, and GATS commitments made, in other sectors (e.g. financial services). Other sectors are subject to a common policy, but no GATS commitments were made. These include maritime transport and audiovisual services, the latter being a sector where EU protectionist tendencies are particularly strong, owing to a perceived threat to European cultural identity from low-cost American products (WTO, 1996a).

The GATS provides very incomplete coverage of service sectors, but it contains provisions for continued negotiations to liberalize services trade progressively. It was decided specifically to extend the negotiations on financial services, basic telecommunications and maritime transport. An agreement was reached on telecommunications in February 1997, entering into force for most signatories on 1 January 1998, according to which 69 WTO members grant each other (and most other WTO countries) national treatment in all forms of telecommunication services, thus covering over 90% of the global telecommunication. This sector is of considerable relevance to the EU: telecom revenues accounted for roughly 2% of GDP in 1995 and the sector's product is an important input to most other economic activities. The WTO estimates that telecoms liberalization could mean cumulative global income gains of some one trillion dollars over the next decade, which represents about 4% of world GDP (*WTO Focus*, February 1997). The successful completion of these negotiations is significant therefore in its own right, and it also sets a precedent for other sectoral WTO negotiations to follow.

Quantification of the effects of liberalizing services trade is subject to a wide margin of error. However, the GATS has placed access to service markets firmly on the multilateral trade-policy agenda, and the 1997 agreement on telecommunications bodes well for further progress in this field. The EU has a particular interest in promoting this agenda, given its strong competitive position in services. In addition, the EU's own experience of slow liberalization under the Single Market programme is a lesson that international agreements alone cannot ensure the opening of the complex regulatory systems which segment service markets, and that consistent implementation of rule changes at the national level can be more difficult to attain than declarations of intent at international fora.

21.4.2 Trade and intellectual property rights

Services are not the only kind of intangible commodity whose share in trade as well as in economic output at large is increasing. *Knowledge goods*, ranging from computer programs to pop songs, and *reputation goods* such as trade marks or appellations of origin, account for an unquantifiable but undeniably growing share of the value embodied in traded products. The nature of trade policy with respect to such knowledge and reputation goods differs radically from policy aimed at liberalizing merchandise trade, since the main concern is not to abolish obstacles to imports (as countries are generally keen to attract knowledge goods), but to safeguard owners' property rights. Negotiations on intellectual property rights therefore do not consist of bargaining on abolition of barriers, but agreements to set up minimum standards of ownership protection.

From a theoretical viewpoint, the enforcement of intellectual property rights is a double-edged sword (see Primo Braga, 1995). In the short run, protecting owners of *knowledge goods* (e.g. through patents) violates the rule that public goods, whose marginal usage cost is zero, should be free. Static efficiency considerations therefore advocate a lax implementation of such property rights, to allow maximum dissemination. In the long run, however, the generation of additional knowledge goods is costly: resources have to be invested in research and development, and this will only occur if a future pecuniary return on such an investment can be safely expected. A zero price of knowledge goods is therefore socially suboptimal in a dynamic sense, because it discourages innovation.

Property rights on *reputation goods* also have their advantages and drawbacks in equity terms. Trade mark protection on the one hand increases the monopoly power of owners, and thereby restricts competition, but on the other hand it can increase consumer welfare by allowing product differentiation and facilitating product information.

The two sides of the theoretical argument have been advanced in multilateral negotiations on intellectual property rights. Since developed countries, including the EU, tend to be the owners and exporters of intellectual property, while developing countries are net importers, the former generally argue in favour of stricter property-right enforcement than the latter. This was particularly evident during the Uruguay Round. These negotiations culminated in the Agreement on Trade-Related Aspects of Intellectual Property Rights (the TRIPS Agreement), which, alongside the GATT and GATS, forms one of the three pillars of the WTO. TRIPS negotiations were championed mainly by the United States and the EU against much initial opposition from developing countries. Agreement was eventually secured on the basis of a trade-off with concessions in negotiations on agricultural market access and the MFA (see Hoekman and Kostecki, 1995).

Under the TRIPS accord, signatories have to establish minimum standards of intellectual property right protection, implement procedures to enforce these rights and extend the traditional GATT principles of national treatment and most-favoured-nation practice to intellectual property. It was agreed that 20-year patent protection should be available for all inventions, whether of products or processes, in almost all fields of technology. Copyright on literary works (including computer programs), sound recordings and films is made available for at least 50 years. Under the agreed transition period, developed countries had to take on full TRIPS obligations since 1996, while developing countries may postpone application of most provisions until the year 2000 and least-developed countries until 2006.

The TRIPS Agreement impinges on competencies held by the EU as well as by national authorities. Both the EU and member states therefore had to ratify the agreement and were subsequently responsible for the required legal adaptations. Relatively few changes were necessary for the EU (see WTO, 1995b), since all member countries had long been signatories to the Paris Convention on patents and trademarks and the Berne Convention on copyright, which constitute the basis of the TRIPS framework.

The EU is one of the main beneficiaries of the TRIPS Agreement and is likely to remain one of its most committed promoters. In particular, the EU has an interest in the protection of geographical indications and enthusiastically promotes ongoing negotiations on a multilateral registration system of such indications for wines and spirits. Exporters of technology-intensive goods as well as owners of high-street brand names stand to gain substantially from stricter patent protection and a clampdown on trade in counterfeit goods.

21.4.3 Trade and the environment

Environmental policy has moved to a prominent position on the trade agenda relatively recently (see Chapter 19). Until the early 1980s, virtually the only environmental concern to affect trade policy was the protection of endangered species. With the rise of ecological awareness and transfrontier pollution problems such as ozone depletion, acid rain and global warming, trade policy came to be seen as a significant element in a country's overall environmental policy.

The main trade policy issue in this debate relates to the use of import restrictions on goods whose production creates negative transborder environmental externalities. Economic theory suggests that in such circumstances the most efficient remedy is to apply direct environmental policy at the source of the externality (e.g. through pollution taxes, eco-subsidies or regulation; see Chapter 19). This is termed the *first-best* policy (see Corden, 1997). However, environmental policies, particularly in the LDCs, are often rudimentary at best, as well as difficult to enforce, so the first-best option may not be feasible. In that case, import restrictions may be the only practicable, albeit less efficient, policy tool. The main drawback of import restrictions against polluting countries is that they provide protection to domestic producers of the importable good, and ecological arguments are therefore vulnerable to abuse by domestic protectionist lobbies. For this reason, trade measures should be temporary and accompanied by efforts to implement environmental policies in the polluting countries.

Even if the externalities are dealt with by environmental policies adopted at the source, new problems can still emerge. Environmental policies affect the competitiveness of open economies. Thus, countries with lax environmental legislation are blamed for 'ecological dumping', and import-competing industries in countries with stringent laws may lobby for protection to ensure a 'level playing field'. As before, the first-best way of ensuring a level playing field is by achieving some degree of coordination in environmental policies across countries. This does not necessarily mean that all countries must adopt exactly the same environmental regime, but it provides a powerful rationale for negotiating environmental policies in multilateral fora such as the WTO. Yet, even if 'ecological dumping' cannot be eradicated through regulatory harmonization, it remains questionable whether trade restrictions are the most appropriate remedy. First, as mentioned above, restricting imports can be counterproductive, as it promotes the domestic activities which the environmental policy is attempting to constrain (Hoekman and Kostecki, 1995). Second, import restrictions tend to apply rather indiscriminately to all imports of a product irrespective of whether its production has met environmental standards or not.

Another issue in this debate is that trade *per se* can damage the environment. Oil leakage from tankers and pollution from increased road haulage are classical examples. Again, trade restrictions will be inefficient in most cases, and a policy aimed at the source of the problem is preferable (e.g. taxation of oil shipments and use of polluting fuels by lorries). Some controversy has arisen in this context between the EU and Switzerland. In bilateral negotiations about extending parts of the Single Market to Switzerland, the EU has pressed for free Alpine road haulage transit. The Swiss, concerned by air and noise pollution from increased freight traffic in narrow mountain valleys, are pursuing the strategic policy of redirecting all transit freight traffic onto railways, both by increasing rail transport capacity and by levying high taxes on road transit. The EU argues that the restrictive Swiss policy diverts traffic onto Austrian and French routes. Ideally, this problem should be solved through international coordination of environmental rules. The use by the EU of trade policy, through withholding Single Market freedoms, or by the Swiss using a blanket ban on road freight transit, are inferior ways to resolve this highly complex issue.

Trade policy, therefore, is an inefficient instrument to protect the environment. It also emerges that international dialogue is particularly important both to address transborder externalities and to defuse protectionist pressures. The main platform for such negotiations is the WTO Committee on Trade and Environment, which was established in 1995. Discussions in this committee have so far been a mere stocktaking exercise, and its report to the Singapore WTO Ministerial Conference in December 1996 contained no specific proposals. The EU has been an active participant in these negotiations, championing in particular the cause of multilateral environmental agreements as a means of discouraging the use of more trade disruptive and less environmentally efficient unilateral measures.

21.4.4 Trade and labour standards

Similarly to concerns that lax environmental rules can be used as a strategy to secure economic competitiveness in traded industries, it is often feared that countries neglect the protection of workers' rights to attain a cost advantage ('social dumping'). This argument has sometimes been invoked in trade relations among developed countries, for instance after the UK's opt-out from the Social Chapter in the Maastricht Treaty (a policy which was reversed by the new Labour government in May 1997), but it appears with much greater frequency in relationships between developed and developing countries.

The theoretical implications of this issue resemble closely those discussed in the context of 'ecological dumping'. The first-best policy is to seek agreement on minimum international labour standards directly rather than via the detour of trade sanctions, be they real or threatened. It is therefore often suggested that the issue should be left to the International Labour Organization (ILO) and kept separate from the trade talks at the WTO (Leary, 1994; OECD, 1996a). A more pragmatic view, however, points to the fact that the ILO has only moral powers to enforce its rules, and that trade sanctions might be the only source of leverage over countries offending against core labour standards (Oxfam, 1996).

The issue of labour standards was introduced in the final stages of the Uruguay Round at the insistence of France and the United States. Strong resistance from LDCs obstructed a 'social clause' in the WTO legal code, but agreement was found that signatories would abide by 'core labour standards' as defined by the ILO. These core standards include:

- the elimination of child labour exploitation;
- prohibition of forced labour;
- freedom of association;
- the right to organize and bargain collectively; and
- non-discrimination in employment.

These aspirations, however, are not backed by any WTO rules allowing countries to impose trade restrictions on exporters who are deemed to be violating the core labour standards.

The EU is likely to continue pressing for some multilateral rules on labour (and environmental) standards. The EU Commissioner for trade policy, Sir Leon Brittan, stated in his address to the Singapore WTO Conference in 1996 that 'labour standards and environmental protection remain important. ... The results of the WTO's work to date fall short of our expectations. The WTO's credibility is at stake, and there is much to do.'

21.5 Conclusions

An 'open' market is an elusive goal, and this chapter has shown that the EU still mans strong defences against many imports. The fortifications have not been razed to the ground, and it is unlikely that the gates will be opened completely for all potential entrants. Even under an optimistically liberal scenario, it will be a considerable time before Australia and New Zealand will be able to sell agricultural produce or China textile and clothing products into the EU market without let or hindrance. However, this chapter documents that the direction of change has leaned, and will probably continue to lean, towards easier access. In this sense, the 'Fortress Europe', which some had feared would be erected around the Single Market, has not materialized.

The Union is trade dependent and continues to rely on extra-EU countries as a source of trade gains. Its policy will be dictated by a number of factors in the years ahead.

First, the maintenance of a strong growth performance remains crucial. Enthusiasm for integration within and outside the EU gathers momentum when the economy is doing well. To some extent European integration and external liberalization are fair weather phenomena. It is also true that the process of liberalization itself tends to improve the weather. Estimates of the EU's economic gains from the Uruguay Round range as high as US$164 billion (1990 prices, not including services; GATT, 1994), which is equivalent to almost one-half of the maximum estimate of gains from the Single Market (ECU 257bn in 1988 prices; Emerson *et al.*, 1988).

Second, within the context of a strong EU economy, the maintenance of regional balance is important in order to prevent the emergence of protectionist lobbies. The long-run effects of European integration on the EU's less developed regions remains a matter of controversy (see Chapter 17). The Commission's Single Market Review (1996) notes an overall tendency of income convergence among EU member countries and regions, but it points to the large variance in regional performance, and it is agnostic as to the cause of observed convergence trends. Protectionist pressure might also be maintained because of Europe's high level of unemployment and its lower degree of labour mobility.

Third, there is now a prospect of increasing heterogeneity among EU members in terms of their status within the Union. Such heterogeneity can be expected to result from the staggered adoption of the single currency, from the 'flexibility clause' in the 1997 Amsterdam treaty and from the accession of new members in Central and Eastern Europe with large transition periods in key policy areas. These developments are likely to increase the difficulty of reaching consensus on trade policy, and protectionist minority interests may have better prospects of success if the process of political bargaining within the EU becomes even more complex and piecemeal.

Fourth, awareness of the cost of protection has increased, not only in relation to manufacturing, but also in the case of agriculture. At the same time, economists and business strategists have developed new perspectives on the potential gains from trade. The new trade theories stress the importance of economies of scale, product variety and competition, all of which require large, open markets for their full realization. Extensive though the EU market already is, economic efficiency requires global competition through a market system seconded by adequate international institutions. Awareness of these requirements has set the agenda for the liberalization of the EU, both among member states and with the outside world.

chapter twenty-two

The Lomé Agreement

A. MARIN

22.1 Background

The first Lomé Agreement was signed in Lomé, the capital of Togo, in 1975 between the EC and a group of forty-six developing countries (LDCs) known as the ACP – the Afro-Caribbean–Pacific group. The name ACP seems an odd way of describing a group of countries, but, as shown in Table 22.1, the countries in the group (which has now expanded by a steady accretion of new members to seventy) have little in common except their underdeveloped status and the fact that almost all are ex-colonies of EC states.[1] However, the Asian ex-colonies of the EC states are excluded. The choice of the ungainly and unrevealing description Afro-Caribbean–Pacific was itself a reflection of the background to the signing of the agreement, the neutrality of the purely geographical terminology reflecting both an attempt to differentiate the agreement from its predecessors and officially a hope for an entirely new type of relationship between developed countries and the LDCs which would prove to be a desirable model for others to follow.

The initial predecessor of the Lomé Agreement was Part IV of the Treaty of Rome, entitled 'Association of the Overseas Countries and Territories'. This part of the Treaty referred to the colonies of the original member states, of which the French were by far the most numerous.[2] Many commentators, in fact, viewed the association of the colonies as being in one respect like the Common Agricultural Policy (CAP) – part of the price (what economists now often call a 'side payment') paid to the French for agreeing to join a Community which was likely to be economically dominated by the Germans. In this case, the payment took the form of enabling France to maintain its close economic relationship with its colonies, while obtaining EC help with its aid burden – see Chapters 2 and 10.

In addition to the securing of the aid, which was achieved by the establishment of a European Development Fund (EDF) as well as by some finance from the European Investment Bank (EIB), the Treaty laid down that the associated colonies should be able to export to all the EC states on the same free trade terms as the member states themselves. Although the colonies could keep tariffs where these were necessary for revenue raising (but, by implication, not for protection), they could not discriminate between member states, and this ruled out any preferential

Table 22.1 ⬤ **The ACP countries in 1994.**

Country	Population (millions)	GNP per Capita (US $)	Country	Population (millions)	GNP per Capita (US $)
Angola	10.442	na	Lesotho[a]	1.900	720
Antigua &			Liberia[a]	2.719	na
Barbuda	0.067	6,770	Madagascar	13.100	200
Bahamas[a]	0.272	11,800	Malawi	9.500	170
Barbados[a]	0.260	6,560	Mali	9.500	256
Belize	0.211	2,530	Mauritania	2.200	480
Benin[a]	5.300	370	Mauritius	1.100	3,150
Botswana[a]	1.400	2,800	Mozambique	15.500	90
Burkina Faso[a]	10.100	300	Namibia	1.500	1,970
Burundi[a]	6.200	160	Niger[a]	8.700	230
Cameroon[a]	13.000	680	Nigeria[a]	108.000	280
Cape Verde	0.372	930	Papua New		
Central African			Guinea[a]	4.200	1,240
Republic[a]	3.200	370	Rwanda[a]	7.800	800
Chad[a]	6.300	180	St. Kitts & Nevis	0.041	4,760
Comoros	0.485	510	St. Lucia	0.166	3,130
Congo[a]	2.600	620	St. Vincent &		
Côte D'Ivoire[a]	13.800	610	Grenadines	0.110	2,140
Djibouti	0.603	na	Sao Tome &		
Dominica	0.072	2,800	Principe	0.125	250
Dominican			Senegal[a]	8.300	600
Republic	7.600	1,330	Seychelles	0.072	6,680
Equatorial			Sierra Leone[a]	4.400	160
Guinea[a]	0.386	430	Solomon Islands	0.365	810
Eritrea	3.482	na	Somalia[a]	8.775	na
Ethiopia[a]	54.900	100	Sudan[a]	27.364	na
Fiji[a]	0.767	2,250	Surinam	0.407	860
Gabon[a]	1.300	3,880	Swaziland[a]	0.906	1,100
Gambia[a]	1.100	300	Tanzania[a]	28.800	140
Ghana[a]	16.600	410	Togo[a]	4.000	320
Grenada[a]	0.092	2,630	Tonga[a]	0.101	1,590
Guinea[a]	6.400	520	Trinidad & Tobago[a]	1.300	3,740
Guinea			Tuvalu	0.010	na
Bissau[a]	1.000	240	Uganda[a]	18.600	190
Guyana[a]	0.826	536	Western Samoa[a]	0.164	1,000
Haiti	7.000	230	Vanuatu	0.165	1,150
Jamaica[a]	2.500	1,540	Zaire[a]	42.540	na
Kenya[a]	26.000	250	Zambia[a]	9.200	350
Kiribati	0.078	740	Zimbabwe	10.800	500

EC GNP per capita in 1994 was $19,600.

[a] Original signatory of Lomé I.

Source World Bank, *World Development Report 1996*.

access for imports from the 'mother country' of a colony.[3] Nor could they discriminate against colonies of another member state.

In the 1957–62 period, many colonies achieved independence. With one exception (Guinea), the ex-colonies wished to maintain the sort of relationship they had had with the EC under Part IV of the Treaty of Rome. As independent states, they were now able to negotiate on their own behalf and to sign agreements for themselves, whereas they had not been involved either in the negotiations leading up to Part IV of the Rome Treaty or in acceptance of its application to them. Nevertheless, the new agreement did not differ greatly from its predecessor. The agreement was reached in December 1962 and formally signed in 1963. It was known as the Yaoundé Convention, since it was signed in Yaoundé, Cameroon.

There were in fact two Yaoundé Conventions: 1963–68 and 1969–74.[4] Officially, the signatories were to 'cooperate on a basis of complete equality', but the document recognized that the aim was 'to maintain their association'. The eighteen ex-colonies even continued to use the word 'association' in their name: Association of African and Malagasy States (AAMS).

Most of the apparent changes between Part IV of the Treaty of Rome and the Yaoundé Agreements were institutional changes arising from the independence of the associates; for example, a Council of the Association and other joint bodies were formed. There were also some changes in the trade/aid provisions, though these were minor in practice. One such change was that although the associates were still allowed to levy tariffs on imports from the EC only when these were for revenue raising,[5] and although such tariffs could still not discriminate between EC states, the associates could levy protective tariffs against imports from each other. This provision aroused hostility from some other countries, especially the United States: unlike the association under the Treaty of Rome, when the associated territories could be considered part of a wide free trade area together with the EC, the new provision meant that the EC–AAMS was clearly not a single free trade area. Hence the United States and others claimed that there was no justification for EC exports to the (now independent) associates to receive preferential access by facing lower tariffs than their own exports to the associates.

As well as the problem over the 'reverse preferences' granted by the AAMS to the EC, by the early 1970s there were other reasons why a simple extension to a Yaoundé III was no longer viewed as adequate. One change specific to the EC was the accession of the United Kingdom, which had its own ex-colonies, some of which had already signed agreements with the EC (the Lagos and Arusha Agreements).

Another change was a result of broader changes in world political/economic relationships. Partly inspired by the success of the OPEC countries in reversing their dependence on the West,[6] there was a general increase in assertiveness by the LDCs. They wanted a more equal relationship. This was often summarized in the call for a NIEO – a New International Economic Order. On the whole, British ex-colonies were more sensitive to arrangements that maintained them in a blatantly dependent status than were the ex-French colonies.[7] Because of the general mood of the times, reinforced by the inclusion of the British ex-colonies, any new relationship with the

EC would have to appear to be signed between equals. Hence the dropping of the word 'Associated' in the AAMS to the simple, unqualified, ACP as the designator of the new, broader group.

Another change in the early 1970s as a result of the OPEC oil price rises, and the strategic embargo by its Arab members in 1973, was a fear by some in the West that the LDCs might successfully cartelize some other raw materials. This provided the EC with an extra motive for tightening links with a group of countries that included some major mineral and other raw material producers.

As part of the background, the 1970s also saw the increasing importance of a particular group of LDCs – the newly industrialized economies (NIEs; see Chapter 21). The ACP countries excluded these 'success stories'. The non-oil African countries in particular, but the ACP countries as a whole, were falling behind the NIEs both in their development and in their ability to sell manufactured goods to developed countries.

The exclusion of the NIEs has not just been a matter of chance. The Lomé agreements follow the Yaoundé wording in limiting applications for new membership to countries 'whose economic structure and production are comparable with those of the ACP States' ('Associated States' in Yaoundé). The countries which are already signatories have to approve the new accessions. Furthermore, according to Matthews (1977) even in 1963, during the United Kingdom's first attempt to join the EC, the United Kingdom realized that the association was unlikely to be extended to the non-African members of the Commonwealth. By the time the United Kingdom actually joined, a Protocol and Declaration of Intent to the 1972 Treaty of Accession explicitly distinguished the 'developing Commonwealth countries situated in Africa, the Indian Ocean, the Pacific Ocean and the Caribbean' (listed by name in an annex) from those in 'Asia (India, Pakistan, Singapore, Malaysia and Ceylon)'. The countries of the former, but not the latter, group were offered the choice of joining Yaoundé or arranging some other formal relationship with the EC. The reasons for the exclusions should be clear from the discussions below on aid (given the populations of India and Pakistan) and trade (NIEs, including Singapore).

The new agreement was signed in Lomé in February 1975. It became known as Lomé I (1975–79) and was followed by Lomé II (1980–84), Lomé III (1985–89) and Lomé IV (1990–99).[8] As shown in Table 22.1, there is a wide disparity in the population and income of the ACP. Even now, with twenty-four more members than in 1975, Nigeria on its own has about a fifth of the total population of the ACP, and for much of the time since 1974 (though not most recently) has contributed more than a third of all ACP–EC trade, both of ACP exports and imports.[9] The ACP includes many of the poorest LDCs and many of those with the least successful growth record, since it includes all the Sahel countries which were hit so badly by drought in the 1980s.

All of these factors, as well as others, are seen by some as relevant to the desire for a new agreement, and to its form and content. However, various assessments of the purposes and results of the Lomé agreements are split by fundamental political disagreements. The preamble to the first Lomé Agreement stated that the contracting states:

Anxious to establish, on the basis of complete equality between partners, close and continuing co-operation in a spirit of international solidarity ... resolved to establish a new model for relations between developed and developing States, compatible with the aspirations of the international community towards a more just and more balanced economic order.

The last phrase is probably to be taken as referring to the NIEO. Some commentators have seen this preamble as a genuine expression of the true intentions of both sides: 'The EEC–ACP partnership represents a symbol of hope in a divided world'.[10]

From the beginning, there have been others who took a diametrically opposed view and saw Lomé as a neo-colonialist successor to Part IV of the Treaty of Rome. That is, despite the apparent recognition of the ex-colonies as independent and equal partners in a joint agreement, the underlying motive of the EC states was to keep the ACP linked to them, yet still in a dependent position, at the least cost to themselves. It would always be the EC which made the decisions in its own interest and the ACP which had to go along with them.[11] One statement of this view is: 'The Lomé Convention was neo-colonial because it was a path chosen for the ACP by the European Community' (Lister, 1988, p. 216).

A third view is that of Ravenhill (1985b) whose notion of 'collective clientism' views Lomé as an agreement between unequals, but where the dependent party (the ACP) was eager for the agreement. On this approach, the ACP countries knew that they were weak, even as compared with other LDCs, i.e. the NIEs. They attempted to construct an arrangement to preserve their position in the EC. This involved trying to place constraints on EC policy making in relevant areas, whereas the EC wanted to maintain its position in the ACP states at low cost (this part is not so far removed from the neocolonialist position, although the first part is). To satisfy both sides there were ambiguities in Lomé; the ACP in 1975 thought that it had achieved a patronage relation whereby the EC would protect its interests even where Lomé was not specific. An alternative description of 'collective clientism' would be a kind of feudalism – the vassal pledged fealty in return for protection against outsiders and reassurance that the superior would not take untoward advantage of his power. Ravenhill sees the leaders of the ACP countries as feeling disappointed, even cheated, at the failure of the EC to fulfil what the ACP countries had expected its side of the bargain to be.

One way of classifying these views is in terms of what they see as the balance of the relative weight given to self-interest, altruism, frankness and consistency by the EC and by the ACP. The following sections will deal with the major provisions of the Lomé agreements, in the two main areas, which are trade and aid. In these sections, I shall try to deal with the issues in a way that does not pre-judge where the truth lies.

22.2 General aid

The aid provisions of the Lomé agreements fall into two groups. One is the traditional sort of aid, provided by the EDF and the EIB under Part IV of the Rome Treaty, Yaoundé and then under Lomé. In order to protect ACP sensitivities (preserve the illusion of equality even where it is obviously inapplicable?), the relevant section of the Lomé Agreement is entitled 'Financial and Technical Co-operation'. As always, aid programmes are subject to differing opinions. On the one hand, since poverty and underdevelopment have continued in the ACP, and worsened in some of its members, aid has 'obviously' been insufficient and ineffective. On the other hand, any aid at all is 'obviously' better than nothing and could be said to represent generosity. Neither argument is necessarily convincing: to support the first argument one would need to know what would have happened otherwise. For the second argument, not only are there the moralists who would say that the ex-colonial members of the EC have a moral debt to their ex-colonies, but there is also the neocolonialist analysis which sees minimal aid as a way of tying the recipients to the donors – against the best long-term interests of the former. There are also some economists who see all aid as a harmful distraction from the true need of the LDCs.[12]

As well as the general problems associated with aid generally, there have been specific charges against EC aid programmes under Lomé. It is often alleged that delays in approving and then disbursing aid are excessive. Even by the bureaucratic standards of many EC institutions, the procedures for EDF aid seem particularly cumbersome. Although the ACP governments can submit proposals for aid projects, they are investigated by an EC 'delegate' accredited to the ACP country concerned. They then require approval by the EDF committee and by the EC Commission. The resulting delays can be considerable. For example, six years after the signing of Lomé III, only 42% of Lomé III aid had been disbursed and for Lomé IV the equivalent figure was 37%.[13] Nevertheless, it is only fair to mention that other multinational aid donor bodies can be as slow as the EDF.[14]

Those who criticize the Lomé agreements as merely having a facade of equality point to the requirement for appraisal and approval by the EC member states (the EDF committee) and the Commission (for example, Lister, 1988, and Ravenhill, 1985a). The Lomé Treaty states: 'The Community shall be responsible for taking financing decisions on projects and programmes.' However, it could be argued that not only is the EC no worse than other donors in its unilateral right of decision, but that it has been criticized for being more willing to accept ACP proposals and less demanding in its assessments than other aid bodies, such as the World Bank. Within the EC, in 1982, the Development Commissioner, Pisani, criticized the EDF for agreeing to fund too many 'cathedrals in the desert', i.e. isolated grandiose projects pushed for prestige reasons by ACP governments.

Partly as a result of the last criticism, and partly as a result of changing ideas among all Western donor bodies generally, over the course of the four Lomé agreements there have been changes in the approach of the EC to aid projects. The sectoral allocation has always tended towards agriculture rather than industry, but under Lomé III there was a switch to promoting more agricultural self-sufficiency and away from a stress on agricultural export goods for the world market.[15] There was a change in orientation to financing linked programmes and sectors, rather than discrete (and, therefore, possibly isolated) projects. Within this there is also an increased emphasis on 'micro-projects'.

In Lomé IV, the EC followed the World Bank, and devoted EDF funds for 'structural adjustment support'. It also stressed the development of services sectors, while the 1995 revision (in a section with the title 'Decentralised Cooperation') stressed integrating NGOs into the aid use.

Whether or not these changes are sensible, some of the ACP countries resented what they saw (whether correctly or not) as an attempt by the EC member states to dictate to them what their development strategy and priorities should be, as if they could not be trusted to decide for themselves where the money they received should be spent. This resentment was even stronger over another change in the EC approach between Lomé I and Lomé III, which was the attempt to introduce a 'policy dialogue' into aid administration. In the account of the President of the Commission, Gaston Thorn (with emphasis added):

> the 'policy dialogue'. What passions were aroused, what anxiety and what misunderstandings caused by this idea, which the Community had put forward with the sole purpose of making aid more effective ... some thought they could detect in it a move by the Community to make its aid conditional upon the adoption by its *partners* of policies decided elsewhere. (*The Courier*, No. 89, January/February 1985)

In the end, the ACP accepted 'cooperation' between the ACP recipient of aid and the EC in setting up programmes and in evaluating and checking how the money was being spent and its results. Quite clearly, as the above quote shows, the fundamental divisions in views about Lomé apply here. On the one set of views, the EC was signalling its determination to keep total control, and/or showing that it did not trust the competence (and possibly the honesty) of the ACP governments. References to 'partners' and 'equal relationships' were just facades. On the other set of views, given the shortage of trained, often of even literate, manpower in most ACP countries, it was sensible to make use of EC expertise to help ensure the most effective use of scarce funds.

22.3 STABEX and SYSMIN

Many of the ACP countries are heavily dependent on the exports of a few raw materials – sometimes, as in the case of Ghana, of a single product (cocoa). Many of these commodities have aggregate market supplies which are inelastic in the short run, whereas demand in the industrialized countries may swing sharply with the state of the business cycle. Furthermore, as non-differentiated products with highly competitive markets, they are what is now often called 'flex-price'. As a result, their prices tend to swing widely from year to year. Exporters therefore suffer wide *variability* in their earnings. An extra source of instability in earnings occurs when the raw material is agricultural rather than mineral: weather conditions during the growing season can lead to wide fluctuations in yield in any one area. Since any one ACP country may not dominate the market, a drop in yield there is unlikely to lead to an offsetting rise in price; thus, there are two independent causes of variability in earnings.

A major innovation of Lomé I[16] was a scheme to compensate ACP countries when their earnings from commodity exports fell. The system was called STABEX, and although formally not part of the aid package, is clearly aid rather than trade. Under Lomé I the scheme covered twenty-nine products in twelve commodity groups; more products have been added to the list in the later Lomé agreements. There are now fifty products, all agriculture-based commodities (now including shrimps, prawns and squid) and primarily tropical (though now including peas and beans).[17]

The compensation is available to an ACP country where the product, or product group, is responsible for at least 5% of the country's export earnings, and where the earnings from the product have fallen by 4.5%.[18] The compensation is normally payable only on the country's exports to the EC.[19] The maximum funds available to the EDF for STABEX payments are laid down in advance by each Lomé Agreement. Particularly in 1981–82 and 1988–91, there were serious shortfalls of funds due to slumps in commodity prices in the preceding years (payment is usually a year in arrears). In 1981 only 52.8% and in 1982 only 40.4% of legitimate ACP claims could be met. The 1987 meeting of ACP–EEC ministers reported that:

> The ACP States also continue to maintain that the Community is obliged to pay them the balance of the requests for the 1980 and 1981 years of applications, which were not met in full because of lack of resources. The Community disagrees.

There is still disagreement.

As the system has developed, a major source of conflict between the ACP and the EC has been over the use of receipts under STABEX.[20] The payments are given to the ACP government and, according to Lomé I (Article 20), 'the recipient ACP State shall decide how the resources will be used', and it merely had *ex post* to 'inform the Commission annually of the use to which it has put the resources transferred'. Despite this freedom given to the ACP – which in this way was treated as a responsible equal of the EC – many in the EC felt that the receipts should be used to help the producers adversely affected by the drop in their earnings. However, many ACP governments used much of the receipts from STABEX as part of their government revenue, using them to fund various of their general programmes, including development programmes, with the product covered by STABEX benefiting, at most, as part of the general gains expected from the projects.

Despite complaints by the EC at this 'diversion' of funds to the ACP governments, it can be argued that this is not an obviously inferior use of the STABEX receipts. For many of the ACP countries, given their low levels of literacy and thus the lack of formal accounting of domestic transactions, revenues from tariffs and from taxes on exports are necessarily a major part of government revenue.[21] Under such circumstances, a shortfall in the proceeds from export taxes and the revenues of the export marketing boards represents a major problem in the orderly running of government-financed projects and services.

However, the argument has also been made that this justification is unconvincing. Firstly, the amounts received under STABEX are only very loosely related to shortfalls in government revenues – essentially because the implicit tax rate on exports of commodities covered by STABEX varies greatly between ACP countries. In some it is so low that STABEX receipts 'appropriated' by the government are greater than their tax revenue lost because of declines in the value of the exports. Secondly, the lag between the decline in export values and the actual payment of STABEX money means that the increase in government revenue because of the STABEX receipts may come just when revenues have recovered anyway. This is destabilizing to government budgets and to the effects of their fiscal policies.[22]

Although, as just discussed, the issue is not clear cut, the EC succeeded (against the initial wishes of the ACP, for the same reasons as with general aid 'cooperation') in altering Lomé III. This has continued in Lomé IV, and STABEX transfers are now to be devoted either to the sector 'that recorded the loss of export earning and be used there for the benefit of the economic operators adversely affected by the loss' or to promote diversification to other appropriate agricultural or agricultural processing sectors – see the previous section on the switch in Lomé III to food self-sufficiency. In the 1995 revision, non-agricultural diversification is allowed where there is an ongoing 'adjustment programme' in place. Not only is the purpose of the use of the receipts now removed from the discretion of the ACP governments, but the actual request by an ACP government for a payment now has to include 'substantial analysis ... on the programmes and operations to which the ACP State *undertakes to allocate* the funds' (emphasis added). Lomé IV has further insisted on a closer and more rigorous joint monitoring of the use of the funds.

The commodities covered by STABEX do not include any mineral-based ones (see note 17). In the second Lomé Agreement, this omission was dealt with by a somewhat similar scheme known as SYSMIN which covered copper, phosphate, manganese, bauxite and alumina, tin and iron (and now includes uranium). There were, however, some differences between the two schemes.

Although the statement of aims for SYSMIN in the Lomé II Agreement mentioned export earnings, the context made it clear that the main aim was to enable the ACP states to maintain 'their capacity to export mining products to the Community'. The focus was to avoid the loss of mining capacity when income fell. In general, many mineral extraction facilities (especially underground) deteriorate if there is insufficient maintenance. The receipts from SYSMIN were to be used for maintaining the facilities.

Unlike STABEX, the trigger was 'a substantial fall in production or export *capacity*' (emphasis added). There was no figure given for the fall in export earnings, and the necessary fall was, in practice, assessed by the Commission.[23] Similarly, the actual amount of SYSMIN aid needed was to be assessed by the Commission, and is not directly related to the drop in earnings. Less relevant for an analysis of the intentions and effects of SYSMIN, the substantial fall in capacity was taken to be 10%, while the required proportion of export earnings from the commodity was generally 15% (reduced to 10% for the poorest ACP states).

In the late 1970s the sharp fall in the real price of commodities and the excess capacity in mining industries was thought to be a temporary cyclical phenomenon, since the minerals involved were primarily industrial raw materials. As the 'temporary' price depression and excess capacity stretched on into the 1980s, views changed and fears of an imminent shortage of raw materials receded. By Lomé III there was a loosening of the aims and conditions of SYSMIN payments to include other development projects which the ACP states had intended to finance from their mining revenue, provided that the viability of the mineral industry is not endangered by the shortfall in earnings, or where maintenance or restoration of the viability is impossible. As with STABEX, the spending of any receipts under SYSMIN now requires EC agreement.

Assessments of the STABEX and SYSMIN programmes vary widely, with the differences in opinion often related to the fundamental differences in approaching Lomé that have been discussed above. On the one hand, these are schemes of a type that have often been strongly advocated by LDCs heavily dependent on primary product exports whose price fluctuates widely. Thus, the compensation when export earnings fall can be seen as an attempt by the EC to meet the worries, and demands, of the ACP.

The sceptical view sees these two programmes as an attempt to tie in the ACP states to the EC market. On this view, it is not coincidental that they were introduced when the West was worrying about the possibility of shortages of raw materials. Because STABEX and SYSMIN payments are usually linked to the recent exports to the EC (under Lomé IV this has been somewhat relaxed), the ACP countries have an incentive to direct their exports of the commodities to the EC and not to other countries. Hence the EC was ensuring its shares of the supplies of raw materials in the face of the worries just mentioned.[24] This view concentrates especially on the provisions of SYSMIN, under Lomé II, with its stress on 'maintaining capacity to export mining products to the *Community*' (Article 49, emphasis added). Only when the fears of not having sufficient access to the raw materials had disappeared was the EC prepared to consider diversification of output in the ACP, and a possible relaxation to cover exports to non-EC countries.

Whatever one's assessment of the *aims* of the EC side in the Lomé Conventions, as a question of economic analysis, it should be noted that STABEX and SYSMIN do provide an incentive to produce the commodities covered by the schemes. Those economists who think that LDCs would do better in terms of their long-term standards of living if their resources were reallocated away from the production of primary products for exports to other types of output (whether to manufactured output or to home food output) would consider the incentives inherent in STABEX–SYSMIN as undesirable. Economists who think that concentration on efficient production of primary products for export is a viable route of development for countries with a comparative advantage in those sectors will see the innovations under Lomé as beneficial.

22.4 Total aid

Because of the increase in the number of ACP countries, the increases in their population and the declines in the purchasing power of the European Currency Unit (ECU; EUA – European Unit of Account – for Lomé I–II), it is not easy to decide the level in real terms of total EC aid to the ACP. The problem is complicated by the existence of some payments that are not straightforward grants, and by the treatment of administrative costs.[25]

The majority opinion is that there was a definite fall in the real per capita aid agreed at Lomé II. For Lomé III and IV the aid was probably not quite as far below the Lomé II level. Table 22.2 gives an example of the sorts of results obtained.[26]

Although it is possible that the individual EC member states would have given more aid to some (at least) of the ACP if they had not been contributing to the EDF, there is no evidence. Ravenhill (1985b), although generally sceptical about the benefits the ACP has received from the Lomé agreements, has analyzed the various bilateral aid flows and concluded that probably no diversion occurred and that EDF donations were additional to the other aid grants of the EC member states.

It might also be interesting to note, to put the figures into perspective, that during 1990–94 the EU countries gave total official grants of 110 billion ECU to developing countries (data from CEU 1996d, converted from $ by the author). Thus their EDF committments through Lomé were about 10% of their total aid in the form of grants (of the 12 billion ECU aid under Lomé IV, 10.9 was from the EDF.).

Table 22.2 ⬤ Comparisons of aid under Lomé I, II, III, IV and IV revision.

	Lomé I	Lomé II	Lomé III	Lomé IV	Lomé IV revision
At current prices (millions EUA–ECU)	3,466[a]	5,227[a,b]	8,500[b]	12,000[c]	14,625[c]
Percentage change from previous		50.1	+62.6	+41.2	+21.9
Deflated for price change (%)		+5[a]	+15.7[b]	+14.8[c]	+0.9[c]
Real per capita change (%)		−7[a]	−5[b]	+3[c,d]	−10[c,d]

[a] Ravenhill (1985), Table 8.11.
[b] Stevens (1984), Table 2.
[c] Author, based on EC figures. As a proportion of *EC–GDP* in the first year of the Agreements, there was a 5% fall in aid between Lomé III and Lomé IV and a 10% fall between Lomé IV and its revision. The latter allows for the increase in EU membership.
[d] The 1990 meeting of ACP–EEC Council pointed out that the *level* (not change) of aid per capita of population in the ACP under Lomé IV would amount to less than 5 ECU per capita per year.

Even if there were falls in the real per capita value of the aid received by the ACP as a result of the Lomé agreements, the period of the 1980s and early 1990s was one in which the total real aid given by the West was relatively stagnant, and the real aid per capita is considered to have dropped sharply. The relatively minor falls in Lomé aid combined with its probable additionality suggest that, judged in terms of receipts, whatever the motives of the donors and the long-term implications of the procedures of implementation, the ACP countries gained from Lomé. This conclusion is reinforced by the fact that whatever their complaints, and whatever the

Table 22.3 ⬭ Shares of ACP countries in EC imports from developing countries.

Year	EC imports from ACP (million ECU)	EC imports from ACP as percentage of EC imports from developing countries	EC imports from non-oil ACP[a] as percentage of EC imports from non-oil developing countries[b]
1960	2,896	24	27
1965	3,812	23	29
1970	5,515	23	30
1975	9,867	16	25
1977	13,644	16	25
1978	12,846	16	22
1979	15,878	16	20
1980	20,889	16	19
1981	18,960	13	16
1982	20,273	14	16
1983	22,083	16	15
1984	27,931	18	16
1985	30,509	20	16
1986	19,762	18	18
1987	16,510	15	15
1988	17,541	15	13
1989	19,597	14	13
1990	20,125	14	12
1991	19,134	13	10
1992	17,954	12	10
1993	14,570	10	9

[a] 'Non-oil ACP' is 69 ACP countries minus Nigeria, Cameroon, Gabon, Congo, Angola, Bahamas and Trinidad and Tobago.
[b] 'Non-oil developing countries' is all developing countries minus OPEC members and Cameroon, Congo, Angola, Bahamas and Trinidad and Tobago (Nigeria and Gabon are in OPEC).
Source EC External Trade Statistics Yearbook, 1987, 1992, 1994.

views of commentators about the ultimate effects of Lomé on long-term patterns of development, no ACP countries have dropped out of the agreements (or even re-fused particular payments they were entitled to), and there has been a steady stream of new applicants.

22.5   Trade

Lomé I followed the Yaoundé agreements in giving the LDCs involved tariff-free access to the EC market. It went further, and did not require the ACP to provide tariff-free access to EC exports – the only requirement was that each ACP state should provide the same terms of access to all EC exports, with no discrimination favouring any particular EC country.

Nevertheless, the ACP has expressed strong dissatisfaction with the trade results of Lomé. In this section we first consider the actual export record of the ACP to the EC, and then consider why the record seems disappointing despite the apparent preferential access given to the ACP.

There are major difficulties in assessing how far, if at all, ACP exports have benefited. One difficulty is the high proportion that oil exports formed of the total (about 40% in some years). The major swings of oil prices over the Lomé period can thus give misleading impressions of changes in the pattern of trade. Even if oil is considered separately, there are two major trends which could affect the data. On the one hand, over the period from 1975 to date, the EC has grown less fast than developed countries in general (particularly Japan and the United States). On the other, the African countries, which form the bulk of the ACP (see Table 22.1) have performed noticeably worse than many other LDCs.

Attempts to deal with these problems have been made. Probably the most thorough is a series of studies by Moss and Ravenhill. The first was published in 1982 and they have been updated, the most recent being 1987. They use two methods, each of which deals with one of the two problems mentioned above. The first is dealt with by looking at the proportion of ACP imports in total imports by the EC from the LDCs. This could still show a poor performance by the ACP owing to the depressing effect of the second trend, even if the ACP were doing better in the EC than it would have done without the preferential access granted under Lomé. Conversely, the poor export performance of the ACP compared with other LDCs should not affect the second measure, which is the share of ACP exports that go to the EC as a proportion of their total exports. However, this measure would still be biased down, as a measure of the effects of Lomé, because of the relatively slow growth of the EC as a market. Taken together, however, the two measures might provide some indication of whether preferential access to the EC has helped ACP exports, even though if both biases were important one could still mistakenly reject the hypothesis of benefits to trade.

An example of the type of results is given in Table 22.3, where I have followed the approach of Moss and Ravenhill, though with slight differences on some details of the calculations. The table covers 69 ACP and 12 EC countries over the whole period (all of the current ACP except for Eritrea). Because of the expansion in both the ACP and EC membership over the period, if Lomé had any effect at all this should push the figures upwards. The downwards trend actually found shows that at the very least Lomé failed to outweigh the other forces diminishing the ACP's share of EC imports. Moss and Ravenhill's findings on their other measures generally suggest a similar lack of impact of Lomé on ACP exports going to the EC.[27]

However, there is some evidence for a diversification within the EC market. Although total ACP non-oil exports have not kept their share of the EC market, Moss and Ravenhill's findings show that there was a tendency for the British Commonwealth members of the ACP to send less of their exports to the United Kingdom and more to the other EC countries. Earlier analyses of the Yaoundé agreements had shown a similar tendency: the AAMS countries tended to diversify their exports away from what has been their previous colonial 'parent country' towards the other EC states.[28] Finally, it might be noted that there is some evidence of slight improvement in exports to the EC of a few processed and manufactured products from a few ACP countries, but these are still a small proportion of ACP exports (see McQueen and Stevens, 1989; Davenport et al, 1995 or *The Courier*, March–April 1997, p. 19).

There are a large number of possible reasons for these disappointing results (disappointing, at least, from the viewpoint of the ACP states). One point to notice is that, because the ACP depends so heavily on exports of primary products, most of its exports would have been free of tariffs anyway since the EC does not impose any duties on these imports, whatever their origin. The exact proportions differ according to the period covered, but an EC estimate was that in the late 1980s about two-thirds of ACP exports to the EC would have been zero rated regardless of origin (*The Courier*, May–June 1988).

Even if the ACP has no special advantage over other primary producers through Lomé, one might have thought that as a result of Lomé the countries involved would switch to higher-value agricultural products, processed foods or manufactured goods, where their tariff-free access would provide them with an advantage over competitors. However, this possibility is limited by several factors, some of which relate to provisos and exceptions in the Lomé agreements.

One such limit on the usefulness of Lomé to the ACP is that a specific exception is made for products that are supported within the EC by the CAP. The EC has often pointed out that over 99% of ACP exports enter the EC duty free: less than 1% are CAP products. This, however, is irrelevant – what is relevant is what ACP exports of these products would be if they could enter the EC without any constraints or tariffs, not what they are if deterred. Even where some special arrangements have been made, for example, for Botswana beef, critics have alleged that the concessions have been grudging, insufficient and trivial from the EC's point of view.[29]

This applies not only to the obvious CAP products but also to such items as Kenyan strawberries and cut flowers. As already mentioned, there are special, although limited, arrangements for a few products. For example, a quota of sugar is purchased at a guaranteed price, intended to compensate the ACP sugar producers for the trade diversion from their cane sugar to EC sugar beet when the United Kingdom entered the EC. Nevertheless, this does not compensate the ACP (and other) sugar cane producers for the disastrous drop in world sugar prices, largely caused by the massive EC surplus of inefficient sugar beet production induced by the CAP.[30]

One contentious set of limits on the ability of the ACP to export processed–manufactured products to the EC is due to the 'rules of origin' as to what constitutes an ACP product. It may be reasonable for the EC to avoid entry of 'screwdriver' factory products, where an ACP country would be used to give a label entitling tariff-free access to the EC for products, nearly all of whose costs and profits of production accrue to a non-ACP, truly originating, country – as discussed in Chapter 21, the issue is applicable to a wider set of EC trade relationships. However, the actual rules of origin in the Lomé Treaties are particularly complex. There are different rules of origin for different products. Some are by detailed description of the stages of production which must occur within an ACP country. Others are by percentage of value-added: for many manufactured products, 50% or 60% of the value must accrue within the ACP; for some processed food, the processing must add 70% to be counted an originating product.

There are also possibilities for derogations for ACP industries where value-added in the ACP state is at least 45% of the value of the finished product and which cannot cause serious injury to an EC industry. As this has been revised under Lomé IV, it is too early to say whether it will prove to be a significant relaxation.

Although the idea of rules of origin might seem reasonable, the ACP countries have argued, bitterly at times, that the rules are too stringent. They, and those economists who support their view, say that for countries at their stage of development it is natural for industrialization to occur in the form of using cheap labour to do the routine stages of assembly, etc., on products where the sophisticated higher-technology/capital-intensive stages take place in countries that are currently relatively scarce in unskilled labour but relatively abundant in capital (human and non-human). This is a sensible use of comparative advantage (compare the Hecksher–Ohlin theory). It is also the route apparently taken by some NIEs, which have now moved on.[31]

The final reason we shall mention for the ACP failure to export non-raw materials to the EC is a mixture of Lomé itself and other factors. The latter are the system of EC preferential relationships with other groups discussed in Chapter 21, as well as the gradual reductions in tariffs agreed in the GATT rounds. Attention is most often drawn to the generalized system of preferences (GSP), as applying to the obvious competitors to the ACP, but many of the other agreements listed in Table 21.2 cover countries producing some, at least, of the products the ACP might be expected to try to export to the EC. The ACP has protested against extension of the GSP, and also against other tariff cuts which erode its advantage. An example is a bitter row between ACP and EC delegates in 1992, over the possibility of improved access to the EC for products coming from the former communist countries.[32]

In response, the EC has often drawn attention to the various ceilings and complex NTBs limiting the value of the GSP and other agreements. The EC has said that the ACP receives preferential treatment because it is exempt from these ceilings and non-tariff barriers. However, the interaction with Lomé itself mentioned in the previous paragraph is that the ACP is also subject to the proviso that if ACP exports 'result in serious disturbance in a sector of the economy of the Community or of one or more of its Member States' the Community may take 'safeguard measures'.

Although the EC has never actually implemented the safeguard clause, it has threatened to do so.[33] The issue arose in a 'sensitive' sector: textiles. General warnings were issued to the ACP in 1977 not to expand too far in this area, and indicative quotas were set up on the ACP in areas covered by the MFA. The crunch came with Mauritius. Under pressure from the French (who used a technique of delaying customs clearance that was later perfected on Japanese videocassette recorders), Mauritius agreed to a VER on its shipments to France. It then switched much of its textile exports to the United Kingdom and Ireland. Both complained to the Commission in 1979. The United Kingdom invoked the 'safeguard clause'. Under threat of imposition of the 'safeguard clause', Mauritius then agreed to a VER on its exports to the United Kingdom and Ireland.

Even if the safeguard clause has never actually been imposed, the possibility of its imposition, especially after the Mauritian case, is alleged to have created enough uncertainty to have inhibited investment in ACP production capacity directed at exports of manufactured goods which could fall foul of the safeguard. The nature of the EC sectors which face the most problems, and where the safeguard might be invoked, is that those are precisely the sectors where the LDCs are likely to have a comparative advantage: EC problem sectors are those facing 'cheap' competition.

The assessment of the EC defence against ACP complaints of erosion of preferential advantage is thus uncertain. Probably the ACP has been subject to fewer VERs and other barriers than the LDCs relying on the GSP. The ACP itself, however, has not been unaffected either by actual barriers or by the threat of further barriers if they were to become more successful. Game theory would predict that threats which are credible can affect actions, without the threat having to be implemented.[34]

22.6 Conclusion

In this chapter I have discussed the outcome of the Lomé agreements, and to some extent discussed the motivations of the two sides to the agreements. I have not dealt with the actual negotiations themselves and the relative cohesion and bargaining power of each side. The last sentence of the previous section suggests that an alternative method of analysis would be to examine the whole process in terms of the concepts from game theory: aims, threat points, possible strategies, degrees of information about the other players, learning, and likely pay-offs. Although such an analysis would be interesting and probably productive, as far as I know it has not been attempted so far.

Although I briefly outlined some of the different assessments of the motives of the two groups – the EC and the ACP – I have tried in analyzing the mechanisms and outcomes of the Lomé agreements to be as objective as possible and not to let my own views intrude too much. Complete objectivity on contentious issues is obviously impossible.

The conclusion of the discussions of the effects of the trade and aid provisions of the Treaties would seem to be that the ACP has gained more, at least in terms of receipts, from the aid than from the trade concessions. However, a comparison of the top row of Table 22.2 and the first column of Table 22.3 (remembering that Table 22.2 covers five-year periods) strongly suggests that trade results are quantitatively far more important to the ACP than aid payments, and small percentage increases in trade receipts would outweigh much larger percentage increases in aid.[35] Indeed, ultimately, Lomé agreements will be successful only if they effectively encourage the ACP to increase its possibility of producing, and of exporting (whether to the EC or elsewhere), enough to increase its standard of living and to escape from the poverty summarized in Table 22.1.

Notes

1. At the time of writing, South Africa is a partial, not full, member of the ACP.

2. France distinguished between its colonies and its 'overseas departments', of which, in 1957, Algeria was the most important. The latter were dealt with separately in Article 227. Many of the subsequent developments, culminating in the Lomé agreements, did not apply to them.

3. Although where the colony's protection was by quota, discrimination between EC member states was still allowed. Some authors view this as a particular concession to French exporters to its colonies. There are several books which provide a detailed account of the pre-Lomé relationships of the EC and the associated Territories. Examples are Lister (1988) and Grilli (1993).

4. For reasons connected with the first UK attempt to join the EC, the Yaoundé convention did not enter into force until July 1964.

5. Also, quantitative restrictions on imports from the EC were not allowed.

6. There is no single term which exactly covers the most developed countries. For convenience we shall use the 'West', even though it includes Japan and even though the EC is to the east of the Caribbean members of the ACP.

7. See, for example, Lister (1988) and Grilli (1993) for an account of the ideological underpinnings of the French approach to their colonies, and the resulting effects on the relationships.

8. Although these dates are often given, Lomé I officially came into force in April

1976 and was due to expire in March 1980. Lomé II was signed in October 1979 but did not formally come into force until January 1981 and was due to expire in February 1985. Lomé III was signed in December 1984, only formally came into force in May 1986 and was due to expire in February 1990. Some sources refer to Lomé I as 1975–80, and Lomé II as 1980–85. Lomé IV was signed in December 1989, came into force in September 1991 and is due to expire in 2000, with a renegotiation signed in November 1995 but not yet ratified. The aid funds are for five years.

9. Moss and Ravenhill (1988). Data on country-by-country trade can be found in the EC *External Trade Statistical Yearbooks*. As Moss and Ravenhill also point out, during 1979–83 71% of ACP exports came from ten of the sixty-four countries, while 70% of EC exports went to eleven of the countries.

10. Cosgrove Twitchett (1978), p. xv. The title of the book is revealing.

11. The first leader of Ghana after independence wrote: 'The essence of neo-colonialism, is that the State which is subject to it is, in theory, independent and has all the trappings of international sovereignty. In reality its economic system and thus its political policy is directed from outside.' Nkrumah (1965), quoted in Lister (1988).

12. The whole issue of whether any aid is appropriate and, if it is, in which form it should be given is one which has caused sharp debates among development economists. A sceptic might well claim that ideas on types of aid, as on suitable paths of development, have changed simply to reflect the failure of each idea in turn to actually improve the position of the least developed countries.

13. *The Courier*, No. 132 (March–April 1992), *OJC* 12.11.96, p. 291. For Lomé I and II, see Stevens (1984), who also gives a short summary of other aspects of the implementation of the Lomé funds.

14. See, for example, Ravenhill (1985b), Chapter 8, or Lister (1988), p. 139. She, like others, points out that since the funds are fixed in nominal terms, the delays mean a real loss when inflation reduces the purchasing power of the ECU.

15. This particular switch may owe something to analyses of the Sahel famines, and possibly to Sen's analysis of famines generally, which stresses the risk of relying for purchasing power on sales to a (fluctuating) market rather than producing for own consumption. Note 12 is relevant for the change in sectoral emphasis and for the following points in the text. The emphasis on programmes and away from projects is parallelled by equivalent changes in the purely internal EC 'structural funds' such as the ERDF as well as the EIB.

16. Although before the formation of the EC, France guaranteed to buy some raw materials from its colonies at prices above world levels, and there had been a partial precursor under Yaoundé.

17. Iron ore, which was the only exception and an anomaly, was shifted to SYSMIN.

18. In Lomé I both thresholds were 7.5%, they were 6.5% under Lomé II and 6%

under Lomé III. There are lower thresholds for the poorest, landlocked or island ACP states (2.5% under Lomé I, now 1.0%), while sisal has a lower fluctuation threshold (5% under Lomé I, now 4.0%). Under the new 1995 revision, there may be limits on the amount of compensation when exports fall by more than 20%.

19. Because STABEX was supposed to be a *stabilization* scheme, not just a minimum floor, in theory most ACP countries could have had to repay their STABEX receipts when earnings recovered, but the relevant criteria were both complex and vague in parts and were not generally triggered. Under Lomé IV, repayment is no longer required even in principle. Also under Lomé IV, there was a possibility of compensation on exports which are not to the EU.

20. A detailed account of Lomé I and II is in Hewitt (1983).

21. Compare the situation in pre-industrial Britain. Not only does the whole genre of smugglers' tales reflect this reality, but disputes between King and Parliament over who was to have the right to the proceeds from the sale of the rights to international trading were one of the sources of conflict leading up to the Civil War.

22. This is similar to the familiar arguments in macroeconomics between monetarists and Keynesians over the possible destabilizing effects of attempted stabilization policies in the presence of lags. It is also possible for some 'advance payments' to be made under STABEX, but this provision has rarely been used.

23. According to Daniel (1984). In Lomé IV a 10% drop in export earnings is required, but this is a necessary, not a sufficient, condition for aid to be given. There must also be 'serious difficulties' as a result of the drop in earnings.

24. Daniel (1984), p. 66, summarizes a 1976 submission by a group of EC mining companies to the Commission which is quite explicit on this point.

25. EU statements imply that the aim of the 1995 revision was to keep the real value of aid unchanged. This holds, as in Table 22.2, if the consumer price index is used to deflate current prices. If the more appropriate 'implicit GDP deflator' were used, the real change from 1990 to 1995 would be +7.6% and the real per capita change −4%.

26. Stevens (1984) finds a much sharper fall in annual real per capita aid between Lomé I and II. In arriving at this conclusion, he made an allowance for the late implementation of Lomé I, which meant that its aid was effectively spread over four years, not five.

27. There is a more econometrically sophisticated analysis of this and related issues in Babarinde (1994). His results indicate no particular trade advantage or disadvantage for the ACP relative to non-ACP countries.

28. The analysis can be found in the 1975 edition, *ACP: Yearbook of Foreign Trade Statistics 1968–73* (published 1975), and is shown in graphs in Gandia (1981).

29. See Moss and Ravenhill (1982), chapter 4, for further details. They quote an EC spokesman during one set of arguments over access for CAP products as saying, 'You must not ask us to scorn our own interest, that is not possible.' An annex to Lomé IV lists some further promises of 'concessions' e.g., for strawberries and figs during the winter (when EC products are not marketed).

30. See Roarty (1985) for details of the sugar problem, in the context of the CAP, more generally. At the time of writing, another important special arrangement, for bananas, will have to be discontinued in its present form because of a WTO ruling. This has resulted from a complaint by the US on behalf of its multinational companies which grow bananas in Latin America.

31. Some, e.g. Ravenhill (1985a), also point to the waiver of the rules for the part of the value-added in an EC member state as being a way of giving EC firms an advantage over those from other developed countries, or NIEs.

32. Estimates of the limited relative advantages of Lomé on exports by the Sub-Saharan African ACP countries can be found in Davenport (1992), and discussion of the effects of the GATT in Page and Davenport (1994) and Davenport *et al.* (1995).

33. The following account is based on Ravenhill (1985b), chapter 4.

34. In Chapter 21 it is suggested that the relationship between NTBs (including safeguards on 'sensitive' products) and success is not straightforward. The greater use against other LDCs may merely reflect their greater success, as compared with the ACP, in exporting manufactured goods to the EC.

35. The figures only strongly suggest, rather than prove, the advantage of percentage increases in 'trade over aid' because there will typically be some opportunity costs to increasing exports.

chapter twenty-three

EU enlargement

D. G. MAYES

Enlargement of the EU and its more effective operation as a larger unit are the key issues of the current policy agenda; indeed the Commission's new forward look *Agenda 2000* (CEU, 1997) is built around this. Enlargement is now entirely a matter of looking eastwards.[1] Although the previous round of enlargement ended up with rather less than expected, as only Austria, Finland and Sweden of the EFTA countries joined on 1 January 1995, there are no immediate plans to explore closer relationships with the remainder – Switzerland, (Liechtenstein), Norway and Iceland. Of these, Norway and Iceland are in the European Economic Area (EEA) which effectively brings them into the 'internal market', with the exception of agriculture.

The next steps that are planned in enlargement were spelt out in the Amsterdam summit and in *Agenda 2000*. In particular the appendices to *Agenda 2000* set out the Commission's opinion on the applications from ten central and eastern European countries (CEECs): Bulgaria, Czech Republic, Estonia, Hungary, Latvia, Lithuania, Poland, Romania, Slovakia and Slovenia. The way forward for negotiation over membership is now open for the Czech Republic, Estonia, Hungary, Poland and Slovenia – in addition to Cyprus, which was agreed earlier. The others on the list are for later consideration, as indeed is Turkey.

When the EFTA countries were being considered for membership, there was no real question as to whether they met the appropriate criteria, with the exception of the issue of political neutrality. The question was merely whether they were willing to accept the conditions of joining, and in the case of Norway and Switzerland the answer was negative. The negotiation process was very one sided (see chapter 9 in Mayes (1997) by Brewin for an exposition). Now, since there have been real concerns over whether the Union could cope with the particular applicants, it has become necessary to spell out the criteria for membership much more explicitly.[2] Thus, it is now possible to explore the full political economy of the process of enlargement much more clearly. Furthermore, as the extent of enlargement has progressed, the EU has reached the point that it has to make changes in its administrative structure and finances if it is not to find the system becoming increasingly unworkable and the cost unacceptable.[3]

23.1 The process of enlargement

Even from its earliest stages the European Community hoped to embrace the whole of 'Europe':

> The high contracting parties, determined to lay the foundations for an ever-closer union among the peoples of Europe, resolved to ensure the economic and social progress of their countries by common action to eliminate the barriers which divide Europe ... and calling upon the other peoples of Europe who share their ideal to join in their efforts. (preamble to the Treaty of Rome)

However, it took sixteen years from its foundation in 1957 before the Community was first expanded in 1973, with the addition of the United Kingdom, Denmark and the Irish Republic. The delay was not because others did not want to join. The UK applied unsuccessfully in both 1963 and 1967, but it was not until the beginning of the 1970s that a set of terms could be found that was acceptable both to the UK and to all the existing members.

This problem of achieving a balance between what the applicants would like and what the existing members are prepared to concede is inevitable in such circumstances. The expansions to include Greece in 1981 and Portugal and Spain in 1986 were not without their difficulties, but the problems of the applicants were dealt with by having extended periods of transition in sensitive areas and by having explicit arrangements to assist in the structural development of disadvantaged regions, which in the case of Portugal meant the whole country. Even at that stage, it was clear that the process of enlargement presented problems for the Common Agricultural Policy (CAP), which was (and still is to a lesser extent) the major area of expenditure in the EU. Since the structure of the CAP was aimed largely at Northern European temperature products, it did not offer an easy balance of gain for the applicants and new explicit expenditures were necessary to offset this (through the structural funds).

The fourth enlargement in 1990 offered no such problems as no new treaty was required. When the former DDR joined the Federal Republic, no constitutional change was required as the eastern *Länder* were viewed as in effect being temporarily under a different administration. The questions to be resolved related to assistance with structural change and the timing of the transition periods for applying Community law. The speed of change during that period meant that there was little time to consider any wider implications. The EC was in the middle of the main phase of implementing the completion of the internal market following the Single European Act of 1986 and was considering the steps to be taken towards Economic and Monetary Union and forming the EEA.

Up until the collapse of the former Soviet Union and the regime changes in central Europe, the remainder of EFTA – following the exit of the UK, Denmark and the Irish Republic – faced various constraints in joining the EC or indeed in developing closer relations with it. Despite negotiating entry along with the UK, Denmark and the Irish Republic, Norway had rejected membership in a referendum, and hence there was difficulty in mobilizing political enthusiasm for membership. Iceland is not only very small in population, even compared with Luxemburg, but also has been relatively slow in participating in European integration and has an economy of a very different character, dominated by fishing. Austria, Finland, Sweden and Switzerland all had concepts of neutrality built into their policy or constitutions. In the last two cases it was largely a matter of independent choice, whereas in the former it was a consequence of the construction of Europe after the Second World War. These states were therefore either unwilling or unable to contemplate membership while the cold war continued. Liechtenstein has also followed a path very similar to that of Switzerland. The changes further east led to a major reappraisal. Finland in particular was very keen to find means of strengthening itself with respect to its eastern neighbour, first because the collapse of trade with the FSU led to a drastic cut in Finnish GDP and second because of the political instability. Finland only gained full independence from Russia in 1917 and had been forced into losing territory at the end of the war.

However, economic motivation was appearing in addition to the political attractions. As it became clear that the completion of the Single European Act would mean a substantial step towards closer economic integration for the EC, there was an incentive, both for the EC and for EFTA, to try to deepen their relationship. Unless the EFTA countries adopted the conditions of the single market there was a danger that they could gain a substantial cost advantage through their free trade agreements with the EC. Hence the EC had a clear incentive for a closer agreement. By the same token, if the EFTA countries wanted equal access for services a new agreement was required.[4] This led to the formation of the EEA in parallel with the Treaty on European Union in 1993.

Whereas the free trade agreements between the EFTA countries and the EC had all been bilateral, the EEA agreement was a single document which applied to all of the countries. Or rather, almost all, as Switzerland rejected membership of the EEA in a referendum in December 1992.

One might have expected the EEA to be a very good compromise for the EFTA countries as it brought the gains of access to the Single Market without broaching the sensitive subject of agriculture and without the need to participate in the bureaucratic mechanisms of the EU. The Cohesion Fund which was set up to provide a transfer from the better-off parts of the EEA to the relatively disadvantaged regions was a relatively small price for the EFTA countries to pay. However, two facets of the process encouraged a different view. First of all the EU was simultaneously taking another step towards integration with economic and monetary union, which might again place the EFTA countries at a disadvantage. Secondly, the negotiation of the EEA had not been a very happy experience for the EFTA countries (see Brewin, in Mayes, 1997).[5] The process had been very one sided, with the EC only being prepared to discuss variations in the timetable for transferring the relevant parts of the *acquis communitaire* into the EFTA countries' domestic law. At the last moment the European Court added to the rather one-sided nature by insisting that jurisdiction over the agreement could not be shared as originally negotiated.

Thus the EFTA countries found themselves having not just to accept most of the EEA terms as a *fait accompli* but having relatively little opportunity to influence the development of future legislation. They thus had many of the responsibilities of the EU members but without the same rights. It was not even a matter of accepting the *status quo*. The EU was moving on. The Maastricht Treaty made it clear that deepening was to come before further widening of the EU. There would therefore be further steps which could put the EFTA countries at a disadvantage. Furthermore, there was even the danger that some of the central European countries, such as Hungary, Poland and the Czech and Slovak Republics might overtake them in the process of achieving membership, as the focus of interest, in Germany, in particular, had clearly moved towards the east.

From the EU side, membership by the well-off EFTA countries was likely to provide few problems and could result in clear benefits in terms of increased resources to deal with the concerns of structural change. They were likely to be net contributors to the EU budget, not net recipients, and if they were to accept all the existing *acquis communitaire* there was very little downside. The market would be widened and the usual range of efficiency and dynamic gains would be available. There was therefore no need to draw up detailed rules or justifications to determine which countries were to be admitted to membership. At the same time, the CEECs were undergoing such trauma in their transition to market economies that they were clearly not in a position to cope with membership, and nor indeed could the EU have coped readily had they joined.

The process of enlargement was therefore divided rapidly into two streams, without outright negotiations for membership being undertaken with the four EFTA applicants, but a range of other agreements for a slower pace of integration being concluded with the central and eastern European countries. The Visegrad countries, Hungary, Poland and the Czech and Slovak Republics, were given the fastest initial track, with separate Europe Agreements in 1993–94, Free Trade Agreements were concluded with the Baltic states of Estonia, Lithuania and Latvia in 1994 and new Partnership and Cooperation Agreements with Russia and the Ukraine in the same year. The negotiations were shorter than for any of the previous enlargements, lasting only some 13 months, and Austria, Finland and Sweden joined in January 1995 after the referendum in Norway rejected membership, just 38,000 votes swinging the result. It is interesting to note that public enthusiasm in all of the applicants was not overwhelming, implying that the popular view did not coincide with either the idea of clear economic benefits or that of obvious political imperatives.[6] Perhaps the memory of the less than enthusiastic support for EMU in France, the rejection of the Maastricht Treaty at the first poll in Denmark and the reservations of the United Kingdom helped temper the deliberation.

The negotiations themselves, which followed those on the Maastricht Treaty with only a gap of a few months,[7] were relatively straightforward, with agriculture, fisheries, energy and regional problems being the main stumbling blocks. A five-year phase-in period was agreed for the most difficult parts of the CAP, while a new Objective 6 on low population density regions was included for the structural funds to accommodate the Nordic countries' particular regional problems. Voting within the enlarged Council caused some debate among the existing members and it is interesting to note that the member states only agreed to let the total budget for agriculture expand by 74% of the rise merited by the increase in EU GDP, a prelude for the more difficult negotiations now envisaged.

23.2 Deciding on a wider membership

Deciding upon admitting other applicants on this occasion was a much more difficult task than in the case of the EFTA countries, as in the short run admitting any of them would involve net costs for the existing members. It was therefore necessary to have some criteria which would help to keep the costs and difficulties within manageable bounds. In effect these were that the applicants should be economically and politically ready, in the sense that they could meaningfully adopt the principles of the Treaty on European Union and adapt their economies within a reasonably short timetable to the full vigours of the EU market. The Copenhagen Council in June 1993 adopted three key principles to express this by stating that membership requires that the candidate country:

- has achieved stability of institutions guaranteeing democracy, the rule of law, human rights and respect for and protection of minorities;
- the existence of a functioning market economy as well as the capacity to cope with competitive pressure and market forces within the Union;
- the ability to take on the obligations of membership, including adherence to the aims of political, economic and monetary union.[8]

Agenda 2000 takes a step forward by assessing all the 10 CEECs listed at the beginning of this chapter in a single comparative framework. Thus it is not only possible to see the assessment of where the five selected for negotiation now lie, but where others would lie in the future. The individual country assessments are each around 120 pages in length.

The assessments try to go beyond a simple listing of the measures that have been adopted into a view of how they actually operate in practice. However, they do not represent an attempt to assess the costs and benefits to either the applicants or the existing member states. While this could have been done along the lines of, say, the *European Economy* (1996) evaluation of the internal market, the outcomes would depend upon which and how many of the applicants joined at any one time. It was, therefore, probably wise to neglect the cost–benefit approach and stick to assessment of a group of indicators. One consequence, of course, is that the assessment is relatively imprecise.

The countries not deemed ready yet for negotiation for membership (Bulgaria, Latvia, Lithuania, Romania and the Slovak Republic) are promised a further report by the end of 1998 and assistance with making the changes. Indeed, the countries

Table 23.1 ● Basic data for applicant CEECs and EU member states, 1995.

	Area (1000 km²)	Population (millions)	Population density (inhabit- ants/km²)	GDP at current market prices				GDP at purchasing power standards		Agriculture	
				(billion ECU)	(ECU per head)	(ECU per head as % of EU average)	(billion ECU at PPP rates)	(ECU per head at ppp rates)	(ECU per head as % of EU average)	(% of total gross value added)	(% of total employment)
	1	2	3	4	5	6	7	8	9	10	11
Hungary	93	10.2	110	33.4	3,340	19	64.6	6,310	37	6.2	8.0
Poland	313	38.6	123	90.2	2,360	14	203.3	5,320	31	7.6	26.9
Romania	238	22.7	95	27.3	1,200	7	94.3	4,060	23	20.5	34.4
Slovakia	49	5.4	110	13.1	2,470	14	38.0	7,120	41	6.3	9.7
Latvia	65	2.5	38	3.4	1,370	8	7.9	3,160	18	9.9	18.5
Estonia	45	1.5	33	2.8	1,850	11	5.9	3,920	23	8.1	13.1
Lithuania	65	3.7	57	3.5	930	5	15.3	4,130	24	9.3	23.8
Bulgaria	111	8.4	76	9.9	1,180	7	35.4	4,210	24	13.9	23.2[a]
Czech Republic	79	10.3	130	36.1	3,490	20	97.2	9,410	55	5.2	6.3
Slovenia	20	2.0	100	14.2	7,240	42	20.1	10,110	59	5.0	7.1
CE-10	1,078	105.3	98	234.0	2,220	13	582.0	5,530	32	8.6	22.5
As % of EU-15	33	28	85	4	13		9	32		358	425

Table 23.1 ● *continued*

Belgium	31	10.1	332	205.9	20,310	118	196.0	19,340	112	1.7	2.7
Denmark	43	5.2	121	132.1	25,260	146	104.4	19,960	116	3.7	4.4
Germany	357	81.5	228	1,845.2	22,600	131	1,556.8	19,070	110	1.0	3.2
Greece	132	10.4	79	87.4	8,360	48	118.4	11,320	66	14.7	20.4
Spain	506	39.2	77	428.1	10,920	63	518.8	13,230	77	3.7	9.3
France	544	58.0	107	1,174.3	20,200	117	1,076.5	18,520	107	2.5	4.9
Ireland	70	3.6	51	49.2	13,740	80	57.4	16,020	93	7.5	12
Italy	301	57.3	190	831.4	14,250	83	1,036.8	17,770	103	2.9	7.5
Luxembourg	3	0.4	157	13.3	32,370	187	11.9	29,140	169	1.5	3.9
Netherlands	42	15.4	371	302.5	19,570	113	284.3	18,390	107	3.6	3.8
Austria	84	8.0	96	178.4	22,180	128	155.5	19,320	112	2.4	7.3
Portugal	92	9.9	108	77.1	7,770	45	115.2	11,620	67	5.1	11.5
Finland	338	5.1	15	95.6	18,720	108	84.5	16,550	96	5.2	7.8
Sweden	450	8.8	20	176.3	19,970	116	153.5	17,390	101	2.1	3.3
United Kingdom	244	58.5	240	844.8	14,410	83	971.7	16,580	96	1.6	2.1
EU-15	3,236	371.6	115	6,441.5	17,260	100	6,441.5	17,260	100	2.4	5.3

Exact compatibility of CEEC Statistical Institutes data with EU standards on statistics and thus the comparability with EU figures cannot be guaranteed. For calculating the per capita GDP data, the populations according to national account definition are used. Purchasing power parity (PPP) exchange rates are commonly used in place of official exchange rates to estimate relative standards of living. They therefore take into account cost differences between countries.

ᵃ The figure is for 1994.

Sources: CEECs, columns 1–10 *Eurostat*, based on data from the CEEC Statistical Institutes, column 11 *Statistical Yearbooks* from the CEEC Statistical Institutes; EU Member States, *Eurostat*.

recommended for membership negotiations are to get continuing assistance to prepare for membership during the period before accession (assuming the negotiation is successful) and these funds are built into the revised EU budgetary proposals in Part 3 of *Agenda 2000*.

Table 23.1 shows the extent to which factors beyond simple income per head have been taken into account in making the judgements about readiness for membership.[9] The Slovak Republic, which has the third highest GDP per head (after Slovenia and the Czech Republic) is not included in the first-round list, primarily because of lack of progress under the first, political, condition. Estonia, on the other hand, which has the second lowest GDP per head, is included because it has made good progress on all three fronts. With a GDP per head around a third of that prevailing in Portugal and Greece and less than a quarter of the EU average, clearly the adjustment process is likely to be long and could be dramatic. It is also the smallest applicant with a population of only 1.5 million.[10]

The EU is progressing steadily with enlargement and is not at present having to face any awkward discussions over where the word 'European' reaches its technical or, more likely, political limits. From an economic point of view there is no particularly good reason why boundaries should be drawn on the basis of centuries' old decisions by geographers as to where the continents should be thought to start and end. The Russian Federation spans the Urals and, although there are various divisions in the Federation, particularly in the South, there are strong economic links across the Urals. The economic resources in Siberia are such that European Russia attaches a very strong importance to the region and drawing that particular division would make little sense to them. The Far Eastern zone is already being drawn into the Asian economy and its development will probably be strongly influenced by the other parts of Asia Pacific (Bollard and Mayes, 1991).

Similarly, if we look southwards, in Roman times it made more sense to think of the Mediterranean as a region – a region based on sea rather than land mass. Travel was easier by boat than by land and there was considerable economic interdependence across the region. The same line of argument can be advanced for the Baltic. The links between Finland and Estonia are one of the reasons why Estonia has moved to a position suitable for membership rather more quickly than many other central European countries.

Most current definitions of 'Europe' therefore tend to depend on a combination of economic, political, cultural and geographic links and divisions.[11] However, it is only the eastwards definition which appears to have given the EU much of a problem. Even westwards could have included Greenland had its inhabitants decided differently. In any case, non-European parts of France and Spain already form part of the EU. Turkey's application has been deferred, not because it is not 'European', part of Turkey is clearly European in terms of traditional geographic definitions, but for political and economic reasons, particularly relating to human rights.[12] Turkey also poses a problem because of its size. It is more than half as large as all the CEECs considered in *Agenda 2000* and similar in size to the last two enlargements taken together. GDP per head is in the same league as that of most members of the CEECs which have not been selected in the first round of negotiations.[13] Furthermore, the very agrarian nature of Turkey, with around a half of the population still working in that sector, could pose major budgetary strains on the EU unless the basis of expenditure were altered. Calculations made by the UK Foreign and Commonwealth Office in 1992 suggested that Turkey would have been a recipient on the then rules of some 12 billion ECU a year, which would have been equivalent to 15% of its GDP and 5% of the total EU budget (House of Lords, 1992). The calculations by the Commission in *Agenda 2000* for all the potential applicants and the likely cost for those which become members is an order of magnitude smaller, reaching only 19 billion ECU per year in 1997 prices by 2006.

The EU has, however, shown itself willing to tackle some of the hard political questions in enlargement by agreeing that accession negotiations with Cyprus should start by the end of 1997. This means that negotiations are likely to begin before a political solution is found to Cyprus's continuing divisions. This presents several problems, not least the lack of recognition of a legal authority for the Turkish-speaking north. So it is not fully clear with whom negotiations would be undertaken. The imminence of the accession negotiations may in itself help to resolve some of the dispute. The issue of Malta becoming a member has been removed from the agenda for the time being as Malta withdrew its application in early 1997. Given the degree of integration already existing between Malta and the EU, some 75% of trade is with the EU, and the fact that the level of GDP per head is similar to that of Portugal and Greece it would have been difficult to exclude Malta from the next round of applications to be considered.

Assuming that the negotiations succeed for at least a few of the next group, the point at which the fiscal and organizational issues highlighted in *Agenda 2000* have to be addressed will have been reached. However, difficult questions such as the position of Russia can be put on one side for the time being as Russia advances up the ladder of closer association.[14]

23.3 Coping with a larger Union

Somewhat surprisingly, *Agenda 2000* suggests that the EU will be able to absorb the budgetary consequences of enlargement reasonably readily and budgets are set out on an annual basis out to 2006. For example, the Commission concludes (vol. 1, p. 74) 'Maintaining the current agricultural guideline would not pose any difficulty in covering identified agricultural expenditure needs.' Initially this seems to be at variance with calculations about the impact of full membership by all ten countries on the EAGGF Guarantee section of 11 billion ECU per year by 2005 (vol. 2, p. 42). However, by staggering membership and phasing in the introduction of the full CAP (as seems likely) and positing structural changes in the applicant countries, this sum is massively reduced.

Even the structural measures are an order of magnitude larger than can be accommodated without breaking through the current 'own resources' ceiling for EU expenditure of 1.27% of EU GDP (see Chapter 15). According to the Commission's calculations, the maximum, reached in 1999, is 1.25% and 1.22% is projected for 2002–6. These conclusions are of course based on a variety of assumptions and would be violated if, for example, economic growth in the existing EU-15 were slower than the 2.5% a year assumed. However, this is not a particularly optimistic assumption by comparison with the growth that has actually been recorded over recent years.

The new member states would, however, be absorbing around 30% of the structural funds by the end of the period. Reorganization of the funds would be required, with restriction in the current Objective 1 recipients and reduction in the expenditure on other Objectives (see Chapter 17). A review of the eligibility for the cohesion fund is also implied.

The Commission even concludes (vol. 1, p. 84) that it will not be appropriate to reappraise the rebates to the UK until after the first further enlargement. One might question the optimistic assertion – 'The next enlargement ... will inevitably provoke a deterioration in the budgetary positions of all the current member states. This cannot come as a surprise and should not give rise to claims for compensation.'

It is not at all clear that wider enlargement will not impose more substantial strains than those posed by the enlargements of 1981 and 1986 simply because of the extent of the income differentials. In the first place it is possible that the nature of the integration will exploit interindustry trade rather than intraindustry trade as has been the case until now. There maybe a tendency to concentrate more labour-intensive and lower value-added activities in central and eastern Europe. In these circumstances, differentials between the different parts of the EU may not converge quite as fast as they otherwise would have done.

An alternative scenario is that the extent of the differentials results in a degree of labour mobility that has hitherto not been too much of a concern for the EU. Substantial unemployment differentials have persisted in Europe (Mayes *et al.*, 1993, and Chapter 20) not just between member states but within them. The economic incentives to move are not as effective as they are in the United States, for example, where the population is much more mobile. In part this is a function of history. A large proportion of families in the US do not have roots in the same location going back more than a short period. In Europe, on the other hand, many families have lived in the same place for centuries and therefore have much stronger ties.

With very large income differentials, the incentive to move, even if only for part of the working life, may be sufficiently strong to overcome the inertia which has prevailed in western Europe. It is noticeable in Finland, for example, where urbanization has been largely a function of the present century, that many city dwellers still have family homes in the country or have built cottages there so as to be able to return.[15] Mobility from east to west to work may therefore be substantial by comparison with the past.

The Commission has already recognized its own need to restructure as the EU continues with a set of institutions designed for a Community of six. If the next round of negotiations is successful, six further countries will be added to the list. All of them use at least one major new language. They will want their stake in the running of the Union. Despite suggestions to the contrary, the expansion to 15 member states occurred without major changes except the splitting up of portfolios. The Commission is already proposing to restructure its own procedures, with decentralization, rationalization and simplicity as the three watchwords. It is suggesting that it should concentrate on the core functions and hive off the others to executive agencies which can be nearer the customers. It is recommending that the number of Commissioners be reduced to one per member state and that the Council needs to reconsider its voting rules. However, *Agenda 2000* suggests 'that a new Intergovernmental Conference be convened as soon as possible after 2000 to produce a thorough reform of the provisions of the Treaty concerning the composition and functioning of institutions'. The pace of change is thus not going to be exactly precipitate.

The proposals for the structure of the ECB set a precedent whereby it is possible to operate at the highest level without one person drawn from each member state. Nevertheless, there will always be a reluctance both to give up any existing powers and to give up a seat at the table. Other institutions such as the World Bank and the IMF have had to handle this problem a long time ago to prevent administrative complexities getting out of hand, but experience in such organizations is not a particularly optimistic indicator of the likelihood of a very successful reorganization. The need for rationalization, of course, applies not just to the Commission but to all of the institutions.

23.4 Coping without enlargement

One question which is not well addressed in the existing literature is how well the aspiring applicant countries could cope without membership of the EU. Indeed, there might be benefits from staying out. The reason that the question is largely ignored is simply that these countries have found it very difficult to attract inward investment, whether from private sources or through governmental or intergovernmental agencies. Such investment usually requires considerable conditionality either explicitly or implicitly. The requirements for loans and project finance at the governmental or related level tend to include elements concerning fiscal and monetary prudence, the creation of market mechanisms, frameworks for property rights, etc. In the case of funds from the EU, the necessary framework is much more explicit and comprehensive. Furthermore, that framework does not usually conflict with that required by other public sector lenders or donors. There is therefore an incentive to adopt the framework irrelevant of other considerations because it offers the fastest and most substantial route to achieving satisfactory structural change.

The private sector inflow, on the other hand, has a wide variety of motives (Nam and Reuter, 1992). While these will normally include an adequate infrastructure framework and some certainty about being able to enjoy the return on the investment, the same requirements for market openness may not be present as the investor may well wish to gain from exploiting a monopoly position. In some respects, a less open and integrated market may appeal to the investor because it offers a greater certainty of maintaining cost advantages and privileged market access.

It might appear a rather short-sighted approach to permit such distortions to emerge, but the starting point is not an open market. The attraction of inward investment can be greater where there is the opportunity to buy existing incumbent firms with monopolies or near monopolies. This has been revealed very clearly in the case of New Zealand (Mayes, 1996), where inward investment over the years 1989–95 exceeded that of the whole of the Visegrad countries, despite the fact that their combined population is about 20 times as large. New Zealand sold a large range of public sector enterprises: airline, railway, telecoms, steelworks, banks, insurance, hotel chain, forestry and many more as existing enterprises. Although the New Zealand competitive framework requires that industries be contestable (Mayes, 1997c), the practice is that the incumbents have a very strong position. Hence there is a good prospect of a strong profit stream. The domestic resources of the host country possess neither the financial capital necessary to make the investments to become internationally competitive nor the access to the necessary technological expertise and market contacts to make such investments successful.

As a result New Zealand has achieved a very rapid turnaround during the last decade, moving more swiftly into recovery than the CEECs, and enduring a much smaller loss of GDP in the process. Of course, the circumstances are not directly comparable as the extent of distortions and lack of competitiveness were far greater in Europe. Nevertheless, there could be advantages in allowing the transformation of existing enterprises in a process of more measured transition (Mayes, 1997a) as the social costs need to be balanced against the rate of exploitation of the economic gains. Achieving this balance between 'cohesion' and competition has been a key feature governing the use of the structural funds inside the EU. There is a limit to which regional divergences are politically acceptable. Beyond that limit people vote against the process of change even though the longer-run outcome from change is clearly better, because they find the short-run costs too high.

The EU's approach as expounded in *Agenda 2000* seeks to address this point both by assistance to the countries not yet accepted for membership and by the transitional aid for those ready for membership. The irony in this arrangement is, however, that the further advanced in the process of integration a country is, then the greater assistance it receives from the EU. If, however, one was to take a view on the extent of need, then those furthest from being able to cope with membership might be thought to be those with the greatest need for assistance in the process of transformation. In part, this is a question of absorptive capacity (as the economy progresses so it is able to cope with more projects and faster structural change), but it is also a question of incentives. If less conditionality were to be attached to EU help then the degree of transformation of the recipient economies might be lower.

Altering the process of adjustment to full membership of the EU, particularly by delaying the point at which labour mobility can be freer, may also affect the structure of the applicant economies. As discussed in Baldwin *et al.* (1995), it is not immediately clear which way a less integrated economy might develop. It will be less attractive to investors as a base for production for the whole market insofar as there are barriers to export, but then it will need a wider range of production itself because of the same barriers. Insofar as there is a minimum time needed to establish viable firms with a higher value-added product then there may be some attraction in a more measured pace of change. However, the history of 'infant industry' and related arguments for slower transition is very mixed, with considerable success stories to point to in Asia Pacific and much more disastrous experiences in much of the rest of the world. It is thus not clear whether there are any clear steps, other than the process of rapid opening towards the EU model, which would diminish the risk of getting locked into a rather unattractive form of interindustry specialization.

23.5 Concluding remarks

One cannot help but be impressed with the rate of change in the EU over the last decade and with the changes proposed for the coming five years: the enlargement to include Spain and Portugal, the Single European Act, the Maastricht Treaty, the European Economic Area, the agreements and programmes with central and eastern Europe, the enlargement to include Austria, Finland and Sweden, completion of Stage 3 of EMU and a further enlargement ... One might have expected that something or other would have collapsed along the way, particularly given some of the political difficulties with agreeing the Maastricht Treaty.

Furthermore, this major expansion of programmes has been accompanied by a substantial budgetary expansion, but not one on the scale envisaged a decade or so earlier when the McDougall Report (1977) for example looked at what would be the minimum size for a budget with a more federal feel to it (see Chapter 15). For more than two decades it has been thought that the Common Agricultural Policy would have to change markedly, but while it has indeed changed it is still the dominant area of expenditure. It is merely that the structural funds have added a second major category. *Agenda 2000* suggests that the Union will be able to cope financially with the existing ceilings, despite the size of these programmes, through to 2006.

One must ask whether there is a stage at which the process will have to change its character. Taking a purely 'European' definition of the Union, the limits to size are beginning to come within the horizon for thought if not for actual long-term planning. Beyond Stage 3 of EMU the process of closer integration in other areas of economic, political and social affairs appears to be relatively slow (by comparison at least). However, it remains to be seen how much the member states will find that, for example, existing fiscal diversity is sustainable under monetary union. The temptation is always to think that the next stage in enlargement or indeed in 'deepening' the Union will be the one that triggers a more major change in the character of the institutions and the nature of the common policies and expenditures. To some extent such a change is likely within the next five years with another enlargement, but reluctance to change thus far suggests that the member states may prefer to accept the complexities and consequent inefficiencies for rather longer.

At the time of writing there is still a question mark over the timing, country composition or perhaps even occurrence of Stage 3 of EMU. This will clearly interact with enlargement, but at some stage one or the other will surely result in the EU having to restructure itself in a major way.

Notes

1. This is not literally true in the sense of moving the easternmost point in the European Union. Currently that is in Finland (as is the northernmost point). Of those countries under current consideration for membership, it is only Cyprus which is further east. Otherwise the Union would have to include Belarus, Moldova, Russia, Turkey or the Ukraine for it to stretch further eastwards. With the withdrawal of the application by Malta there is now no proposal to extend further southwards, although Spanish and French islands might make the claim for the boundary to be further south already.

2. The application from Turkey was not a real test either as Turkey is so large and at such a low relative income level that there was never any doubt that the Union would be unwilling to bear the cost. Similarly, Cyprus and Malta are sufficiently small that they would not pose a difficulty for the EU's resources. Any grounds for decision would be largely political rather than economic.

3. However, I notice I made this same observation in 1993 with a view to the intergovernmental conference which was concluded with the Amsterdam Treaty in June 1996. It may be possible to evade much of the issue again as it falls in the 'too hard' tray on many people's desks.

4. Baldwin *et al.* (1997) show that under imperfect competition the incentive to join a grouping of similar structured economies increases as the size of the grouping increases.

5. The Austrian application for membership was made in July 1989, antedating the EEA negotiations, while the Swedish application was made in June 1991 before the negotiations were complete. The Finnish, Swiss and Norwegian applications were made in March, May and November of 1992, respectively.

6. The Austrian result in June was clear with 66.4% voting in favour and support in Finland in October was 57%. However, the Swedish voted only 52.2% for and 46.9% against on 13 November and the outcome was in doubt right up to the end. The Norwegian vote came only a fortnight later but this time the 52.2% were against.

7. The Commission produced its favourable 'Opinions' on each of the applicants

rapidly. (Norway's entry to the negotiations was officially delayed until April 1993 to allow the Opinion to be completed, although it had been involved in aspects of the negotiations earlier.)

8. The 'EFTA' group negotiations were already in progress at the time.

9. The accuracy of these GDP per head comparisons across is of course limited but they are not so wrong as to invalidate the qualitative argument.

10. But with a land area bigger than Belgium, the Netherlands or Denmark.

11. Sometimes the arguments over the appropriate boundary have been put in terms of the limits of the former Austro-Hungarian empire, sometimes the extent of Christianity and sometimes the limits of Catholicism (Crouch and Marquand, 1992).

12. The 1964 Ankara Association Agreement with Turkey made clear that it was in principle eligible for membership. The question was merely when would it be ready. *Agenda 2000* makes it clear that Turkey will be judged on the same criteria as any other applicant and is also receiving assistance from the EU to help it with the transition.

13. Being able to avoid discussing Turkish membership has other political advantages as it is not necessary to face the question of whether Greece would in any case veto Turkish membership.

14. In Mayes (1993), I described the EU as having almost a series of concentric circles of closer affiliation for countries depending upon their geographic nearness. Since 1995 the EU has had a common border with Russia. If the negotiations with all of the next group of applicants succeed, that boundary will be increased and both Belarus and the Ukraine will then have common borders with the EU. The 'nearness' will thus continue to increase in geographic terms.

15. In part, this may be a special feature of the slow development of forests, where important proportions of rural family wealth can lie. It may take three generations to be able to reap the benefit from planting.

Conclusions

chapters

chapter twenty-four

The development of the EU

A. M. EL-AGRAA

The aim of this chapter is to provide a brief review of the progress made by the EU in terms of establishing a common market and moving towards an economic union. However, such a summary of events would not be complete without an adequate re-statement of the most significant political developments that have taken place; indeed it could be argued that a list of EU accomplishments would be pointless without also explaining the political context within which they have been achieved. The first section of this chapter is therefore devoted to these develop-ments while the remaining sections tackle the periods before and after the first en-largement of the EU, and the present. The future, being speculative and subject to many personal prejudices, is left to the final chapter.

24.1 Political developments

As stated in Chapter 2, at the beginning the EU created a number of institutions to execute the tasks it had been entrusted with. These revolved around a legislative body (the Council of Ministers) and an initiator of policies (the Commission, which is also the administrator, mediator and police force of the EU), backed up by an ad-visory body (the European Parliament, with recently increased powers) and a guardian of the treaties (the Court of Justice). However, by the 1970s, it had become clear that the EU was entering a period of political change for which these institu-tions were less suitable than had initially been envisaged and for which they lacked adequate strength. However, rather than promoting a strengthening of the existing institutions, a method was found to bring national political leaders more closely into EU affairs by the introduction of summit meetings. As we have seen, these were formalized under the name of the European Council in 1974.

The first major summit was held in The Hague in December 1969. At that summit, the original six member nations effectively recognized that they were so closely in-terdependent that they had no choice other than to continue as a united group. They were thus compelled to settle matters such as the Common Agricultural Policy (CAP) and changes in the general budget. A point of vital importance was the recognition that the EU possessed the political will to work for enlargement and hence had to confront the question of relations with the United Kingdom more positively.

The summit also recognized that the EU needed to reconsider its position in the world. The EU's responsibilities neither matched its economic weight nor allowed effective consideration of the political aspects of its external economic relations. Individual member nations still conducted external affairs themselves and could, therefore, undermine EU interests. The attraction of bringing foreign policy into the EU sphere was the greater effectiveness this might bring in international affairs; but the idea raised such sensitive issues as the relations with the United States and the USSR as well as defence matters.

In the end The Hague summit requested the foreign ministers to study the best way of achieving further political integration, within the context of commitment to EU enlargement, and to present a report. The later efforts made to achieve political cooperation, with emphasis upon international affairs, have been important in helping the EU identify its common aims and making the nature of the group coherent. Political cooperation has itself led to institutional innovation. This has occurred alongside the original institutions of the EU and not as part of them, although they are increasingly coming closer together.

In 1972 an important summit was held in Paris. This was attended by the three new members – Denmark, Ireland and the United Kingdom. The summit devoted considerable attention to the need to strengthen the social and regional aims of the EU. Furthermore, the deterioration in the international climate and the preoccupation of member governments with economic matters at home seemed to require frequent meetings of heads of government to ensure that the EU remained an effective economic unit.

The different philosophies and approaches of the governments of member countries to new problems made summit meetings essential for establishing the extent of common ground and for ensuring that this was used as the basis for action by the member nations. Initially, this seemed to strengthen the intergovernmental structure of the EU at the expense of the supranational element. However, it was also a reflection of the reality that the member nations had realized that their future aims were closely interdependent and required the formulation of joint goals and policies over a very wide field indeed. Informal discussion of general issues, whether economic or political, domestic or international, was a necessary preliminary to further, formal integration, and through the summit meetings and the political cooperation procedure the scope of the subject matter for the EU was steadily enlarged.

By the time of the Paris summit meeting in 1972 the member nations had laid down for themselves an ambitious programme of activity designed to lead to a 'European Union'. Much remained to be defined, but a number of external issues had been clearly identified. These included the following:

1. The need to maintain a constructive dialogue with the United States, Canada and Japan.

2. The need to act jointly in matters of external trade policy.

3. The need for member nations to make a concerted contribution to the 'Conference on Security and Cooperation in Europe'.

Foreign ministers were to meet more frequently in order to handle this last theme.

The global economic difficulties of the 1970s, triggered by the first oil shock, created a harsh environment within which the EU had to strive to establish its identity, future goals and executive responsibilities. It is easy to understand why progress was extremely slow during this period.

The Paris summit of 1974 formally agreed that the distinction between EU affairs and political cooperation was untenable, and in 1981 the foreign ministers agreed that political cooperation between the member nations had become central to their foreign policies. Proceedings became formalized and relations were established with the Commission.

The same summit asked the then Belgian prime minister (Leo Tindemans) to consult the governments of the member nations and to write a report on the concept of European union. This brought out into the open the long-standing question of whether the member nations did, or could, constitute an effective economic whole or whether progress as a two-tier EU might be preferable.

The concept of a two-tier EU means that those member nations which have the will and ability to forge ahead towards such a union should do so. The others would lag behind, but would not be relieved from the need to achieve the ultimate goal. As Swann (1988) has argued, this could be interpreted pessimistically: the fact that the concept is discussed at all suggests lack of cohesion between the member nations. It could also be interpreted optimistically: in the absence of majority voting, some member nations could still forge ahead despite the disagreement of the rest of the member nations – the European Monetary System (EMS) was launched on such a basis since the United Kingdom refused to take part in the exchange-rate aspect of the scheme (see Chapter 16) at the time. Although this question was avoided in favour of special measures (financed by the structural funds) within the EU to help the weaker member nations (see Chapter 15), it has surfaced again with respect to a single EU currency and further developments.

A further proposition was that the EU should take steps towards making itself more of a citizens' Europe by including action in matters such as consumer rights, environmental protection and the safeguarding of fundamental rights – see Chapters 18 and 19.

Two further ideas were discussed:

1. A common stand in foreign policy, which could then be applied by the member states.

2. A tentative start on defence issues.

Institutional reform would be required in several directions. The interrelated issues of constitutional development and institutional reform continued to occupy the attention of those concerned with the EU, but for a number of years little progress was made. The EU appeared to be in danger of reaching a dead end:

1. The deepening of the integrative process required action that the member nations found controversial.
2. New member nations introduced their own problems and perspectives.
3. The recession meant that the attitudes of the member nations hardened towards the necessary compromise which is needed if cooperative solutions to problems were to be found.

A particular constraint was presented by the limits on EU finance (the size of the EU General Budget) which prevented the development of EU policies and led to the bitter arguments about the resources devoted to the CAP (see Chapter 15).

Internal divisions were compounded by fears of a lack of dynamism in the EU economy which threatened a relative decline in international terms. Such worries suggested that a significant leap forward was needed to ensure a real 'common market' and to encourage new growth. However, to move the EU in this direction and to modernize EU institutions so that they worked more efficiently proved a laborious process. While member nations could agree upon the aims, in practice they fought hard to ensure that the reform incorporated measures favourable to themselves.

As the debate continued, a major division emerged between those who were primarily interested in the political ideal of European union and who wished to see institutional reform which would strengthen the EU's capacity to act, and those who had a more pragmatic approach which stressed the need for new policies, especially those directed to stimulating the EU economy. The idea of European union was developed further by an Italian–German proposal for a European Act (the Genscher–Colombo Plan) and by the European Parliament which adopted a 'Draft treaty on European union' in 1984.

In the meantime a series of summit meetings was keeping the momentum going at the level of heads of state or government. The Stuttgart summit meeting of 1983 agreed on an impressive work programme of issues which needed solution, and produced a 'Solemn declaration on European union'.

The vehement discussions of the following two years, often complicated by the need to solve more immediate problems, meant that it was not until the Luxemburg summit meeting of 1985 that lines of the agreement could be settled. These were brought together in the Single European Act (SEA) which became operative on 1 July 1987 (see Chapters 2 and 7). They were reinforced and extended through the adoption of the Delors Report on EMU and, provided that the Maastricht Treaty of December 1991 is fully implemented, by the creation of an EU common defence policy, a single currency and a common central bank before the end of this century (see Chapters 2 and 5), but the Amsterdam summit of June 1997 shied away from the idea of a common defence policy and institutional reform and settled for the membership of the expanded NATO.

24.2 The period from 1958 to 1969

Between 1958 and 1969, when the transition period came to an end, the original six member nations were preoccupied with the construction of the 'community' envisaged in the Treaty of Rome. Here, it is not necessary to describe all the measures that were undertaken during this period since these have been fully discussed earlier in this book. It is enough to state that the basic elements of the customs union (i.e. the removal of the internal tariffs, the elimination of import quota restrictions and the creation of the common external tariffs (CETs)) were established ahead of schedule – see Tables 24.1 and 24.2. Initial steps were undertaken and measures proposed to tackle the many non-tariff barriers to the free movement of goods, services and factors of production so that by 1969 a recognizably common market could be said to exist.

Progress was uneven in the area of common policies. Because of French demands,

Table 24.1 ⬭ EC intra-area tariff reductions (%).

Acceleration of reduction	Individual reductions made on the 1 January 1957 level	Cumulative
1 January 1959	10	10
1 July 1960	10	20
1 January 1961	10	30
1 January 1962	10	40
1 July 1962	10	50
1 July 1963	10	60
1 January 1965	10	70
1 January 1966	10	80
1 July 1967	5	85
1 July 1968	15	100

Source Commission of the European Communities, *First General Report on the Activities of the Communities* (EC Commission: Brussels), p. 34.

Table 24.2 ⬤ The establishment of the CET (%).

Acceleration of	Industrial products adjustment	Cumulative adjustment	Agricultural products adjustment	Cumulative adjustment
1 January 1961	30	30		
1 January 1962			30	30
1 July 1963	30	60		
1 January 1966			30	60
1 July 1968	40	100	40	100

Source Commission of the European Communities, *First General Report on the Activities of the Communities* (EC Commission: Brussels), p. 34.

sometimes bordering on threats, the CAP was almost fully operational by 1969. However, as McGowan clearly shows in Chapter 13, the common transport policy was slow to evolve. Moreover, Collins has demonstrated in Chapters 2 and 18 that the European Social Fund (ESF) and the European Investment Bank (EIB) were duly established and were fully operational at an early stage. Furthermore, as McAleese and Brülhart argue in Chapter 21, steps were taken to create a Common Commercial Policy (CCP), and, as Marin clearly shows in Chapter 22, the original six undertook appropriate trade and aid arrangements in respect of their colonial and increasingly ex-colonial dependencies. A rudimentary system of macroeconomic policy coordination was also devised (see Chapter 5).

Although during this period progress was evident and optimism about the success of the EU was much enhanced, there were some disappointments. From a 'federalist' point of view, perhaps the greatest was the French refusal to accept the supranational element in the Treaty decision-making system, hence the 'Luxemburg compromise'. When the member nations signed the Treaty of Rome, they opted for an EU Council of Ministers which could take decisions on the basis of a supranational majority voting system, but the Luxemburg compromise meant that any member state could insist that nothing should happen unless it agreed that it should happen, i.e. a veto system was adopted.

24.3 The period from 1969 to the early 1980s

When the transition period came to an end in 1969, it would have been possible for the original six to state that their mission had been accomplished. However, there were several reasons why it was neither possible nor appropriate for the EU to stop there. Firstly, the creation of common policies in such fields as agriculture and competition required an administration to operate them. This is because decisions regarding agricultural prices had to be taken on a seasonal or annual basis and markets had to be continuously manipulated in order that those prices should be received by farmers. The activities of businessmen and governments had to be continuously monitored in order that factors which would otherwise prevent, restrict or distort competitive trade should be eliminated. Secondly, although substantial progress had been made in achieving the aims listed in Article 3 of the Treaty, when the transition period was approaching its end it had to be admitted that substantial policy gaps still remained to be filled before it could be claimed that a truly common market existed.

Be that as it may, it would have been possible for the member nations to state that, subject to the need to operate existing policies and to fill obvious policy gaps, no further economic integration or institutional development should be attempted. In fact the EU decided quite the contrary: new areas of economic policy were opened up and old ones were substantially changed.

In 1969, during The Hague summit, the original six decided that the EU should progressively transform itself into an economic and monetary union (EMU). Although important measures were subsequently introduced in order to achieve the EMU, the goal of reaching this aim eventually failed. This was due to the global economic difficulties of the early 1970s and to the first enlargement of the EU. Nevertheless, the idea did not go away since in the late 1970s a more modest scheme was successfully introduced – EMS. Moreover, in 1989, the member nations endorsed the Delors Report, committing themselves to achieving an EMU in three stages: as we have seen (Chapter 5) the first began on 1 July 1990, the second in 1994 and third will begin in 1999 for the member nations which pass the strict conditions specified for this purpose.

The EMU proposal was only one of a succession of new policy initiatives during 1969–72. Indeed, this period can be described as one of great activity. First, in 1970, the original six reached a common position on the development of a Common Fisheries Policy (CFP – see Chapter 11), although total agreement was not to be achieved until 1983. Second, at the Paris summit of 1973, agreement was reached on the development of new policies in relation to both industry and science and research. Third, the summit also envisaged a more active role for the EU in the area of regional policy, and decided that a European Regional Development Fund (ERDF) was to be established to channel EU resources into the development of the backward regions (see Chapter 17). Fourth, as we saw in Chapter 18, the summit also called for a new initiative in the field of social policy. Fifth, later in the 1970s, the relationship between the EU and its ex-colonial dependencies was significantly reshaped in the form of the 'Lomé Convention' (see Chapters 21 and 22). Finally, there was the series of institutional developments which we discussed briefly in the first section of this chapter (and, fully, in Chapter 2), especially the summit meetings and their formalization into the European Council.

It is obvious from all these developments that the EU needed financial resources not only to pay for the day-to-day running of the EU but also to feed the various funds that were established: the ESF, ERDF and, most important of all, the European Agricultural Guidance and Guarantee Fund (EAGGF). As we have seen, in 1970 the EU took the important step of agreeing to introduce a system that would provide the EU, and specifically the General Budget, with its own resources, thus relieving it of the uncertainty of annual decisions regarding its finances as well as endorsing its political autonomy (see Chapter 15). Another step of great importance was the decision that the European Parliament should be elected directly by the people, not by the national parliaments. In addition, the EU decided to grant the European Parliament significant powers over the General Budget; as we saw in Chapter 2, this proved to be a very significant development. Finally, but by no means least, was the development of the political cooperation mechanism. It is important not to forget that the dedicated Europeans had always hoped that the habit of cooperation in the economic field would spill over into the political arena, i.e. into foreign policy matters. As we have seen, that has indeed happened: the political cooperation that we see today can be said to date from The Hague summit of 1969 and was formally inaugurated in 1970, and, when the Maastricht Treaty is fully implemented, the EU will come very close to having a common defence policy (the 1997 Amsterdam summit's qualification, stressing NATO, cannot be the permanent reality), thus it will have to have a common foreign policy on defence and security matters.

Although there have been a series of institutional developments, the relationship between the member nations has undergone a significant change. When the member nations signed the Treaty of Rome, they opted for an EU Council of Ministers which could take decisions on the basis of a supranational majority voting system. However, the insistence of the French led to the Luxemburg compromise. In addition, and especially after 1969, the centre of gravity of decision making within the EU became the European Council.

The method of operation of the European Council is cast in the traditional intergovernmental mould. As Swann (1988) argues, the development of intergovernmentalism might have been expected to slow down the pace of progress within the EU: the unanimity principle would always force the EU to adopt the lowest common denominator and that might mean little or even no change whatever. However, that was certainly not the case in the early 1970s: as we have seen, a number of new initiatives were launched and in the main those initiatives were designed to further the process of integration.

Intergovernmentalism was still strong in the 1980s, but the performance of the intergovernmental EU of the early 1980s was markedly less dynamic than that of the early 1970s. A good deal of activity within the EU then centred around quarrels over matters such as the reform of the CAP and the General Budget, especially the United Kingdom's contribution to it.

At this juncture it may be useful to stress two conclusions. The first is that, despite developments in foreign policy cooperation, unless the Maastricht Treaty is *fully* implemented, the EU would continue to lack two essential attributes of a state.

These are responsibility for external affairs and defence. Thus, as Collins argues in Chapter 2, the EU has a great gap in its competences, but its weight makes it highly significant in world economics and thus in world politics. The second is that the significant achievements of the EU during the post-1969 period made it very attractive. This attraction is demonstrated by:

1. Its first round of enlargement to include Denmark, Ireland and the United Kingdom in 1973.

2. The adhesion of Greece in 1981.

3. Its second round of enlargement to include Portugal and Spain in 1986.

4. Its third round of enlargement to include Austria, Finland and Sweden in 1995.

5. The recent applications for membership by several nations, including Cyprus, Hungary, Malta, Poland, Switzerland and Turkey, and most of the eastern European countries, especially the Czech and Slovak Republics.

Tables 24.3 and 24.4 give the timetable for the adjustments in the common external tariffs (CETs) and the dismantling of the internal tariffs for the three countries involved in the first enlargement: Denmark, Ireland and the United Kingdom. The tables do not cover all groups of commodities. For example, tariffs on coal imports were abolished from the day of accession, and tariffs on certain groups of commodities given in Annex III of the Treaty of Accession were abolished on 1 January 1974, etc. In the case of the CETs, those tariffs that differed by less than 15% were adjusted on 1 January 1974. Import quota restrictions were also abolished from the date of accession. Measures having equivalent effects to the import quota restrictions were eliminated by the deadline of 1 January 1975. All three new member nations had no difficulties in achieving these changes.

Table 24.3 ⬤ New members' intra-tariff reductions (%).

	Individual reductions made on 1 January 1972	Cumulative reduction
1 April 1973	20	20
1 January 1974	20	40
1 January 1975	20	60
1 January 1976	20	80
1 July 1977	20	100

Source Bulletin of the European Communities, no. 8, 1978.

Table 24.4 ⬤ **Approaching the CET (%).**[a]

	Individual adjustments made on 1 January 1972	Cumulative adjustment
1 January 1974	40	40
1 January 1975	20	60
1 January 1976	20	80
1 July 1977	20	100

[a] For products which differ by more than 15% from the CET.
Source Bulletin of the European Communities, no. 8, 1978.

In the case of Greece's membership, a five-year period was agreed for the progressive dismantling of residual customs duties on Greek imports of products originating in the EU and for the progressive alignment of Greek tariffs to the CET. Customs duties on Greek imports from the EU were to be reduced in six stages commencing on 1 January 1981, with a reduction of 10 percentage points followed by a further reduction of the same percentage points on 1 January 1982 and four annual reductions of 20 percentage points so that all customs duties on Greek intra-EU trade should have been removed by 1 January 1986. Alignment of the CET was to follow the same timetable.

Quantitative restrictions between Greece and the EU were to be abolished on adhesion, with the exception of fourteen products for which Greece was authorized to maintain transitional quotas. These quotas were to be progressively increased during the five-year transitional period and to be completely eliminated by 31 December 1985. As a general rule, the minimum rate of increase for such quotas was 25% at the beginning of each year for quotas expressed in value terms and 20% at the beginning of each year for quotas expressed in volume terms. Measures having equivalent effect to quantitative restrictions were to be eliminated upon adhesion, except for the Greek system of cash payments and import deposits which were to be phased out over three years (see *Bulletin of the European Communities*, no. 5, 1969, for these and further details).

In the case of Portugal and Spain, a ten-year transitional period was agreed. For Portugal, this is divided into two equal (five-year) stages for the majority of products and a basic seven-year period for other products, although some measures would apply for the full ten years. For Spain, there are some variations, but the essentials are basically the same.

It can be stated that Greece, Portugal and Spain have navigated their transition periods successfully. With regard to the three members joining in 1995, there is practically no transition period since they were members of EFTA, and, as we have seen, EFTA and the EU have had free trade between them for a very long time through the arrangement now known as the EEA. Indeed, the only derogation from immediate implementation of all EU legislation is a four-year transitional period during which the new members can maintain their higher than EU health, safety and environmental standards.

So far there has been one withdrawal. The position of Greenland was renegotiated in 1984 but it remains associated under the rules of 'Overseas countries and territories'. A special agreement regulates mutual fishing interests.

Of course, one should point out that, in contrast to this rosy picture, a number of non-tariff barriers remained. However, as we have seen (Chapters 2 and 7), the aim of the 'internal market' is to abolish these either directly or indirectly via the harmonization of technical specifications which will promote the right environment for getting rid of them. All these non-tariff barriers are fully set out in Chapter 7.

24.4 The present

The present begins in the mid-1980s. Without a shadow of doubt, its stars must be the SEA which now regulates all the activities of the EU and, provided that it is fully implemented, the Maastricht Treaty since the Amsterdam Treaty of June 1997 does not incorporate major changes. In the section on political developments, we examined the factors which led to the birth of the SEA. As Collins has shown in Chapter 2, the SEA contains policy development which is based upon the intention of having a true single market in place by the end of 1992 with free movement of capital, labour, services and goods rather than the patchy arrangements of the past. The SEA also introduces, or strengthens, other policy fields. These include the following:

1. Responsibility towards the environment.
2. The encouragement of further action to promote health and safety at work.
3. Technological R&D.
4. Work to strengthen economic and social cohesion so that weaker members may participate fully in the freer market.
5. Cooperation in economic and monetary policy.

In addition, the SEA brings foreign policy cooperation into scope and provides it with a more effective support that it has had hitherto, including its own secretariat to be housed in the Council building in Brussels.

Institutionally, as we have seen, it was agreed that the European Council would take decisions on qualified majority vote in relation to the internal market, research, cohesion and improved working conditions and that, in such cases, the European Parliament should share in decision making. These developments were followed later by agreement regarding the control of expenditure on the CAP (which, as we have seen in Chapters 10 and 15, has been a source of heated argument for a number of years) and, most importantly, a fundamental change in the EU General Budget (see Chapter 15).

Before turning to the other star, the Maastricht Treaty, recall that a three-stage timetable for EMU started on 1 July 1990 with the launching of the first phase of intensified economic cooperation during which all the member states were to submit their currencies to the *exchange rate mechanism* (ERM) of the EMS. The main target of this activity was the United Kingdom whose currency was not subject to the ERM discipline; the United Kingdom joined in 1991 while Mrs (now Baroness) Thatcher was still in office, but withdrew in 1992 when the UK could not maintain the ERM parity for the pound. During the second stage, which started in 1994, the EU created the *European Monetary Institute* (EMI) to prepare the way for a European Central Bank which started operating on 1 January 1997. As we have seen, the Treaty allows Denmark and the United Kingdom to opt out of the final stage when the EU currency rates will be permanently and irrevocably fixed and a single currency (the Euro) floated.

Here is a sketch of the agreement:

1. The EC will be given an appropriate title: the 'European Union'.

2. A single currency, to be managed by an independent European Central Bank, will be introduced as early as 1997 if seven of the present twelve nations pass the strict economic criteria (see Chapter 5) required for its successful operation, and in 1999 at the latest.

3. The EC states are to move towards a joint foreign and security policy, but with most decisions requiring unanimity voting. The *Western European Union* (WEU; launched in 1954 as an intergovernmental organisation to enable the ending of the occupation of Germany, but has been dormant ever since – see Chapter 2) will become the equivalent of an EC defence force. Thus for the first time the EC is set to have a common defence policy with the implication that the WEU will eventually be responsible for implementing the decisions of an inevitable EC political union. Appreciation for (or is it accommodation of?) NATO was reiterated by stating that the revival of the long-dormant WEU is to be linked to NATO, thus ensuring a continued alliance with the United States and Canada for the defence of Europe; an essential compromise for reaching agreement. The EC is given jurisdiction in specific areas with the member states voting to implement decisions. These areas include industrial affairs, health, education, trade, environment, energy, culture, tourism and consumer and civil protection. Also, social affairs will become an EC jurisdiction in all the member countries except the United Kingdom which rejected EC-imposed legislation on workers' rights on the pretext that this would undermine EC competitiveness. Increased political cooperation will be carried out under a new name: the European Union (EU). The EC will also create a permanent diplomatic network of senior political officials in the EC capitals. Finally, the European Parliament will get a modest say in the shaping of some EC legislation, but this falls short of their demand for 'an equitable sharing of the right to make EC laws with the EC governments'.

4. A European police intelligence agency (Europol), to fight organized crime and drug trafficking, will be created.

5. Greece, Ireland, Portugal and Spain, the less-developed members of the EC, will receive increased support from the remaining partners to assist them in the process of catching up with the average level of development in the EC as a whole. For this purpose, the EC will create a special fund (*Cohesion Fund*) in 1993.

To up-date on these aims, one should point out that the stipulated earlier (1997) floating of a single currency had to be waived, the new British government has decided to participate in the 'social chapter' and to run a referendum on the single currency, and membership of NATO has been extended to the eastern European nations with the endorsement of Russia, which signed an agreement to that effect in May 1997.

24.5 Conclusion

The main conclusion is that the EU has been successful not only in achieving *negative* integration (see Chapter 1), but also in adopting a host of *positive* integration measures. Indeed, when the Maastricht Treaty becomes a reality, the EU would be heading towards the dream of its 'founding fathers', the creation of a *United States of Europe*, despite the vehement utterances, by *some* member nations to the contrary.

chapter twenty-five

The future of the EU

A. M. EL-AGRAA

To give a meaningful answer to the question of what the future will bring to the EU, one needs a specification of what the future means. Is it the immediate future? Or is it the indefinite future? Of course, the future is both of these, but, as will become apparent in this chapter, one needs to deal with these periods separately. However, the indefinite future is easy to tackle; hence it is discussed first and briefly in the following section.

25.1 The indefinite future

The long-term future of the EU is quite clear. As has been consistently and persistently indicated, the founding fathers, and more recently those who suggested a two-tier Europe, dreamt of the creation of a United States of Europe. The main reason for this is the achievement of eternal peace in an area with a long history of deep conflict and bloody wars. The political and economic dimensions came later and in a reinforcing manner: Europe stood no chance to be on par with the United States and Japan in terms of economic excellence and say in world affairs without being united on both fronts. Thus, until a single European nation becomes a reality, the energies of those dedicated to this cause will still be devoted to finding ways of doing so. The recent Franco-German efforts to speed up the unity process are consistent with this, and so is the statement by Mr Jacques Delors (ex-President of the EU Commission) that a two-speed Europe means that if and when those countries fit and able to make fast progress go ahead, this will not retard the integrative process, since the countries left behind will find themselves in a worse situation than before; hence they will hasten their catching-up process. Indeed, in doing so, they may actually enhance the speed of the integrative process for all the countries concerned.

This might sound like a bold and peculiar statement, given that the new government of the United Kingdom, led by Mr Tony Blair of the Labour Party, has clearly indicated that although it intends to play a full and cooperative part with its EU partner nations, it will do so within the clear context of independent, sovereign, states. However, this sentiment is certainly shared neither by the two largest countries behind the real drive for EU integration, France and Germany, nor by the BENELUX countries, Italy or Spain; indeed, the closest ally to the UK in this respect is Denmark. Also, and as we have seen, it is consistent with the attitude adopted by Britain towards European integration throughout the post-WW II period. Therefore, even if a multitier scenario became the reality, at least one substantial tier would continue with its pursuit of the cherished dream.

25.2 The next millennium

However, if by the future one is concerned with what will happen between now and the early part of the next millennium (i.e. will the opening up of the EU internal market and the full implementation of the Maastricht Treaty – the Amsterdam Treaty of June 1997 does not incorporate any major deviations – be ends in themselves or merely staging posts on the way to greater economic and political union?), then, as stated in the previous edition of this book, the answer requires a consideration of some interchanges that took place between British ex-Prime Minister Margaret Thatcher (now Baroness Thatcher), the President of the Commission during the late 1980s (Mr Jacques Delors) and Germany's Chancellor Helmut Köhl as well as the developments incorporated into the Maastricht Treaty. Let us examine these in turn.

During the middle of the summer of 1988, Mr Delors predicted that 'in ten years' time 80 per cent of economic, and perhaps social and tax, legislation will be of Community origin'. In early September of the same year, he followed this with a speech to the United Kingdom's Trade Union Congress (TUC) in which he spoke strongly of the 'social dimension' of the internal market, and called for a 'platform of guaranteed social rights', including the proposal that every worker should be covered by a collective agreement with his or her employer; a proposal which is close to the hearts of most, if not all, British trade unionists.

Later, during the same month (on 20 September), Mrs Thatcher, speaking in Bruges at the College of Europe (where else!), responded in very strong terms: 'We have not rolled back the frontiers of the state in Britain only to see them re-imposed at a European level, with a European super-state exercising a new dominance from Brussels.' Since then, she repeated the same emotive phrases regarding the 'nightmare of an EC government' on many occasions. She did this in Luxemburg and Madrid, alongside Lake Maggiore in Italy during a summit meeting, and before the Conservative Party Conference in Brighton in the United Kingdom. Nor did she confine her attacks to broad policy issues. She also did so with regard to every single practical measure by which her fellow EU leaders sought to achieve progress within the EU. She told a somewhat bemused Italian Prime Minister (then Ciriaco De Mita) at Lake Maggiore, 'I neither want nor expect to see a European central bank or a European currency in my lifetime or ... for a long time afterwards'. Recently, the Baroness has declared that she has regretted having signed the Maastricht Treaty, and backed Mr William Hague for the leadership of the Conservative Party simply because he had vehemently announced that qualification for membership in his shadow cabinet will require unwavering commitment to ensuring that the Euro will have no place in Britain.

The first rebuttals of Mrs Thatcher's vehement utterances came not from the 'socialist' leaders of the other EC member nations at the time, such as President Francois Mitterand of France, Prime Minister Phillipie Gonzalez of Spain or Prime Minister Andreas Papandreou of Greece. They sensibly kept their feelings to themselves, and left it to the more right-wing prime ministers, Germany's Chancellor Helmut Köhl, Italy's Ciriaco De Mita, Holland's Ruud Lubbers and Belgium's Wilfred Martens, to respond to her.

The most outspoken was Chancellor Köhl, hitherto Mrs Thatcher's closest ally. He declared flatly in Brussels in November of the same year that:

1. All internal frontiers within the EC must disappear by 1992.
2. Tax harmonization is indispensable.
3. A European police force is the answer to crime and terrorism.
4. By pooling sovereignty the EC states will gain and not lose.
5. The EC must have (in alliance with the United States) a common defence policy, leading to a European army.

He did not mention Mrs Thatcher by name, but every point he emphasized is one on which she is on record as taking the opposite view.

It should be stressed that Mrs Thatcher's stance on these matters suggests that she believes that the EU is predominantly a zero sum game: every increase in the EU's sovereignty is at the expense of that of the member nations, especially of the United Kingdom. However, most of the other EU leaders have fewer illusions about what the medium-sized member countries of the EU can achieve by themselves: they believe this is very little indeed. They reckon that by 'pooling sovereignty' they increase the range of possibilities for the EU as a whole and thus indirectly for their own countries as well. Hence, Chancellor Köhl's carefully considered remarks on this subject should be much appreciated, particularly since Germany is not one of the smaller EU nations; indeed it is the largest country in the EU in terms of both population and GDP.

In short, it can be claimed that the other EC leaders saw Mrs Thatcher following the example of Charles de Gaulle, whose anti-EC policies in the 1960s held back the development of the EC, ironically including the admission of the United Kingdom. The comparison is almost certainly one which Mrs Thatcher herself may find flattering; but does she realize that de Gaulle's intransigence eventually did much to undermine French influence for a long time both within the EC and outside it?

Although Mrs Thatcher was in a minority of one within the EC, she put herself in that position entirely by her own doing – her isolation was self-inflicted. She had been in that situation before, when she fought her long and hard battle to reduce the United Kingdom's contribution to the EC General Budget, but then attracted much grudging admiration from the leaders of the other member nations. Although they objected to her tactics, they recognized that she was protecting a vital British interest and was seeking to remedy an evident injustice. However, their sympathy for the position she adopted in the late 1980s (and continues to espouse today) was non-existent. She was seen as acting out of sheer perversity or, at least, out of nationalism of the narrowest possible kind.

However, what is intriguing is the fact that being in a minority of one does not offer much hope for the majority. Although the other eleven member states were reasonably united in their opposition to Mrs Thatcher, there was little they could do to get their way without asking the United Kingdom to forgo its membership of the EC. As we have seen, majority voting does not extend to such vital issues as the admission of new member nations, tax harmonization, the creation of a common central bank and one currency, and banking in general; these are still subject to unanimity. Had Mrs Thatcher chosen to veto any proposed reforms in these fields, or any other moves towards a political union, there would have been no way to prevent her from doing so. I argued in the third edition of this book that the fact that she surprised everyone by endorsing the Delors Report, subject to some provisos (see Chapter 5), 'is neither here nor there since she may still drag her feet over the second and final stages of the EMU and may even slow down the first stage by making a real issue of every problem encountered over those innocent provisos' (p. 492). That prediction came true since, as we have seen, the UK obtained special protocols in the Maastricht Treaty for opting out of the single EU currency and the social charter.

In the fourth edition, I added that the EC leaders could not have waited until Mrs Thatcher's retirement from the political scene. She told *The Times* (London) then that she would like to complete a fourth term of office, which could have taken her to 1997 or beyond. Given the divided state of Britain's opposition parties at the time, this could have been no idle boast; the results of the elections for the European Parliament then may have cast only a shadow of doubt on this (see Chapter 2). Few, if any, of the EC's other leaders had much hope of still being around then; two had already disappeared from the scene.

I asked: what could have been the way out of this impasse? To answer this question, I quoted from the third edition of this book:

> One may well ask who could change Mrs Thatcher's mind or coerce her into taking a different view? In theory, at least, her own political party could. The British Conservative Party led the United Kingdom into the EC and remained overwhelmingly committed when the Labour Party swung violently against. Moreover, the Conservative Party has a long tradition of being uncompromising in its choice of leader; therefore, if they agree that Mrs Thatcher is completely out of line, they are most likely to let her go. However, as discussed below, there is a recent twist to this argument.
>
> The irony now is that the Labour Party is at least warming to the EC (the Labour Party's manifesto for the 1983 general election contained withdrawal from the EC as one of its four major issues), and President Jacques Delors of the EC Commission was given a rapturous reception when he spoke to the TUC in September 1988. There is no reason to believe that the bulk of the Conservative Party has changed its mind about the EC, but there

has been hardly a whisper of criticism of Mrs Thatcher's stance against the further development of the EC. Of course, it is still possible that the results of the recent (1989) elections for the European Parliament and one by-election in the United Kingdom may have a positive influence; indeed, it could be argued that Mrs Thatcher's endorsement of the EMU was entirely the result of this.

The reason for this state of affairs was cruelly exposed by a recent satirical television broadcast in the United Kingdom, which reported that a man had crawled on his hands and knees for 27 miles just to get into the *Guinness Book of Records*. The TV commentator suggested that 'if he had crawled another three miles, he might have got into the Cabinet'. That Mrs Thatcher has surrounded herself with yes-men is one of Britain's worst-kept secrets. These yes-men now dominate the Conservative Party, and that is why the party is less likely to sack Mrs Thatcher from her position over the question of the future of the EC, or indeed any other issue. However, one of the future contenders (Michael Heseltine) for the leadership of the party has recently published a book fully endorsing the future envisaged for the EC by the most demanding of its advocates [see Heseltine, 1989]; but he is out of the Cabinet at the moment.

As the years have gone by, there have become fewer and fewer people to whom she has been prepared to listen. One of them has certainly been ex-President Ronald Regan, but he is now gone. Will Mr Bush command her attention and persuade this superpatriotic leader that in diminishing the EC she is also diminishing her own country? If not, the EC faces the dim prospect of another decade of lost opportunities. However, Mr Bush is not likely to attempt to do so, given the present confrontation between the United States and the EC over agricultural and other matters, which is making progress very difficult indeed in the present round of GATT negotiations (see Baldwin *et al.*, 1988). Moreover, Mr Bush is more likely to be concerned with the Canada–US free trade area arrangement and the 'special relationship between the USA and Japan', i.e. he sees the centre of gravity to be increasingly moving towards the Pacific region, particularly with the USSR reducing its military forces in Europe and diverting them to the east.

Given this background, I argued in that edition that, in spite of the endorsement of the EMU, all signs seemed to suggest either that the achievement of the internal market by the end of 1992 would be the final goal or that an EC without the United Kingdom would be the inevitable way forward. I saw this, and continue to see it, as a matter of vital importance, not only because it would have had to be contemplated if Mrs Thatcher had continued in office and insisted on her declared position, but also because the EC had no precedent on this matter and its constitution is completely silent on it. I urged that the legal implications of this had to be investigated, but in the meantime hoped that, if this issue became a reality, the United Kingdom would to the honourable thing and simply withdraw from the EC.

I did not leave this matter there. I added the following:

> Of course, one should also consider what would happen if Mrs Thatcher managed to persuade some of the other member nations of the EC to adopt her position. If this did happen, the outcome then would most certainly be a two-tier EC. However, all the signs indicate that the majority of the member nations will forge ahead with political integration, with the second of the two-tiers comprising no more than the United Kingdom. The result would be a United States of Western Europe minus the United Kingdom. That might not be a bad thing because the British would then have to consider their position

seriously, and such a reconsideration would inevitably result in the United Kingdom applying to rejoin the EC, but then fully committed to a one-nation EC. Hence, in trying to prevent the further progress of the EC towards economic and political union, Mrs Thatcher may actually cause the EC to achieve this goal much sooner than its vehement supporters ever hoped for.

If the circumstances change so much as to enable the United Kingdom to secure the support of more EC member states, then the two-tier Europe would become a reality. Such an outcome would be most disappointing, given our discussion of the history of European unity. However, one cannot leave it there since as long as the European movement remains strong, the past suggests that a way out, and forward, will be found. Indeed, this may prove inevitable since the erosion of the illusionary sovereignty that Mrs Thatcher is worried about will certainly occur after the internal market has been achieved in 1992. By then:

1. The member nations of the EC will have to agree on a joint trade policy towards the rest of the world...

2. The ability of governments to set their own rates of VAT will become extremely limited...

3. The continued success of the EMS will ensure that the member states will move smoothly towards the second and final stages of the EMU (the complete fixity of exchange rates, the creation of an EC central bank and the adoption of a single currency). Putting it differently, the success of the EMS will force them to align their monetary policies more closely if they are to keep their promise of allowing capital to move freely across the borders of member nations; this may prove impossible without a common central bank.

Thus, whichever way one looks at it, the inevitable conclusion is that Mrs Thatcher is bound to fail and the EC is set to achieve the cherished aims of its founding fathers. The sovereignty that Mrs Thatcher is so reluctant to compromise has already been subjected to that process. Those who think in terms of absolute sovereignty live in an imaginary world.

In the fourth edition, I stated that I need hardly add that although some of the detail in this argument may not have stood the test of the time between then and 1994, my main predictions came true. Mrs Thatcher was forced to resign by her own Conservative Party over the issue of the EC, and this was made possible because one of her closest allies in the Cabinet (Sir Geoffrey Howe) decided enough was enough by openly declaring his opposition to her attitude towards the EC. Although her recommendation for successor, Mr John Major, triumphed, he did not follow closely in her footsteps, and, apart from a brand new Labour Party, some would call it a neo-Conservative Party, his government's downfall was partly due to deep division within the Conservatives over the role of Britain within the EU; a division made starkly clear by the two who contested the final for his (Major's) replacement: Kenneth Clarke, a committed pro-European, and William Hague, a devout anti-European. Moreover, the EC has made great progress since Mrs Thatcher by ratifying the Maastricht Treaty, to which I now turn, albeit briefly simply because it has been covered in full in Chapters 3 and 5, and throughout the whole book.

I added that, as we have seen, the original Maastricht Treaty provided for the creation of a single EU currency by as early as 1997 if seven of the then twelve member countries pass the agreed strict, yet flexible, five criteria on price stability, interest rates, budget deficits, public debt and currency stability (see Chapter 5), or by 1999 at the latest. The earlier date was later waived, somewhat vindicating 'flexibility'. The Treaty also called for the establishment of a common central bank to be in charge of the common currency. These two plus the common defence policy, if it became a reality, although the Amsterdam Treaty of June 1997 seemed to suggest otherwise for the time being, would bring the EU much closer to a political union. Thus, the EU, but not in its entirety, seemed to be set on the road leading to the final destination.

I suggested that, against this rosy picture, one had to emphasize that full ratification became a thorny issue: Denmark had to have a second referendum in May 1993, and a favourable outcome there was needed to pave the way for approval by the United Kingdom. Ironically, what complicated the ratification process in the United Kingdom was the insistence of the Labour Party on British participation in the Social Act, one of the opt-out protocols negotiated by the British government. Moreover, some items of the Maastricht Treaty were watered down during the Edinburgh Summit in December 1992 with the aim of pleasing the Danes in order to enable a positive outcome for their referendum (see Chapter 3), and some would argue that the resulting dilution ensured that political integration had been relegated to the distant future.

I did add that this pessimism could not be justified. First, the subsidiarity principle was not a diluting of the Maastricht Treaty since it simply clarified what should be attempted at the EU level (the central government) and at the national level (the local government). Second, as we have seen in the case of Mrs Thatcher, member countries such as France and Germany were not likely to adhere to this for long: they would go for a Delors-type two-tier EU, with the majority constituting one tier and Denmark and the United Kingdom as the other. Again, this could happen for only a short time because sooner or later, the Danes and the British would have no alternative but to return to the fold. A well-seasoned European tried to provide the rationale for this:

> if we had not had the European Community, the Danes, who have a large agricultural production, would have had great difficulty exporting agricultural products to the other European countries. In the Community there is a common market for agriculture. The Danes knew that, with their agricultural strength, they would be competitive in the common market. They did not want to join because of the ideas of European union. They wanted to join for economic reasons. This was predominantly the British motive as well. Those two countries have difficulties with European union because they never fully understood the concept of European union...

> The European union can live without Denmark ..., even without Great Britain. The Community existed before the British wanted to be part of it. The British did not join the Community at the beginning because they thought it would never work. They only joined when they saw that it works. If they left, the Community would continue to work. (Warner Ungerer, Rector, College of Europe at Bruges, *Japan Update*, no. 17, February 1993).

I reiterated that (as we have seen in Chapters 1, 2 and 24) this was no more than a very partial and distorted explanation. The British did not join from the start simply because they were torn between their Empire and Commonwealth obligations and a commitment to a Europe determined to have a common policy for agriculture which ran against their own interests as well as against those of their partners in the Commonwealth. Of course, there was also another reason. At that time, Britain still thought of itself as a world superpower; hence it was equally torn between this delusion and being relegated to one of three important nations in just Europe. Nevertheless, Britain did change its mind when it realized that its superpower status was no more than a figment of its own imagination and that the EC member countries were growing fast economically when Britain was hovering at the zero per cent level. Thus, the explanation is not purely economic; it is economic within the context of diminished international importance. With regard to Denmark, the economic rationale is nearer to the truth, but, as we have also seen in the above chapters, Denmark simply followed in the British footsteps. These two countries seem to have a great deal in common, hence their insistence on the subsidiarity principle even though it has no direct bearing on the real substance of the integrative process, and their antics during the ratification for the Maastricht Treaty should be quite understandable.

I concluded that Ungerer's explanation left a lot to be desired. As has been emphasized again and again, the aim of the founding fathers is the creation of a United States of Europe. Thus, although it is true to argue that the EC can succeed without Britain and Denmark, such an argument misses this important dimension. In order to unite Europe, we need to accommodate these two countries, but not at the expense of the other EC nations. Attempts at such an accommodation may actually lead to the sacking of the British and the Danes from the EC, but the door must always be left open for them since, as argued above, they will have no alternative but to return, and then fully committed. This is especially so when one recalls (see Chapters 5 and 23) that the countries which are expected to join the EC in about 1995 will come fully committed not only to the Maastricht Treaty but to everything the EC stands and aims for.

I repeat that although the above analysis, in its entirety, may not have stood the test of time, it remains essentially true. However, the real message from the interchanges and developments is that because politicians, on the whole, stay at the helm for short durations, it should be understandable that their preoccupations are with their survival in office; hence they will endeavour to please the masses in accordance with the sentiments of the time. The ones who have the vision and commitment to its pursuit come once in a while, but they are the ones that really matter for European integration. Hence, one should not be distracted with petty squabbles between politicians at particular moments in time.

25.3 Conclusion

Thus, one seems to have gone round in a full circle: the immediate future led back to the indefinite future. However, although this is inevitable, it misses the real message that the road is not only long and winding, but also has ups and downs: the summit may be clear, but reaching it means not falling off the precipices. To put it differently, economics has never been the driving force behind European integration, it has been only a vehicle to that end. Economic problems are simply obstacles on the way, but the European movement will ensure that they are no more than that. Thus, it is inevitable that the two futures should come together.

Bibliography

Throughout this book, reference is made to numerous Communications by the Commission of the European Communities/Union to the Council. These are not given in full here because the EC/EU system of referencing is quite clear. For example, COM (88) 491 means Communication number 491, issued in 1988. Reference is also frequently made to the Treaties of the European Communities. Some of these are published by Her Majesty's Stationery Office (HMSO) in the United Kingdom, but the most comprehensive set is issued by Sweet & Maxwell, which is listed here.

Throughout the book, *EU Bulletin* is used to refer to the Commission of the European Communities' *Bulletin of the Economic Communities* (various issues), and *OJC*, *OJL* or *OJCL* (where L stands for legal) refer to the Commission's *Official Journal of the European Communities*. Again the EC/EU's own system of referencing is clear.

Adams, W. and **Stoffaes, C.** (eds) (1986) *French Industrial Policy*, The Brookings Institution, Washington.

Aho, C. M. and **Bayard, T. O.** (1982) 'The 1980s: twilight of the open trading system?', *The World Economy*, vol. 5, no. 4.

Agence Europe (pamphlet), various dates.

Aitken, N. D. (1973) 'The effects of the EEC and EFTA on European trade: a temporal cross-secion analysis', *American Economic Review*, vol. 68.

Albert, M. (1991) *Capitalisme contre Capitalisme*, Seuil.

All Saints Day Manifesto (1975) *The Economist*.

Allais, M., Duquesne de la Vinelle, L., Oort, C. J., Seidenfuss, H. S. and **del Viscoro, M.** (1965) 'Options in transport policy', *EEC Studies, Transport Series*, no. 1.

Allen, D. (1983) 'Managing the Common Market: the Community's competition policy', in H. Walllace, W. Wallace and C. Webb (eds), *Policy Making in the European Community*, Wiley, second edition.

Allen, G. H. (1972) *British Agriculture in the Common Market*, School of Agriculture, Aberdeen.

Allen, P. R. (1983) 'Cyclical imbalance in a monetary union', *Journal of Common Market Studies*, vol. 21, no. 2.

Allen, P. R. and **Kenen, P.** (1980) *Asset Markets, Exchange Rates and Economic Integration*, Cambridge University Press.

Alting von Geusau, F. A. (1975) 'In search of a policy', in M. Adelman and F. A. Alting von Geusau (eds), *Energy in the European Communities*, Sijthoff.

Ardy, B. (1988) 'The national incidence of the European Community budget', *Journal of Common Market Studies*, vol. 26, no. 4.

Argyris, N. (1989) 'The EEC rules of competition and the air transport sector', *Common Market Law Review*, vol. 26, no. 1.

Argyris, N. (1993) 'Regulatory reform in the electricity sector', *Oxford Review of Economic Policy*, vol. 19, no. 1.

Armington, P. S. (1969) 'A theory of demand for products distinguished by place of production', *IMF Staff Papers*, March.

Armington, P. S. (1970) 'Adjustment of trade balances: some experiments with a model of trade among many countries', *IMF Staff Papers*, vol. 17.

Armstrong, H. W. (1978) 'European Economic Community regional policy: a survey and critique', *Regional Studies*, vol. 12, no. 5.

Armstrong, H. W. (1985) 'The reform of European Community regional policy', *Journal of Common Market Studies*, vol. 23.

Armstrong, H. W. (1994) 'Regional problems and policies', in B. F. Duckham *et al.* (eds), *The British Economy Since 1945*, Oxford University Press.

Armstrong, H. W. (1995a) *Growth Disparities and Convergence Clubs in Regional GDP in Western Europe, USA and Australia*, Report for DG16, European Commission, Brussels.

Armstrong, H. W. (1995b) 'Convergence among regions of the European Union', *Papers in Regional Science*, vol. 40.

Armstrong, H. W. and **Taylor, J.** (1978) *Regional Economic Policy and Its Analysis*, Philip Allan.

Armstrong, H. W. and **Taylor, J.** (1993) *Regional Economics and Policy*, Routledge.

Arndt, H. W. and **Garnaut, R.** (1979) 'ASEAN and the industrialisation of East Asia', *Journal of Common Market Studies*, vol. 17, no. 3.

Arndt, S. W. (1968) 'On discriminatory versus non-preferential tariff policies', *Economic Journal*, vol. 78.

Arndt, S. W. (1969) 'Customs unions and the theory of tarrifs', *American Economic Review*, vol. 59.

Artis, M. J. (1981) 'From monetary to exchange rate targets', *Banca Nazionale del Lavoro Quarterly Bulletin*, September.

Artis, M. J. and **Currie, D. A.** (1981) 'Monetary targets and the exchange rate: a case for conditional targets', in W. A. Eltis and P. J. N. Sinclair (eds), *The Money Supply and the Exchange Rate*, Oxford University Press.

Artus, J. R. and **Crockett, A. D.** (1978) 'Floating exchange rates and the need for surveillance', *Essays in International Trade*, Allen & Unwin.

Asch, P. (1970) *Economic Theory and the Antitrust Dilemma*, Wiley.

Auboin, M. and **Laird, S.** (1997) 'EU import measures and the developing countries', mimeo, World Trade Organization, Geneva.

Audretsch, D. B. (1989) *The Market and the State: Government policy towards business in Europe, Japan and the United States*, Harvester Wheatsheaf.

Aujac, C. (1986) 'An introductiron to french industrial policy', in W. Adams and C. Stoffaes (eds), *French Industrial Policy*, The Brookings Institution, Washington.

Babardine, O. A. (1994) *The Lomé Convention and Development*, Avebury.

Bacchetta, M. (1978) 'Oil refining in the European Community', *Journal of Common Market Studies*, vol. 11.

Bacon, R., Godley, W. and **McFarquhar, A.** (1978) 'The direct cost to Britain of belonging to the EEC', *Cambridge Economic Policy Review*, vol. 4.

Balassa, B. (1961) *The Theory of Economic Integration*, Allen & Unwin.

Balassa, B. (1967) 'Trade creation and trade diversion in the European Common Market', *Economic Journal*, vol. 77.

Balassa, B. (1974) 'Trade creation and trade diversion in the European Common Market: an appraisal of the evidence', *Manchester School*, vol. 42.

Balassa, B. (1974) *European Economic Integration*, North-Holland.

Baldwin, R. E. (1971) *Non-tariff Distortions of International Trade*, Allen & Unwin.

Baldwin, R. E. (1989) 'The growth effect of 1992', *Economic Policy*, no. 9.

Baldwin, R. E. (1994) *Towards an Integrated Europe*, Centre for Economic Policy Research, London.

Baldwin, R. E. *et al.* (eds) (1988) *Issues in US–EC Trade Relations*, University of Chicago Press.

Baldwin, R. E. *et al.* (1992) *Is Bigger Better? The Economics of EC Enlargement*, Centre for Economic Policy Research, London.

Baldwin, R., Haaparanta, P. and Kiander, J. (1995) *Expanding Membership of the European Union*, Cambridge University Press.

Ball, R. J., Burns, T. and Laury, J. S. E. (1977) 'The role of exchange rate changes in balance of payments adjustments – the UK case', *Economic Journal*, vol. 87.

Baneth, J. (1993) 'Fortress Europe and other myths about trade', *World Bank Discussion Papers*, no. 225.

Bangemann, M. (1992) *Meeting the Global Challenge: Establishing a successful European industrial policy*, Kogan Page.

Banister, D. and Button, K. J. (eds) (1991) *Transport in a Free Market Economy*, Macmillan.

Bank for International Settlements (1979) *Annual Report 1978*, Basle.

Bank for International Settlements (1989) *International Banking and Financial Market Developments*, February.

Bank of Canada (1983) 'The European Monetary System: the foreign exchange mechanism', *Bank of Canada Monthly Review*, August.

Bank of England (1979) 'Intervention arrangement in the European Monetary System', *Bank of England Quarterly Bulletin*, June.

Bank of England (1982) *Quarterly Bulletin*, March.

Barker, E. (1971) *Britain in a Divided Europe*, Weidenfeld & Nicolson.

Barrell, R. and Pain, N. (1993) 'Trade restraints and Japanese direct investment flows', mimeo, National Institute of Economic and Social Research, London.

Barro, R. J. and Sala-i-Martin, X. (1991) 'Convergence across states and regions', *Brookings Papers*, no. 1.

Barten, A. P. (1970) 'Maximum likelihood estimation of a complete system of demand equations', *European Economic Review*, vol. 1.

Barten, A. P. *et al.* (1976) 'COMET: a medium-term macroeconomic model for the European Economic Community', *European Economic Review*, vol. 7.

Baumol, W. J. and Oates, J. E. (1988) *The Theory of Environmental Policy*, Cambridge University Press, second edition.

Bayliss, B. T. (1973) 'Licensing and entry to the market', *Journal of Transport Planning and Technology*, vol. 2, no. 1.

Bayliss, B. T. (1979) 'Transport in the European Communities', *Journal of Transport Economics and Policy*, vol. XIII, no. 1.

Begg, I. (1989) 'European integration and regional policy', *Oxford Review of Economic Policy*, vol. 5, no. 2.

Begg, I. (1992) 'The spatial impact of the EC internal market for financial services', *Regional Studies*, vol. 26.

Begg, I., Cripps, F. and Ward, T. (1981) 'The European Community problems and prospects', *Cambridge Economic Policy Review*, vol. 7, no. 2.

Belcredi, M., Caprio, L. and Ranci, P. (1988) *The Aid Element in State Participation to Company Capital*, report to the Commission, Office for Official Publications of the European Communities.

Bellamy, C. and Child, G. (1987) *Common Market Law on Competition*, Sweet & Maxwell.

Bellis, J. F. (1976) 'Potential competition and concentration policy: relevance to EEC antitrust', *Journal of World Trade Law*, vol. 10, no. 1.

Berglas, E. (1979) 'Preferential trading theory – the *n* commodity case', *Journal of Political Economy*, vol. 81.

Berglas, E. (1981) 'Harmonisation of commodity taxes', *Journal of Public Economics*, vol. 16.

Berglas, E. (1983) 'The case for unilateral tariff reactions: foreign tariffs reconsidered', *AER*, vol. 73.

Bergman, D. *et al.* (1970) *A Future for European Agriculture*, Atlantic Institute, Paris.

Berkhout, F., Boehmer Christiansen, S. and **Skea, J. F.** (1989) 'Deposit and repositories: electricity wastes in the UK and West Germany', *Energy Policy*, vol. 17.

Best, M. (1990) *The New Competition: Institutions of industrial restructuring*, Polity.

Beveridge, W. (1940) *Peace by Federation?*, Federal Tract no. 1, Federal Union, London.

Bhagwati, J. N. (1965) 'On the equivalence of tariffs and quotas', in R. E. Baldwin *et al.* (eds), *Trade, Growth and the Balance of Payments*, North-Holland.

Bhagwati, J. N. (1969) *Trade, Tariffs and Growth*, Weidenfeld & Nicolson.

Bhagwati, J. N. (1971) 'Customs unions and welfare improvement', *Economic Journal*, vol. 81.

Bhaskar, K. (1990) *The Effect of Different State Aid Measures on Inter Country Competition*, report to the Commission, Office for Official Publications of the European Communities.

Bieber, R. *et al.* (1988) *1992: One European Market? A critical analysis of the Commission's internal market strategy*, Nomos Verlagsgesellschaft.

Black, J. and **Dunning, J. H.** (eds) (1982) *International Capital Movements*, Macmillan.

Black, R. A. (1977) 'Plus ça change, plus c'est la même chose: 9 governments in search of a common energy policy', in H. Wallace, W. Wallace and C. Webb (eds), *Policy-Making in the European Communities*, Little Brown.

Blackoby, F. T. (1980) 'Exchange rate policy and economic strategy', *Three Banks Review*, June.

Blancus, P. (1978) 'The Common Agricultural Policy and the balance of payments of the EEC member countries', *Banca Nazionale del Lavoro Quarterly Review*, vol. 5, no. 3.

Bluet, J. C. and **Systermanns, Y.** (1968) 'Modèle gravitionel d'échanges internationaux de produits manufacturés', *Bulletin du CEPREMAP*, vol. 1, January (new series).

Boardman, R. *et al.* (1985) *Europe, Africa and Lomé III*, University Press of America.

Bodenheimer, S. (1967) *Political Union, a Microcosm of European Politics*, Sijthoff.

Boehmer-Christiansen, S. and **Skea, J.** (1990) *Acid Politics: Environmental and energy policies in Britain and Germany*, Pinter.

Bohme, H. (1983) 'Current issues and progress in European shipping policy', *The World Economy*, vol. 6.

Bollard, A. E. and **Mayes, D. G.** (1991) 'Regionalism and the Pacific Rim', *Journal of Common Market Studies*, vol. 30.

Bootle, R. (1983) 'Foreign exchange intervention: a case of ill-founded neglect', *The Banker*, May.

Booz, A. and **Booz, H.** (1989) *The Effects of the Internal Market on Greece, Ireland, Portugal and Spain*, a study carried out for the EC Commission.

Bork, R. (1978) *The Antitrust Paradox: A policy at war with itsef*, Basic Books.

Bos, M. and **Nelson, H.** (1988) 'Indirect taxation and the completion of the internal market of the EC', *Journal of Common Market Studies*, vol. 27, no. 1.

Boulding, K. E. (1966) 'The economics of the coming spaceship Earth', in H. Jarret (ed.), *Environmental Quality in a Growing Economy*, Johns Hopkins.

Bourgeois, J. and **Demaret, P.** (1995) 'European Industrial, Competition and Trade Policies: Legal Aspects', in P. Buigues, A. Jacquenain and A. Sapir (eds), *European Policies on Competition, Trade and Industry*, Edward Elgar.

Bourguignon, F., Gallais-Hamonno, G. and **Fernet, B.** (1977) *International Labour Migrations and Economic Choices: the European case*, Development Centre of the OECD.

Bowers, J. K. (1972) 'Economic efficiency in agriculture', in Open University, *Decision Making in Britain III*, Parts 1–6.

Bowers, J. K. (ed.) (1979) *Inflation, Development and Integration: Essasys in honour of A. J. Brown*, Leeds University Press.

Brada, J. C. and **Méndez, J. A.** (1985) 'Economic integration among developed, developing and centrally planned economies: a comparative analysis', *Review of Economics and Statistics*, vol. 67.

Brander, J. (1981) 'Intra-industry trade in identical commodities', *Journal of International Economics*, vol. 11.

Brander, J. and **Spencer, B.** (1984) 'Tariff protection and imperfect competition', in H. Kierzkowski (ed.), *Monopolistic Competition and International Trade*, Oxford University Press.

Brazier, M., Lovecy, J. and **Morgan, M.** (1993) 'Professional regulation and the single European market: a study of the regulation of doctors and lawyers in England and France', mimeo, University of Manchester.

Breckling, J. *et al.* (1978) *Effects of EC Agricultural Policies: A general equilibrium approach*, Bureau of Agricultural Research, Canberra.

Bredimas, A. E. and **Tzoannos, J. G.** (1983) 'In search of a common shipping policy for the EC', *Journal of Common Market Studies*, vol. 20.

Breton, A. and **Scott, A.** (1978) 'The assignment problem in federal structures', in M. S. Feldstein and R. P. Inman (eds), *The Economics of Public Services*, Macmillan.

Brewin, C. (1987) 'The European Community: a union of states without unity of government', *Journal of Common Market Studies*, vol. XXVI, no. 1.

Brewin, C. C. (1992) 'Participation of non-member states in shaping the rules of the European Community's single market', Economic and Social Research Council report, Swindon.

Brittan, L. (1992) *European Competition Policy: Keeping the playing field level*, CEPS.

Britton, A. and **Mayes, D. G.** (1992) *Achieving Monetary Union*, Sage.

Brown, A. J. (1961) 'Economic separatism versus a common market in developing countries', *Yorkshire Bulletin of Economic and Social Research*, vol. 13.

Brown, A. J. (1977) 'What is wrong with the British economy?', *The University of Leeds Review*, vol. 20.

Brown, A. J. (1979) 'Inflation and the British sickness', *Economic Journal*, vol. 89.

Brown, A. J. (1980) 'The transfer of resources', in W. Wallace (ed.), *Britain in Europe*, Heinemann, Chapter 7.

Brülhart, M. (1994) 'Marginal intra-industry trade: measurement and relevance for the pattern of industrial adjustment', *Weltwirtschaftliches Archiv*, vol. 130.

Brülhart, M. and **Elliot, R.** (1998) 'Adjustment to the European single market: inferences from intra-industry trade patterns', *Journal of Economic Studies*, forthcoming.

Bruppacher, F. (1988) 'How European electricity trade is conducted', paper presented in the *Financial Times* World Electricity Conference.

Bryant, R. C. (1980) *Money and Monetary Policy in Independent Nations*, The Brookings Institution, Washington.

Buck, T. (1975) 'Regional policy and economic integration', *Journal of Common Market Studies*, vol. 13.

Buckley, P. J. and **Casson, M.** (1976) *The Future of the Multinational Enterprise*, Macmillan.

Buckwell, A., Harvey, D. R., Thomson, K. J. and **Parton, K.** (1982) *The Costs of the Common Agricultural Policy*, Croom Helm.

Buigues, P. and **Sapir, A.** (1992) 'Community industrial policy', paper presented at an EIPA conference.

Buigues, P.-A. and **Martínez Mongay, C.** (1997) 'The European Union internal market in implementation: how single is the single European market for the LDCs?', mimeo, European Commission, Brussels.

Bundesbank (1979) *Monthly Review*, March.

Burrows, B., Denton, G. R. and **Edwards, G.** (1977) *Federal Solutions to European Issues*, Macmillan.

Butt Philip, A. (1981) 'The harmonisation of industrial policy and practices', in C. Cosgrove Twitchett (ed.), *Harmonisation in the EEC*, Macmillan.

Butt Philip, A. (1988) 'Implementing the European internal market: problems and prospects', *Discussion Paper*, no. 5, Royal Institute of International Affairs.

Butt Philip, A. (1992) *Report to the European Commission*, presented to the Royal Economic Society Industry Seminar, Shell Centre, London.

Button, K. J. (1982) *Transport Economics*, Heinemann.

Button, K. J. (1993) *Transport, the Environment and Economic Policy*, Edward Elgar.

Button, K. J. and **Gillingwater, D.** (1976) *Case Studies in Regional Economics*, Heinemann.

Button, K. J. and **Pitfield, D.** (eds) (1991) *Transport Deregulation: An international movement*, Macmillan.

Byé, M. (1950) 'Unions douanières et données nationales', *Economie Appliquée*, vol. 3. Reprinted (1953) in translation as 'Customs unions and national interests', *International Economic Papers*, no. 3.

Cairncross, A. *et al.* (1974) *Economic Policy for the European Community: The way forward*, Macmillan.

Calingaert, M. (1988) *The 1992 Challenge from Europe: Development of the European Community's internal market*, National Planning Association, Washington DC.

Cambridge Economic Policy Group (1981) *Cambridge Economic Policy Review*, vol. 7, no. 2.

Cameron, G. C. (1974) 'Regional economic policy in the United Kingdom', in N. M. Hansen (ed.), *Public Policy and Regional Economic Development*, Saxon House.

Camps, M. (1964) *Britain and the European Community 1955–63*, Oxford University Press.

Canenbley, C. (1972) 'Price discrimination and EEC cartel law: a review of the Kodak decision of the Commission of the European Communities', *The Antitrust Bulletin*, vol. 17, no. 1.

Carraco, C. and **Sinisalco, D.** (eds) (1993) *The European Carbon Tax: An economic assessment*, Klawer.

Carrier Licensing Report of the Geddes Committee, HMSO.

Cawson, A., Morgan, K., Webber, D., Holmes, P. and **Stevens, A.** (1990) *Hostile Brothers Competition and Closure in the European Electronics Industry*, Oxford University Press.

Cecchini, P. (1988) *The European Challenge 1992: The Benefits of a Single Market*, Wildwood House.

Central Bank of Ireland (1979) 'A guide to the arithmetic of the EMS exchange rate mechanism', *Central Bank of Ireland Quarterly Bulletin*, Autumn.

Central Statistical Office (1981) *Britain in the European Community*, Reference Pamphlet 137, HMSO.

CEPS (1995) *European Telecommunications Policy – How to Regulate a Single Market, Working Party Report 13*.

Choi, J.-Y. and **Yu, E. S. H.** (1984) 'Customs unions under increasing returns to scale', *Economica*, vol. 51.

Chard, J. S. and **Macmillen, M. J.** (1979) 'Sectoral aids and Community competition policy: the case of textiles', *Journal of World Trade Law*, vol. 13, no. 2.

Choufoer, J. H. (1982) 'Future of the European Energy Economy', address to the Conference of European Petroleum and Gas, Amsterdam.

Clark, C. (1962) *British Trade in the Common Market*, Stevens.

Clark, C., Wilson, F. and **Bradley, J.** (1969) 'Industrial location and economic potential in Western Europe', *Regional Studies*, vol. 3, no. 2.

Clauvaux, F. J. (1969) 'The import elasticity as a yardstick for measuring trade creation', *Economia Internazionale*, November.

Cleutinx, C. (1996) 'Is there a future for coal in Europe?', *Energy in Europe*, no. 27, December.

Cmnd. 8212 (1981) *Statement on the Defence Estimates*, vol. 1, HMSO.

Cnossen, S. (1986) 'Harmonisation of indirect taxes in the EEC', *British Tax Review*, vol. 4.

Cobham, D. (1982) 'Comments on Peeters and Emerson', in M. T. Sumner and G. Zis (eds), *European Monetary Union: Progress and prospects*, Macmillan.

Cobham, D. (1996) 'Causes and effects of the European monetary crises of 1996–93', *Journal of Common Market Studies*, vol. 34.

Cockfield, Lord (1986) Address to the International Management Institute, Geneva.

Coffey, P. (1976) *The External Relations of the EEC*, Macmillan.

Coffey, P. (1977) *Europe and Money*, Macmillan.

Coffey, P. (1979) *Economic Policies of the Common Marker*, Macmillan.

Coffey, P. (1987) *The European Monetary System: Past, present and future*, Kluwer.

Coffey, P. and **Presley, J.** (1971) *European Monetary Integration*, Macmillan.

Cohen, B. J. (1981) 'The European Monetary System', *Essays in International Finance*, no. 142, Princeton University.

Cohen, C. D. (ed.) (1983) *The Common Market – Ten Years After*, Philip Allan.

Cohen, W. and Levin, R. (1989) 'Empirical studies of innovation and market structure', in R. Schmalensee and R. D. Willig (eds), *Handbook of Industrial Organization*, North-Holland.

Collier, P. (1979) 'The welfare effects of customs union: an anatomy', *Economic Journal*, vol. 89.

Collins, C. D. E. (1975) *The European Communities: the Social Policy of the first phase*, Martin Robertson.

Collins, C. D. E. (1980) 'Social policy', in A. M. El-Agraa (ed.), *The Economics of the European Community*, Chapter 15, Philip Allan.

Comanor, W. S. (1990) 'United States antitrust policy: issues and institutions', in W. S. Comanor *et al.*, *Competition Policy in Europe and North America: Economic issues and institutions*, Harwood Academic.

Comanor, W. S. *et al.* (1990) *Competition Policy in Europe and North America: Economic issues and institutions*, Harwood Academic.

Comité intergouvernemental créé par la conférence de Messina (1956) *Rapport des chefs de délégation aux Ministres des Affaires Etrangères*, Brussels.

Commission of the European Communities (various issues) *Bulletin of the European Communities*, or EC Bulletin.

Commission of the European Communities (various years) *Social Report*.

Commission of the European Communities (various issues and items) *Official Journal of the European Communities* (referred to throughout as *OJC, OJL* or *OJCL*, where L stands for Legal).

Commission of the European Communities (three times a year) *Social Europe*. Also, Supplements.

Commission of the European Communities (annual) *Report on Social Developments*.

Commission of the European Communities (annual) *Employment in Europe*.

Commission of the European Communities (1953) *Report on Problems raised by the Different Turnover Tax Systems Applied within the Common Market* (the Tinbergen Report).

Commission of the European Communities (1960) *Community Energy Policy Objectives for 1985* (COM (74) 60).

Commission of the European Communities (1961) *Memorandum on the General Lines of a Common Transport Policy*.

Commission of the European Communities (1962) *Action Programme of the Community for the Second Stage*.

Commission of the European Communities (1963) *Report of the Fiscal and Financial Committee* (the Neumark Report).

Commission of the European Communities (1966) *Report on the Situation of the Fisheries Sector in the Member States and the Basic Principles for a Common Policy*.

Commission of the European Communities (1967) *Tenth Annual Report of the Activities of the Communities*, Brussels.

Commission of the European Communities (1968) 'Premieres Orientatirons pour une politique energetique communautaire', *Communication de la Commission presente au Conseil le 18 December 1968*, Brussels.

Commission of the European Communities (1969) 'Memorandum on the Report of Agriculture in the European Economic Community', *Bulletin of the European Communities*, Supplement, January.

Commission of the European Communities (1970a) 'Report to the Council and the Commission on the realisation by stages of economic and monetary union in the Community', *Bulletin of the European Communities*, Supplement, no. 11 (the Werner Report).

Commission of the European Communities (1970b) *Industrial Policy in the Community: Memorandum from the Commission to the Council*.

Commission of the European Communities (1970c) *Corporation Tax and Income Tax in the European Communities* (the van den Tempel Report).

Commission of the European Communities (1970d) *Industrial Policy in the Community*, Office of Official Publications of the European Communities.

Commission of the European Communities (1971a) 'Preliminary guidelines for a social policy', *Bulletin of the European Communities*, Supplement 2/71.

Commission of the European Communities (1971b) 'General regional aid systems', *Official Journal, OJ* C111 of 4 November 1971.

Commission of the European Communities (1972a) *Competition Law in the European Economic Community and in the European Coal and Steel Community*.

Commission of the European Communities (1972b) *First Report on Competition Policy*.

Commission of the European Communities (1973a) 'Proposals for a Community regional policy', *Official Journal, OJ* C68 of 16 October 1973, and *OJ* C106 of 6 December 1973.

Commission of the European Communities (1973b) *Programme of Action in the Field of Technological and Industrial Policy*, SEC (73) 3824 final, October.

Commission of the European Communities (1973c) *Communication from the Commission to the Council on the Development of the Common Transport Policy*, COM (73).

Commission of the European Communities (1974a) 'Social Action Programme', *Bulletin of the European Communities*, Supplement 2/74.

Commission of the European Communities (1974b) *Third Report on Competition Policy*.

Commission of the European Communities (1975a) 'Report and proposal decision on a programme of action for the European aeronautical sector', *Bulletin of the European Communities*, Supplement 11/75.

Commission of the European Communities (1975b) 'Council Regulation (EEC) 724/75 of 18 March 1975 establishing a European Regional Development Fund', *Official Journal, OJ* L73 of 21 March 1975.

Commission of the European Communities (1975c) *Report of the Study Group 'Economic and Monetary Union 1980'*, March (the Marjolin Report).

Commission of the European Communities (1976a) *Fifth Report on Competition – EEC*.

Commission of the European Communities (1976b) 'Action Programme in favour of migrant workers and their families', *Bulletin of the European Communities*, Supplement 3/76.

Commission of the European Communities (1977a) *Guidelines for Community Regional Policy*, COM (77) 195 final.

Commission of the European Communities (1977b) 'Regional concentration in the countries of the European Community', *Regional Policy Series*, no. 4.

Commission of the European Communities (1977c) *Report of the Study Group on the Role of Public Finance in European Integration*, 2 vols (the McDougall Report).

Commission of the European Communities (1977d) 'Community regional policy: new guidelines', *Bulletin of the European Communities*, Supplement, June.

Commission of the European Communities (1978a) 'Council Decision of 16 October 1978 empowering the Commission to contact loans for the purpose of promoting investment in the Community', *Official Journal, OJ* L298 of 25 October 1978.

Commission of the European Communities (1978b) *Twelfth General Report of the Activities of the European Communities in 1978*.

Commission of the European Communities (1978c) 'Regional aid systems', *Official Journal, OJ* C31 of 3 February 1979.

Commission of the European Communities (1978d) *Report on Some Structural Aspects of Growth*.

Commission of the European Communities (1979a) 'Regional incentives in the European Community', *Regional Policy Series*, no. 15.

Commission of the European Communities (1979b) 'The Regional Development Programmes', *Regional Policy Series*, no. 17.

Commission of the European Communities (1979c) 'Air Transport – a Community Approach', *Bulletin of the European Communities*, Supplement 5/79.

Commission of the European Communities (1979d) *Proposals for Reform of the Commission of the European Communities and its Services* (the Spierenburg Report).

Commission of the European Communities (1979e) *Eighth Report on Competition Policy.*

Commission of the European Communities (1980a) *Lá Suisse et la Communauté.*

Commission of the European Communities (1980b) *Official Journal of the European Communities*, Legislation, no. C149.

Commission of the European Communities (1980c) *Tenth Report on Competition Policy.*

Commission of the European Communities (1980d) 'Commission Directive 80/723/EEC of 25 June 1980 on the transparency of financial relations between Member States and public undertakings', *Official Journal, L195*, 29 July.

Commission of the European Communities (1981a) *Communication to the Council on the Categories of Infrastructure to which the ERDF may Contribute in the Various Regions aided by the Fund*, COM (81) 38 final.

Commission of the European Communities (1981b) *Principal Regulations and Decisions of the Council of the European Communities on Regional Policy.*

Commission of the European Communities (1981c) 'Proposal for a Council Regulation amending Regulation (EEC) 724/75 establishing a European Regional Development Fund', *Official Journal, OJ* C336 of 23 December 1981.

Commission of the European Communities (1981d) *New Regional Policy Guidelines and Priorities*, COM (81) 152 final.

Commission of the European Communities (1981e) 'Deglomeration policies in the European Community – a comparative study', *Regional Policy*, no. 18.

Commission of the European Communities (1981f) 'Study of the regional impact of the Common Agricultural Policy', *Regional Policy Series*, no. 21.

Commission of the European Communities (1981g) 'Commission recommendation of 9.10.1981 on transfrontier coordination for regional development', *Offical Journal, OJ* L321 of 10 November 1981.

Commission of the European Communities (1981h) *The Regions of Europe: First periodic report on the social and economic situation in the regions of the Community.*

Commission of the European Communities (1981i) 'The European Community's Transport Policy', Periodical 2/1981, EC Documentation.

Commission of the European Communities (1982a) *Fifteenth General Report of the Activities of the European Communities in 1981.*

Commission of the European Communities (1982b) *The Agricultural Situation in the Community – 1981 Report.*

Commission of the European Communities (1982c) *Ten Years in Europe.*

Commission of the European Communities (1983a) 'Memorandum of evidence to the House of Lords Select Committee on the European Communities', *House of Lords Report*, q.v.

Commission of the European Communities (1983b) *Twelfth Report on Competition Policy.*

Commission of the European Communities (1983c) *Seventeenth General Report on the Activities of the European Communities.*

Commission of the European Communities (1983d) *European Political Cooperation*, European File 13/83.

Commission of the European Communities (1984a) *Eighteenth General Report on the Activities of the European Communities.*

Commission of the European Communities (1984b) *Review of Member States' Energy Policies* (COM (84) 88).

Commission of the European Communities (1984c) *Social Report.* Also, for other years.

Commission of the European Communities (1984d) *Civil Aviation Memorandum No. 2: Progress towards the development of a Community air transport policy*, COM (84) 72.

Commission of the European Communities (1985a) *Completing the Internal Market* (White Paper from the EC Commission to the EC Council) – COM (85) 310.

Commission of the European Communities (1985b) *The European Community and its Regions.*

Commission of the European Communities (1985c) *14th Report on Competition Policy.*

Commission of the European Communities (1985d) *Community Energy Policy Objectives for 1985,* (COM (74) 1960).

Commission of the European Communities (1985e) *Fourteenth Report on Competition Policy.*

Commission of the European Communities (1985f) *Nineteenth General Report on the Activities of the European Communities.*

Commission of the European Communities (1985g) 'Commission Directive 85/413/EEC of 24th July 1985 amending Directve 80/723/EEC on the transparency of financial relations between Member States and public undertakings', *Official Journal, L229,* 28 August.

Commission of the European Communities (1986a) *Official Journal of the European Communities,* Legislation, no. C241.

Commission of the European Communities (1986b) *Communication on Natural Gas,* COM (86) 518.

Commission of the European Communities (1986c) *Twentieth General Report on the Activities of the European Communities.*

Commission of the European Communities (1987a) *Efficiency, Stability and Equity* (the Padoa–Schioppa Report).

Commission of the European Communities (1987b) *Completion of the Internal Market: Approximation of indirect tax rates and harmonisation of indirect tax structure,* Global Communication from the EC Commission, COM (87) 320.

Commission of the European Communities (1987c) *European Environmental Policy,* Economic and Social Committee and Consultative Assembly.

Commission of the European Communities (1987d) *Sixteenth Report on Competition Policy.*

Commission of the European Communities (1987e) (Green Paper) *Development of the Common Market for Telecommunications Services and Equipment,* COM (87) 290.

Commission of the European Communities (1988a) *Bulletin of the European Communities,* Supplement 4/47.

Commission of the European Communities (1988b) *Review of Member States' Energy Policies – the 1995 Energy Objectives,* COM (88) 174.

Commission of the European Communities (1988c) *Proposal for a Council Recommendation to the Member States to Promote Cooperation between Public Electricity Supply Companies and Private Generators of Electricity,* COM (88) 225.

Commission of the European Communities (1988d) *An Internal Market for Energy,* COM (88) 234.

Commission of the European Communities (1988e) *The Internal Energy Market,* COM (88) 238.

Commission of the European Communities (1988f) *Review of the Community Oil Industry,* COM (88) 491.

Commission of the European Communities (1988g) *Report on the Application of the Community Rules for State Aid to the Coal Industry in 1987,* COM (88) 541.

Commission of the European Communities (1988h) *Completing the Internal Market: An area without internal frontiers,* COM (88) 650.

Commission of the European Communities (1988i) *Research on the Cost of Non-Europe: Basic findings,* 16 vols (the Cecchini Report).

Commission of the European Communities (1988j) *22nd General Report of the Activities of the European Communities.*

Commission of the European Communities (1988k) *Community R&TD Programmes,* special issue.

Commission of the European Communities (1988l) *Commission Directive on Competition in Telecommunications Terminal Equipment,* 88/301.

Commission of the European Communities (1989a) *Transparency in Energy Prices*, COM (89) 123.

Commission of the European Communities (1989b) *Energy in Europe.*

Commission of the European Communities (1989c) *ESPRIT Workprogramme.*

Commission of the European Communities (1989d) *A Framework for Community R&D Actions in the 90s.*

Commission of the European Communities (1989e) *Guide to the Reform of the Community's Structural Funds.*

Commission of the European Communities (1989f) *Survey of State Aids*, Office for Official Publications of the European Communities.

Commission of the European Communities (1989g) *Communication on a Community Railway Policy*, COM (89) 564.

Commission of the European Communities (1989h) *Energy and the Environment*, COM (89) 369.

Commission of the European Communities (1990a) *Second Survey on State Aids in the EC in Manufacturing and Certain Other Sectors.*

Commission of the European Communities (1990b) 'The impact of the internal market by industrial sector', *European Economy*, special edition.

Commission of the European Communities (1990c) 'One market, one money: an evaluation of the potential benefits and costs of forming an economic and monetary union', *European Economy.*

Commission of the European Communities (1990d) *Second Survey of State Aids*, Office for Official Publications of the European Community.

Commission of the European Communities (1990e) *Industrial Policy in an Open and Competitive Environment*, COM (90) 556.

Commission of the European Communities (1990f) *Commission Directive on Competition in the Markets for Telecommunications Services*, 90/388.

Commission of the European Communities (1991a) *The Regions in the 1990s: Fourth Periodic Report on the Social and Economic Situation and Development of the Regions of the Community.*

Commission of the European Communities (1991b) *Europe 2000: Outlook for the Development of the Community's Territory*, Communication from the Commission to the Council and European Parliament, Brussels–Luxemburg.

Commission of the European Communities (1991c) *Twentieth Report on Competition Policy.*

Commission of the European Communities (1991d) *Communication from the Commission to the Council on the European Energy Charter*, COM (91) 36.

Commission of the European Communities (1991e) *Opening up the Internal Market.*

Commission of the European Communities (1991f) *European Economy.*

Commission of the European Communities (1992a) *Community Structural Policies: Assessment and outlook*, COM (92) 84 final.

Commission of the European Communities (1992b) *From the Single Act to Maastricht and Beyond: The means to match our ambitions*, COM (92) 2000 final.

Commission of the European Communities (1992c) *The Community's Finances Between Now and 1997*, COM (92) 2001 final.

Commission of the European Communities (1992d) *Third Survey of State Aids*, Office for Official Publications of the European Communities.

Commission of the European Communities (1992e) *Transport and the Environment – Towards sustainable mobility*, COM (92) 80.

Commission of the European Communities (1992f) *21st Report on Competition Policy 1991*, Office of Official Publications of the European Communities.

Commission of the European Communities (1992g) *The Future Development of the Common Transport Policy*, COM (92) 494.

Commission of the European Communities (1992h) *The European Maritime Industries*, COM (92) 490.

Commission of the European Communities (1992i) *Proposal for a Council Directive Concerning Common Rules for the Internal Market in Electricity*, COM (91) 548.

Commission of the European Communities (1992j) *A Community Strategy to Limit Carbon Dioxide Emissions and to Improve Energy Efficiency*, COM (92) 246.

Commission of the European Communities (1992k) 'A view to the future', in *Energy in Europe*, special edition.

Commission of the European Communities (1992l) *Report of the Committee of Independent Experts on Company Taxation*.

Commission of the European Communities (1993a) *European Economy: the European Community as a World Trade Partner*.

Commission of the European Communities (1993b) *Growth Competitiveness, Employment – the Challenges and Ways Forward into the 20th Century*.

Commission of the European Communities (1994) *For a European Union Energy Policy – Green Paper*, COM (94) 659.

Commission of the European Communities (1995a) *A Common Policy on the Organisation of the Inland Waterway Transport Market and Supporting Measures*, COM (95) 199.

Commission of the European Communities (1995b) *Action Programme and Timetable for Implementation of the Action Announced in the Communication on an Industrial Competitiveness Policy for the European Union*, COM (95) 87.

Commission of the European Communities (1995c) *An Energy Policy for the European Union – White Paper of the European Commission*, COM (95) 682.

Commission of the European Communities (1995d) *Citizens Network*, COM (95) 601.

Commission of the European Communities (1995e) *Communication on a common policy on the Organisation of the Inland Waterway Transport Market and Supporting Measures*, COM (95) 199.

Commission of the European Communities (1995f) *Green Paper on Innovation*, COM (95) 688.

Commission of the European Communities (1995g) *High Speed Europe*.

Commission of the European Communities (1995h) *Short Sea Shipping*.

Commission of the European Communities (1995i) *The Citizens' Network Fulfilling the Potential of Public Passenger Transport in Europe, European Commission Green Paper*, COM (95) 601.

Commission of the European Communities (1995j) *The Common Transport Policy Action Programme 1995–2000*, COM (95) 302.

Commission of the European Communities (1995k) *The Development of Short Sea Shipping in Europe*, COM (95) 317.

Commission of the European Communities (1995l) *The Development of the Community's Railways*, COM (95) 337.

Commission of the European Communities (1995m) *Trans European Networks*.

Commission of the European Communities (1995n) *Green Paper Towards Fair and Efficient Pricing in Transport*, COM (95) 691.

Commission of the European Communities (1996a) *Benchmarking of the Competitiveness of European Industry*, COM (96) 463.

Commission of the European Communities (1996b) *Energy for the Future. Renewable Sources of Energy – Green Paper for a Community Strategy*, COM (96) 576.

Commission of the European Communities (1996c) *Impact of the Third Package of Air Transport Liberalisation Measures*, COM (96) 514.

Commission of the European Communities (1996d) *Proposal for a Council Decision Concerning the Organisation of Cooperation Around Agreed Community Energy Policy Objectives*, COM (96) 431.

Commission of the European Communities (1996e) *Report from the Commission on the Application of the Community Rules on Aid to the Coal Industry in 1994*, COM (96) 575.

Commission of the European Communities (1996f) *Services of General Interest in Europe*, COM (96) 443.

Commission of the European Communities (1996g) *The First Action Plan for Innovation in Europe*, COM (96) 589.

Commission of the European Communities (1996h) *The Situation of Oil Supply Refining and Markets in the European Community*, COM (96) 143.

Commission of the European Communities (1996i) *Towards a New Maritime Strategy*, COM (96) 81.

Commission of the European Communities (1996j) *Towards an International Framework of Competition Rules*, COM (96) 284.

Commission of the European Communities (1996k) *White Paper – a Strategy for Revitalising the Community's Railways*, COM (96) 421.

Commission of the European Communities (1996l) *Research and Technological Development Activities of the European Union Annual Report 1996*, COM (96) 437.

Commission of the European Communities (1997a) *An Overall View of Energy Policy and Actions*, COM (97) 167.

Commission of the European Communities (1997b) *Fifth Survey on State Aid in the European Union in the Manufacturing and Certain Other Sectors*, COM (97) 170.

Commission of the European Communities (1997c) *Towards the Fifth Framework Programme: Scientific and Technological Objectives*, COM (97) 47.

Commission of the European Communities (1997d) *Results of the Altener Programme*, COM (97) 122.

Commission of the European Union (1995) *Competitiveness and Cohesion: Fifth periodic report on the social and economic situation in the regions of the community*, Office for Official Publications of the European Communities.

Commission of the European Union (1996a) *First Cohesion Report*, COM(96) final, Brussels.

Commission of the European Union (1996b) *The Structural Funds and Cohesion Fund 1994–1999*, CEU, Brussels.

Commission of the European Union (1996c) 'The 1996 single market review', *Commission Staff Working Paper*, SEC(96)2378, Brussels.

Commission of the European Union (1996d) 'Green paper on relations between the European Union and the ACP countries on the eve of the 21st century', CEU/DG VIII, Brussels.

Commission of the European Union (1996e) *XXVth Report on Competition Policy 1995*, CEU.

Commission of the European Union (1997) *Agenda 2000: For A Stronger and Wider Union*, Brussels, July.

Commission of the European Union (1997b) *XXVIth Report on Competition Policy 1996*, CEU.

Commission of the European Union (1997c) *Report on the Competitiveness of European Industry*, CEU.

Community of European Railways (1988) *Towards a European High Speed Rail Network*, Paris, CER.

Community of European Railways (1995) *High Speed Europe*.

Congress of the United States, Office of Technology Assessment (1991) *Competing Economies America, Europe and the Pacific Rim*.

Congress of the United States, Office of Technology Assessment (1992) *Competing Economies*, USGPO.

Congressional Budget Office (USA) (1987) *The GATT Negotiations and US Trade Policy*.

Coombes, D. (1970) *Politics and Bureaucracy in the European Community*, Allen & Unwin.

Cooper, C. A. and Massell, B. F. (1965a) 'A new look at customs union theory', *Economic Journal*, vol. 75.

Cooper, C. A. and Massell, B. F. (1965b) 'Towards a general theory of customs unions in developing countries', *Journal of Political Economy*, vol. 73.

Corbett, H. (1979) 'Tokyo Round: twilight of a liberal era or a new dawn?', *National Westminster Quarterly Review*, February.

Corden, W. M. (1965) 'Recent developments in the theory of international trade', *Special Papers in International Finance*, Princeton University Press.

Corden, W. M. (1972a) 'Economies of scale and customs union theory', *Journal of Political Economy*, vol. 80.

Corden, W. M. (1972b) 'Monetary integration', *Essays in International Finance*, no. 93, Princeton University.

Corden, W. M. (1973) 'The adjustment problem', in L. B. Krause and W. S. Salant (eds), *European Monetary Unification and Its Meaning for the United States*, The Brookings Institution, Washington.

Corden, W. M. (1974) *Trade Policy and Economic Welfare*, Oxford University Press.

Corden, W. M. (1976) 'Monetary union', *Trade Policy Research Centre Paper on International Issues*, no. 2, December.

Corden, W. M. (1977) *Inflation, Exchange Rates and the World Economy*, Oxford University Press.

Corden, W. M. (1988) 'Trade policy and macroeconomic balance in the world economy', *IMF Working Paper*, November.

Corden, W. M. (1997) *Trade Policy and Economic Welfare*, Oxford University Press.

Cosgrave, C. A. (1969) 'The EEC and developing countries', in G. R. Denton (ed.), *Economic Integration in Europe*, Weidenfeld & Nicolson.

Cosgrove Twitchett, C. (1978) *Europe and Africa: From association to partnership*, Saxon House.

Cosgrove Twitchett, C. (ed.) (1981) *Harmonisation in the EEC*, Macmillan.

Council of the European Communities (various years) *Review of the Council's Work*.

Council of the European Communities (1986) *Report by the Chairman of the Fiscal Borders Abolition ad hoc Group*.

Council of the European Communities (1990) *Council Directive of 28th October 1990 on the Transit of Electricity Through Transmission Grids (90/547/EEC)*.

Council of the European Communities (1991) *Council Directive on the Development of the Community's Railways, 91/440*.

Cowling, K. (1989) 'New directions for industrial policy', in Cowling, K. and Tomann, H., *Industrial Policy After 1992*, Anglo-German Foundation for the Study of Industrial Society.

Cowling, K. and Tomann, H. (1989) *Industrial Policy After 1992*, Anglo-German Foundation for the Study of Industrial Society.

Cox, A. W. (ed.) (1982) *Politics, Policy and the European Recession*, Macmillan.

Crouch, C. and Marquand, D. (1992) *Towards Greater Europe: A continent without an Iron Curtain*, Basil Blackwell.

Crowley, J. (1992) 'Inland transport in the European Community following 1992', *The Antitrust Bulletin*, vol. 37, no. 2.

Cruickshank, A. and Walker, W. (1981) 'Energy research development and demonstration policy in the European Communities', *Journal of Common Market Studies*, vol. 20, no. 1.

Culem, C. G. (1988) 'The locational determinants of direct investment among industrialised countries', *European Economic Review*, vol. 32.

Cunningham, S. and Young, J. A. (1983) 'The EEC Fisheries Policy: retrospect and prospect', *National Westminster Bank Quarterly Review*, May.

Curzon, G. and Curzon, V. (1971) 'New-colonialism and the European Community', *Yearbook of World Affairs*, Institute of World Affairs, London.

Curzon, G. and Curzon Price, V. (1987) 'Follies in European trade relations with Japan', *World Economy*, June.

Curzon, G. and Curzon Price, V. (1989) 'The GATT, non-discrimination principles and the rise of "material reciprocity" in international trade', mimeo, Collège de Bruges.

Curzon Price, V. (1974) *The Essentials of Economic Integration*, Macmillan.

Curzon Price, V. (1981) *Industrial Policies in the European Community*, Macmillan for the Trade Policy Research Centre.

Curzon Price, V. (1982) 'The European Free Trade Association', in A. M. El-Agraa (ed.), *International Economic Integration*, Macmillan.

Curzon Price, V. (1988) '1992: Europe's last chance? From Common Market to single market', *Occasional Paper*, no. 81, Institute of Economic Affairs, London.

Cuthbertson, K. *et al.* (1980) 'Modelling and forecasting the capital account of the balance of payments: a critique of the "Reduced Form Approach",' *National Institute Discussion Paper*, no. 37.

Daintith, T. and Hancher, K. (eds.) (1986) *Energy Strategy in Europe: The legal framework*, de Gruyter.

Dam, K. W. (1970) *The GATT: Law and international economic organization*, Chicago University Press.

Daniel, P. (1984) 'Interpreting mutual interest: non-fuel minerals in EEC–ACP relations', in C. Stevens (ed.), *EEC and the Third World: A survey. 4: Regenerating Lomé*, London.

Dauphin, R. (1978) *The Impact of Free Trade in Canada*, Economic Council of Canada, Ottawa.

Davenport, M. (1986) *Trade Policy, Protectionism and the Third World*, Croom Helm.

Davenport, M. (1992) 'Africa and the unimportance of being preferred', *Journal of Common Market Studies*, vol. 29.

Davenport, M., Hewitt, A. and Koning, A. (1995) *Europe's Preferred Partners*, Overseas Development Institute, London.

Davies, E. *et al.* (1989) *1992 Myths and Realities*, Centre for Business Strategy, London.

Davies, G. (1982) 'The EMS: its achievements and failures', *Special Analysis*, Simon & Coates.

Dayal, R. and Dayal, N. (1977) 'Trade creation and trade diversion: new concepts, new methods of measurement', *Weltwirtschaftliches Archiv*, vol. 113.

Deacon, D. (1982) 'Competition policy in the Common Market: its links with regional policy', *Regional Studies*, vol. 16, no. 1.

De Grauwe, P. (1973) *Monetary Interdependence and International Monetary Reform*, Saxon House.

De Grauwe, P. (1975) 'Conditions for monetary integration: a geometric interpretation', *Weltwirtschaftliches Archiv*, vol. 111.

De Grauwe, P. and Peeters, T. (1978) 'The European Monetary System after Bremen: technical and conceptual problems', paper delivered to the International Economics Study Group at the London School of Economics and Political Science.

De Grauwe, P. and Peeters, T. (1979) 'The EMS, Europe and the Dollar', *The Banker*, April.

De Vries, T. (1980) 'On the meaning and futures of the EMS', *Essays in International Finance*, no. 138, Princeton University.

Deaton, A. S. and Muellbauer, J. (1980a) 'An almost ideal demand system', *American Economic Review*, vol. 70.

Deaton, A. S. and Muellbauer, J. (1980b) *Economics and Consumer Behaviour*, Cambridge University Press.

Defrennes, M. (1996) 'The European nuclear industry in the context of the European Union', *Energy in Europe*, no. 27.

Degli Abbati, C. (1987) *Transport and European Integration*, Office for Official Publications of the European Community.

Dell, E. and Mayes, D. G. (1989) *1992 and Environment for European Industry*, Centre for European Policy Studies.

Demekas, D. G. *et al.* (1988) 'The effects of the Common Agricultural Policy for the European Community: A survey of the literature', *Journal of Common Market Studies*, vol. 27, no. 2.

Denison, E. F. (1967) *Why Growth Rates Differ: Post-war experience in nine Western countries*, The Brookings Institution, Washington.

Dennis, G. E. J. (1979) 'German monetary policy and the EMS', mimeo, December.

Dennis, G. E. J. (1981) 'The United Kingdom's monetary interdependence and membership of the European Monetary System', in J. P. Abraham and M. Van den Abeele (eds), *The European Monetary System and International Monetary Reform*, College of Europe, Brussels.

Dent, C. M. (1997) *The European Economy: The global context*, Routledge, London.

Denton, G. R. (ed.) (1969) *Economic Integration in Europe*, Weidenfeld & Nicolson.

Denton, G. R. (ed.) (1974) *Economic and Monetary Union in Europe*, Croom Helm.

Denton, G. R. (1981) 'How can the EEC help to solve the energy problem?', *The Three Banks Review*, March.

Department of Industry (1982) *Inward Investment and the IIB 1977–82*.

Deringer, A. (1964) 'The interpretation of Article 90(2) of the EEC Treaty', *Common Market Law Review*, vol. 2, no. 2.

Deutsche Bundesbank (1979) 'The European Monetary System', *Deutsche Bank Monthly Bulletin*, March.

Diebold, W. (1959) *The Shuman Plan: A study in economic cooperation, 1950–1959*, Praeger.

Diebold, W. (1980) *Industrial Policy as an International Issue*, McGraw-Hill.

Digby, C., Smith, M. A. M. and Venables, A. (1988) 'Counting the cost of voluntary export restrictions in the European car market', *Discussion Paper Series*, no. 249, Centre for Economic Policy Research.

Dixit, A. (1975) 'Welfare effects of tax and price changes', *Journal of Public Economics*, vol. 4.

Donges, J. B. *et al.* (1982) *The Second Enlargement of the Community: Adjustment requirements and challenges for policy reform*, Mohr.

Dore, R. and de Bauw (1995) *The European Energy Charter*, RIIA.

Dosser, D. (1966) 'The economic analysis of tax harmonisation', in C. S. Shoup (ed.), *Fiscal Harmonisation in Common Markets*, vol. 2, Columbia University Press.

Dosser, D. (1971) 'Taxation', in J. Pinder (ed.), *The Economics of Europe*, Knight.

Dosser, D. (1973) *British Taxation and the Common Market*, Knight.

Dosser, D. (1975) 'A federal budget for the Community', in B. Burrows *et al.* (eds), *Federal Solutions to European Issues*, Macmillan.

Dosser, D. and Hans, S. S. (1968) *Taxes in the EEC and Britain – the Problem of Harmonisation*, PEP/Institute of International Affairs.

Doyle, M. F. (1989) 'Regional policy and European economic integration', in *Report on Economic and Monetary Union in the European Community* (Delors Report), Commission of the European Communities, Luxemburg.

Dreyer, P. (1980) 'The outlook for steel', in Helleiner, G. K. *et al.*, *Protectionism or International Adjustment*, Atlantic Institute for International Affairs.

Deuchene, F. and Shepherd, G. (eds) (1987) *Managing Industrial Change in Western Europe*, Pinter.

Dunning, J. H. (1977) 'Trade, location of economic activity and the MNE: a search for an eclectic approach' in B. Ohlin *et al.* (eds), *The International Allocation of Economic Activity*, Macmillan.

Dunning, J. H. (1982) 'Explaining the internal direct investment position of countries: towards a dynamic or developmental approach', in J. Black and J. H. Dunning (eds), *International Capital Movements*, Macmillan.

Economic and Social Committee of the European Communities (1977) *EEC's Transport Problems with East European Countries*, EC Commission.

The Economist Intelligence Unit (1957) *Britain and Europe*, The Economist.

The Economist (1973) 'Europe and Britain's regions', *The Economist*, vol. 247, no. 6765, pp. 55–60.

Edwards, G. and Wallace, H. (1977) *The Council of Ministers of the European Community and the President-in-Office*, Federal Trust, London.

Eeckhout, J. C. (1975) 'Towards a common Europe industrial policy', *Irish Banking Review*, December.

EFTA Secretariat (1968) *The Effects on Prices of Tariff Dismantling in EFTA*.

EFTA Secretariat (1969) *The Effects of the EFTA on the Economies of Member States*.

EFTA Secretariat (1972) *The Trade Effects of the EFTA and the EEC 1959–1967*.

Ehlermann, C. D. (1993) 'Managing monopolies: the role of the state in controlling market dominance in the European Community', *European Competition Law Review*, vol. 14, no. 2.

El-Agraa, A. M. (1978) 'On trade creation' and 'On trade diversion', *Leeds Discussion Papers*, nos 66 and 67, University of Leeds, School of Economic Studies.

El-Agraa, A. M. (1979a) 'Common markets in developing countries', in J. K. Bowers (ed.), *Inflation, Development and Integration: Essays in honour of A. J. Brown*, Leeds University Press.

El-Agraa, A. M. (1979b) 'On tariff bargaining', *Bulletin of Economic Research*, vol. 31.

El-Agraa, A. M. (1979c) 'On optimum tariffs, retaliation and international cooperation', *Bulletin of Economic Research*, vol. 31.

El-Agraa, A. M. (1981) 'Tariff bargaining: a correction', *Bulletin of Economic Research*, vol. 33.

El-Agraa, A. M. (1982a) 'Professor Godley's proposition: a theoretical appraisal', *Leeds Discussion Papers*, no. 105.

El-Agraa, A. M. (1982b) 'Professor Godley's proposition: a macroeconomic appraisal', *Leeds Discussion Papers*, no. 113.

El-Agraa, A. M. (ed.) (1982c) *International Economic Integration*, Macmillan.

El-Agraa, A. M. (1982d) 'Comments on Rybczynski', in M. T. Sumner and G. Zis (eds), *European Monetary Union*, Macmillan.

El-Agraa, A. M. (ed.) (1983a) *Britain within the European Community: The way forward*, Macmillan.

El-Agraa, A. M. (1983b) *The Theory of International Trade*, Croom Helm.

El-Agraa, A. M. (1984a) 'Is membership of the EEC a disaster for the UK?', *Applied Economics*, vol. 17, no. 1.

El-Agraa, A. M. (1984b) *Trade Theory and Policy: Some topical issues*, Macmillan.

El-Agraa, A. M. (ed.) (1987) *Conflict, Cooperation, Integration and Development: Essays in honour of Professor Hiroshi Kitamura*, Macmillan and St Martin's.

El-Agraa, A. M. (1988a) *Japan's Trade Frictions: Realities or Misconceptions?*, Macmillan and St Martin's.

El-Agraa, A. M. (ed.) (1988b) *International Economic Integration*, second edition, Macmillan and St Martin's.

El-Agraa, A. M. (1989a) *The Theory and Measurement of International Economic Integration*, Macmillan and St Martin's.

El-Agraa, A. M. (1989b) *International Trade*, Macmilland and St Martin's.

El-Agraa, A. M. (1990) 'EC Budgetary politics: the rationality of the EC Commission being undermined by the irrationality of the member nations', *Review of Commercial Sciences*, vol. 38, no. 2.

El-Agraa, A. M. (1995) 'VERs as a prominent feature of Japanese trade policy: their rationale, costs and benefits', *The World Economy*, vol. 18.

El-Agraa, A. M. (1997) *Economic Integration Worldwide*, Macmillan and St Martin's.

El-Agraa, A. M. and Goodrich, P. S. (1980) 'Factor mobility with specific reference to the accounting profession', in A. M. El-Agraa (ed.), *The Economics of the European Community*, first edition, Philip Allan, Chapter 16.

El-Agraa, A. M. and Jones, A. J. (1981) *The Theory of Customs Unions*, Philip Allan.

El-Agraa, A. M. and Majocchi, A. (1983) 'Devising a proper fiscal stance for the EC', *Revista Di Diritto Finznziario E Scienza Delle Finanze*, vol. 17, no. 3.

Ellis, F., Marsh, J. and Ritson, C. (1973) *Farmers and Foreigners – The impact of the Common Agricultural Policy on the associates and associables*, Overseas Development Institute, London.

Emerson, M. (1979) 'The European Monetary System in the broader setting of the Community's economic and political development', in P. H. Trezise (ed.), *The European Monetary System: Its promise and prospects*, Brookings Institution, Washington.

Emerson, M. (1988) 'The economics of 1992', *European Economy*, no. 35.

Emerson, M. and Dramais, A. (1988) *What Model for Europe?*, MIT Press.

Emerson, M. et al. (1988) *The Economics of 1992: The EC Commission's assessment of the economic effects of completing the internal market*, Oxford University Press.

Emmiger, O. (1979) 'The exchange rate as an instrument of policy', *Lloyds Bank Review*, July.

Erdmenger, J. (1983) *The European Community Transport Policy: Towards a common transport policy*, Gower.

ESPRIT Review Board (1985) *The Mid-term Review of ESPRIT*, EC Commission.

Ethier, W. and **Bloomfield, A. J.** (1975) 'Managing the managed float', *Essays in International Finance*, no. 122, Princeton University.

European Economy (1982) 'Documents relating to the European Monetary System', no. 12, July.

European Economy (1996) 'Economic evaluation of the internal market', *Reports and Studies*, no. 4.

European Investment Bank (1981) *Annual Report 1980*.

European Parliament (1980) *European Taxation 1980/81*, Energy Commission.

European Parliament (1986) 'Report on the relations between the European Community and the Council for Mutual Economic Assistance', DOC AZ187/86, 19 December.

European Parliament (1993) 'The economic impact of dumping and the community's anti-dumping policy', *EP Directorate General for Research Working Papers*, Economic Series E-1, Luxemburg.

European Round Table (1985) *Missing Links*, ERT.

Eurostat (annual) *Basic Statistics of the Community*.

Eurostat (annual) *Statistical Review*.

Eurostat (1980) *Review 1970–1979*, EC Commission.

Eurostat (1982) *Farm Accountancy Data Network*, microfiche.

Eurostat (1995) *Panorama of EU Industry 1995/96*, Luxemburg.

Eurostat (1997) 'External and intra-EU trade', *Monthly Statistics*, Luxemburg.

Farrands, C. (1983) 'External relations: textile politics and the Multi-Fiber Arrangement', in H. Wallace, *et al.*, *Policy Making in the European Community*, second edition, John Wiley.

Federal Reserve Bank of New York (1981) *Quarterly Review*, Summer.

Federal Trust (1974) *Economic Union in the EEC*, Federal Trust.

Fee, D. (1992) 'A new proposal in the framework of the Save Programme to limit carbon dioxide emissions by improving energy efficiency', *Energy in Europe*, no. 20.

Fennell, R. (1979) *The Common Agricultural Policy of the European Community*, Granada.

Fielding, L. (1991) 'Europe as a global partner', *UACES Occasional Paper*, no. 7.

Finger, J. M. and **Olechowski, A.** (1987) *The Uruguay Round: A handbook on the multilateral trade negotiations*, World Bank.

Finon, D. (1990) 'Opening access to European grids in search of common ground', *Energy Policy*, vol. 18, no. 5.

Finon, D. and **Surèy, J.** (1996) 'Does energy policy have a future in the European Union', in F. McGowan, *Energy Policy in a Changing Environment,* Physica Verlag.

Fitzmaurice, J. (1988) 'An analysis of the European Community's Co-operation Procedure', *Journal of Common Market Studies*, vol. 26, no. 4.

Fleming, J. M. (1971) 'On exchange rate unification', *Economic Journal*, vol. 81.

Flockton, C. (1970) *Community Regional Policy*, Chatham House.

Fogarty, M. (1975) *Work and Industrial Relations in the European Community*, Chatham House/PEP.

Foot, M. D. (1979) 'Monetary targets; nature and record in the major economies', in B. Griffiths and G. Wood, *Monetary Targets*, Macmillan.

Forsyth, M. (1980) *Reservicing Britain*, Adam Smith Institute, London.

Forte, F. (1977) 'Principles for the assignment of public economic functions in a setting of multi-layer government', in Commission of the European Communities, *Report of the Study Group on the Role of Public Finance in European Integration*, vol. II (the MacDougall Report).

Francioni, F. (1992) *Italy and EC Membership Evaluated*, Pinter.

Franzmeyer, F. *et al.* (1991) *The Regional Impact of Community Policies*, Regional Policy and Transport Series 17, European Parliament.

Frazer, T. (1992) *Monopoly, Competition and the Law: the regulation of business activity in Britain, Europe and America*, second edition, Harvester/Wheatsheaf.

Freeman, R. B. (1995) 'Are your wages set in Beijing?', *Journal of Economic Perspectives*, vol. 9.

Freeman, C. and Oldman, C. (1991) 'Introduction: beyond the Common Market', in C. Freeman, M. Sharp and W. Walker (eds), *Technology and the Future of Europe; Global competition and the environment in the 1990s*, Pinter.

Freeman, C., Sharp, M. and Walker, W. (eds) (1991) *Technology and the Future of Europe: Global competition and the environment in the 1990s*, Pinter.

Friedman, M. (1975) *Unemployment versus Inflation? An Evaluation of the Philips Curve*, Institute of International Affairs (London).

Gandia, D. M. (1981) *The EEC's Generalised System of Preferences and the Yaounde and Other Agreements*, Allenhead, Osmun & Co.

Gatsios, K. and Seabright, P. (1989) 'Regulation in the European Community', *Oxford Review of Economic Policy*, vol. 5, no. 2.

GATT (1991) *Trade Policy Review: The European Communities*, vols I and II.

GATT (1993) *Trade Policy Review: The European Communities*, Geneva.

GATT (1994) *Market Access for Goods and Services: Overview of the Results*, Geneva.

Gehrels, F. (1956–7) 'Customs unions from a single country viewpoint', *Review of Economic Studies*, vol. 24.

George, K. (1990) 'UK competition policy: issues and institutions', in W. S. Comanor *et al.* (eds), *Competition Policy in Europe and North America: Economic issues and institutions*, Harwood Academic.

George K. and Jacquemin, A. (1990) 'Competition policy in the European Community', in W. S. Comano *et al.* (eds), *Competition Policy in Europe and North America: Economic issues and institutions*, Harwood Academic.

George, K. D. and Joll, C. (eds) (1975) *Competition Policy in the United Kingdom and the European Economic Community*, Cambridge University Press.

Geroski, P. A. (1989a) 'European industrial policy and industrial policy in Europe', *Oxford Review of Economic Policy*, vol. 5, no. 2.

Geroski, P. A. (1989b) 'The choice between diversity and scale', in E. Davis *et al.* (eds) *1992 Myths and Realities*, Centre for Business Strategy.

Geroski, P. A. (1990) 'Procurement policy as a tool of industrial policy', *International Review of Applied Economics*, vol. 4, no. 2.

Giavazzi, F. and Pagano, M. (1986) 'The advantage of tying one's hands: EMS discipline and central bank credibility', *European Economic Review*, vol. 28.

Giavazzi, F., Micossi, S. and Miller, M. (eds) (1988) *The European Monetary System*, Cambridge University Press.

Giersch, H. *et al.* (1975) 'A currency for Europe', *The Economist*, 1 November.

Gilchrist, J. and Deacon, D. (1990) 'Curbing subsidies', in P. Montagnon (ed.), *European Competition Policy*, RIIA.

Gillingham, J. (1991) *Coal, Steel, and the Rebirth of Europe, 1945–1955: The Germans and French from Ruhr conflict to economic community*, Cambridge University Press.

Godley, W. (1980a) 'Britain and Europe', *Cambridge Economic Policy Review*, vol. 6, no. 1.

Godley, W (1980b) 'The United Kingdom and the Community Budget', in W. Wallace (ed.), *Britain in Europe*, Heinemann, Chapter 4.

Godley, W. and Bacon, R. (1979) 'Policies of the EEC', *Cambridge Economic Policy Review*, vol. 1, no. 5.

Gourevitch, P. (1986) *Politics in Hard Times*, Cornell University Press.

Gramlich, E. (1994) 'Infrastructure investment', *Journal of Economic Literature*, vol. 32.

Grant, W. (1982) *The Political Economy of Industrial Policy*, Butterworth.

Grant, W. and Sargent, J. (1987) *Business and Politics in Britain*, Macmillan.

Graubard, S. (ed.) (1964) *A New Europe?*, Oldbourne Press.

Greenaway, D. and Hindley, B. (1985) 'What Britain pays for voluntary export restraints', *Thames Essays*, no. 43, Trade Policy Research Centre.

Grilli, E. R. (1993) *The European Community and the Developing Countries*, Cambridge University Press.

Grinols, E. L. (1984) 'A thorn in the lion's paw: has Britain paid too much for Common Market membership?', *Journal of International Economics*, vol. 16.

Guieu, P. and **Bonnet, C.** (1987) 'Completion of the internal market and indirect taxation', *Journal of Common Market Studies*, vol. 25, no. 3.

Guruswamy, I. D., Papps, I. and **Storey, D.** (1983) 'The development and impact of an EC directive: the control of discharges of mercury to the aquatic environment', *Journal of Common Market Studies*, vol. 22, no. 1.

Guy, K. *et al.* (1991) *Evaluation of the Alvey Programme for Advanced Information Technology*, HMSO.

Gwilliam, K. M. (1980) 'Realism and the common transport policy of the EEC', in J. B. Polak and J. B. van der Kemp (eds), *Changes in the Field of Transport Studies*, Martinus Nijhoff.

Gwilliam, K. M. (1985) 'The Transport Infrastructure Policy of the EEC', in S. Klatt (ed.), *Perspektwm verkehrswissenschaftlicher Forshung: Festschrift für Fritz Voigt*, Berlin.

Gwilliam, K. M. and **Allport, R. J.** (1982) 'A medium term transport research strategy for the EEC – Part 1: context and issues', *Transport Review*, no. 3.

Gwilliam, K. M. and **Mackie, P. J.** (1975) *Economics of Transport Policy*, Allen & Unwin.

Gwilliam, K. M., Petriccione, S., Voigt, F. and **Zighera, J. A.** (1973) 'Criteria for the coordination of investments in transport infractructure', *EEC Studies, Transport Series*, no. 3.

Haas, E. B. (1958 and 1968) *The Uniting of Europe*, Stevens.

Haas, E. B. (1967) 'The uniting of Europe and the uniting of Latin America', *Journal of Common Market Studies*, vol. 5.

Haberler, G. (1964) 'Integration and growth in the world economy in historical perspective', *American Economic Review*, vol. 54.

Hager, W. (1982) 'Industrial policy, trade policy and European social democracy', in J. Pinder (ed.), *National Industrial Strategies and the World Economy*, Croom Helm.

Haigh, N. (1987) *EEC Environmental Policy and Britain*, second edition, Longman.

Hall, R. and **Van Der Wee, D.** (1992) 'Community regional policy for the 1990s', *Regional Studies*, vol. 26.

Han, S. S. and **Leisner, H. H.** (1970) 'Britain and the Common Market', *Occasional Paper*, no. 27, Department of Applied Economics, University of Cambridge.

Hancher, L and **van Slot, P.** (1990) 'Article 90', *European Competition Law Review*, vol. 11, no. 1.

Hansard (1972), vol. 831, 15 February.

Hansen, N. M. (1977) 'Border regions: a critique of spatial theory and a European case study', *Annals of Regional Science*, vol. XI, no. 1.

Hardach, K. W. (1980) *The Political Economy of Germany in the Twentieth Century*, University of California Press.

Hart, J. (1992) *Rival Capitalists*, Cornell University Press.

Hayek, F. A. (1989) *The Fatal Conceit*, University of Chicago Press.

Hazlewood, A. (1967) *African Integration and Disintegration*, Oxford University Press.

Hazlewood, A. (1975) *Economic Integration: the East African Experience*, Heinemann.

Heidensohn, K. (1995) *Europe and World Trade*, Pinter, London.

Heidhues, T. *et al.* (1978) *Common Prices and Europe's Farm Policies*, Thames Essays, no. 14, Trade Policy Research Centre.

Heitger, B. and **Stehn, J.** (1990) 'Japanese direct investment in the EC: response to the internal market 1993?', *Journal of Common Market Studies*, vol. 29.

Helleiner, G. K. *et al.* (1980) *Protectionism or International Adjustment*, Atlantic Institute for International Affairs.

Hellman, R. (1977) *Gold, the Dollar and the European Currency System*, Praeger.

Helm, D. R. and **McGowan, F.** (1989) 'Electricity supply in Europe: lessons for the UK', in D. R. Helm, J. A. Kay and D. J. Thompson (eds), *The Market for Energy*, Oxford University Press.

Helm, D. R. and **Smith, S.** (1989) 'The assessment: integration and the role of the European Community', *Oxford Review of Economic Policy*, vol. 5, no. 2.

Helm, D. R., **Kay, J. A.** and **Thompson, D. J.** (eds) (1989) *The Market for Energy*, Oxford University Press.

Helpman, E. (1981) 'International trade in the presence of product differentiation, economies of scale and monopolistic competition', *Journal of International Economics*, vol. 11.

Henderson, D. (1989) *1992: The external dimension*, Group of Thirty, New York.

Henry, C. (1993) 'Public service and competition in the European Community approach to communications networks', *Oxford Review of Economic Policy*, vol. 9, no. 1.

Heseltine, M. (1989) *The Challenge of Europe: Can Britain win?*, Weidenfeld & Nicolson.

Hewitt, A. (1983) 'Stabex: analysing the effectiveness of an institution', in C. Stevens (ed.), *EEC and the Third World: a survey*, 3, *The Atlantic Rift*, Hodder & Stoughton.

Hill, C. and **Wallace, W.** (1979) 'Diplomatic trends in the European Community', *International Affairs*, January.

Hindley, B. (1974) *Theory of International Trade*, Weidenfeld & Nicolson.

Hindley, B. (1984) 'Empty economics in the case for industrial policy', *The World Economy*, vol. 7, no. 3.

Hindley, R. (1992) 'Trade policy of the European Community', in P. Minford (ed.), *The Cost of Europe*, Manchester University Press.

Hine, R. C. (1985) *The Political Economy of European Trade*, Wheatsheaf.

HMSO (1967) *Treaty Setting up the European Economic Community.* The original was published in Rome in 1957 by the EDC, and Sweet & Maxwell publish a regularly updated comprehensive set on the *European Community Treaties*.

HMSO (1985) *Employment: the Challenge to the Nation*, Cmnd. 9474.

Hocking, R. D. (1980) 'Trade in motor cars between the major European producers', *Economic Journal*, vol. 90.

Hodges, M. (ed.) (1972) *European Integration*, Penguin.

Hodges, M. (1977) 'Industrial policy: a directorate general in search of a role', in H. Wallace, W. Wallace and C. Webb (eds), *Policy-making in the European Communities*, John Wiley.

Hodges, M. (1983) 'Industrial policy: from hard times to great expectations', in H. Wallace, W. Wallace and C. Webb (eds), *Policy Making in the European Communities*, John Wiley.

Hoekman, B. and **Djankov, S.** (1996) 'Intra-industry, foreign direct investment and the reorientation of East European exports', *CEPR Discussion Paper*, no. 1377, Centre for Economic Policy Research, London.

Hoekman, B. and **Kostecki, M.** (1995) *The Political Economy of the World Trading System*, Oxford University Press.

Hofstadter, R. (1965) *The Paranoid Style in American Politics, and Other Essays*, Knopf.

Holland, S. (1976a) *The Regional Problem*, Macmillan.

Holland, S. (1976b) *Capital versus the Regions*, Macmillan.

Holland, S. (1980) *Uncommon Market: Capital, class and power in the European Community*, Macmillan.

Holloway, J. (1981) *Social Policy Harmonisation in the European Community*, Gower.

Holmes, P. and **Shepherd, G.** (1983) 'Protectionist policies of the EEC', paper presented to the International Economics Study Group conference at Sussex University.

House of Commons (1985) *The European Monetary System*, Select Committee on the Treasury and Civil Service, report of a sub-committee.

House of Commons (1987) *Indirect Taxes: Harmonisation*, Select Committee on European Legislation, Eighth Report, HMSO.

House of Lords (1983) *European Monetary System*, report of the Select Committee on the European Communities, Fifth Report, 1983–4, HMSO.

House of Lords (1985–6) 'Single European Act and parliamentary scrutiny', in *12th Report of the House of Lords Select Committee on the European Communities*, no. 149.

House of Lords (1992) *Enlargement of the Community*, Select Committee on the European Communities, Session 1991–2 10th Report, HL55, HMSO.

House of Lords Select Committee on the European Communities (1986) *European Maritime Transport Policy*, 9th Report, HL 106.

Hu, Y.-S. (1979) 'German agricultural power: the impact on France and Britain', *The World Today*, vol. 35.

Hufbauer, G. C. (1990) *Europe 1992: An American Perspective*, The Brookings Institution, Washington.

Hughes, M. (1982) 'The consequences of the removal of exchange controls on portfolios and the flow of funds in the UK', in D. C. Corner and D. G. Mayes (eds), *Modern Portfolio Theory and Financial Institutions*, Macmillan, Chapter 9.

Hughes, T. P. (1983) *Networks of Power*, Johns Hopkins.

Hull, C. (1979) 'The implication of direct elections for European Community regional policy', *Journal of Common Market Studies*, vol. 17, no. 4.

IFO (1990) *An Empirical Assessment of the Factors Shaping Regional Competitiveness in Problem Regions*, study carried out for the EC Commission.

Ingram, J. C. (1959) 'State and regional payments mechanisms', *Quarterly Journal of Economics*, vol. 73.

Ingram, J. C. (1962) 'A proposal for financial integration in the Atlantic Community', in *Factors Affecting the US Balance of Payments*, Joint Economic Committee Print, 87th Congress, 2nd Session, Washington.

Ingram, J. C. (1973) 'The case for European monetary integration', *Essays in International Finance*, no. 98, Princeton University.

International Coal Report, 1992.

International Energy Agency (1980) *Energy Policies and Programmes of IEA Countries, 1979 Review*, OECD.

International Energy Agency (1988a) *Coal Prospects and Policies in IEA Countries 1987*, IEA/OECD.

International Energy Agency (1988b) *Coal Information 1988*, IEA/OECD.

International Monetary Fund (various issues) *Balance of Payments Manual*.

International Monetary Fund (1974) *Guidelines for Floating Exchange Rates*, IMF, Washington.

International Monetary Fund (1979) 'The EMS', *IMF Survey*, Supplement.

International Monetary Fund (1989) *IMF Survey*.

International Monetary Fund (1991) *IMF Survey: The coming emergence of three grant trading blocks*, IMF, Washington.

Inukai, I. (1987) 'Regional integration and development in Eastern and Southern Africa', in A. M. El-Agraa (ed.), *Protection, Cooperation, Integration and Development: Essays in honour of Professor Hiroshi Kitamura*, Macmillan and St Martin's.

Irving, R. W. and **Fearne, H. A.** (1975) *Green Money and the Common Agricultural Policy*, Centre for European Agricultural Studies, Wye College, Ashford, Kent.

Ishikawa, K. (1990) *Japan and the Challenge of Europe 1992*, Printer Publishers.

Jacquemin, A. P. (1974) 'Application to foreign firms of European rules on competition', *The Antitrust Bulletin*, vol. 19, no. 1, Spring.

Jacquemin, A. P. (1988) 'Cooperative agreements in R&D and European antitrust policy', *European Economic Review*, vol. 32.

Jacquemin, A. (1990) 'Discussion of Neven's chapter', *Economic Policy*, April.

Jacquemin, A. P. and **de Jong, H. W.** (1977) *European Industrial Organisation*, Macmillan.

Jacquemin, A. and **Sapir, A.** (1991) 'Competition and imports in the European Market', in L. A. Winters and A. J. Venables (eds), *European Integration: Trade and Industry*, Cambridge University Press.

Janssen, L. H. (1961) *Free Trade, Protection and Customs Union*, Economisch Sociologisch Institut, Leiden.

Jenkins, R. (1977) 'Europe's present challenge and future opportunity', *Bulletin of the European Communities*, vol. 10.

Jenkins, R. (1978) 'European Monetary Union', *Lloyds Bank Review*, January.

Jenkins, R. (ed.) (1983) *Britain and the EEC*, Macmillan.

Jenny, F. (1990) 'French competition policy in perspective', in W. S. Comanor *et al.*, *Competition Policy in Europe and North America: Economic issues and institutions*, Harwood Academic.

Johnson, D. G. (1972) *World Agriculture in Disarray*, Macmillan, for the Trade Policy Research Centre.

Johnson, H. G. (1965a) 'Optimal trade intervention in the presence of domestic distortions', in R. E. Baldwin *et al.* (eds), *Trade, Growth and the Balance of Payments*, North-Holland.

Johnson, H. G. (1965b) 'An economic theory of protectionism, tariff bargaining and the formation of customs unions', *Journal of Political Economy*, vol. 73.

Johnson, H. G. (1971) *Aspects of the Theory of Tariffs*, Allen & Unwin.

Johnson, H. G. (1973) 'Problems of European Monetary Union', in M. B. Krauss (ed.), *The Economics of Integration*, Allen & Unwin.

Johnson, H. G. (1974) 'Trade diverting customs unions: a comment', *Economic Journal*, vol. 81.

Johnson, H. G. and **Krauss, M. B.** (1973) 'Border taxes, border tax adjustments, comparative advantage and the balance of payments', in M. B. Krauss (ed.), *The Economics of Integration*, Allen & Unwin.

Joilet, R. (1971) 'Resale price maintenance under EEC antitrust law', *The Antitrust Bulletin*, vol. 16, no. 3, Fall.

Jones, A. J. (1979) 'The theory of economic integration', in J. K. Bowers (ed.), *Inflation Development and Integration: Essays in honour of A. J. Brown*, Leeds University Press.

Jones, A. J. (1980) 'Domestic distortions and customs union theory', *Bulletin of Economic Research*, vol. 32.

Jones, A. J. (1982) 'A macroeconomic framework for customs union theory', *Leeds Discussion Papers*, no. 112.

Jones, A. J. (1983) 'Withdrawal from a customs union: a macroconomic analysis', in A. M. El-Agraa (ed.), *Britain within the European Community: The way forward*, Macmillan, Chapter 5.

Jones, K. (1983) 'Impasse and crisis in steel trade policy', *Thames Essay*, no. 35, Trade Policy Research Centre.

Jones, R. T. (1976) 'The relevance to the EEC of American experience with industrial property rights', *Journal of World Trade Law*, vol. 10, no. 6.

Jones, R. W. and **Raune, F.** (1990) 'Appraising the options for international trade in services', *Oxford Economic Papers*, vol. 42.

Josling, T. (1969) 'The Common Agricultural Policy of the European Economic Community', *Journal of Agricultural Economics*, May.

Josling, T. (1979a) 'Agricultural policy', in P. Coffey (ed.), *Economic Policies of the Common Market*, Macmillan, Chapter 1.

Josling, T. (1979b) 'Agricultural protection and stabilisation policies: analysis of current and neomercantilist practices', in J S, Hillman and A. Schmitz (eds), *International Trade and Agriculture: Theory and policy*, Westview Press.

Josling, T. and **Harris, W.** (1976) 'Europe's Green Money', *The Three Banks Review*, March

Josling, T. *et al.* (1972) *Burdens and Benefits of Farm-support Policies*, Trade Policy Centre, London.

Kaldor, N. (1966) *Causes of the Slow Rate of Economic Growth of the United Kingdom*, Cambridge University Press.

Kaldor, N. (1971) 'The dynamic effects of the Common Market', in D. Evans (ed.), *Destiny or Delusion: Britain and the Common Market*, Gollancz.

Katz, M. and **Ordover, J.** (1990) 'R&D cooperation and competition', *Brookings Papers on Economic Activity*, special issue.

Katzenstein, P. (ed.) (1989) *Industry and Politics in West Germany*, Cornell University Press.

Kay, J. A. and Keen, M. (1987) 'Alcohol and tobacco taxes: criteria for harmonisation', in S. Cnossen (ed.), *Tax Coordination in the European Community*, Kluwer.

Kay, J. A. and King, M. A. (1996) *The British Tax System*, Oxford University Press.

Kay, J. and Silbertson, A. (1984) 'The new industrial policy: privatisation and competition', *Midland Bank Review*, Spring.

Kelly, M. *et al.* (1988) 'Issues and developments in international trade policy', *Occasional Papers*, no. 63, IMF.

Kelman, S. (1981) *What Price Incentives?*, Auburn House.

Kenen, P. (1988) *Managing Exchange Rates*, Routledge.

Kern, D. (1978) 'An international comparison of major economic trends, 1958–76', *National Westminster Bank Quarterly Review*, May.

Kierzkowski, H. (1987) 'Recent advances in international trade theory', *Oxford Review of Economic Policy*, vol. 3, no. 1.

Kirchner, E. (1982) 'The European Community and the economic recession: 1973–79', in A. Cox (ed.), *Politics, Policy and the European Recession*, Macmillan.

Klou, F. and Mittlestädt (1986) 'Labour market flexibility', *OECD Economic Studies*.

Klodt, H. (1989) 'European integration: how much scope for national industrial policy', in K. Cowling and H.Tomann (eds), *Industrial Policy After 1992*, Anglo-German Foundation for the Study of Industrial Society.

Klom, A. (1996) 'Electricity deregulation in the European Union', *Energy in Europe*, no. 27, December.

Knox, F. (1972) *The Common Market and World Agriculture*, Praeger.

Koester, U. (1977) 'The redistributional effects of the Common Agricultural Financial System', *Economic Review of Agricultural Economics*, vol. 4, no. 4.

Kol, J. (1987) 'Exports from developing countries: some facts and scope', *European Economic Review*, vol. 29.

Korah, V. (1988) 'Research and development, joint ventures and the European Economic Community competition rules', *International Journal of Technology Management*, vol. 3, nos. 1/2.

Korah, V. (1990) *An Introductory Guide to EEC Competition Law and Practice*, ESC Publishing, fourth edition.

Kouevi, A. F. (1965) 'Essai d'application prospective de la methode RAS au commerce international', *Bulletin du CEPREL*, vol. 5.

Krause, L. B. (1962) 'US imports, 1947–58', *Econometrica*, April.

Krause, L. B. (1968) *European Economic Integration and the United States*, The Brookings Institution, Washington.

Krause, L. B. and Salant, W. S. (eds), (1973a) *European Economic Integration and the United States*, The Brookings Institution, Washington.

Krause, L. B. and Salant, W. S. (eds), (1973b) *European Monetary Unification and Its Meaning for the United States*, The Brookings Institution, Washington.

Krauss, M. B. (1972) 'Recent developments in customs union theory: an interpretative survey', *Journal of Economic Literature*, vol. 10.

Krauss, M. B. (ed.) (1973) *The Economics of Integration*, Allen & Unwin.

Kreinin, L. B. (1967) 'Trade arrangements among industrial countries', in B. Balassa (ed.), *Studies in Trade Liberalisation*, Johns Hopkins University Press.

Kreinin, M. E. (1961) 'The effects of tariff changes on the prices and volumes of imports', *American Economic Review*, vol. 51.

Kreinin, M. E. (1964) 'On the dynamic effects of a customs union', *Journal of Political Economy*, vol. 72.

Kreinin, M. E. (1969) 'Trade creation and diversion by the EEC and EFTA', *Economia Internazionale*, May.

Kreinin, M. E. (1972) 'Effects of the EEC on imports of manufactures', *Economic Journal*, vol. 82.

Kreinin, M. E. (1975) 'European integration and the developing countries', in B. Balassa (ed.), *European Economic Integration*, North Holland.

Kreinin, M. E. (1979) *International Economics: A policy approach*, Harcourt Brace Jovanovich (also subsequent editions).

Kreis, H. W. R. (1992) 'EC competition law and maritime transport', *The Antitrust Bulletin*, vol. 37, no. 2.

Kreuger, A. O. (1974) 'The political economy of the rent-seeking society', *American Economic Review*, vol. 64.

Krugman, P. R. (1979) 'Increasing returns, monopolistic competition and international trade', *Journal of International Economics*, vol. 9.

Krugman, P. R. (1983) New theories of trade among industrial countries', *AER Papers and Proceedings*, May.

Krugman, P. R. (1986) *Strategic Trade Policy and the New International Economics*, MIT Press.

Krugman, P. R. (1988) 'EFTA and 1992', *Occasional Papers*, no. 23, EFTA Secretariat.

Krugman, P. (1990) 'Policy problems of a monetary union', in P. de Grauwe and L. Papademos (eds), *The European Monetary System in the 1990s*, Longman, Harlow.

Kruse, D. C. (1980) *Monetary Integration in Western Europe: EMU, EMS and beyond*, Butterworth.

Kuhn, U., Seabright, P. and Smith, A. (1992) *Competition Policy Research*, CEPR.

Laidler, D. E. W. (1982) 'The case for flexible exchange rates in 1980', in M. T. Sumner and G. Zis (eds), *European Monetary Union: Progress and prospects*, Macmillan.

Laird, S. (1997) 'Quantifying commercial policies', in J. F. Francois and K. Reinert, *Applied Trade Policy Modelling: A handbook*, Cambridge University Press.

Laird, S. and Yeats, A. (1990a) 'Trends in nontariff barriers of developed countries, 1966–1986', *Weltwirtschaftliches Archiv*, vol. 126.

Laird, S. and Yeats, A. (1990b) *Quantitative Methods for Trade-barrier Analysis*, Macmillan.

Lamfalussy, A. (1963) 'Intra-European trade and the competitive position of the EEC', *Manchester Statistical Society Transactions*, March.

Lancaster, K. (1980) 'Intra-industry trade under monopolistic competition', *Journal of International Economics*, vol. 10.

Lange, O. (1938) *On the Economic Theory of Socialism*, Minnesota University Press.

Lantzke, U. (1976) 'International cooperation in energy', *The World Today*, March.

Larre, B. (1995) 'The impact of trade on labour markets: an analysis by industry', *OECD Jobs Study Working Paper*, OECD, Paris.

Laurent, P. (1996) 'Anti-dumping policies in a globalising world', European Commission DGI, Brussels.

Laury, J. S. E., Lewis, G. R. and Omerod, P. A. (1978) 'Properties of macroeconomic models of the UK economy: a comparative study', *National Institute Economic Review*, no. 83.

Layton, C. (1969) *European Advanced Technology: A programme for integration*, Allen & Unwin.

Leary, V. A. (1995) 'Workers' rights and international trade: the social clause', in J. Bhagwati and R. Hudec (eds), *Fair Trade and Harmonization: Prerequisites for free trade?*, MIT Press.

Lehner, S. and Meiklejohn, R. (1990) 'Fair competition in the Internal Market: Community state and policy', *European Economy*, no. 48.

Lenior, R. (1974) *Les Exclus: un Francais sur Dix*, Editions du Seuil.

Lévi-Sandri, L. (1968) 'Pour une politique sociale moderne dans la Communauté Européenne', reprint of speech to the European Parliament, March.

Lincoln, E. J. (1990) *Japan's Unequal Trade*, The Brookings Institution, Washington.

Lindberg, L. N. (1963) *The Political Dynamics of European Economic Integration*, Standford University Press.

Lindberg, L. N. and Scheingold, S. A. (1970) *Europe's Would-be Policy Patterns of Change in the European Community*, Prentice Hall.

Linnemann, H. (1966) *An Econometric Study of International Trade Flows*, North-Holland.

Lipgens, W. (1968) *Europa-Föderationspäne der Widerstandsbewegungen 1940–45*, R. Oldenbourg Verlag for the Forschungsinstitut der Deutschen Gesellschaft für Auswärtige Politik.

Lipgens, W. (1982) *A History of European Integration*, vol. 1, *1945–47: The formation of the European Unity Movement*, Clarendon Press.

Lippert, A. (1987) 'Independent generators and the public utilities', paper presented to the *Financial Times* World Electricity Conference.

Lippert, B. and Stevens-Strohmann, R. (1993) *German Unification and EC Integration*, RIIA.

Lipsey, R. G. (1957) 'The theory of customs unions, trade diversion and welfare', *Economica*, vol. 24.

Lipsey, R. G. (1960) 'The theory of customs unions: a general survey', *Economic Journal*, vol. 70.

Lipsey, R. G. (1975) *An Introduction to Positive Economics*, Weidenfeld & Nicolson.

Lipsey, R. G. (1977) 'Comments', in F. Machlup (ed.), *Economic Integration, Worldwide, Regional, Sectoral*, Macmillan.

Lister, L. (1960) *Europe's Coal and Steel Community: an experiment in European union*, New York, Twentieth Century Fund.

Lister, M. (1988) *The European Community and the Developing World*, Gower.

Llewellyn, D. T. (1980) *International Financial Integration: The limits of sovereignty*, Macmillan.

Llewellyn, D. T. (1982a) 'European monetary arrangements and the international monetary system', in M. T. Sumner and G. Zis (eds), *European Monetary Union*, Macmillan.

Llewellyn, D. T. (1982b) in D. T. Llewellyn *et al.*, *The Framework of UK Monetary Policy*, Chapter 1, Heinemann.

Llewellyn, D. T. (1983) 'EC monetary arrangement: Britain's strategy', in A. M. El-Agraa (ed.), *Britain within the European Community: The way forward*, Macmillan.

Lloyd, P. L. (1992) 'Regionalism and World trade', *OECD Economic Studies*, Spring.

Loewenheim, U. (1976) 'Trademarks and free competition within the European Community', *The Antitrust Bulletin*, vol. 21, no. 4.

Lucas, N. J. D. (1977) *Energy and the European Communities*, Europa Publications for the David Davies Memorial Institute of International Studies, London.

Ludlow, P. (1982) *The Making of the European Monetary System: A case study of the politics of the European Community*, Butterworth.

Lunn, J. L. (1983) 'Determinants of US direct investment in the EEC revisted again', *European Economic Review*, vol. 21.

McAleese, D. (1990) 'External trade policy', in A. M. El-Agraa (ed.), *The Economics of the European Community*, third edition, Phillip Allan.

McAleese, D. (1991) 'The EC internal market programme: implications for external trade', in N. Wagner (ed.), *ASEAN and the EC: The impact of 1992*, Institute of Southeast Asian studies, Singapore.

McAleese, D. (1993) 'The Community's external trade policy', in D. G. Mayes (ed.), *The External Implications of European Integration*, Simon & Schuster.

MacBean, A. I. (1988) 'The Uruguay Round and the developing countries', paper presented to the annual conference of the International Economics Study Group, Sussex University.

MacBean, A. I. and Snowden, P. N. (1981) *International Institutions in Trade and Finance*, Allen & Unwin.

McCrone, G. (1969) *Regional Policy in Britain*, Allen & Unwin.

McCrone, G. (1971) 'Regional policy in the European Community', in G. R. Denton (ed.), *Economic Integration in Europe*, Weidenfeld & Nicolson.

McDougall Report (1977) *see* Commissioon of the European Communities (1977c).

McFarquhar, A., Godley, W. and Silvey, D. (1977) 'The cost of food and Britain's membership of the EEC', *Cambridge Economic Policy Review*, vol. 3.

McGowan, F. (1990) 'Conflicting objectives in EC energy policy', *Political Quarterly*.

McGowan, F. (1993a) 'Utilities as infrastructures', *Utilities Policy*, vol. 3, no. 4.

McGowan, F. (1993b) *The Struggle for Power in Europe*, RIIA.

McGowan, F. (1994) 'The consequences of competition', *Revue des Affaires Européenes*, no. 2.

McGowan, F. (ed.) (1995) *European Energy Policy in a Changing Environment*, Physica.

McGowan, F. and **Mansell**, R. (1992) 'EC utilities; a regime in transition', *Futures*, vol. 16.

McGowan, F. and **Seabright**, P. (1989) 'Deregulating European airlines', *Economic Policy*, November.

McGowan, F. and **Seabright**, P. (1994) 'Regulation in the European Community', in M. Bishop, J. Kay and C. Mayer (eds), *Privatisation and Regulation in the UK*, second edition, Clarendon.

McGowan, F. and **Thomas**, S. (1990) 'Restructuring the world power plant industry', *The World Economy*, vol. 12.

McGowan, F. and **Trengove**, C. (1986) *European Aviatioon: A Common Market?*, IFS.

McGowan, F. *et al.* (1989) 'A single European market for energy', *Chatham House Occasional Paper*, Royal Institute of International Affairs.

McGowan, F. *et al.* (1993) *UK Energy Policy*, SPRU, University of Sussex.

Machlup, F. (1977a) *A History of Thought on Economic Integration*, Macmillan.

Machlup, F. (ed.) (1977b) *Economic Integration, Worldwide, Regional, Sectoral*, Macmillan.

Mackel, G. (1978) 'Green Money and the Common Agricultural Policy', *National Westminster Bank Review*, February.

McKinnon, R. I. (1963) 'Optimum currency areas', *American Economic Review*, vol. 53.

McLachlan, D. L. and **Swann**, D. (1967) *Competition Policy in the European Community*, Oxford University Press.

MacLaren, D. (1981) 'Agricultural trade and the MCA's: a spatial equilibrium analysis', *Journal of Agricultural Economics*, vol. 32, no. 1.

MacLennan, M. C. (1979) 'Regional policy in a European framework', in D. MacLennan and J. B. Parr, *Regional Policy: Past experience and new directions*, Martin Robertson.

MacMahon, C. (1979) 'The long run implications of the EMS', in P. H. Trezise (ed.), *The European Monetary System: Its promise and prospects*, The Brookings Institution, Washington.

McManus, J. G. (1972) 'The theory of the international firm', in G. Paquet (ed.), *The Multinational Firm and the National State*, Collier Macmillan.

McMillan, J. and **McCann**, E. (1981) 'Welfare effects in customs unions', *Economic Journal*, vol. 91.

McQueen, M. and **Stevens**, C. (1989) 'Trade preferences and Lomé IV: non-traditional ACP exports to the EC', *Development Policy Review*, September.

Magnifico, G. and **Williamson**, J. (1972) *European Monetary Integration*, Federal Trust, London.

Majone, G. (1991) 'Cross national sources of regulatory policy making in Europe and the United States', *Journal of Public Policy*, vol. 11, no. 1.

Major, R. L. (1960) 'World trade in manufactures', *National Institute Economic Review*, July.

Major, R. L. (1962) 'The Common Market: production and trade', *National Institute Economic Review*, August.

Major, R. L. and **Hays**, S. (1963) 'Another look at the Common Market', in *The Market Economy in Western European Integration*, University of Louvain.

Malcor, R. (1970) 'Problèmes posés par l'application pratique d'une unification pour l'usage des infrastructures routières', *EEC Studies, Transport Series*, no. 2.

Maltby, N. (1993) 'Multimodal transport and EC competition law', *Lloyds Maritime and Commercial Law Quarterly*, no. 1.

Manners, G. (1976) 'Reinterpreting the reginal problem', *Three Banks Review*, no. 3.

Mansholt, S. (1969) *Le Plan Mansholt*, EC Commission.

Marenco, G. (1983) 'Public sector and Community law', *Common Market Law Review*, vol. 20, no. 3.

Marer, P. and **Montias**, J. M. (1988) 'The Council for Mutual Economic Assistance', in A. M. El-Agraa (ed.), *International Economic Integration*, Macmillan and St Martin's.

Marin, A. (1979) 'Pollution control: economists' views', *Three Banks Review*, no. 121.

Marjolin Report (1975) *see* Commission of the European Communities (1975c).

Marquand, D. (1982) 'EMU: the political implications', in M. T. Sumner and G. Zis (eds), *European Monetary Union: Progress and prospects*, Macmillan.

Marquand, J. (1980) 'Measuring the effects and costs of regional incentives', *Government Economic Service Working Paper*, no. 32, Department of Industry, London.

Marsh, J. and Ritson, C. (1971) *Agricultural Policy and the Common Market*, Chatham House, PEP European Series, no. 16.

Marsh, J. S. and Swanney, P. J. (1980) *Agriculture and the European Community* (second edition, 1985), Allen & Unwin.

Masera, R. (1981) 'The first two years of the EMS: the exchange rate experience', *Banca Nazionale del Lavoro Review*, September.

Mason, E. S. (1946) *Controlling World Trade: Cartels and commodity agreements*, McGraw-Hill.

Mathijsen, P. S. R. F. (1972) 'State aids, state monopolies, and public enterprises in the Common Market', *Law and Contemporary Problems*, vol. 37, no. 2, Spring.

Mathijsen, P. S. R. F. (1975) *A Guide to European Community Law*, Sweet & Maxwell/Matthew Bender.

Matthews, A. (1986) *The Common Agricultural Policy and the Less Developed Countries*, Gill & Macmillan.

Matthews, A. (1990) *The European Community's Trade Policy and the Third World: An Irish perspective*, Dublin Gill and Macmillan.

Matthews, J. D. (1977) *Association System of the European Community*, Praeger.

Matthews, M. and McGowan, F. (1992) 'Reconciling diversity and scale: some questions of method in the assessment of the costs and benefits of European integration', *Revue d'Economie Industrielle*, no. 59.

Mayes, D. G. (1971) *The Effects of Alternative Trade Groupings on the United Kingdom*, PhD Thesis, University of Bristol.

Mayes, D. G. (1974) 'RASAT, a model for the estimation of commodity trade flows in EFTA', *European Economic Review*, vol. 5.

Mayes, D. G. (1978) 'The effects of economic integration on trade', *Journal of Common Market Studies*, vol. 17, no. 1.

Mayes, D. G. (1981) *Applications of Econometrics*, Prentice Hall.

Mayes, D. G. (1982) 'The problems of the quantitative estimation of integration effects', in A. M. El-Agraa (ed.), *International Economic Integration*, Macmillan.

Mayes, D. G. (1983a) 'EC trade effects and factor mobility', in A. M. El-Agraa (ed.), *Britain within the European Community: The way forward*, Chapter 6, Macmillan.

Mayes, D. G. (1983b) 'Memorandum of Evidence', in House of Lords Select Committee on the European Communities, *Trade Patterns: The United Kingdom's changing trade patterns subsequent to membership of the European Community*, HL (41), 7th Report, Session 1983–84, HMSO.

Mayes, D. G. (1988) Chapter Three, in A. Bollard and M. A. Thompson (eds), *Trans-Tasman Trade and Investment*, Institute for Policy Studies, Wellington, New Zealand.

Mayes, D. G. (ed.) (1990) 'The external implications of closer European Integration', *National Institute Economic Review*, November.

Mayes, D. G. (1997d) 'The problems of the quantitative estimation of integration effects', in A. M. El-Agraa, *Economic Integration Worldwide*, Macmillan and St Martin's.

Mayes, D. G. (1993) *The External Implications of European Integration*, Harvester Wheatsheaf.

Mayes, D. G. (1996) 'The role of foreign direct investment in structural change: the lessons from the New Zealand experience', in G. Csaki, G. Foti and D. Mayes (eds), *Foreign Direct Investment and Transition: The case of the Visegrad countries*, Trends in World Economy, no. 78, Institute for World Economics, Budapest.

Mayes, D. G. (1997a) 'Competition and cohesion: lessons from New Zealand', in M. Fritsch and H. Hansen (eds), *Rules of Competition and East-West Integration*, Kluwer.

Mayes, D. G. (1997b) *The Evolution of the Single European Market*, Edward Elgar.

Mayes, D. G. (1997c) 'The New Zealand experiment: using economic theory to drive policy', *Policy Options*, vol. 18, no. 7.

Mayes, D. G. (1997d) 'The problems of the quantitative estimation of integration effects', in A. M. El-Agraa (ed.), *Economic Integration Worldwide*, Macmillan and St Martins.

Mayes, D. G. and **Britton, A.** (1992) *Achieving Monetary Union*, Sage.

Mayes, D. G., Hager, W., Knight, A. and **Streeck, W.** (1993) *Public Interest and Market Pressures: Problems posed by Europe 1992*, Macmillan.

Mayes, D. G. and **Chapple, B.** (1995) 'The costs and benefits of disinflation: a critique of the sacrifice ratio', *Reserve Bank Bulletin*, vol. 34.

Maynard, G. (1978) 'Monetary interdependence and floating exchange rates', in G. Maynard *et al.*, *Monetary Policies in Open Economics*, SUERF.

Mayne, R. (1970) *The Recovery or Europe*, Weidenfeld & Nicolson.

McAleese, D. (1994) 'EC external trade policy', in Ali M. El-Agraa (ed.) *The Economics of the European Community*, 4th edition, Harvester Wheatsheaf.

Meade, J. E. (1951) *The Balance of Payments*, Oxford University Press.

Meade, J. E. (1973) 'The balance-of-payments problems of a European free-trade area', in M. B. Krauss (ed.), *The Economics of Integration*, Allen & Unwin.

Meade, J. E. (1980) *The Theory of International Trade Policy*, Oxford University Press.

Meade, J. E., Liesner, H. H. and **Wells, S. J.** (1962) *Case Studies in European Economic Union: The mechanics of integration*, Oxford University Press.

Meadows, D. H. *et al.* (1972) *The Limits to Growth*, Earth Island.

Messerlin, P. (1988) 'The Uruguay negotiations on dumping and subsidies', World Bank mimeo.

Messerlin, P. (1989) 'The EC anti-dumping regulations: a first appraisal', *Weltwirtschaftliches Archiv*, vol. 125.

Messerlin, P. A. (1997) 'MFN-based freer trade and regional free trade: what role for the European Community?', mimeo, Institut d'Études Politiques, Paris.

Messerlin, P. A. and **Reed, G.** (1995) 'Anti-dumping policies in the United States and the European Community', *Economic Journal*, vol. 105.

Michalopoulos, G. T. (1991) *Macroeconomic Consequences of the US Dollar Exchange Rate Movements for the EC Economy: An empirical analysis*, unpublished doctoral thesis, University of Reading.

Midland Bank (1970) 'The dollar: an end to benign neglect?', *Midland Bank Review*, Autumn.

Mikesell, R. F. and **Goldstein, H. N.** (1975) 'Rules for a floating rate regime', *Essays in International Finance*, no. 109, Princeton University.

Millward, R. (1981) 'The performance of public and private ownership', in E. Roll (ed.), *The Mixed Economy*, Macmillan.

Mingst, K. A. (1977/78) 'Regional sectoral economic integration: the case of OAPEC', *Journal of Common Market Studies*, vol. 16.

Mishan, E. J. (1967) *The Cost of Economic Growth*, Stables.

Molle, W. (1990) *Economics of European Integration: Theory, Practice, Policy*, Aldershot.

Molle, W. (1994) *The Economics of European Integration*, 2nd edn., Dartmouth, Aldershot.

Molle, W. and **Morsink, R.** (1990) 'Direct investment and European integration', *European Economy*, special issue.

Molle, W. *et al.* (1980) *Regional Disparity and Economic Development in the European Community*, Saxon House.

Monnet, J. (1995) *Les Etats-Unis d'Europe ont Commencé*, Robert Laffont.

Montagnon, P. (1990a) 'Regulating the utilities', in P. Montagnon, *European Competition Policy*, RIIA.

Montagnon, P. (1990b) *European Competition Policy*, RIIA.

Moore, B. and **Rhodes, J.** (1975) 'The economic and Exchequer implications of British regional economic policy', in J. Vaizey (ed.), *Economic Sovereignty and Regional Policy*, Gill & Macmillan.

Morgan, A. D. (1980) 'The balance of payments and British membership of the European Community', in W. Wallace (ed.), *Britain in Europe*, Heinemann, Chapter 3.

Morgan, R. (1983) 'Political cooperation in Europe', in R. Jenkins (ed.), *Britain and the EEC*, Chapter 12, Macmillan.

Morris, C. N. (1980a) 'The Common Agricultural Policy', *Fiscal Studies*, vol. 1, no. 2.

Morris, C. N. (1980b) 'The Common Agricultural Policy: sources and methods', *Institute of Fiscal Studies Working Paper*, no. 6.

Morris, C. N. and Dilnot, A. W. (1981) 'The distributional effects of the Common Agricultural Policy', *Institute of Fiscal Studies Working Paper*, no. 28.

Morris, V. (1979) *Britain and the EEC – the Economic Issues*, Labour, Economic, Finance and Taxation Association, London.

Moss, J. and Ravenhill, J. (1982) 'Trade developments during the first Lomé Convention', *World Development*, vol. 10.

Moss, J. and Ravenhill, J. (1988) 'The evolution of trade under the Lomé Convention: the first ten years', in C. Stevens and J. V. van Themaat (eds), *EEC and the Third World: a survey*, 6, *Europe and the International Division of Labour*, Hodder & Stoughton.

Mundell, R. A. (1961) 'A theory of optimum currency areas', *American Economic Review*, vol. 51.

Mundell, R. A. (1964) 'Tariff preferences and the terms of trade', *Manchester School*, vol. 32.

Munk, K. J. (1989) 'Price support to the EC agricultural sector: an optimal policy?', *Oxford Review of Economic Policy*, vol. 5, no. 2.

Musgrave, R. A. and Musgrave, P. B. (1976) *Public Finance in Theory and Practice*, McGraw-Hill.

National Institute of Economic and Social Research (1971) 'Entry into the EEC: a comment on some of the economic issues', *National Institute Economic Review*, no. 57, August.

National Institute of Economic and Social Research (1983) 'The European Monetary System', *National Institute Economic Review*, February.

National Institute of Economic and Social Research (1991) *A New Strategy for Social and Economic Cohesion After 1992*, a study carried out for the European Parliament, Brussels/Luxemburg.

Nau, H. (1974) *National Politics and International Technology: Nuclear reactor development in Western Europe*, Johns Hopkins University Press.

Needleman, L. and Scott, B. (1964) 'Regional problems and the location of industry policy in Britain', *Urban Studies*, no. 12.

Nello, S. (1991) *The New Europe: Changing economic relations between East and West*, Harvester Wheatsheaf.

Neumark, F. (1963) *Report of the Fiscal and Financial Committee*, EC Commission; see CEC 1963.

Neven, D., Nuttal, R. and Seabright, P. (1993) *Competition and Merger Policy in the EC*, CEPR.

Neven, D. J. (1990) 'Gains and losses from 1992', *Economic Policy*, April.

Neven, E. T. (1988) 'VAT and the European Budget', *The Royal Bank of Scotland Review*, no. 157.

Nicolaides, P. (1990) 'Anti-dumping measures as safeguards: the case of the EC', *InterEconomics*, November/December.

Nijkamp, P., Reichman, S. and Wegener (eds) (1990) *Euromobile: Transport, Communications and Mobility in Europe: A cross national comparative overview*, Avebury.

Nkrumah, K. (1965) *Neo Colonialism: The last stage of imperialism*, Heinemann.

Noel, E. (1975) *Working Together*, EC Commission.

Oates, W. E. (1972) *Fiscal Federalism*, Harcourt Brace.

O'Donnell, R. (1992) 'Policy requirements for regional balance in economic and monetary union', in A. Hannequart (ed.), *Economic and Social Cohesion in Europe: a New Objective for Integration*, Routledge.

O'Donnell, R. and Murphy, A. (1994) 'The relevance of the European union and European integration to the world trade regime', *International Journal*, vol. 49.

OECD (various years) *Economic Survey of Europe*.

OECD (1979) *The Case of Positive Adjustment Policies: A compendium of OECD documents 1978/79*, OECD.

OECD (1983) *The OECD Interlink Model.*

OECD (1985 and various years) *OECE Economic Outlook*, no. 38.

OECD (1985) *Costs and Benefits of Protection.*

OECD (1988) *The Newly Industrialising Countries: Challenges and opportunity for OECD industries.*

OECD (1990) *Competition Policy and the Deregulation of Road Transport*, OECD.

OECD (1992) *Regulatory Reform, Privatisation and Competition Policy*, OECD.

OECD (1994) *The OECD Jobs Study, Part I: Labour Market Trends and Underlying Forces of Change*, OECD, Paris.

OECD (1995) *Environmental Taxes in OECD Countries*, OECD, Paris.

OECD (1996a) *Employment Outlook*, July 1996, OECD, Paris.

OECD (1996b) *Indicators of Tariff and Non-tariff Trade Barriers*, OECD, Paris.

Oliver, H. (1960) 'German neoliberalism', *Quarterly Journal of Economics*, vol. 74.

Oort, C. J. (1975) *Study of Possible Solutions for Allocating the Deficits which may Occur in a System of Charging for the Use of Infrastructures aiming at Budgetary Equilibrium*, EC Commission.

Open University (1973) *The European Economic Community: History and institutions, national and international impact*, Open University Press.

Oppenheimer, P. M. (1981) 'The economics of the EMS', in J. R. Sargent (ed.), *Europe and the Dollar in World-wide Disequilibrium*, Sijthoff and Noordhoff.

Ordover, J. (1990) 'Economic foundations of competition policy', in W. S. Comanor *et al.* (eds), *Competition Policy in Europe and North America: Economic issues and institutions*, Harwood Academic.

Osborne, F. and Robinson, S. (1989) 'Oil', in F. McGowan *et al.*, *A Single European Market for Energy*, Chatham House Occasional Paper, Royal Institute of International Affairs.

Oughton, C. and Whittam, G. (1997) 'Competitiveness, EU industrial strategy and subsidiarity', in P. Devine, Y. Katsoulacos and R. Sugden (eds), *Competitiveness, Subsidiarity and Industrial Policy.*

Owens, S. and Hope, C. (1989) 'Energy and the environment – the challenge of integrating European policies', *Energy Policy*, vol. 17.

Owen-Smith, E. (1983) *The West German Economy*, Croom Helm.

Oxfam (1996) 'Protecting workers' rights: the case for a social clause', Oxfam Report, Dublin.

Oxford Review of Economic Policy (1987), vol. 3, no. 1.

PA Cambridge Economic Consultants (1989) *The Regional Consequences of the Completion of the Internal Market for Financial Services*, study carried out for the EC Commission.

Padoa-Schioppa, T. (1983) 'What the EMS has achieved', *The Banker*, August.

Padoa-Schioppa, T. (1985) 'Policy cooperation in the EMS experience', in W. H. Buiter and R. C. Marston (eds), *International Economic Policy Coordination*, Cambridge University Press.

Padoa-Schioppa, T. *et al.* (1987) *Efficiency, Stability and Equity: A strategy for the evolution of the economic system of the European Community*, report of a study group appointed by the EC Commission.

Page, S. A. B. (1979) 'The management of international trade', *National Institute Discussion Papers*, no. 29.

Page, S. A. B. (1981) 'The revival of protectionism and its consequences for Europe', *Journal of Common Market Studies*, vol. 20, no. 1.

Page, S. A. B. (1982) 'The development of the EMS', *National Institute Economic Review*, November.

Page, S. and Davenport, M. (1994) *World Trade Reform: Do developing countries gain or lose?*, Overseas Development Institute, London.

Palmer, M. and Lambert, J. (1968) *European Unity*, Allen & Unwin.

Panic´, M. (1982) 'Some longer term effects of short-run adjustments policies: behaviours of UK direct investment since the 1960s', in J. Black and J. H. Dunning (eds), *International Capital Movements*, Macmillan.

Papaconstantinou, H. (1988) *Free Trade and Competition in the EEC: Law, policy and practice*, Routledge.

Pappalardo, C. (1991) 'State measures and public undertakings: Article 90 of the EEC Treaty revised', *European Competition Law Review*, vol. 12, no. 1.

Parkin, J. M. (1976) 'Monetary union and stabilisation policy in the European Community, *Banca Nazionale del Lavoro Review*, September.

Pauly, M. V. (1973) 'Income redistribution as a local public good', *Journal of Public Economics*, vol. 2.

Paxton, J. (1976) *The Developing Common Market*, Macmillan.

Peacock, A. T. (1972) *The Public Finance of Inter-allied Defence Provision: Essays in honour of Antonio de Vito de Marco*, Cacucci Editore.

Peacock, A. T. and **Wiseman, J.** (1967) *The Growth of Public Expenditure in the UK*, Allen & Unwin.

Pearce, D. W. (1976) 'The limits of cost–benefit analysis as a guide to environmental policy', *Kyklos*, vol. 29.

Pearce, D. W. and **Westoby, R.** (1983) 'Energy and the EC', in A. M. El-Agraa (ed.), *Britain within the European Community: The way forward*, Chapter 10, Macmillan.

Pearce, J. and **Sutton, J.** (1985) *Protection and Industrial Policy in Europe*, Routledge & Kegan Paul.

Pearce, J. and **Sutton, J.** (1986) *Protection and Industrial Policy in Europe*, Routledge.

Pearson, M. and **Smith, S.** (1991) *The European Carbon Tax*, Institute for Fiscal Studies, London.

Peeters, T. (1982) 'EMU: prospects and retrospect', in M. T. Sumner and G. Zis (eds), *European Monetary Union: Progress and prospects*, Macmillan.

Pelkmans, J. (1984) *Market Integration in the European Community*, Martinus Nijhoff.

Pelkmans, J. (1987) 'The European Community's trade policy towards developing countries', in C. Stevens and J. V. van Themaat, *EEC and the Third World: a survey, 6, Europe and the International Division of Labour*, Hodder & Stoughton.

Pelkmans, J. (1991) 'Completing the EC internal market: an update and problems ahead', in N. Wagner (ed.), *ASEAN and the EC: The impact of 1992*, Institute of Southeast Asian Studies, Singapore.

Pelkmans, J. and **Carzaniga, A. G.** (1996) 'The trade policy review of the European Union', *World Economy*, special edition on 'Global trade policy, 1996'.

Pelkmans, J. and **Brenton, P.** (1997) 'Free trade with the EU: driving forces and effects of "me-too" ', mimeo, Centre for European Policy Studies, Brussels.

Pelkmans, J. and **Murphy, A.** (1992) 'Strategies for the Uruguay Round', in P. Ludlow (ed.), *Europe and North America in the 1990s*, Centre for European Policy Studies, Brussels.

Pelkmans, J. and **Robson, P.** (1987) 'The aspirations of the White Paper', *Journal of Common Market Studies*, vol. 25, no. 3.

Pelkmans, J. and **Winters, L. A.** (1988) *Europe's Domestic Market*, Routledge.

Peterson, J. (1991) 'Technology policy in Europe: explaining the framework programme and Eureka in theory and practice', *Journal of Common Market Studies*, vol. 29, no. 3.

Petith, H. C. (1977) 'European integration and the terms of trade', *Economic Journal*, vol. 87.

Phelps, E. S. (1968) 'Money–wage dynamics and labour market equilibrium, *Journal of Political Economy*, vol. 76.

Phillips, A. W. (1958) 'The relation between unemployment and the rate of change of money wages in the United Kingdom', *Economica*, vol. 25.

Pinder, J. (1968) 'Positive integration and negative integration', *The World Today*, March.

Pinder, J. (1969) 'Problems of European integration', in G. R. Denton (ed.), *Economic Integration in Europe*, Weidenfeld & Nicolson.

Pinder, J. (ed.) (1971) *The Economics of Europe*, Knight.

Pinder, J. (1982) 'Industrial policy in Britain and the European Community', *Policy Studies*, vol. 2, part, 4, April.

Pinder, J. (1991) *European Community: The building of a union*, Oxford University Press.

Pintado, X. *et al.* (1988) 'Economic aspects of European economic space', *Occasional Papers*, no. 25, EFTA Secretariat.

Platteau, K. (1991) 'Article 90 EEC Treaty after the court judgement in the telecommunications (1991) terminal equipment case', *European Community Law Review*, vol. 12, no. 3.

Political and Economic Planning (PEP) (1962) *Atlantic Tariffs and Trade*, Allen & Unwin.

Political and Economic Planning (PEP) (1963) 'An energy policy for the EEC', *Planning*, vol. 29.

Pomfret, R. (1986) *Mediterranean Policy of the European Community: Study of discrimination in trade*, Macmillan.

Porter, M. (1990) *The Competitive Advantage of Nations*, Macmillan.

Poyhonen, P. (1963a) 'Towards a general theory of international trade, *Ekonomista Samfundets Tidskrift*, no. 2.

Poyhonen, P. (1963b) 'A tentative model for the volume of trade between countries, *Ekonomista Samfundets Tidskrift*, no. 2.

Prais, S. J. (1982) *Productivity and Industrial Structure*, Cambridge University Press.

Presley, J. R. and Coffey, P. (1974) *European Monetary Integration*, Macmillan.

Press, A. and Taylor, C. (1990) *Europe and the Environment*, The Industrial Society.

Prest, A. R. (1972) 'Governent revenue, the national income and all that', in R. M. Bird and J. G. Read, *Modern Fiscal Issues*, Toronto University Press.

Prest, A. R. (1975) *Public Finance in Theory and Practice*, Weidenfeld & Nicholson.

Prest, A. R. (1979) 'Fiscal policy', in P. Coffey (ed.), *Economic Policies of the Common Market*, Chapter 4, Macmillan.

Prewo, W. E. (1974) 'Integration effects in the EEC', *European Economic Review*, vol. 5.

Primo Braga, C. A. (1995) 'Trade-related intellectual property issues: the Uruguay Round agreement and its economic implications', in W. Martin and L. A. Winters (eds) 'The Uruguay Round and the developing economics', *World Bank Discussion Papers*, no. 307, Washington, DC.

Pryce, R. (1962) *The Political Future of the European Community*, Marshbank.

Pryce, R. (1973) *The Politics of the European Community*, Butterworth.

Pryce, R. (ed.) (1987) *The Dynamics of European Union*, Croom Helm.

Pulliainen, K. (1963) 'A world trade study: an econometric model of the pattern of commodity flows in international trade 1948–1960', *Ekonomista Samfundets Tidskrift*, no. 2.

Quevit, M. (1992) 'The regional impact of the internal market: a comparative analysis of traditional industrial regions and lagging regions', *Regional Studies*, vol. 26.

Raisman Report (1961) *East Africa: Report of the Economic and Fiscal Commission*, Cmnd 1279, Colonial Office.

Ravenhill, J. (1985a) 'Europe and Africa: an essential continuity', in R. Boardman *et al.*, *Europe, Africa and Lomé III*, University Press of America.

Ravenhill, J. (1985b) *Collective Clientism: the Lomé Convention and North–South Relations*, Columbia University Press.

Resnick, S. A. and Truman, E. M. (1975) 'An empirical examination of bilateral trade in Western Europe', *Journal of International Economics*, vol. 3.

Richonnier, M. (1984) 'Europe's decline is not irreversible', *Journal of Common Market Studies*, vol. 22, no. 3.

Riezman, R. (1979) 'A 3×3 model of customs unions', *Journal of International Economics*, vol. 9.

Ritson, C. (1973) *The Common Agricultural Policy*, in *The European Economic Community: Economics and agriculture*, Open University Press.

Ritson, C. (1980) 'Self sufficiency and food security centre for agricultural strategy', *Discussion Paper*, no. 8, University of Reading.

Ritson, C. and Tangermann, S. (1979) 'The economics and politics of Monetary Compensatory Amounts', *European Review of Agricultural Economics*, vol. 6.

Ritter, L. and **Overburg, C.** (1977) 'An attempt at a practical approach to joint ventures under the EEC rules on competition', *Common Market Law Review*, vol. 14, no. 4.

Roarty, M. J. (1985) 'The EEC's Common Agricultural Policy and its effects on less developed countries', *National Westminster Bank Quarterly Review*, February.

Robinson, P. W., Webb, T. R. and **Townsend, M. A.** (1979) 'The influence of exchange rate changes on prices: a study of 18 industrial countries', *Economica*, February.

Robson, P. (1980 and 1985) *The Economics of International Integration*, Allen & Unwin.

Robson, P. (1983) *Integration, Development and Equity: Economic integration in West Africa*, Allen & Unwin.

Robson, P. (1987) 'Variable geometry and automaticity: strategies for experience of regional integration in West Africa', in A. M. El-Agraa (ed.), *Conflict, Cooperation, Integration and Development: Essays in honour of Professor Hiroshi Kitamura*, Macmillan and St Martin's.

Rogers, S. T. and **Davey, B. H.** (eds) (1973) *The Common Agricultural Policy and Britain*, Saxon House.

Rollo, J. N. C. and **Warwick, K. S.** (1979) 'The CAP and resource flows among EEC member states', *Government Economic Service Working Paper*, no. 27, Ministry of Agriculture, Fisheries and Food, London.

Roy, R. (1994) 'Investment in transport infrastructure: the recovery in Europe', *ECIS Report*.

Royal Institute of International Affairs (1953) *Documents on International Affairs, 1949–50*, RIIA.

Rybczynski, T. (1982) 'Fiscal Policy under EMU', in M. T. Sumner and G. Zis (eds), *European Monetary Union*, Macmillan.

Sachs, J. D. and **Shatz, H. J.** (1994) 'Trade and jobs in US manufacturing', *Brookings Papers on Economic Activity*, vol. 1.

Sachs, J. D. and **Shatz, H. J.** (1996) 'US trade with developing countries and wage inequality', *American Economic Review*, papers and proceedings, vol. 86.

Sala-i-Martin, X. (1996) 'Regional cohesion: evidence and theories of regional growth and convergence', *European Economic Review*, vol. 40.

Sapir, A. (1996) 'The effects of Europe's internal market programme on production and trade: a first assessment', *Weltwirtschaftliches Archiv*, vol. 132.

Sapir, A. and **Winter, C.** (1994) 'Services trade', in D. Greenaway and L. A. Winters (eds), *Surveys in International Trade*, Blackwell, Oxford.

Sargent, T. J. and **Wallace, N.** (1976) 'Rational expectations and the theory of economic policy', *Journal of Monetary Economics*, April.

Sarna, A. J. (1985) 'The impact of a Canada–US free trade area', *Journal of Common Market Studies*, vol. 23, no. 4.

Sawyer, M. (1992) 'Reflections on the nature and role of industrial policy', *Metroeconomica*, vol. 43.

Sayigh, Y. (1982) *The Arab Economy*, Oxford University Press.

Scaperlanda, A. and **Balough, R. S.** (1983) 'Determinants of US direct investment in the EEC revisited', *European Economic Review*, vol. 21.

Schindler, P. (1970) 'Public enterprises and the EEC Treaty', *Common Market Law Review*, vol. 7, no. 1.

Schmalensee, R. and **Willig, R. D.** (eds) (1989) *Handbook of Industrial Organization*, North-Holland.

Schuknecht, L. (1992) *Trade Protection in the European Community*, Harwood Academic.

Schumacher, D. and **Mobius, U.** (1991) 'Eastern Europe and the EC: trade relations and trade policy with regard to industrial products', paper presented to Joint Canada/Germany Symposium, November 1990, revised 1991, Berlin Deutsches Institüt fur Wirtschaftforschung (DIW).

Scitovsky, T. (1958) *Economic Theory and Western European Integration*, Allen & Unwin.

Secretariat of the European Parliament (1983) *The European Parliament, Its Powers*.

Sellekaerts, W. (1973) 'How meaningful are empirical studies on trade creation and diversion?, *Weltwirtschaftliches Archiv*, vol. 109.

Shanks, M. (1977) *European Social Policy, Today and Tomorrow*, Pergamon Press.

Sharp, M. L. (1987) 'Collaboration in the high technology sectors', *Oxford Review of Economic Policy*, vol. 3, no. 1.

Sharp, M. L. (1991) 'The single market and European technology policies', in C. Freeman, M. L. Sharp and W. Walker (eds), *Technology and the Future of Europe*, Pinter.

Sharp, M. L. and **Pavitt, K.** (1993) 'Technology policy in the 1990s: old trends and new realities', *Journal of Common Market Studies*, vol. 31, no. 2.

Sharp, M. L. and **Shearman, C.** (1987) *European Technological Collaboration*, RIIA.

Sharp, M. L. and **Walker, W. B.** (1991) 'The policy agenda – challenges for the new Europe', in C. Freeman, M. L. Sharp and W. Walker (eds), *Technology and the Future of Europe*, Pinter.

Shlaim, A. and **Yannopoulos, G. N.** (eds) (1976) *The EEC and the Mediterranean Countries*, Cambridge University Press.

Shonfield, A. (1965) *Modern Capitalism: The changing balance of public and private power*, Oxford University Press.

Short, J. (1978) 'The regional distribution of public expenditure in Great Britain, 1969/70–1973/74', *Regional Studies*, vol. 12, no. 5.

Short, J. (1981) *Public Expenditure and Taxation in the UK Regions*, Gower.

Shoup, C. S. (ed.) (1966) *Fiscal Harmonisation in Common Markets*, 2 vols, Columbia University Press.

Shoup, C. S. (1972) 'Taxation aspects of international integration', in P. Robson (ed.), *International Economic Integration*, Penguin.

Shourd, M. (1980) *The Theft of the Countryside*, Temple Smith.

Smith, A. J. (1977) 'The Council of Mutual Economic Assistance in 1977: new economic power, new political perspectives and some old and new problems', in US Congress Joint Economic Committee's *East European Economics Post-Helsinki*.

Smith, S. (1988) 'Excise duties and the internal market', *Journal of Common Market Studies*, vol. 27, no. 2.

Spaak Report (1987) *The Single European Act: a New Frontier – Programme of the Commission for 1987*. Supplement 1/87 of the *Bulletin of the European Communities*.

SPRU–RIIA (1989) *A Single European Market for Energy*, RIIA.

Starkie, D. (1993) 'Train service coordination in a competitive market', *Fiscal Studies*, vol. 14, no. 2.

Steenbergen, J. (1980) 'The Common Commercial Policy', *Common Market Law Review*, May.

Stern, J. (1989) 'Natural gas', in F. McGowan *et al.*, *A Single Market for Energy*, Chatham House Occasional Paper, Royal Institute of International Affairs.

Stern, J. (1992) *Third Party Access in European Gas Markets*, RIIA.

Stern, R., Francis, S. and **Schumacker, B.** (1976) *Price Elasticities in International Trade: An annotated bibliography*, Macmillan.

Stevens, C. (1984) 'The new Lomé Convention: imperfections for Europe's Third World policy', Paper No. 16, Centre for European Policy Studies.

Stevens, C. and **Watson, A.** (1984) 'Trade diversification: has Lomé helped?', in C. Stevens (ed.)., *EEC and the Third World: a survey, 4, Renegotiating Lomé*, Hodder & Stoughton.

Stevens, C. and **van Themaat, J. V.** (eds) (1988) *EEC and the Third World: A Survey, 6, Europe and the International Division of Labour*, Hodder & Stoughton.

Stewart, J. A. and **Begg, H. M.** (1976) 'Towards a European regional policy', *National Westminster Bank Quarterly Review*, May.

Stigler, G. J. (1971) 'The theory of economic regulation', *Bell Journal of Economics and Management Science*, vol. 2.

Stoeckel, A. B. (1985) *Intersectoral Effects of the CAP: Growth, Trade and Unemployment*, Bureau of Agricultural Research (Canberra).

Stoffaes, C. (1986) 'Postscript', in W. Adams and C. Stoffaes (eds), *French Industrial Policy*, The Brookings Institution, Washington.

Stokes, B. (1996) *Open for Business: Creating a transatlantic marketplace*, Council of Foreign Relations, New York.

Stone, J. K. N. and **Brown, J. A. C.** (1963) 'Input–output relationships', in *A Programme for Growth*, no. 3, Chapman & Hall.

Stoneman, P. (1989) 'Technology policy in Europe', in Cowling, K. and Tomann, H., *Industrial Policy After 1992*, Anglo-German Foundation for the Study of Industrial Society.

Strange, S. and **Tooze, R.** (eds) (1981) *The International Politics of Surplus Capacity: Competition for market shares in the world recession*, Allen & Unwin.

Strasser, D. (1981) 'The finances of Europe', *The European Perspective Series*, EC Commission.

Sturmey, S. G. (1962) *British Shipping and World Competition*, Athlone.

Sumner, M. T. and **Zis, G.** (eds) (1982) *European Monetary Union: Progress and prospects*, Macmillan.

Sundelius, B. and **Wiklund, C.** (1979) 'The Nordic Community: the ugly duckling of regional cooperation', *Journal of Common Market Studies*, vol. 18, no. 1.

Swann, D. (1973) *The Economics of the Common Market*, first edition, Penguin.

Swann, D. (1978) *The Economics of the Common Market*, second edition, Penguin.

Swann, D. (1983) *Competition and Industrial Policy in the European Community*, Methuen.

Swann, D. (1988) *The Economics of the Common Market*, fourth edition, Penguin.

Swann, D. (1992) *The Economics of the Common Market*, seventh edition, Penguin.

Sweet & Maxwell (regularly updated) *European Community Treaties*, Sweet & Maxwell.

Swinbank, A. and **Ritson, C.** (1988) 'The Common Agricultural Policy, customs unions and the Mediterranean basin', *Journal of Common Market Studies*, vol. 27, no. 2.

Swoboda, A. K. (1983) 'Exchange rate regimes and European–US policy interdependence', *International Monetary Fund Staff Papers*, March.

Symons, E. and **Walker, I.** (1989) 'The revenue and welfare effects of fiscal harmonisation for the UK', *Oxford Review of Economic Policy*, vol. 5, no. 2.

Talbot, R. B. (1978) 'The European Community's regional fund', *Progress in Planning*, vol. 8, no. 3.

Tharakan, P. K. M. (ed.) (1991) *Policy Implications of Antidumping Measures*, North-Holland.

Tharakan, P. K. M. (1995) 'Political economy and contingent protection', *Economic Journal*, vol. 105.

Tharakan, P. K. M. and **Waelbroeck, J.** (1994) 'Anti-dumping and countervailing duty decisions in the EC and in the US', *European Economic Review*, vol. 38.

Thomas, S. D. (1984) *The Realities of Nuclear Power*, Cambridge University Press.

Thomas, S. D. (1988) 'Power plant life extension', *Energy the International Journal*.

Thomson, G. (1973) 'European regional policy in the 1970s', *CBI Review*, no. 10, Autumn.

Thomson, G. (1989) *Industrial Policy: USA and UK debates*, Routledge.

Thomson, K. J. (1983) 'CAP budget projections to 1988', *Discussion Paper*, no. 4, Department of Agricultural Economics and Department of Agricultural Marketing, University of Newcastle.

Thorbecke, E. and **Pagoulatos, E.** (1975) 'The effects of European economic integration on agriculture', in B. Balassa (ed.), *European Economic Integration*, North-Holland.

Thurow, L. C. (1971) 'The income distribution as a public good', *Quarterly Journal of Economics*, vol. 85.

Thygesen, N. (1979) 'EMS: precursors, first steps and policy options', in R. Triffin (ed.), *The EMS: the emerging European Monetary System*, National Bank of Belgium.

Thygesen, N. (1981a) 'Are monetary policies and performance converging?', *Banca Nazionale del Lavoro Quarterly Review*, September.

Thygesen, N. (1981b) 'The EMS: an approximate implementation of the Crawling Peg?', in J. Williamson (ed.), *Exchange Rate Rules*, Macmillan.

Tiberi, U. and **Cardoso**, F. (1992) 'Specific actions towards greater penetration of renewable energy sources (ALTENER)', *Energy in Europe*, no. 20.

Timberg, S. (1972) 'Antitrust in the Common Market: innovation and surprise', *Law and Contemporary Problems*, vol. 37, no. 2.

Tinbergen, J. (1952) *On the Theory of Economic Policy*, North-Holland.

Tinbergen, J. (1953) *Report on Problems Raised by the Different Turnover Tax Systems Applied within the Common Market* (the Tinbergen Report), European Coal and Steel Community.

Tinbergen, J. (1954) *International Economic Integration*, Elsevier.

Tindemans, L. (1976) 'European Union', *Bulletin of the European Communities*, Supplement.

Toulemon, R. (1972) 'Etal d'advancement des travaux en mataiè re de politique industrielle dans la Communauté', paper presented to the conference organised by the European Communities on 'Industrie et sociéte dans la Communauté Européene', Venice.

Trela, I. and **Walley**, J. (1990) 'Unraveling the threads of the MFA', in C. B. Hamilton (ed.), *Textiles Trade and the Developing Countries: Eliminating the Multi-Fibre Agreement in the 1990s*, World Bank.

Trezise, P. H. (ed.) (1979) *The European Monetary System: Promise and prospects*, The Brookings Institution, Washington.

Truman, E. M. (1969) 'The European Economic Community: trade creation and trade diversion', *Yale Economic Essays*, Spring.

Truman, E. M. (1972) 'The production and trade of manufactures products in the EEC and EFTA: a comparison', *European Economic Review*, vol. 3.

Truman, E. M. (1975) 'The effects of European economic integration on the production and trade of manufactured products', in B. Balassa (ed.), *European Economic Integration*, North-Holland.

Tsoukalis, L. (1981) *The European Community and its Mediterranean Enlargement*, Allen & Unwin.

Tsoukalis, L. (ed.) (1982) *The European Community Past, Present and Future*, Basil Blackwell.

Tsoukalis, L. (1991) *The New European Economy: The politics and economics of integration*, Oxford University Press.

Tullock, G. (1967) 'The welfare costs of tariffs, monopolies and theft', *Western Economic Journal*, vol. 5.

Tyson, L. D. (1992) *Who's Bashing Whom?: Trade conflict in high technology industries*, IIE.

Ungerer, H., **Evans**, O. and **Nyberg**, P. (1983) 'The European Monetary System: The experience, 1979–82', *International Monetary Fund Occasional Papers*, no. 19, May.

Ungerer, H. *et al.* (1986) 'The European Monetary System – recent developments', *Occasional Papers*, no. 48, IMF.

Ungerer, W. (1993) 'EC: one step back, two steps forward', *Japan Update*, no. 17, February.

United Nations (1982) 'Standardised input–output tables of EEC countries for years around 1975', *Statistical Standards and Studies*, no. 34.

United Nations Economic Commission for Africa (1984) *Proposals for Strengthening Economic Integration in West Africa*, UNECA (Addis Ababa).

University of Louvain (1963) *The Market Economy in West European Integration*, Editions Nauwelaerts.

Uribe, P., **Theil**, H. and **De Leeuw**, C. G. (1966) 'The information approach to the prediction of interregional trade flows', *Review of Economic Studies*, July.

van der Linde, J. G. and **Lefeber**, R. (1988) 'IEA captures the development of European Community energy law', *Journal of World Trade*, vol. 22.

van Doorn, J. (1975) 'European regional policy: an evaluation of recent developments', *Journal of Common Market Studies*, vol. 13, no. 3.

van Gent, H. and **Nijkamp**, P. (1991) 'Devolution of transport policy in Europe', in K. Button and D. Pitfield (eds), *Transport Deregulation: An international movement*, Macmillan.

van Miert, K. (1996) 'The proposal for a European competition agency', *Competition Policy Newsletter*, vol. 2, no. 2.

van Themaat, J. V. and **Stevens, C.** (1987) 'The division of labour between competition and the Third World', in C. Stevens and J. V. Themaat, *EEC and the Third World: a survey*, 6, *Europe and the International Division of Labour*, Hodder & Stoughton.

Vanhove, N. and **Klaassen, H.** (1987) *Regional Policy: a European approach*, second edition, Gower.

Vaubel, R. (1978) *Strategies for Currency Unification*, J. C. B. Mohr/Paul Siebeck.

Verdoorn, P. J. (1954) 'A customs union for Western Europe: advantages and feasibility', *World Politics*, vol. 6.

Verdoorn, P. J. and **Schwartz, A. N. R.** (1972) 'Two alternative estimates of the effects of EEC and EFTA on the pattern of trade', *European Economic Review*, vol. 3.

Verdoorn, P. T. and **Meyer zu Schlochtern, F. J. M.** (1964) 'Trade creation and trade diversion in the Common Market', in H. Brugmans (ed.), *Integration Europeene et Realité Économique*, Collège d'Europe, Bruges.

Vernon, R. (1966) 'International investment and international trade in the product cycle', *Quarterly Journal of Economics*, vol. 80.

Vickerman, R. W. (ed.) (1991) *Infrastructure and Regional Development*, Pion.

Vickerman, R. (1995) 'The regional impacts of trans-European networks', *Annals of Regional Science*, vol. 29.

Vickers, J. and **Yarrow, G.** (1988) *Privatization: An economic analysis*, MIT Press.

Viner, J. (1950) *The Customs Union Issue*, Carnegie Endowment for International Peace, New York.

von Geusau, F. A. (1975) 'In search of a policy', in F. A. Geusau (ed.), *Energy Strategy in the European Communities*, Sijthoff.

Waelbroeck, J. (1964) 'Le commerce de la communauté Européene avec les pays tieiers', in H. Brugmans (ed.), *Integration Européene et Réalité Economique*, Collége d'Europe, Bruges.

Waelbroeck, J. (1977) 'Measuring the degree of progress of economic integration', in F. Machlup (ed.), *Economic Integration, Worldwide, Regional, Sectoral*, Macmillan.

Waelbroeck, M. (1976) 'The effect of the Rome Treaty on the exercise of national industrial property rights', *The Antitrust Bulletin*, vol. 21, no. 1, Spring.

Waeterloos, C. (1991) 'Why a European energy charter?', *Energy in Europe*, no. 17.

Wagner, N. (1991) 'The EC internal market and ASEAN: an overview', in N. Wagner (ed.), *ASEAN and the EC: The impact of 1992*, Institute of Southeast Asian Studies, Singapore.

Wallace, H. and **Ridley, A.** (1985) 'Europe: the challenge of diversity', *Chatham House Papers*, no. 29, Routledge & Kegan Paul.

Wallace, H., Wallace, W. and **Webb, C.** (eds) (1977) *Policy-making in the European Communities*, John Wiley.

Wallace, W. (ed.) (1980) *Britain in Europe*, Heinemann.

Wallace, W. (ed.) (1990) *The Dynamics of European Integration*, Pinter.

Walter, I. (1967) *The European Common Market*, Praeger.

Walter, N. (1982) 'The EMS: performance and prospects', in M. T. Sumner and G. Zis (eds), *European Economic Union: Progress and prospects*, Macmillan.

Walton, R. J. (1988) 'ECU financial activity', *Quarterly Bulletin*, Bank of England, November.

Webb, C. (1977) 'Variations on a theoretical theme', in H. Wallace, W. Wallace and C. Webb (eds), *Policy-making in the European Communities*, Wiley.

Weber, A. A. (1991) 'EMU and asymmetrics and adjustment problems in the EMS – some empirical evidence', *European Economy*, special edition, no. 1.

Weidemann, R. (1990) 'The anti-dumping policy of the European Communities', *Inter Economics*, January/February.

Weiss, F. D. (1988) 'A political economy of European trade policy against the less developed countries?, *European Economic Review*, vol. 30.

Weiss, F. D. (1992) 'Public procurement in the EC Internal Market, 1992: the second coming of the European champion', *The Antitrust Bulletin*, vol. 37, no. 2.

Wemelsfelder, J. (1960) 'The short term effects of lowering import duties in Germany', *Economic Journal*, vol. 70.

Wenban-Smith, G. C. (1981) 'A study of the movement of productivity in individual industries in the United Kingdom 1968–79', *National Institute Economic Review*, no. 3.

Werner Report (1970) *see* Commission ofthe European Communities (1970a).

West, E. G. (1973) ' "Pure" versus "Operational" economics in regional policy', in G. Hallet (ed.), *Regional Policy for Ever?*, London Institute of Economic Affairs.

Weyman Jones, T. (1986) *Energy in Europe*, Methuen.

Whalley, J. (1979) 'Uniform domestic tax rates, trade distortions and economic integration', *Journal of Public Economics*, vol. 11.

Whalley, J. (1985) *Trade Liberalisation among Major World Trading Areas*, MIT Press.

Whitelegg, J. (1988) *Transport Policy in the EEC*, Routledge.

Whitney, S. N. (1958) *Antitrust Policies: American experience in twenty industries*, Twentieth Century Fund.

Williamson, J. and **Bottrill, A.** (1971) 'The impact of customs unions on trade in manufactures', *Oxford Economic Papers*, vol. 25, no. 3.

Williamson, O. E. (1987) 'Economies as an antitrust defense: the welfare trade-offs', in O. E. Williamson, *Antitrust Economics*, Blackwell.

Winters, L. A. (1984a) 'British imports of manufactures and the Common Market', *Oxford Economic Papers*, vol. 36.

Winters, L. A. (1984b) 'Separability and the specification of foreign trade functions', *European Economic Review*, vol. 27.

Winters, L. A. (1987) 'Britain in Europe: a survey of quantitative trade studies', *Journal of Common Market Studies*, vol. 25.

Winters, L. A. (1988) 'Completing the European Internal Market: some notes on trade policy', *European Economic Review*, vol. 32.

Winters, L. A. (1991) 'International trade and 1992', *European Economic Review*, vol. 2.

Winters, L. A. (ed.) (1992) *Trade Flows and Trade Policy after 1992*, Cambridge University Press.

Winters, L. A. (1994a) 'The EC and protection: the political economy', *European Economic Review*, vol. 38.

Winters, L. A. (1994b) 'Intégration européene et bin-etre économique dans le Reste du Monde', *Économie Internationale*, vol. 65.

Wise, M. (1984) *The Common Fisheries Policy of the European Community*, Methuen.

Wolf, M. (1983) 'The European Community's trade policy', in R. Jenkins (ed.), *Britain in the EEC*, Macmillan.

Wolf, M. (1987) 'An unholy alliance: the European Community and the developing countries in the international trading system', *Aussenwirtschaft*, vol. 1. Also in L. B. Mennes and J. Kol, *European Trade Policies and the Developing World*, Croom Helm.

Wonnacott, G. P. and **Wonnacott, R. J.** (1981) 'Is unilateral tariff reduction preferable to a customs union? The curious case of the missing foreign tariffs', *American Economic Review*, vol. 71.

Wood, A. (1994) *North–South Trade, Employment, and Inequality*, Oxford University Press.

Wood, A. (1995) 'How trade hurt unskilled workers', *Journal of Economic Perspectives*, vol. 9.

Woodland, A. D. (1982) *International Trade and Resource Alllocation*, North Holland.

Woolley, P. K. (1975) 'The European Investment Bank', *Three Banks Review*, no. 105, March.

World Bank (1981) *World Development Report*, Oxford University Press.

World Bank (1988) *World Development Report, 1987*.

WTO (1995a) *Regionalism and the World Trading System*, Geneva.

WTO (1995b) *Trade Policy Review: European Union 1995*, vols I and II, Geneva.

WTO (1996) *Annual Report 1996*, Geneva.

Yannopoulos, G. N. (1985) 'EC external commercial policies and East–West trade in Europe', *Journal of Common Market Studies*, vol. 24, no. 1.

Yannopoulos, G. N. (1988) *Customs Unions and Trade Conflicts: The enlargement of the European Community*, Routledge.

Yannopoulos, G. N. (1990) 'The effects of the single market on the pattern of Japanese investment', *National Institute Economic Review*, November.

Yarrow, G. (1985) 'Strategic issues in industrial policy', *Oxford Review of Economic Policy*, vol. 1, no. 3.

Young, S. Z. (1973) *Terms of Entry: Britain's negotiations with the European Community, 1970–1972*, Heinemann.

Ypersele de Strihou, J. van. (1979) 'Operating principles and procedures of the European Monetary System', in P. H. Trezise (ed.), *The European Monetary System: Promise and prospects*, The Brookings Institution, Washington.

Yuill, D. and **Allen, K.** (1982) *European Regional Incentives – 1981*, Centre for the Study of Public Policy, University of Strathclyde Press.

Author index

Subject index

Page numbers in italics indicate tables or figures. These are only shown separately when there is no textual reference on the page. A list of abbreviations used is given on pages xxiii–xxix